Lecture Notes of the Institute for Computer Sciences, Social Informatics and Telecommunications Engineering 398

More information about this series at http://www.springer.com/series/8197

Joaquin Garcia-Alfaro · Shujun Li ·
Radha Poovendran · Hervé Debar ·
Moti Yung (Eds.)

Security and Privacy in Communication Networks

17th EAI International Conference, SecureComm 2021
Virtual Event, September 6–9, 2021
Proceedings, Part I

Springer

Editors
Joaquin Garcia-Alfaro (iD)
Télécom SudParis,
Institut Polytechnique de Paris
Palaiseau, France

Radha Poovendran (iD)
University of Washington
Seattle, WA, USA

Moti Yung (iD)
Google Inc.
New York, NY, USA

Shujun Li (iD)
University of Kent Canterbury
Canterbury, Kent, UK

Hervé Debar (iD)
Télécom SudParis,
Institut Polytechnique de Paris
Palaiseau, France

ISSN 1867-8211 ISSN 1867-822X (electronic)
Lecture Notes of the Institute for Computer Sciences, Social Informatics
and Telecommunications Engineering
ISBN 978-3-030-90018-2 ISBN 978-3-030-90019-9 (eBook)
https://doi.org/10.1007/978-3-030-90019-9

This Springer imprint is published by the registered company Springer Nature Switzerland AG
The registered company address is: Gewerbestrasse 11, 6330 Cham, Switzerland

Preface

We are delighted to introduce the proceedings of the 17th EAI International Conference on Security and Privacy in Communication Networks (SecureComm 2021). This conference brought together cybersecurity scholars from all around the world, advancing the state of the art and knowledge of cybersecurity and privacy by proposing new methods and tools to address the major cybersecurity challenges faced by our digital systems.

These proceedings contain 43 papers from the main conference, which were selected out of 126 submissions (with an acceptance rate around 34%) from authors in universities, national laboratories, and the private sector from the Americas, Europe, Asia, Australasia, and Africa. All submissions went through an extensive review process undertaken by 82 internationally-recognized experts in cybersecurity. The accepted papers are authored by researchers from 16 countries, with the USA and China being the top two countries with the most papers (18 and 12, respectively).

These proceedings also contain the following papers from two co-located workshops and two other tracks of the conference: five papers accepted to the International Workshop on Post-quantum Cryptography for Secure Communications (PQC-SC), two papers accepted to the International Workshop on Cyber-Physical Systems Strategic and Technical Security (CPS-STS), and four papers to the PhD and Poster Tracks. Submissions to these workshops and tracks were organized by the separate (co-)chairs: Kalpana Singh, Elisa Lorenzo Garcia, Rajeev Anand Sahu, Gaurav Sharma, and T. Chithralekha who co-chaired PQC-SC, Ali Ismail Awad, Charalambos Konstantinou, and Mohammed M. Alani who co-chaired CPS-STS, and Roger A. Hallman who chaired the PhD and Poster Tracks. The accepted papers in these workshops and tracks are authored by researchers from seven different countries (USA, China, Brazil, Italy, South Korea, UAE, and UK).

Any successful conference relies on the contribution of multiple stakeholders, who have volunteered their time and energy in disseminating and publicizing the call for papers, submitting original research results, participating in the reviewing process, and in the end contributing altogether to a great program. First and foremost, we would like to offer our gratitude to the entire Organizing Committee for guiding the entire process of the conference, keeping everything organized and in check. We are also deeply grateful to all the Technical Program Committee (TPC) members for their time and effort in reading, commenting, debating, and finally selecting the papers. We also thank the (co-)chairs, TPC members, and external reviewers of the co-located workshops and the PhD/Poster Tracks for their contributions to the conference. Last but not least, we also thank all the authors who submitted papers to the conference and all participants who attended the conference to support the conference and make it a successful event. Support from the Steering Committee and EAI staff members was also crucial in ensuring the success of the conference. It was a great privilege to work with such a large group of dedicated and talented individuals.

We had hoped for a physical event, and it is unfortunate that we once more had to revert to an online one. We nevertheless hope that you found the discussions and interactions at SecureComm 2021 enjoyable and that the proceedings will simulate further research.

August 2021

Shujun Li
Radha Poovendran
Hervé Debar
Moti Yung

Conference Organization

Steering Committee

Imrich Chlamtac	University of Trento, Italy
Guofei Gu	Texas A&M University, USA
Peng Liu	Pennsylvania State University, USA
Sencun Zhu	Pennsylvania State University, USA

Organizing Committee

General Chair

Shujun Li — University of Kent, UK

General Co-chair

Radha Poovendran — University of Washington, USA

Technical Program Committee Chair and Co-chair

Hervé Debar	Télécom SudParis/Institut Polytechnique de Paris, France
Moti Yung	Google Inc./Columbia University, USA

Sponsorship and Exhibit Chair

Theodosios Dimitrakos — Munich Research Centre, Huawei Technologies Ltd, Germany

Local Chairs

Budi Arief	University of Kent, UK
Gareth Howells	University of Kent, UK

Workshops Chair

David Arroyo Guardeño — CSIC, Spain

Publicity and Social Media Chairs

Jason Nurse	University of Kent, UK
Kaitai Liang	TU Delft, The Netherlands

Publications Chair

Joaquin Garcia-Alfaro   Télécom SudParis/Institut Polytechnique de Paris,
                                     France

Web Chair

Christophe Kiennert   Télécom SudParis/Institut Polytechnique de Paris,
                                     France

Posters and PhD Track Chair

Roger A. Hallman   Naval Information Warfare Center
                                     Pacific/Dartmouth College, USA

Panels Chairs

Julio Hernandez-Castro   University of Kent, UK
Sanjay Bhattacherjee   University of Kent, UK

Tutorials Chair

Anyi Liu   Oakland University, USA

Technical Program Committee

Magnus Almgren   Chalmers University of Technology, Sweden
Elias Athanasopoulos   University of Cyprus, Cyprus
Gregory Blanc   Télécom SudParis/Institut Polytechnique de Paris,
                                     France
Sébastien Bardin   CEA LIST, France
Lorenzo Cavallaro   Kings College London, UK
Lucas Davi   University of Duisburg-Essen, Germany
Gabi Dreo   Bundeswehr University Munich, Germany
Sven Dietrich   City University of New York, USA
Daniel Gruss   Graz University of Technology, Austria
Christophe Hauser   University of Southern California, USA
Vasileios Kemerlis   Brown University, USA
Andrea Lanzi   University of Milan, Italy
Fabio Martinelli   CNR, Italy
Michael Meier   University of Bonn/Fraunhofer FKIE, Germany
Marius Muench   Vrije Universiteit Amsterdam, The Netherlands
William Robertson   Northeastern University, USA
Thomas Schreck   Munich University of Applied Sciences, Germany
Seungwon Shin   KAIST, South Korea
Angelos Stavrou   George Mason University, USA

Gianluca Stringhini	Boston University, USA
Giovanni Apruzzese	University of Liechtenstein, Liechtenstein
Urko Zurutuza	Mondragon University, Spain
Fabio Di Franco	ENISA, Greece
Platon Kotzias	NortonLifeLock Research Group, Greece
Sokratis Katsikas	NTNU, Norway
Razvan Beuran	JAIST, Japan
Youki Kadobayashi	NAIST, Japan
Franco Chiaraluce	UNIVPM, Italy
Igor Kotenko	St. Petersburg Federal Research Center of the Russian Academy of Sciences, Russia
Evangelos Markatos	FORTH, Greece
Silvia Bonomi	Sapienza University of Rome, Italy
Apostolis Zarras	TU Delft, The Netherlands
Jan Hajný	Brno University of Technology, Czech Republic
Gabriele Restuccia	CNIT, Italy
Jacques Traore	Orange, France
Jouni Viinikka	6Cure, France
Pavel Laskov	University of Lichtenstein, Lichtenstein
Michal Choras	ITTI, Poland
Olivier Thonnard	Amadeus, France
Roland Rieke	Fraunhofer SIT, Germany
Ali Abbasi	Ruhr University Bochum, Germany
Claudio Canella	TU Graz, Austria
Jun Xu	Stevens Institute of Technology, USA
Cristian-Alexander Staicu	CISPA, Germany
Guillaume Hiet	CentraleSupelec, France
Sharif Abuadbba	Data61, CSIRO, Australia
Mohiuddin Ahmed	Edith Cowan University, Australia
Nadeem Ahmed	Cyber Security Cooperative Research Centre, Australia
Ehab Al-Shaer	Carnegie Mellon University, USA
Budi Arief	University of Kent, UK
Anirban Basu	Hitachi, Ltd, Japan/University of Sussex, UK
Sanjay Bhattacherjee	University of Kent, UK
Liquan Chen	Southeastern University, China
Jinguang Han	Nanjing University of Finance and Economics, China
Debiao He	Wuhan University, China
Julio Hernandez-Castro	University of Kent, UK
Darren Hurley-Smith	Royal Holloway University of London, UK
Zahid Islam	Charles Sturt University, Australia

Helge Janicke	Cyber Security Cooperative Research Centre, Australia
Shancang Li	University of the West of England, UK
Yingjiu Li	University of Oregon, USA
Kaitai Liang	TU Delft, The Netherlands
Anyi Liu	Oakland University, USA
Zhe Liu	Nanjing University of Aeronautics and Astronautics, China
George Loukas	University of Greenwich, UK
Xiapu Luo	Hong Kong Polytechnic University, Hong Kong
Leandros Maglaras	De Montfort University, UK
Kalikinkar Mandal	University of New Brunswick, Canada
Mark Manulis	University of Surrey, UK
Carsten Maple	University of Warwick, UK
Wojciech Mazurczyk	Warsaw University of Technology, Poland
Weizhi Meng	Technical University of Denmark, Denmark
Nour Moustafa	UNSW Canberra, Australia
Toni Perković	University of Split, Croatia
Siraj Ahmed Shaikh	University of Coventry, UK
Chunhua Su	University of Aizu, Japan
Zhiyuan Tan	Edinburgh Napier University, UK
Ding Wang	Nankai University, China
Wei Wang	Beijing Jiaotong University, China
Yongdong Wu	Jinan University, China
Xiaosong Zhang	University of Electronic Science and Technology of China, China
Deqing Zou	Huazhong University of Science and Technology, China
Sushmita Ruj	Data61, CSIRO, Australia/ISI, Kolkata, India
Guomin Yang	University of Wollongong, Australia
Louis Rilling	Inria Rennes - Bretagne Atlantique, France

Contents – Part I

Cyber Threats and Defence

DeepHunter: A Graph Neural Network Based Approach for Robust Cyber
Threat Hunting 3
   Renzheng Wei, Lijun Cai, Lixin Zhao, Aimin Yu, and Dan Meng

SIEMA: Bringing Advanced Analytics to Legacy Security Information
and Event Management 25
   Pejman Najafi, Feng Cheng, and Christoph Meinel

Automatic Generation of Malware Threat Intelligence from Unstructured
Malware Traces 44
   Yuheng Wei and Futai Zou

Towards Automated Assessment of Vulnerability Exposures in Security
Operations 62
   Philip Huff and Qinghua Li

Repeatable Experimentation for Cybersecurity Moving Target Defense 82
   Jaime C. Acosta, Luisana Clarke, Stephanie Medina, Monika Akbar,
   Mahmud Shahriar Hossain, and Frederica Free-Nelson

MPD: Moving Target Defense Through Communication Protocol Dialects 100
   Yongsheng Mei, Kailash Gogineni, Tian Lan, and Guru Venkataramani

Blockchain and P2P Security

GuardedGossip: Secure and Anonymous Node Discovery in Untrustworthy
Networks 123
   Andriy Panchenko, Asya Mitseva, Torsten Ziemann, and Till Hering

An Extensive Security Analysis on Ethereum Smart Contracts 144
   Mohammadreza Ashouri

A Distributed Ledger for Non-attributable Cyber Threat Intelligence
Exchange 164
   Philip Huff and Qinghua Li

AI and Security/Privacy

Understanding ε for Differential Privacy in Differencing Attack Scenarios 187
  Narges Ashena, Daniele Dell'Aglio, and Abraham Bernstein

Explanation-Guided Diagnosis of Machine Learning Evasion Attacks 207
  Abderrahmen Amich and Birhanu Eshete

ToFi: An Algorithm to Defend Against Byzantine Attacks in Federated
Learning 229
  Qi Xia, Zeyi Tao, and Qun Li

TESLAC: Accelerating Lattice-Based Cryptography with AI Accelerator 249
  Lipeng Wan, Fangyu Zheng, and Jingqiang Lin

Research of CPA Attack Methods Based on Ant Colony Algorithm 270
  Xiaoyi Duan, You Li, Jianmin Tong, Xiuying Li, Siman He,
  and Peishu Zhang

Local Model Privacy-Preserving Study for Federated Learning 287
  Kaiyun Pan, Daojing He, and Chuan Xu

Applied Cryptography

Cryptonite: A Framework for Flexible Time-Series Secure Aggregation
with Non-interactive Fault Recovery 311
  Ryan Karl, Jonathan Takeshita, and Taeho Jung

Cryptonomial: A Framework for Private Time-Series Polynomial
Calculations 332
  Ryan Karl, Jonathan Takeshita, Alamin Mohammed, Aaron Striegel,
  and Taeho Jung

Provably Secure Contact Tracing with Conditional Private Set Intersection 352
  Jonathan Takeshita, Ryan Karl, Alamin Mohammed, Aaron Striegel,
  and Taeho Jung

Origin Attribution of RSA Public Keys 374
  Enrico Branca, Farzaneh Abazari, Ronald Rivera Carranza,
  and Natalia Stakhanova

Network Security

Fine-Grained Intra-domain Bandwidth Allocation Against DDoS Attack 399
Lijia Xie, Shuang Zhao, Xiao Zhang, Yiming Shi, Xin Xiao,
and Zhiming Zheng

TMT-RF: Tunnel Mixed Traffic Classification Based on Random Forest 418
Panpan Zhao, Gaopeng Gou, Chang Liu, Yangyang Guan, Mingxin Cui,
and Gang Xiong

CROCUS: An Objective Approach for SDN Controllers Security
Assessment 438
Carlos Silva, Bruno Sousa, and João P. Vilela

Controlling Network Traffic Microstructures for Machine-Learning Model
Probing 456
Henry Clausen, Robert Flood, and David Aspinall

Using NetFlow to Measure the Impact of Deploying DNS-based Blacklists 476
Martin Fejrskov, Jens Myrup Pedersen, and Emmanouil Vasilomanolakis

Digital Forensics

A Forensic Tool to Acquire Radio Signals Using Software Defined Radio 499
M. A. Hannan Bin Azhar and German Abadia

SEMFLOW: Accurate Semantic Identification from Low-Level System Data 513
Mohammad Kavousi, Runqing Yang, Shiqing Ma, and Yan Chen

Author Index 537

Contents – Part II

Web/OSN Security and Privacy

Analyzing Security Risks of Ad-Based URL Shortening Services Caused
by Users' Behaviors 3
*Naoki Fukushi, Takashi Koide, Daiki Chiba, Hiroki Nakano,
and Mitsuaki Akiyama*

XHunter: Understanding XXE Vulnerability via Automatic Analysis 23
Zhenhua Wang, Wei Xie, Jing Tao, Yong Tang, and Enze Wang

Anonymous Short Communications over Social Networks 43
*Francesco Buccafurri, Vincenzo De Angelis, Maria Francesca Idone,
and Cecilia Labrini*

A Sybil Detection Method in OSN Based on DistilBERT
and Double-SN-LSTM for Text Analysis 64
*Xiaojie Xu, Jian Dong, Zhengyu Liu, Jin Yang, Bin Wang,
and Zhaoyuan Wang*

ePayment Security

An Empirical Study on Mobile Payment Credential Leaks and Their
Exploits 79
*Shangcheng Shi, Xianbo Wang, Kyle Zeng, Ronghai Yang,
and Wing Cheong Lau*

System-Wide Security for Offline Payment Terminals 99
Nikolay Ivanov and Qiben Yan

Horus: A Security Assessment Framework for Android Crypto Wallets 120
Md Shahab Uddin, Mohammad Mannan, and Amr Youssef

Systems Security

Leakuidator: Leaky Resource Attacks and Countermeasures 143
Mojtaba Zaheri and Reza Curtmola

JABBIC Lookups: A Backend Telemetry-Based System for Malware Triage ... 164
*Octavian Ciprian Bordeanu, Gianluca Stringhini, Yun Shen,
and Toby Davies*

Facilitating Parallel Fuzzing with Mutually-Exclusive Task Distribution 185
  Yifan Wang, Yuchen Zhang, Chenbin Pang, Peng Li,
  Nikolaos Triandopoulos, and Jun Xu

Flowrider: Fast On-Demand Key Provisioning for Cloud Networks 207
  Nicolae Paladi, Marco Tiloca, Pegah Nikbakht Bideh, and Martin Hell

Mobile Security and Privacy

Mobile Handset Privacy: Measuring the Data iOS and Android Send
to Apple and Google 231
  Douglas J. Leith

Who's Accessing My Data? Application-Level Access Control
for Bluetooth Low Energy 252
  Pallavi Sivakumaran and Jorge Blasco

HTPD: Secure and Flexible Message-Based Communication for Mobile
Apps 273
  Yin Liu, Breno Dantas Cruz, and Eli Tilevich

Smartphone Location Spoofing Attack in Wireless Networks 295
  Chengbin Hu, Yao Liu, Zhuo Lu, Shangqing Zhao, Xiao Han,
  and Junjie Xiong

IoT Security and Privacy

Compromised Through Compression: Privacy Implications of Smart
Meter Traffic Analysis 317
  Pol Van Aubel and Erik Poll

iDDAF: An Intelligent Deceptive Data Acquisition Framework for Secure
Cyber-Physical Systems 338
  Md Hasan Shahriar, Mohammad Ashiqur Rahman,
  Nur Imtiazul Haque, Badrul Chowdhury, and Steven G. Whisenant

PhD and Poster Track

Encouraging the Adoption of Post-Quantum Hybrid Key Exchange
in Network Security 363
  Alexandre Augusto Giron

Quantitative and Qualitative Investigations into Trusted Execution
Environments 372
  Ryan Karl

Phishing Web Page Detection with Semi-Supervised Deep Anomaly
Detection   384
    Linshu Ouyang and Yongzheng Zhang

Poisoning Attack for Inter-agent Transfer Learning   394
    Zelei Cheng and Zuotian Li

PQC-SC Workshop

An Efficient Post-Quantum PKE from RLWR with Simple Security Proof   407
    Parhat Abla and Mingsheng Wang

Kyber on ARM64: Compact Implementations of Kyber on 64-Bit ARM
Cortex-A Processors   424
    Pakize Sanal, Emrah Karagoz, Hwajeong Seo, Reza Azarderakhsh,
    and Mehran Mozaffari-Kermani

Compressed SIKE Round 3 on ARM Cortex-M4   441
    Mila Anastasova, Mojtaba Bisheh-Niasar, Reza Azarderakhsh,
    and Mehran Mozaffari Kermani

A Quantum Circuit to Speed-Up the Cryptanalysis of Code-Based
Cryptosystems   458
    Simone Perriello, Alessandro Barenghi, and Gerardo Pelosi

Hardware Deployment of Hybrid PQC: SIKE+ECDH   475
    Reza Azarderakhsh, Rami Elkhatib, Brian Koziel,
    and Brandon Langenberg

CPS-STS Workshop

Towards Stealing Deep Neural Networks on Mobile Devices   495
    Shashank Reddy Danda, Xiaoyong Yuan, and Bo Chen

Phishing Website Detection from URLs Using Classical Machine Learning
ANN Model   509
    Said Salloum, Tarek Gaber, Sunil Vadera, and Khaled Shaalan

Author Index   525

Cyber Threats and Defence

DeepHunter: A Graph Neural Network Based Approach for Robust Cyber Threat Hunting

Renzheng Wei[1,2], Lijun Cai[1(✉)], Lixin Zhao[1], Aimin Yu[1], and Dan Meng[1]

[1] Institute of Information Engineering, Chinese Academy of Sciences, Beijing, China
[2] School of Cyber Security, University of Chinese Academy of Sciences, Beijing, China
{weirenzheng,cailijun,yuaimin,mengdan}@iie.ac.cn

Abstract. Cyber Threat hunting is a proactive search for known attack behaviors in the organizational information system. It is an important component to mitigate advanced persistent threats (APTs). However, the attack behaviors recorded in provenance data may not be completely consistent with the known attack behaviors. In this paper, we propose DeepHunter, a graph neural network (GNN) based graph pattern matching approach that can match provenance data against known attack behaviors in a robust way. Specifically, we design a graph neural network architecture with two novel networks: *attribute embedding networks* that could incorporate Indicators of Compromise (IOCs) information, and *graph embedding networks* that could capture the relationships between IOCs. To evaluate DeepHunter, we choose five real and synthetic APT attack scenarios. Results show that DeepHunter can hunt all attack behaviors, and the accuracy and robustness of DeepHunter outperform the state-of-the-art method, Poirot.

Keywords: Cyber threat hunting · Robustness · Provenance analysis · Graph neural network · Graph pattern matching

1 Introduction

Threat hunting is a proactive search for intruders who are lurking undetected in the organizational information system. A typical task for a threat hunter is to match system events against known adversarial behavior gained from CTI (Cyber Threat Intelligence). Threat hunting is increasingly becoming an important component to mitigate the Advanced Persistent Threats (APTs), as large enterprises or organizations seek to stay ahead of the latest cyber threats and rapidly respond to any potential attacks.

Existing threat hunting tools (e.g., Endpoint Detection and Response tools, namely EDR) rely on matching low-level Indicators of Compromise (IOCs) or TTP rules (i.e., adversarial Tactics, Techniques, and Procedures). However, simple rules matching methods are prone to high volumes of false alarms, which

© ICST Institute for Computer Sciences, Social Informatics and Telecommunications Engineering 2021
Published by Springer Nature Switzerland AG 2021. All Rights Reserved
J. Garcia-Alfaro et al. (Eds.): SecureComm 2021, LNICST 398, pp. 3–24, 2021.
https://doi.org/10.1007/978-3-030-90019-9_1

leads to the "threat alert fatigue" problem. To overcome this problem, recent works [13,16,31] start to focus on the relationship between IOCs or the correlation among threat alerts. One approach [16] to hunt the ransomware takes advantage of the sequential relationship among IOCs, but the mined sequential patterns typically can not capture long-term attack behaviors.

Recent research suggests that the *provenance graph* can incorporate the long-term historical context and facilitate threat investigation. Based on the provenance graph, many works [13,31] have made advancements to improve the performance of threat hunting. For example, RapSheet [13] leverages dependency relations in the provenance graph to correlate the threat alerts generated by EDR tools, then drops the alerts that do not conform to the APT "kill chain". Poirot [31] improves the accuracy of threat hunting by designing a graph pattern matching algorithm to search the provenance graph for the *query graph* that represents the known attack behavior.

Although the provenance graph can greatly facilitate threat hunting tasks, there still exist several limitations in the existing approaches:

- **Expert knowledge needed.** Existing threat hunting tools or methods need analysts with expert knowledge on known attacks and target systems (e.g., Windows, Linux, macOS, etc.). For example, one needs to estimate the number of entry points of APT attacks when setting Poirot's threshold.
- **Efficiency.** The size of the provenance graph is very large because of the presence of long-term attacks. So the provenance graph-based approaches (i.e., graph matching/searching algorithms) must be efficient.
- **Lack of robustness (most important).** In practice, real attack activities recorded in provenance data are not completely consistent with the known attack behaviors due to auditing/monitoring systems, attack mutations, and random noise. For example, one or more attack steps in CTIs might disappear in the provenance graph. This sort of inconsistency weakens the ability of provenance graph-based methods [13,31,32] to correlate threat alerts. Even worse, the attack provenance graphs might be disconnected, which will bring errors into path-based approaches, i.e., Poirot [31]. We will detail this scenario in Sect. 3.3.

In recent years, graph neural networks (GNNs) have shown great success in handling graph data. Inspired by that, our idea is to view the threat hunting task as a graph pattern matching problem and leverage the powerful GNN model to estimate the matching score between the provenance graph and the given query graph. The graph neural networks have several advantages on the graph pattern matching problem: (1) The graph neural networks naturally excel at efficiency, since modern GPUs can largely accelerate matrix computations by parallel processing. (2) No additional expert knowledge about attacks and target systems is needed, as the graph neural network is trained in an end-to-end manner. What we need is to learn a GNN-based graph pattern matching model that could extract robust graph patterns that are resistant to the inconsistency mentioned earlier. Basically, if both the node attributes (i.e., IOC information) and the graph structures (i.e., dependency relations between IOCs) in the query graph are largely matched in the provenance graphs, the model should output a high matching score and raise alarms.

Unfortunately, there is no off-the-shelf GNN-based architecture that can be simply applied to solve our problem due to two reasons. First, indicators are the entity with multiple attributes (i.e., file names, IP addresses, ports, process names, etc.). Different attributes may have different importance to the graph pattern matching task. Second, the two input graphs for graph pattern matching have different characteristics: The query graph is small and noise-free; The provenance graph is bigger and contains redundant nodes, as the provenance graph represents low-level system events.

To solve these problems in threat hunting, we propose two novel graph neural network structures: the *attribute embedding network* and the *graph embedding networks*. The attribute embedding network encodes attributes into vectors. In particular, we add the attention mechanism to the attribute embedding network. So it could assign higher weights to those attributes that are important to the graph matching task. The graph embedding networks are used for representing graph structures. To better represent distinct input graphs, we employ two different graph embedding networks to encode them, respectively. Specifically, we design one graph embedding network to represent the provenance graph and adopt GCN [22] to represent the query graph. At last, we utilize a powerful relation learning network (i.e., NTN [45]), instead of the traditional Siamese network, to learn a metric for computing the matching score. With this new design practice, we could build the GNN model for graph pattern matching, which is robust against different degrees of inconsistency between the query graph and the provenance graph in threat hunting.

We implemented our proposed technique as **DeepHunter**, a GNN-based graph pattern matching model for threat hunting. To evaluate the accuracy and robustness of DeepHunter, we choose 5 APT attack scenarios with different degrees of inconsistency. Particularly, one of these scenarios (Q5) contains disconnected attack provenance graphs. Experimental results show that Deep-Hunter can identify all of the attack behaviors in 5 APT scenarios, and it is resistant to various degrees of inconsistency and the disconnected attack provenance graphs. The robustness of DeepHunter outperforms the state-of-the-art APT threat hunting method, Poirot. Moreover, DeepHunter could find attacks that Poirot can not identify under the specific complex attack scenario, Q5+ETW. We also compare DeepHunter with other graph matching approaches, including a non-learning approach and GNN-based approaches. Results show that the performance of DeepHunter is superior to these methods.

In summary, this paper makes the following contributions:

- We propose DeepHunter, which is a GNN-based graph pattern matching approach for cyber threat hunting. DeepHunter can tolerate the inconsistency between the real attack behaviors recorded in provenance data and the known attack behaviors to some extent.
- We design a graph neural network architecture with two novel networks: *attribute embedding networks* and *graph embedding networks*. These two

networks could capture complex graph patterns, including IOC information and the relationships between IOCs.

– We choose 5 APT attack scenarios with different degrees of inconsistency between the provenance graph and the query graph, including 3 real-life APT scenarios and 2 synthetic APT scenarios, to evaluate our approach.
– Our evaluation illustrates that DeepHunter outperforms the state-of-the-art APT threat hunting approach (i.e., Poirot) in accuracy and robustness. Meanwhile, DeepHunter, as a graph pattern matching model, is superior to other graph matching methods (i.e., non-learning-based and GNN-based) in the threat hunting task.

2   Related Work

2.1   Threat Hunting Approaches

In this work, we mainly focus on the threat hunting methods. Poirot [31] is a related work to DeepHunter. We will introduce and compare it with DeepHunter in the evaluation (Sect. 7.2). RapSheet [13] is an approach that could improve EDR's threat hunting ability using the provenance graph analysis. But RapSheet [13] requires complete paths remained in the provenance graph to correlate alerts. Obviously, the disconnected attack provenance graphs will undermine the performance of RapSheet.

For APT detection and investigation, both Holmes [32] and NoDoze [14] correlate alerts using the provenance graphs. To hunt stealthy malware, ProvDetector [49] proposes a graph representation learning approach to model process' normal behavior in provenance graphs. However, these methods assume an accurate normal behavior database for reducing false alarms. We know that the normal behavior model may create a risk of the poisoning attack due to concept drift as benign usage changes. Additionally, all of these methods are path-based approaches. So their robustness could be influenced by the disconnected provenance graphs.

Some methods use IOCs or threat alerts as a clue to identify attack behaviors (i.e., zero-day attack [47] and C&C [35]). However, these methods overlook the relationship between indicators or alerts. So it could bring high false positives.

2.2   Provenance Graph Analysis

Provenance graph analysis is widely applied to the APT attack detection [51], forensic analysis [18], and attack scenario reconstruction [17,38], etc. Recent works [15,32] seek to bridge the semantic gap between low-level system events and high-level behaviors. Many recent works (i.e., Morse [18], BEEP [24], MPI [28], and OmegaLog [15], etc.) are proposed to address the dependency explosion problem in provenance graphs. StreamSpot [29] views the provenance graph as a temporal graph with typed nodes and edges, then proposes a graph sketching algorithm for anomaly detection.

2.3   Graph Matching Approaches

Graph pattern matching and graph similarity computation have been studied for many real applications [9, 25]. The graph pattern match problem is NP-complete. NeMa [21] is a neighborhood-based heuristic algorithm, which uses optimization techniques to improve the efficiency. Other works [31, 39, 48] are path-based approaches, which could not resistant to disconnected attack provenance graphs. Recently, many graph neural networks [4, 5, 26, 50] have been proposed for graph pattern matching. However, these approaches do not take into account the size difference between the query graph and the provenance graph. Additionally, the graph characteristics present new challenges to existing graph neural networks, such as being typed, directed. We compare three of them in the evaluation.

3   Background and Motivation

In this section, we first introduce the background knowledge of the provenance graph and the query graph (Sect. 3.1). Then, we briefly illustrate several common motivating situations where the threat hunting approach calls for high robustness (Sect. 3.2). Finally, taking an APT attack scenario with disconnected attack graphs as an example, we illustrate how this scenario affects existing methods and explain why DeepHunter can resist this situation (Sect. 3.3).

3.1   Background

Provenance Graph. Provenance graph is generally a directed acyclic graph (DAG) [11], where the nodes represent system entities, and the edges represent the dependency relation between these entities. There are two types of nodes in provenance graphs: subjects, which represent processes, and objects, which represent other system entities such as files, Windows registry, and network sockets, etc. Subject node's attributes include process name, command line arguments. Object node's attributes include file names, IP addresses, ports, etc. Table 1 shows the nodes and edges we consider in this work. Provenance graph can represent dependencies between system events.

Table 1. A summarization of nodes and edges in provenance graphs and query graphs.

Subject type	Object type	Attributes	Relations
Process	Process	Name, Augments	Fork, Start
	File	File name	Read, ImageLoad, Write
	Socket	Src/dst IP, Src/dst port	Recv, Send
	Registry	Key name	Write

Query Graph. The query graph G_q in our work can be constructed by manually or automatically [19,27,53] extracting IOCs together with the relationships among them from CTIs (including human-written reports or other threat intelligence feeds with structured standard formats (e.g., STIX [34], OpenIOC [8] and MISP [33])). Both nodes and edges of the query graph are the same as the provenance graph, as shown in Table 1. We set the node's or edge's attributes to null if CTIs do not include the corresponding information.

3.2   Motivating Situations

To motivate our work, we introduce several common situations that could lead to inconsistency or disconnected provenance graphs, which will weaken the existing methods' threat hunting ability. Firstly, provenance systems (e.g., Spade [10]) that are developed for recording system events in the application layer may overlook certain attack activities. For instance, Spade does not trace system activities until user space is started. Hence, if the attack occurred before the tracing of Spade, an incomplete attack provenance graph would be generated. Fortunately, the whole-system provenance trackers (like Hi-Fi [40], LPM [6], and CamFlow [36]) can overcome this problem. Indeed these whole-system provenance trackers begin recording system activities in the early boot phase as the *INIT* process starts.

Secondly, even if the whole-system provenance system is applied, some targeted attacks could also lead to inconsistency or disconnected attack provenance graphs. Taking the microarchitectural side-channel attack as an example, there is no connection between the attacker process and the victim process in the provenance graph. Coordinated attacks could generate disconnected attack provenance graphs as well. If attackers control multiple entry points of a compromised system and coordinate to achieve an operational goal, each entry point may correspond to an isolated attack graph.

Finally, attack mutations (or inaccurate CTIs) are another reason that incurs the inconsistency or disconnected attack provenance graphs. In the next section, we present an APT scenario with attack mutations to illustrate its influence to threat investigation.

3.3   An APT Attack Scenario

Recently, cryptocurrency mining malware is one of the most prevalent threats in the wild. Figure 1 describes a typical cryptominer's progression, including the EternalBlue exploitation stage, the persistence stage, and the cryptocurrency mining stage. At its exploitation stage, *wininit* is responsible for configuring and reconnaissance scans. *svchost* exploits the EternalBlue vulnerability for propagation. At the persistence stage (persistence I), *spoolsv.exe* creates an executable binary and adds its path to the "run keys" in the Windows registry. At the last stage, the cryptominer process *minner.exe* is started.

Now, let's consider what happens if the attacker changes the persistence techniques. For example, the attacker adopts an alternative persistence technique II

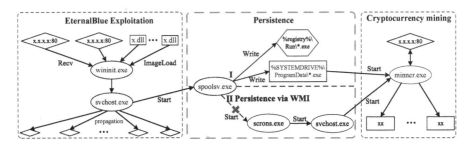

Fig. 1. Query graph of synthetic APT attack scenarios illustrated in Sect. 3.3. Ovals, diamonds, rectangles, and hexagons represent processes, sockets, files, and registry entries, respectively. Many nodes and relations are not shown in the figure for clarity.

(persistence via WMI in Fig. 1). WMI is a preinstalled system tool and it can achieve fileless attacks [12, 30]. We further assume that the running provenance system (not a whole-system provenance system) can not capture the dependency between the *spoolsv.exe* process and the *scrons.exe* process (which is the host process of WMI script). Hence, the connection between the EternalBlue exploitation stage and the cryptocurrency mining stage is broken in attack provenance graphs.

Note that the query graph used by analysts is the EternalBlue exploitation stage, the cryptocurrency mining stage, and the upper part of the persistence stage (persistence technique I) in Fig. 1. So the behavior recorded in the attack provenance graph is inconsistent with the given query graph. Besides, the attack provenance graph is disconnected. This situation makes both threat hunting and forensic investigation more difficult. In Sect. 7.2, we will show that this attack mutation can seriously impair the existing threat hunting approach (i.e., Poirot). Additionally, existing provenance graph-based threat correlation methods, like [13, 14, 32], will definitely lose the correlation between the alerts of the exploitation stage and the alerts of the cryptocurrency mining stage. And the path-based anomaly scores (e.g., rareness score [14, 49] and threat score [13]) may also be affected by disconnected attack provenance graphs.

In contrast, DeepHunter is robust against this attack mutation. Intuitively, although there exist inconsistencies and disconnected attack graphs in this scenario, most node attributes and the main graph structures are preserved. DeepHunter can learn robust graph patterns from training data which are resistant to inconsistencies. We detail the design of DeepHunter in Sect. 5.

4   Design Overview and Challenges

4.1   Graph Pattern Matching for Cyber Threat Hunting

We aim to determine if a provenance graph and a given query graph represent the same attack behaviors for a threat hunting task. In this work, we formulate the threat hunting task as a graph pattern matching problem.

Given a query graph G_q, the output is a matching score s of (G_q, G_p^i), where $G_p^i \in S = \{G_p^1, G_p^2, \ldots, G_p^N\}$, S is the set of provenance graphs. Our goal is to learn a graph matching model $\mathcal{M}$, where $\mathcal{M}(G_p, G_q) = 1$ indicates that the provenance graph G_p and the query graph G_q represent the identical behavior; otherwise, $\mathcal{M}(G_p, G_q) = -1$ indicates that they are different. The graph pattern matching model $\mathcal{M}$ must meet three requirements: ① No expert knowledge needed; ② High efficiency (Graph pattern matching is NP-complete in the general case.); ③ High robustness.

As aforementioned, using a graph neural network to extract graph patterns and further compute matching scores is particularly appealing, since it can learn a graph matching model without expert knowledge. Also, once the graph matching model is learned, the matching score can be efficiently computed, and thus we no longer rely on any expensive graph pattern matching algorithms.

4.2   Challenges and Solutions

It has been demonstrated that graph neural networks can learn complex graph patterns for downstream tasks, such as binary code similarity detection [52] and memory forensic analysis [46]. In this work, we need the graph neural network to extract graph patterns for matching two graphs. In particular, the graph patterns should be composed of node attributes and graph structures. We show the challenges of designing graph neural networks and our corresponding solutions as follows.

Challenge 1. How to represent node attribute information effectively? There are multiple node types in graphs, each node has many attributes, and different attributes may have different importance to the graph pattern matching task. Previous work [29] considers the provenance graph as a heterogeneous graph and searches the heterogeneous graph following the meta-paths. However, constructing the meta-path needs expert knowledge on the target systems.

We propose the attribute embedding network (detailed in Sect. 5.1) to represent the node's attributes. We treat the node type (e.g., process, file, socket, etc.) as one of a node's attributes and employ the attention mechanism to automatically learn which attributes contribute most to the graph matching task.

Challenge 2. How to represent graph structures effectively? Previous graph pattern matching models [4, 25, 50] utilize the same neural network structure to represent both input graphs. But the characteristics of two input graphs for threat hunting are distinct, as mentioned in Sect. 1.

We adopt two different graph neural networks: One is GCN for the query graph, and the other is specially designed to represent the provenance graph structure. We introduce them as the graph embedding networks, as detailed in Sect. 5.2.

5   DeepHunter's Graph Pattern Matching Model

5.1   Attribute Embedding Network for Encoding Node's Attributes

The goal of the attribute embedding network is to obtain the input feature h_u^0 for each node u, which incorporates $u's$ attributes information. Specifically, we first generate an embedding v_i for each attribute i of the node u (as depicted on the left of Fig. 2), and then compute $u's$ input feature h_u^0 by aggregating $u's$ attribute embeddings (as depicted on the right of Fig. 2).

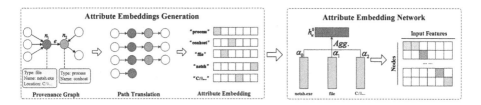

Fig. 2. The process of generating input features.

To obtain the attribute embedding v_i, inspired by the path embedding method of ProvDetector [49], we view a path in the provenance graph as a sentence and then adopt an unsupervised NLP model (word2vec [23]). Specifically, we first translate paths in the provenance graphs into sentences which consist of attributes. For example, the colored nodes n_1, n_2, and the edge e between them in the provenance graph of Fig. 2 can be translated into a sentence as follows: Process *conhost* reads file *netsh.exe* in $C : \backslash\backslash Windows \backslash\backslash System32$. Then we feed the sentences into a word2vec model to learn the vector representation v_i for each attribute i.

We represent a node $u's$ input feature as the aggregation of its attribute embeddings v_i. Common aggregation functions include *sum* and *average*. However, for the graph pattern matching task, the importance of each node attribute may be different. Hence, we use the attention mechanism to learn the weight for each attribute of a node. Specifically, we compute node $u's$ input feature h_u^0 by

$$h_u^0 = \sum\nolimits_{i \in A_u} \alpha_i v_i, \tag{1}$$

where A_u is the attribute set of the node u, α_i is the weight of the $i-th$ attribute, v_i is the embedding of attribute i.

5.2   Graph Embedding Networks for Encoding Graph Structures

Graph embedding networks aim to represent graph structures of both the query graph and the provenance graph. There are two stages in the graph embedding networks: the node-level embedding stage and the graph-level embedding stage. We use two different graph embedding networks to encode the provenance graph G_p and the query graph G_q respectively.

Stage 1: Node-Level Embedding. It is the node embedding method that leads to the difference between the query graph embedding network and the provenance graph embedding network. We adopt the existing graph convolutional network (GCN) [22] to embed the nodes in the query graph. As a matter of fact, the query graph is usually small and noise-free, which can be handled by GCN. To embed the nodes in the provenance graphs, we design a provenance graph embedding network (shown in Fig. 3) which is capable of dealing with the redundant nodes while remaining the key information for matching the query graph. The provenance graph node embedding network is detailed as follows.

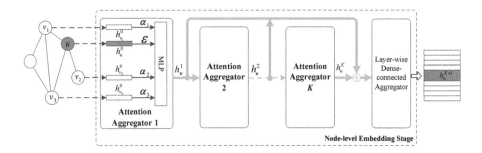

Fig. 3. Provenance graph node-level embedding network structure.

Firstly, we design a GNN layer, called *attention aggregator*, which could aggregate information from neighbors for the target node. Note that, for a node u in the provenance graph, different neighbors may have different importance for graph matching when incorporating their node features into node u. In particular, the redundant neighbors should be assigned a lower importance value to reduce their impact on $u's$ hidden representation h_u, while the nodes that can match the corresponding ones in the query graph should be assigned a higher importance value. For this purpose, we adopt another attention mechanism that can learn weights for neighbors of node u. Formally, the hidden representation h_u outputted by the layer k can be computed via a neural aggregation function that is achieved by

$$h_u^k = MLP(\epsilon^{(k)} h_u^{k-1} + \sum_{v \in N_u} \alpha_v h_v^{k-1}), \tag{2}$$

where h_u^k is the output of layer k of the provenance graph embedding network, and it is the hidden representation of node u; α_v is the attentional weight of node v ($v \in N_u$, where N_u is the set of node $u's$ neighbors).

To aggregate the information into h_u from distant nodes, we then add more layers defined by Eq. 2. The number of layers, K, means that the GNN can aggregate information from u's $K - hops$ neighbors. However, simply adding layers may squash exponentially-growing information (including noise) into fixed-size vectors. To address this issue, we adopt the Layer-wise Dense-connected Aggregator which is proposed by [50]. This strategy is formulated as follows:

$$h_u^{K+1} = MLP([h_u^0; h_u^1; \ldots h_u^K]), \tag{3}$$

where $[\cdot; \cdot]$ is the feature concatenation operation.

Stage 2: Graph-Level Embedding. Now we obtain the node embedding h for each node in both the query graph and the provenance graphs. How to generate a low-dimensional embedding vector for a graph using node embeddings? In this work, we adapt the Global Context-Aware Attention strategy proposed in SimGNN [4] to obtain the graph-level embedding h_G. Intuitively, nodes that are similar to the global context will be assigned larger weights, which allows the corresponding node embeddings to contribute more to the graph-level embedding. Different from SimGNN, we normalize the weights into 1, because we do not want the graph size to affect the calculation of the matching score. Hence, we replace the sigmoid function in SimGNN with a softmax function $\sigma(\boldsymbol{z})_i = \frac{e^{z_i}}{\sum_{j=1}^K e^{z_j}}$. This graph-level embedding is formally represented by the following equation:

$$\begin{aligned} h_G &= \sum_{u=1}^{N} \sigma(h_u c) h_u \\ &= \sum_{u=1}^{N} \sigma(h_u \tanh((\frac{1}{N} \sum_{m=1}^{N} h_m) W)) h_u, \end{aligned} \tag{4}$$

where N is the number of nodes in a graph, $\tanh(\cdot)$ is a activation function, W is the trainable parameters.

5.3   GNN-Based Architecture for Graph Pattern Matching

Based on the attribute embedding network and the graph embedding network, DeepHunter's graph pattern matching model could learn robust graph patterns. The framework of DeepHunter's graph pattern matching model is shown in Fig. 4. It consists of two branches. The upper branch of Fig. 4 deals with CTI information, and the lower one is for provenance data. At the beginning of each branch, the query graph and the provenance graph are constructed. Then both of them are fed into our GNN-based models.

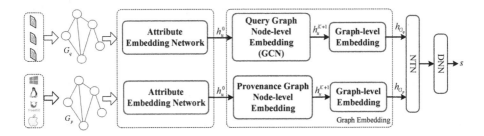

Fig. 4. The framework of DeepHunter's graph pattern matching model.

Given the output of two branches, h_{G_q} and h_{G_p}, many existing graph matching models adopt the Siamese architecture [7] to learn the relation between them. However, the Siamese architecture that directly computes the inner product of h_{G_q} and h_{G_p} is too simple to model the complex relation. Instead, we employ Neural Tensor Network (NTN), which is a powerful relation learning network, to replace the inner product operation. We compare NTN and the traditional Siamese architecture in Sect. 7.3.

After the NTN layer, we connect multi-layer dense neural networks (DNNs) and output the graph matching score s. At last, to compute the loss, we compare s against the ground-truth label using the following mean squared error loss function:

$$\mathcal{L} = \sum_{(G_{p_i}, G_{q_i}) \in \mathcal{D}} (\hat{s} - s(h_{G_{p_i}}, h_{G_{q_i}}))^2, \tag{5}$$

where $D = \{(G_{p_1}, G_{q_1}), (G_{p_2}, G_{q_2}), ...\}$ is the training dataset.

We train the proposed model in an end-to-end way. We leverage stochastic gradient descent to estimate parameters. After a number of training epochs, the loss value will be small and stable, the accuracy of validation data will be high, which demonstrates that the model is trained well.

6   Implementation

6.1   Provenance Graph Reduction

In practice, due to hosting long-term system logs is prohibitively expensive, analysts attempt to reduce the provenance graph and yet preserve the quality of threat hunting [13]. In this work, we prune the provenance graph as follows.

First, we leverage the MITRE ATT&CK TTPs and the IOCs to generate suspicious events. Specifically, DeepHunter uses the EDR tool (i.e., BLUES-PAWN [44]), which provides matching rules to detect MITRE ATT&CK TTPs. Besides, DeepHunter also matches the IOCs (extracted from threat intelligence, such as APT reports) using regular expressions. The events identified by both the EDR tool and the IOC matching are regarded as suspicious events.

We then propose the provenance graph reduction algorithm (Algorithm 1), which could prune the provenance graphs based on the suspicious events. Inspired by Poirot [31], we select *seed nodes* from the nodes that match the IOCs. For example, suppose IOC α has x matched nodes in provenance graphs, IOC β has y matched nodes, and IOC γ has z matched nodes. If $z = min\{x, y, z\}$, then these z nodes are *seed nodes*. We start from a *seed node* and execute *adaptiveBFS* searching on the provenance graphs. A suspicious subgraph generated by the graph reduction algorithm could cover all IOCs' alerts.

The *adaptiveBFS* is an adapted Breadth-First Search (BFS) algorithm. Specifically, during BFS on the provenance graph, only the nodes related to suspicious events and the process node could be visited.

Algorithm 1: Provenance Graph Reduction Algorithm

Input: Provenance Graphs: G_p, Indicators Set: I, Matched Nodes Set: P;
Output: Suspicious Subgraphs: $SuspGraphs$
Function ExpandSearch($SeedNodes$, $Susp$):
    foreach $node \in SeedNodes$ **do**
        $start\_node \leftarrow node$; $subgraph \leftarrow adaptiveBFS(start\_node, P)$;
        $Susp \leftarrow ComposeGraph(Susp, subgraph)$;
        if $Susp$ contains all indicators in I **then**
            | Add $Susp$ to $SuspGraphs$
        else
            $remain\_nodes \leftarrow seed$ nodes from P that are not matched with any
            indicators in I; $ExpandSearch(remain\_nodes, Susp)$;
        end
    end
    return $SuspGraphs$

Obviously, the suspicious subgraphs generated by our provenance graph reduction algorithm contain lots of false positives (the threat alert fatigue problem). Therefore, it is still necessary for analysts to use our graph pattern matching model (Sect. 5) to calculate the matching score.

6.2 Training Data Generation

Training DeepHunter requires a large number of positive samples (G_{p_i}, G_{q_i}) $(\mathcal{M}(G_{p_i}, G_{q_i}) = 1)$ and negative samples (G_{p_i}, G_{q_i}) $(\mathcal{M}(G_{p_i}, G_{q_i}) = -1)$. The query graph can be considered as a summarization of its corresponding provenance graph. Therefore, we use the graph summarization techniques to generate the matched query graph G_q for each provenance graph G_p. We also add random noise to improve the robustness. We detail the training data generation method as follows.

Firstly, we extract a subgraph as G_{p_i} from the provenance graphs. Specifically, we start from a process node and use DFS on the provenance graph. We limit the length of the paths, which is less than 4. Then we refine the G_{p_i} using two graph summarization rules as follows:

- Merge process nodes that have the same process name;
- Remove duplicate paths. If two paths are duplicates (i.e., two sequences of node name are equal), only one is reserved.

Then we add noise to G_{p_i} by:

- randomly dropping edges or object nodes on G_{p_i};
- randomly removing one or more attributes of a node.

After the above two steps, we generate a G_{q_i} for the G_{p_i}. So (G_{q_i}, G_{p_i}) is a positive sample for training.

Table 2. APT attack scenarios description and the source of query graphs.

Scenario	Short description	Query graph source
Q1+CADETS	A Nginx server was exploited and a malicious file was downloaded and executed. The attacker tried to inject into sshd process, but failed	DARPA TC 3 reports
Q2+TRACE	The Firefox process was exploited and established a connection to the attacker's operator console. The attacker downloaded and executed a malicious file	DARPA TC 3 reports
Q3+TRACE	A Firefox extension (a password manager) was exploited. A malicious file was downloaded and executed to connect out to the C&C server	DARPA TC 3 reports
Q4+ETW	Detailed in Sect. 3.3	Fig. 1 with persistence I
Q5+ETW	The attack mutation of scenario Q4	Fig. 1 with persistence II

At last, we construct the negative sample (G_{q_j}, G_{p_i}) by randomly combining G_{p_i} and G_{q_j}, where $i \neq j$. By doing this, we simulate the situation where most of the node attribute information and the main graph structure of G_{p_i} is preserved in G_{q_i}.

7   Evaluation

7.1   Attack Scenarios and Experimental Setup

To evaluate the efficacy of DeepHunter, we utilize provenance data which contain 5 APT attack scenarios, including 3 real-life APTs(DARPA TC engagement 3) and 2 synthetic APTs. For each of the attack scenarios, the corresponding query graph is also provided. To simulate real-world threat hunting, the query graphs we used in the evaluation are either generated by the third-party or constructed based on the public APT reports. The description of APT scenarios and the source of corresponding query graphs are shown in Table 2.

Inconsistency Scores. Before evaluating robustness, we define three inconsistency scores to quantify the degree of the inconsistency between the query graph and the corresponding provenance graph. Specifically, we compute graph edit distance (GED) and the number of *missing nodes* and *missing paths*. GED measures the cost that transforms G_q into G_p. We adopt a graph matching toolkit [20,43] to calculate GED and normalize [41] the GED scores for different graph sizes. The *missing node* of the query graph is the node that we cannot find its alignments in provenance graphs. The *missing path* means that for an edge from node i to j in the query graph, there is no path from the nodes aligned to i to the nodes aligned to j in provenance graphs. Table 3 shows the inconsistency scores of the scenarios in Table 2. We can see from Table 3 that the chosen scenarios contain different degrees of inconsistency.

Table 3. Inconsistency scores of different scenarios. The values in parentheses on the second and third columns are the number of missing nodes and paths, respectively.

Scenario	Missing nodes (%)	Missing paths (%)	GED
Q1+CADETS	0	0	0.192
Q2+TRACE	0	6.25%(1)	0.303
Q3+TRACE	0	16%(4)	0.504
Q4+ETW	3.8%(1)	4%(1)	0.454
Q5+ETW	21.4%(6)	20%(7)	0.557

Experimental Setup. The provenance data from DARPA are collected by two provenance systems: CADETS [2] and TRACE [3]. Besides, we synthesized attacks in scenarios Q4+ETW and Q5+ETW on Windows 7 32 bit systems. The provenance data of Q4+ETW and Q5+ETW, including benign system activities and attack behaviors, were collected by our provenance system which is based on Windows ETW [1].

We employed the gensim [42] Python library to obtain the attribute embeddings v_i (detailed in Sect. 5.1). We implemented the proposed graph neural network model using PyTorch [37]. We trained whole neural network-based models using 2 Nvidia Tesla P4 GPU. Other experiments (e.g., provenance graph construction, graph reduction, etc.) are conducted on a server with two Intel Xeon E5-2630 v3 CPUs and 128 GB memory running CentOS system.

Datasets. We generated a dataset for each provenance system and named the dataset after the provenance system. We used the graph reduction method illustrated in Sect. 6.1 to prune the provenance graph. The generated subgraphs (i.e., test graphs) were manually labeled based on the corresponding reports' timestamp. We also generated training graph pairs using the method detailed in Sect. 6.2. The characteristics of our datasets are shown in Table 4.

Table 4. The characteristics of graph datasets used in our evaluation.

Dataset	Raw graph size	# of test graphs		# of training graphs
		Benign	Attack	
CADETS	904 MB	10	1	150,000
TRACE	22.5 GB	9	6	150,000
ETW	40 GB	105	10	300,000

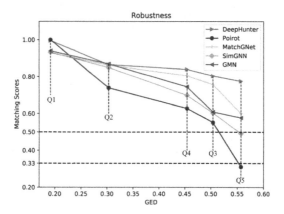

Fig. 5. Axis x: graph edit distance between G_q and G_p of each scenario in Table 2; Axis y: matching scores between G_q and G_p of each scenario. Q1–Q5 represent attack scenarios

7.2   Robustness

We evaluate the impact of inconsistency on DeepHunter and the state-of-the-art Poirot. We also analyze why Poirot fails in scenario Q5+ETW which contains disconnected attack provenance graphs.

State-of-the-Art Poirot. Poirot is a heuristic graph pattern matching algorithm that can compute the graph alignment score between the query graph and the provenance graph. Poirot searches for aligned nodes in the provenance graphs according to the *information flows* in the query graph. During the search, Poirot omits the paths that are impossible to be adopted by attackers.

Experimental Results. We compare DeepHunter with Poirot using all scenarios in Table 2. The matching scores calculated by Poirot, DeepHunter, and other GNN-based graph matching models are shown in Fig. 5. We can see that all matching scores calculated by DeepHunter are greater than the threshold (which is 0.5). This result shows that the accuracy of DeepHunter can be guaranteed in scenarios where there exist various degrees of inconsistency.

Moreover, as the degree of the inconsistency increases, all matching scores decrease. But the curve of DeepHunter is more stable. On the contrary, the curve of Poirot drops faster than the GNN-based graph matching models. Even worse, the matching score calculated by Poirot is less than its threshold in the most inconsistent scenario Q5+ETW , which means that Poirot fails to identify this attack.

Additionally, we detail the false positive results of DeepHunter and Poirot in Table 5. The results can demonstrate that the high robustness of DeepHunter is not built upon false positives.

Why Does Poirot Fail? When searching on the disconnected attack provenance graphs in Q5+ETW, the paths which start from nodes belonging to the

Table 5. False positive results of DeepHunter and Poirot.

Dataset	CADETS	TRACE	ETW
# of test graphs	11	15	115
# of FPs (DeepHunter)	0	0	1
# of FPs (Poirot)	0	1	2

EternalBlue exploitation stage to nodes belonging to the cryptocurrency mining stage can not be found. So the *graph alignment score* computed using the Eq. (2) in Poirot [31] becomes smaller (The *influence scores* of the missing paths are all equal to 0. And the denominator of Eq. (2) in Poirot [31], $|F(G_q)|$, which is the number of *flows* in the query graph, remains unchanged). As a result, this type of inconsistency in Q5+ETW leads to the invalidation of Poirot. On the contrary, DeepHunter does not rely on complete connectivity remained in the provenance graph. As long as most node attribute information and the main graph structure information between the query graph and the traceability graph are matched, DeepHunter can recognize that the two graphs represent the same attack behavior. Therefore, DeepHunter has a more robust cyber threat hunting ability.

7.3   Comparison with Other Graph Matching Models

We compare DeepHunter with a non-learning graph matching approach and other GNN-based graph matching models. Note that these GNN-based models are not specifically designed for threat hunting. We evaluate all the graph matching approaches using the AUC value, since it is a strict metric. If a small mistake is made, the error would be obvious.

DeepHunter vs. Non-learning Approach. We compare DeepHunter with the Weisfeiler Lehman (WL) kernel, a non-learning method for calculating the graph similarity. We set the number of iteration of the WL kernel from 1 to 10 and put the best results in Table 6. The result of the WL kernel is not desirable because it is designed for graph isomorphism testing. In contrast, the graph matching in a threat hunting task is more similar to determining whether a query graph can be regarded as an abstraction of the provenance graph.

DeepHunter vs. GNN-based Graph Matching Models. We compare DeepHunter's graph matching model with other GNN-based graph matching networks: MatchGNet [50], SimGNN [4] and GMN [26]. MatchGNet proposed a Hierarchical Attentional Graph Neural Encoder (HAGNE) which could embed the provenance graph. Given the graph-level embeddings, MatchGNet employs the Siamese network to learn the similarity metric. We believe that the Siamese network is not enough to learn the complex relationship between the two graphs.

Hence, we substitute the Siamese network of MatchGNet with the NTN layer. We call the modified model MatchGNet-NTN. By comparing DeepHunter and MatchGNet-NTN, we can evaluate the effectiveness of our graph embedding networks. As can be seen in Table 6, the performance of DeepHunter outperforms MatchGNet and MatchGNet-NTN.

We also evaluate the effectiveness of the attribute embedding network. Instead of the attribute embedding network, we directly use the one-hot encoding of attributes as the node's input feature. We call this model DeepHunter-wo-AEN. Table 6 shows that DeepHunter-wo-AEN is inferior to DeepHunter, which demonstrates the attribute embedding network is necessary for our graph matching task.

At last, we evaluate the other two graph matching networks: SimGNN and GMN. Like DeepHunter, SimGNN also leverages GNN to represent input graphs and then utilizes NTN to learn the similarity between two graph-level embeddings. But the graph neural networks in SimGNN are not specifically designed for representing the provenance graphs. Besides, SimGNN believes that if there is a difference in the size of the two input graphs, then the two graphs are not similar. GMN takes into account the node correlation across graphs to model the relation. The results of SimGNN and GMN are shown in Table 6. We can see that the performance of DeepHunter is superior to both SimGNN and GMN.

Table 6. AUC values of graph matching models on three datasets.

Dataset	CADETS	TRACE	ETW
DeepHunter	1	**0.951**	**0.916**
MatchGNet [50]	1	0.880	0.805
MatchGNet-NTN	1	0.932	0.844
MatchGNet-wo-AEN	1	0.891	0.820
SimGNN [4]	1	0.906	0.805
GMN [25]	1	0.846	0.830
WL kernel	1	0.492	0.301

8   Conclusions

We propose DeepHunter, a GNN-based graph pattern matching approach for cyber threat hunting. More importantly, DeepHunter is robust against the inconsistency between real attack behaviors recorded by provenance data and known attack behaviors to some extent. Our extensive evaluations show that DeepHunter can tolerate various scenarios with different inconsistency scores, including disconnected attack provenance graphs. In our synthetic APT attack scenario, DeepHunter is superior to the state-of-the-art APT threat hunting approach Poirot. Our research showcased a successful application of the graph neural network on the threat hunting task.

Acknowledgment. This work is supported by the Strategic Priority Research Program of Chinese Academy of Sciences, Grant No. XDC02040200.

References

1. Event tracing. https://docs.microsoft.com/en-us/windows/win32/etw/event-tracing-portal
2. Causal, adaptive, distributed, and efficient tracing system (cadets) (2018). https://www.cl.cam.ac.uk/research/security/cadets/. Accessed 21 Sept 2020
3. Trace: Preventing advanced persistent threat cyberattacks (2018). https://archive.sri.com/work/projects/trace-preventing-advanced-persisten-threat-cyberattacks. Accessed 21 Sept 2020
4. Bai, Y., Ding, H., Bian, S., Chen, T., Sun, Y., Wang, W.: SimGNN: a neural network approach to fast graph similarity computation. In: Proceedings of the Twelfth ACM International Conference on Web Search and Data Mining, pp. 384–392 (2019)
5. Bai, Y., Ding, H., Gu, K., Sun, Y., Wang, W.: Learning-based efficient graph similarity computation via multi-scale convolutional set matching. In: AAAI, pp. 3219–3226 (2020)
6. Bates, A., Tian, D.J., Butler, K.R., Moyer, T.: Trustworthy whole-system provenance for the linux kernel. In: 24th {USENIX} Security Symposium ({USENIX} Security 15), pp. 319–334 (2015)
7. Bromley, J., Guyon, I., LeCun, Y., Säckinger, E., Shah, R.: Signature verification using a "siamese" time delay neural network. In: Advances in Neural Information Processing Systems, pp. 737–744 (1994)
8. FireEye (2018). https://openioc.org. openIOC
9. Fyrbiak, M., Wallat, S., Reinhard, S., Bissantz, N., Paar, C.: Graph similarity and its applications to hardware security. IEEE Trans. Comput. **69**(4), 505–519 (2019)
10. Gehani, A., Tariq, D.: SPADE: support for provenance auditing in distributed environments. In: Narasimhan, P., Triantafillou, P. (eds.) Middleware 2012. LNCS, vol. 7662, pp. 101–120. Springer, Heidelberg (2012). https://doi.org/10.1007/978-3-642-35170-9_6
11. Gibson, T., Schuchardt, K., Stephan, E.G.: Application of named graphs towards custom provenance views. In: Workshop on the Theory and Practice of Provenance (2009)
12. Graeber, M.: Abusing Windows Management Instrumentation (WMI) to Build a Persistent, Asyncronous, and Fileless Backdoor. Black Hat, Las Vegas (2015)
13. Hassan, W.U., Bates, A., Marino, D.: Tactical provenance analysis for endpoint detection and response systems. In: Proceedings of the IEEE Symposium on Security and Privacy (2020)
14. Hassan, W.U., et al.: NODOZE: combatting threat alert fatigue with automated provenance triage. In: NDSS (2019)
15. Hassan, W.U., Noureddine, M.A., Datta, P., Bates, A.: OmegaLog: high-fidelity attack investigation via transparent multi-layer log analysis. In: Proceedings NDSS (2020)
16. Homayoun, S., Dehghantanha, A., Ahmadzadeh, M., Hashemi, S., Khayami, R.: Know abnormal, find evil: frequent pattern mining for ransomware threat hunting and intelligence. IEEE Trans. Emerg. Top. Comput. **8**, 341–351 (2017)

17. Hossain, M.N., et al.: {SLEUTH}: real-time attack scenario reconstruction from {COTS} audit data. In: 26th {USENIX} Security Symposium ({USENIX} Security 17), pp. 487–504 (2017)

18. Hossain, M.N., Sheikhi, S., Sekar, R.: Combating dependence explosion in forensic analysis using alternative tag propagation semantics. In: 2020 IEEE Symposium on Security and Privacy (SP). IEEE (2020)

19. Husari, G., Al-Shaer, E., Ahmed, M., Chu, B., Niu, X.: TTPDrill: automatic and accurate extraction of threat actions from unstructured text of CTI sources. In: Proceedings of the 33rd Annual Computer Security Applications Conference, pp. 103–115 (2017)

20. Kaspar, R.: https://github.com/dzambon/graph-matching-toolkit (2018). mig-logcleaner-resurrected

21. Khan, A., Wu, Y., Aggarwal, C.C., Yan, X.: NeMa: fast graph search with label similarity. Proc. VLDB Endowment **6**(3), 181–192 (2013)

22. Kipf, T.N., Welling, M.: Semi-supervised classification with graph convolutional networks. arXiv preprint arXiv:1609.02907 (2016)

23. Le, Q., Mikolov, T.: Distributed representations of sentences and documents. In: International Conference on Machine Learning, pp. 1188–1196 (2014)

24. Lee, K.H., Zhang, X., Xu, D.: High accuracy attack provenance via binary-based execution partition. In: NDSS (2013)

25. Li, Y., Gu, C., Dullien, T., Vinyals, O., Kohli, P.: Graph matching networks for learning the similarity of graph structured objects. In: Chaudhuri, K., Salakhutdinov, R. (eds.) Proceedings of the 36th International Conference on Machine Learning. Proceedings of Machine Learning Research, Long Beach, California, USA, 09–15 Jun 2019, vol. 97, pp. 3835–3845. PMLR (2019). http://proceedings.mlr.press/v97/li19d.html

26. Li, Y., Gu, C., Dullien, T., Vinyals, O., Kohli, P.: Graph matching networks for learning the similarity of graph structured objects. arXiv preprint arXiv:1904.12787 (2019)

27. Liao, X., Yuan, K., Wang, X., Li, Z., Xing, L., Beyah, R.: Acing the IOC game: toward automatic discovery and analysis of open-source cyber threat intelligence. In: Proceedings of the 2016 ACM SIGSAC Conference on Computer and Communications Security, pp. 755–766 (2016)

28. Ma, S., Zhai, J., Wang, F., Lee, K.H., Zhang, X., Xu, D.: {MPI}: Multiple perspective attack investigation with semantic aware execution partitioning. In: 26th {USENIX} Security Symposium ({USENIX} Security 17), pp. 1111–1128 (2017)

29. Manzoor, E., Milajerdi, S.M., Akoglu, L.: Fast memory-efficient anomaly detection in streaming heterogeneous graphs. In: Proceedings of the 22nd ACM SIGKDD International Conference on Knowledge Discovery and Data Mining, pp. 1035–1044 (2016)

30. Micro, T.: cryptocurrency Miner Uses WMI and EternalBlue To Spread Filelessly (2017). https://blog.trendmicro.com/trendlabs-security-intelligence/cryptocurrency-miner-uses-wmi-eternalblue-spread-filelessly/. Accessed 4 May 2020

31. Milajerdi, S.M., Eshete, B., Gjomemo, R., Venkatakrishnan, V.: POIROT: aligning attack behavior with kernel audit records for cyber threat hunting. In: Proceedings of the 2019 ACM SIGSAC Conference on Computer and Communications Security, pp. 1795–1812 (2019)

32. Milajerdi, S.M., Gjomemo, R., Eshete, B., Sekar, R., Venkatakrishnan, V.: HOLMES: real-time apt detection through correlation of suspicious information flows. In: 2019 IEEE Symposium on Security and Privacy (SP), pp. 1137–1152. IEEE (2019)

33. MISP: Open Source Threat Intelligence Platform & Open Standards For Threat Information Sharing (2019). https://www.misp-project.org/

34. Mitre: Structured Threat Information eXpression (STIX) (2018). https://stixproject.github.io

35. Oprea, A., Li, Z., Yen, T.F., Chin, S.H., Alrwais, S.: Detection of early-stage enterprise infection by mining large-scale log data. In: 2015 45th Annual IEEE/IFIP International Conference on Dependable Systems and Networks, pp. 45–56. IEEE (2015)

36. Pasquier, T., et al.: Practical whole-system provenance capture. In: Proceedings of the 2017 Symposium on Cloud Computing, pp. 405–418 (2017)

37. Paszke, A., et al.: Pytorch: an imperative style, high-performance deep learning library. In: Wallach, H., Larochelle, H., Beygelzimer, A., d'Alché-Buc, F., Fox, E., Garnett, R. (eds.) Advances in Neural Information Processing Systems, vol. 32, pp. 8024–8035. Curran Associates, Inc. (2019). http://papers.neurips.cc/paper/9015-pytorch-an-imperative-style-high-performance-deep-learning-library.pdf

38. Pei, K., et al.: HERCULE: attack story reconstruction via community discovery on correlated log graph. In: Proceedings of the 32nd Annual Conference on Computer Security Applications, pp. 583–595 (2016)

39. Pienta, R., Tamersoy, A., Tong, H., Chau, D.H.: MAGE: matching approximate patterns in richly-attributed graphs. In: 2014 IEEE International Conference on Big Data (Big Data), pp. 585–590. IEEE (2014)

40. Pohly, D.J., McLaughlin, S., McDaniel, P., Butler, K.: Hi-fi: collecting high-fidelity whole-system provenance. In: Proceedings of the 28th Annual Computer Security Applications Conference, pp. 259–268 (2012)

41. Qureshi, R.J., Ramel, J.-Y., Cardot, H.: Graph based shapes representation and recognition. In: Escolano, F., Vento, M. (eds.) GbRPR 2007. LNCS, vol. 4538, pp. 49–60. Springer, Heidelberg (2007). https://doi.org/10.1007/978-3-540-72903-7_5

42. Řehůřek, R., Sojka, P.: Software framework for topic modelling with large corpora. In: Proceedings of the LREC 2010 Workshop on New Challenges for NLP Frameworks, Valletta, Malta, pp. 45–50. ELRA, May 2010. http://is.muni.cz/publication/884893/en

43. Riesen, K., Emmenegger, S., Bunke, H.: A novel software toolkit for graph edit distance computation. In: Kropatsch, W.G., Artner, N.M., Haxhimusa, Y., Jiang, X. (eds.) GbRPR 2013. LNCS, vol. 7877, pp. 142–151. Springer, Heidelberg (2013). https://doi.org/10.1007/978-3-642-38221-5_15

44. Smith, J. (2021). https://libraetd.lib.virginia.edu/public_view/5138jf509. Accessed 4 Mar 2021

45. Socher, R., Chen, D., Manning, C.D., Ng, A.: Reasoning with neural tensor networks for knowledge base completion. In: Advances in Neural Information Processing Systems, pp. 926–934 (2013)

46. Song, W., Yin, H., Liu, C., Song, D.: DeepMem: learning graph neural network models for fast and robust memory forensic analysis. In: Proceedings of the 2018 ACM SIGSAC Conference on Computer and Communications Security, pp. 606–618 (2018)

47. Sun, X., Dai, J., Liu, P., Singhal, A., Yen, J.: Using bayesian networks for probabilistic identification of zero-day attack paths. IEEE Trans. Inf. Forensics Secur. **13**(10), 2506–2521 (2018)

48. Tong, H., Faloutsos, C., Gallagher, B., Eliassi-Rad, T.: Fast best-effort pattern matching in large attributed graphs. In: Proceedings of the 13th ACM SIGKDD International Conference on Knowledge Discovery and Data Mining, pp. 737–746 (2007)
49. Wang, Q., et al.: You are what you do: Hunting stealthy malware via data provenance analysis. In: Proceedings of the Symposium on Network and Distributed System Security (NDSS) (2020)
50. Wang, S., et al.: Heterogeneous graph matching networks for unknown malware detection. In: Proceedings of the 28th International Joint Conference on Artificial Intelligence, pp. 3762–3770. AAAI Press (2019)
51. Xiong, C., et al.: CONAN: a practical real-time APT detection system with high accuracy and efficiency. IEEE Trans. Depend. Secur. Comput. (2020)
52. Xu, X., Liu, C., Feng, Q., Yin, H., Song, L., Song, D.: Neural network-based graph embedding for cross-platform binary code similarity detection. In: Proceedings of the 2017 ACM SIGSAC Conference on Computer and Communications Security, pp. 363–376 (2017)
53. Zhu, Z., Dumitras, T.: ChainSmith: automatically learning the semantics of malicious campaigns by mining threat intelligence reports. In: 2018 IEEE European Symposium on Security and Privacy (EuroS&P), pp. 458–472. IEEE (2018)

SIEMA: Bringing Advanced Analytics to Legacy Security Information and Event Management

Pejman Najafi$^{(\boxtimes)}$, Feng Cheng, and Christoph Meinel

Hasso Plattner Institute, University of Potsdam, Potsdam, Germany
{pejman.najafi,feng.cheng,christoph.meinel}@hpi.de

Abstract. Within today's organizations, a Security Information and Event Management (SIEM) system is the centralized repository expected to aggregate all security-relevant data. While the primary purpose of SIEM solutions has been regulatory compliance, more and more organizations recognize the value of these systems for threat detection due to their holistic view of the entire enterprise. Today's mature Security Operation Centers dedicate several teams to threat hunting, pattern/correlation rule creation, and alert monitoring. However, traditional SIEM systems lack the capability for advanced analytics as they were designed for different purposes using technologies that are now more than a decade old. In this paper, we discuss the requirements for a next-generation SIEM system that emphasizes analytical capabilities to allow advanced data science and engineering. Next, we propose a reference architecture that can be used to design such systems. We describe our experience in implementing a next-gen SIEM with advanced analytical capabilities, both in academia and industry. Lastly, we illustrate the importance of advanced analytics within today's SIEM with a simple yet complex use case of beaconing detection.

Keywords: Reference architecture · Next-gen SIEM · Advanced analytic · Big data · Cybersecurity

1 Introduction

Nowadays, an indispensable tool in any organization's arsenal is a Security Information and Event Management (SIEM) system, used as a centralized repository of all aggregated security-related data. The primary source of these data is log data, produced by IT systems across the enterprise's landscape, such as security devices, network infrastructure, host and endpoint systems, applications, and cloud services. Other sources of data include network telemetry, information about inventories, users, assets, and vulnerabilities.

Although originally, the primary purpose of SIEM solutions was to meet regulatory and compliance requirements (e.g., PCI DSS, HIPAA, and SOX), their capability to assist in heterogeneous data correlation, threat hunting, and

© ICST Institute for Computer Sciences, Social Informatics and Telecommunications Engineering 2021
Published by Springer Nature Switzerland AG 2021. All Rights Reserved
J. Garcia-Alfaro et al. (Eds.): SecureComm 2021, LNICST 398, pp. 25–43, 2021.
https://doi.org/10.1007/978-3-030-90019-9_2

monitoring [16] would soon come to play, having more and more companies realizing their ability to detect early, targeted attacks and advanced persistent threats [11]. This would become increasingly important as the years passed since cyber attacks had advanced in sophistication and complexity, rendering the perimeter defenses used by companies at the time insufficient. Therefore, SIEM solutions would come to fill that gap by providing visibility when the traditional defenses (e.g., Antivirus, Firewalls, Intrusion Detection Systems, etc.) are insufficient.

The assumption here is that if a threat has managed to bypass traditional defense perimeters, we expect to see traces of its activities somewhere in the events and logs captured within the SIEM system. Thus, the analysis of such data can be the last safety net to catch potential threats that might slip through.

In the last few years, there has been an increasing interest in analyzing such data for malware detection, both in academia and industry. The industry has taken a more heuristic-based approach [4]. For instance, defining specific patterns and rules such as *alert if Microsoft Word spawns Command-line*. In comparison, the research community has been evaluating statistical, machine learning [18,31] as well as data [28] and graph mining-based approaches [8,13,14].

While these approaches have proven to be effective and successful in academia, their adaptation is yet to be done by industry. The majority of today's SIEM solutions are unable to perform the necessary data analysis. Their architectures are based on proprietary technologies designed in the early 2000s. Since then, we have experienced significant technological advancement, especially in the realm of big data analytics and deep learning. Technologies such as Spark and Hadoop can support heavy data computation and processing and have found application in many industries. Many of today's organizations utilize big data pipelines and analytics to enable data-driven decision making, e.g., LinkedIn [26], Facebook [27]. Therefore, the translation of such work in the cybersecurity industry could be proven invaluable in meeting the ever-changing threat landscape.

In this paper, we outline the requirements needed to build a next-generation SIEM system that would enable advanced analytics whilst supporting traditional SIEM capabilities (Sect. 4.1). Subsequently, we describe the reference architecture allowing individuals to build such systems (Sect. 4.2). Next, we present our experimental setups in two scenarios: an in-house research workbench and a real-world enterprise setup (Sect. 5). Lastly, we discuss a case study highlighting the need for next-gen SIEM with advance analytical capabilities (Sect. 6).

The main contributions of this paper are summarized below:

- Describing the main requirements for a next-gen SIEM with advanced analytical capabilities, hence, Security Information/Event Management and Analytics (SIEMA).
- Outlining the Reference Architecture (RA) for SIEMA with the description of the main components.
- Providing our learnings when implementing and deploying a SIEMA system in a real-world setting.
- Presenting beaconing detection as a case study to highlight the need and value of a SIEM system with analytical capabilities.

2   Background

2.1   Intrusion Detection System

An Intrusion Detection System (IDS) is a monitoring system that is typically installed on a single system attempting to detect suspicious activities and generates alerts that will be consumed by a Security Operator Center (SOC) analysts for further investigation. IDS systems are usually categorized into Host-Based IDS (HIDS) and Network-Based IDS (NIDS) [19]. While HIDs are typically installed on endpoints (hosts) to monitoring operating system resources, NIDs are typically deployed on intermediary network nodes to monitor network traffic.

2.2   Security Information and Event Management

A SIEM system integrates two formerly heterogeneous systems, a Security Information Management (SIM) system and a Security Event Management (SEM) system. SEM systems were originally designed as a tool to provide real-time monitoring for security events and alerts oriented to identify and manage threats. In comparison, SIM systems were designed as a log management tool for record-keeping and reporting of security-related events supporting compliance, forensic investigation, and analysis of security threats [1]. SIEM systems were raised as the result of integrating SIM and SEM to simplify the IT landscape. Since then, these systems have evolved to support a wide variety of needs.

One of the limitations of IDS systems is their limited ability to have a holistic view of the IT landscape to support better decision making, i.e., event correlation. For instance, while a failed login event is nothing to concern with, multiple failed logins to a different host by a single user is concerning. This can only be recognized while correlating events from various endpoints. That is why over time, SIEM systems have evolved to also act as an IDS system supporting threat detection as the last perimeter of defense.

Gartner research group [24] characterized the main requirements for Security Information and Event Management systems as follows:

- **Information and Event Management:** The main requirement for SIEM systems remains as the collection and storage of events and logs from heterogeneous devices in the organization, allowing SOC analysts to monitor the landscape, providing visualization, reporting, and alerting mechanisms. These trends can be created based on real-time and/or historical data to identify patterns that can aid in gaining insight into high-risk behavior. The report can also be used to measure the status against compliance regulations and standards such as PCI DSS, GDPR, HIPAA, and SOX.
- **Threat Hunting and Investigation:** SIEM systems are expected to be the centralized repository holding all security-relevant information and event. These systems are used by SOC analysts to freely explore and analyze data, hunting for threats, or investigating known security incidents. Thus the search features and functionality is fundamental in a SIEM tool. This requires the platform to run efficient ad-hoc queries against massive amounts of data.

– **Rule-based Pattern Matching for Signature-Based Threat Detection:** Today's SIEM systems are highly utilized for threat detection using a rule-based correlation engine [16]. These rules (patterns and signatures) can be as simple as: "alert if there are more than k authentication failures" or as sophisticated as multi-step patterns with dynamic conditions.

– **Automated Correlation and Enrichment:** One of the other most essential features of SIEM systems is the capability to correlate events from disparate sources allowing analysts to see the bigger picture. While the SOC analyst may correlate and join data as part of their hunting/investigation, the ability of the system to automatically enrich certain data points with others may enhance the SOC hunting and investigation activities. For example, the real-time correlation of proxy logs, asset/user information, and DHCP logs would significantly assist during incident handling and response.

– **Cyber Threat Intelligence (CTI) and Open-Source Intelligence (OSINT):** Due to the value of OSINT and CTI, the majority of today's SIEM systems have evolved to support the ingestion of Cyber Threat Intelligence, such as lists of known malicious file hashes, IPs, domains, or other Indicators of Compromise (IOCs), as well as Open-Source Intelligence such as vulnerability data, common weaknesses, domain registrars, etc. The ingested CTI and OSINT enable the development of additional use cases, such as correlation rules based on the IOCs or risk assessment via vulnerability analysis.

3   Related Work

There are numerous commercial SIEM tools. Gartner [16] provides a good overview of the major providers in the SIEM market. The majority of the leading solutions are still based on legacy technologies and architectures. Nevertheless, there are those new players that attempt to bring big data architectures and analytics into Security Information and Event Management.

Gartner [16] identifies Exabeam[1] and Securonix[2] as the top contender for complex security monitoring use cases with advanced threat detection capabilities. The community also identifies these SIEM systems as one of the first truly scalable next-gen SIEM systems, as they both utilize big data technologies such as Hadoop, Apache Spark, Apache Kafka, and trends such as Data Lake, Lambda architecture, stream and batch processing, advanced analytics, and User and Entity Behavior Analytics (UEBA).

There also several open-source attempts to bring SIEM and big data architectures and analytics closer together. Excellent examples of such projects are: Apache Metron [6], Wazuh [32], Apache Spot [7], and Apache Eagle [5].

SANS Institute provides an overview and a guide for the critical features of next-gen SIEM [11]. Menges et al. [20] discuss the shortcoming of traditional SIEM systems such as advanced forensic analysis and propose an extended architecture addressing those shortcomings. Wheelus et al. [33] propose and evaluate

---

[1] Exabeam, https://www.exabeam.com/.

[2] Securonix, https://www.securonix.com/.

a big data architecture for real-time network traffic processing. The authors discuss several case studies highlighting the potential values in big data analytics in the context of cybersecurity.

In this paper, we provide a reference architecture that abstracts the majority of the above works' capabilities. Ullah et al. [29] provides a comprehensive systematic literature review of frequently reported quality attributes and architectural tactics for big data cybersecurity analytic systems. Each of these tactics can be abstracted by the proposed RA in this paper.

To the best of our knowledge, there are no previous efforts in addressing the limitation of today's SIEM systems, particularly in terms of advanced analytical capabilities.

4   SIEMA

In this section, we first provide an overview of the next-gen SIEM system's main business and architectural requirements. Having covered the main requirements, we provide our reference architecture while highlighting the main components of the blueprint for anyone who wishes to design such systems.

4.1   Requirements

Before proceeding to the reference architecture, it is crucial to outline the added requirements for the next-gen SIEM system. We categorized the main requirements into two groups: Business requirements (BR) and Architectural Requirements (AR).

BR1. Data Science (Advanced Analytics): One of the main limitations of traditional SIEM systems is their reliance on signature/heuristic-based threat detection, limiting the detection only to previously known threats. Finding truly unknowns requires the utilization of state-of-the-art data science (statistics, machine learning, and data mining algorithms). In this regard, the platform should acknowledge state-of-the-art data science tools and techniques [3].

Data science can also be used to eliminate static rules which pose high false-positive rates. For example, instead of looking at 10 authentication failures within 1 min (i.e., attempt to find brute force attacks), one could learn the threshold per user and endpoint, thus reducing false positives.

BR2. Data Engineering (Complex Data Processing): As different use cases may require different shapes of data, the platform should be able to handle data engineering pipelines. This can include data aggregation, correlation, enrichment, normalization, parsing, validation, tagging, duplication, and transformation. In this regard, a next-gen SIEM should allow data scientists, data engineers, and SOC analysts to seamlessly develop, combine, manage, and maintain different data processing pipelines.

AR1. Distributed, Scalable, and Fault-Tolerant: A next-gen SIEM is expected to handle big data with 3Vs: large *volume*, high rate of generation (*velocity*), and heterogeneity of the types of structured and unstructured data (*variety*). Hence, to cope with the volume, velocity, and variety of data produced by today's enterprises, the platform should be scalable and elastic. To achieve this, the best practices in distributed systems (e.g., distributed storage and processing) should be followed and adhered across all architectural levels of the platform.

In a distributed setting, availability and resilience to failure become a challenging yet crucial aspect of the system. In this regard, the platform is also expected to be fault-tolerant and available during a failure/outage, such as network outages or hardware failures.

AR2. Extensible: Today's technology landscape is evolving faster than ever. The most relevant technologies or solutions of today may be irrelevant in a few years. A next-gen SIEM should be able to undergo numerous modifications and extensions to stay relevant in an ever-changing technological world, e.g., able to adopt a new distributed processing framework.

AR3. Open: Today's open-source community is very active and often ahead of its commercial competitors. Therefore, the platform needs to respect open-source solutions and technologies by allowing the adoption of open-source. This will ensure the system's relevance with state-of-the-art technologies.

Furthermore, one of the main criticisms of today's legacy SIEMs is their locked-in data model. A next-gen SIEM should have an open data model respecting the users and data portability.

AR4. Integration: The platform should have standard methods to interface and integrate with other external tools or systems via APIs. This allows other tools to better appreciate the values provided by the next-gen SIEM.

AR5. Data Lake for All Storage Requirements: Storage is a core aspect of a next-gen SIEM. Different use cases require different storage systems, from a relational database to a distributed file store. Particularly, to enable advanced analytics, new data lake architectures are needed.

AR6. Modular Data Ingestion: A next-gen SIEM is expected to ingest a variety of data. These data can be from external sources, such as vulnerability data, indicators of compromise, related OSINT. It can also be from internal sources, such as event logs from network and security systems (e.g., Intrusion

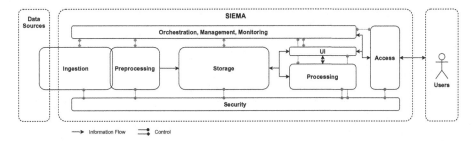

Fig. 1. Module decomposition of the reference architecture

detection systems, endpoint security, firewalls, VPN, proxy, DNS), applications, endpoints, assets, network topologies, security configuration, and policies. Thus, a next-gen SIEM is expected to ingest data from both external and internal sources. The ingestion should mainly expect authenticated incoming data and the possibility of crawling or collecting, e.g., to crawl related OSINT.

AR7. Security and Privacy: A next-gen SIEM is also expected to guarantee security (security by design). This includes but is not limited to: privilege separation, access control, encryption at rest and transit, privacy, anonymization/pseudonymization, least privilege principle, access, and audit logging.

4.2 Reference Architecture

We design our RA based on decade-long experience and knowledge revolving around the best practices in designing big data architectures and pipelines, e.g., LinkedIn [26], Facebook [27], and other reference architectures [17]. Figure 1 shows the high-level reference architecture for the proposed SIEM. Figure 2 illustrates the system workflow consisting of five main stages.

Fig. 2. SIEMA proposed workflow

Data Ingestion and Collection: This layer is expected to consist of a collection of extendable ingestors and collectors, each designed to ingest a particular data source. Data sources can be *internal* data, such as event logs, telemetries, inventories, or *external* data, such as OSINT, and vulnerability data.

These modules can either accept authenticated data being forwarded (push model) or pull particular data points. Data being forwarded can either come directly from the data sources or being forwarded by a remote ingestor node. The pull mechanism is expected to be limited due to the lack of a dedicated agent.

In Sect. 7, we discuss the extension of SIEMA to allow better collection and response, hence introducing Security Orchestration, Automation and Response (SOAR) like capabilities.

Pre-processing: The next stage in the system is pre-processing, i.e., data validation, cleansing, optimization (e.g., de-duplication), parsing, and basic transformation (e.g., standardizing the timestamps), and basic enrichment/tagging (e.g., tagging the events according to their type and source).

All pre-processing steps are expected to be simple, efficient, and scalable. Further enrichment and correlation are expected to be carried out by the analytic/processing modules.

After pre-processing, the data shall be dumped on messaging queues or directly to file storage where the primary data processing pipelines could take the lead for more advanced data processing (e.g., normalization), storage (e.g., ETL, indexing, etc.) or analytics.

Storage: Similar to the data lake architectural pattern, storage is a key and fundamental component for RA. The main objective of the data storage layer is to provide reliable and efficient access to persisted data. Part of this is to offer multiple representations for single data records to accommodate different use cases, e.g., OLAP style data analytics, OLTP queries, or string searches.

Note that the storage system of such next-gen SIEM is expected to be highly scalable and agile. This is integral, as organizational and business needs change over time, calling for adjustments in technologies and environment setups.

One can categorize storage needs based on latency, throughput, access patterns, and data type. Some examples of storage needs in the context of a next-gen SIEM are: NoSQL transactional database for results. Index store and search engine to allow string search on event logs for efficient ad-hoc threat hunting and investigation. A Distributed file/object-store to satisfy data lake requirements for advanced and distributed analytics and machine learning models. A queuing mechanism to enable the reliable transmission of data across different processing layers. For instance, a messaging queue that enables an enrichment module to enhance the result of an anomaly detection algorithm, i.e., outliers are pushed to a queue, where the enrichment module is subscribing to, enriching the outliers with related contexts. An in-memory caching mechanism to allow multiple executors or workers within a processing module to exchange data efficiently. A graph database to store the relationships between various internal and external entities.

Processing: The Processing layer is responsible for efficient, scalable, distributed, and reliable processing. At a high level, it can serve two main purposes: *data engineering* and *data science*. The data engineering sub-layer is responsible for data processing and transformation, e.g., event correlation and enrichment, normalization, ETL pipelines, storage optimization (compression, partitioning, bucketing), pattern matching, etc. On the other hand, the data science-based modules are concerned with knowledge extraction from the data, e.g., machine learning, data mining, statistical analysis, graph analytics, etc. It is worth noting that analytical processing can be interactive, batch, and stream.

Access: The access layer is the interaction point of the system with external actors. These actors can be SOC analysts, data scientists, data engineers, administrators, managers, or external APIs. Each actor is expected to require interaction with a specific part of the platform for a particular reason. The access layer is responsible for managing these interactions while ensuring security and load balancing. For example, a SOC analyst requiring an interactive interaction with the platform's search capabilities to investigate threats, defining rules for the correlation engine and dashboard to view the alert, and visualizing the trends.

UI: The user interface layer is responsible for abstracting actors' interactions with storage or processing modules. For instance, a UI that enables SOC analysts to run their query against the storage system, or the data science notebooks designed to allow the data scientist to interactively analyze data loaded from the storage layer in the processing layer.

Orchestration, Management, and Monitoring: This layer has three main responsibilities: orchestration, management (administration), and monitoring.

The orchestration module is responsible for providing configuration, management, and coordination between the various platform layers and their modules. This includes job submission, collectors configurations, data engineering pipelines, etc. In addition, this module is also expected to provide monitoring capabilities for every module within each layer, e.g., monitoring the analytical jobs and their status.

The administration/management module is responsible for the configuration, provisioning, and control of the underlying infrastructure and the platform itself, e.g., managing the underlying storage system.

Lastly, the platform auditing module supports the health monitoring of the system and its underlying heterogeneous systems. For instance, it is expected that the storage layer will consist of multiple systems, e.g., distributed files system, NoSQL database, a messaging queue. In this regard, this module should allow administrators to monitor the health and performance of these systems.

Security: Given the nature of our next-gen SIEM system, there are concerns around the security and privacy of such big data platforms. In this regard, this layer is responsible for the security of the platform and its underlying data. This includes enforcement of access rules, restricting access based on classification or need-to-know, and securing data at rest or in transit.

5   Experimental Setup and Deployments

We have endeavored two implementations of the proposed RA, in-house academic research workbench and real-world experimental setup in an international enterprise's infrastructure.

5.1   In-House Research Workbench

Our first attempt to develop and deploy a SIEMA system according to the proposed RA was done on a cluster consisting of two Dell PowerEdge (R730, R820) and five Fujitsu Primergy RX600 with a total of 1,864 GB RAM, 24 CPUs (200 total cores), and 4 TB storage interconnected via 10 Gb optical fiber. In addition, an external Network Attached Storage (NAS) connected to the cluster via 3× 10 Gb optical fiber. Table 1 presents the leading underlying technologies used for this setup.

Table 1. In-house SIEMA as first research POC.

Technology	Reference	Usage
Kubernetes	Orchestration/Management	Backbone system and orchestrator
Ansible	Orchestration/Management	Platform operation and administeration
Zookeeper	Orchestration	Configuration maintenance and synchronization
Apache Spark	Processing	Distributed processing and analytics engine
Presto	Processing	Distributed processing (SQL query engine)
Apache Livy	Management	Multi-tenancy and job management
Apache Kafka	Storage	Distributed messaging and queueing
Hadoop HDFS	Storage	Distributed file system and object store
Elasticsearch	Storage	Search engine, index store
Prometheus	Storage	Time series database for metrics regarding the platform health
HBase	Storage	Distributed NOSQL data store on top of HDFS
Apache Nifi	Processing, UI	Orchestration and data preprocessing
Kibana	UI	UI for interaction with the search engine
Grafana	UI	UI for platform health monitoring
Zeppelin	UI	Notebook for ad-hoc data science
CMAK	UI, Orchestration	Cluster manager for Apache Kafka
Hue	UI	Hadoop interface

The platform designed was utilized during multiple successful research to apply different data mining and machine learning approaches to the problem of malicious Domain/IP detection using proxy and DNS logs, resulting in multiple publications [21, 22].

5.2 Real-World Enterprise Setup

We also had the opportunity to explore a SIEMA system in a real-world setting with a large international company with quite a mature cyber defense. This company had a cloud-based legacy SIEM continuously utilized for threat hunting, monitoring, and rule-based threat detection. We attempted to build around it with analytical capabilities to explore the potential values. We utilized available cloud-based services compliant with the companies policies, such as Azure Data Factory, Azure Data Lake Storage, and Databricks, to enable advanced data engineering and science.

The first significant value of this platform was the ability to run basic aggregation, correlation, and statistical queries over larger time frames (over 100 terabytes of data) which would not be possible with traditional SIEM systems as they were designed for only interactive investigation and searches.

The next value was the ability to create successful advanced use cases using the underlying data (EDR, proxy, DNS). Examples of such use cases are beaconing detection, malicious processes detection, suspicious DNS and proxy requests, windows logon anomalies, and user behavior analytics over weeks of data. The result of these use cases led to the rise of multiple incidents missed by traditional rule-based detections.

Lastly, the ability to train a model to rate and prioritize traditional SIEM alerts according to past experiences. Most of today's organizations receive $17,000$ alerts per week where more than 51% of the alerts are false positives, and only 4% of the alerts get adequately investigated [2]. Therefore, prioritization of alerts can help the SOC analyst to focus their efforts better. This was the last use case, designed to read past investigated alerts, their artifacts, and the associated responses (thus labels) to train a model that attempts to prioritize the new alerts according to their potential to be true positives. This prioritization was achieved by adding a confidence score to the alert passed to the traditional SIEM dashboard. The initial impression and qualitative evaluation of this use case seemed promising.

6   Case Study: Beaconing Detection

To better understand the need for advanced analytical capabilities within today's SIEM, we decided to prepare a simplified experiment performed on our real-world setup. Particularly a heavy yet straightforward use case of beaconing detection.

One of the characteristics of sophisticated cyber threats, such as Advanced Persistent Threats (APTs), is periodic attempts to reach out to the command and control (C&C) infrastructure controlled by the adversary to receive further instructions. Such heartbeat and callback behavior is known as beaconing.

Malware beaconing is typically characterized by two main configurations: sleep time and jitter (variations from central value). The beaconing frequency can vary from slow and stealth to fast and aggressive (from a few seconds to hours or even days sleep time). Nevertheless, generally, it is expected that the adversaries maintain regular beacons for better visibility and control of the infected machines [15].

While at first glance, beaconing detection seems simple, it is quite challenging:

- **Temporal Analysis in Big Data**: In order to detect beaconing, one has to analyze the traffic behavior of all source and destination pairs over an extended period of time. This makes beaconing detection a big data problem.
- **Intentional Randomness and Jitter**: One of the other challenges with beaconing detection is the adversarial strategies to hid the beaconing behavior. One of the common ways the adversaries attempt to prevent detection is by varying the sleep time to make it appear as normal traffic. Other methods can include omitting certain beacons or injecting additional random beacons.
- **False Positives (Benign Applications)**: While we discussed the maliciousness of beaconing behavior, there are several scenarios in which beaconing is an integral part of the communication and does not indicate maliciousness. For instance, Network Time Protocol (NTP), automated software patching, mailing clients, updates, or keep alive traffic in long-lived sessions may also appear as beacons.
- **External Factors**: There can be unanticipated external factors that can introduce errors while looking at the periodicity, such as the host (endpoint) going offline or network interruptions.

6.1   Detection Approach

Beaconing detection has been studied widely in the literature [12, 15, 25, 30], and while there are many ways to develop a beaconing detection approach, here we present one of the simplest ones using statistical methods.

(i) *Data Preparation*: We start by pre-processing the network connection events keeping only the source (host unique identifier), the destination (e.g., IP address and port), and the timestamp fields. One could also validate to ensure the destinations are valid and timestamps are in Unix Timestamp format.

(ii) *Delta Time Calculations*: Next, we group connections by source and destination and sort them by their timestamp. This will allow us to calculate the time deltas between connections of each source and destination pair. For instance, if host *H1* connects to destination *D1* at the time *t1* and *t2*, the time delta between these two connections is $t2 - t1$.

(iii) *Clean Time Deltas*: To ensure the detection quality, we need to filter out bad entries, e.g., border time delta (nulls) - indicating no previous connections, or time deltas equal to zero - indicating network issues resulting in multiple connections in a very short time.

As mentioned, one of the challenges with beaconing detection can also be external factors such as network interruptions or the host going offline (host shutting down). We tackle this challenge by filtering out outliers in time deltas for each source and destination pair using Interquartile Range [34]. This ensures that when the host has gone offline, the time delta showing the big gap is treated as an outlier, hence eliminated from further calculations.

(iv) *Periodicity via Average and Standard Deviations*: While there are more sophisticated ways to detect periodicity [9,10,23], here we take the simplest approach. We calculate the average and the standard deviation of time deltas for each source and destination pair to estimate the periodicity of connections.

(vi) *Destination's Reputation*: To tackle the false positives (i.e., benign applications), we also calculate the prevalence of each destination, i.e., how many hosts (sources) have connected to this destination during the analysis period. This can be achieved by simple grouping and counting.

(vii) *Scoring*: At this point, for each source and destination, we have the average and standard deviation of time deltas, number of connections (beacons), and the prevalence of the destination. One can now define certain heuristics to score the beaconing behavior to prioritize the alerts. For this case study, we simplify our scoring to three main functions:

- Low Coefficient of Variation: The coefficient of variation is defined as the ratio of the standard deviation to the mean.
  While a low standard deviation of time deltas means perfect periodicity (almost all time deltas are the same), it does not consider how big the average is. That is why the relative standard deviation (coefficient of variation) can help by looking at the ratio.
  We utilize an exponential function (Eq. 1) to transform the coefficient of variation into a score. The reasoning here is that all low ratios (an indication of better periodicity and beaconing behavior) should be scored closer to 1, and as the ratio gets bigger, it should have a decaying effect (logarithmic) in the scores, getting closer to 0.

$$S_{cv} = e^{-\sqrt{\frac{\sigma}{\mu}}} \tag{1}$$

  where μ and σ is the average and standard deviation of time deltas respectively, and S_{cv} is the score derived from the coefficient of variation.

- Low Destination Reputation: Destinations with high reputations (largely accessed by the majority of the endpoint) typically indicate benignness. That is why we would prioritize those beaconing alerts whose destination is rarely observed. More specifically:

$$S_{rep} = e^{-\frac{p(dest)}{k}} \tag{2}$$

  where $p(dest)$ indicates the prevalence of the destination (i.e., how many hosts have been observed connecting to this destination). k is a numerical constant internally determined based on domain knowledge as the threshold to smooth the curve (i.e., after k the scores should smoothen as we don't care anymore). For example, if k is set to 100 that means as

$p(dest)$ gets closer and pass the threshold of 100 hosts, the score should be low, and there is no significant difference between 300 to 600 to 1000, as we only care for low numbers (e.g., 1 or 10 hosts).

- Beaconing Consistency: Sometimes, just the destination prevalence is insufficient to filter out benign applications, particularly updates. In this regard, one could take yet another attempt to eliminate those beaconing-like behaviors. A malicious beaconing could be characterized by its consistency, whereas some benign behavior such as an update will only appear for a certain time. Thus, one could analyze the consistency of the beaconing behavior by looking at the ratio of the number of the beacons and their average delta time to the analysis range.

$$S_{con} = \frac{b \cdot \mu}{t_e - t_s} \tag{3}$$

where b is the number of beacons, μ is the average, $t_e - t_s$ is the analysis range (e.g., 86400 s).

Note that while here we discussed only three simple scoring functions on top of the information available with our case study, one could design multiple other heuristics to reduce the false-positive rate. Lastly, we aggregate the scores via an aggregator function such as weighted average to derive a single score.

(vii) *Alerting*: Having a final score for each source and destination pair, we could sort the alerts descending and take the first k items (where k is set by the rate the analyst can handle). One could also do further analysis for the distributions of the scores to dynamically set k.

6.2 Experiment Setup

We carried out our experiment for this case study within the premise of a large international organization. Particularly, we implemented the described methodology for beaconing detection as a use case within the enterprise SIEM system as well as our analytical platform (discussed in Sect. 5.2). Therefore, the implementations were identical in terms of their logic.

While we cannot discuss the details of the traditional SIEM system used by the enterprise due to NDA, we can confirm that the SIEM system is among the top SIEM leaders identified by the Gartner Research Group [16]. Furthermore, the setup is among one of the largest enterprise SIEM setups, designed to handle the ingestion of more than 10 TB per day.

Our analytical platform for this experiment was configured on Databricks with 5 "Standard_D32s_v3" workers. Thus, having a big data platform backed up by Apache Spark with a total of: 640-GB Memory, 160 vCPU Cores, 1280 GB temp SSD storage.

We ran our main experiment on one day of network connections collected from an EDR tool (172.5 million events) which spanned to approximately 102 GB.

6.3   Results

Running the described beaconing detection on the traditional SIEM took 45 min to go over 89 million events before reaching the disk usage limit (set by the enterprise) and return 246 events. This is because traditional SIEMs are not designed for large-scale analysis (i.e., distributed processing). They tend to aggregate the events of interest into a single server where the calculations take place. In contrast, our analytical environment supported by Databricks and Apache Spark was able to go through all 172.5 million events and finishing the use case within only 26 s.

Although there are many variables in place that make this comparison unfair (e.g., the clusters sizes not being the same, the implementations of a simple calculation such as mean, etc.), one can observe the enormous gap between the capabilities.

One of the other expectations of such analytical platforms is their ability to scale out. Figure 3 shows the runtime of beaconing detection as we add more workers to the run the use case.

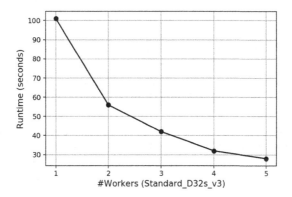

Fig. 3. Beaconing detection use case run-time on databricks based on the number of workers.

Lastly, while we could not run the use case for 5 weekdays on the traditional SIEM, we could run it in the analytical environment. In this regard, the described setup (with 5 "Standard_D32s_v3" workers) could analyze approximately 960 million events (over 550 GB) in 126 s.

6.4   Discussion and Lessons Learnt

With a simple statistical-based use case, we highlighted that traditional SIEM systems are not designed for advanced analytics. One could imagine how more sophisticated analytics, e.g., machine learning, data mining, and graph analytics, will further challenge traditional SIEMs.

As highlighted by most related work, the ability to run complex data analytics is one of the most critical capabilities required for the next-gen SIEM systems to give us a fighting chance against previously unknown threats.

Nevertheless, we cannot underestimate the need for legacy SIEMs, particularly when investigating incidents and alerts. While the analytical platform will take a long time to search, as it requires touching almost all files, the legacy SIEMs are designed for optimized searching, allowing a SOC analyst to run ad-hoc queries investigating incidents and correlating data on-demand. For instance, in our example, while the legacy SIEM took 23 s to search the context of one of the alerts, the analytical platform took more than 1 min. Note that the searches are on one day of data; as the time frame gets bigger, the analytical platform will take even longer (for random searches). Although one could argue that there are ways to speed up the search, e.g., partitioning, bucketing, indexing, and adding meta-data, it still will not be comparable to traditional SIEMs (i.e., index stores) that are designed for optimized searches.

This highlights the need for next-gen SIEM systems that integrate the capabilities of both big data platforms and legacy SIEMs to provide ultimate value to today's SOCs.

7 Future Work

Today's organizations require more than just a SIEM - they require a fully managed system that can interact and respond. That is why many vendors try to close the gap between SIEM systems and Security Orchestration, Automation, and Response (SOAR) systems.

SOAR systems' capabilities mainly include automation that usually occurs through playbooks, runbooks, and incident response capabilities such as triage, containment, and remediation. However, to provide this automation and response capability, there is a need for a dedicated agent running on each endpoint.

In this work, we explicitly focused on SIEM and analytical capabilities, thus putting data collection and incident response out of the scope. However, in our future work, we would like to extend the reference architecture with an assumption of dedicated agents managed by the platform. This agent can enable new capabilities, such as better event collection, event pre-processing on the edge, asset discovery, vulnerability assessment and scanning, policy and configuration checking, file integrity, service availability monitoring, software inventory, and incident response.

Lastly, we would like to better benchmark and evaluate our implemented SIEMA system's capabilities compared to traditional SIEMs.

8 Conclusion

In this paper, we discussed the limitations of the current SIEM systems, in particular, their ability to perform advanced analytics and utilize state-of-the-art data mining, machine learning, and graph mining approaches. With that in mind, we described the requirements for a next-generation SIEM system with advanced analytical capabilities, hence SIEMA (Security Information/Event Management and Analytics). Next, provided the reference architecture for SIEMA, considering best practices and patterns in big data architectures and pipelines. Next, we described our implementation of such SIEMA under two settings. One, as a research workbench with all open-sources technologies. Second, a version of the proposed architecture in a real-world setting next to an international organization's traditional SIEM system. We also highlighted the value added by the analytical capabilities of such a system to not only help in pushing the research in data mining for threat detection but also developing successful advanced use cases in an industrial setting leading to the detection of genuine threats and incidents. Lastly, we presented beaconing detection as a case study highlighting the limitations of the traditional SIEM systems in comparison to those with analytical capabilities.

We believe the cybersecurity domain, particularly in the industry, is falling behind when it comes to the advancement in data-driven decision-making and data science. One of the main contributing factors to this is the long-delayed evolution of the security systems holding the data (SIEMs), thus limiting the capabilities of SOC analysts to explore statistical and machine learning approaches for threat detection. We hope this paper motivates the design and implementation of next-gen SIEM systems giving more power to SOC analysts, closing the gap between traditional threat hunters and today's data scientists/engineers.

References

1. A Practical Guide to Next-Generation SIEM, Tech. Rep. SENSAGE
2. How many alerts is too many to handle? https://www2.fireeye.com/StopTheNoise-IDC-Numbers-Game-Special-Report.html
3. Improve Threat Detection with Big Data Analytics and AI, Tech. Rep. Databricks
4. Anthony, R.: Detecting security incidents using windows workstation event logs. SANS Institute, InfoSec Reading Room Paper (2013)
5. Apache Software Foundation: Apache eagle. https://eagle.apache.org/
6. Apache metron. https://metron.apache.org/
7. Apache spot. https://spot.apache.org/
8. Chau, D.H.P., Nachenberg, C., Wilhelm, J., Wright, A., Faloutsos, C.: Polonium: tera-scale graph mining and inference for malware detection. In: Proceedings of the 2011 SIAM International Conference on Data Mining, pp. 131–142. SIAM (2011)
9. Elfeky, M.G., Aref, W.G., Elmagarmid, A.K.: Periodicity detection in time series databases. IEEE Trans. Knowl. Data Eng. **17**(7), 875–887 (2005)
10. Elfeky, M.G., Aref, W.G., Elmagarmid, A.K.: Warp: time warping for periodicity detection. In: Fifth IEEE International Conference on Data Mining (ICDM 2005), p. 8. IEEE (2005)
11. Filkins, B.: An Evaluator's Guide to Nextgen SIEM. SANS Institute, Information Security Reading Room (2013)
12. Gardiner, J., Cova, M., Nagaraja, S.: Command & control: understanding, denying and detecting-a review of malware c2 techniques, detection and defences. arXiv preprint arXiv:1408.1136 (2014)

13. Hassan, W.U., Bates, A., Marino, D.: Tactical provenance analysis for endpoint detection and response systems. In: IEEE Symposium on Security and Privacy (SP), vol. 2020, pp. 1172–1189. IEEE (2020)
14. Hassan, W.U., et al.: NODOZE: combatting threat alert fatigue with automated provenance triage. In: Network and Distributed Systems Security Symposium (2019)
15. Hu, X., et al.: Baywatch: robust beaconing detection to identify infected hosts in large-scale enterprise networks. In: 2016 46th Annual IEEE/IFIP International Conference on Dependable Systems and Networks (DSN), pp. 479–490. IEEE (2016)
16. Kavanagh, K., Bussa, T., Sadowski, G.: Magic Quadrant for Security Information and Event Management. Gartner Group Research Note (2020)
17. Klein, J., Buglak, R., Blockow, D., Wuttke, T., Cooper, B.: A reference architecture for big data systems in the national security domain. In: IEEE/ACM 2nd International Workshop on Big Data Software Engineering (BIGDSE), vol. 2016, pp. 51–57. IEEE (2016)
18. Kolosnjaji, B., Zarras, A., Webster, G., Eckert, C.: Deep learning for classification of malware system call sequences. In: Kang, B.H., Bai, Q. (eds.) AI 2016. LNCS (LNAI), vol. 9992, pp. 137–149. Springer, Cham (2016). https://doi.org/10.1007/978-3-319-50127-7_11
19. Liao, H.-J., Lin, C.-H.R., Lin, Y.-C., Tung, K.-Y.: Intrusion detection system: a comprehensive review. J. Netw. Comput. Appl. 36(1), 16–24 (2013)
20. Menges, F., et al.: Introducing DINGfest: an architecture for next generation SIEM systems (2018)
21. Najafi, P., Mühle, A., Pünter, W., Cheng, F., Meinel, C.: MalRank: a measure of maliciousness in SIEM-based knowledge graphs. In: Proceedings of the 35th Annual Computer Security Applications Conference, pp. 417–429 (2019)
22. Najafi, P., Sapegin, A., Cheng, F., Meinel, C.: Guilt-by-association: detecting malicious entities via graph mining. In: Lin, X., Ghorbani, A., Ren, K., Zhu, S., Zhang, A. (eds.) SecureComm 2017. LNICST, vol. 238, pp. 88–107. Springer, Cham (2018). https://doi.org/10.1007/978-3-319-78813-5_5
23. Rasheed, F., Alhajj, R.: STNR: a suffix tree based noise resilient algorithm for periodicity detection in time series databases. Appl. Intell. 32(3), 267–278 (2010)
24. Sadowski, G., Bussa, T., Kavanagh, K.: Critical Capabilities for Security Information and Event Management. Gartner Group Research Note (2020)
25. Shalaginov, A., Franke, K., Huang, X.: Malware beaconing detection by mining large-scale DNS logs for targeted attack identification. In: 18th International Conference on Computational Intelligence in Security Information Systems. WASET (2016)
26. Sumbaly, R., Kreps, J., Shah, S.: The big data ecosystem at linkedin. In: Proceedings of the 2013 ACM SIGMOD International Conference on Management of Data, pp. 1125–1134 (2013)
27. Thusoo, A., et al.: Data warehousing and analytics infrastructure at Facebook. In: Proceedings of the 2010 ACM SIGMOD International Conference on Management of Data, pp. 1013–1020 (2010)
28. Ucci, D., Aniello, L., Baldoni, R.: Survey of machine learning techniques for malware analysis. Comput. Secur. 81, 123–147 (2019)
29. Ullah, F., Babar, M.A.: Architectural tactics for big data cybersecurity analytics systems: a review. J. Syst. Softw. 151, 81–118 (2019)
30. Van Splunder, J.: Periodicity detection in network traffic. Technical Report, Mathematisch Instituut Universiteit Leiden (2015)

31. Wang, Q., et al.: You are what you do: hunting stealthy malware via data prove-
    nance analysis. In: Symposium on Network and Distributed System Security
    (NDSS) (2020)
32. Wazuh: The open source security platform. https://wazuh.com/
33. Wheelus, C., Bou-Harb, E., Zhu, X.: Towards a big data architecture for facilitat-
    ing cyber threat intelligence. In: 2016 8th IFIP International Conference on New
    Technologies, Mobility and Security (NTMS), pp. 1–5. IEEE (2016)
34. Yang, J., Rahardja, S., Fränti, P.: Outlier detection: how to threshold outlier
    scores? In: Proceedings of the International Conference on Artificial Intelligence,
    Information Processing and Cloud Computing, pp. 1–6 (2019)

Automatic Generation of Malware Threat Intelligence from Unstructured Malware Traces

Yuheng Wei and Futai Zou[✉]

School of Cyber Science and Engineering, Shanghai Jiao Tong University,
Shanghai, China
{geralweiyh,zoufutai}@sjtu.edu.cn

Abstract. Sharing plenty and accurate structured Cyber Threat Intelligence (CTI) will play a pivotal role in adapting to rapidly evolving cyber attacks and malware. However, the traditional CTI generation methods are extremely time and labor-consuming. The recent work focuses on extracting CTI from well structured Open Source Intelligence (OSINT). However, many challenges are still to generate CTI and Indicators of Compromise(IoC) from non-human-written malware traces. This work introduces a method to automatically generate concise, accurate and understandable CTI from unstructured malware traces. For a specific class of malware, we first construct the IoC expressions set from malware traces. Furthermore, we combine the generated IoC expressions and other meaningful information in malware traces to organize the threat intelligence which meets open standards such as Structured Threat Information Expression (STIX). We evaluate our algorithm on real-world dataset. The experimental results show that our method achieves a high average recall rate of 89.4% on the dataset and successfully generates STIX reports for every class of malware, which means our methodology is practical enough to automatically generate effective IoC and CTI.

Keywords: Malware · Threat intelligence · Indicators of compromise

1 Introduction

Malware (short for malicious software) has been used as a weapon by the threat actors. Many types of malware, including computer virus, trojans, worms, ransomware, rootkit, and bots, are now active on the Internet, posing threats to Internet users [30]. We can see the crazy malware number growth year by year, referring to many security company's annual reports. Unfortunately, it is hard to win the security war with the rapidly growing and evolving malware using traditional malware analysis methods.

Plenty and accurate structured Cyber Threat Intelligence (CTI) will play a pivotal role in adapting to the rapidly evolving cyber attacks and malware [13]. However, the traditional CTI generation method is extremely time and labor-consuming. Various techniques have been developed for improving malware

J. Garcia-Alfaro et al. (Eds.): SecureComm 2021, LNICST 398, pp. 44–61, 2021.
https://doi.org/10.1007/978-3-030-90019-9_3

detection algorithms and methods, but not for reporting. Traditional CTI generation methods rely on security experts to summarize the massive, easy-to-get but low-value basic data, such as Hash, network traces, and host information. Such an inefficient method is impossible to deal with the rapid development and growth of malware. Security industries or organizations may have collected a large number of malware samples from the Internet; what they need is an effective and robust method to automatically summarize the features of these samples and then generate usable CTI. To address this issue, we need to find a reliable technology or system to analyze threat information and generate structured threat intelligence automatically.

There is extensive research on machine learning based CTI generation methods, especially IoC generation methods based on artificial intelligence algorithms. Many of these machine learning based methods use online security articles or malware analysis results, for example, Symantec's malware or APT reports, as their information sources. Under the intuition that some information that can be used to generate a structured CTI will be presented in a similar way in these articles or malware reports, researchers try to use artificial intelligence algorithms like NLP to extract this useful information. Of course, these machine learning based methods can generate high-quality IoC, however, they only cover well-organized malware analysis reports, which means these are not available methods for those security industries and organizations that only have a large number of raw malware samples. When we try to use machine learning methods like decision tree to generate IoC from malware static analysis and dynamic analysis results, they may generate too complex signatures, and it is hard to use in real malware detection.

This work will introduce a practical methodology to automatically generate concise, accurate, and understandable CTI from unstructured malware traces. Using malware samples collected from the Internet, we obtain malware traces through sandbox analysis. Since IoC is one of the most important parts of CTI, we first propose a method to generate IoC from malware traces. Furthermore, we combine the generated IoC and other meaningful strings in malware traces, such as malware class information, attacker's IP address, and observed intrusion action, to organize a CTI meeting certain standards.

Contributions. Our contributions are as follows:

- We develop a practical and easy-to-deploy methodology to generate structured CTI from raw malware traces automatically. We first get traces of malware samples by sandbox analysis, then generate accurate and concise IoC after data preprocessing. We finally integrate generated IoC and other meaningful information in malware traces to generate well-structured CTI.
- We study the malware sandbox analysis report structure and design several rules for removing low-value strings from it. Usually, the malware traces consist of static analysis and dynamic analysis results, but not all of the strings in the reports help generate IoC and CTI. We design rules to remove meaningless strings in malware traces and only select those features that can represent characteristics well.

- We propose an effective Greedy IoC Generation algorithm, *GIG* for short, to generate concise, accurate, and understandable IoC from malware traces. For a specific class of malware, we first add up all the possible IoC candidates and merge similar expressions into one regular expression based IoC. After that, we use a greedy feature selection algorithm to generate the best IoC for this malware.
- We introduce the method to generate structured CTI following STIX standard, using information from the unstructured malware traces.

2   Background

In this section, we will first introduce the format of IoC and then introduce the OpenIoC standard using in our IoC generation process. We then explain terms of CTI and the Structured Threat Information Expression (STIX).

2.1   Indicators of Compromise

Indicators of compromise is a set of proofs that can be used to identify intrusion on a host or network [19], and now has become one of the most potent threat events detection weapons [26]. An IoC expression consists of *IndicatorItem*, two kinds of condition "`is`" and "`contains`" and a corresponding value field. IoC use operators "`AND`" or "`OR`" to combine several IoC expressions, making it possible to describe the abnormal traces in multiple dimensions. We can identify an intrusion if the traces or logs obtained from the network or host match the IoC condition. OpenIoC is a simple XML based IoC describing schema advised by MANDIANT. It is convenient for us to generate structured IoC following OpenIoC standard, as it only requires six necessary XML tags and simple express grammar. Also can we transform OpenIoC expression into other IoC describing standard.

Besides using hundreds of pre-defined *IndicatorItem* to describe behavior or threat in detail, OpenIoC allows users to define their *IndicatorItem*. This also convenience our IoC generation process, as not all the features can be classified into suitable pre-defined *IndicatorItem* in the analysis of malware traces.

2.2   Cyber Threat Intelligence and STIX

Cyber Threat Intelligence (CTI) is defined as "evidence-based knowledge, including context, mechanisms, indicators, implications, and actionable advice, about an existing or emerging menace or hazard to assets that can be used to inform decisions regarding the subject's response to that menace or hazard", according to Gartner [20].

To convenience the sharing of CTI and let CTI can be understood by the machine, there are many CTI describe languages like STIX [24], CybOX [4], and MAEC [5] is created. STIX is one of the most expressive CTI describe standards created by MITRE. Users can describe different elements in a cyber threat, including basic network features, IoC, TTP and exploited vulnerabilities. All these messages can be organized in a `json` file. STIX2.0 defines 12 types of

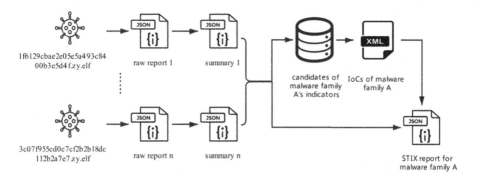

Fig. 1. Overview of generating CTI from malware samples obtained from the Internet

STIX Domain Objects (SDOs) to describe different types of threat intelligence, and 2 STIX Relationship Objects (SROs) to describe the relationship between different SDOs. STIX is more expressive than OpenIoC, as STIX can involve more information except threat indicators.

3   Overview

In this part we will give an overview of how we generate CTI following STIX from malware obtained from the Internet. Figure 1 illustrates how our system works. For one kind of malware class, we are first using sandbox analysis to obtain the malware traces. We then perform our IoC generation algorithm after malware traces processing, in which we select several kinds of strings and transform them into IoC expressions. Finally, we use generated IoC expressions and other useful information in the summary of traces to organize a STIX report. Works done in each step will be described below.

Malware Analysis. We use a sandbox to finish our malware analysis mission. It is worth noting that the structure and content in the sandbox reports will not influence our system and results. Though a sandbox can not simulate all the running conditions of malware samples, the information we can get from sandbox reports is enough to extract malware features. For every malware sample that belongs to the same class, we get its running traces through sandbox simulation. The sandbox analysis result will be written in a `json` file.

Data Preprocessing. There are two kinds of information in the malware traces: static analysis results and dynamic analysis results. The static analysis results include basic file information like file name, file MD5, YARA matching results, and strings obtained from reverse analysis; The dynamic analysis results are logs of interaction between malware sample and host or network, for example, network traces, process creation, file creation and delete behavior and register modify.

Not all the strings extracted from malware are useful for IoC generation. Figure 2 shows part of the sandbox analysis result which are organized in a `json` file. The **string** block gives the result of static string extraction, in which we observe that only a very small part of these string extraction outputs like command or DLL name is meaningful and useful. Most of these extracted strings are hard to understand and meaningless; therefore, we choose to discard these meaningless or repeated strings in malware traces preprocessing.

```
"static_info": {
  "scan": {...},
  "strings": [
      "+UntAsyncTask",
      "SetWindowPlacement",
      "pmCopy",
      "TIntConst",
      "VarMul",
      "WaitForSingleObject",
      "TSampleGrabberCBInt",
      "RUSSIAN_CHARSET",
      "OnContextPopup",
      ...]
}
"behavior": {
  "basic_behavior": {...},
  "behavior_sequence": [...],
  "other_behavior": [...]
}
```

Fig. 2. Part of sandbox analysis result

On the other hand, not all the analysis results have the same value. When we try to generate concise and robust IoC and CTI, we should discard those low-value strings in malware traces. File MD5 is undoubtedly efficient and accurate in malware detection, but file MD5 based malware detection needs many active samples and has a short life circle. If we use MD5 as our indicator, the attacker can bypass this IoC detection at ease [6]. Although most open source IoC use file MD5 as their indicator, we will not use it in our work. Similar low-value information also includes file compilation time and file size.

IoC Generation. After data preprocessing, we obtain a shorter version of malware traces, leaving only strings that can better characterize the behaviors or features of malware in the sandbox simulation. In order to generate structured IoC, we first transform strings in sandbox analysis result into IoC expression. For a single piece of malware behavior description or static characteristic information, we select appropriate *IndicatorItem* according to the content and construct a IoC expression. We will talk about the transformation rules in Sect. 4.1.

We then count all the IoC expressions in each malware trace to build a candidate list for each malware class. For those IoC expressions which have similar value field, we generate a regular expression to replace them. We will describe why and how we construct the candidate list in Sect. 4.2. In the last phase of IoC generation, we choose the most suitable IoC expression subset from the candidate list through a feature selection algorithm. Our target here is to select a subset that has the best performance on the dataset. We will introduce our algorithm and metrics in Sect. 4.3.

STIX Report Generation. Besides the information we used to generate IoC, there are also other strings like network traffic and basic observation in the malware analysis report, which can help understand and characterize certain type of malware. Furthermore, we can summarize malicious behavior set from malware traces, which can help the malware detection and build a better defense system. We organize analysis results of a malware class following STIX standard. We select several SDOs suitable for our task, including *Indicator, Observed Data, Malware, Threat Actor, Identify, Intrusion Set* and *Report*. We design several SROs to describe the relationship between different SDOs and provide a visualization version of the STIX report. Details about how we construct SDOs and design the SROs will be shown in Sect. 5.

4   IoC Generation

In this section, we will describe how we generate IoC from malware traces in detail.

4.1   Expression Transform

Transforming strings in malware traces into a standardized form will benefit the candidate list building process. To transform static and dynamic features in malware traces into IoC expression, we first build the conversion relationship between feature strings and *IndicatorItem*. OpenIoC provides 27 pre-defined *IndicatorItem*, each of them can be divided into more detailed indicators according to specific behavior or feature. Table 1 gives several examples of expression-*IndicatorItem* conversion.

For every string in malware traces, search the corresponding *IndicatorItem* and use its content to fill the value field of IoC expression. There are also some descriptions in malware traces that cannot be expressed with only one simple *IndicatorItem*, as we showed in Table 1. In this case, we find out all the corresponding *IndicatorItem* and use **AND** to connect these IoC expressions.

The predicate(*is, contains* or *matches*) should be used in the IoC expression can be determined once we choose a specific *IndicatorItem*. As a result, it is not necessary to use the predicate *not* in our IoC expression.

4.2   Candidate List Generation

We design a candidate list for certain malware classes to record the IoC expressions and their occurrence frequency. Every IoC expression converted from the

Table 1. Examples of expression conversion

Description in malware traces	OpenIoC *IndicatorItem*
MD5	FileItem/File MD5
filename	FileItem/File Filename
file_behavior add	FileItem/File Filename Created
reg_behavior new	RegistryItem/Registry Key Path **AND** RegistryItem/Registry Value **AND** RegistryItem/Registry Value Name
process created	ProcessItem/Process PID **AND** ProcessItem/Process

malware traces will be stored in a `.csv` file in the form of (logical predicate, indicator type, indicator subdivision type, expression value type, expression value, frequency) six-tuple form. The constructed candidate list can facilitate the classification and matching of IoC expressions. Besides, malware may produce variants shortly, with means generated IoC may not maintain high efficiency. With the help of IoC expressions candidate list, we can easily add newly obtained data in after initialization. This design guarantees that our generated IoC can indicate latest malware sample and its attack behavior.

It is challenging to detect and handle those highly similar IoC expressions when building a candidate list. Since malware samples may have different versions, not all of their behaviors are entirely consistent. For instance, malware in a specific class may all write data into other processes, but the target process may not exactly be the same. This will result in two different IoC expressions after our data preprocessing and expression transform, however, the two IoC expressions are representing the same kind of behavior or malware characteristic, with only very little difference in the target process name. Recent studies have proposed several methods to solve this problem using cluster algorithm [28] or multi-granular regular expression extraction [11]. We find that these methods, especially clustering based methods, may not distinguish different kinds of behaviors, and eventually result in bad performance.

Similar IoC expressions seldom appear in our obtained malware traces. To address this challenge, we divide IoC expressions in the candidate list according to their types(for example, file behavior, register edit and so on). In every divided subset, select the expressions with high frequency as the aggregation center, then calculate the *Levenshtein Distance* between high-frequency expressions and other expressions in the same subset. If the calculated distance between two expressions smaller than our prescribed threshold, use a regular expression to merge them. We use a heuristic method to decide the threshold for each class of malware, which mainly depends on the average length of IoC expressions' value field.

Figure 3 shows an example of how we use regular expression to merge similar IoC expressions. As we mentioned before, we will only calculate the Levenshtein

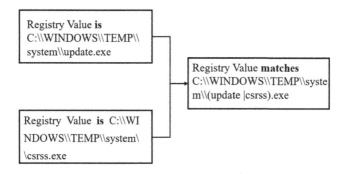

Fig. 3. A sample of using regular expression to merge similar IoC expressions

Distance for those IoC expressions with high frequency to reduce the computational cost. When we use a regular expression to replace the value field in IoC expression, we use *matches* as the predicate. To control the complexity of IoC expressions, we only use — to construct a regular expression.

4.3   IoC Expression Selection

Effective IoC should have properties that only identify attacker's activities, easy to evaluate and expensive for attackers to evade, according to MANDIANT [19]. In other words, the IoC we expected should have a high true positive rate and low false positive rate, and the indicators and value field we designed should be concise and easy for a machine to understand.

IoC subset selection is similar to the feature selection problem. Suppose there are N candidate IoC expressions in the candidate list; our goal is to select a subset which has the best performance and the highest quality on our malware traces dataset. In this problem, the search space will be $2^N - 1$. We can easily evaluate one specific IoC subset, but we may need to test all combinations to find the best one. By using a suitable algorithm, we can obtain an approximate optimal solution of this problem. For example, [28] builds a keyword tree base on the frequency of IoC attributes and find out IoC from the root node to specific leave nodes; [11] designs a submodular function to evaluate the performance of IoC, and generates IoC through maximizing the submodular function [12].

Compared with feature selection problem in machine learning tasks, we have a priori knowledge about the frequency of candidate IoC expressions, which can represent the importance of this IoC expression, in other words, the higher frequency an IoC expression has, the better the IoC including this expression perform precision and recall. We design a heuristic IoC selection algorithm *GIG* which starts the selection from the IoC expression with the highest frequency:

Function $p()$ in the algorithm will evaluate the precision performance of current IoC subset on the test set, n represents the current scale of generated IoC subset $\mathcal{C}$. Our algorithm first adds one of the IoC expressions with the highest frequency into IoC subset, then continuously adds expressions that can improve

Algorithm 1. Greedy IoC Generation

Input: Dataset $\mathcal{D}$, Candidate list $\mathcal{I}$, maximum expression number m, precision threshold θ

Output: IoC subset $\mathcal{C}$

1: **function** EXPRESSION SELECTION$(\mathcal{D}, \mathcal{I}, m, \theta)$
2:     add the most frequent $i \in \mathcal{I}$ to $\mathcal{C}$
3:     $n \leftarrow 1$
4:     $\mathcal{I} \leftarrow \mathcal{I} - i$
5:     **while** $(p(\mathcal{C}) <= \theta \; || \; n < m)$ **do**
6:         find i from $\mathcal{I}$ until $p(\mathcal{C} \cup i) > p(\mathcal{C})$
7:         **if** successfully find i **then**
8:             $\mathcal{C} \leftarrow \mathcal{C} \cup i$
9:             $\mathcal{I} \leftarrow \mathcal{I} - i$
10:             $n \leftarrow n + 1$
11:         **end if**
12:         **if** can not find any i **then**
13:             **return** $\mathcal{C}$
14:         **end if**
15:     **end while**
16:     **return** $\mathcal{C}$
17: **end function**

IoC subset's performance, until the IoC expressions in IoC subset hit the prescribed maximum expression number m or the IoC subset is good enough. When we find more than one IoC expression which brings the same precision increase in one iteration, we randomly add one of them into our IoC. We set the maximum expression number m to control the conciseness of the final IoC. Our experiment shows that we can get concise and effective IoC through fixing a suitable m.

With the help of *IoC writer* [18], we can easily export the IoC from tabular data to an OpenIoC format .IoC file. The selected expressions $(i_1, i_2, ...i_n)$ will be connected with OR, and the final IoC for a specific kind of malware will be like $(i_1||i_2||...||i_n)$. Figure 4 shows the IoC our algorithm generated for DarkComet family.

(Service API **matches** (SeDebugPrivilige—SeLoadDriverPrivilige))
OR (Hook Hooked Module **matches** C:\\WINDOWS\\TEMP\\(csrss—msdcsc).exe)
OR (Registry Key Path **contains** HKEY_LOCAL_MACHINE\\Software\\Microsoft
\\Windows NT\\CurrentVersion\\Winlogon
AND Registry Key Value name **contains** UserInit
AND Registry Key Value **matches** C:\\WINDOWS\\TEMP\\system\\(update—csrss
—msdcsc).exe)

Fig. 4. Generated IoC for DarkComet following OpenIoC standard

5   STIX Report Construction

When constructing a STIX report, we first fill each SDOs, and then define SROs between SDOs to describe their relationship. This section will show the details of how we select SDOs and SROs for STIX report generation task and discuss how to use information in malware traces to construct SDOs and SROs.

5.1   SDOs Selection and Construction

Document [24] defines the description scope and format of all 12 types of SDOs. As we mentioned before, to organize these scattered and unstructured malware traces, we need to select SDOs suitable for our description scenario. Specifically, we choose the following SDOs to construct STIX report:

– *Observed Data:* This SDO contains a series of monitored basic behavior or information like file name, IP address and network traces. For specific malware class, we directly write corresponding basic observation in all sandbox reports into an Observed Data object after merging similar items.
– *Malware:* Malware object describes malware category and its common characteristics. Though the Malware object itself can only describe some general characteristics, we can link it to other SDOs we use to depict a vast landscape of malware attacks.
– *Threat Actor:* This SDO can describe the information about individuals or organizations related to threat events. We treat each malicious IP address as an attacker in our malware description task and write an IP address list into threat actor object. Malware likes bots [27] may try to connect back to the control side during the sandbox simulation, we can record those malicious IP addresses by analyzing the network traces. There is another SDO in STIX, Identity, which can describe the information of attackers. However, the Identify object should contain information of victims at the same time, as a result, Threat Actor is the better choice for our description task.
– *Indicator:* Indicator is an essential component in the malware CTI, consistent and well structured IoC can help to automate some processes in malware detection. STIX provides more expressive IoC describe grammar, compare to OpenIoC. Using the API developed by OASIS [23], we can transform our generated IoC into STIX's Indicator format.
– *Intrusion Set:* Intrusion Set summarizes the malicious behavior of malware during the sandbox simulation, such as process hijacking, registry modification. We infer malicious behavior from the malware traces and use these results to construct an Intrusion Set object in our CTI report.
– *Report:* The Report object in STIX organizes all the related SDOs together. A list of references and descriptions to other SDOs will be written in.

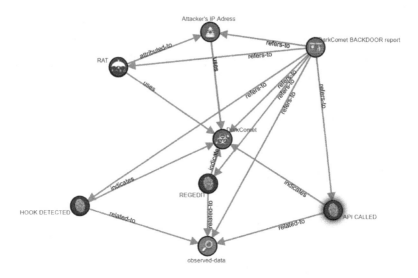

Fig. 5. Visualized STIX report of DarkComet

5.2 SROs Construction

In our malware CTI generation process, we first obtain unstructured malware traces from sandbox analysis, then we finish work like malware signature and indicator construction, attacker identify and malicious behavior analysis. Our SROs established based on this scenario are as follows:

- Observed Data **related-to** Indicator;
- Indicator **indicates** malware;
- Threat Actor **uses** malware;
- Intrusion Set **uses** malware;
- Intrusion Set **attributed-to** Threat Actor.

The **related-to, indicates, uses** are connection types defined by STIX [24]. Finally we get a malware CTI heterogeneous information network consists of SDOs and SROs with the help of a STIX visualization toolkit [22], as showed in Fig. 5.

6 Evaluation

In this section, we will introduce a series of experiments to evaluate whether our IoC generation algorithm can produce concise and effective IoC for specific malware class. We will first introduce our dataset and settings. After that we will introduce our evaluation methodology and give our experiment results.

6.1 Evaluation Setup

We deploy a honeypot system to collect malware samples from the Internet from May 2019 to June 2020. We use ANTIY's [1] sandbox service to get malware traces. We build a Windows XP 32 bit and a centos 6.5 32 bit virtual machine as the sandbox analysis environment. The structure and content in the sandbox reports has been described in Sect. 3 and Sect. 4. Table 2 summarizes the malware samples used in our experiment, and shows the analysis environment we use. We label these malware samples with the help of YARA rules.

Table 2. Malware samples used in IoC generation algorithm evaluation

Malware	Size	Environment
njRat	259	win XP 32 bit
DarkComet	113	win XP 32 bit
NanoCore	174	win XP 32 bit
Setag	172	centos 32 bit
Gafgyt	252	centos 32 bit

To evaluate the detection efficiency of our generated IoCs, we split these malware samples into two parts to simulate a real-world malware detection scene. The first part, namely the training set, consists of 80% of malware samples; we will use them to generate IoC for each malware class. We use the rest of malware samples as testing objects.

The analyzer machine runs only one malware sample at the same time to avoid interference, and the running report will be written in a `json` file. We build a candidate list for each malware class with our method using samples in the training set. We then perform *GIG* to generate one IoC for each malware class; Fig. 4 shows one generation result. We run all the experiments on 8 cores Intel(R) Xeon(R) CPU E5-2630 v4 @ 2.20 GHz with 16 GB RAM.

In the first part of the evaluation, we will investigate whether IoCs generated from the training set can detect unknown testing objects. After data preprocessing, we judge whether a testing object belongs to specific malware classes using generated IoCs. We also evaluate whether our IoCs can achieve the same classification efficiency as other methods, especially machine learning based methods.

6.2 IoC Generation Evaluation

In this experiment, we first use the training set to generate IoC for each malware class, then we evaluate those IoC on the test set consisting of all five types malware samples. The evaluation of IoC can be considered a binary classification problem, and we should be concerned about the precision and recall rate of generated IoC. An IoC with high precision and recall rates means lower false positive and false negative in real world malware detection, which better meets our needs.

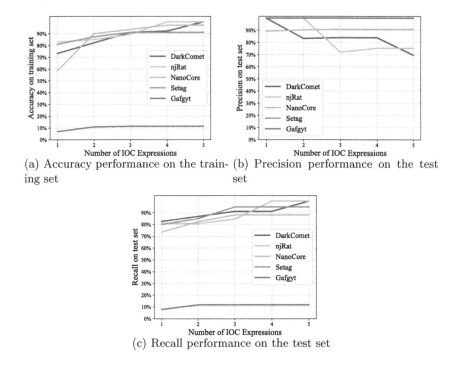

(a) Accuracy performance on the train- (b) Precision performance on the test
ing set   set

(c) Recall performance on the test set

Fig. 6. The performance of generated IoC w.r.t. number of IoC expressions

Figure 6 illustrates the performance of generated IoC w.r.t. number of IoC
expressions on different dataset. Not all the malware samples will have dynamic
behavior during the sandbox simulation due to the imperfection of the sandbox
running mechanism. For traces obtained from these inactive malware samples,
since we choose to discard most of the static characteristics in the traces preprocessing, there will be very few strings in it and lack of common feature, which
may lead to bad algorithm performance. For example, we find that nearly all the
Gafgyt samples in our experiment are inactive during the sandbox simulation;
as a result we get a lousy curve for it.

For other malware classes, as we generate our IoC respectively, the accuracy
performance on the training set is the same as precision performance. Our algorithm continuously adds expression into IoC, we can see in Fig. 6(a) that the
more expressions we use, the higher accuracy we achieve. As we mentioned in
Sect. 4.1, we generate candidate IoC expressions from every malware trace. To
evaluate generated IoC on test set, we compare it with every sample's IoC expressions to see whether this IoC can detect target malware sample. Figure 6(b) and
6(c) show the performance of generated IoC on test set. Similar to the accuracy
performance on training set, the more expressions we use, the higher recall rate
we get. However, more expressions may not bring higher precision performance,
since the more expressions we use, the more false positive will appear. According
to our experiment result, if we add no more than 3 expressions into the IoC, we

can get concise and effective IoC. Table 3 shows the performance of 3 item IoC on our test set. In conclusion, our system is practical enough to generate effective malware threat intelligence and help malware detection.

Table 3. Recall performance on test set of 3 items IoC

Malware	Recall
njRat	91.31%
DarkComet	84.62%
NanoCore	88.24%
Setag	95.00%

6.3 Algorithm Comparison

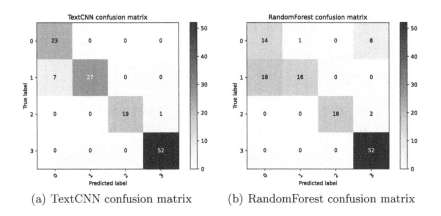

(a) TextCNN confusion matrix   (b) RandomForest confusion matrix

Fig. 7. Classification performance of machine learning based algorithms

Detection accuracy is one of the critical metrics for IoC. Generally, machine learning based malware classification model can utilize implicit features to achieve better classification performance, comparing to coarse-grained method likes expression and regular expression based model. In this comparison, we will investigate whether IoC generated by *GIG* can achieve the same classification performance as machine learning methods, with the help of data preprocessing and fine-grained feature selection.

To compare our algorithm's classification performance with machine learning based method, we set up Random-Forst [2] and TextCNN [10] models on our dataset as the opponents. The TextCNN used in our experiment has four kernels of different sizes (2, 3, 4 and 5) and has 800 kernel in total. In the embedding layer, we first train a word2vec model [21] to generate word vector from malware traces and change every trace into a matrix. On the other hand, we treat each expression in candidate list as a feature to build feature vector and train a RandomForest classifier with 100 estimators. Figure 7 shows the confusion matrix of RandomForest and TextCNN models in the classification task.

Table 4 shows the recall rate comparison between different algorithms; we run our algorithm to generate IoC with three expressions in the comparison. The results indicate our method performs at least not worse than general machine learning based algorithms. Simultaneously, our method has the obvious advantage of generating reliable, concise and easy for machine to understand IoC which can help the malware detection in the real environment. On the contrary, those machine learning based algorithms can only work like a black box classifier, which the classification criteria behind is hard to explain.

Table 4. Recall rate comparison

Method	Malware			
	DarkComet	NanoCore	Setag	njRat
GIG	91.31%	88.24%	95%	84.62%
TextCNN	100%	79.41%	95%	100%
RandomForest	60.87%	47.06%	90%	100%

7 Related Work

Cyber Threat Intelligence. Traditional CTI generation methods rely on security experts to summarize the large amount but low-value basic network traces or system logs, which is inefficient and labor-consuming. More and more research is focusing on automatically generating CTI, especially IoC extraction using different methods. Published works like [15] explore how IoC related information is described in security articles and reports, and develop a NLP model to automatically extract IoC from them; [31] designs a multi-granular attention based IoC recognition system based on BiLSTM and CRF to extract IoC entities from security blogs and articles. Many works try to extract IoC from Open Source Intelligence(OSINT), though their data source may be different and may develop different generation models based on machine learning and regular expression [3]. These OSINTs are somehow well structured and IoC information will be described in a particular format; as a result, it is possible to extract them through NLP algorithms. If we want to obtain IoC as timely as possible, we may need to extract them from unstructured malware or threat event traces, and we need further study to automate this process.

Besides IoC, there is still lots of information in malware or network traces that can help depict a complete picture of threat events. Related work like [9] try to automatically construct attack pattern messages from OSINT and organize them into CTI expression standards. In our work, we extract threat information about attackers and intrusion sets from malware traces and organize them following STIX standard.

Another point in CTI research is to evaluate the actual effect of those automatically generated IoC or CTI and utilize them in real world threat action detection. [14] designs a set of evaluation metrics and measures a broad range of Threat Intelligence(TI) and concludes that there are still many challenges and limitations in using existing IoC and CTI.

Malware Detection. Pioneer work has made remarkable improvements in malware detection. The malware detection process can be divided into feature selection and classification/clustering [30]. In the feature selection stage, fine-grained features are extracted to improve detection performance. For example, [17] summarizes three characteristics in bots' network traces and designs signature for detection; [25] focuses on HTTP-based malware and defines similarity metrics to build a network level malware clustering system. In the classification and clustering stage, researchers introduce different models in recent years. For example, [8,16] build a heterogeneous information network based on host logs, and use graph embedding algorithm to construct eigenvector for every node, then find out malicious log entries through clustering; [29] first derives the CFGs of malware file and use graph based algorithm to finish malware classification.

We use sandbox analysis reports as our source data to make up for the lack of static characteristics in malware detection and IoC generation [7]. We generate IoC and CTI from malware traces analysis, of course the generated IoC can be used to finish the malware classification task.

8 Conclusion

This paper introduces a system to automatically generate IoC and CTI following STIX standard from unstructured malware traces. Different from OSINT based CTI or IoC extraction research, we design our system to generate them directly from malware samples' sandbox analysis reports. In the IoC generation phase, we first define rules for the transformation between strings in malware traces and IoC expression. After that, for a specific class of malware, we build an IoC expressions candidate list. Finally we propose *GIG* to select the most effective IoC from the candidate list. Our experiment of IoC generation achieves a 89.4% recall rate on average. In conclusion, our system is practical enough to generate concise and effective malware IoC and threat intelligence, which can help the real world malware detection and security operation.

Acknowledgement. We thank the anonymous reviewers for the valuable comments and suggestions. This work is supported by National Key Research and Development Program of China [No. 2020YFB1807500] and National Natural Science Foundation of China [No. 61831007].

References

1. ANTIY. https://www.antiy.cn/
2. Breiman, L.: Random forests. Mach. Learn. **45**(1), 5–32 (2001)
3. Catakoglu, O., Balduzzi, M., Balzarotti, D.: Automatic extraction of indicators of compromise for web applications. In: Proceedings of the 25th International Conference on World Wide Web, WWW 2016, International World Wide Web Conferences Steering Committee, Republic and Canton of Geneva, CHE, pp. 333–343 (2016). https://doi.org/10.1145/2872427.2883056
4. Corporation, T.M.: CybOX: cyber observable expression. https://cyboxproject.github.io
5. Corporation, T.M.: Malware attribute enumeration and characterization (MAEC). https://maecproject.github.io/documentation/overview/
6. David, B.: The pyramid of pain: Intel-driven detection & response to increase your adversary's cost of operation. Technical Report, FireEye. https://rvasec.com/slides/2014/Bianco_Pyramid
7. Firdausi, I., Erwin, A., Nugroho, A.S., et al.: Analysis of machine learning techniques used in behavior-based malware detection. In: 2010 Second International Conference on Advances in Computing, Control, and Telecommunication Technologies, pp. 201–203. IEEE (2010)
8. Gao, Y., Li, X., Peng, H., Fang, B., Yu, P.: HinCTI: a cyber threat intelligence modeling and identification system based on heterogeneous information network. IEEE Trans. Knowl. Data Eng., 1 (2020)
9. Husari, G., Al-Shaer, E., Ahmed, M., Chu, B., Niu, X.: TTPDrill: automatic and accurate extraction of threat actions from unstructured text of CTI sources. In: Proceedings of the 33rd Annual Computer Security Applications Conference, pp. 103–115 (2017)
10. Kim, Y.: Convolutional neural networks for sentence classification. arXiv preprint arXiv:1408.5882 (2014)
11. Kurogome, Y., et al.: EIGER: automated IOC generation for accurate and interpretable endpoint malware detection. In: Proceedings of the 35th Annual Computer Security Applications Conference. ACSAC 2019, pp. 687–701. Association for Computing Machinery, New York (2019). https://doi.org/10.1145/3359789.3359808
12. Lakkaraju, H., Bach, S.H., Leskovec, J.: Interpretable decision sets: a joint framework for description and prediction. In: Proceedings of the 22nd ACM SIGKDD International Conference on Knowledge Discovery and Data Mining, pp. 1675–1684 (2016)
13. Li, J.: Cyberspace threat intelligence perception, sharing and analysis technology: A survey. Chin. J. Netw. Inf. Secur. **2**(002), 16–29 (2016)
14. Li, V.G., Dunn, M., Pearce, P., McCoy, D., Voelker, G.M., Savage, S.: Reading the tea leaves: a comparative analysis of threat intelligence. In: 28th {USENIX} Security Symposium ({USENIX} Security 19), pp. 851–867 (2019)
15. Liao, X., Yuan, K., Wang, X., Li, Z., Xing, L., Beyah, R.: Acing the IOC game: toward automatic discovery and analysis of open-source cyber threat intelligence. In: Proceedings of the 2016 ACM SIGSAC Conference on Computer and Communications Security, pp. 755–766 (2016)
16. Liu, F., Wen, Y., Zhang, D., Jiang, X., Xing, X., Meng, D.: Log2vec: a heterogeneous graph embedding based approach for detecting cyber threats within enterprise. In: Proceedings of the 2019 ACM SIGSAC Conference on Computer and Communications Security, pp. 1777–1794 (2019)

17. Liu, L., Chen, S., Yan, G., Zhang, Z.: BotTracer: execution-based bot-like malware detection. In: Wu, T.-C., Lei, C.-L., Rijmen, V., Lee, D.-T. (eds.) ISC 2008. LNCS, vol. 5222, pp. 97–113. Springer, Heidelberg (2008). https://doi.org/10.1007/978-3-540-85886-7_7

18. MANDIANT: IOC writer. https://github.com/mandiant/ioc_writer

19. MANDIANT: Sophisticated indicators for the modern threat intelligence: an introduction to openIOC. Technical Report, MANDIANT. https://www.academia.edu/31820654/An_Introduction_to_Open_IOC

20. McMillan, R., Pratap, K.: Market guide for security threat intelligence services. Technical Report, Gartner (2014). https://www.gartner.com/en/documents/2874317

21. Mikolov, T., Chen, K., Corrado, G., Dean, J.: Efficient estimation of word representations in vector space. arXiv preprint arXiv:1301.3781 (2013)

22. OASIS: Lightweight visualization for STIX 2.0 objects and relationships. https://github.com/oasis-open/cti-stix-visualization/

23. OASIS: openIOC-to-SITX. https://github.com/STIXProject/openioc-to-stix

24. OASIS: STIX version 2.0. part 2: STIX objects. Technical Report. https://docs.oasis-open.org/cti/stix/v2.0/stix-v2.0-part2-stix-objects.pdf

25. Perdisci, R., Lee, W., Feamster, N.: Behavioral clustering of http-based malware and signature generation using malicious network traces. In: NSDI, vol. 10, p. 14 (2010)

26. SANS: The sans state of cyber threat intelligence survey: CTI important and maturing. Technical Report. https://www.sans.org/reading-room/whitepapers/analyst/state-cyber-threat-intelligence-survey-cti-important-maturing-37177

27. Stinson, E., Mitchell, J.C.: Characterizing bots' remote control behavior. In: M. Hämmerli, B., Sommer, R. (eds.) DIMVA 2007. LNCS, vol. 4579, pp. 89–108. Springer, Heidelberg (2007). https://doi.org/10.1007/978-3-540-73614-1_6

28. Xu, W., Wang, Y., Xue, Z.: Automatic generation of IOC for threat intelligence. Commun. Technol. **50**(1), 116–123 (2017)

29. Yan, J., Yan, G., Jin, D.: Classifying malware represented as control flow graphs using deep graph convolutional neural network. In: 2019 49th Annual IEEE/IFIP International Conference on Dependable Systems and Networks (DSN), pp. 52–63. IEEE (2019)

30. Ye, Y., Li, T., Adjeroh, D., Iyengar, S.S.: A survey on malware detection using data mining techniques. ACM Comput. Surv. (CSUR) **50**(3), 1–40 (2017)

31. Zhao, J., Yan, Q., Liu, X., Li, B., Zuo, G.: Cyber threat intelligence modeling based on heterogeneous graph convolutional network. In: 23rd International Symposium on Research in Attacks, Intrusions and Defenses ({RAID} 2020), pp. 241–256 (2020)

Towards Automated Assessment of Vulnerability Exposures in Security Operations

Philip Huff[✉] and Qinghua Li

University of Arkansas, Fayetteville, AR 72701, USA
{phu,qinghual}@uark.edu

Abstract. Current approaches for risk analysis of software vulnerabilities using manual assessment and numeric scoring do not complete fast enough to keep pace with the maintenance work rate to patch and mitigate the vulnerabilities. This paper proposes a new approach to modeling software vulnerability risk in the context of the network environment and firewall configuration. In the approach, vulnerability features are automatically matched up with networking, target asset, and adversary features to determine whether adversaries can exploit a vulnerability. The ability of adversaries to reach a vulnerability is modeled by automatically identifying the network services associated with vulnerabilities through a pipeline of machine learning and natural language processing and automatically analyzing network reachability. Our results show that the pipeline can identify network services accurately. We also find that only a small number of vulnerabilities pose real risks to a system. However, if left unmitigated, adversarial reach to vulnerabilities may extend to nullify the effect of firewall countermeasures.

Keywords: Software vulnerability · Risk analysis · Artificial intelligence

1 Introduction

The actual number of software vulnerabilities has become more evident with bug bounty programs, automated code analysis, and increased reporting by software vendors. In 2017, the number of vulnerabilities reported annually through the National Vulnerability Database (NVD) doubled and currently continues an upward trend [5]. Vulnerability mitigation for servers and other autonomous devices requires extensive planning, coordination, and testing. Consequently, the burden to maintain secure operations in organizations often exceeds the available resources.

To address this problem, defenders in an organization need a more contextual understanding of the actual risk posed by a vulnerability. Contextual risk assessment requires understanding (i) an adversary's tactics, capabilities, and access to a targeted vulnerability and (ii) the effectiveness of existing mitigation in the organization. Moreover, defenders need the risk information quickly.

© ICST Institute for Computer Sciences, Social Informatics and Telecommunications Engineering 2021
Published by Springer Nature Switzerland AG 2021. All Rights Reserved
J. Garcia-Alfaro et al. (Eds.): SecureComm 2021, LNICST 398, pp. 62–81, 2021.
https://doi.org/10.1007/978-3-030-90019-9_4

For example, in a 2017 Equifax breach, a months-old unpatched Apache Struts vulnerability was identified as the initial attack vector [13]. If the degree of risk became evident upon release of the vulnerability, operators could have immediately patched the software.

A commonly used defense is a firewall. Thus, one promising solution for providing contextual risk information to operators in determining whether an adversary has the needed network access to exploit given vulnerabilities under firewall rules. The challenge is mapping the many applicable software vulnerabilities of a system to the firewall rules. Currently, operators can only perform this manually.

Our work bridges this gap by automating the identification of network services used to exploit vulnerabilities through a pipeline of machine learning (ML) and natural language processing (NLP) methods. The machine learning method uses standard vulnerability features from the NVD data feed to predict the associated network service. The NLP method further boosts the overall prediction accuracy with information from vulnerability descriptions. Experiments show that the pipeline can identify network services for 97% of vulnerabilities with an accuracy of 95%.

The joining of firewall and vulnerability data allows identifying which vulnerabilities are accessible outside of their segmented network zone. It then becomes possible to model an adversary's external view of the vulnerability. To do this, we model the placement of adversaries in the Internet and enterprise network zones and develop methods for network reachability analysis under firewall rules.

Once the adversary's ability to reach the vulnerability is determined, the system's security state can be precisely assessed. Using standard features for access, capability, and impact in the Common Vulnerability Scoring System (CVSS), we model safety as a function of set dominance between the vulnerability, target asset, and adversary.

The approach demonstrates that over a realistic sample system only a small portion of vulnerabilities are unsafe. The practical result signifies a reduced effort for the defender to maintain a system's secure state. The model can also recursively iterate to show how adversaries might extend their reach using already reached software vulnerabilities. We refer to vulnerabilities in this path as gateway vulnerabilities and demonstrate the detriment they may have on the entire system's safety.

Our contributions are summarized as follows:

- A formal definition of system state safety when combining vulnerability, adversary, and target asset features, and an automation framework for assessing the system security, which includes data modeling, extraction of network service information from vulnerability features/descriptions, network reachability analysis under firewall rules, and model checking vulnerability safety.
- An artificial intelligence pipeline including ML and NLP methods to identify the network services associated with vulnerabilities based on vulnerability features and descriptions enables automating the association between vulnerabilities and firewall policies.
- Evaluation of the solution based on vulnerabilities from the NVD and identification of gateway vulnerabilities that can flip the network attack modeling in favor of the adversary.

Section 2 reviews related work. Section 3 introduces data modeling. Section 4 describes how to identify the network service associated with vulnerabilities. Section 5 presents network reachability analysis under firewall rules. Section 6 presents the safety model for vulnerability exposure checking. The last two sections present evaluation results and conclusions.

2   Related Work

The concept of assessing software vulnerability risk in terms of adversarial capability has its roots in the broader field of attack trees. Attack Trees, initially pioneered by Schneier [28], are practical and well-established modeling tools for automatically assessing risk by refining the ultimate goal of an attacker into a granular tree of actions to quantify the risk of an attack. Later research provides a formal specification for attack trees [24]. Attack-Defense Trees (AD-Trees) add the analysis of defense mitigation in the presence of attack methodologies to assess both mitigation approaches and risk of attack [19]. Recent solutions in automated AD-Tree generation [12], multi-parameter risk optimization [15] and automatically relating attacks to attack tree goals [23] continue to propel AD-Trees as a practical tool to optimize vulnerability mitigation. Our approach differs from AD-Trees by focusing only on software vulnerabilities from the perspective of a defender. In assessing software vulnerabilities, we model the simple attacker goal to exploit the system and use standard atomic attributes to measure the attacker's capability.

Network attack graphs have similar objectives to attack trees in identifying adversarial capability to attack but focus on the target reachability by the attacker. The use of modeling the physical network as a graph to assess an attacker's capability to exploit vulnerabilities originated in work [27] and [11]. In [33], they provide a grammar for defining connectivity in a network and propose a model-checking safety invariant for assessing vulnerabilities. This approach is expanded in [31] to include a more general safety condition against unknown or zero-day attacks.

Several papers have suggested approaches to automating the software vulnerability assessment using network attack graphs. In [17,34], they propose metrics for a qualitative security score based on vulnerabilities present in the network. Similarly, [26] combines vulnerability metric data with firewall topology to provide an overall view of risk using various metrics, including connectivity and length of network paths. A more recent approach involves scoring network path edges using applicable vulnerability metrics to host data to calculate risk as a function of the path cost [16].

AD-Trees and attack graphs have the same nuisance of overwhelming the security analyst with risk metrics and attack scenarios. Our approach overcomes this obstacle by focusing more narrowly on the common problem of software vulnerability management using standard data features (i.e., CVSS) well understood by practitioners. Instead of outputting a graph or risk score which still needs much manual analysis to decide whether vulnerabilities need mitigation or not, our model generates a deterministic output as to whether vulnerabilities are safe from attackers or not. We abstract much of the complexity in decision making using set dominance similar to other areas of formal models in computer security such as access control [20] and, more recently, in trusted computing [35]. Also, existing work does not address the automated extraction of network services from vulnerability features and descriptions.

Some studies have used the NVD data for security purposes. [21] uses NLP over vulnerability descriptions for extracting new entities (i.e., Named-Entity Recognition or NER) to generally describe vulnerabilities in terms of cause, consequence analysis, and impact estimation. [32] uses ML models for attack classification and improved impact scoring, and [22] uses concept drift in NLP to assess vulnerabilities based on their descriptions. [36], and [37] use machine learning to recommend remediation actions for and predict the probabilistic risk levels of vulnerabilities, and [25] uses natural language processing over vulnerability descriptions to identify mitigation information. [18] studies how to map software assets to vulnerabilities. See [9] for a repository of work in this domain. However, these existing studies do not automatically extract network services from vulnerability features and descriptions, and they do not consider firewall policies as our work does.

3   Data Modeling

Our safety model seeks to understand whether and how a set of adversaries can exploit a given vulnerability. This section describes the relevant data for understanding adversarial interaction. A significant portion of the input data comes from the NVD as distinct attributes, which provides a consistent and timely source for real-time vulnerability analysis.

3.1   Vulnerability Features, Asset Features, and Adversary Capabilities

The NVD provides a full data feed of twelve attributes associated with the CVSS. CVSS is an open standard maintained by a special interest group under the Forum of Incident Response and Security Teams (FIRST) [3]. Software publishers broadly use it to describe security vulnerabilities in their software.

Here, we describe the attributes related to the adversarial capability necessary to exploit vulnerabilities as a function of state labeling propositions that we use for modeling. Each feature labels a distinct capability, representing a cumulative set hierarchy for deterministically calculating adversarial interaction requirements.

Features in the NVD have an abbreviation convention, which we conveniently adopt with state labeling. The Attack Vector, AV, label defines the access necessary for an exploit. The propositions *Physical* (P), *Local* (L), *Network* (N) and *Adjacent* (A) are an ordered set $AV = \{N, A, L, P\}$ in terms of decreasing exploit opportunity with respect to the vulnerability and increasing exploit difficulty for the adversary. An attack vector of N implies that the adversary can exploit the vulnerability directly through a network service. In contrast, an attack vector of L implies the adversary needs to interact with the device for exploitation. Local attacks do not necessarily mean an adversary cannot perform the attack remotely. For example, an adversary can interact through VNC or SSH to exploit a vulnerability with an attack vector of L.

Attack Complexity, AC, describes the difficulty required to develop an exploit for a given vulnerability. Propositions include *Low*, L, and *High*, H, with the ordered set $AC = \{L, H\}$. For example, low attack complexity would indicate an adversary's greater opportunity to exploit the vulnerability.

Privileges, PR, describes the level of privileges necessary to exploit the vulnerability and is similar to AC with the additional possibility of no privileges, N required. Thus, the ordered set would be $PR = \{N, L, H\}$ in terms of decreasing opportunity for exploitation.

The User Interaction label, UI, indicates the degree to which a human must be involved to exploit the vulnerability. Propositions include *Required*, R, and *None*, N, with the ordered set as $UI = \{R, N\}$. When R applies to a device, it would indicate regular user interaction and have more exploit opportunities.

The temporal metric of exploitability, EX, describes the current availability of code to exploit a vulnerability. The label EX propositions include *High*, H, meaning exploit code is widely available, *Functional*, F, meaning exploit code is available but may require additional work, *Proof-of-concept*, P, and *Unproven*, U, where the exploit code is not known to be developed. The ordered set is $EX = \{H, F, P, U\}$ with decreasing exploitability of a vulnerability.

Although the CVSS attributes describe vulnerability features, we make a key observation that these features apply to both (i) target assets associated with the vulnerability and (ii) a prospective adversary's capability. Table 1 describes the relationship of the CVSS capability features. We capitalize on these relationships in Sect. 6 to precisely define capability in terms of safety.

Table 1. CVSS-based data features

CVSS feature	Vulnerability	Adversary	Asset
Attack Vector	The physical or network access for exploit	The ability of an adversary to use the path	The location of an asset
Privileges	The logical access necessary for exploit	The level of privileges available to the adversary	
User Interaction	Whether an exploit needs interaction with a human		Whether humans interact on the asset
Exploitability	The availability and ease of developing exploit code	The ability of an adversary to use or develop exploit code	

Impact Gradient Labels. Impact gradient labels describe the impact an exploited vulnerability might have on a target device, and they only apply to the vulnerability and target device. The labels of *Confidentiality*, *C*, *Integrity*, *I* and *Availability*, *A*, describe the functionality of the vulnerability and the security requirements of the target device. For each *C*, *I* and *A*, the labels include *None*, *N*, *Low*, *L*, and *High*, *H*, with the same ordered set $\{N, L, H\}$.

3.2   Adversarial Data

We primarily consider scenarios in which adversaries have access outside of a targeted network zone. Otherwise, if an adversary has internal access, they likely could use credentials rather than software vulnerabilities for attacks. However, we do model an insider threat in Sect. 7, but we do so from a network zone on the fringe of the targeted system.

Adversary objects have capability labels assigned from Table 1, and these should be selected to match the real adversarial capability closely. For example, a threat actor on the Internet may have the capability to exploit vulnerabilities with *High* attack complexity, *Low* privilege, and *Unproven* exploitability. An insider threat may have *High* privileges, but only have exploit capability for *Low* attack complexity and *High* exploitability.

3.3   Network Service and Network Reachability

Vulnerabilities that remote adversaries could exploit are usually associated with specific network services, e.g., a web service. The network service information is critical for associating vulnerability exposure with the firewall policy, which governs access to network services. Currently, the network service associated with a vulnerability is not released/reported in any standard format. Instead, security operators usually need to manually dig it out by reading vulnerability descriptions such as those released in the NVD. We will describe how to extract the network service information from vulnerability data in Sect. 4, and how to explore an adversary's network reachability to the target device and service in Sect. 5.

4   Network Service Extraction

The enabling factor for defining an adversary's ability to reach a vulnerability is the extraction of network service information from the vulnerability's features and descriptions. We first use machine learning to extract network services for vulnerabilities and then apply natural language processing (NLP) to boost results. This section describes the machine learning approach, the NLP approach, and how they are combined into one pipeline to identify network services.

4.1   Machine Learning-Based Extraction

The machine learning portion of the pipeline uses a predictive decision-tree model over standard feature data from the NVD to predict the network services associated with vulnerabilities. Standard features include (i) Common Product

Enumeration (CPE) [1], (ii) Common Vulnerability Scoring System (CVSS) [2] features, and (iii) the Common Weakness Enumeration (CWE) [4]. All of these features are regularly updated and made available by the NVD [6].

We initially tried using machine learning to predict for all network services. Machine learning by itself performs well for the *web* services and *client* services involving user interactions. However, it performs much worse for other network services, probably because there are relatively few vulnerabilities for other network services in the NVD dataset. Inspired by this observation, we use machine learning to classify vulnerabilities into three categories, *CLIENT*, *WEB*, and *INCONCLUSIVE*, for better accuracy. The *CLIENT* category represents the broad class of vulnerabilities in which either the adversary must exploit locally (e.g., local input) or must initiate client network traffic for a remote exploit (e.g., browser-based vulnerabilities). The *WEB* category represents vulnerabilities with web services. The *INCONCLUSIVE* category represents all other vulnerabilities in which machine learning does not accurately determine network services and which requires further processing by NLP.

We labeled network services for 19,433 vulnerabilities sampled from the 2017–2019 NVD dataset as our training data. The samples were shuffled and randomly partitioned into an 80% to 20% training-testing split. The model uses a decision-tree classifier using the features from the CVSS, CPE, and CWE described above and a Gini-index for branching. As shown in Table 2, the prediction is very accurate.

Table 2. Machine learning classification results for network services

Network service type	Precision	Recall	F-score	Support
CLIENT	100%	100%	100%	3,764
WEB	99%	100%	100%	591
INCONCLUSIVE	99%	99%	99%	504

4.2   Natural Language Processing-Based Extraction

We then use NLP to further process the vulnerabilities within the *INCONCLU-SIVE* category of the machine learning prediction. One approach is to directly classify each vulnerability description with a label identifying the network service. However, there are thousands of network services which makes it very challenging to get a high accuracy based on the currently available data. Instead, we build semantic meaning from the vulnerability descriptions in the NVD through named-entity recognition (NER), which locates and classifies named entities in a text into pre-defined categories such as organizations and products. For example, NER would classify "Google LLC" in a sentence as an Organization. For a complete description of NER, refer to [8,14]. We use NER to extract standard features in vulnerability descriptions.

Inspired by existing work on cybersecurity ontologies [10,29,30], we define the following named entities for classifying network services:

1. **SERVICE** - Service affected by the vulnerability. Examples include HTTP, VNC, ssh, and CLI. These entities often map directly to network services.
2. **SOFTWARE** - Software product affected by the vulnerability. Software products often have network service requirements. For example, a vulnerability affecting WordPress maps to a web service and Google Chrome vulnerabilities require client interactions.
3. **THREAT** - Method used to exploit the vulnerability. This entity is most helpful in identifying web services. Descriptions of attack vectors commonly use HTTP and HTML terms such as POST, URI, and cookie. These adjectives often follow the preposition "via" in the description.
4. **WEAKNESS** - Software failure causing the vulnerability. Examples include web attack references such as CSRF, SSRF, and path traversal. These weaknesses commonly precede the term *vulnerability* as an adjective.

We annotated approximately 4,000 vulnerability descriptions from the 2017 through 2019 NVD dataset. Then a convolutional neural network (CNN) model for recognizing named entities was trained based on these vulnerabilities with a random 80% to 20% training-testing split. Table 3 shows the results.

We then build a set of rules for mapping vulnerabilities to network services using named entities. Each rule tags a specific network service based on the named entities extracted from vulnerability descriptions.

Table 3. NLP named-entity recognition scores

NLP	NER results summary		
NER category	*Precision*	*Recall*	*F1-score*
SERVICE	76%	68%	72%
SOFTWARE	63%	64%	63%
THREAT	72%	61%	66%
WEAKNESS	70%	54%	61%

4.3   The Service Extraction Pipeline

The entire pipeline of network service extraction is as follows. We first use the above machine learning method to identify a set of vulnerabilities associated with the *WEB* and *CLIENT* services. For other vulnerabilities that fall into the *INCONCLUSIVE* category, the above NLP-based rule matching identifies the specific network services. Vulnerabilities that do not match any NLP-based rules are left for manual analysis by security operators.

We tested the pipeline over 3,841 vulnerabilities published in the NVD in 2020. We used the 2020 NVD dataset for testing because both the machine-learning and NLP models trained over data features from 2017 through 2019. The results are shown in Fig. 1.

The left-most column shows the results of *machine-learning only* where service classification is derived for 88% of vulnerabilities with a 97% classification accuracy (for the remaining 12% of vulnerabilities, the machine learning method

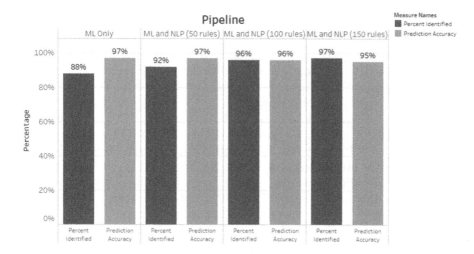

Fig. 1. Performance of network service extraction

alone is not able to generate any service classification). The following three columns show the classification results of *machine learning and NLP* when the number of NLP rules changes from 50 to 100 and 150. When there are 50 NLP rules, more vulnerabilities' network services are classified than machine learning only while the overall classification accuracy maintains at the same level. By adding NLP rules from 50 to 150, vulnerabilities with identified network services increase from 92% to 97%. As a trade-off, there is a slight reduction in the overall classification accuracy (from 97% to 95%) since some NLP rules generate wrong service mappings. However, the accuracy is still high.

3,529 (92%) of the identified network services were categorized as either *WEB* or *CLIENT*, with 3,353 (87%) identified by machine learning and 404 (10%) by

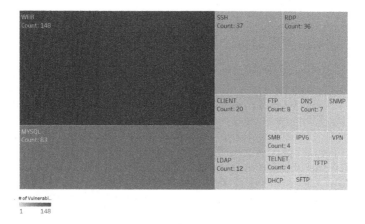

Fig. 2. Additional network services identified through NLP

NLP. Figure 2 shows the diversity of network services identified solely by NLP. The treemap shows the number of network services in both color and area.

Each network service maps to a set of transport-layer network ports. The ports directly associate with firewall rules to automatically assess network reachability, as we show in the next section.

5   Network Reachability

Network reachability means an adversary's ability to access a target device over a network. Firewalls between the adversary and target device serve as the principal inhibitor of access for most server environments. Determining the combined and effective access permitted by the set of firewalls is tantamount to establishing whether an adversary can reach a given vulnerability. Reach analysis includes an assessment of both i) direct network service access and ii) interactive access, in which an adversary extends its reach into the network through the possession of authentication credentials and vulnerability exploits.

This step aims to identify combinations of adversaries, target devices, and vulnerabilities for safety analysis. As shown in Fig. 3, target devices reside in network zones, and adversaries get placed in network zones based on some realistic approximation of where an adversary may already reside in the network. In this diagram, the outmost firewall may block the state-sponsored adversary from the Internet to the target operator's workstation. However, the internal firewall policies may allow an insider threat to reach the target operator workstation.

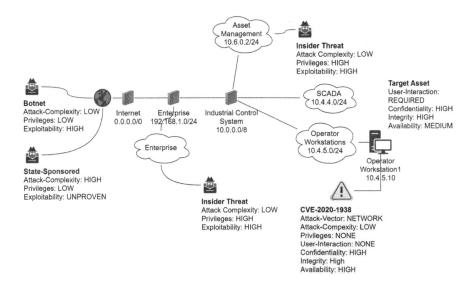

Fig. 3. Reachability analysis combining Adversaries, Targets, and Vulnerabilities

The reachability model answers the question, "can an adversary reach a target asset and exploit a vulnerability?" Armed with each vulnerability's network service information, the model can use a firewall configuration analyzer (e.g., NP-View[1]) to parse out network topology and accessibility between network zones and determine whether a given adversary has an opportunity to exploit a given vulnerability.

Firewall configuration in the network can be parsed to produce paths represented as a five-tuple variable of protocol, source and destination IP address, and source and destination transport-layer port. The set of path tuples serve as an effective firewall ruleset between all network zones. We also further categorize firewall rules related to interactive services (e.g., SSH, RDP). This subset of rules allows the adversary to have authenticated access in a network zone, thereby extending its reach and pivot toward its target. In contrast, non-interactive services (e.g., HTTP, SMB) do not provide a direct opportunity for pivoting into a network zone.

We can now model adversarial reach by placing adversaries in network zones such as the placement shown in Fig. 3. For assessing an adversary's ability to pivot between networks, the model uses an undirected graph because interactive access can occur between any network zones in a routed network. The network services used to permit interactive access, $\Psi \in \Gamma$, include those which permit the adversary to have local interactive access to the target operating system.

A depth-first-search with cycle detection traverses the graph to associate adversaries with network zones. Suppose an adversary can interact with a device in a different network zone because of permitted interactive access. In that case, the model assumes the adversary can obtain credentials in the existing zone. By recursively traversing the graph, adversaries copy over into each network zone to which it may pivot.

6   Model Checking Vulnerability Safety

Network reachability represents a significant obstacle for the adversary, but adversarial access to the vulnerability is not the end of the story. This section presents a definition of safety with respect to a vulnerability, adversary, and its target device. Throughout the model discussion, we refer to the transition system in the following definition:

Definition 1. *Software Vulnerability Transition System*

- *S - Set of states*
- *$R \subseteq S \times S$ - Transition functions*
- *$S_0 \subseteq S$ - The set of initial states*
- *AP - Set of atomic propositions*
- *$L : S \to 2^{AP}$ - Labeling of states formula*
- *$\Phi = AG(\neg unsafe)$ - Invariant condition defining an secure state*
- *S_s - Set of final accepting states*

---

[1] https://www.network-perception.com/.

The safety invariant, Φ, indicates the model cannot reach an unsafe state, which means the adversary cannot exploit the vulnerability. The labels apply to the three model objects: (i) vulnerabilities denoted as v, (ii) target devices denoted as τ, and (iii) adversaries denoted as ϵ. These objects are the basic building blocks for assessing system safety. Together, these objects provide the propositional labels applying to a system state, such that $AP = \{v, \tau, \epsilon\}$.

Figure 4 provides an example of how object labels combine in a final state, S_s, to calculate both the safety invariant and the overall impact. In this example, the vulnerability dominates the attack complexity (AC) of the adversary. A high AC for a vulnerability means an adversary with low AC could not successfully exploit the vulnerability. Therefore, as we show later in this section, the final state is safe. Because the final state is considered safe, the model does not assess impact. However, if the final state was unsafe, the calculated impact gradient label (see Sect. 3.1) of *medium* would apply.

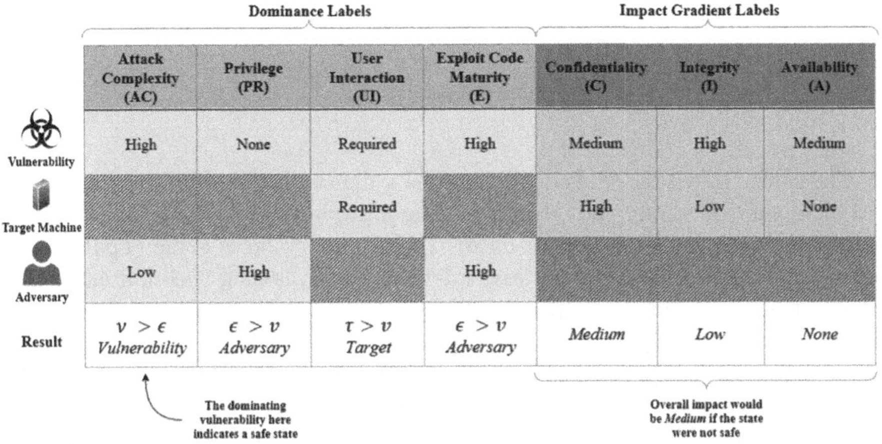

	Dominance Labels				Impact Gradient Labels		
	Attack Complexity (AC)	Privilege (PR)	User Interaction (UI)	Exploit Code Maturity (E)	Confidentiality (C)	Integrity (I)	Availability (A)
Vulnerability	High	None	Required	High	Medium	High	Medium
Target Machine			Required		High	Low	None
Adversary	Low	High		High			
Result	$v > \epsilon$ Vulnerability	$\epsilon > v$ Adversary	$\tau > v$ Target	$\epsilon > v$ Adversary	Medium	Low	None

The dominating vulnerability here indicates a safe state

Overall impact would be *Medium* if the state were not safe

Fig. 4. Example final state labeling

6.1 Dominance Relation in Capability State Labels

We now formally describe each capability label and how the labeling function applies to the vulnerability in the final state.

Definition 2 (Dominance Labels). *A vulnerability state label grouping in which the following properties hold:*

- *Distinct labels in the group can order in terms of increasing difficulty and decreasing opportunity of exploitation*
- *A cumulative set hierarchy represents attacker capability on the ordered labels.*
- *The label group defines a necessary condition for exploitation.*

This definition holds for the CVSS exploitability and temporal metrics. Labels have order applied as described below in this section. The cumulative set hierarchy follows from the ordered set, in which the capabilities accrue based on the order. Then, finally, the necessity for exploitation should be evident in the description of each label group.

We can now formally define safety in terms of the dominance relation between v, τ and ϵ. For a given state $s \in S$, $L(s)$ includes labels for $\{v, \tau, \epsilon\}$ in the capability categories of each $Cap = \{AC, PR, UI, EX\}$. We symbolize a state label for some category $c \in Cap$ with respect to an object as v_s^c, τ_s^c and ϵ_s^c. For brevity, Cap is also split as Cap_ϵ for labels applying to adversaries and Cap_τ for labels applying to targets. The dominance relation is defined for vulnerability dominance as:

$$(v_s)dom(\epsilon_s, \tau_s) \iff$$
$$\exists c \in Cap_\epsilon, v_s^c > \epsilon_s^c$$
$$\vee \exists c \in Cap_\tau, v_s^c > \tau_s^c$$

And dominance for the adversary and target is defined as:

$$(\epsilon_s, \tau_s)dom(v_s) \iff$$
$$\forall c \in Cap_\epsilon, \epsilon_s^c > v_s^c$$
$$\wedge \forall c \in Cap_\tau, \tau_s^c > v_s^c$$

The safety invariant, Φ, is defined as the vulnerability dominating the target and adversary, meaning the adversary cannot exploit the target using the vulnerability. Likewise, a *safe* state means the adversary lacks some capability to exploit the vulnerability on the target device. The following theorem associates the dominance property to our definition of model safety.

Theorem 1. *if $(v_s)dom(\epsilon_s, \tau_s)$, then the state, $s \in S_s$ is safe.*

Proof. We begin proving this by assuming the dominance relation holds between vulnerabilities and adversaries. Each capability-based category forms an ordered set which is also a cumulative set hierarchy with respect to v, ϵ and τ.

$$\forall c \in Cap \mid 0 \leq i < |c|,$$
$$v^{c_i} \subseteq v^{c_{i+1}}, \epsilon^{c_{i+1}} \subseteq \epsilon^{c_i}, \tau^{c_{i+1}} \subseteq \tau^{c_i}$$

Recall that the set order indicates both (i) increasing difficulty and (ii) decreasing exploit opportunity. For v, lower ordered categories are a subset of those higher-ordered. The ordering means an unsafe vulnerability based on v^{c_i} remains unsafe for any lower ordered capability. In contrast, ϵ and τ have a reverse hierarchical set because capability at a higher level would suffice to exploit any vulnerability with v at a lower order.

Because v is dominating, we know there is at least one $c \in Cap$ in which v is greater than either ϵ or τ. Through the cumulative set hierarchy, it follows that:

$$\exists c \in Cap \mid v^c \cap \epsilon^c \in \emptyset \vee v^c \cap \tau^c \in \emptyset \tag{1}$$

Therefore, the adversary cannot exploit the vulnerability on the target in at least one category, and by Definition 2, v is safe. The proof ends.

The converse is not necessarily true because some other capability category may exist outside of the CVSS metric.

6.2   Measuring Impact

Impact gradient labels apply when the final state of a system is not safe. These labels provide further context for assessing the vulnerable state of a system and prioritizing risk mitigation work. The set of risk gradient categories are $G = \{C, I, A\}$. Similar to dominance labels, we also define each label category as a cumulative set hierarchy in which:

$$\forall g \in G \mid 0 \le i < |g|, g_i \subseteq g_{i+1} \tag{2}$$

For example, if the vulnerability label for confidentiality were H (or high), then $v^C = \{L, M, H\}$. Now, a simple impact gradient calculation provides the combined result of v and τ:

Definition 3. *A calculated impact gradient label applies to final states S_s in which $\Phi = AG(\neg safe)$ as:*

$$Impact(S_s) = max(\bigcup_{g \in G} v^g \cap \tau^g)$$

The impact calculation bounds the impact of the target device label.

7   Evaluations

Open data sets for firewall and vulnerability management are not available due to the highly sensitive nature of the data and industry-specific compliance obligations. To overcome these barriers, we generate a realistic sample system. We adopt an approach to generate the requisite system data using network service exploration. The applications required to run on the system determine the required network services. We identified the required applications through interviews, assessments, and exploration of industry compliance obligations. These applications are decomposed into classes of commonly used computing assets and further decomposed into individual assets and software.

In particular, our sample system derives from applications and compliance obligations required for a power grid control center, but the approach works for other critical infrastructure domains as well. We derive it using elements of the computing environment required by the North American Electric Reliability Corporation (NERC) Critical Infrastructure Protection (CIP) regulatory standards [7]. The standard sufficiently references specific types of technology related to security and reliability for creating a representative sample. The resulting system contains 124 devices organized into 25 asset groups, e.g., Web Servers and Operator Workstations, as shown in Fig. 5. The data set also includes 4,894 combined software assets mapped to the NVD.

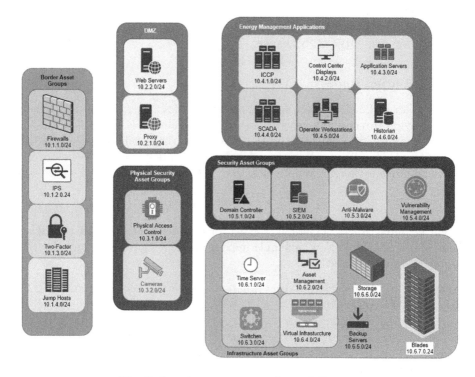

Fig. 5. Sample system network zonal diagram

We tested the implementation of network reachability and safety analysis on the above asset dataset using the vulnerabilities from the NVD for January 2017 through July 2020 that match the assets. Vulnerabilities map to software and computer assets using a combination of Common Product Enumeration (CPE) applicability matching, Microsoft vulnerability reports, and Red Hat vulnerability reports. In that timeframe, we found a total of 106,313 vulnerabilities applicable to the assets.

To generate firewall rules, we analyze each asset by identifying its listening network services, client services, and remote access services and then generate firewall rules for these services. The generated firewall ruleset has a realistic basis in the system's common sector-specific services. We generated 1,156 distinct firewall rules by traversing the network graph and filling in the required services.

Adversaries had access to the Internet network zone, enterprise network zone, and an asset management zone internal to the control system in the model. The Internet adversaries modeled a state-sponsored adversary (i.e., skillful with minimum internal privileges) and an automated botnet (i.e., minimally capable with minimum internal privileges). The two internal adversaries modeled inside threats that hold highly privileged access but are minimally capable of exploiting vulnerabilities.

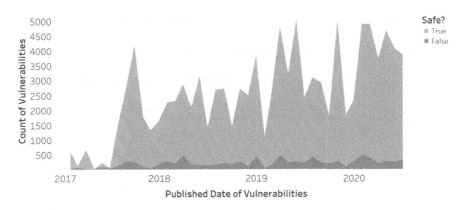

Fig. 6. Monthly safety analysis of all applicable vulnerabilities

Each network zone's data structure included all adversaries having interactive reach into the zone based on the generated firewall ruleset. Network services were extracted for all the vulnerabilities as well.

Finally, each of the 106,313 vulnerabilities received an assessment using the presented model-checking safety analysis. The assessment included modeling each adversary with interactive access to the device and assessing adversaries having reach associated with the vulnerability's network service. A particular case also occurs for vulnerabilities requiring user interactions. Our model mainly considers inbound reachability from the Internet to a target server device. However, we model outbound user interaction by assuming the worst-case scenario, in which a state-sponsored adversary has backdoor interactive access to an asset.

Figure 6 presents the results. This graph shows the monthly count of both safe and unsafe vulnerabilities for the sampling period. Those vulnerabilities assessed as safe account for approximately 92% of the vulnerabilities overall, whereas those assessed as unsafe remain consistently below 500 applicable vulnerabilities per month. *This implies security operators informed by safety analysis can use their limited resources to address unsafe vulnerabilities.*

The model checking also allows iterative exploration where the adversary's reach extends through unsafe vulnerabilities, which we term gateway vulnerabilities. Gateway vulnerabilities allow full access or privilege escalation on a reachable target such that exploitation would extend the adversary's reach into additional network zones. The model checking increases reachability only for unsafe vulnerabilities having *High* integrity impact. In contrast, vulnerabilities with only denial of service effects (i.e., availability impact) or information disclosure effects (i.e., confidentiality impact) do not extend adversary reach.

Figure 7 shows the results of extending reachability using gateway vulnerabilities. The first graph/iteration is a copy of Fig. 6, and the second graph/iteration shows the number of increased vulnerabilities after extending adversarial reach from the first iteration. The third graph is the third iteration. It is the full extension of adversarial reach since there are no additional gateway vulnerabilities beyond the third iteration. The number of unsafe vulnerabilities rises from

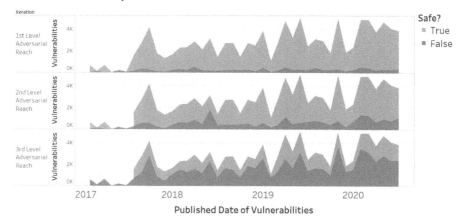

Fig. 7. Iterative safety analysis for all applicable vulnerabilities

8% in the first iteration to 20% in the second, and then 60% in the final iteration and maximum adversarial reach.

The data would suggest an adversarial advantage in unsafe vulnerabilities, but a countermeasure strategy to immediately mitigate gateway vulnerabilities would maintain the defense advantage of minimal unsafe vulnerabilities. The graph in Fig. 8 shows the number of gateway vulnerabilities per month, which remains minuscule compared to the overall number of vulnerabilities.

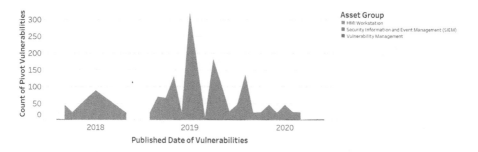

Fig. 8. Vulnerabilities allowing extension of adversarial reach

8 Conclusion

We proposed a new scheme of automatically evaluating software vulnerabilities for state safety using firewall configuration data. It involves automated identification of network services associated with vulnerabilities and connects that to firewall rules, target devices, and adversarial attributes under one formal framework. Tests on a realistically simulated sample system showed only 8% of the applicable vulnerabilities are unsafe. We further modeled the dynamic threat movement to pivot deeper into the network using gateway vulnerabilities and found the presence of gateway vulnerabilities, when left unmitigated, remarkably changes the number of unsafe vulnerabilities. The results suggest new strategies in cybersecurity operations to apply limited resources better.

Acknowledgement. This material is based upon work supported by the Department of Energy under Award Number DE-CR0000003.

References

1. Common product enumeration standard. https://nvd.nist.gov/products/cpe. Accessed 28 Jan 2020
2. Common vulnerability scoring system specification. https://www.first.org/cvss/v3.1/specification-document. Accessed 28 Jan 2020
3. Common vulnerability scoring system v3.1: Specification document. https://www.first.org/cvss/v3.1/specification-document. Accessed 1 Feb 2020
4. Common weakness enumeration. https://cwe.mitre.org/. Accessed 28 Jan 2020
5. National vulnerability database data feed. https://nvd.nist.gov/general/visualizations/vulnerability-visualizations/cvss-severity-distribution-over-time. Accessed 1 Feb 2020
6. National vulnerability database data feed. https://nvd.nist.gov/vuln/data-feeds. Accessed 28 Jan 2020
7. North American electric reliability corporation (NERC) critical infrastructure protection (CIP) standards. https://www.nerc.com/pa/Stand/Pages/CIPStandards.aspx. Accessed 1 Feb 2020
8. Spacy and prodigy network language processing tools. https://explosion.ai/. Accessed 2 Feb 2020
9. Vulnerability and patch management resources. http://cybersecurity.ddns.uark.edu/vpm/. Accessed 25 June 2021
10. Stix version 2.1, March 2020. https://docs.oasis-open.org/cti/stix/v2.1/cs01/stix-v2.1-cs01.html. Accessed 9 Mar 2021
11. Ammann, P., Wijesekera, D., Kaushik, S.: Scalable, graph-based network vulnerability analysis. In: ACM Conference on Computer and Communications Security, pp. 217–224 (2002)
12. Audinot, M., Pinchinat, S., Kordy, B.: Guided design of attack trees: a system-based approach. In: 2018 IEEE 31st Computer Security Foundations Symposium (CSF), pp. 61–75, July 2018
13. Collins, K.: The hackers who broke into Equifax exploited a flaw in open-source server software. Quartz. https://qz.com/1073221/the-hackers-who-broke-into-equifax-exploited-a-nine-year-old-security-flaw/
14. Collobert, R., Weston, J., Bottou, L., Karlen, M., Kavukcuoglu, K., Kuksa, P.: Natural language processing (almost) from scratch. J. Mach. Learn. Res. **12**(ARTICLE), 2493–2537 (2011)
15. Fila, B., Wide, W.: Efficient attack-defense tree analysis using pareto attribute domains. In: 2019 IEEE 32nd Computer Security Foundations Symposium (CSF), June 2019
16. Gamarra, M., Shetty, S., Nicol, D.M., Gonzalez, O., Kamhoua, C.A., Njilla, L.: Analysis of stepping stone attacks in dynamic vulnerability graphs, pp. 1–7, May 2018
17. Ghosh, N., Ghosh, S.K.: An approach for security assessment of network configurations using attack graph. In: International Conference on Networks & Communications, pp. 283–288 (2010)

18. Huff, P., Li, Q.: A recommender system for tracking vulnerabilities. In: International Workshop on Next Generation Security Operations Centers (NG-SOC) (2021)
19. Kordy, B., Mauw, S., Radomirović, S., Schweitzer, P.: Foundations of attack–defense trees. In: Degano, P., Etalle, S., Guttman, J. (eds.) FAST 2010. LNCS, vol. 6561, pp. 80–95. Springer, Heidelberg (2011). https://doi.org/10.1007/978-3-642-19751-2_6
20. Landwehr, C.E.: Formal models for computer security. ACM Comput. Surv. (CSUR) **13**(3), 247–278 (1981)
21. Le, H.T., Loh, P.K.K.: Using natural language tool to assist VPRG automated extraction from textual vulnerability description. In: 2011 IEEE Workshops of International Conference on Advanced Information Networking and Applications, March 2011
22. Le, T.H.M., Sabir, B., Babar, M.A.: Automated software vulnerability assessment with concept drift. In: 2019 IEEE/ACM 16th International Conference on Mining Software Repositories (MSR), pp. 371–382 (2019)
23. Mantel, H., Probst, C.W.: On the meaning and purpose of attack trees. In: 2019 IEEE 32nd Computer Security Foundations Symposium (CSF), pp. 184–18415, June 2019
24. Mauw, S., Oostdijk, M.: Foundations of attack trees. In: Won, D.H., Kim, S. (eds.) ICISC 2005. LNCS, vol. 3935, pp. 186–198. Springer, Heidelberg (2006). https://doi.org/10.1007/11734727_17
25. McClanahan, K., Li, Q.: Automatically locating mitigation information for security vulnerabilities. In: IEEE International Conference on Communications, Control, and Computing Technologies for Smart Grids (SmartGridComm) (2020)
26. Noel, S., Jajodia, S.: Metrics suite for network attack graph analytics. In: Proceedings of the 9th Annual Cyber and Information Security Research Conference, pp. 5–8 (2014)
27. Phillips, C., Swiler, L.P.: A graph-based system for network-vulnerability analysis. In: Proceedings of the 1998 Workshop on New security paradigms, pp. 71–79 (1998)
28. Schneier, B.: Attack trees. Dr. Dobb's J. **24**(12), 21–29 (1999)
29. Sikos, L.F.: OWL ontologies in cybersecurity: conceptual modeling of cyber-knowledge. In: Sikos, L.F. (ed.) AI in Cybersecurity. ISRL, vol. 151, pp. 1–17. Springer, Cham (2019). https://doi.org/10.1007/978-3-319-98842-9_1
30. Syed, Z., Padia, A., Finin, T., Mathews, L., Joshi, A.: UCO: a unified cybersecurity ontology. In: UMBC Student Collection (2016)
31. Wang, L., Jajodia, S., Singhal, A., Noel, S.: k-zero day safety: measuring the security risk of networks against unknown attacks. In: Gritzalis, D., Preneel, B., Theoharidou, M. (eds.) ESORICS 2010. LNCS, vol. 6345, pp. 573–587. Springer, Heidelberg (2010). https://doi.org/10.1007/978-3-642-15497-3_35
32. Wang, P., Zhou, Y., Sun, B., Zhang, W.: Intelligent prediction of vulnerability severity level based on text mining and XGBboost. In: 2019 Eleventh International Conference on Advanced Computational Intelligence (ICACI), pp. 72–77 (2019)
33. Wing, J.M., et al.: Scenario graphs applied to network security. In: Information Assurance: Survivability and Security in Networked Systems, pp. 247–277 (2008)
34. Xie, A., Wen, W., Zhang, L., Hu, J., Chen, Z.: Applying attack graphs to network security metric. In: Proceedings of the 2009 International Conference on Multimedia Information Networking and Security, vol. 01, pp. 427–431 (2009)
35. Xu, M., et al.: Dominance as a new trusted computing primitive for the internet of things. In: 2019 IEEE Symposium on Security and Privacy (SP) (2019)

36. Zhang, F., Huff, P., McClanahan, K., Li, Q.: A machine learning-based approach for automated vulnerability remediation analysis. In: IEEE Conference on Communications and Network Security (CNS) (2020)
37. Zhang, F., Li, Q.: Dynamic risk-aware patch scheduling. In: IEEE Conference on Communications and Network Security (CNS) (2020)

Repeatable Experimentation for Cybersecurity Moving Target Defense

Jaime C. Acosta[1]([✉]), Luisana Clarke[2], Stephanie Medina[2], Monika Akbar[2], Mahmud Shahriar Hossain[2], and Frederica Free-Nelson[1]

[1] DEVCOM Army Research Laboratory, Adelphi, USA
jaime.c.acosta.civ@mail.mil
[2] University of Texas at El Paso, El Paso, USA

Abstract. The scientific method emphasizes that repeatable experimentation is critical for several reasons; to facilitate comparative analysis, to recreate experiments, to re-validate reported results, to critique and propose improvements, and to augment the work. In the field of cybersecurity moving target defense, where assets are shuffled to thwart attackers, it is critical to know what strategies work best, the success factors, and how these strategies may impact system performance. While some researchers make their algorithms, models, and tools available as open source, it is difficult and, in some cases, impossible to recreate studies due to the lack of the original operating environment or no support for software components used within that environment.

In this paper, we present the repeatable experimentation system (RES), which aids in creating and recreating networked virtual environments to conduct comparative network studies. Experiments are composed of virtual machines, containers, automation scripts, and other artifacts that are needed to recreate and re-run a study. This includes data collection and analysis. We provide a case study where we incorporate two publicly available moving target defense implementations that use different underlying software components. We present how RES can be used for fully automated experimentation along with an analysis on the results obtained from parallel and sequential executions. We have packaged the case study into a RES file that can be used by other researchers to repeat, modify, and improve on these and other works.

Keywords: Cybersecurity · Repeatable experimentation · Dynamic defense · Moving target defense

1 Introduction

Moving target defense (MTD) is a technique that holds much promise; it reduces the attack surface by making changes to system configurations when certain conditions are met. Network MTD approaches may change IP addresses at certain time intervals or based on observed throughput [6]. At the operating system

© ICST Institute for Computer Sciences, Social Informatics and Telecommunications Engineering 2021
Published by Springer Nature Switzerland AG 2021. All Rights Reserved
J. Garcia-Alfaro et al. (Eds.): SecureComm 2021, LNICST 398, pp. 82–99, 2021.
https://doi.org/10.1007/978-3-030-90019-9_5

level, a prominent technique in wide use is address space layout randomization (ASLR), where the mapping of memory for processes is meant to be ever-changing and unpredictable [11]. Application-level MTD algorithms may, for example, attempt to randomize the code execution paths of a binary [23].

Attackers, especially those that are experienced or members of an organizations, follow certain tactics, techniques, and procedures (TTPs) depending on their objectives [22]. MITRE and others [27] have documented some of these attack scenarios through analyses of breaches and other incidents. TTPs consist of steps that include the gathering of information, such as the network devices and addresses on an internal network. An attacker that gains access will be more prepared, and likely need to reveal less (for example, eliminating the need for a noisy port scan) based on what they know beforehand. Using the IP Shuffling technique [3], a defender can attempt to eliminate this overmatch by dynamically changing the addresses of network nodes.

There are many considerations that must be addressed before claiming security measures as successful. Rigorous investigations are required to study the impact of a security measure in concrete scenarios and their effectiveness against the adversary's intentions. Additionally, a single solution will not likely work in all circumstances. For example, in a network where situational awareness is occasionally transmitted using short messages in a small network, high-frequency shuffling may not be an issue. This solution may not be suitable in scenarios where there is high-latency and high throughput. In short, a characterization of the impact of the algorithm in a relevant scenario must be performed. These results must be compared and analyzed against other relevant studies in relevant domains.

In this paper, we present the repeatable experimentation system (RES)[1] with the objective of enabling widely-accessible and shareable MTD experimentation. In summary, our contributions are the following.

- An open source and extensible tool, RES, along with demonstrations showing how it can be used to package experiments to facilitate repeatability.
- A case study in which we incorporate a MTD implementation[2] that uses software-defined networking and a randomized IP shuffling technique (similar to those reported in [5]).
- An analysis that shows that using RES and its parallel execution does not impact execution results and a characterization of the MTD implementation when used against port scans.

Section 2 outlines the literature relevant to this paper. We explain our Repeatable Experimentation System (RES) in Sect. 3. Section 4 provides the design of the case study we conducted in this paper. We provide experimental analyses with MTD characterization in Section 5. Section 6 concludes the paper with a brief discussion on future directions of the work.

---

[1] Available at: https://github.com/ARL-UTEP-OC/res.
[2] Available at: https://github.com/ARL-UTEP-OC/res-ryu-mtd.

2   Related Work

Many approaches have been proposed to create variability for achieving moving target defense. Some of these approaches work on reducing attack surfaces [15, 21, 33], some focus on randomizing the network components [16, 24], others propose randomizing types of services [28], or switching operating systems [4]. Among these, the software-defined network (SDN) has gained attention in randomizing network components by programmatically changing network configurations [2, 20, 32].

Given the rise in MTD research, there are usually multiple different MTDs to choose from under any given threat scenario. However, there is no standard metric for evaluating MTDs, which makes it difficult to estimate the cost or assess the effectiveness of MTDs when deciding the best or most suitable MTD. Several projects used attack surface [7, 21] and attack graphs [13] to evaluate MTDs. Others used security [18], performance [8], and various network and system properties [14, 29] to assess MTDs.

When it comes to measuring the effectiveness or evaluating the performance of an MTD, most MTDs present a customized approach. There are a few ongoing efforts towards building theoretical assessment frameworks for MTDs [6, 31]. However, much of these efforts are geared towards specific types of attacks or MTDs. There are no standard mechanisms for analyzing different MTDs and evaluating and comparing their effectiveness, to the best of our knowledge.

3   Repeatable Experimentation System

The development of RES is based on several interactions with cybersecurity professionals and previous experience in developing cybersecurity-inclusive moving target defense network scenarios. Even when moving target defense algorithms are made available, it still takes a significant amount of work to replicate the experiments described in scientific papers — to allow building upon the work. This is primarily due to software dependencies or software being inoperable; where newer versions of packages are incompatible with other software, including the operating system. Other reasons include gaps in the intricate details related to set up and configuration that are omitted, possibly due to paper length constraints. We developed a novel software tool – RES – to mitigate these issues and to facilitate the scientific experimentation process.

3.1   Capabilities

RES is available as open source software to encourage its wide use and to allow analysts to share their experiments without having to purchase software licenses. It is extensible and it leverages several other tools including Oracle VirtualBox [30], Apache Guacamole [10], and, optionally, HashiCorp Vagrant [12]. Python 3 is the primary implementation language and we use the PyQt5 module for the graphical frontend. RES runs on Linux, Mac, and Windows with only minimal graphical differences. The underlying base code is the same.

Expansion and flexibility are critical for repeatable MTD experiments, especially due to the ever-changing and ever-improving underlying virtualization technologies. To support expansion and flexibility of existing virtual environments, we used a plugin design to allow analysts to add, swap, and improve interfaces to underlying components such as the hypervisor, remote desktop provider, and packaging system.

To ease the process of replicating experiments – including those developed by other analysts – RES allows analysts to import a single all-inclusive file that contains all the required artifacts necessary for an experiment. This includes the virtual machines (VMs), which are automatically loaded into the hypervisor, as well as any other instructional materials associated with the experiment. After import, the number of steps required to repeat the experiment are minimal. Exporting of experiments is trivial. Users are able to specify virtual machines, materials, and also their experiment configurations (number of experiments, scripts, remote display information) and then create an all-inclusive package.

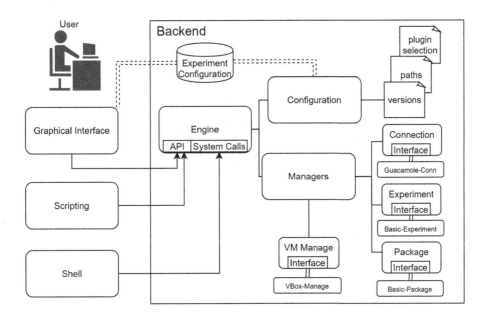

Fig. 1. RES architecture

Experiments may be cloned to enable the parallel or sequential execution of multiple runs. An analyst may include specific commands that run on start. As an example, a user may have an experiment that requires Mininet [17] to run with certain arguments; pointing to the scenario that will execute. The scenario needs to run for a certain length of time, then quit and copy the resulting data to a network attached storage device. All of these commands can be added to the experiment during configuration. All of the hypervisor invocations are multi-threaded, including calls to start, stop, pause, snapshot, and delete clones; this is done to improve performance.

Lastly, we focused on giving analysts the ability to interact with RES using different modes of operation. The system can be invoked through a graphical interface, but also through Python scripting that communicates directly with the backend as shown in Fig. 1.

3.2   Design

The system, shown in Fig. 1, consists of a segregated frontend and backend. The frontend is a way to abstract and facilitate access to backend capabilities. Users of the graphical application can run an experiment using the point-and-click interface; the developer of an experiment can create a script that automates all of the actions required to execute and collect data; an interactive shell provides a user with an interactive terminal-session to conduct the same actions available through the graphical interface. Communication between the frontend and backend occurs through either a Python application programming interface, essentially function calls with results provided through return values, or by executing a companion application that makes calls to the engine and writes results to standard output. Examples are provided with the application; including unit tests and a fully working graphical user interface that implements the system capabilities.

The graphical interface (shown in Fig. 2) contains a mechanism to create and modify experiment configurations (each is stored as a XML file). When started, RES displays the Configuration tab (shown in the left window) where a user may select, import, and export experiments. They can also specify a server IP address (used for remote display), group name, number of clones (or instantiations of the experiment), among several others. It is also possible to add virtual machines and any additional files that should belong to the experiment from this view. Selecting a virtual machine (shown in the bottom window) will display additional configuration options, including whether remote display should be enabled for the machine, commands that should be run on the machine when it first starts, and the interfaces on the machine. Specifying network interface names that match across other virtual machines will connect the machines together (similar to them being on a shared network switch). In Fig. 2, the Ubuntu18-core-cdes machine has 8 different interfaces; the first is intnet1. The ATTACKER_10.0.0.2 machine has only a single interface called intnet1. These two machines, when cloned, will share a common interface and can therefore communicate directly. This functionality is preserved across clones so that each set will only be able to communicate amongst themselves. This allows for building larger, complex networks when combined with network emulation software such as the Common Open Research Emulator [1] or Mininet. In this case, machine's traffic can be forced to traverse through the emulated network, which can be e.g., an SDN, before reaching a

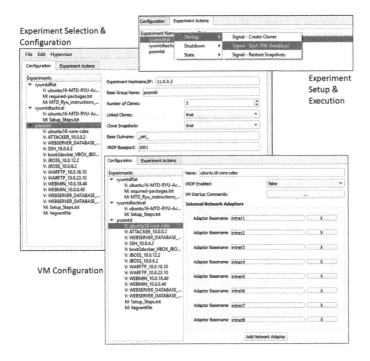

Fig. 2. RES graphical interface

recipient. The second GUI tab (shown in the top window) invokes various functions of the Experiment Manager. It is worth noting that these XML files can be manually created and modified; the GUI is merely a convenient way to do so. The backend modules are included in Fig. 1.

The Configuration module reads and parses the XML experiment files and then makes data structures available to the Managers. The Configuration module also reads and writes information related to specific plugins (e.g., the concrete VirtualBox implementation), paths to external programs (such as the path to VBoxManage), and values representative of specific versions of packages associated with the system.

The Managers module uses a plugin design to enable flexible integration with external components. The VMManage interface module consists of all of the tasks associated with virtualization components at the virtual machine level; including starting, pausing, stopping, snapshot, and restoring of individual virtual machines. The software currently implements these functions with VirtualBox plugins, but it can easily be extended to support others, such as VMWare, ESX, XenServer, and Proxmox; as these all have mechanisms for controlling virtual machines as well as several interfaces and concrete implementation classes to handle remote desktop functions. We also chose to implement VMManage at this granularity to enable concurrent execution; e.g., to allow several virtual machines to snapshot, clone, start, stop, etc. simultaneously; many of which are not concurrent through the standard VirtualBox GUI.

The Package interface module primarily handles importing and exporting. Using the information associated with the experiment, provided by the Experiment Configuration, it calls the VMManage module to trigger the backend hypervisor to execute its specific import/export functions. In the case of VirtualBox, open virtual appliances (OVAs) are created for virtual machines. In addition to this, any material files that are part of the experiment are included in the exported file. The result is a compressed file with the *RES* file extension. This module is also extensible; we provide the behavior described above as the fundamental and basic, however, developers are able to extend this module and provide additional functionality, e.g., to import and export remotely, implement authentication, secure with encryption, and others.

Behaviors related to experiments, such as cloning, starting, and stopping occur through the Experiment interface module. As with the other modules, experiment information is read from the Configuration and then batch operations are executed through this component. Specifically with our VirtualBox implementation, we use the guest control feature; which requires that the virtual machines are running the same version of guest additions as the host. We provided basic functionality, but as with the Package interface, developers may choose to extend functionality to include additional scripting, such as integration with other provisioning software including Vagrant and Ansible.

During the execution and setup of experiments, it's important to allow users to see the running systems. We developed the Connection interface module for this reason. Currently, it uses Apache Guacamole to broker remote desktop connections that are accessible using HTML5 with any modern web browser. User creation is also automated, using the guacapy REST API Python module.[3] Developers may write extensions to connect to virtual machines instead through VNC, add capabilities such as key-based authentication, or even swap out the guacamole module entirely with another remote desktop broker.

4   Case Study Design

To demonstrate and test the utility of RES, we developed a case study with the following process.

1. Recreate the execution environment for a network MTD algorithm and modify for use in a set of experiments (Sects. 4.1 and 4.2).
2. Construct and execute experiments several times in parallel using RES. Afterwards, the experiments and results are packaged into self-contained, archives that can be redistributed (Sects. 4.2 and 4.3).
3. Analyze the differences in the results when using RES versus manual execution. Characterize the scanning success rate when using different MTD shuffling time intervals (Sect. 5).

---

[3] Available at https://github.com/pschmitt/guacapy.

4.1   MTD Algorithm Implementation

We started by looking for free and open-source implementations of network MTD algorithms. We selected a Ryu controller-based SDN implementation [9] because it shared similarities with more sophisticated algorithms such as the Flexible Random Virtual IP Multiplexing [26]. The Ryu controller is written in the Python language, it provides access to its backend processes using an API, and it runs on Linux. Ryu is prominently used today and supports newer versions of the OpenFlow protocol. Rohitaksha and Rajendra [25] provide an in-depth study of the advantages and disadvantages of Ryu and other controllers such as Pox.

The Ryu implementation uses Python dictionaries to keep track of current mappings between real and virtual IPs and uses rules and flow tables to restrict communication to and from virtual IPs. The Ryu implementation was developed as a homework assignment for a course that teaches software-defined networking concepts. We made several modifications to the original code and introduced features that make it usable in our experiments. We refer to this modified implementation as mtd-ryu. Figure 3 shows the high-level processes that compose mtd-ryu.

Mtd-ryu inherits it's dependencies from the original implementation. It runs on an Ubuntu 16 VM, and it works with the latest version of Mininet (2.3.0d4). It requires Python2 (which is deprecated) and Ryu-manager version 4.3.2. The controller uses OpenFlow 1.3 to communicate with the switches, which run Open vSwitch version 2.5.5. Address resolutions are stored as flow entries on each switch and packet header field values are modified to use virtual IPs instead of real IPs.

Many MTD scenarios in the literature shuffle IP mappings in such a way that all established connections, even seemingly legitimate ones, are dropped indiscriminately. This seems impractical for a realistic scenario; important services would be interrupted and the stateful connections would constantly be restoring address resolutions and re-establishing connections after every shuffle. Non-stateful connections would at a minimum have to constantly resolve node addresses. These could cause significant delays in communications.

Rather than having flow tables simply cleared every specified number of seconds and dropping all connections, we used the concept of authorized and unauthorized entities. Connections that originate and are destined for authorized entities (based on IP Addresses) are considered legitimate connections. These are ignored during shuffling which eliminates disruptions. Connections that are not considered legitimate are dropped and must be re-established after every shuffle. In the code, we implement this behavior by having two separate flow tables on each switch; managed by the controller. The authorized flow tables contains legitimate connections and they are never cleared. Both tables use only virtual IP addresses. This does not affect the legitimate connections because ARP entries are persistent and domain name resolution only happens once; when the nodes communicate for the first time. Lastly, we added a throughput monitor that can be used in future work to base shuffles on anomalous traffic load.

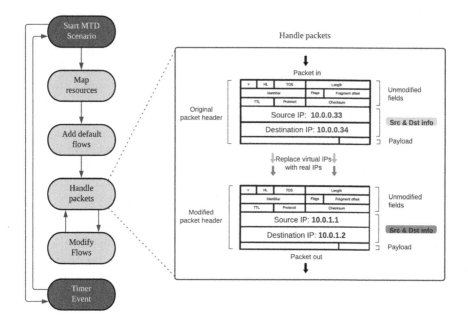

Fig. 3. Mtd-ryu high-level process

4.2   Scenario

The following is the scenario that we constructed for the case study. The network consists of two switches, four host nodes and one controller (as shown in Fig. 4.)

Each switch is running Open vSwitch and gets flow updates through the controller. The four nodes are segregated into two subnets (h1 and h2; h3 and h4). Nodes can communicate across the subnetworks through the switch nodes. Subnet s1 and s2 are using a moving target defense algorithm for all traffic; nodes that reside within the s1 subnetwork are considered trusted entities and all others are untrusted. The moving target defense algorithm is configured to change all node virtual IP addresses shuffle at some given interval (ranging from 20 s to 230 s). The algorithm uses a pre-defined set of virtual IP addresses, all within a /24 subnetwork, (resulting in 255 possible IP addresses) for assignment. It is possible that a node receives a previously used virtual IP multiple times during execution. Any traffic across trusted entities is never interrupted by shuffles.

At the start of the scenario, h1 runs a script that opens 20 disperse ports from 22–9999 using the netcat software. Nodes h3 and h2 both run an Nmap scan against node h1, particularly looking for any open ports in the range 0–9999. Nodes use Nmap's template level 4, which ranges from 0–5, where 0 is the slowest and 5 is the fastest. This template is suggested for use on ethernet-connected networks [19]. All nodes write observed traffic to a network packet capture file (pcap) and scanning nodes write nmap results to text files; h2 and h3 write unauth_scan_output and auth_scan_output respectively.

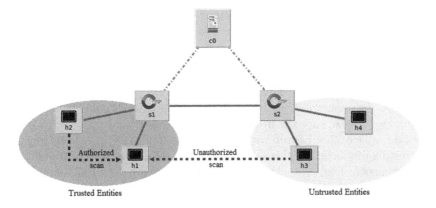

Fig. 4. Experiment scenario

To run mtd-ryu, we used Mininet [17], a virtual networking Linux-based emulator that uses process isolation to enable analysts to create multi-node scenarios on a single system. Mininet scales very well (demonstrating more than 4096 individual nodes on a single Linux Kernel) and its main purpose is to create OpenFlow applications [17]. While not perfect (e.g., in practice, it can only be used on systems running Linux) it is a useful tool for testing and experimentation of SDNs, such as those used for MTD. Mininet also allows analysts to specify technologies to use for switches and controllers. We used Miniedit, Mininet's graphical user interface, to construct the scenario as shown in Fig. 4.

We set up the entire scenario in a Virtual Machine and then automated the execution and data transfer with RES.

4.3 Experiment Construction with RES

We used the RES graphical interface to create a new experiment and added the Ubuntu VM along and a README file that documents the steps required to run the experiment manually. We configured the VM to allow remote connections and specified the localhost as the address. We configured the system to create 10 clones and to use the link-cloned option for speed.

In order to fully automate the experiment, we iteratively added 6 commands to be executed 60 s after the machines are instantiated. This process required some fine-tuning through trial during which time we used VBoxManage. The commands are as follows.

1. Start the controller
2. Sleep for 10 s to allow time for the controller to start and the virtual IPs to be generated and mapped
3. Start the topology; including all scripts for packet capture, opening ports, and nmap scans
4. Sleep for 3600 s to allow the scans to complete

5. Stop the scenario by killing all associated processes (python2 in this case)
6. Copy all data collected from the scenario to a unique path on the host.

A special construct, {{RES_CloneNumber}}, is used to specify a unique number associated with experiment instances. This is useful especially when specifying the directory where data should be copied from the instances to the host (step 6 above). For example specifying ryu-out30s_{{RES_CloneNumber}} denotes the directory ryu-out30s_1 for the first instance.

At first, a Dell 7700 Laptop with 8 processors running Windows 10 was used as our testing platform, but this was not well-suited for running the 10 simultaneous experiments. The CPU utilization consistently stayed at 100% throughout the executions and after a short while, the system was unusable. To alleviate this issue, we created a RES file using the export feature and then imported and re-ran the experiments on a Rack Mounted Desktop Server with two 1.80 GHz Eight Core Intel Xeon Silver 4108 Processors - 11 MB Cache processors and 128 GB RAM. This system was running Linux. Performance is shown later in Fig. 5 and Fig. 6. VirtualBox and RES were installed on the remote system; no modifications to the experiment were needed. Using the remote display features allowed us to use a Remote Desktop Client to occasionally and remotely connect to the virtual machines.

5   Ryu Experiment Analysis

5.1   Impact of RES Parallel Execution

We first wanted to test if executing several instances of virtual machines, running the individual scenarios, had any impact on the results. We proceeded with two paths; first we executed the network scans without shuffling manually and sequentially 10 times. Afterwards, we used RES to run a 10-set simultaneous execution. We recorded the times required to complete the scans of all 20 open ports. When using no shuffling, in every case, all 20 ports were identified. Table 1 shows the results.

Overall, the timings observed between the manual and automated scans are relatively close, considering the inherent variability associated with networking scanning in general. It is worth noting, that while the results vary across the runs, they consistently fall within a general range. The average, min, and max values between the manual and automated runs are all close, within 5.25 s. The behavior can, therefore, be characterized and used when making decisions about defenses. Running these in sequence is time consuming, but the parallelization of RES alleviates this issue.

Table 1. Manual vs. automated timings without shuffles (in seconds)

	Intra-Subnet		Inter-Subnet	
Run	Manual	Auto	Manual	Auto
1	29.34	29.5	204.81	196.31
2	56.5	18.25	131.33	105.56
3	49.43	30.72	198.7	126.13
4	21.16	27.78	198.89	208.03
5	19.58	16.51	150.86	100.16
6	75.21	62.52	136.63	216.65
7	69.59	40.01	201.62	138.41
8	35.04	35.97	102.62	202.70
9	30.34	22.91	159.08	123.85
10	27.15	76.61	119.4	225.90
Avg	41.33	36.08	160.39	164.37
Std. Dev.	19.05	18.36	36.25	47.20
Min	19.58	16.51	102.62	100.16
Max	75.21	76.61	204.81	225.9

The somewhat high standard deviation is due to some of Nmap's non-deterministic scanning behavior as well as complexities in the underlying network stack. This exemplifies the need for experimentation that emphasizes characterization of behaviors across several executions versus assumptions based on limited-samples.

Nmap completion time was on average four times greater when the scans originated from a remote node (inter-subnet scans) than from an intra-subnet node. This is due to the additional network device between the nodes: the switch. The switch may also cause delays e.g., when it queries the controller for a flow table addition, removal, or modification.

With respect to execution performance (as shown in Fig. 5), the total CPU load was stable at 4–6% at rest. In the case of a single experiment (with a single virtual machine), load spiked to roughly 12%; when the virtual machines were first instantiated by RES. This subsided when the VMs finish booting (when the VMs reached their login screens). When the scenarios and scans started, the load stayed between 10 and 16% (averaging 13%) and when scans complete, at roughly 240 s, the load decreased until the data transfer (pulling the results from the VMs to the host) and then VM shutdown. Very similar behavior was observed during the parallel executions, except at a higher magnitude. Memory utilization was stable at 8 GB for the single run and 26 GB for the parallel run throughout execution; this is because each VM was allocated 2 GB of memory and the host used roughly 6 GB.

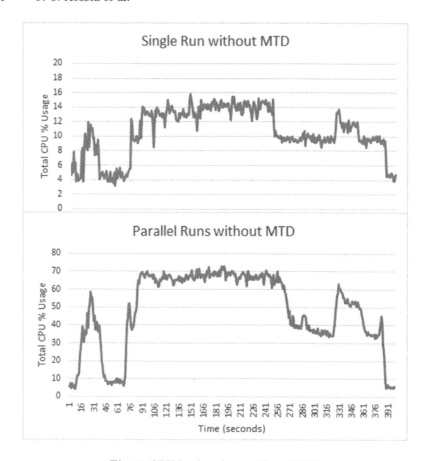

Fig. 5. CPU load on host without MTD

5.2   MTD Characterization

To demonstrate the utility of RES in characterizing behaviors of scanning and defense technologies, we tested the impact of the Ryu-MTD algorithm against Nmap completion times and accuracy in the inter-subnet case. More specifically, we observed the time it would take for a scan to complete as well as the number of ports correctly identified as open when IPs are shuffled at different time intervals. The algorithm is not suited for the intra-subnet case due to the short completion times (as shown in Table 1). Every scan was executed using RES, configured to run 10 instances simultaneously. We report the statistics for these runs in Table 2.

Table 2. Scan times (t) and port identification accuracy (p) with varying shuffle times

Shuffle	Avg		Std. Dev.		Min		Max	
Time(s)	t	p	t	p	t	p	t	p
20	1459.49	10	583.52	4.69	450.63	4	2200.48	20
50	1676.81	12.5	794.10	5.12	98.64	4	2464.63	20
80	1553.80	12.1	809.00	2.70	687.95	9	3244.14	18
110	762.067	15.6	328.51	2.11	250.43	13	1249.41	20
140	777.35	15	597.84	2.24	227.36	12	2242.52	20
170	556.182	17	243.14	1.90	214.25	14	951.03	20
200	353.29	18.9	320.07	1.64	155.65	15	1050.85	20
230	164.37	20	47.20	0	100.16	20	225.9	20

The 230 s shuffle time is a duplicate of the case with no shuffling (the last column in Table 1), since all scans were completed before the shuffle occurred. All other scan time averages are at least twice as long, and as much as 10 times as long (50 s shuffle), compared to when no shuffling is used. The trend is for time to complete the shuffle to decrease and for the accuracy of port identification to rise as shuffle times increase. Additionally, the standard deviation for completion times and port identifications decrease as the shuffle times increase. An interesting outcome of these results is that in all cases except 1 (80 s) the maximum number of correctly identified ports found is 20 of the possible 20. This means that there is always a risk, even when using the mtd-ryu implementation that a port scan will succeed in identifying all open ports correctly. However, the time taken to do so will very likely be higher, giving a defender more time to detect and react, than without MTD.

The CPU execution load during the shuffle experiments is shown in Fig. 6. As with the observations without MTD, the load times during the single and parallel runs are very similar, except at different scales. The experiments were run for one hour using 20 s shuffles. The same spikes were observed during boot. During the single run, the CPU load averaged 7%; this is less than the case with no MTD. The reason is because Nmap scans are slowed due to the shuffles. When a host is identified, a probe is sent and a reply is awaited; this delay causes a decreased load on the system. Memory usage did not change: 8 GB for the single run and 26 GB for the parallel run.

As mentioned previously, the experiment file containing all assets required to recreate the experiment executions is available for download.

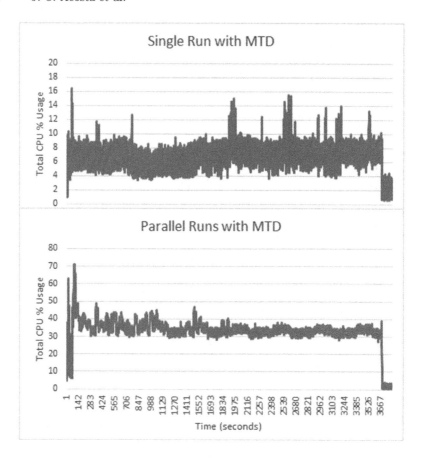

Fig. 6. CPU load on host with MTD

6   Future Work

We plan to make incremental improvements to RES based on community feed-back. More importantly, we plan to use this tool to conduct comparative analysis on different defense techniques. The data generated from the executions of different defense mechanisms will become inputs to an autonomous decision support system that will provide insights into which mechanisms may work better under different conditions.

We built RES and we provide it to the community with hope that it will encourage distribution of, not only of written scientific results, but of entire studies; including materials, results, and mechanisms required to reconstruct and improve on the research.

References

1. Ahrenholz, J., Danilov, C., Henderson, T.R., Kim, J.H.: CORE: a real-time network emulator. In: MILCOM 2008–2008 IEEE Military Communications Conference, pp. 1–7 (2008)
2. Al-Shaer, E., Duan, Q., Jafarian, J.H.: Random host mutation for moving target defense. In: Keromytis, A.D., Di Pietro, R. (eds.) SecureComm 2012. LNICST, vol. 106, pp. 310–327. Springer, Heidelberg (2013). https://doi.org/10.1007/978-3-642-36883-7_19
3. Carroll, T.E., Crouse, M., Fulp, E.W., Berenhaut, K.S.: Analysis of network address shuffling as a moving target defense. In: 2014 IEEE International Conference on Communications (ICC), pp. 701–706 (2014)
4. Carter, K.M., Riordan, J.F., Okhravi, H.: A game theoretic approach to strategy determination for dynamic platform defenses. In: Proceedings of the First ACM Workshop on Moving Target Defense, MTD 2014, pp. 21–30 (2014). https://doi.org/10.1145/2663474.2663478
5. Cho, J.H., et al.: Toward proactive, adaptive defense: a survey on moving target defense. arXiv preprint arXiv:1909.08092 (2019)
6. Clark, A., Sun, K., Poovendran, R.: Effectiveness of IP address randomization in decoy-based moving target defense. In: 52nd IEEE Conference on Decision and Control, pp. 678–685 (2013)
7. Crouse, M., Prosser, B., Fulp, E.W.: Probabilistic performance analysis of moving target and deception reconnaissance defenses. In: Proceedings of the Second ACM Workshop on Moving Target Defense, MTD 2015, pp. 21–29 (2015). https://doi.org/10.1145/2808475.2808480
8. Dishington, C., Sharma, D.P., Kim, D.S., Cho, J., Moore, T.J., Nelson, F.F.: Security and performance assessment of IP multiplexing moving target defence in software defined networks. In: 2019 18th IEEE International Conference On Trust, Security And Privacy In Computing And Communications/13th IEEE International Conference On Big Data Science And Engineering (TrustCom/BigDataSE), pp. 288–295 (2019)
9. Gangappa, G.S.: Moving target defense RHM using SDN (2018). https://github.com/girishsg24/Moving-Target-Defense-RHM-using-SDN. Accessed 20 Feb 2021
10. Apache guacamole. https://guacamole.apache.org, https://guacamole.apache.org. Accessed 20 Feb 2021
11. Hamlet, J.R., Lamb, C.C.: Dependency graph analysis and moving target defense selection. In: Proceedings of the 2016 ACM Workshop on Moving Target Defense, MTD 2016, pp. 105–116 (2016). https://doi.org/10.1145/2995272.2995277
12. Vagrant by HashiCorp. https://www.vagrantup.com, https://www.vagrantup.com. Accessed 20 Feb 2021
13. Hong, J.B., Kim, D.S.: Scalable security models for assessing effectiveness of moving target defenses. In: 2014 44th Annual IEEE/IFIP International Conference on Dependable Systems and Networks, pp. 515–526 (2014)
14. Huang, C., Zhu, S., Yang, Y.: An evaluation framework for moving target defense based on analytic hierarchy process. EAI Endorsed Trans. Secur. Saf. 4, e4 (2018)
15. Huang, Y., Ghosh, A.K.: Introducing diversity and uncertainty to create moving attack surfaces for web services. In: Jajodia, S., Ghosh, A.K., Swarup, V., Wang, C., Wang, X.S. (eds.) Moving Target Defense: Creating Asymmetric Uncertainty for Cyber Threats, pp. 131–151 (2011). https://doi.org/10.1007/978-1-4614-0977-9_8

16. Jafarian, J.H., Al-Shaer, E., Duan, Q.: OpenFlow random host mutation: transparent moving target defense using software defined networking. In: Proceedings of the First Workshop on Hot Topics in Software Defined Networks, HotSDN 2012, pp. 127–132 (2012). https://doi.org/10.1145/2342441.2342467

17. Kaur, K., Singh, J., Ghumman, N.S.: Mininet as software defined networking testing platform. In: International Conference on Communication, Computing & Systems (ICCCS), pp. 139–42 (2014)

18. Kyi Oo, W.K., Koide, H., Vasconcellos Vargas, D., Sakurai, K.: A new design for evaluating moving target defense system. In: 2018 Sixth International Symposium on Computing and Networking Workshops (CANDARW), pp. 561–563 (2018)

19. Lyon, G.F.: Nmap network scanning: the official Nmap project guide to network discovery and security scanning. Insecure. Com LLC (US) (2008)

20. MacFarland, D.C., Shue, C.A.: The SDN shuffle: creating a moving-target defense using host-based software-defined networking. In: Proceedings of the Second ACM Workshop on Moving Target Defense, MTD 2015, pp. 37–41 (2015). https://doi.org/10.1145/2808475.2808485

21. Manadhata, P.K.: Game theoretic approaches to attack surface shifting. In: Jajodia, S., Ghosh, A.K., Subrahmanian, V., Swarup, V., Wang, C., Wang, X.S. (eds.) Moving Target Defense II, pp. 1–13 (2013). https://doi.org/10.1007/978-1-4614-5416-8_1

22. MITRE ATT&CK (2019). https://attack.mitre.org/. Accessed 20 Feb 2021

23. Paulos, A., Pal, P., Schantz, R., Benyo, B.: Moving target defense (MTD) in an adaptive execution environment. In: Proceedings of the Eighth Annual Cyber Security and Information Intelligence Research Workshop, CSIIRW 2013 (2013). https://doi.org/10.1145/2459976.2460045

24. Duan, Q., Al-Shaer, E., Jafarian, H.: Efficient random route mutation considering flow and network constraints. In: 2013 IEEE Conference on Communications and Network Security (CNS), pp. 260–268 (2013)

25. Rohitaksha, K., Rajendra, A.B.: Analysis of POX and Ryu controllers using topology based hybrid software defined networks. In: Karrupusamy, P., Chen, J., Shi, Y. (eds.) ICSCN 2019. LNDECT, vol. 39, pp. 49–56. Springer, Cham (2020). https://doi.org/10.1007/978-3-030-34515-0_6

26. Sharma, D.P., Kim, D.S., Yoon, S., Lim, H., Cho, J.H., Moore, T.J.: FRVM: flexible random virtual IP multiplexing in software-defined networks. In: 2018 17th IEEE International Conference On Trust, Security And Privacy In Computing And Communications/12th IEEE International Conference On Big Data Science And Engineering (TrustCom/BigDataSE), pp. 579–587 (2018)

27. Strom, B.E., Applebaum, A., Miller, D.P., Nickels, K.C., Pennington, A.G., Thomas, C.B.: MITRE ATT&CK: design and philosophy. MITRE Product MP, pp. 18–0944 (2018)

28. Vadlamud, S., et al.: Moving target defense for web applications using Bayesian stackelberg games. In: AAMAS 2016 - Proceedings of the 2016 International Conference on Autonomous Agents and Multiagent Systems, pp. 1377–1378 (2016)

29. Van Leeuwen, B.P., Stout, W.M.S., Urias, V.E.: Empirical assessment of network-based moving target defense approaches. In: MILCOM 2016–2016 IEEE Military Communications Conference, pp. 764–769 (2016)

30. VirtualBox. https://www.virtualbox.org/, https://www.virtualbox.org/. Accessed 20 Feb 2021

31. Xu, J., Guo, P., Zhao, M., Erbacher, R.F., Zhu, M., Liu, P.: Comparing different moving target defense techniques. In: Proceedings of the First ACM Workshop on Moving Target Defense, MTD 2014, pp. 97–107 (2014). https://doi.org/10.1145/2663474.2663486
32. Yoon, S., Cho, J.H., Kim, D.S., Moore, T.J., Free-Nelson, F., Lim, H.: Attack graph-based moving target defense in software-defined networks. IEEE Trans. Netw. Serv. Manage. **17**(3), 1653–1668 (2020)
33. Zhuang, R., DeLoach, S.A., Ou, X.: Towards a theory of moving target defense. In: Proceedings of the First ACM Workshop on Moving Target Defense, pp. 31–40 (2014). https://doi.org/10.1145/2663474.2663479

MPD: Moving Target Defense Through Communication Protocol Dialects

Yongsheng Mei[✉], Kailash Gogineni, Tian Lan, and Guru Venkataramani

The George Washington University, Washington, D.C., USA
{ysmei,kailashg26,tlan,guruv}@gwu.edu

Abstract. Communication protocol security is among the most significant challenges of the Internet of Things (IoT) due to the wide variety of hardware and software technologies involved. Moving target defense (MTD) has been adopted as an innovative strategy to solve this problem by dynamically changing target system properties and configurations to obfuscate the attack surface. Nevertheless, the existing work of MTD primarily focuses on lower-level properties (e.g., IP addresses or port numbers), and only a limited number of variations can be generated based on these properties. In this paper, we propose a new approach of MTD through communication protocol dialects (MPD) - which dynamically customizes a communication protocol into various protocol dialects and leverages them to create a moving target defense. Specifically, MPD harnesses a dialect generating function to create protocol dialects and then a mapping function to select one specific dialect for each packet during communication. To keep different network entities in synchronization, we also design a self-synchronization mechanism utilizing a pseudo-random number generator with the input of a pre-shared secret key and previously sent packets. We implement a prototype of MPD and evaluate its feasibility on standard network protocol (i.e., File Transfer Protocol) and internet of things protocol (i.e., Message Queuing Telemetry Transport). The results indicate that MPD can create a moving target defense with protocol dialects to effectively address various attacks - including the denial of service attack and malicious packet modifications - with negligible overhead.

Keywords: Protocol dialect · Moving target defense

1 Introduction

The Internet of Things (IoT) refers to the concept of a large number of smart objects and devices connected to the Internet, offering diverse capabilities, such as sensing, actuating, processing, and communication. It integrates and relies on various enabling components, e.g., software, application libraries, middleware, embedded systems, and network artifacts. Any vulnerability in these components would lead to exploitations to create serious threats - such as the denial of service attack and reconnaissance attack- to the IoT system.

© ICST Institute for Computer Sciences, Social Informatics and Telecommunications Engineering 2021
Published by Springer Nature Switzerland AG 2021. All Rights Reserved
J. Garcia-Alfaro et al. (Eds.): SecureComm 2021, LNICST 398, pp. 100–119, 2021.
https://doi.org/10.1007/978-3-030-90019-9_6

The Moving Target Defense (MTD) has been developed as an effective defense strategy to dynamically (and randomly) change the properties of configurations of a target system while maintaining its essential functionalities to diversify its defense mechanism and obfuscate the resulting attack surfaces. It significantly increases the work factor of an adversary to launch an effective attack towards a constantly evolving defense. System attributes (and thus the potential attack surfaces) that can be dynamically changed to confuse attackers include instruction sets, address space layouts, IP addresses, port numbers, proxies, virtual machines, and operating systems [5]. Existing work on MTD has primarily focused on low-level attributes, such as instruction set randomization [4,13] and address space layout randomization [11,30]. Some other MTD methods target network-level features, such as IP address randomization [2,12], virtualization-based MTD [26] and software-defined networking based MTD [19,34]. However, considering the security of communication protocols in IoT, these MTD methods cannot achieve desired defense diversity against potential attacks, as the low-level protocol properties to be mutated (e.g., IP addresses or port numbers) are minimal.

In this paper, we propose a new approach for communication protocol MTD through protocol dialects, denoted by MPD. Our key idea of MPD is to automatically create many protocol dialects, which are variations of the target protocol created by mutating its handshake and message formats while keeping the communication functionalities unchanged. By selecting different protocol dialects and switching between them on the fly, we craft an MTD solution with substantially boosted diversity in communication. In order to enable easy management of dialects, our proposed solution also leverages distributed hash and keyspace partitioning to allow adding, removing, modifying any protocol dialect independent of others in MPD. We show that MPD requires very low overhead and is suitable for lightweight communication protocols in IoT using client-server architecture, e.g., File Transfer Protocol (FTP) and Message Queuing Telemetry Transport (MQTT). These protocols are usually lightweight and focus on data exchange efficiency while offering very limited security mechanism [3,24]. We argue that vigilantly customizing protocol dialects for higher-level features such as handshake and message format is crucial for directly protecting IoT security from potential attacks, especially for insecure communication channels in IoT that adversaries frequently target.

At the core of creating customized packet dialects, the critical problem is to design appropriate dialect generating functions that are easy to implement and will not introduce a high computational cost. Manually creating dialect templates is costly and also unrealistic for a huge program. Apart from that, we need to consider how to make the automatically created dialect applied on each packet vary following a random and unpredictable pattern. Only by increasing the uncertainty of the moving target can our approach help improve communication security. We propose two types of dialect generating functions - targeting at handshake and message format, respectively - to automatically create a number of protocol dialects as candidates for MTD. During communication, different dialects will be selected by a mapping function and applied to every handshake to dynamically change the defense properties, thus varying the attack surface on the fly. Furthermore, to deal with potential disruptions and attacks on the communication channel, we design the self-synchronization mechanism motivated by the self-synchronizing stream cipher [23] to ensure that the server and clients in an IoT system always return to a synchronized state after a limited error propagation.

The main contributions of our work are as follows:

- We propose MPD , an automated and self-synchronous framework for creating and leveraging protocol dialects for effective MTD in IoT communications. Given a specific protocol, MPD can automatically generate enough dialects per user needs and apply them to certain packets/handshakes during communication to improve security.
- MPD leverages distributed hash and keyspace partition for easy dialect management. It also implements a self-synchronization mechanism. Packets are cached and used in conjunction with a pseudo-random generator to ensure the randomness and unpredictability of dialects.
- Evaluation using two communication protocols, namely FTP and IoT protocol MQTT, shows that MPD can efficiently generate a large number of dialects and dynamically select the dialects for a round of communication for improved security in IoT systems.

2   Motivation

In this paper, we focus on IoT communication protocols that adopt a server-client architecture and employ packets for a communication, e.g., FTP and MQTT. Such protocols often emphasize communication efficiency and offer limited protection and security. We consider a threat model in which adversaries in an IoT system can dominate all communications, erase, replay, and replace arbitrary control packets between the client and server. In particular, an attacker can launch the Denial of Service (DoS) attack to exhaust the resources available at a victim network entity (e.g., a server or a client). This type of attack can be easily implemented by replaying the system with numerous connection requests [8] or intentionally keeping all the connections alive on the network busy [32]. Besides, in our threat model, we also consider malicious modification of communication. Given a pre-owned privilege, an attacker can modify genuine control packets or inject malformed control packets to launch the command injection attack [17,33], and this could undermine the system's integrity by maliciously disrupting handshakes or guiding a victim to execute unauthorized code. These attacks can also be indicated by the documented real-world vulnerabilities such as CVE-2019-9760 on FTP and CVE-2016-10523 on MQTT. We note that the above-mentioned threat models support a proof-of-concept for MPD as a promising new direction of MTD in communication security without being over-aiming for an all-encompassing solution. Therefore, this work serves as an initial step toward a comprehensive solution based on MTD through protocol dialects.

Moving target defense (MTD) [25] enables us to create, analyze, evaluate, and deploy mechanisms and strategies that are diverse and that continually shift and change over time to increase complexity and cost for attackers, limit the exposure of vulnerabilities and opportunities for attacks, and increase system resiliency. Current MTD methods are limited in increasing complexity against potential attacks because low-level system attributes (e.g., IP addresses and port numbers) only offer a limited degree of freedom for mutation. Due to the above reasons, we design MPD , an MTD technique combined with protocol dialect that leverages more application-layer properties of communication protocols and efficiently increases the number of variations that we can create.

The goal of MPD is to customize a standard protocol and create a moving target defense by (i) fabricating desired protocol dialects and (ii) allowing servers/clients to dynamically select dialects for communication in a synchronous fashion. We first introduce our definition of protocol dialects as follows:

Definition 1. *Protocol Dialect.* *Given a standard communication protocol, a dialect in this paper is a variation created by mutating its packets and handshakes while keeping the communication functionalities unchanged. More precisely, let $\mathcal{D}$ be a set of possible packet mutation functions, such as byte swapping and obfuscation. If the standard protocol employs packets $\{m_1, m_2, \ldots\}$, then the protocol dialect corresponding to $d_n \in \mathcal{D}$ (denoted as a dialect generating function) uses packets $\{d_n(m_1), d_n(m_2), \ldots\}$ for communication under the same communication rules. Thus, each protocol dialect is uniquely defined by a distinct dialect generating function $d_n \in \mathcal{D}$.*

From the given definition, protocol dialect can increase the variation of system attributes to improve communication security. We design a protocol dialect customization scheme to ensure the evolving of dialects used for every handshake. MPD allows the client and server, who are aware of the same protocol dialect varying pattern to communicate with each other correctly. Any infiltrated malicious packets sent by an attacker will be detected and discarded by the client/server without noticing the mutation pattern.

In order to develop a moving target defense using protocol dialects, the critical challenge is keeping both client and server synchronized during communication. Under the ideal circumstance, both sides will follow the same protocol dialect variation pattern. Thus, the client/server can send and receive packets using the same dialect during one handshake. However, supposing there are disruptions in the channel (e.g., losing packets in transmission), the client and server will lose synchronization without an appropriate synchronization mechanism, leading to the disorder of selecting dialects within coming handshakes. This paper borrows the idea from the self-synchronizing stream cipher and redesigns

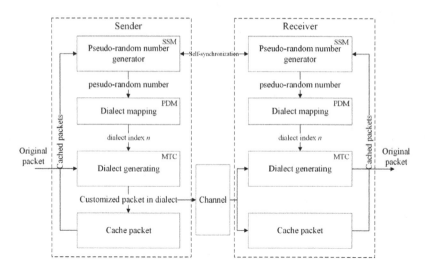

Fig. 1. MPD system diagram.

its key mechanism in MPD. We use previously sent packets as the reference to guarantee that the dialect selected by the client and server will rematch after a limited time of error propagation when disruptions or attacks happen.

3   System Design

MPD consists of three major modules: (i) Moving Target Customization (MTC), (ii) Self-Synchronization Mechanism (SSM), and (iii) Protocol Dialect Management (PDM). Its architecture is illustrated in Fig. 1. When commands (e.g., GET command to retrieve a file or LS command to display a local directory in FTP) are received by a client, PDM automatically selects a protocol dialect (with a dialect index n) for the corresponding packets, and SSM ensures that the server and the client remain synchronized with respect to the dialect they decide to use. We note the dialect selections must be unpredictable to eves-droppers in order to prevent attacks on the protocol dialect, such as the denial of service attacks and command injection attacks. To this end, a pair of pseudo-random number generators that are self-synchronous are employed by SSM at the server and the client, respectively. Then, the consistent hashing mapping function is used in PDM to map the output of such pseudo-random number generators to proper dialect index n. Next, PDM instructs MTC to generate customized communication packets using the selected dialect generating function d_n – which are pre-installed on the server and the client – and send those packets to the receiver. In particular, the sender's MTC module applies d_n on each out-going packet while the receiver's MTC module employs its inverse function d_n^{-1} to destruct the dialect and recover the standard packets for processing at the receiver.

3.1 Moving Target Customization

In our system, the MTC module can utilize any function d_n to create protocol dialects, as long as (i) d_n can sufficiently (i) mutate any communication packets m and (ii) the inverse d_n^{-1} exists and can be used to recover the original packets m, i.e.,

$$m' = d_n(m) \text{ and } m = (d_n)^{-1}(m'), \forall m, \tag{1}$$

where m and m' are the original and customized packets containing application layer information. To demonstrate the key ideas, we design two groups of dialects which are (i) shuffling dialect and (ii) packet-splitting dialect.

Shuffling: The shuffling function aims to generate various protocol dialects by switching randomly selected segments from the original packet. Assuming a total number of s switching-available segments within one packet, the mutations that we can create are the permutation of the s segments. Each of these permutations is considered as one specific dialect. In practice, we often carefully select the subset of mentioned permutations to achieve better performance, as not the shuffling of every available segment will be valid given the possibility that some segments contain the same information or vital information that cannot be arbitrarily moved.

Example 1. In this example, we illustrate byte-shuffling by defining three parameters, i.e., position, length and offset. *Position* decides starting byte of first segment. *Offset* is the distance between starting bytes of two segments. *Length* determines the length of two segments. We used p, l and o to denote those three parameters accordingly. The dialect index n for bytes-shuffling maps to the available combination of three mentioned parameters, noted as $n(p, l, o)$, which is predefined. Meanwhile, letting m be a packet of k bytes, we denote its i byte by $m(i)$ for $i = 1, 2, \ldots, k$. A segment of the packet m from i^{th} to j^{th} is denoted as $m(i, j)$. Therefore, we describe the bytes-shuffling function as following:

$$\begin{aligned} d_{n(p,l,o)}(m) &= [m(1, p)||m(p + o, p + o + l)||m(p + l, p + o)|| \\ &\quad m(p, p + l)||m(p + o + l, k)] \\ &= m', \end{aligned} \tag{2}$$

where $||$ denotes the separation of two segments within a packet. In equation, $m(p, p + l)$ and $m(p + o, p + o + l)$ are the two segments shuffled by function $d_{n(p,l,o)}$. The final result is the customized packets m'. In order to destruct the dialect and retrieve original packet m on receiver side, we need to employ an inverse function of $(d_{(p,l,o)})^{-1}$, which is:

$$\begin{aligned} (d_{n(p,l,o)})^{-1}(m') &= [m(1, p)||m(p, p + l)||m(p + l, p + o)|| \\ &\quad m(p + o, p + o + l)||m(p + o + l, k)] \\ &= m. \end{aligned} \tag{3}$$

Since three parameters will be synchronous for both sides during communication, we can locate two segments we need to shuffle back and then recover the original packets. By using the bytes-shuffling function and its inverse function, we can automatically generate the desired number of dialects for packets.

Packet-Splitting: The second type of dialect is packet-splitting dialect. This will generate protocol dialects by splitting a single packet into several sub-packets of any length (smaller than the original packet). In each sub-packet, the lower-layer header remains, but it only carries part of the application layer information of the original packet. Considering that each sub-packet will receive its corresponding response from the receiver, it breaks one handshake into several handshakes. Therefore, the packet-splitting dialect will change the original handshake pattern into a customized one with multiple handshakes.

Example 2. In this example, we split one single packet into four sub-packets. We introduce three predefined parameters t_1, t_2 and t_3 to denote the length of first three sub-packets correspondingly. Since the original packet has the fixed message length k, the length of the last sub-packets is equal to $k - t_1 - t_2 - t_3$. The combination of every four sub-packets is a new dialect. Therefore, we describe the packet-splitting function as following:

$$
\begin{aligned}
d_{n(t_1,t_2,t_3)}(m) &= d_{n(t_1,t_2,t_3)}([m(1,t_1)||m(t_1,t_1+t_2)|| \\
&\quad m(t_1+t_2,t_1+t_2+t_3)||m(t_1+t_2+t_3,k)]) \\
&= [m_1'||m_2'||...||m_4'],
\end{aligned}
\tag{4}
$$

where m_i' denotes each sub-packet created by function $d_{n(t_1,t_2,t_3)}$. Each sub-packet accordingly contains a segment of the information from original packet. In order to retrieve the original packet m from each sub-packet, receiver need to leverage inverse function $(d_{n(t_1,t_2,t_3)})^{-1}$ to merge all received sub-packets, which is:

$$
\begin{aligned}
(d_{n(t_1,t_2,t_3)})^{-1}([m_1'||m_2'||...||m_4']) &= (d_{n(t_1,t_2,t_3)})^{-1}([m(1,t_1)||m(t_1,t_1+t_2)|| \\
&\quad m(t_1+t_2,t_1+t_2+t_3)||m(t_1+t_2+t_3,k)]) \\
&= m.
\end{aligned}
\tag{5}
$$

Each index indicates one specific combination of three defined parameters t_1, t_2 and t_3. With different dialect index n, the length of the sub-packets will be different. Due to the synchronization mechanism of protocol dialect, both sides will synchronize and generate the same dialect index n during the communication. Hence, we can collect all the sub-packets and merge them to recover original packets.

3.2   Self-synchronization Mechanism

Dialect selection by the server and client must be unpredictable to any eves-droppers and yet remain synchronized to ensure the proper functioning of the communication protocol. To this end, we propose a mechanism that leverages a pseudo-random number generator to create randomness for selecting random

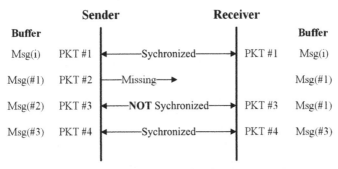

*Buffer: store the previously sent packet. If we allows n packets to be stored in buffer, the error propagation will be n.

Fig. 2. An illustration of the proposed self-synchronization mechanism.

dialects. Similar to the idea of self-synchronizing stream ciphers, we make future dialect indexes depend on past packet values to allow the server and client to self-synchronize even under packet erasures/modifications.

We cache one past packet (denoted by m_{i-1}) in a local buffer at the server and the client, i.e.,

$$M_i = m_{i-1}. \tag{6}$$

The Keyed-hash function is widely used in the keyed-hash message authentication code (HMAC). However, we note that rather than using the keyed-hash value for message authentication, we consider it as a pseudo-random number that can be securely generated by the client and server and compute the current dialect index from the keyed-hash value. Therefore, next, we leverage the keyed-hash function to produce a pseudo-random number based on a shared secret key K known to both the server and client. For a current cached message M_i and shared secret K, the keyed-hash function will generate a pseudo-random number S from M_i.

More precisely, we present the keyed-hash function we used in our implementation as following:

$$\begin{aligned} S &= H((K \oplus opad)\|H(K \oplus ipad)\|M_i) \\ &= H((K \oplus opad)\|H(K \oplus ipad)\|m_{i-1}), \end{aligned} \tag{7}$$

where H is cryptographic hash function such as MD5, and $\oplus$ denotes bitwise exclusive or (XOR). According to RFC 2104, outer padding $opad$ consists of repeated bytes valued 0x5c, and inner padding $ipad$ consists of repeated bytes valued 0x36. As shown in Eq. 7, the input becomes shared secret key K and cached past packet M_i, and those work as random seed for each iteration.

The modified keyed-hash function used in this paper is just one among many possible candidates from the available pseudo-random functions family. Due to the security properties provided by keyed-hash functions, the resulting pseudo-random number S is unpredictable to any eves-dropper who does not have access to the shared secret key K. It is also apparent that the server and the client will eventually resume synchronization even under packet erasures and modification. As illustrated in Fig. 2, as long as the past packets stored in local buffers are the same for both client and server, their pseudo-random number generator would compute the same pseudo-random number. Now the self-synchronous property is realized between client and server and can always be achieved if making the final dialect index depend on past packet values.

We note that similar to self-synchronizing stream ciphers, caching more than one previous packet and concatenate them as new M_i will leverage the contents of previously sent packets, which increases the complexity of modified keyed-hash function (i.e., Eq. 7) and efficiency against brute force attacks aiming at the self-synchronizing mechanism. In contrast, it takes longer to re-synchronize the server and the client under network errors.

3.3 Protocol Dialect Management

Finally, we need to map the pseudo-random number got from Eq. 7 to dialect index n. We implement the idea borrowed from consistent hashing in keyspace partitioning. Keyspace partitioning originally aims at mapping keys to nodes in a distributed hash table. We keep the concept but replace the keys with the pseudo-random number we had and nodes with protocol dialect indexes. Therefore, we design consistent hashing mapping that treats protocol dialect indexes as points on a circle, and $\delta(n, n+1)$ is the distance between two points, which is traveling clockwise around the circle from index n to $n+1$, as shown in Fig. 3. Assuming the pseudo-random number value is S and distance δ between every two indexes are equally distributed, in this case, consistent hashing mapping is presented as following:

$$n = S//(S_{max}//n_{max} + 1) + 1, \tag{8}$$

where S_{max} is the maximum pseudo-random number value we can generate, and $//$ denotes floor division. Considering that the total number of protocol dialects is n_{max}, we can decide the certain dialect with index n that should be applied to the current packet by computing Eq. 8.

Due to the different protocol dialects that we created, consistent hashing mapping gives us the flexibility to add new dialects or drop existing dialects. Without making significant changes in the mapping function, we can minimize the update of Eq. 8 and thereby increase the efficiency of the design.

Example 3: Given the example illustrated in Fig. 3, the circle in this figure represents the range of pseudo-random numbers ranging from 0 to S_{max}. We have four existed dialects in use shown in Fig. 3(a), and each of them takes a quarter of the circle. Assuming that we add a new dialect 5 as a candidate, in Eq. 8, the only changed parameter is the total number of protocol dialects n_{max}, which should increase from 4 to 5. Representing in Fig. 3(b), the distance δ will decrease to δ' which is one-fifth of the circle. Therefore, we can update n_{max} value in the equation without modifying any parameters else and thereby mitigate the impact made by adding/dropping of dialect in our system.

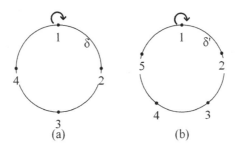

Fig. 3. Consistent hashing mapping before (a) and after (b) adding new dialect.

3.4   Security Analysis

IoT protocol MQTT is widely applied in many popular IoT applications, such as IBM Watson IoT Platform and AWS IoT services. Four phases are in an MQTT session: (i) connection, (ii) authentication, (iii) communication, and (iv) termination. After establishing the connection by creating a TCP/IP connection with the server (broker) on a predefined port, the client will send the *CONNECT* packet that includes user identification to start the MQTT communication. In this step, an attacker can launch a Denial of Service (DoS) attack by sending many *CONNECT* requests continuously and thereby maliciously making the server busy as in requests flooding, which impairs the availability of the system [7]. As the server is not able to differentiate the normal *CONNECT* and the malicious *CONNECT* packets, on receiving the flooding request messages, the broker starts to acknowledge all with *CONNACK* message. Assuming many connection requests that arrive simultaneously, the server's buffer will be drained out, and the server will not be capable of processing new incoming requests. In our design, we will apply the MPD on *CONNECT* packets. Before the server receiving incoming *CONNECT* packets from the client, the system will check whether the dialect index of the current packet matches that of the server. For malicious *CONNECT* packets, no dialect will be applied, and therefore they will fail the dialect index check. In this case, the server will refuse to start MQTT communication when receiving malicious request messages, saving its resources for processing valid requests.

Attacks such as command injection attacks and cipher suite downgrade attacks can intentionally erase or alter the communication packets on a public channel, damaging the integrity of communication. In the light-weight controller area network (CAN) protocol, a message-based IoT protocol designed to allow microcontrollers and devices to communicate with each other's applications, no encryption or authentication is initially applied due to their high cost. Thus, it is vulnerable and threatens by safety issues such as command injection attack [17]. In this type of attack, attackers will use reprogrammed electronic control units (ECU) to send malicious packets to the CAN bus. These malicious packets are fabricated and injected with forged ID and data to distract victim ECUs or make them execute malformed actions. For some other protocols, a standard mechanism such as SSL/TLS can be used to protect communication security. However, aiming to vulnerability existed in SSL/TLS, man in the middle (MITM) attackers can launch cipher suite downgrade attacks by abandoning the *ClientHello* packet sent by the genuine client and replacing it with a malformed packet containing lower-version TLS [16,31]. In consequence, the server will start the communication with the client using insecure lower-version TLS. We propose the MPD that will guarantee the evolution of packet dialect patterns during communication. Even though an attacker leverage the fetched information to launch an attack, malicious packets such as command injection packet or lower-version *ClientHello* packet will not be processed by the target because they cannot match the dialect evolution pattern of the receiver without acquiring knowledge of MPD.

In the above threat models, if packets are missing in an unstable communication channel or maliciously erased/altered by an attacker, it will affect the current packet in communication and drive the moving target defense of the client and server into an asynchronous state. The self-synchronization mechanism in our proposed solution guarantees the resilience of our system under packet erasures and modifications. Supposing there is a packet missing or modified, according to Eq. (7), it will only affect the dialect selection of the next packet (i.e., causing the server and the client to select different dialects for the next packet). Thus, such an error only propagates once. The server and the client will resume synchronization after a short, finite, and predictable transient time (when the erased or corrupted packet moves out of the local buffer).

As shown in Fig. 2, supposing the packet *PKT #2* is missing/erased, when transferring the *PKT #3*, previously cached packets stored in the local buffer of both sides are different. The sender assumes *PKT #2* was successfully sent and updates it into its local buffer, while the cached packets in the receiver's local buffer remain unchanged. The total number of past packets we cached is one, and therefore the error will propagate for only one handshake from *PKT #2* to *PKT #3*. After that, the sender and receiver return to a synchronous state again as the cached error packets move out of their local buffers. We note that if expanding the total number of cached packets in the local buffer to h, the error will propagate for h handshakes accordingly.

4   Implementation

We implement a prototype of MPD on FTP and MQTT, which includes the following main components.

Table 1. Examples of byte-shuffling dialect evolution pattern, including dialect index and parameters for the dialect generating function, computed for different FTP GET commands.

Original packet	Customized packet	Index	Position	Length	Offset
rget,sample.txt	r,etgsample.txt	8	1	1	3
rget,sample.txt	tger,sample.txt	7	0	1	3
rget,blog.css	etrg,blog.css	4	0	2	2
rget,template.pdf	etrg,template.pdf	4	0	2	2

Table 2. Examples of packet-splitting dialect evolution pattern, including dialect index and parameters for the dialect generating function, computed for different FTP GET commands.

Original packet	Customized sub-packets	Index	Length			
			Pkt1	Pkt2	Pkt3	Pkt4
rget,sample.txt	[r][ge][t,][sample.txt]	6	1	2	2	10
rget,sample.txt	[r][ge][t][,sample.txt]	2	1	2	1	11
rget,blog.css	[r][ge][t][,blog.css]	2	1	2	1	9
rget,template.pdf	[rg][et][,][template.pdf]	4	2	2	1	12

Dialect Customization and Management: We implement our dialect customization functions (e.g., shuffling-byte) in FTP and MQTT. Its input parameters are predefined and bundled together. We use indexes to indicate those parameter combinations. The index is decided by the consistent hashing mapping function in the PDM module. It determines which dialect is used for each communication packet.

Pseudo-random Number Generator: We implement a keyed-hash function as the pseudo-random number generator. The output pseudo-random number will be fed into the consistent hashing mapping function to compute the corresponding dialect index.

Self-synchronization Module: We implement our SSM module and cache one previous packet, which implies that any network errors will propagate for only one cycle during communication. The buffer will be filled with one predefined initial packet at the beginning of the program execution.

5   Evaluation

In this section, we evaluate the performance of MPD and the effectiveness of the proposed moving target defense.

Experiment Setup: Our experiments are conducted on a 2.60 GHz Intel(R) Core(TM) CPU i7-9750H machine with 16 Gigabytes of memory. The operating

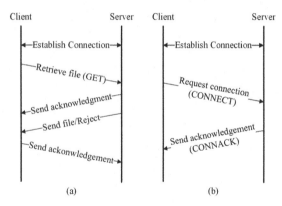

Fig. 4. Timing diagram of GET command in FTP (a) and CONNECT action in MQTT (b).

Fig. 5. Results of establishing connection with server by genuine FTP client (a) and attacker FTP client (b).

system is Ubuntu 18.04 LTS. We perform MTC, SSM, and PTD modules on the selected communication protocol.

Target Protocol: FTP. FTP is a standard network protocol used for the transfer of computer files between the client and the server. Many FTP clients and automated utilities have been developed for desktops, servers, mobile devices, and hardware. As a target protocol for our proof of concept evaluation, FTP offers two main benefits: (i) It is a lightweight protocol having better performance and easier to test, and (ii) it does not have many complex features, making it easier to customize and analyze.

FTP packet format contains IP header, TCP header, and FTP message contents. We programmed a standard FTP client and server and applied our implementation to them. For instance, when a GET command is received on the server, the corresponding file (if file exists) or rejection message (if the file does not exist) will be sent to the client via four handshakes, as shown in Fig. 4(a). After adding the MTC module on both server and client, the packet for transferring the GET command will be cast into a proper dialect during each handshake.

Protocol	Length	Info
33 FTP	80	Request: r,etgdummy.txt
39 FTP	83	Request: rgte,etmplate.pdf
41 FTP	71	Request: 59801
46 FTP	79	Response: Exists,261215
48 FTP	71	Request: Ready
68 FTP	81	Request: Received,261215
70 FTP	73	Response: Success
76 FTP	79	Request: etrg,blog.css
78 FTP	71	Request: 45047
83 FTP	78	Response: Exists,45386
85 FTP	71	Request: Ready
93 FTP	80	Request: Received,45386
95 FTP	73	Response: Success

Fig. 6. Packets captured by Wireshark showing error propagation equal to the total number of previously sent packets cached in the buffer.

Table 3. Self-synchronization mechanism demonstration with missing Pkt #1.

Iteration	Client	Cached Pkt	Server	Cached Pkt	Status
1	Pkt #1	[Pkt #p]	—	[Pkt #p]	Synchronized, Nothing received
2	Pkt #2	[Pkt #1]	Pkt #2	[Pkt #p]	Not synchronized
3	Pkt #3	[Pkt #2]	Pkt #3	[Pkt #2]	Synchronized
4	Pkt #4	[Pkt #3]	Pkt #4	[Pkt #3]	Synchronized

[1] We assume *Pkt #1* is erased/missing during communication.

[2] *Pkt #p* is previously sent packet that has already been cached in local buffer.

Tables 1 and 2 show byte-shuffling dialect and packet-splitting dialect as well as the evolution process of key parameters during four consecutive file transfers. Due to the different pseudo-random numbers being generated for each message/packet, the PDM module will map the number into different dialect indexes, resulting in different dialect selections and different input parameters of the MTC module for customizing packets. On the server-side, after performing the inverse process, the original packets are recovered, and the server will send the requested file to the client, as shown in Fig. 5(a).

To demonstrate the effectiveness of our moving target defense, we create an attacker FTP client that implements a spoofed (and fixed) dialect of the FTP. The attacker client connects to the FTP server equipped with our moving target defense and starts fabricating and sending the malicious command to the server to launch the command injection attack. The result are presented in Fig. 5(b). It is obvious that the command injection attack fails to work. Since the attacker's client protocol dialect pattern is fixed, it is unable to understand the dialect evolution pattern generated in our moving target defense applied on the GET command. We prove that our method can effectively defend the system from such attacks.

Next, we evaluate the effectiveness of our self-synchronization mechanism under erased/missing packets. In particular, we choose to store only one past packet in the buffer for self-synchronization. As is shown in Fig. 6, suppose that, due to some network error or intentional attack, one GET command packet before frame #33 gets lost during communication (Thus, this missing packet cannot be captured by Wireshark in the screenshot). As we can observe, for the

Table 4. Evaluating the overhead of designed moving target defense in FTP.

Performance index	Original FTP	Modified FTP
System time/sec	0.57	0.60
Elapsed time/sec	42.64	44.53
Percent of CPU this job got	1%	1%
Maximum resident set size/KB	6402	7683

[1] System time: time spent in kernel mode while running the program.
[2] Maximum resident set size: Maximum memory space occupied while running the program.

second GET command packets that the client sent, which in Fig. 6 corresponds to frame #33, the server generates no response. Till now, the dialect selection at the client and the server are not synchronized because the previously sent packet cached in the local buffer is different, resulting in selecting different dialect for *Pkt #2* as shown in Table 3 Row 3. However, starting from the third packet, which is frame #39 in Fig. 6 and Row 4 in Table 3, both sides are successfully re-synchronized, as the different packets move out of their local buffers after one (network) cycles, and as a result, the same previously sent packets are again shared between them. It demonstrates MPD 's ability to self-synchronize under packet erasures or in an unstable communication channel.

Finally, we evaluate the overhead of MPD , by comparing it with the execution overhead of a standard FTP implementation on the server-side, concerning the network, CPU, and memory overhead. To this end, we use the *time* command in the terminal to monitor several performance indexes such as running time and maximum resident set size. To avoid potential statistical bias, we run each experiment four times and record the average overhead in Table 4. For each test, we write a script to execute one billion FTP commands randomly (e.g., using GET to continuously retrieve a small text file from the server to the client).

As it is shown in the Table 4, while a number of functions (including dialect generating function, pseudo-random function, and consistent hashing mapping function) are added in FTP to support our moving target defense, the overhead is almost negligible as compared to a standard FTP program. More precisely, the execution overhead (as measured by elapsed time) increases by 4.43%, while the maximum resident set size we need compared to standard FTP implementation increase by 1281 KB.

Target Protocol: MQTT. MQTT is a standard lightweight IoT protocol for transporting messages among IoT devices. Due to its small size, it is designed to provide efficient message delivery for the network where the bandwidth is limited. Apart from the similar reasons we mentioned for choosing FTP, we select MQTT as another target protocol for analysis because it is the typical IoT protocol used by many IoT devices, and shares many common characters compared with other IoT protocols.

Fig. 7. Results of establishing connection with server (broker) by genuine MQTT client (a) and attacker MQTT client (b).

MQTT usually runs over TCP/IP. Besides IP header and TCP header, an MQTT packet also contains a fixed header (including control field, e.g., *CON-NECT/CONNACK*, and packet length field), variable length header, and payload on the application layer. We programmed a standard MQTT client and server (broker) and applied MPD on them. The timing diagram of establishing the MQTT connection is shown in Fig. 4(b). The client will send the *CON-NECT* to the server to request MQTT communication. After receiving *CON-NECT* packet, server will response with *CONNACK* to confirm the connection. We add the MTC module using the byte-shuffling function on both sides, and thus the *CONNECT/CONNACK* packet will be cast into an appropriate dialect during each handshake.

To demonstrate the capability of the modified MQTT system in defending the DoS attack, we implement an attacker MQTT client that tries to flush the modified server by continuously sending *CONNECT* packets with different identities. The MTC module uses the byte-shuffling function, which will shuffle the control field with other fields in the *CONNECT* packet. As shown in Fig. 7(b), the attacker fails to use multiple malicious *CONNECT* packets to exhaust the server's buffer space because these packets will fail the dialect index check before getting accepted. In contrast, as shown in Fig. 7(a), the genuine client is able to successfully start communication and publish information on the server due to their having the synchronized dialect evolution pattern. Therefore, we can apply MPD on IoT protocol MQTT to prevent the system from some types of DoS attacks.

6   Related Work

Pseudo-random Number Generator: Pseudo-random number generator (PRNG) is an algorithm for generating a sequence of numbers that have properties approximating the properties of random-number sequences. Since we need to implement MPD with randomly varying moving targets, the basic idea is using PRNG to output a random number for self-synchronization and dialect selection. Many previous works [1,15,29,35] provide us with insight of choosing PRNG, such as PRNG based on logistic chaotic system [35] and elliptic curve PRNG [15].

Self-synchronizing Stream Cipher: Stream cipher [10,20,28] is a symmetric key cipher where the digits of plain text are combined with a pseudo-random cipher digit stream (which is the keystream), including two types: (i) synchronous stream cipher (SSC), and (ii) self-synchronizing stream cipher (SSSC). The latter uses previous ciphertext digits to compute the keystream. In paper [21], several alternative design approaches for SSSCs are proposed that are superior to the design based on the block cipher with respect to encryption speed and security. Joan Daemen et al. introduce another design approach for hardware-oriented SSSCs named Moustique [6]. Besides, many other discussions are about SSSCs, which can be found in papers [14,23].

Moving Target Defense (MTD): Plenty of previous works about MTD have different areas of focus respectively. Some of them are about leveraging lower-level system configurations, which provide insights into our design. In Open-Flow random host mutation [12], Jafarian et al. provided an MTD architecture that transparently mutates IP addresses with randomness. RPAH [18] achieved MTD by constantly changing IP addresses and ports to realize random port and address hoping. On protocol level, Ghost-MTD [27] applied mutation on protocols to achieve MTD, while the protocol mutation pattern should be pre-defined and pre-shared between client and server.

Security Risks of IoT Protocols: Internet of things is growing rapidly and reaches a multitude of different domains such as environmental monitoring, smart home, and automatic driving. However, many low-end IoT products do not usually have strong security mechanisms embedded [7,9]. Hence, threats such as leakage of sensible information, DoS attacks, and unauthorized network access attacks bring a severe safety issue to the IoT system [22]. Some researches are conducted previously to mitigate the threat of attacks targeting IoT protocols and devices. Besides, in the survey [24], Nebbione et al. provided some basic ideas for solving the security issues in many IoT protocols.

7   Conclusion

We design and evaluate a novel moving target defense framework, MPD, which aims to generate customized dialects during communication and dynamically select different dialects in a self-synchronous manner. Our experiment results using FTP and MQTT indicate that MPD is able to harden the security while incurring low execution overhead effectively.

References

1. Akhshani, A., Akhavan, A., Mobaraki, A., Lim, S.C., Hassan, Z.: Pseudo random number generator based on quantum chaotic map. Commun. Nonlinear Sci. Numer. Simul. **19**(1), 101–111 (2014)
2. Al-Shaer, E.: Toward network configuration randomization for moving target defense. In: Jajodia, S., Ghosh, A., Swarup, V., Wang, C., Wang, X. (eds.) Moving Target Defense. Advances in Information Security, vol. 54, pp. 153–159. Springer, New York (2011). https://doi.org/10.1007/978-1-4614-0977-9_9
3. Andy, S., Rahardjo, B., Hanindhito, B.: Attack scenarios and security analysis of MQTT communication protocol in IoT system. In: 2017 4th International Conference on Electrical Engineering, Computer Science and Informatics (EECSI), pp. 1–6. IEEE (2017)
4. Barrantes, E.G., Ackley, D.H., Forrest, S., Palmer, T.S., Stefanovic, D., Zovi, D.D.: Randomized instruction set emulation to disrupt binary code injection attacks. In: Proceedings of the 10th ACM Conference on Computer and Communications Security, pp. 281–289 (2003)
5. Cho, J.H., et al.: Toward proactive, adaptive defense: a survey on moving target defense. IEEE Commun. Surv. Tutorials **22**(1), 709–745 (2020)
6. Daemen, J., Kitsos, P.: The self-synchronizing stream cipher MOUSTIQUE. In: Robshaw, M., Billet, O. (eds.) New Stream Cipher Designs. LNCS, vol. 4986, pp. 210–223. Springer, Heidelberg (2008). https://doi.org/10.1007/978-3-540-68351-3_16
7. Firdous, S.N., Baig, Z., Valli, C., Ibrahim, A.: Modelling and evaluation of malicious attacks against the IoT MQTT protocol. In: 2017 IEEE International Conference on Internet of Things (iThings) and IEEE Green Computing and Communications (GreenCom) and IEEE Cyber, Physical and Social Computing (CPSCom) and IEEE Smart Data (SmartData), pp. 748–755. IEEE (2017)
8. Haripriya, A., Kulothungan, K.: Secure-MQTT: an efficient fuzzy logic-based approach to detect dos attack in MQTT protocol for internet of things. EURASIP J. Wirel. Commun. Netw. **2019**(1), 90 (2019)
9. Hartzell, S., Stubel, C.: Automobile can bus network security and vulnerabilities. Univ. Washington, Seattle, WA, USA, Technical report (2017)
10. Hell, M., Johansson, T., Meier, W.: Grain: a stream cipher for constrained environments. Int. J. Wirel. Mobile Comput. **2**(1), 86–93 (2007)
11. Hund, R., Willems, C., Holz, T.: Practical timing side channel attacks against kernel space ASLR. In: 2013 IEEE Symposium on Security and Privacy, pp. 191–205. IEEE (2013)
12. Jafarian, J.H., Al-Shaer, E., Duan, Q.: Openflow random host mutation: transparent moving target defense using software defined networking. In: Proceedings of the First Workshop on Hot Topics in Software Defined Networks, pp. 127–132 (2012)
13. Kc, G.S., Keromytis, A.D., Prevelakis, V.: Countering code-injection attacks with instruction-set randomization. In: Proceedings of the 10th ACM Conference on Computer and Communications Security, pp. 272–280 (2003)

14. Khazaei, S., Meier, W.: New directions in cryptanalysis of self-synchronizing stream ciphers. In: Chowdhury, D.R., Rijmen, V., Das, A. (eds.) INDOCRYPT 2008. LNCS, vol. 5365, pp. 15–26. Springer, Heidelberg (2008). https://doi.org/10.1007/978-3-540-89754-5_2
15. Lee, L., Wong, K.: An elliptic curve random number generator. In: Steinmetz, R., Dittman, J., Steinebach, M. (eds.) Communications and Multimedia Security Issues of the New Century. ITIFIP, vol. 64, pp. 127–133. Springer, Boston, MA (2001). https://doi.org/10.1007/978-0-387-35413-2_12
16. Lee, S., Shin, Y., Hur, J.: Return of version downgrade attack in the era of TLS 1.3. In: Proceedings of the 16th International Conference on Emerging Networking Experiments and Technologies, pp. 157–168 (2020)
17. Liu, J., Zhang, S., Sun, W., Shi, Y.: In-vehicle network attacks and countermeasures: Challenges and future directions. IEEE Netw. **31**(5), 50–58 (2017)
18. Luo, Y.B., Wang, B.S., Wang, X.F., Hu, X.F., Cai, G.L., Sun, H.: RPAH: random port and address hopping for thwarting internal and external adversaries. In: 2015 IEEE Trustcom/BigDataSE/ISPA, vol. 1, pp. 263–270. IEEE (2015)
19. MacFarland, D.C., Shue, C.A.: The SDN shuffle: creating a moving-target defense using host-based software-defined networking. In: Proceedings of the Second ACM Workshop on Moving Target Defense, pp. 37–41 (2015)
20. Mannai, O., Becheikh, R., Rhouma, R.: A new stream cipher based on nonlinear dynamic system. In: 2018 26th European Signal Processing Conference (EUSIPCO), pp. 316–320. IEEE (2018)
21. Maurer, U.M.: New approaches to the design of self-synchronizing stream ciphers. In: Davies, D.W. (ed.) EUROCRYPT 1991. LNCS, vol. 547, pp. 458–471. Springer, Heidelberg (1991). https://doi.org/10.1007/3-540-46416-6_39
22. Meneghello, F., Calore, M., Zucchetto, D., Polese, M., Zanella, A.: IoT: Internet of threats? A survey of practical security vulnerabilities in real IoT devices. IEEE Internet Things J. **6**(5), 8182–8201 (2019)
23. Millérioux, G., Guillot, P.: Self-synchronizing stream ciphers and dynamical systems: state of the art and open issues. Int. J. Bifurcation Chaos **20**(09), 2979–2991 (2010)
24. Nebbione, G., Calzarossa, M.C.: Security of IoT application layer protocols: challenges and findings. Future Internet **12**(3), 55 (2020)
25. NITRD, C.: IWG: cybersecurity game-change research and development recommendations (2013)
26. Okhravi, H., Comella, A., Robinson, E., Haines, J.: Creating a cyber moving target for critical infrastructure applications using platform diversity. Int. J. Crit. Infrastruct. Prot. **5**(1), 30–39 (2012)
27. Park, J.G., Lee, Y., Kang, K.W., Lee, S.H., Park, K.W.: Ghost-MTD: moving target defense via protocol mutation for mission-critical cloud systems. Energies **13**(8), 1883 (2020)
28. Paul, G., Maitra, S.: RC4 Stream Cipher and its Variants. CRC Press, New York (2011)
29. Salmon, J.K., Moraes, M.A., Dror, R.O., Shaw, D.E.: Parallel random numbers: as easy as 1, 2, 3. In: Proceedings of 2011 International Conference for High Performance Computing, Networking, Storage and Analysis, pp. 1–12 (2011)
30. Seibert, J., Okhravi, H., Söderström, E.: Information leaks without memory disclosures: Remote side channel attacks on diversified code. In: Proceedings of the 2014 ACM SIGSAC Conference on Computer and Communications Security, pp. 54–65 (2014)

31. Sjoholmsierchio, M., Hale, B., Lukaszewski, D., Xie, G.G.: Strengthening SDN security: protocol dialecting and downgrade attacks. arXiv preprint arXiv:2010.11870 (2020)
32. Vaccari, I., Aiello, M., Cambiaso, E.: Slowite, a novel denial of service attack affecting MQTT. Sensors **20**(10), 2932 (2020)
33. Vuong, T.P., Loukas, G., Gan, D., Bezemskij, A.: Decision tree-based detection of denial of service and command injection attacks on robotic vehicles. In: 2015 IEEE International Workshop on Information Forensics and Security (WIFS), pp. 1–6. IEEE (2015)
34. Wang, K., Chen, X., Zhu, Y.: Random domain name and address mutation (RDAM) for thwarting reconnaissance attacks. PloS One **12**(5), e0177111 (2017)
35. Wang, L., Cheng, H.: Pseudo-random number generator based on logistic chaotic system. Entropy **21**(10), 960 (2019)

Blockchain and P2P Security

GuardedGossip: Secure and Anonymous Node Discovery in Untrustworthy Networks

Andriy Panchenko[1(✉)], Asya Mitseva[1], Torsten Ziemann[1], and Till Hering[2]

[1] Brandenburg University of Technology, Cottbus, Germany
{andriy.panchenko,asya.mitseva,torsten.ziemann}@b-tu.de
[2] RWTH Aachen University, Aachen, Germany
till.hering@rwth-aachen.de

Abstract. Node discovery is a fundamental service for any overlay network. It is a particular challenge to provide unbiased discovery in untrustworthy environments, e.g., anonymization networks. Although a major line of research focused on solving this problem, proposed methods have been shown to be vulnerable either to active attacks or to leak routing information, both threatening the anonymity of users. In response, we propose GuardedGossip—a novel gossip-based node discovery protocol—that achieves an unbiased random node discovery in a fully-decentralized and highly-scalable fashion. It is built on top of a Chord distributed hash table (DHT) and relies on witness nodes and bound checks to resist active attacks. To limit routing information leakages, GuardedGossip uses gossiping to create uncertainty in the process of node discovery. By incorporating the principles of DHTs with the unstructured nature of gossiping in a subtle way, we profit from the strengths of both techniques while carefully mitigating their shortcomings. We show that GuardedGossip provides a sufficient level of security for users even if 20% of the participating nodes are malicious. Concurrently, our system scales gracefully and provides an adequate overhead for its security and privacy benefits.

Keywords: Node lookup · DHT · Tor · Onion routing · Anonymity

1 Introduction

The Internet has become the most powerful medium for communication and information retrieval. Concurrently, an increasing number of repressive governments and other dominant entities endangers the free circulation of speech and information on the Internet by using censorship methods to restrict the open access to online content or even by prosecuting citizens who exercise their right to freedom of expression. For many people, the use of anonymization techniques is the only way to hide their identity (i.e., IP address) on the Internet and to bypass country-level censorship. Currently, Tor [11] is the most popular low-latency anonymization network comprising over 8,000 nodes run by volunteers and more than two million users daily [3]. Despite its continuous evolution, Tor still struggles with a

J. Garcia-Alfaro et al. (Eds.): SecureComm 2021, LNICST 398, pp. 123–143, 2021.
https://doi.org/10.1007/978-3-030-90019-9_7

limited scalability caused by its centralized node discovery method, i.e., a small set of trusted nodes keeps track of all active volunteer nodes. To preserve anonymity, each Tor user is required to have a complete network view and detailed information for at least 60% of the nodes (i.e., the current default value [2] versus 100% in the initial specification of Tor). The distribution of the global network view to each user creates at least three major problems. First, the maintenance of a consistent complete network view introduces a significant bandwidth overhead on Tor nodes and users. This overhead is foreseen to increase into such a level in near future that Tor would spend more bandwidth for maintaining a global network view than for anonymizing user connections [14]. Second, the list of all active volunteer nodes (except a special set of *hidden* volunteer nodes, called *bridges*), can be easily fetched by anybody. This makes them trivially blockable by any-level attackers [1]. Third, the small set of trusted nodes creates a single point of trust and failure, which makes them an attractive target for attacks from repressive governments and other dominant entities.

Several works focused on solving the scalability problem of Tor [14,18,20,23] or even proposed alternative anonymization systems with improved node discovery methods [12,19,21]. These methods are often divided into client-server based and peer-to-peer (P2P) based approaches [18,23]. While the client-server based methods provide an easy-deployable solution how to extend the capabilities of the current node discovery mechanism in Tor, they create additional hardware dependencies [23], increased computational costs to Tor nodes [18], and do not prevent the blocking of nodes by Internet censors. P2P-based node discovery services rely on either structured topologies, e.g., distributed hash tables (DHTs), or random walks and, thus, enable an efficient and scalable search of other nodes without having a global network view. However, these methods have been shown to be vulnerable to active attacks [6,24,27] (e.g., eclipse attack) and to passive information leakages, threatening the anonymity of users [16]. Despite the evolution of the proposed P2P-based node discovery methods, none of them provides a practical solution for a fully decentralized and scalable secure node discovery.

To address this challenge, we propose *GuardedGossip*—a novel gossip-based node discovery protocol, which achieves an unbiased random node discovery in a fully decentralized and highly scalable fashion. It is built on top of a Chord DHT and relies on witness nodes and bound checking to resist active attacks. To limit routing information leakages, GuardedGossip applies gossiping to introduce uncertainty in the process of node discovery. By incorporating the principles of structured topologies with the unstructured nature of gossiping, we aim to profit from the strength of both types of techniques while mitigating their shortcomings by carefully distributing the task. We provide a prototypic implementation and an evaluation of our method and show its superiority over existing approaches.

2   Problem Description and Attacker Model

Problem Description. A node discovery system aims to enable a random and unbiased selection of nodes from the set of all active peers in the network. A straightforward solution would be to use a centralized directory, from which one fetches the list of available nodes and locally performs the random choice. Thus, the attacker has no influence on the selection process (except by deploying more malicious nodes) and there is no information leakage as all users have the same knowledge base for node selection. However, this solution creates several issues: (i) the need to trust a central directory keeping track of active nodes, (ii) the central directory is a single point of failure, (iii) it is easy to block such a system by either blocking the directory or the addresses of all the nodes, and, most notably, (iv) the use of a central directory limits scalability. To overcome these issues, it is appealing to use distributed methods, where each peer knows only a small portion of the network. However, this partial knowledge imposes new challenges. First, the randomness of the selection should not be affected by malicious peers (this is usually referred to as an *active attack*). In particular, the fraction of malicious nodes in lists discovered by users should not be significantly higher than their overall fraction in the network. Second, if only a small set of nodes gets discovered, it should be kept secret which node knows which other nodes. Otherwise, *bridging* and *fingerprinting* attacks [9] can be mount, in which the attacker restricts the set of possible users for (partially) observed anonymization connections based on user's knowledge about active nodes (these are known as *passive attacks*).

Attacker Model. In our work, we assume the attacker to be an observer and an active participant in the network that can generate, drop, or modify transmitted node discovery information. The attacker has a limited view on the network by controlling a restricted number of *colluding* nodes participating the network. We also assume that the fraction of the malicious nodes is static, i.e., the adversary cannot compromise other peers in the wild, and is below 30%—a typical hypothesis in the field of anonymous node discovery research [11,26].

3   Related Work

In the following, we review previously proposed secure node discovery systems.

P2P Solutions. Tarzan [12] is the only state-of-the-art method relying on gossiping for node discovery. In Tarzan, nodes need to maintain a complete network view [8], which was shown to not scale beyond 10,000 nodes [19]. Contrary to Tarzan, our system is built on top of a DHT and does not aim at discovering the whole network. We use gossiping to create uncertainty in the node discovery and to limit passive attacks against our underlying DHT-based methods. Other early proposed node discovery methods [28] rely on plain DHTs without any security mechanisms [6–8]. In response, Castro et al. [7] propose a set of defenses including a secure assignment of node identifiers (IDs) by using certificates and a secure message forwarding by using routing failure tests and redundancies. Mislove et al. [15] incorporate the secure lookup mechanism of [7] in a Pastry DHT [22]. Still, these methods remain vulnerable to active attacks [8,13].

More recent works [4,13,19] rely on redundant searches to build a secure node discovery system. The goal here is to execute several redundant searches for a single target, which traverse different nodes and, thus, reduce the impact of malicious nodes trying to sabotage the lookup. Salsa [19] uses a custom DHT that has been shown to be insecure [6]. Kapadia and Triandopoulos [13] argue that the use of custom DHTs increases the overhead and propose to use a Chord DHT with indirect lookups. While being effective against active attacks, Mittal and Borisov [16] raise the issue that these methods leak routing information due to the redundancy and are prone to passive attacks. Panchenko et al. [20] show that redundant routing does not scale in terms of security. To mitigate routing information leakages while keeping resistance against active attacks, NISAN [20] relies on a Chord DHT, where each node retrieves and processes entire finger tables (FTs) of other nodes locally to keep the lookup destination hidden. Each NISAN node further applies bound checking to assess the plausibility of the retrieved FT. As in [20], Backes et al. [5] aims to hide the identity of the requested node by using oblivious transfer. Instead of adding anonymity into the lookup itself, Torsk [14] executes random walks to select secret buddy nodes for each peer. Each Torsk node uses one of its secret buddies as a proxy to perform a lookup on its behalf and, thus, hides the relationship between itself and the lookup destination. However, neither NISAN nor Torsk provide a sufficient level of security against passive and active attacks [27]. Octopus [26] aims to overcome known security issues by using redundancy, proactive identification of malicious peers, and dummy lookup requests to limit passive attacks. However, it still requires trusted third party and creates high communication overhead and complexity.

To prevent information leakage, other works use random walks for node discovery. In MorphMix [21] each node knows only a few neighbors. The user initiates a connection and each subsequent intermediate node is randomly selected by the next hop along the path. Each MorphMix node relies on witness nodes and a collision detection mechanism to detect manipulations. However, the collision detection method of MorphMix has been shown to be broken [25] and, hence, MorphMix does not have direct practical impact on new designs anymore. Unlike MorphMix, where witness nodes are used to select the next hop along the path, we rely on them in a passive way (to detect malicious replacements of node IDs in a fetched FT). ShadowWalker [17] is another proposal using random walks. To avoid a compromise of the walk, it organizes the nodes in a DHT and relies on a set of shadow nodes for each peer in the network. The goal of the shadows is to check the node's neighborhood information by signing the FT of that node. However, ShadowWalker is vulnerable to eclipse and DoS attacks [24].

Client-Server Solutions. Tor [10,11] relies on a set of predefined trusted nodes, called *directory authorities* (DAs), to maintain a global network view on available nodes, known as onion relays (ORs). The ORs periodically report their parameters to the DAs in a self-signed *relay descriptor*. Based on this data, the DAs agree on a network view and publish a list of active ORs together with their description in the form of a *consensus* document once per hour [2]. When joining Tor, users download the consensus to select ORs for their connections. Next, they fetch complete descriptors of at least 60% of all ORs (as long as it is not stated otherwise by the Tor users or instructed by the DAs). The fallback from initially 100% to 60% is one of the workarounds done to address the scalability issues faced by Tor. To reduce the load on the DAs, ORs can act as *directory caches* (DCs) that fetch copies of the consensus and node descriptors from the DAs and host them for global distribution to the users and other ORs. The Tor Project further introduced the use of a *microdescriptor consensus* [2] and diffs of consensuses. While these countermeasures slow down the scalability issues, they do not provide a long-term solution for Tor's problem. Therefore, several works [18,23] focused on designing improved centralized methods combined with private information retrieval (PIR) techniques or Oblivious RAMs with trusted execution environments to allow users to obtain information about only a few ORs in an anonymous way. Mittal et al. [18] suggest PIR-Tor, where DCs can act as PIR servers and clients retrieve individual ORs from these caches. While PIR-Tor significantly decreases the network load, it puts additional computational overhead on the DAs and DCs due to the operation mode of the applied PIR methods. In response to the latter, Sasy and Goldberg [23] propose the use of Oblivious RAMs with trusted execution environments to reduce this bandwidth and computational overhead. However, in both methods the DAs still need to be trusted and to keep a global network view and handle joining and leaving nodes.

4 GuardedGossip: Secure and Anonymous Node Lookup

The evolution of P2P-based node discovery systems indicates a constant conflict between their increased level of security against active attacks and their reduced level of anonymity due to the efficacy of passive attacks [16,27]. To address the latter, we propose *GuardedGossip*—a novel gossip-based node discovery protocol that incorporates the use of a Chord DHT with witness nodes and bound checking to resist active attacks and the concept of gossip communication to add uncertainty in the process of node discovery and, thus, prevent passive attacks.

4.1 Design Overview

We assume that all nodes in GuardedGossip are organized in a Chord DHT with IDs generated by a pseudo-random function with a seed based on deterministic, node-specific input (as it will be described below). Thus, the nodes get distributed uniformly at random over the ID space of Chord and cannot influence their placement. In GuardedGossip, each node periodically sends gossip requests to get information about other nodes in the network. The use of the Chord DHT ensures that peers can send and receive gossip messages from a restricted set of other peers. Next, nodes directly collected though gossiping are neither considered for user connections nor for further distribution via gossiping. The reason for this is that gossiping is vulnerable to active attacks where malicious nodes share knowledge preferably about other malicious peers. To avoid this, we perform two additional checks to verify the trustworthiness of the collected peers. As in [20], we first retrieve the complete FTs of the nodes collected via gossiping and apply bound checking over them, i.e., we check whether the distance observed between optimal nodes (as if all IDs in the Chord would be occupied) and active nodes (an actually occupied optimal ID or the nearest existing successor of that optimal ID in the direction of the Chord ring) in a FT corresponds to the average distance between any two nodes in the network. In the second verification step—witness check—we use nodes that have already been received by gossiping as witnesses to recognize malicious replacements in the newly obtained FTs (whether some nodes were skipped). Finally, only peers passing both security checks are used to transmit user traffic or to be further propagated via gossiping. Overall, the key principles of our method can be summarized as follows:

(*i*) *Limit Your Contacts.* The use of a Chord DHT ensures that gossip messages are sent or received by a limited number of nodes. A peer accepts gossip requests only from nodes that have it in their FTs and sends requests and accepts gossip replies only from nodes that are in its FT. This limits active attacks and allows to maintain scalability while using gossiping. Contrary to the common gossip concept [12], in GuardedGossip nodes *actively request* gossip information instead of passively listening for it. As gossips are coming only from nodes that were asked for, the number of potential gossip messages exchanged between peers is reduced. This ensures a moderate communication overhead in the network. The requestee can also limit the rate of answering gossip queries to protect against DoS attacks by another peer flooding it with a large number of gossip messages.

(*ii*) *Never Trust Your Gossips.* As gossiping is vulnerable to active attacks where the attacker primarily sends IDs of other malicious nodes, our method does not use the peers collected via gossiping directly for user connections and further propagation, but relies on them as a source to retrieve information about other network participants. GuardedGossip fetches the whole FTs of nodes received via gossiping and verifies their plausibility. Only if the check of a FT is successful, a random subset of peers from that FT is considered for further use (i.e., either for user connections or for further propagation via gossiping). Finally, after the FT was processed, the gossiped source peer becomes obsolete and is discarded.

(*iii*) *Know Your Witnesses.* GuardedGossip combines a distance check between nodes in a FT with a novel witness check. The witness check keeps track of nodes already observed via gossiping (including a timestamp of a last-seen event) and verifies whether any node in a FT was bypassed (i.e., there exist a node between an optimal node ID and the reported one), which indicates a manipulation.

(*iv*) *Spawn Uncertainty.* Once the collected FTs are successfully validated, nodes from these FTs are used either for user connections or for further distribution via gossiping. To further obscure which set of nodes is used, GuardedGossip spawns additional uncertainty by selecting only a *random subset* of newly learned nodes for further processing (except for the witness list, where all nodes are kept, as this list is used in a passive way only). Thus, we guard from passive attacks, in which one tries to estimate the search target range by evaluating information about the requested FTs [20,27].

4.2   Protocol Details

Figure 1 illustrates the operation of GuardedGossip. Here, we assume that each node has already joined the Chord DHT and has correctly built its FT. Later, we

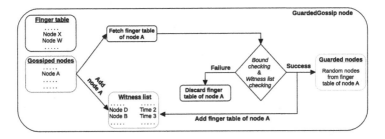

Fig. 1. GuardedGossip protocol workflow.

will discuss how to achieve this assumption. Beside its FT, each GuardedGossip node keeps track of three additional lists: *gossiped nodes*, *guarded nodes*, and *witness nodes*. While the list of gossiped nodes contains the set of new peers retrieved via gossip requests, the list of guarded nodes comprises those nodes that can be used for anonymizing user connections and for further propagation via gossiping. Initially, the list of gossiped nodes is empty, the list of witness nodes consists of all nodes seen during bootstrapping, and the list of guarded nodes contains peers, retrieved by performing secure lookups (i.e., using redundancies and bound checking as described below and in [20]) for random node IDs. Once a sufficient number of inputs for the list of guarded nodes is collected by the regular protocol workflow, the initial bootstrapping nodes (retrieved from secure lookups for random node IDs) become obsolete and are removed from the list. The bootstrapping nodes are never used for anonymizing user connections.

Exchange of Gossip Information. To keep the list of gossiped nodes and the list of guarded nodes loosely in sync and to reduce a potential linkability of both lists, the maintenance of these lists happens in regular random intervals initiated by the GuardedGossip node. To update its list of gossiped nodes, the GuardedGossip node picks one of its fingers (i.e., other nodes comprising the FT of that node) uniformly at random, and sends it a gossip request. The finger returns a set of node IDs in the interval $[0, 2]$, established experimentally as a reasonable trade-off between system security and performance. Only nodes that have received gossip requests and are included in the FT of the GuardedGossip node are allowed to send gossips. Thus, we limit possible gossip information exchange and keep a moderate communication overhead in the network. Next, for each received peer the GuardedGossip node checks whether the ID of that peer is already in the witness list. If it was last-seen recently, the peer is discarded (to avoid an adversary from repeatedly sending the same nodes via gossiping) and the last-seen timestamp of that peer in the witness list is updated. Otherwise, the peer is added to the list of gossiped nodes and the witness list with the current timestamp. After all node IDs retrieved via gossiping are processed, the GuardedGossip node checks whether the length of the gossiped list is within a predefined range and, if not, random elements are deleted (to spawn additional uncertainty about further use of nodes). The size of the witness list is limited by the timestamp of last-seen events. Outdated witness nodes are removed.

On the other side, the node receiving a gossip request checks if the requester is eligible to ask for gossips, i.e., it has that node in its FT. It replies only after successful check. Each of the to-be-sent node IDs are randomly chosen from the list of guarded nodes and, simultaneously, deleted from that list with a probability $p_r = \frac{1}{3}$. Thus, we limit the information leakage about the nodes that can be used for anonymizing user connections. Simply removing all sent IDs would make the receiver aware that these IDs are definitely no longer known by the sender and not used by it for user connections.

Verification of Collected Gossip Information. To build and maintain the list of guarded nodes, we rely on information collected via gossiping. However, the data in gossip messages is not trustworthy. As a consequence, an adversary could bias the lookup process by propagating mostly other malicious nodes if we would directly use gossiped nodes. Instead, we use the gossip information in an indirect way. We arbitrarily choose a set of nodes $\{v_0, \ldots, v_m\}$ from the list of gossiped nodes, where $m \in [0, 3]$ is a random number. We established this interval experimentally as a reasonable trade-off between system security and performance. Simultaneously, the selected nodes are removed from the list of gossiped nodes. Next, each of these nodes v_j, $j = 0, \ldots, m$, is requested to provide its full FT. Every received FT is validated using *bound checking* and *witness list checking*. If and only if both checks succeed, a uniformly random subset of nodes of size up to $n_o = 10$ is selected from the FT and added to the list of guarded nodes (we identified the boundary of 10 as a reasonable trade-off between the uncertainty gain and the frequency of newly collected guarded nodes). Otherwise, the FT is discarded. Thus, we achieve two key properties. First, only nodes from verified FTs are added to the list of guarded nodes. This significantly reduces the probability of biased selection of nodes due to manipulated FTs. Second, we create uncertainty in our choice as the node, from which the FT was fetched, does not get any information which of its fingers are selected for further usage. On average, five nodes are added to the list of guarded nodes for each peer selected from the list of gossiped nodes. As shown in Sect. 5, this ensures a system stability, i.e., at any given time a sufficient number of nodes are available to execute gossiping and to build anonymized user connections. Moreover, all nodes seen in a validated FT are also added to the witness list (or, if already present, their timestamps are updated).

Bound Checking. GuardedGossip uses the same bound checking method applied in NISAN [20]. Due to space constrains, we do not describe the operation of bound checking but refer interested readers to Appendix A for more details.

Witness List Checking. Although bound checking significantly reduces the probability for a biased node selection, it cannot completely eliminate the possibility of manipulating some node IDs in a FT. Therefore, we propose a second verification step, called witness check. Each GuardedGossip node maintains a witness list containing active nodes that have been seen before. On the receipt of a new FT from a gossiped node that has already passed the bound checking, the witness list is next used to further verify the plausibility of this FT. To this end, the optimal IDs of the given FT are initially computed. Then, we search in the witness list for nodes whose IDs are closer to one of the optimal IDs than the nodes currently presented in that FT, i.e., a peer that has been skipped in favor of another node located more far away in the DHT. If such a peer is discovered, this is an indication for a potential malicious manipulation of the FT under verification. In this case, we either silently discard the complete FT with probability $p_c = \frac{1}{2}$ or further investigate this incident with probability $(1 - p_c)$. For our additional verification, we contact the closer node found in our witness list and check its availability. If the availability check succeeds, we discard this FT completely and update the timestamp of our witness node in the witness list. If the availability check fails, we remove the witness node from our witness list and accept the FT. The goal of the non-deterministic incident checking is to reduce the information leakage. It becomes uncertain for the adversary if a (possibly) slightly manipulated FT is accepted or not. Moreover, without non-determinism, one would possibly reveal the reason (i.e., the presence of an active witness node) for rejecting the manipulated FT and, thus, the attacker would gain intelligence about the content of client's witness list. Finally, an extended canonical Chord stabilization is periodically executed. Except Chord update, it purges all outdated nodes in the witness list according to their timestamps.

Creation of Anonymized User Connections. In GuardedGossip, the first node used for an anonymized user connection is selected from the list of guarded nodes. The nodes in this list have passed both bound checking and witness list checking. To further obscure the choice of nodes for anonymized user connections, the initiator of a transmission first creates a one-hop connection to the selected node. Then, the extension of this connection is executed via tunneling. This means that the initiator of the connection randomly selects a node from its list of gossiped nodes and performs a regular GuardedGossip operation via the tunnel to the first node. A random node from the validated FT is further used to extend the anonymized user connection. This process protects from inferences based on destinations of initiator's queries that can be observed by an adversary and is repeated until the necessary path length is reached. Typically, three nodes are used for a path creation in onion routing [11].

Bootstrapping New Nodes. When a new node joins the network, it first gets assigned a pseudo-random, unused ID from the ID space of the underlying DHT. However, the node should not be able to deterministically influence the selection of its ID and, thus, its placement at a certain position, e.g., close to another specific node. To this end, one can use a combination of an IP address and a global consensus, e.g., the hash of a public blockchain. Besides getting an ID, the newly joining node has to know an initial set of *bootstrapping* nodes. The IDs of these nodes are usually obtained out-of-band, e.g., announced by trusted third parties, received via email or from a friend-to-friend network, or distributed together with the software (as in Tor). As in related work [17,26], we assume that at least one of these nodes is not malicious. Next, the newly joining node uses a slightly modified version of NISAN node lookup [20] to bootstrap and introduce itself in the network. It uses its node ID to compute optimal node IDs for its FT and sends lookup requests for them (to fill in its own FT) and randomly selected

IDs (to fill in its guarded list) through its bootstrapping nodes. All nodes that are discovered during this lookup process and passed the bound checking are added to the witness list, together with a timestamp. If a peer already exists in the witness list, only its timestamp will be updated. Moreover, a randomly selected subset of nodes retrieved from the verified FTs is used to initialize the list of guarded nodes. During bootstrapping, the list of gossiped nodes is empty. This list is getting filled once the regular operation of GuardedGossip has started.

5   Evaluation

GuardedGossip aims to provide scalable node discovery while resisting active, e.g., route capture, and passive, i.e., information leakage, attacks. Here, we analyze whether GuardedGossip achieves these goals by means of simulations. As it relies on partial knowledge about active nodes in the network to gain scalability (i.e., each node knows only a portion of the whole network), it is important that this knowledge is unbiased, i.e., every node has equal chance to get known by a particular discovering peer. To this end, we also analyze the randomness of the node discovery process and the impact of churn on our method. We show that GuardedGossip achieves a sufficient level of security for users even if 20% of the participating nodes are malicious. Concurrently, our system scales gracefully and provides an adequate overhead for its security and privacy benefits.

Experimental Setup. The simulation of GuardedGossip is implemented in Python. All interactions between nodes are executed in discrete time steps. We repeated each experiment up to several hundred times to increase the significance of our measurements, presenting mean values together with 95% confidence intervals. The ID space size $N = 2^{32}$ of the Chord ring and the total number of nodes n in GuardedGossip, comprising up to $n = 10^5$ active nodes, are chosen as a trade-off between the goal to simulate as large network sizes as possible, and simultaneously limiting the amount of computational resources needed to handle our simulations. Our setup includes significantly more nodes compared to Tor, and the ID space is sufficiently sparsely populated to model realistic conditions.

Protection against Active Attacks. In GuardedGossip, the indicator for a successful protection against active attacks is the fraction of malicious nodes in the guarded list of each node, which should be similar to the overall fraction of malicious nodes in the network. On the other hand, the attacker aims to maximize the fraction of malicious nodes contained in the guarded lists of other honest nodes. To do this, the adversarial nodes respond on gossip requests with a random sample of IDs belonging to other malicious nodes instead of reporting nodes from their guarded lists. To avoid this, GuardedGossip uses witness list and bounds checking. To simulate a strong adversary, we assume global knowledge of the FT tolerance factor γ for bound checking (see Appendix A). Thus, malicious nodes can optimally maximize the fraction of colluding nodes FTs without being immediately detected. This simulates the worst-case active attacker scenario.

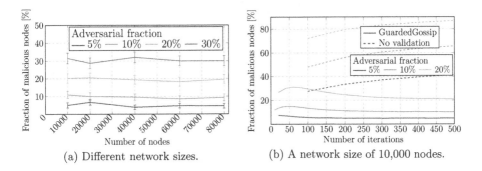

Fig. 2. Fraction of malicious nodes in guarded lists of honest nodes.

Figure 2a shows that the combination of both checking methods is an effective measure against active attacks. The fraction of malicious nodes in the guarded lists remains stable for different network sizes and fractions of malicious nodes. We also see that in each of the considered cases the fraction of malicious nodes contained in the lookup results is close to the theoretical minimum, i.e., the overall attacker fraction in the network. Figure 2b shows the dependency on the number of iterations (i.e., a single run of our method as shown in Fig. 1) and highlights the impact of FT checks. While without any validation the fraction of malicious nodes in guarded lists dramatically increases over time, our checking methods can stabilize the fraction of malicious nodes to a steady state close to the theoretical minimum. It is recommended to stay for at least 100 (or even 200) iterations in the system before starting building anonymized user connections to benefit from an effective witness check and filled guarded lists, as also suggested in Appendix C.

The witness check itself mainly depends on the size of the witness list measured relatively to the total number of nodes in the network (let ω denote this fraction). Given the ID space of size N, n active nodes, and a fraction f of malicious nodes in the system, the total number of adversarial nodes is $f \cdot n$ and the number of nodes in honest node's witness list is $n_\omega = \lfloor n \cdot \omega + 0.5 \rfloor$. Then, the number of possible witness lists of size n_ω is $t = \binom{N}{n_\omega}$. The average distance between two consecutive malicious nodes can be calculated as $\frac{N}{f \cdot n}$. Assuming uniform distribution of nodes in the ID space, the average distance between a randomly selected node and the next (in the direction of the Chord ring) malicious node is in the expectation value on the half of the distance between two consecutive malicious nodes, i.e., $n_m = \lfloor \frac{N}{2 \cdot f \cdot n} + 0.5 \rfloor$. On the other hand, this is exactly the average number of possible witnesses that would reveal a manipulation (as each of the nodes counted by the distance is a potential witness). Each witness list that contains at least one of these witnesses helps to reveal the manipulation. Let the number of these lists be d. First, we compute the number of all possible witness lists that do not have a single member to detect the manipulation $\overline{d} = \binom{N - n_m}{n_\omega}$. We then derive the detection probability that uses of the number of all possible witness lists having at least one member that reveals the

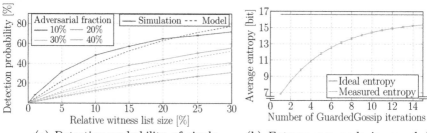

(a) Detection probability of single manipulated FT entries.

(b) Entropy per node in guarded lists for 100,000 active nodes.

Fig. 3. Detection of single manipulated FT entries and entropy of guarded lists.

manipulation of a FT: $p_{\text{detection}}(N, n, f) = \frac{d}{t} = 1 - \frac{\bar{d}}{t} = \frac{\binom{N}{\lfloor nw+0.5\rfloor} - \binom{N - \lfloor \frac{N}{2 \cdot f \cdot n} + 0.5\rfloor}{\lfloor n \cdot w + 0.5\rfloor}}{\binom{N}{\lfloor n \cdot w + 0.5\rfloor}}$.

Figure 3a shows the effectiveness of this check in detecting a single manipulated member of a FT using the previous mathematical model and simulations. The success probability increases with the size of the witness list. However, a single manipulation is detected effectively only when the adversarial fraction in the network is low. While to achieve a detection probability of 50%, a relative witness list size of 15% is sufficient for 10% attacker fraction, we need a relative witness list size of 25% to achieve the same result for 20% attacker fraction. Overall, the witness check does not scale well with respect to the attacker fraction when only a single FT entry is manipulated. However, the situation becomes much better if the adversary replaces more than one entry. As shown in Fig. 4, if the attacker manipulates the FT in a random manner, a replacement of more than three entries will be detected with probability over 60% using a relative witness list size of 15% only. If the adversary replaces FT entries with the closest malicious nodes, changing less than five entries is still hard to detect with a reasonable relative witness list size, e.g., less than 30% of the total nodes. A good detection is achieved by changing at least seven nodes and assuming relative witness list size of 15%. Even a relatively small witness list size of 5%-10% already helps to detect manipulations. Still, as we saw before, the use of both witness checking and bound checking is the most effective protection against active attacks.

Network Churn. We analyze the resistance of our method to network churn. We performed a simulation where 0.5% and 1%, respectively, of all nodes leave the network per iteration, while the same number of new nodes joins the network. Hence, the network size remains stable. Please note that the change of 0.5% and 1% of the entire network per iteration implies is a huge fluctuation of the nodes. Figure 5 shows the impact of churn on the fraction of malicious nodes in the FTs of honest nodes. Here, we distinguish between honest nodes including or excluding the newly joined ones. Due to a deterministic bootstrapping process without gossiping, the newly joined nodes have more secure FTs and, hence, lower number of malicious nodes in their guarded lists. However, it is wrong to deduce that it is better to freshly join the network instead of staying within for some

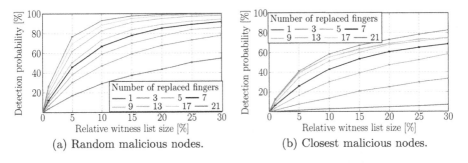

(a) Random malicious nodes.　　　　(b) Closest malicious nodes.

Fig. 4. Probability to detect a malicious replacement of FT entries using witness checking in a network of size 10,000 nodes with 20% malicious nodes.

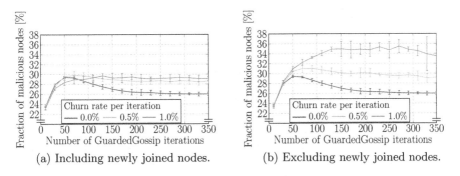

(a) Including newly joined nodes.　　(b) Excluding newly joined nodes.

Fig. 5. Fraction of malicious nodes in guarded lists of honest nodes for different levels of churn in a network of size 5,000 nodes with 20% malicious nodes.

time. Though performing a good job against active attacks, the nodes contained in the guarded lists of freshly joined nodes are deterministic in the beginning and do not provide protection against passive attacks (our method starts using the guarded list for anonymizing user connections only after the bootstrapping nodes are replaced by those obtained from a regular protocol behavior). High churn mostly impacts the witness list as many of the witness nodes become outdated. In this case, the major protection is achieved by the bound checking. Even under extremely high churn rate of 1% per iteration, honest nodes have a controllably stable fraction of malicious nodes in their guarded lists over the number of iterations (see Fig. 5a). Although the churn negatively influences the level of protection against active attacks, its impact is almost negligible as it is just 3% above the steady state of the system without churn.

Protection against Passive Attacks. We aim to obscure the identity of nodes that will be used for anonymizing connections. To measure the difficulty of estimating the nodes in the guarded list of other honest nodes, we evaluate the entropy of the lists elements. The theoretical maximum possible entropy of an element in a guarded list is given by $H_{\max} = \log_2(n)$. This ideal entropy could be achieved by assuming that lists are sampled uniformly at random from all

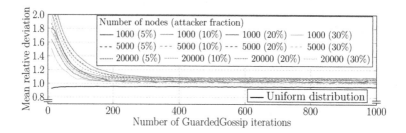

Fig. 6. Mean relative deviation of distances between nodes in lists of guarded nodes and the expected distances based the uniform distribution.

active nodes in the network. The average entropy per guarded node list member is monotonously converging to the ideal value above mentioned (see Fig. 3b). An acceptable value of entropy is already reached after only 15 iterations of our method. Hence, GuardedGossip leads to fast network information propagation and achieves sufficiently large entropy to render passive attacks impossible.

Randomness of Node Discovery. During bootstrapping, GuardedGossip undergoes deterministic measures to achieve its security properties. To identify the duration of the bootstrapping phase for different number of malicious nodes (i.e., how long does it take to achieve a sufficient level of node randomness in a guarded list), we analyze the distribution of nodes collected in individual guarded lists. Figure 6 shows the mean relative deviation of distances between nodes collected in guarded lists and the expected distances based on the uniform distribution. To compute the mean relative deviation, we first calculate the optimal average distance $\overline{d}$ between nodes in our Chord DHT, i.e., $\overline{d} = \frac{N}{e}$, where e is the size of a guarded list and N is the size of the ID space in the DHT. Then, we obtain the mean relative deviation of distances $mrd = \sqrt{\frac{1}{e} \sum_{j=0}^{e} \left(\frac{d_j - \overline{d}}{\overline{d}} \right)^2}$, where d_j, $j = 1, \ldots, e$, are the actual distances between members in guarded lists. Initially, the mean relative deviation is very high, compared to the uniform distribution. However, almost independently on the network size and the fraction of malicious nodes, the mean relative distance decreases significantly within the first 200 iterations. Then, the relative mean distance behave stable, being only slightly above the optimum deviation defined theoretically by the uniform distribution. Thus, the distribution of nodes in guarded lists is well normalized over time and it is safe to use these nodes after about 200 iterations. We also explore the average number of nodes in both, the gossiped list and the guarded list, and show that the number of nodes in both lists becomes sufficient after approximately 150 iterations. For more details about our results, see Appendix C.

To sum up, our method effectively hampers active attacks while being able to cope with churn and, thanks to its gossiping component, achieves high entropy in the guarded lists, rendering passive attacks impractical.

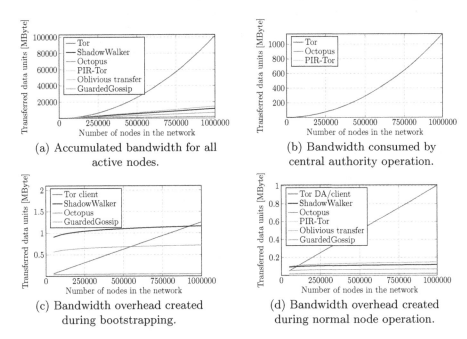

(a) Accumulated bandwidth for all active nodes.

(b) Bandwidth consumed by central authority operation.

(c) Bandwidth overhead created during bootstrapping.

(d) Bandwidth overhead created during normal node operation.

Fig. 7. Bandwidth overhead of GuardedGossip and other node discovery systems.

Overhead. We compare the amount of bandwidth overhead created by the most popular prior node discovery systems the Tor's node discovery method [11], ShadowWalker [17], Octopus [26], oblivious transfer [5], and PIR-Tor [18] to GuardedGossip. Here, we assume that GuardedGossip operates in a churn rate of 0.1% per iteration, whereas the total number of available nodes is kept constant by letting join the same number of nodes that have left the network. Each GuardedGossip node is assumed to perform 200 iterations before start building anonymization connections to ensure that the bootstrapping of that node is complete and it has a sufficient number of guarded nodes. For Tor, we assume the existence of 10 DAs, which agree on a new consensus every time step. All parts of the Tor directory protocol that are not needed for path construction are omitted and the distribution of node descriptors is done using *microdescriptors* to ensure higher bandwidth efficiency. ShadowWalker is simulated using 40 shadow nodes as in [24] to achieve sufficient security. Octopus uses a path length of four nodes as in [26] and is configured according to the original experimental setup in [26]. PIR-Tor uses three PIR servers providing the network consensus. For oblivious transfer, we use the method in [5] with a quorum size of 100 nodes.

Figure 7a shows the bandwidth overhead accumulated for all active nodes. While the amount of bandwidth required by Tor for increasing network sizes rises dramatically, the bandwidth consumption of the other methods remains nearly constant over the different network sizes. GuardedGossips achieves lower level of bandwidth overhead compared to ShadowWalker and oblivious transfer.

Although Octopus still creates the smallest amount of bandwidth overhead, it is not a pure P2P approach as it relies on a centralized mechanism for the detection of active attacks and the blacklisting of malicious nodes. Thus, the scalability of its centralized mechanism needs to be further explored for increasing network sizes. We also analyze the bandwidth overhead created due to the use of centralized servers. We focus on Tor, Octopus, and PIR-Tor, as they are the only node discovery systems that rely on centralized mechanisms. As shown in Fig. 7b, the bandwidth overhead created by the operation of Tor DAs rises almost quadratically for increasing network sizes. In contrast, the amount of bandwidth consumed by the centralized servers of Octopus and PIR-Tor is negligible.

Figure 7c shows the amount of bandwidth created during the bootstrapping phase of each method for different network sizes. GuardedGossips has comparably high bandwidth costs during bootstrapping due to the security checks applied when nodes join the network. Octopus consumes two orders of magnitude less bandwidth for bootstrapping compared to GuardedGossips. The amount data units transferred by Tor, ShadowWalker, and oblivious transfer during bootstrapping is in the same order of magnitude. We also observe that the bandwidth overhead created during bootstrapping depends on the node discovery method used and is not influenced by the network size. This, in turn, promises a graceful scalability in case of GuardedGossip and makes it an attractive candidate for larger network sizes. Finally, Fig. 7d shows the bandwidth consumption created during normal node operation (i.e., once the bootstrapping phase completes). While the amount of bandwidth overhead created by GuardedGossip and Octopus is similar, the bandwidth consumption of PIR-Tor and oblivious transfer is slightly higher. In contrast, the amount of bandwidth required by Tor rises dramatically for all network sizes.

6   Discussion and Conclusion

Contrary to Tor [11] and PIR-Tor [18], GuardedGossip is a pure P2P approach. Hence, it weakens the trust assumption and does not require any trusted third party and a single point of failure (even if it is distributed over several nodes). Although Octopus is also P2P based, it requires the use of a trusted authority actively involved in node operations. The major advantage of GuardedGossip is its scalability as its underlying structure is a well-studied scalable DHT. The gossiping component is influenceable by the nodes themselves. Depending on their demands and capacities, they can limit or increase the gossiping rate. As in Tor, in GuardedGossip it is easy to collect the complete list of available nodes (see Appendix B). Though not having this property would be beneficial to allow for better blocking resistance, our method and, to the best of our knowledge, all the prior related work fail to achieve this. Future work is required to design mechanisms that would make it difficult to enumerate all active nodes.

Since GuardedGossip, as a DHT-based approach, allows for secure and scalable node lookups in P2P designs, an interested reader could wonder how it can be integrated into Tor. If Tor would switch to a P2P concept, which would be from the authors' perspective the preferred option for getting rid of trusted DAs and improving scalability, then the GuardedGossip could serve as a good design candidate for node lookups. In the current Tor concept, a possible solution could be to let users select their trusted entry OR (similar to the secret buddy concept in Torsk [14]) as a proxy to execute the GuardedGossip protocol on their behalf. This trusted entry OR should be used for longer time period (as the guard ORs in Tor). Although such a mechanism offers less security than in a P2P design, this method would allow for scalable network information distribution without requiring to trust the same third party (i.e., the Tor DAs) by all users.

To sum up, node discovery and lookup methods form an integral part of any overlay network. Their use in untrustworthy environments—such as the Internet—brings additional challenges with respect to possible attacks. Especially in anonymous communication, it is important to provide secure and unbiased discovery as otherwise the anonymity of millions of people using these networks and reling on their properties can be compromised. In this paper, we proposed GuardedGossip—a secure, decentralized network information distribution system based on the combination of gossiping with a Chord DHT. This is done without trusting any third party. Our system scales gracefully and provides an adequate overhead for achieving its superior security properties.

Acknowledgments. Parts of this work have been funded by the EU and state Brandenburg EFRE StaF project INSPIRE.

A   Bound Checking

Given a FT, bound checking is performed as follows: Initially, the node density d is computed. Ideally, this can be done by deriving $d = \frac{N}{n}$, where N is the ID space size of the DHT and n is the number of active nodes. However, n is usually not known. Thus, each peer computes means of the distance between the actual IDs in its FT and optimal IDs (as if all IDs would exist). The mean distance is then multiplied with a *finger table tolerance factor* $\gamma > 0$. Finally, to verify the plausibility of a given FT g the GuardedGossip node applies the following constraint $d_g < \gamma d$ to check whether the FT g is manipulated. In our work, we use $\gamma = \sqrt{\frac{1}{f}}$, where f is the (supposed) fraction of colluding malicious nodes. As the actual fraction of colluding malicious nodes is not known by the users, γ corresponds to the estimated maximum fraction of malicious nodes that is supposed to be tolerated by our approach.

To assess the optimal value of γ, we rely on the approach used to detect routing failures in [7]. As the value of γ depends on the false positives rate α (i.e., a correct FT is falsely detected as manipulated) and the false negatives rate β (i.e., a manipulated FT is detected as correct), here we aim to minimize both, α and β, simultaneously. To this end, we deal with the total number n of all uniformly sampled active nodes within the ID space N. According to [7], the distances between consecutive node IDs within a FT can be modeled by independent exponentially distributed random variables with a mean of $\frac{N}{n}$. Similarly, the distance between consecutive malicious nodes can be modeled using exponential distribution with a mean of $\frac{N}{f \cdot n}$, where f is the fraction of malicious nodes. We construct a new random variable by summing up the distances between nodes in the FT of the verifying node (denoted as S_o) and the distances between nodes in the retrieved FT to be verified by that node (denoted as S_v). Given that k denotes the FT size, the values of $\frac{1}{k} \cdot S_o$ and $\frac{1}{k} \cdot S_v$ measure the mean distances between node IDs in the FT of the verifying node and the retrieved FT to be verified by that node using bound checking. Now, the false positive rate α can be expressed by the probability $\alpha(k, \gamma, f) = Pr\left(\frac{1}{k} \cdot S_v > \gamma \frac{1}{k} \cdot S_o\right)$. Similarly, the false negative rate β is computed as follows: $\beta(k, \gamma, f) = Pr\left(\frac{1}{k} \cdot S_v < \gamma \frac{1}{k} \cdot S_o\right)$. According to [7], the false positives and false negatives get minimized if $\alpha = \beta$. Thus, we obtain the following equation: $\alpha(k, \gamma, f) = \beta(k, \gamma, f)$, from which γ can be computed. Moreover, S_o and S_v, are γ-distributed with a shape parameter k and scale parameters $\frac{n}{N}$ and $\frac{f \cdot n}{N}$, correspondingly. The use of the gamma distribution and solving the equation by γ finally yields $\gamma = \sqrt{\frac{1}{f}}$.

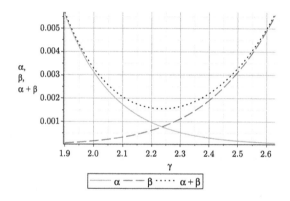

Fig. 8. Bounds checking false positive rate α, false negative rate β, and objective function for optimization $\alpha + \beta$ over the FT tolerance factor γ for $f = 0.2$.

We performed experiments to check these theoretical results. Figure 8 shows the bounds checking false positive rate α, the false negative rate β and the objective function for the optimization of $\alpha + \beta$, which is intended for minimization over the threshold $\gamma > 0$. As suggested in [7], the minimal cumulated error is achieved in case of $\alpha = \beta$, which justifies our computation of γ.

B   Completeness of Node Discovery

To achieve a sufficient level of anonymity, GuardedGossip should deliver random nodes from the set of all active nodes in the network. Thus, the attacker cannot influence the selection of nodes for anonymized user connections except by injecting more peers in the network. As the list of guarded nodes is the only source in our approach providing nodes for building user connections, we analyze its content with respect to its completeness. Figure 9 shows the fraction of nodes collected in individual lists of guarded nodes during the operation of GuardedGossip over time. For an increasing number of iterations, the fraction of nodes observed in guarded lists (measured by 95% quantiles) converges to 100%. Already after 1000 iterations, almost all GuardedGossip nodes have seen other active nodes forming the half of the network. This also confirms the expectation that staying longer in the network increases the coverage of discovered nodes. Every node also gets a chance to be discovered by all network participants.

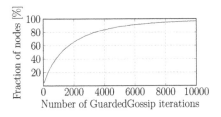

Fig. 9. Fraction of nodes in guarded lists measured by 95% quantiles for a network of size 2,000 nodes.

C   Number of Nodes in Gossiped and Guarded Lists

We also explore the average number of nodes contained in both the gossiped list and the guarded list. Figure 10 shows that the size of the guarded list rapidly increases already in the beginning of operation of our approach, i.e., after 20 iterations. On the other hand, the number of nodes in the gossiped list increases slower, i.e., after 100 iterations it becomes stable. The guarded list grows faster as it gets filled by the whole FTs whereas the gossiped list only by single entries. We observe that the size of the network does not influence the bootstrapping process of the guarded list and has only a moderate impact on the size of gossiped list. Naturally, for an increasing network size the steady state of the gossiped list is reached earlier as more nodes participate in the gossiping process. However, even for small networks with 1000 nodes we achieve a sufficient number of nodes after

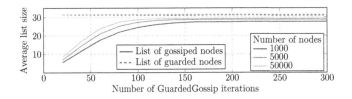

Fig. 10. Average number of nodes in gossiped and guarded lists for different network sizes with 10% adversarial nodes.

approximately 150 iterations. This ensures fluctuations within the lists (once both lists are completely filled, some nodes are discarded in favor of new nodes) so that it becomes more difficult for an attacker to promote favorable nodes due to the constant rotation of nodes in the gossiped list.

References

1. Torproject.org Blocked by GFW in China: Sooner or Later? (2008). https://blog. torproject.org/torprojectorg-blocked-gfw-china-sooner-or-later
2. Tor Directory Protocol, Version 3 (2018). https://gitweb.torproject.org/torspec. git/tree/dir-spec.txt
3. Tor Metrics (2021). https://metrics.torproject.org/
4. Artigas, M.S., et al.: Cyclone: a novel design schema for hierarchical DHTs. In: P2P (2005)
5. Backes, M., et al.: Adding query privacy to robust DHTs. In: ASIA CCS (2012)
6. Borisov, N., et al.: Denial of service or denial of security? How attacks on reliability can compromise anonymity. In: CCS (2007)
7. Castro, M., et al.: Secure routing for structured peer-to-peer overlay networks. In: OSDI (2002)
8. Danezis, G., Clayton, R.: Route fingerprinting in anonymous communications. In: P2P (2006)
9. Danezis, G., Syverson, P.: Bridging and fingerprinting: epistemic attacks on route selection. In: Borisov, N., Goldberg, I. (eds.) PETS 2008. LNCS, vol. 5134, pp. 151–166. Springer, Heidelberg (2008). https://doi.org/10.1007/978-3-540-70630-4_10
10. Dingledine, R., Mathewson, N.: Tor Protocol Specification (2018). https://gitweb. torproject.org/torspec.git/plain/tor-spec.txt
11. Dingledine, R., et al.: Tor: the second-generation onion router. In: USENIX Security Symposium (2004)
12. Freedman, M.J., Morris, R.: Tarzan: a peer-to-peer anonymizing network layer. In: CCS (2002)
13. Kapadia, A., Triandopoulos, N.: Halo: high-assurance locate for distributed hash tables. In: NDSS (2008)
14. McLachlan, J., et al.: Scalable onion routing with Torsk. In: CCS (2009)
15. Mislove, A., et al.: AP3: cooperative, decentralized anonymous communication. In: ACM SIGOPS European Workshop (2004)
16. Mittal, P., Borisov, N.: Information leaks in structured peer-to-peer anonymous communication systems. In: CCS (2008)
17. Mittal, P., Borisov, N.: ShadowWalker: peer-to-peer anonymous communication using redundant structured topologies. In: CCS (2009)
18. Mittal, P., et al.: PIR-Tor: scalable anonymous communication using private information retrieval. In: USENIX Security Symposium (2011)
19. Nambiar, A., Wright, M.: Salsa: a structured approach to large-scale anonymity. In: CCS (2006)
20. Panchenko, A., et al.: NISAN: network information service for anonymization networks. In: CCS (2009)
21. Rennhard, M., Plattner, B.: Introducing MorphMix: peer-to-peer based anonymous internet usage with collusion detection. In: WPES (2002)

22. Rowstron, A., Druschel, P.: Pastry: scalable, decentralized object location and routing for large-scale peer-to-peer systems. In: IFIP/ACM Middleware (2001)
23. Sasy, S., Goldberg, I.: ConsenSGX: scaling anonymous communications networks with trusted execution environments. In: PETS (2019)
24. Schuchard, M., et al.: Balancing the shadows. In: WPES (2010)
25. Tabriz, P., Borisov, N.: Breaking the collusion detection mechanism of MorphMix. In: PETS (2006)
26. Wang, Q., Borisov, N.: Octopus: a secure and anonymous DHT lookup. In: ICDCS (2012)
27. Wang, Q., et al.. In search of an anonymous and secure lookup: attacks on structured peer-to-peer anonymous communication systems. In: CCS (2010)
28. Zhuang, L., et al.: Cashmere: resilient anonymous routing. In: NSDI (2005)

An Extensive Security Analysis on Ethereum Smart Contracts

Mohammadreza Ashouri$^{(\boxtimes)}$ iD

Department of Cyber Security, Saint Pölten University of Applied Sciences,
Saint Pölten, Austria
mohammadreza.ashouri@fhstp.ac.at

Abstract. Smart contracts have extensive applications in various emerging domains such as IoT, 5G networks, and finance. In this regard, the Ethereum platform has provided the capability of running smart contracts on its distributed infrastructure. Smart contracts are small programs that describe a set of rules for supervising associated funds, often written in a Turing-complete programming language called Solidity. Furthermore, Ethereum is currently one of the most extensive cryptocurrencies next to Bitcoin. This provides an extraordinary opportunity for attackers to exploit potential zero-day vulnerabilities in this ecosystem that are tightly twisted with financial gain. Consequently, this paper introduces a practical framework called "EthFuzz" to identify vulnerabilities and generate concrete exploits for the Ethereum ecosystem. Our system works through a graph-based method in combination with dynamic symbolic execution. Moreover, our proposed framework can tackle the path explosion problem in its symbolic execution engine. To prove our approach's usefulness, we could successfully identify and generate *26,015* exploits out of *207,412* exploitable paths, within *1,000,000* real-world smart contracts on the Ethereum live blockchain network.

Keywords: Smart contract · Security · Analysis · Ethereum · Exploit

1 Introduction

Blockchain is a distributed ledger technology that designates exchanges of value between individuals securely, permanently, and in a simply provable manner [19]. It is also the underlying technology for cryptocurrencies such as Bitcoin and Ethereum. Even though initially used for financial transactions, applications of blockchain extend beyond finance and can affect a wide variety of industries such as 5G and beyond networks [23]. For example, smart contracts can enable applications to communicate with Things in the IoT [16], in a way similar to how hardware drivers allow applications to cooperate with devices. Moreover, smart contracts can provide high security for the 5G networks involved in decentralized ledgers.

The programmability of the Ethereum platform is predicated on its ability to build and perform smart contracts [19]. The term "smart contract" was introduced by Nick Szabo in 1996 [29], when he described it as "a set of promises,

J. Garcia-Alfaro et al. (Eds.): SecureComm 2021, LNICST 398, pp. 144–163, 2021.
https://doi.org/10.1007/978-3-030-90019-9_8

specified in digital form, including protocols within which the parties perform on these promises". Smart contracts are agreements between transacting parties that are written using computer code and programmed to self-execute when specific conditions are met. These can be integrated into a blockchain platform like Ethereum to implement the verification and integrity required for such an automated system to work.

However, creating trustworthy and secure smart contracts can be remarkably complicated due to the complex semantics of the underlying domain-specific languages and their testability. There have been high-profile incidents suggesting that certain blockchain smart contracts could accommodate various code-security vulnerabilities which can potentially lead to financial harm [26]. This is especially challenging given the notion that smart contracts are supposed to be "immutable". In other words, once a contract code is deployed, it cannot be changed anymore, which makes patching identified vulnerabilities impossible.

In this paper, we introduce a practical and scalable framework for performing in-depth security analysis and automatic exploit generation for commercial off-the-shelf (COTS) smart contracts available on the blockchain network. We call our system "EthFuzz", and it can identify and exploit zero-day vulnerabilities, exploits and runtime attacks based on user specifications in Datalog [31]. Our approach works based on a backward slicing method to classify and control the safety of critical execution paths with a combination of static and dynamic analysis in lockstep with a symbolic execution engine.

We made the following contributions in this work:

1. **Generating concrete exploits.** EthFuzz automatically generates concrete exploits for detected vulnerabilities in smart contracts without access to the source code. Hence, we created a symbolic execution engine based on the Z3 SMT solver to trigger critical executable paths in given Ethereum smart contracts and create exploit inputs.
2. **The low cost of specifying new vulnerabilities.** While previous work [12, 15,17,30] has relied on literal hard-coded configurations, which produce a high maintenance cost and a high cost per vulnerability controlled, in EthFuzz's design, new vulnerability and attack patterns can be specified by the end users in Datalog files, provided by an auxiliary API in our framework. This allows users and developers to upgrade the framework for new attacking patterns without struggling with low-level structures and recompilation process.
3. **Controlling false positives.** In contrast to previous work, EthFuzz proactively separates exploitable from non-exploitable paths with the help of a dynamic execution module in order to prune useless paths from further analysis and symbolic execution operations. In consequence, the final result is more reliable and the exploit generation is faster and less error-prone.
4. **Real-world evaluation.** We have gathered and investigated COTS smart contracts derived from the Ethereum network to find current trends in security issues in the Ethereum ecosystem and regulate the effectiveness of EthFuzz for real-world applications.

2   Background

Smart contracts are only controlled by code that can handle transactions fully autonomously. Moreover, smart contract code is executed when a user submits a transaction along with a smart contract as the recipient. Users add payload data in transactions, which in turn is provided as input to the subject smart contract. More specifically, a contract is established as a collection of functions, which users can invoke. A contract can also trigger the execution of another contract through *CALL* instruction. This critical instruction transfers a message similar to Remote Procedure Call (RPC) in other programming paradigms [11].

In order to execute a smart contract, a sender has to send a transaction to the subject contract and pay a charge, which is called "GAS" (it will be acquired from the contract's computational cost.). The contracts themselves can also call other contracts present on the Ethereum blockchain [26]. Note that every contract is tied to an account and the contract code can be triggered by calls or transactions received from other contracts. However, accounts cannot launch new transactions on their own, which means they can only respond to other transactions they receive. Since smart contracts are generally designed to manipulate and hold funds designated in Ether, they are considered to be highly attractive targets for cybercriminals [27].

2.1   Smart Contract Vulnerabilities

There are multiple well-known security issues reported in the smart contract ecosystem that all have been comprehensively described in various references such as [7,26]. However, we briefly introduce some of the most prevalent vulnerability classes that we frequently mention throughout this paper. For the sake of saving space, we present a two-letter acronym for each vulnerability.

Integer Overflow (IO) and Underflow (IU). Integer overflow (and underflow) is a common error in numerous programming languages but in the context of Ethereum it can have serious outcomes. In Solidity "Integer" data types have no built-in security against integer overflow (IOF) and underflow (UOF) attacks [17,30]. For example, if a loop counter were to overflow, generating an infinite loop, the funds of a contract would become fully frozen. Thus, attackers can exploit this bug by increasing the number of iterations of a loop, for example, by introducing new users to a vulnerable contract [30].

Re-Entrancy (RE). This is a well-known attack that has taken Ethereum security communities by storm, particularly after the notorious DAO hack [28]. This vulnerability will be exploited when a contract attempts to send Ether before having updated its internal state. If the target address is a different contract, the contract code will be executed and can invoke the function to ask Ether again and again, which results in generating funds.

Unhandled Exceptions (UE). Some low-level operations in Solidity (e.g. *send*), which is used to transfer Ether, do not throw an exception on failure, instead they report the status by returning a Boolean. If this returns value were to be unchecked, a contract would continue its execution even if the payment failed, which could lead to inconsistencies [22].

Transaction Order Dependency (TOD). In Ethereum, different transactions are carried in a single block, which means that the state of a contract can be updated many times in the same block. If the order of two transactions calling the same contract changes the final outcome, adversaries can exploit this property. For example, in the case of a smart contract that expects members to submit the resolution to a puzzle in exchange for a bonus, an adversary member could decrease the amount of the bonus when the transaction is submitted.

Locked Ether (LE). Ethereum smart contracts can also have a function labelled as payable that allows the contract to receive Ether and to increase its balance. The contract can also have a function which sends Ether. For example, a contract might have a payable function called *deposit*, which receives Ether, and a function called *withdraw*, which sends Ether. However, there are several reasons why the withdraw function may become unable to send funds any longer. One reason could be that the contract may depend on another contract which has been destructed using the *SELFDESTRUCT* instruction of the EVM—i.e. its code has been removed and its funds transferred. It is also possible that the withdraw function requires an external contract to send Ether. However, if the dependence contract has already been destructed, the *withdraw* function will not be able to actually send the Ether anymore and lock the funds of the contract. This case occurred in the Parity Wallet bug in November 2017, which resulted in a loss of millions of USD worth of Ether [25].

3   Security Analysis Method

Critical Operation. To have a better understanding of the security exploitation in the smart contract ecosystem, we studied all reports available on the National Vulnerability Database (NVD) in order to extract and specify the most critical EVM instructions that are commonly involved in cyber attacks. As a result, we concluded that there are a number of EVM instructions involved in most of the exploits that are essentially linked to value transformation operations. For example, creating transactions (*CALL*), transaction termination (*SELF-DESTRUCT*), code injections (*CALL CODE*), and (*DELEGATECALL*) are some of the most repeated instructions that the public exploits databases. Listing 1.1 represents some of the critical instructions in the abstract level, and Table 1 shows the details of the instructions.

Listing 1.1. A sample generated exploit in Slick (for easier reading the sample contract is shown at the source level)

```
<address>.call(bytes memory) returns (bool, bytes memory)
<address>.delegatecall(bytes memory) returns (bool, bytes memory)
<address>.staticcall(bytes memory) returns (bool, bytes memory)
```

Accordingly, we found that smart contract attackers often steal Ether by exploiting these critical instructions or in some cases, they attempt to interrupt target contracts by triggering errors in the code logic. Consequently, to implement our security analysis mechanism, we are particularly interested in analyzing the runtime behavior of the EVM bytecode instructions associated with critical operations that can be potentially involved in suspicious activities during the code execution.

Table 1. The most critical instructions in the EVM bytecode

OPCODE	INSTRUCTION	DESCRIPTION
0x55	SSTORE	Save word to storage
0xe2	SSTOREBYTES	Only referenced in pyethereum
0xf1	CALL	Message-call into an account
0xf2	CALLCODE	Message-call into this account with alternative account's code
0xf3	RETURN	Halt execution returning output data
0xf4	DELEGATECALL	Message-call into this account with an alternative account's code
0xfa	STATICCALL	Similar to CALL, but does not modify state
0xff	SELFDESTRUCT	Halt execution and register account for later deletion

Accordingly, we aim to introduce an efficient analysis system that identifies not only zero-day vulnerabilities and unseen attacks but also generates reliable exploits the identified bugs without human intervention. Hence, we combine a hybrid approach based on "static call graph analysis", "dynamic execution", and symbolic execution in order to gain accurate results with maximum coverage.

Figure 1 represents the abstract architecture of our introduced approach, which is called "EthFuzz". To deploy our system without special firmware modifications or root privileges on different platforms, we implemented EthFuzz in an isolated and portable execution environment working on top of Ubuntu kernel 16.04 64 bit inside the QEMU emulator [10], which is a fast dynamic translator. Moreover, to evade accessing the contracts' source code for the analysis, EthFuzz functions based on the EVM bytecode instrumentation through leveraging "Parity Ethereum Client" [5]. This feature also enables us to perform bytecode instrumentation for real-world smart contracts.

As illustrated in the abstract of EthFuzz, our approach works based on the following three main stages:

1. Code Property Graphs Analysis
2. Dynamic Execution
3. Symbolic Testing

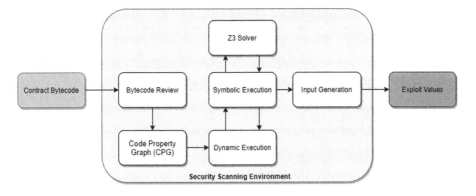

Fig. 1. The overview architecture of EthFuzz.

3.1   Step 1: Call Graph Analysis

In order to interpret and identify potentially exploitable execution paths within the bytecode of smart contracts, we generate a graph model of the target smart contract in a first step. Our graph model is based on *Code Property Graphs (CPGs)* [32], which is an extensible and language-agnostic representation of program code designed for incremental and distributed code analysis. The CPGs are constructed based on the EVM bytecode to help us to distinguish critical instructions and the relevant execution paths. Note that a critical instruction in a generated CPGs can be managed to find data dependency paths between the variables. After finding these paths, we later execute them symbolically to reproduce their corresponding exploits. In order to generate the call graph we used "Porosity" [2], which is an open-source tool. However, the available source code contained many bugs. For example, it stopped the call graph at *STOP* and *REVERT* instructions and did not treat *STATICALL* as call instructions. Porosity only recognized *JUMPI* as jump instruction and thus ignored *JUMP* instructions.

Backward Slicing. In order to generate concrete exploits, we also need to gain the correct entry point (we call it "source") so that a potential generated exploit can reach the critical instructions and perform an attack in the target contract successfully. To do so, EthFuzz performs a hybrid technique that comprises two steps, namely backward slicing" and non-exploitable path pruning (introduced in [6]), which is shown in Algorithm 1.

Algorithm 1: Performing backward-slicing to extract exploitable paths

---

Input: Sensitive Instructions
Result: Exploitable Paths

1 initialization;
2 $SensitiveNodes \leftarrow FINSensitiveIntructionNode(SensitiveInstructions)$;
3 **foreach** $sn \in SensitiveNodes$ **do**
4      $ExploitableEVMPaths = ANALYZECRITICALNODE(sn)$;
5 **end**
6 **return**$ExploitableEVMPaths$;
7 **Function** ANALYZECRITICALNODE($vertex$):
8      $ExploitableEVMPaths \leftarrow []$;
9      $paths = BackwardSLC(sn)$;
10   **foreach** $path \in paths$ **do**
11   **if** $pathhasasource$ **then**
12           $ExploitableEVMPaths \leftarrow path$;
13   **else**
14           $callPaths = ANALYZECRITICALNODE(callVertex)$;
15           $ExploitableEVMPaths \leftarrow path + callPaths$;
16   **end**
17   **end**
18   **return** $ExploitableEVMPaths$;
19 **Function** BackwardSLC($vetex$):
20     $IntraPaths \leftarrow []$;
21   **while** $vertex$ is not a source vertex is not a func. argument **do**
22        $Incvertices = GETINCOMINGDDVERTEX(vertex)$;
23        $UnsanVertics = FILTERSANNVERTICS(Incvertices)$;
24        $vertex \leftarrow unsanVertixs$;
25   **end**
26     $IntraPaths = GETPATHSTO(vertex)$;
27   **return** $IntraPaths$;

The backward-slicing algorithm starts by investigating the nodes (presenting EVM instructions) in the generated graph in order to draw critical instructions (line 2). For each node showing an instruction in the graph, EthFuzz explores its data dependency links in a backward way. *ANALYZECRITICALNODE* calls *BackSLC* in order to succeed all data dependency paths from an instruction node either to a source or a function argument. If the path drops at a function argument, *ANALYZECRITICALNODE* is called recursively over the points denoting the call-sites of that particular function. The function *BackSLC* then analyzes intra-procedural paths between sources and the critical nodes. It also controls safety functions (e.g., SafeMath in OpenZeppelin [3]) in the identified paths and prunes non-exploitable ones. Eventually, *GETPATHSTO* realizes all investigated paths in the graph leading to sources (entry points).

Pruning Non-exploitable Paths. To reduce the overhead caused by analyzing non-exploitable execution paths, we made an assumption. Suppose a detected path cannot reach a critical EVM instruction in the contract under analysis. In that case, we consider the path as a non-exploitable path, which must be excluded from further analysis because it may cause overhead and false-positive results. Algorithm 2 represents the details of the pruning method for non-exploitable paths.

Algorithm 2: Pruning non-exploitable paths

Input: β: candidate path set, exposedCN: explosed critical node
Result: α: set of paths after pruning

1   **foreach** $p \in Path$ **do**
2   **if** $isRelevant() == True$ **then**
3 | $\alpha.push(P)$;
4   **else**
5   **end**
6   **Function** isExploitable(P):
7   **if** $Const.solve() == \emptyset$ **then**
8 | **return** $False$;
9   **else**
10   **if** $P.Succs \cap exposedCN == \emptyset$ **then**
11 | **return** $False$;
12   **else**
13   **return** $True$;

3.2   Step 2: Dynamic Execution

In real-world smart contracts using off-the-shelf libraries for safety enhancement is quite common. For example, *Open Zeppelin SafeMath* is one of the popular libraries for protecting smart contract against Integer overflow/underflow attacks. In our approach, we also need to detect the presence of this type of protection in execution paths in order to reduce the potential of false-positive reports. To do so, we leverage dynamic execution to assess the exploitable target paths with actual runtime data. Thus, in the dynamic execution module, a special input or operation result, and a symbolic variable with a specific name (we call it "Taint Label") is added to the exploitable path. This symbolic variable is initially set by *0* and will be defined *TAINT-PC* (*PC* means program counter). We demonstrate this module in Fig. 2.

The taint label covers to succeeding branches along with the potential dangerous data, engaging in computations but without modifying the results. Our taint tracking method is described as follows:

1. Performing data flow analysis based on the propagation rules that describe which operations can propagate taint message or lead to new taint messages during the execution time (e.g. *ADD, SUB, MUL.*).
2. At some specific program points, security-critical parameters or state variables are supposed to be tainted or not on-demand, according to whether they carry taint labels.
3. If security-critical data of a risky point was tainted, the source entry can also be detected based on the tainted label.

3.3   Step 3: Symbolic Testing and Exploit Input Generation

After identifying exploitable paths, EthFuzz starts to generate concrete exploits for the paths. To avoid path explosion issues, we perform this stage with the help

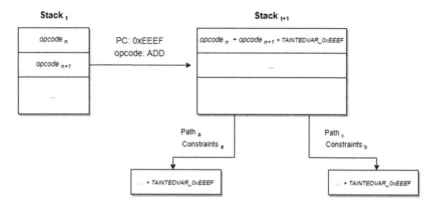

Fig. 2. Dynamic execution allows us to tracks all tainted inputs in the memory during the execution time.

of the collected actual and runtime data during the dynamic execution. Thus, our symbolic engine is not trapped in infinitive loops and infeasible paths. The exploit generation system operates based on a dynamic symbolic execution and Z3 SMT solver [14]. Consequently, we model the exploitable paths as a logical formula "F_{-Xpath}" so that their constraints are derived from the arguments of the extracted source "$F_{-Source}$" and critical instruction "F_{-Crins}" that represent which values after submitting to the target contract can lead to successful attacks.

As a result, the final formula is created as "$F_{-Xpath} \cap F_{-Source} \cap F_{-Crins}$" and will be sent to the Z3 SMT solver. The solver is responsible for executing the exploitable path symbolically and collects a set of path constraints to deliver the values (we call the values "payloads"). In the Z3 engine, we model the arguments of the call sites as "fixed-size" and "bit-vector" expressions. Moreover, we define the "variable-length" elements, such as the arguments by using the array expressions. The outcome of this modelling is actual practical exploits to trigger vulnerabilities inside target EVM bytecode.

Note that EthFuzz generates exploits on a single path first, before seeking more extensive path sequences. Due to the relatively small size of EVM smart contracts, EthFuzz explores path sequences up to length *10*, consisting of at most *8* state-changing paths and one last exploitable path. Listings 1.2 and 1.3 present a vulnerable contract and corresponding exploit generated by EthFuzz. As we stated before, we have implemented our symbolic execution engine based on the Z3 SMT solver.

4   Evaluation Result

We evaluated EthFuzz with *1,000,000* real-world smart contracts available on the Ethereum main blockchain. We collected these benchmarks from the beginning of October 2019 until the end of December 2019 with the help of

Listing 1.2. A generated exploit in EthFuzz in the source code level (for the ease of readers)

```
contract Overflow {
    uint private Balance=0;
    function add(uint value) returns (bool){
        Balance += value; // possible overflow vulnerability
    }
    function secure_add(uint value) returns (bool){
        require(value + Balance >= Balance);
        Balance += value;
    }}
```

Listing 1.3. An example of a EthFuzz's generated exploit for an overflow vulnerability

```
Location: from 22:27 to 22:46
2 numberTokens * COST_PER_TOKEN
3 --------------------
Transaction Sequence:
Tx #1:
Origin: 0xdeadbfefdeadbeefdeadbeefdeadbfefdeadbfee [ ATTACKER ]
Function: buy(uint256) [ d969094a ]
Data: 0xd969094a801000000000000000000000000000000000000000000
00000000000000000000000000
Value: 0x0
```

Etherscan [1]. The details of our collected corpus is shown in Table 2. Figures 3 and 4 also present the average Lines of Code (LoC) and number of functions, contracts and libraries in each categories respectively.

Table 2. Various contract categories in our corpus.

Category	SLOC	LLOC	CLOC
High ETH Moving	450	300	100
High Occurrence	195	150	50
High Interaction	390	225	40
High Origin	500	350	100
High Value	450	275	45

SLOC indicates Source lines of Code, LLOC represents Logical lines of Code, and CLOC represents Comments Line of Code. Our pre-analysis indicates that the average size of the EVM smart contracts on the blockchain is smaller than *400* LLOC. Furthermore, we represented the number of functions, contracts and libraries in the corpus, based one 5 categories including "Higher Moving", "High Occurrence", "High Interaction", "High Origin", and "High Value".

Interestingly, the top *100* contracts (i.e. *0.1%* of the corpus) hold 98.86% of the total Ether value. Hence, this category of the contracts would be an attractive target for hackers (we label them *"High Value Targets"*). Likewise, we define another category as *"High Origin"* that comprises the top *100* contracts that impacted approximately *800k* other contracts in terms of bytecode similarity.

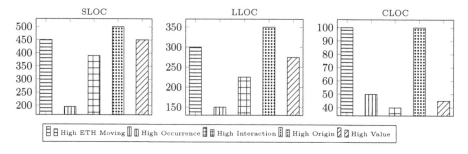

Fig. 3. Average number of Lines of Code (LoC)

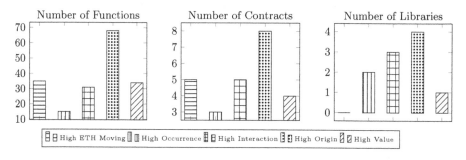

Fig. 4. Presenting the details of our benchmark suite based on the number of functions and libraries in the contracts

Moreover, we presented the top *10* most duplicated contracts in Table 3, and surprisingly one of the contracts, which is called *"User Wallet"*, has been deployed over *651K* times, which reveals the impact that the top *10* contracts have on the whole EVM smart contract blockchain network. Furthermore, only *2* contracts out of these top *10* most duplicated contracts actually have available and verified source code. This is highly surprising, since it raises the question of how a close-sourced contract can be replicated so many times? It seems these *2* contracts have been extensively used by a few certain companies active in the EVM blockchain.

Table 3. Top 10 most duplicated contracts in the corpus.

Address	Source code available	Frequency
2bf69ddcf80f6b24f2e6a8bf1454f662	✓	651930
fa00c5b8d83dbf920aec56d52c1df224	✗	158186
55f0329f9e5dbac461e933c66e0e29b5	✗	115132
dfcc91bcdc37abae7e8e9c82d57fbf6d	✓	99548
702edb219bba3238d55b2b38c759798b	✗	90489
923d7eaf6e90eb272493d3ca5c5859d5	✗	78018
7b63bae3ec81aa70d809a091240dccaa	✗	42868
62dbffb5cce3d14500568320ab6dcd75	✗	40456
1ae99eb3c89152c83cf788a5e7df4532	✗	37534
125fb7c1ad488e0d0b9b034cfd12a977	✗	28255

Experimental Setup. We presumed that the *storage* of each smart contract is initially empty, and that we can therefore handle duplicated contracts at the same time. We eventually made the experiment on an *8 Core Xeon W 3.2* GHz machine with *32* GB RAM running Ubuntu *16.04* LTS. In order to avoid any potential deadlock in analyzing a bytecode excessively, we dedicated *5* min as the maximum analysis time. We yielded this time constrain after multiple configurations of EthFuzz on *1000* arbitrary contracts to reach the maximum path coverage.

4.1   Analysis Results

Performing our in-depth security analysis on the collected corpus has taken approximately *60* days (from the beginning of January 2020 until the end of February 2020). Consequently, EthFuzz could successfully identify and generate *26,015* exploits within one million collected contracts. On the other hand, EthFuzz could not find even a single exploitable execution path inside *681,005* contracts. In other words, we could not detect any critical instructions (e.g., *CALL*, *SSTORE* and *DELEGATECALL*) in the bytecode of these contracts, so we would label them as "secure contracts".

Nevertheless, to check the accuracy of the results, we randomly picked *1,000* of these secure contracts, and we manually controlled their opcode with the aid of the Etherscan dissembler. This tool allowed us to convert the bytecode to the EVM assembly code. Thus, we found only *17* contracts (i.e. *1.7%*) actually contain *CALL* instructions, which are reported secure by EthFuzz mistakenly. This trivial false-negative issue occurred due to the time constraint we had set for the analysis (i.e., *5* min). Hence, by increasing the analysis time to *10* minutes, the issue could be resolved. We consider a *1.7%* false-negative rate for EthFuzz's precision for the strict time constraints. Table 4 presents the vulnerable smart contract with the most popularity on the blockchain network.

Table 4. Results of some vulnerable but popular smart contracts in our analysis.

Contract name	Vulnerability	Address
BeautyChain(BEC)	Integer Overflow	0xC5d105E63711398aF9bbff092d4B6769C82F793D
BlackJack	Bad Randomness	0xA65D59708838581520511d98fB8b5d1F76A96cad
CityMayor	Reentrancy	0x4bdDe1E9fbaeF2579dD63E2AbbF0BE445ab93F10
CNYToken	Integer Overflow	0x041b3eb05560ba2670def3cc5eec2aeef8e5d14b
CNYTokenPlus	Integer Overflow	0xfbb7b2295ab9f987a9f7bd5ba6c9de8ee762deb8
CryptoRoulette	Unitialized Storage Pointers	0x8685631276cFCf17a973d92f6DC11645E5158c0c
DAO	Reentrancy	0xBB9bc244D798123fDe783fCc1C72d3Bb8C189413
EtherLotto	Bad Randomness	0xA11E4ed59dC94e69612f3111942626Ed513cB172
EtherPot	Unchecked External Call	0x539f2912831125c9B86451420Bc0D37b219587f9
Ethraffle v4b	Bad Randomness	0xcC88937F325d1C6B97da0AFDbb4cA542EFA70870
EthStick	Bad Randomness	0xbA6284cA128d72B25f1353FadD06Aa145D9095Af
FirePonzi	Typographical error	0x062524205cA7eCf27F4A851eDeC93C7aD72f427b
G-GAME	Unitialized Storage Pointers	0x3CAF97B4D97276d75185aaF1DCf3A2A8755AFe27
GGToken	Integer Overflow	0xf20b76ed9d5467fdcdc1444455e303257d2827c7
GoodFellas	Function Default Visibility	0x5E84C1A6E8b7cD42041004De5cD911d537C5C007
ICO	Transaction Order Dependance	0xd80cc3550Da18313aF09fbd35571084913Cd5246
KingofTheEtherThrone	Unchecked External Call	0xb336a86e2feb1e87a328fcb7dd4d04de3df254d0
LastIsMe	Transaction Order Dependance	0x5D9B8FA00C16BCafaE47Deed872E919C8F6535BF
Lottery	Bad Randomness	0x80ddae5251047d6CeB29765f38FED1C0013004b7
LuckyDoubler	Bad Randomness	0xF767fCA8e65d03fE16D4e38810f5E5376c3372A8
MESH	Integer Overflow	0x3AC6cb00f5a44712022a51fbace4C7497F56eE31
MTC	Integer Overflow	0x8febf7551eea6ce499f96537ae0e2075c5a7301a
OpenAddressLottery	Unitialized Storage Pointers	0x741F1923974464eFd0Aa70e77800BA5d9ed18902
Rubixi	Function Default Visibility	0xe82719202e5965Cf5D9B6673B7503a3b92DE20be
SMART	Integer Overflow	0x60be37dacb94748a12208a7ff298f6112365e31f

True and False Positives. In our evaluation, we classified and represented true and false positive results based on the attack type. Hence, we believe this helps developers and security experts to take these measurements into perspective in order to design secure test cases before releasing their contracts on the blockchain network. Figure 5 gives the precision of true and false positives in our analysis.

According to descriptions, classical vulnerabilities, e.g., *Integer Overflow* seem to be easier to approach by EVM programmers, particularly by using secure alternative Solidity libraries (e.g. *SafeMath*). However, the more complex operations exist in a code, the higher the chance of receiving intricate security issues in the contract. For example, understanding of some vulnerabilities such as *Re-Entrancy* might require a better comprehension of the Ethereum architecture, which is naturally less likely among junior developers. Consequently, this issue is one of the most common safety flaws in commercial smart contracts.

5   Exploit Generation Precision

In Table 5, we present the breakdown of exploit generation results. While we identified the majority of exploitable paths comprising *CALL* and *SELFDE-STRUCT* critical instructions, only a small number of our generated exploits are based on *CALLCODE* and *DELEGATECALL* opcodes.

Exploit Verification. Considering that every contract account has its own storage that can alter the execution, we checked each exploit upon each concerned account separately. Accordingly, we built a new test Ethereum network including three contracts: a contract under analysis, a normal contract to represent an attacker, and a third contract to play the rule of a proxy for running specific exploits associated with *CALLCODE* and *DELEGATECALL* instructions.

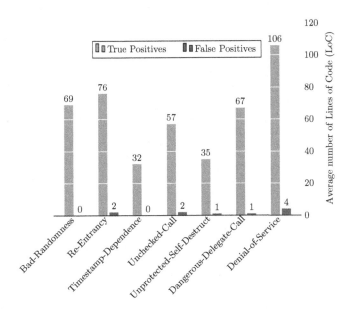

Fig. 5. Distribution of true positives and false positives in each vulnerability class.

Table 5. Showing the break down of the critical paths in the generated exploits (left) and the precision of the generated exploits (right).

#Path type	#Contracts		#Exploits	Precision
Exploitable paths	207,412	TP Exploits	25,703	99%
Non-exploitable paths	701,924	FP. Exploits	312	1%
Generated exploits	26,015	Total	26,015	

Note *CALL* is involved in a value transfer, *SELFDESTRUCT* is involved in contract termination. Moreover, *DELEGATECALL* and *CALLCODE* can allow for code injection

We also provided *100* Ether for the attacker account and *10* Ether for each target contract account. Then, we ran the test network in our simulation on top of the Ethereum Parity client [8], which enabled us to submit the generated exploit transactions to the test network. So, when an exploit succeeded, we submitted its transaction to our test network. In order to avoid transaction reordering, we paused our testing for the miner to process each transaction before yielding the next one.

6   Comparison with Related Work

Security analysis for the smart contract ecosystem is continuously gaining attention of cybersecurity researchers [12,15,18]. In this respect, Oyente [4] is one of the pioneers in performing vulnerability detection that leverages symbolic execution testing for identifying bugs in the Ethereum smart contracts. Similarly, ZEUS [17] works based on a formal verification method to build and verify the correctness of security policies in the contracts.

S-gram [21] and Regaurd [20] both take smart contracts in solidity source code and report potential issues based on static predefined patterns. Securify (v1 and v2) [30] is another static analyzer that takes both source code and the EVM bytecode for performing analysis. Securify v2.0 has also provided Datalog interface to specify new vulnerabilities for the end users. However, both versions are unable to generate exploits.

Although our work was initially inspired by the tools mentioned above, our approach has multiple advantages over previous tools. In this regard, we conducted a comparison measure based on detection efficiency for real-world security analysis, the outcomes of the measurement are shown in Tables 6 and 7.

Table 6. A summary of 100k smart contract analyzed with different tools presented in related work. DSE means "dynamic symbolic execution", the full explanation of various attacks can be found in [26].

Tool	Attack classes	Analysis technique	Source/Bytecode
EthFuzz	20	Hybrid Analysis + DSE	Source + Bytecode
Remix-IDE	7	Static Analysis	Source
SmartCheck	14	Static Analysis	Source
Slither	15	Static Analysis	Source
Oyente	5	Symbolic Execution	Source +Bytecode
Securify	8	Symbolic Execution	Source +Bytecode
Mythril	10	Symbolic Execution	Source +Bytecode

Attack Specification. Because the previous tools detect security problems based on static collection patterns, they are often ineffective in identifying new vulnerabilities and zero-day attacks. EthFuzz, on the other hand, not only supports a wide range of attack patterns but also enables users to easily specify different patterns in the Datalog format.

AEG and Path Explosion. The previous tools do not support automatic exploit generation (AEG). This feature allows developers and contract owners to investigate the safety level of target contracts faster, and therefore, get better prepared to deal with future attacks (e.g., withdrawing their crypto assets). Eth-Fuzz also identifies and prunes non-exploitable paths in the call graphs, thereby reducing analysis overhead and false-positive reports as well as minimizing the risk of a path/state explosion problem occuring during symbolic execution [9].

Table 7. Security issues checked by available tools

Tools	Blockchain				EVM	Solidity												
	TOD	Random number	Timestamp	Unpredictable state	Callstack depth	Lost Ether	Reentrancy	Unchecked call	x.origin	Blockhash	Send	Selfdestruct	Visibility	Unchecked math	Costly pattern	Bad coding pattern	Deprecated	Other
EthFuzz	✓	✓	✓	✓	✓	✓	✓	✓	✓	✓	✓	✓	✓	✓	✓	✓	✓	✓
MAIAN	✗	✗	✗	✗	✓	✗	✓	✗	✗	✗	✓	✗	✗	✗	✗	✗	✗	✗
Mythril	✓	✓	✓	✗	✗	✓	✓	✓	✗	✓	✗	✗	✓	✗	✗	✓	✓	✓
Osiris	✗	✗	✗	✗	✗	✗	✗	✗	✗	✗	✗	✗	✗	✓	✗	✗	✗	✗
Oyente	✓	✗	✓	✗	✓	✗	✗	✗	✗	✗	✗	✗	✗	✓	✗	✗	✗	✗
Porosity	✗	✗	✗	✗	✗	✗	✓	✗	✗	✗	✗	✗	✗	✓	✗	✗	✗	✗
Remix-IDE	✗	✗	✓	✗	✗	✗	✓	✓	✓	✓	✓	✓	✓	✗	✓	✓	✓	✓
Securify	✓	✗	✗	✓	✗	✓	✓	✓	✗	✗	✗	✗	✗	✗	✗	✓	✗	✓
SmartCheck	✗	✗	✓	✓	✗	✓	✓	✓	✓	✗	✓	✗	✓	✗	✓	✓	✓	✓
Solgraph	✗	✗	✗	✗	✗	✗	✗	✗	✗	✗	✓	✗	✓	✗	✗	✗	✗	✓
Vandal	✗	✗	✗	✗	✗	✗	✓	✗	✓	✗	✓	✓	✗	✗	✗	✗	✗	✓

Compared to AEGs. Since EthFuzz is also an AEG tool for smart contracts, we selected MAIAN [24] and Teether [18] because they are the only available AEGs for smart contracts. Hence, we chose these tools as our baseline and compared the result of EthFuzz with them.

We applied MAIAN and Teether to *100,000* of the most popular contracts in our corpus with a timeout of 5 min for each contract. However, Teether and MAIAN could not analyze 11071 and 632 contracts, respectively. This is because of program crashes or timeout. As Table 1 shows, they generated 803 and 497 valid smart contract exploits, respectively. EthFuzz covers 1198 more exploits than Teether and MAIAN in total. It seems that Teether and MAIAN cannot generate valid exploits for contracts.

Moreover, MAIAN is not designed for Code Injection attack; therefore, it missed that type of exploits. Furthermore, in MAIAN's attack model, attackers are not allowed to submit funds into the contracts when trying to find Balance Increment, which causes a loss of coverage. Teether also generates 81 false positives. When Teether tries to solve hash checks, it generates unmatched hash input and output, making the exploits invalid for 81 contracts. Second, different from our definition of Balance In-Crement exploitation, Teether reports exploits once a currency transfer is triggered. However, another 81 false-positive contracts set explicit checks to ensure the in-going fund is larger than the out-going funds. Although the attackers can trigger an outgoing currency transfer, their cost is more than the profit, which is not successful exploitation. Additionally, Teether crashes many times when proceeding contracts, which damage the overall performance as well. Even though EthFuzz produced only 29 false-positives cases in 100,000 contracts, in future work, we plan to extend the attack model to address the false positives. As for time consumption, EthFuzz generates about 25 test cases per second. For generated exploits in this experiment, EthFuzz spends 52 test cases on average, taking several seconds. However, Teether and MAIAN take several minutes to identify an exploit on average.

7   Challenges and Future Work

Since smart contract code is expected to be immutable after deployment and contract owners are anonymous, responsible disclosure is usually infeasible. Hence, dealing with vulnerable contracts seems to be tricky, and there appears to be no way of addressing the errors detected in already deployed contracts [26]. Therefore, the contract owners can only deprecate the vulnerable contract, move all funds out of the contract, use a new contract, and move the funds to the new contract, which is cumbersome since other contracts might reference the address of the vulnerable contract.

However, it seems that designing a runtime shield module in EthFuzz can help not protect in protecting contracts against various runtime attacks and vulnerabilities but also providing a layer of protection for the vulnerable contracts until the contract owners can preserve the funds and the contract developers find a way to fix the issues in the future forks.

8   Conclusion

In this paper, we introduced EthFuzz as a practical and portable security analysis and automatic exploit generation framework for the smart contracts ecosystem. Our approach takes into consideration the complexities of analyzing real-world commercial smart contracts and effectively addresses them. The novelty of the paper is to use an efficient analysis system that identifies zero-day vulnerabilities, unseen attacks, and generates reliable exploits the identified bugs without human intervention by combining a hybrid approach based on "static call graph analysis", "dynamic execution", and symbolic execution in order to gain accurate results with maximum coverage.

Appendix A

Re-Entrancy Attack

Ethereum Virtual Machine (EVM) establishes a machine language called EVM bytecode, which includes approximately *150* opcodes [13]. Unlike memory, storage perseveres beyond the execution history of a contract. Indeed it is stored as a part of the global blockchain state. The EVM also states specific instructions to access transactions' fields, modify the contract's private storage, examine the current blockchain state, and even create additional transactions. It should be highlighted that the original Ethereum paper [28] differentiates between transactions, which are signed by regular accounts, and messages, which are not. Note that the EVM only implements integer arithmetic and cannot handle floating-point values.

In addition to the persistent storage and *256-bit* word stack, the EVM also executes a byte-addressable memory, which serves as an input and output buffer to different instructions. For instance, the *SHA3* instruction, which calculates a *Keccak-256* hash over variable-length data, reads its input from memory, where two stack arguments present both the memory location and length of the input. The memory content is not endured between contract executions, and it is invariably set to "zero" at the opening of each execution.

References

1. Bytecode to opcode disassembler – etherscan. https://etherscan.io/opcode-tool. Accessed 2 Feb 2020
2. Github - comaeio/porosity: *unmaintained* decompiler and security analysis tool for blockchain-based ethereum smart-contracts. https://github.com/comaeio/porosity. Accessed 7 May 2020
3. Openzeppelin/openzeppelin-contracts: Openzeppelin contracts is a library for secure smart contract development. https://github.com/OpenZeppelin/openzeppelin-contracts. Accessed 29 Jan 2021
4. Oyente. https://github.com/melonproject/oyente. Accessed 11 Aug 2019
5. Paritytech/parity-ethereum: The fast, light, and robust EVM and WASM client. https://github.com/paritytech/parity-ethereum. Accessed 2 July 2019
6. Ashouri, M.: Kaizen: a scalable concolic fuzzing tool for scala. In: Proceedings of the 11th ACM SIGPLAN International Symposium on Scala, pp. 25–32 (2020)
7. Atzei, N., Bartoletti, M., Cimoli, T.: A survey of attacks on ethereum smart contracts (SoK). In: Maffei, M., Ryan, M. (eds.) POST 2017. LNCS, vol. 10204, pp. 164–186. Springer, Heidelberg (2017). https://doi.org/10.1007/978-3-662-54455-6_8
8. Parity Authors. Ethereum rust client (2017)

9. Baldoni, R., Coppa, E., D'elia, D.C., Demetrescu, C., Finocchi, I.: A survey of symbolic execution techniques. ACM Comput. Surv. (CSUR) **51**(3), 1–39 (2018)
10. Bellard, F.: QEMU, a fast and portable dynamic translator. In: USENIX Annual Technical Conference, FREENIX Track, vol. 41, p. 46 (2005)
11. Birrell, A.D., Nelson, B.J.: Implementing remote procedure calls. In: Proceedings of the Ninth ACM Symposium on Operating Systems Principles, p. 3 (1983)
12. Brent, L.: Vandal: a scalable security analysis framework for smart contracts. arXiv preprint arXiv:1809.03981 (2018)
13. Dannen, C.: Introducing Ethereum and Solidity. Apress, Berkeley (2017). https://doi.org/10.1007/978-1-4842-2535-6
14. de Moura, L., Bjørner, N.: Z3: an efficient SMT solver. In: Ramakrishnan, C.R., Rehof, J. (eds.) TACAS 2008. LNCS, vol. 4963, pp. 337–340. Springer, Heidelberg (2008). https://doi.org/10.1007/978-3-540-78800-3_24
15. Grech, N., Kong, M., Jurisevic, A., Brent, L., Scholz, B., Smaragdakis, Y.: Madmax: surviving out-of-gas conditions in ethereum smart contracts. Proc. ACM Program. Lang. **2**(OOPSLA), 116 (2018)
16. Huh, S., Cho, S., Kim, S.: Managing IoT devices using blockchain platform. In: 2017 19th International Conference on Advanced Communication Technology (ICACT), pp. 464–467. IEEE (2017)
17. Kalra, S., Goel, S., Dhawan, M., Sharma, S.: Zeus: analyzing safety of smart contracts. In: NDSS, pp. 1–12 (2018)
18. Krupp, J., Rossow, C.: Teether: gnawing at ethereum to automatically exploit smart contracts. In: 27th USENIX Security Symposium (USENIX Security 2018), pp. 1317–1333 (2018)
19. Law, A.: Smart contracts and their application in supply chain management. Ph.D. thesis, Massachusetts Institute of Technology (2017)
20. Liu, C., et al.: ReGuard: finding reentrancy bugs in smart contracts. In: Proceedings of the 40th International Conference on Software Engineering: Companion Proceedings, pp. 65–68. ACM (2018)
21. Liu, H., Liu, C., Zhao, W., Jiang, Y., Sun, J.: S-gram: towards semantic-aware security auditing for ethereum smart contracts. In: Proceedings of the 33rd ACM/IEEE International Conference on Automated Software Engineering, pp. 814–819. ACM (2018)
22. Vivar, A.L., Castedo, A.T., Orozco, A.L.S., Villalba, L.J.G.: Smart contracts: a review of security threats alongside an analysis of existing solutions. Entropy **22**(2), 203 (2020)
23. Nguyen, D.C., Pathirana, P.N., Ding, M., Seneviratne, A.: Blockchain for 5G and beyond networks: a state of the art survey. arXiv preprint arXiv:1912.05062 (2019)
24. Nikolić, I., Kolluri, A., Sergey, I., Saxena, P., Hobor, A.: Finding the greedy, prodigal, and suicidal contracts at scale. In: Proceedings of the 34th Annual Computer Security Applications Conference, pp. 653–663 (2018)
25. Palladino, S.: The parity wallet hack explained, July 2017. https://blog.zeppelin.solutions
26. Perez, D., Livshits, B.: Smart contract vulnerabilities: does anyone care? arXiv preprint arXiv:1902.06710 (2019)
27. Qureshi, H.: A hacker stole 31 m of ether–how it happened, and what it means for ethereum. Freecodecamp.org, 20 July 2017
28. Sirer, E.G.: Thoughts on the DAO hack. Hacking 17 July 2016
29. Szabo, N.: Smart contracts: building blocks for digital markets. EXTROPY J. Transhumanist Thought **16**, 18:2 (1996)

30. Tsankov, P., et al.: Securify: practical security analysis of smart contracts. In: Proceedings of the 2018 ACM SIGSAC Conference on Computer and Communications Security, pp. 67–82. ACM (2018)
31. Whaley, J., Avots, D., Carbin, M., Lam, M.S.: Using datalog with binary decision diagrams for program analysis. In: Yi, K. (ed.) APLAS 2005. LNCS, vol. 3780, pp. 97–118. Springer, Heidelberg (2005). https://doi.org/10.1007/11575467_8
32. Yamaguchi, F., Golde, N., Arp, D., Rieck, K.: Modeling and discovering vulnerabilities with code property graphs. In: 2014 IEEE Symposium on Security and Privacy, pp. 590–604. IEEE (2014)

A Distributed Ledger
for Non-attributable Cyber Threat
Intelligence Exchange

Philip Huff[(✉)] and Qinghua Li

University of Arkansas, Fayetteville, AR 72701, USA
{phuff,qinghual}@uark.edu

Abstract. Cyber threat intelligence (CTI) sharing provides cybersecurity operations an advantage over adversaries by more quickly characterizing the threat, understanding its tactics, anticipating the objective, and identifying the vulnerability and mitigation. However, organizations struggle with sharing threat intelligence due, in part, to the
legal and financial risk of being associated with a potential malware
campaign or threat group. An entity wishing to share threat information or obtain information about a specific threat risks being associated
as a victim of the threat actors, resulting in costly legal disputes, regulatory investigation, and reputational damage. As a result, the threat
intelligence data needed for cybersecurity situational awareness and vulnerability mitigation often lacks volume, quality, and timeliness. We propose a distributed blockchain ledger to facilitate sharing of cybersecurity
threat information and provide a mechanism for entities to have non-
attributable participation in a threat-sharing community. Learning from
Distributed Anonymous Payment (DAP) schemes in cryptocurrency, we
use a new token-based authentication scheme for use in a permissioned
blockchain. The anonymous token authentication allows a consortium
of semi-trusted entities to share the workload of curating CTI for the
community's cooperative benefit.

Keywords: Blockchain · Cyber threat intelligence · Zero-knowledge
proof

1 Introduction

Adversaries have the upper hand in cyber attacks. They benefit from anonymity,
both in person and in purpose. In contrast, targeted entities (e.g., companies) have
difficulty distinguishing everyday benign activities from malicious activities. Thus,
entities spend prodigious efforts to gain actionable threat intelligence. In a recent
survey on Cyber Threat Intelligence (CTI) sharing, security professionals strongly
agree that intelligence sharing supports breach detection/recovery and vulnerability identification/mitigation efforts [40]. However, many technical, trust, legal and
cultural barriers prohibit more widespread threat information sharing [21].

© ICST Institute for Computer Sciences, Social Informatics and Telecommunications Engineering 2021
Published by Springer Nature Switzerland AG 2021. All Rights Reserved
J. Garcia-Alfaro et al. (Eds.): SecureComm 2021, LNICST 398, pp. 164–184, 2021.
https://doi.org/10.1007/978-3-030-90019-9_9

Many cyber threats target critical infrastructures in the private sector. These target entities have the same trust barriers and even more technical and legal barriers due to the limits of qualified security professionals working at each organization. A recent report on cyber threat sharing indicated only 3% of private sector participants shared any threat indicators in 2018 [25].

Furthermore, the value received from CTI is often lacking due to various technical challenges and missing context. In one study [7] 70% of respondents find shared threat data too voluminous and complex for actionable intelligence. Similarly, [8] finds CTI solutions need to enhance their ability to provide context and flexibility to improve the overall value proposition.

1.1 The Current State of Threat Sharing

Organizations are rapidly developing the competency and appetite to participate more in threat-sharing communities. The global rise in security operations centers, through which most CTI exchange occurs, has an expected market growth of 11.5% through 2025 [9]. However, with current approaches heavily focused on classified data and government intelligence services, actionable data is too little and too late. Likewise, as [22] points out, private sector organizations have little motivation to share their threat data sustainably.

Entities share threat data to gain a better understanding of the risk posed to their mission. An average entity may experience tens of thousands of malicious probes from the Internet per day. However, most probes result from automated scanning and do not represent a motivated and intelligent human adversary. Entities participate in threat sharing to distinguish actual danger from benign in hopes of mitigating the threat before it manifests.

Society has an interest in preventing cyber threats from entities that provide critical services and infrastructure. Military and law enforcement agencies would generally provide protection, but they have limited purview into the interaction between adversaries and private entities. Government agencies, national Computer Emergency Response Teams (CERTs), and non-profit Information Sharing and Analysis Centers (ISACs) offer two-way threat-sharing services to address this gap.

However, private entities have many barriers encumbering CTI sharing. A private entity wishing to share threat information risks attribution of the cyber threat, resulting in costly legal disputes, regulatory investigation, and reputational damage. For example, a mistaken analysis of VPN logs to maintain a failed water pump led to a federal investigation of cyber warfare [39]. In [26], legal compliance and limiting attribution are identified as the primary challenges for organizations wishing to share their own CTI with others.

Additional barriers exist with sharing of classified intelligence to private entities. Programs exist to clear private sector entities, but they come at a high cost. Then, moving classified intelligence to actionable threat and vulnerability mitigation cannot keep pace with adversarial intrusion techniques' dynamic nature. Likewise, attempts for fully bidirectional threat sharing have mostly failed.

1.2 Contributions

This paper provides a solution for entities to share observed CTI without attribution using a permissioned blockchain. We propose a novel approach to a Distributed Anonymous Payment (DAP) scheme [33] for permissioned blockchains to allow for anonymous transactions in CTI sharing. This solution also efficiently maintains anonymous authentication and provides revocation services for entities. It does so by splitting maintenance of the Merkle tree used for anonymous authentication between participating peers, which allows for more regular updates of the Merkle Tree across the distributed ledger.

Anonymous transactions address the legal and regulatory barriers organizations have with cyber threat attribution, increasing CTI sharing on the ledger. We then propose a new chaincode to incentivize CTI creation for the cooperative benefit of participating entities. The chaincode targets the barriers preventing bidirectional threat sharing between private sector entities and government agencies by generating timely and actionable CTI without the need for costly declassification.

The chaincode also seeks to reduce volume and increase value in CTI. Human analysts control the volume of threat data through work evaluation functions. Whereas automated log sharing solutions produce data at the speed of machines, the chaincode produces intelligence at the speed of humans. Furthermore, human analysts should find the intelligence actionable because the chaincode originates directly from private entity queries.

1.3 Organization

Section 2 reviews related work. Section 3 introduces the building blocks for our approach. Section 4–6 presents the proposed approach and its major components. Section 7 discusses evaluation results. Section 8 concludes this paper.

2 Background and Related Work

CTI exchange programs fall into three categories:

1. Classified Threat Sharing - Provides automated classified threat indicators to its members. The DHS Enhanced Cybersecurity Services (ECS) is an example of this type of service [4].
2. Data Lakes - Collects a large volume of logs from its members and centrally analyzes the data. The Department of Energy Cyber Risk Information Sharing Program (CRISP) uses the data lake model [3].
3. Analyst to Analyst - Threat hunting analysts exchange data over a shared platform. The European Union Agency for Cybersecurity recommends the Malware Information Sharing Platform for community threat sharing [8].

This paper targets the third category of CTI in which human analysts directly share threat intelligence and indicators between entities. The most commonly shared threat data includes low-level indicators such as IP addresses, URIs, DNS names, and file hashes collected automatically or via threat hunting. Our platform supports sharing of other security information as well, e.g., vulnerability mitigation information. Many services provide one-way data sharing to the entity of known malicious threat indicators.

Stillions' Detection Maturity Levels [35] characterizes this type of data as lower-level evidence of an intrusion attempt. In contrast, higher levels of intelligence include data about how the adversary operates and their motivations.

The work of creating CTI involves tying lower-level indicators to adversarial motivation. However, these indicators exist in the networks of private entities and outside of the direct purview of CTI producers. Timely bidirectional CTI exchange means indicators and resulting CTI are shared freely. The producers receive value by better tracking malicious activity, and consumers receive value through an improved understanding of adversarial risk.

Using a distributed ledger, we can commoditize CTI work as described in Sect. 6 while, at the same time, eliminating trust barriers that preclude the sharing of threat indicators.

2.1 Blockchain Technologies

The permissioned ledger fundamentally uses blockchain as a basis for distributed trust. Blockchain has gained popularity with cryptocurrency technologies like bitcoin [30], and ethereum [38] making possible public distributed transactions with no central authority. Several recent works have suggested using blockchain technologies for CTI exchange [23,24,32]. Our work differs by addressing attribution and targeting CTI sharing communities of trust through a permissioned ledger.

The use of a permissioned blockchain presented in [10] has growing acceptance as a general-purpose distributed ledger. While still public, in the sense of being accessible over the Internet, permissioned blockchains take advantage of partial trust relationships in a system. In the Hyperledger Fabric project, network peers first execute transactions and then order and distribute them onto the blockchain. This approach allows for more complex transactions because peers can detect state and denial of service problems before the chaining operation.

We choose a permissionless blockchain over a public blockchain because of privacy considerations. A CTI sharing community is often open only to participating members from a given sector or nation-state. Although peer entities have no problems with attribution among the community, privacy concerns would likely arise in a public blockchain.

2.2 Zero Knowledge Proofs

The public nature of blockchain systems spotlights the need for anonymity and private information retrieval. Common to most solutions to these problems are zero-knowledge proofs (ZKP), which allow authentication without identification.

In [19], Chaum first developed an e-cash system in which a user could present proof of authentication from some certifying entity without revealing the user. Pseudonym systems in [28] have a similar mechanism to allow entities to operate under a pseudonym untraceable to their original authenticated identity and ultimately form a chain of pseudonyms to conduct anonymous transactions in a system.

Direct Anonymous Authentication (DAA) systems extend and implement ZKP and have widely deployed on trusted platform modules (TPM), and blockchain systems [15–18]. Most recently, the anonymizing idemix library has become available as a core service in Hyperledger Fabric.

However, DAA schemes do not have a mechanism for incentives, and they require additional roles in managing access to the ledger. Instead, we look to recent advancements in cryptocurrency. The explosive growth of cryptocurrencies has ushered in a wave of innovation in anonymizing transactions in the past decade. Anonymous spending in cryptocurrency is made possible through zero-knowledge Succinct Non-Interactive ARgument of Knowledge (zk-SNARKS) presented in [20]. Zerocoin [29] is one of the first systems proposed to support anonymous transactions on top of bitcoin. Zerocash [33] and others [27] made use of zk-SNARKS to make this more feasible and extend the system to prevent tracing the history of a coin and improve efficiency.

Although permissioned blockchains do not require a cryptocurrency incentive, we propose an incentive mechanism for the desired outcome of high quantity and quality threat data. The "gas" or currency of cybersecurity exists in human work and actionable CTI.

3   Building Blocks

Before presenting the approach to non-attributable CTI sharing, we introduce the building blocks used by our approach.

3.1   Sparse Merkle Trees

Merkle trees provide an efficient data structure to authenticate information. They are used on the blockchain to verify transactional integrity. Branches of the tree get formed from the combined secure hashes of its children. In this way, anyone can verify the membership of a tree leaf by comparing the calculated Merkle root with some other valid Merkle root.

Sparse Merkle Trees make use of the property that the path to any given leaf is a function of a small number of branches up to the Merkle root. In the example shown in Fig. 1, we store a minted coin, cm, as a leaf in the Merkle Tree. The leaf's index is determined by the branch direction down the tree, in which a 0 means the left branch, and a 1 means the right branch. Then, for someone to later validate the inclusion of cm, they need only the index and the tree branches along the path indicated by the index, which is necessary to calculate the root.

An sample MISP report with object relationships is shown in Fig. 3. A MISP *Event Report* contains the creating organization (or anonymous), description, and report object, which can range from single threat observation reports to several thousand indicators and sightings of a malware family. There are over 200 open object definitions, and reports can contain multiple objects. Tags describe the report in terms of the information-sharing community. Example tags include the DHS Traffic Light Protocol, malware classifications, IDS rules, and admiralty scale. The tags can be helpful in chaincode for defining access control rules, expiration, and other state transition logic.

Finally, object attributes tie to the reported objects and contain the observable artifacts associated with an event, such as IP addresses, URIs, file hashes, and email addresses. Attributes are the primary search targets for the network. Each network peer stores a document-oriented NoSQL database of existing reports and indexes the attributes for fast searching and correlation.

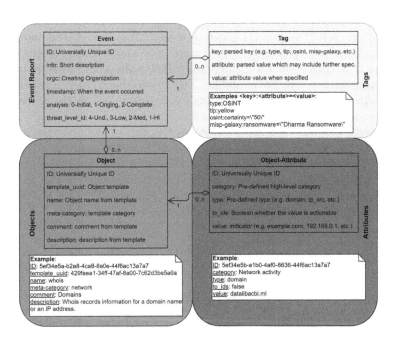

Fig. 3. MISP data object model.

Besides the threat objects, we also define two assets used for managing the quality of threat reports. The *work* asset represents human work and consists of structures for both the problem and the solution. When first submitted, the solution is empty and queued for human analysis. Examples of work may include associating tactics, techniques, and procedures (TTP) to threat artifacts or attribution of a threat report. Other types of work might include validation or annotation of reports to assist in automatic classification, and generation of mitigation actions for vulnerabilities that the adversary tries to exploit.

Finally, a *tree* asset serves to facilitate anonymous authentication and manage the human work by controlling the input, incentivizing the output, and anonymizing the submittal of software artifacts.

5 Non-attributable Token Authentication

For the CTI distributed ledger to function, we must provide its users with anonymization guarantees. We now present the approach for anonymous authentication using a Merkle Tree for zero-knowledge commitment. To start, we present the process of token commitment. Then we show an approach of splitting the tree to support more authentication features such as revocation and value-based spending.

5.1 Anonymous Token Spending

A user receives a token upon the chain code validating some threat intelligence work, or perhaps as part of some bootstrapping process where new users have a limited set of tokens. A user will provide a token to the ledger when performing work for the chaincode to later validate. Then, once the chaincode validates the token, commitment occurs by adding the token as a leaf to the Merkle tree, tree.

The user arbitrarily samples a secret key through the security parameter, λ representing the key length and pseudorandom function $\texttt{Gen}(1^\lambda)$. A user may safely use the secret key repeatedly as a witness to multiple tokens. For each new token, a user arbitrarily generates a serial number, sn, in the same way. Then, using a collision-resistant hash function, $\texttt{CRH} = (0,1)^* \to 0,1^\lambda$, the token is generated as shown in the following functions.

$$
\begin{aligned}
1: \quad & \texttt{sk} \leftarrow \texttt{Gen}(1^\lambda) \\
2: \quad & \texttt{sn} \leftarrow \texttt{Gen}(1^\lambda) \\
3: \quad & \texttt{tk} \leftarrow \texttt{CRH}(\texttt{sk} \parallel \texttt{sn})
\end{aligned}
$$

The sparse Merkle tree then gets calculated with the inclusion of the token as $(\texttt{rt}, \texttt{path})$. The user then has the following public and private data related to the token.

$$
\begin{aligned}
1: \quad & \texttt{tk}_{\texttt{pub}} \leftarrow (\texttt{rt}, \texttt{sn}) \\
2: \quad & \texttt{tk}_{\texttt{pri}} \leftarrow (\texttt{sk}, \texttt{path})
\end{aligned}
$$

Algorithm 1 shows the zk-SNARK circuit for proof and verification. To generate a zk-SNARK proof, a user supplies the public parameters, pp, which includes the common reference string for proving and the zk-SNARK circuit. Public input

---

Algorithm 1 Token Verifier Circuit

    Public Parameters: pp
    Public Input: rt, sn
    Witness: sk, path
    Output: π - proof of inclusion

1: **procedure** TOKEN_VERIFIER
2:     tk $\leftarrow$ CRH(sk $\parallel$ sn)
3:     rt$_{tk}$ $\leftarrow$ the smt calculation using tk and path
4:     **if** rt $=$ rt$_{tk}$ **then**
5:         **return** true
6:     **else**
7:         **return** false
8:     **end if**
9: **end procedure**

---

includes both the Merkle root, rt, demonstrating knowledge of a valid token, and the serial number, sn, formed through the witness. The witness includes the secret key, sk, and the path down the tree to the token.

The chaincode on the distributed ledger verifies the proof represented in Algorithm 2. Here, the public parameters, pp, include the portion of the common reference string used for verification in the ledger. The verification includes (i) checking to ensure the zero-knowledge proof is valid, (ii) verifying the Merkle Root is a valid root for the ledger, and (iii) the serial number represents an unspent coin. The first check uses the zk-SNARK for the network. For the second check, the ledger must include a set of valid roots, and we describe this process in Sect. 5.2. The final check on whether sn exists in SNList prevents a double spend.

Algorithm 2 Verify Token Proof

    Public Parameters: pp
    Input: π, rt, sn
    Output: Valid or Invalid

1: **procedure** VERIFY_PROOF
2:     $valid \leftarrow verify(\text{pp}, \pi, \text{rt}, \text{sn})$ $\triangleright$ zkSNARK verification
3:     **if** $valid \wedge$ rt $\in$ RTList $\wedge$ sn $\notin$ SNList **then**
4:         **return** Valid
5:     **else**
6:         **return** Invalid
7:     **end if**
8: **end procedure**

5.2   Merkle Tree Structure and Root Updates

In the token spending scheme described above, a root update when inserting a batch of new tokens to the tree would make token spending attribution trivial. An entity would only need to search the ledger for the root associated with a token proof to identify the user.

To prevent this attack, we designate an entity to perform the service of sending out root updates at a time interval, t_{new}. Then validation should only include roots published within some time interval, t_{expiry}. Thus, a user wishing to spend a token must wait within a timespan of t_{new} after receiving the validation. Also, a token proof will be valid within a timespan of t_{expiry} from the proof construction. The expiration prevents token attribution because the prover supplies only recent token roots instead of the root calculated at token insertion.

The problem then becomes regularly distributing the tree paths to the network, which we now address. A Merkle tree in a DAP scheme may have token leaves distributed in any order. The location of the leaf in the tree has no association with the identity of the token owner. However, permissioned blockchains have inherent organizational structures, which the ledger can use for more robust authentication features and storage efficiency.

For a Merkle tree of height, h, the branch levels are split into three levels, h_{net}, h_{org}, and h_{user} as shown in Fig. 4. Thus, the tree supports $2^{h_{net}}$ organizations and each organization may have $2^{h_{org}}$ users.

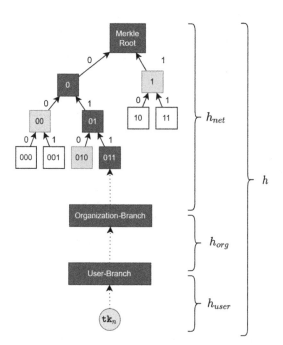

Fig. 4. Merkle tree structure.

By dividing the tree height, we minimize the size of tree updates and storage requirements to only those necessary for the entity's role in the network. As an example, a tree with a height of 32 requires approximately 256 GiB of storage. Also, to keep the siblings, path.S, up to date, the network must distribute a similar-sized update. However, using a permissioned blockchain's organizational structure and setting the h_{net} level at 14, the network updates only require 1 MiB while allowing for 2^{14} organizations.

Each organization is responsible for maintaining its similarly sized sub-tree to distribute path.S updates to its users.

The organizational tree structure supports several other services, which we now describe.

5.3   Revocation of Anonymous Authentication Tokens

Any network peer entity or organization may wish to revoke tokens as users leave, tokens become compromised, or users abuse the network. Since the tree divides into sub-trees of organizations and users, such revocation becomes trivial. User tokens are revoked by setting the desired token sub-tree to null and recalculating the root. Similarly, the network could revoke entire organizations by setting the organization sub-tree to null.

The revocation scheme works because tokens are not anonymous, and the Merkle tree does not need to hide the token holders' identities. A token spend only reveals the serial number, which cannot associate with the token. The network may safely maintain an identity on the token tree while preserving non-attribution in token spending.

The revocation latency ties to the t_{expiry} time interval associated with root updates. Attempts to authenticate using a revoked token will guarantee to fail after t_{expiry} because the proof of token inclusion no longer works with the new root.

5.4   Adding Value to Tokens

In a cryptocurrency, value is an attribute of the coin itself, and spend operations *pour* an old set of coins into a new set with the same value preserved. However, pouring coin value creates problems in the proposed scheme because the primary purpose of the token is for non-attributable authentication, and supporting a large number of token spends adds unnecessary complexity.

Instead, we propose tokens only have a value of 1, and we increase the user Merkle tree height to support a large number of tokens. Only the user only needs to maintain the path siblings for any levels below h_{org}. Knowing these paths allows the user to construct a valid proof without the network or organization having to maintain a tree height to support a large number of possible tokens.

For example, if the network maintained a tree height of 14 at 1 MiB, and each organization maintained a sub-tree height of 18 at 8 MiB, each user could maintain their sparse sub-tree of 64 levels to support a vast number of tokens far beyond the maximum necessary.

5.5   Authentication Without Spending

Finally, by maintaining tokens with revocation services, they provide a useful means of anonymous authentication. There are several scenarios where users might desire anonymity. A user may wish to perform an anonymous search on the network, e.g., searching for a particular IP address. Performing such a search could infer the organization's attribution as a victim of the malware.

To support anonymous authentication only, we make a minor modification to the token spending circuit and remove the serial number as the public verification parameter. Additionally, we hash the timestamp, ts, with the root to prevent replay attacks.

Algorithm 3 Token Authentication Circuit

   Public Input: pp, rt, ts
   Witness: $tk, path$
   Output: Whether the calculated root matches the given root

1: **procedure** TOKEN_AUTH
2:    $rt_{tk} \leftarrow$ the smt calculation using tk and $path$
3:    **if** $CRH(rt \parallel ts) = CRH(rt_{tk} \parallel ts)$ **then**
4:        **return** true
5:    **else**
6:        **return** false
7:    **end if**
8: **end procedure**

---

6   Chaincode for CTI Work

This section presents in detail the state program model used for managing work on the network. Several peer-authenticated transactions occur to update threat reports, which this paper does not formalize. The transactional updates to threat reports are essential but straightforward. Instead, we focus on the *Work* asset transactions to facilitate the expansion of threat knowledge and automation beyond existing services. Recall that a *Work* asset consists of problem and solution data structure which maps to an *Event Report* asset.

Work asset transactions focus both on the problem of submitting CTI anonymously and on validating the quality of the CTI. The cybersecurity community has not extensively considered the use of non-attributable CTI, and the chaincode recognizes this by including a set of evaluation states.

Figure 5 shows a state transition diagram of the workflow from the addition of *Work* to the completion of a solution. Each state transition represents a chaincode function made available to the network for processing the ledger. The ledger must maintain state to support asynchronous processing of transactions and high assurance in the logic of the chaincode.

The object variables for the state program include the following chaincode assets:

$$Var = \{\texttt{event\_record}, \texttt{work}, \texttt{token\_tree}\} \tag{1}$$

A **threat_record** asset includes the complex data structure represented in Fig. 3 and described in Sect. 4.2. Assets for **work** have a problem/solution data structure that stores the proposed problem and maintains a set of proposed solutions for evaluation. The tree asset supports the use of tokens described in Sect. 5.

The program graph over Var is defined as

Definition 1. *State Transaction Program Graph*

- S - *Set of states*
- $Effect : Act \times Eval(Var) \rightarrow Eval(Var)$ - *Transition effect function.*
- $R \subseteq S \times Cond(Var) \times Act \times S$ - *Conditional transition relation*
- $S_0 \subseteq S$ - *The set of initial states*
- $g_0 \in Cond(Var)$ - *The initial condition*

The function $Eval$ comprises the set of evaluations over Var, and the function $Cond$ comprises the set of conditional expressions over Var.

Work state is maintained through the smart contract logic. Valid work states include $S = \texttt{READY\_WORK}, \texttt{IN\_PROGRESS}, \texttt{READY\_EVAL}, \texttt{IN\_EVAL}, \texttt{ADD\_WORK}$.

Anyone with a valid token may submit a **work** record to the network accompanied with a token proof. The chaincode first evaluates the token proof as a guard condition for the work queue. In this way, the **work** has no attribution to an entity, but the entity authenticates as a valid user of the network. Also, the ledger preserves the quality of the work queue by requiring an entity to give up something of value in exchange for work performed.

Each **work** asset gets added to a priority queue on the ledger. The priority queue operates based on priority and time to differentiate work value and prevent starvation for lower priority work requests. Workers should also choose work based on their resources and capabilities, but we leave the optimal dequeuing of work to future research.

Finally, the ledger adds an evaluated solution by i) updating the **event_record** with the added context provided through the work solution, ii) inserting the tokens provided with the work solution and evaluation, and iii) publishing a new root to the network based on the updated tokens.

The entity requesting work will likely search for the work solution periodically. Thus, the network supports authentication-only proofs using tokens to preserve the anonymity of the work requester. An entity need not authenticate with an identity, save only to perform work.

Due to the space limitation, an extended version of this paper will include the algorithms for chaincode.

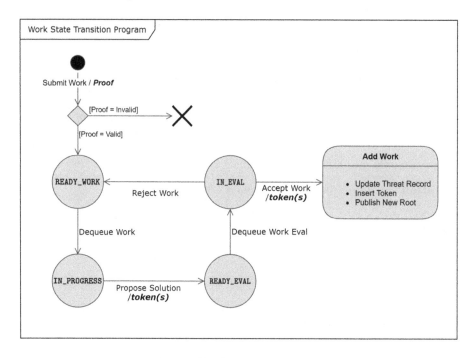

Fig. 5. Work state transition.

7   Implementation

We performed testing to evaluate the Merkle tree maintenance from Sect. 5.2 and token authentication in Sect. 5. Also, we propose implementation guidelines for implementing the blockchain under realistic loading conditions. Our tests of the zk-SNARK proofs use snarkjs and circomlib, and the performance was tested on an Intel Core i5-8356U CPU @1.60 GHz with 16 GB of RAM.

7.1   Token Authentication Performance

The Merkle tree height drives the network performance for token authentication in both storage and time. Authentication allows sparse tree storage at both the organizational, h_{org}, and user levels, h_{user}. However, the network must provide frequent updates at the network level, h_{net}, to support anonymous authentication. Due to the frequency of these updates, we propose setting h_{org} at 15, which for a 256-bit node size, requires 1 MiB of storage.

Users can manage a much deeper portion of the Merkle tree because they only store the sparse tree based on the number of tokens they possess, but the token proof circuit requires a consistent depth. Figure 6 shows the relationship between the depth and proof times. Here, we propose a reasonable tree depth of, at most, 128, which provides ample space for both the foreseeable maximum number of organizational users and the number of tokens allocated for each user.

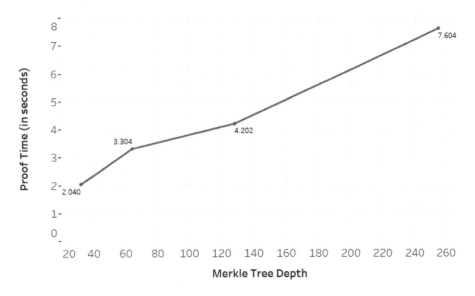

Fig. 6. Proof times relative to Merkle tree height.

The parameters and performance of the algebraic circuit for a tree with this size are shown in Table 1.

7.2   Ledger Operation Guidelines

We developed the chaincode model for use in Hyperledger Fabric, and although a full-scale simulation is in development, we make some observations here about the operation of the network.

There are three types of transactions proposed: i) event reports, ii) work management, and iii) network maintenance activities, including Merkle root updates. To develop a realistic expectation of throughput, we consider the critical infrastructure sectors in the United States. The Department of Homeland Security identifies sixteen critical infrastructure sectors [2]. Using utility data from the Energy Information Administration [1], we find 3,338 individual utility companies in the electric sector. If each organization produced an average of ten transactions per day during a peak of four working hours, we could expect a maximum throughput of 40 transactions per second.

For this level of throughput, Hyperledger Fabric benchmark experiments indicate a latency of approximately 1 s with a block size of 10 transactions [36]. They also indicate that an endorsement policy of up to four network peers for each transaction would have a minimal effect on the overall transaction latency. Overall, the system's theoretical bounds would fall well within the efficient operating conditions of Hyperledger Fabric.

Table 1. Sparse Merkle tree proof circuit parameters and performance

Merkle tree height	128
Number of wires:	32,486
Number of constraints:	32,363
Private inputs:	130
Public inputs:	2
Number of labels:	151,304
Number of outputs:	0
Proof time:	4,200 ms
Verification time:	28.5 ms

8   Conclusion

This paper proposes a new approach for overcoming the trust barriers of inter-organizational threat intelligence sharing using a distributed ledger technology. We have demonstrated a novel use of zk-SNARKs and Sparse Merkle Trees to enable anonymous authentication and anonymous token spending for the ledger's permissioned users. The results pave the way for a new approach to cybersecurity threat intelligence sharing, which commoditizes the work of CTI curation and sharing to produce a greater cooperative value.

Acknowledgement. This work is supported in part by NSF under award number 1751255. This material is also based upon work supported by the Department of Energy under Award Number DE-OE0000779.

References

1. Annual electric power industry report. https://www.eia.gov/electricity/data/eia861/. Accessed 12 Mar 2021
2. Critical infrastructure sectors. https://www.cisa.gov/critical-infrastructure-sectors. Accessed 12 Mar 2021
3. Cyber risk information sharing program (crisp). Tech. rep., Department of Energy, Office of Cybersecurity, Energy Security, and Emergency Response. Accessed 13 Jan 2021
4. Enhanced cybersecurity services (ecs). Tech. rep., Department of Homeland Security. Accessed 13 Jan 2021
5. Hackerone list of bug bounty programs. https://hackerone.com/bug-bounty-programs. Accessed 11 Mar 2021
6. A Common Cyber Threat Framework: A Foundation for Communication (2013)
7. The value of threat intelligence: A study of North American and United Kingdom companies. Tech. rep., Ponemon Institute (July 2016). Accessed 06 Jan 2021
8. Exploring the opportunities and limitations of current threat intelligence platforms. Tech. rep., ENISA (December 2017). Accessed 06 Jan 2021

9. Global security operations center market forecast up to 2025. Business Wire (English) (2019)
10. Androulaki, E., et al.: Hyperledger fabric: a distributed operating system for permissioned blockchains. In: Proceedings of the Thirteenth EuroSys Conference, pp. 1–15 (2018)
11. Banerjee, A., Clear, M., Tewari, H.: Demystifying the role of zk-SNARKs in Zcash. In: 2020 IEEE Conference on Application, Information and Network Security (AINS), pp. 12–19. IEEE (2020)
12. Barnum, S.: Information with the structured threat information expression (STIX) (2013)
13. Bitansky, N., Chiesa, A., Ishai, Y., Paneth, O., Ostrovsky, R.: Succinct non-interactive arguments via linear interactive proofs. In: Sahai, A. (ed.) TCC 2013. LNCS, vol. 7785, pp. 315–333. Springer, Heidelberg (2013). https://doi.org/10.1007/978-3-642-36594-2_18
14. Bowe, S., Gabizon, A., Green, M.D.: A multi-party protocol for constructing the public parameters of the Pinocchio zk-SNARK. In: Zohar, A., et al. (eds.) FC 2018. LNCS, vol. 10958, pp. 64–77. Springer, Heidelberg (2019). https://doi.org/10.1007/978-3-662-58820-8_5
15. Brickell, E., Camenisch, J., Chen, L.: Direct anonymous attestation. In: Proceedings of the 11th ACM Conference on Computer and Communications Security, pp. 132–145 (2004)
16. Camenisch, J., Chen, L., Drijvers, M., Lehmann, A., Novick, D., Urian, R.: One TPM to bind them all: fixing TPM 2.0 for provably secure anonymous attestation. In: 2017 IEEE Symposium on Security and Privacy (SP), pp. 901–920 (2017)
17. Camenisch, J., Drijvers, M., Lehmann, A.: Anonymous attestation using the strong Diffie Hellman assumption revisited. In: Franz, M., Papadimitratos, P. (eds.) Trust 2016. LNCS, vol. 9824, pp. 1–20. Springer, Cham (2016). https://doi.org/10.1007/978-3-319-45572-3_1
18. Camenisch, J., Hohenberger, S., Lysyanskaya, A.: Compact E-cash. In: Cramer, R. (ed.) EUROCRYPT 2005. LNCS, vol. 3494, pp. 302–321. Springer, Heidelberg (2005). https://doi.org/10.1007/11426639_18
19. Chaum, D.: Security without identification: transaction systems to make big brother obsolete. Commun. ACM **28**(10), 1030–1044 (1985)
20. Danezis, G., Fournet, C., Kohlweiss, M., Parno, B.: Pinocchio coin: building zero-coin from a succinct pairing-based proof system. In: Proceedings of the First ACM Workshop on Language Support for Privacy-Enhancing Technologies, pp. 27–30 (2013)
21. Daniel, M., Kenway, J.: Repairing the foundation: how cyber threat information sharing can live up to its promise and implications for NATO. Cyber Threats and NATO 2030: Horizon Scanning and Analysis, p. 178 (2020)
22. Douris, C.: Cyber Threat Data Sharing Needs Refinement. Lexington Institute Arlington, Virginia (2017)
23. Gong, S., Lee, C.: Blocis: blockchain-based cyber threat intelligence sharing framework for sybil-resistance. Electronics **9**(3), 521 (2020)
24. He, S., Fu, J., Jiang, W., Cheng, Y., Chen, J., Guo, Z.: Blotisrt: blockchain-based threat intelligence sharing and rating technology. In: Proceedings of the 2020 International Conference on Cyberspace Innovation of Advanced Technologies, pp. 524–534 (2020)
25. Office of Inspector General: DHS Made Limited Progress to Improve Information Sharing under the Cybersecurity Act in Calendar Years 2017 and 2018 (2020)

26. Johnson, C., Badger, M., Waltermire, D., Snyder, J., Skorupka, C.: Guide to cyber threat information sharing. Tech. rep., National Institute of Standards and Technology (2016)
27. Kosba, A., Miller, A., Shi, E., Wen, Z., Papamanthou, C.: Hawk: the blockchain model of cryptography and privacy-preserving smart contracts. In: 2016 IEEE Symposium on Security and Privacy (SP), pp. 839–858. IEEE (2016)
28. Lysyanskaya, A., Rivest, R.L., Sahai, A., Wolf, S.: Pseudonym systems. In: Heys, H., Adams, C. (eds.) SAC 1999. LNCS, vol. 1758, pp. 184–199. Springer, Heidelberg (2000). https://doi.org/10.1007/3-540-46513-8_14
29. Miers, I., Garman, C., Green, M., Rubin, A.D.: Zerocoin: anonymous distributed e-cash from bitcoin. In: 2013 IEEE Symposium on Security and Privacy, pp. 397–411. IEEE (2013)
30. Nakamoto, S.: Bitcoin: a peer-to-peer electronic cash system. Tech. rep., Manubot (2019)
31. Petkus, M.: Why and how zk-SNARK works: definitive explanation
32. Riesco, R., Larriva-Novo, X., Villagra, V.A.: Cybersecurity threat intelligence knowledge exchange based on blockchain. Telecommun. Syst. **73**(2), 259–288 (2019). https://doi.org/10.1007/s11235-019-00613-4
33. Sasson, E.B., et al.: Zerocash: decentralized anonymous payments from bitcoin. In: 2014 IEEE Symposium on Security and Privacy, pp. 459–474. IEEE (2014)
34. Shen, M., Duan, J., Zhu, L., Zhang, J., Du, X., Guizani, M.: Blockchain-based incentives for secure and collaborative data sharing in multiple clouds. IEEE J. Sel. Areas Commun. **38**(6), 1229–1241 (2020)
35. Stillions, R.: The DML Model (2014)
36. Thakkar, P., Nathan, S., Viswanathan, B.: Performance benchmarking and optimizing hyperledger fabric blockchain platform. In: 2018 IEEE 26th International Symposium on Modeling, Analysis, and Simulation of Computer and Telecommunication Systems (MASCOTS), pp. 264–276. IEEE (2018)
37. Wagner, C., Dulaunoy, A., Wagener, G., Iklody, A.: MISP: the design and implementation of a collaborative threat intelligence sharing platform. In: Proceedings of the 2016 ACM on Workshop on Information Sharing and Collaborative Security, pp. 49–56 (2016)
38. Wood, G., et al.: Ethereum: a secure decentralised generalised transaction ledger. Ethereum Proj. Yellow Pap. **151**(2014), 1–32 (2014)
39. Zetter, K.: Exclusive: comedy of errors led to false 'water-pump hack' report. Wired Threat Level (2011)
40. Zibak, A., Simpson, A.: Cyber threat information sharing: perceived benefits and barriers. In: Proceedings of the 14th International Conference on Availability, Reliability and Security, pp. 1–9 (2019)

AI and Security/Privacy

Understanding ε for Differential Privacy in Differencing Attack Scenarios

Narges Ashena[1]([✉])[iD], Daniele Dell'Aglio[1,2][iD], and Abraham Bernstein[1][iD]

[1] Department of Informatics, University of Zurich, Zurich, Switzerland
{ashena,bernstein}@ifi.uzh.ch
[2] Department of Computer Science, Aalborg University, Aalborg, Denmark
dade@cs.aau.dk

Abstract. One of the recent notions of privacy protection is Differential Privacy (DP) with potential application in several personal data protection settings. DP acts as an intermediate layer between a private dataset and data analysts introducing privacy by injecting noise into the results of queries. Key to DP is the role of ε – a parameter that controls the magnitude of injected noise and, therefore, the trade-off between utility and privacy. Choosing proper ε value is a key challenge and a non-trivial task, as there is no straightforward way to assess the level of privacy loss associated with a given ε value. In this study, we measure the privacy loss imposed by a given ε through an adversarial model that exploits auxiliary information. We define the adversarial model and the privacy loss based on a differencing attack and the success probability of such an attack, respectively. Then, we restrict the probability of a successful differencing attack by tuning the ε. The result is an approach for setting ε based on the probability of a successful differencing attack and, hence, privacy leak. Our evaluation finds that setting ε based on some of the approaches presented in related work does not seem to offer adequate protection against the adversarial model introduced in this paper. Furthermore, our analysis shows that the ε selected by our proposed approach provides privacy protection for the adversary model in this paper and the adversary models in the related work.

Keywords: Differential privacy · Parameter tuning · Differencing attack

1 Introduction

Differential privacy (DP) has changed the very notion of how privacy preservation is being achieved. As such, it has been embraced by industry, governments, and the scientific community. At the core of DP mechanisms, lies the parameter ε, which regulates the amount of noise added to results. ε takes positive values, and as it increases the magnitude of the noise decreases, resulting in less private and more accurate outcomes. ε is, hence, the knob that controls the trade-off

© ICST Institute for Computer Sciences, Social Informatics and Telecommunications Engineering 2021
Published by Springer Nature Switzerland AG 2021. All Rights Reserved
J. Garcia-Alfaro et al. (Eds.): SecureComm 2021, LNICST 398, pp. 187–206, 2021.
https://doi.org/10.1007/978-3-030-90019-9_10

between utility and privacy. In a typical data publishing scenario, data owners desire high privacy and data analysts look for accurate results. Most of the times it is a owner/curator's task to set ε. It is usually straightforward to calculate the error bound that a given value of ε introduces on the data analyst side. However, understanding the role of ε in relation to the formal DP is challenging. After more than a decade since DP's introduction, the literature of DP is sparse in the area of understanding and setting ε. US Census Bureau emphasizes on this very issue for publishing 2020 census data under DP protection [6]. The main objective of this paper is to better support the data owner by defining a more intuitive way of sensing privacy leakages due to inappropriate ε selection. Only a few studies have moved initial steps towards this direction [7,11,13,15].

[13,15] propose interpretations of ε by studying the probability of privacy leak events within a differencing attack scenario. In such a scenario, there is an analyst with permission to investigate a private dataset through various aggregate query submissions. This analyst is an *adversary*, who performs DA (Differencing Attack) to discover the binary secret bit of participants of the dataset. A DA consists of submitting two aggregate queries aiming at the secret bit. The first query addresses a subset of the dataset, while the second addresses the same subset in addition to the target person. The difference between the two query answers can reveal the target person's secret bit. [13,15] assume that the dataset is public (also known by the adversary) except for the secret bits. [13] focuses on the cases where all the participants but one have the secret bit set to 1 (i.e., the privacy leak happens when the identity of the person with secret bit 0 is learnt by the adversary), while [15] targets scenarios where every participant has the secret bit set to either 0 or 1. [15] also assumes that the secret bit set to 1 is more critical than 0, e.g., as being positive to HIV^+.

In this paper, we study the role of *differencing attacks* in a scenario similar to the ones in [13,15], where the privacy threat is the leakage of participants' binary secret bit. However, in contrast to [13,15], we have two different assumptions: (a) an identical level of importance for both values of secret bit and (b) less public knowledge about the dataset. As a solution, we propose to tune ε according to the probability P_{SDA} of successfully performing (where SDA stands for Successful Differencing Attack) a differencing attack on the dataset to be protected.

Hereby, our contributions are:

- the introduction of P_{SDA}, a metric to measure a privacy leakage of a differencing attack under DP protection.
- a method to compute P_{SDA} for different values of ε and three query types: *count*, *sum*, and *average* queries.
- an experimental comparison of P_{SDA} with [13,15]. Our attack strategy performs as successful as [13] for *average* queries, and more successful in *sum* queries. Our approach achieves the same *recall* as [15] in detecting the secret when it is 1, and higher *accuracy* than [15] in detecting both secrets values.

The paper is organized as follows. Section 2 presents a case study that motivates this research. In Sect. 3, we introduce related work. Section 4 provides necessary background knowledge about DP. In Sect. 5, we elaborate on P_{SDA} and the method to compute it for three different aggregate queries. Section 6 provides practical application of P_{SDA} on real data. Section 7 compares the values for ε calculated by our method with state of the art methods. In the end, we present some final remarks and conclusion in Sects. 8 and 9 respectively.

2 Case Study

xyz.abc is an Internet Protocol Television (IPTV) company. xyz.abc users can watch on-air TV programs, choosing between a selection of channels from different European countries. xyz.abc stores users' demographics and viewership data, i.e., whether a user watches a specific channel or not. Table 1 shows a snippet of the xyz.abc dataset. Among viewers from Austria (AT), Alice, identified by the hash ID 3f1fb1c6, is the only English-speaking woman. This data is analyzed by xyz.abc data scientists to showcase to their stakeholders (e.g., advertisement companies) their analytic capabilities. Examples of analyses on viewers' data are aggregate queries such as *count*, *sum*, and *average*, which can be used to compute the market shares of the channels or program ratings.

Even if interested in aggregation queries, xyz.abc is worried about privacy leaks. Bob, an xyz.abc employee and acquaintance of Alice, wants to learn more about her by checking her records in the xyz.abc dataset. From discovering what Alice watches, Bob may obtain information about her political orientation by checking if she watches $Channel\_1$, a conservative news channel. Setting up mechanisms to forbid queries about one specific user (as Alice) and allowing only for aggregate queries does not solve the problem. In this dataset, Alice is in a minority and she is vulnerable to differencing attack. Bob can perform such an attack by submitting two aggregate queries:[1]

Q_1^c. SELECT COUNT(HashID) FROM dataset
    WHERE Gender = 'F' AND $Channel\_1 = 1$
Q_2^c. SELECT COUNT(HashID) FROM dataset WHERE Gender = 'F'
    AND $Channel\_1 = 1$ AND (Language <> 'EN' OR Country <> 'AT').

The difference between the two queries exposes that Alice watched $Channel\_1$, since the result of $Q_1^c - Q_2^c$ is 1. Even banning count queries is not enough, as Bob may decide to attack using other aggregate operators. For example, he could exploit his knowledge about the Alice's age:

Q_1^s. SELECT SUM(Age) FROM dataset WHERE Gender = 'F' AND $Channel\_1 = 1$
Q_2^s. SELECT SUM(Age) FROM dataset WHERE Gender = 'F' AND $Channel\_1 = 1$
    AND (Language <> 'EN' OR Country <> 'AT').

---

[1] One may consider querying directly for Alice's record as
SELECT COUNT(HashID) FROM dataset
WHERE Gender = 'female' AND CHANNEL_1 = 1 AND
Language = 'English' AND Location = 'Austria'.
A Protected dataset may, however, not allow querying over a subset smaller than some threshold. The result is that most differecing attack scenarios in the literature only consider two queries.

Table 1. IPTV dataset of viewer ship. The provided row belongs to Alice. Channel_i is a binary attribute that indicates whether a user has watched the corresponding channel in a given time window or not.

HashID	Age	Gender	Language	Country	Device	Channel_1	Channel_2	...
...	...	F	DE	AT	...	...	...	...
...	...	M	DE	AT	...	...	...	...
...	...	F	DE	AT	...	...	...	...
3f1fb1c6	43	F	EN	AT	Screen	1	0	...
...	...	M	DE	AT	...	...	...	...
⋮	⋮	⋮	⋮	⋮	⋮	⋮	⋮	⋮

$Q_1^s - Q_2^s$ equals to Alice's age if Alice has watched *Channel_1*. For discovering Alice's secret, it suffices that the adversary finds out whether $Q_1 - Q_2 \neq 0$ or not regardless of the query type. One solution to neutralize the differencing attack is to release approximate results of the queries by noise addition, e.g., by using DP. Exploiting the approximate results, the adversary can not make a certain decision about the target person's secret. However, the adversary can have a guess and calculate the correctness probability of such a guess. Hence, the added noise has to be sufficiently large—ε has to be adjusted accordingly—to prevent an adversary from guessing the secret better than guessing randomly.

3   Related Work

Since DP was introduced, most of the research has focused on algorithm design and implementation of DP mechanisms [1,5,9,16,18–20]. Little attention has been dedicated so far to methods and solutions to set the parameter ε. Whilst there have been attempts in explaining DP to non-technical audience such as [22], to date, there are only four thorough studies on this topic [7,11,13,15].

In [22], the increase of probability of a harmful event in general is explained in terms of ε. In this study as well as [13], and [15], however, the probability of a leakage is investigated for a given ε and a specific attack scenario providing probabilities more attuned for these scenarios.

Lee, et al. [13] calculate an upper bound for ε to protect people's secret bit in a dataset. All members have the secret bit value set to 1 except for one individual, whose secret bit is 0. Their threat model assumes that the adversary knows every attribute about every individual, except for the binary secret attribute. The privacy leak happens when the adversary can infer with probability higher than a threshold value who is the person with secret 0. A proper value for ε does not allow the adversary to grow his/her success probability beyond such a threshold. Our method shares the idea of defining privacy loss as the probability of a successful attack while relaxing the assumptions on adversarial knowledge and presence of only one secret attribute value set to 0.

In [15], leakage happens when the adversary infers whether the data of a person contributes into the result of a query or not. This translates to secret bit set to 1 when that person's data is a factor in the query's output and 0 otherwise. To guess the secret bit, the adversary model utilizes the Neyman-Pearson hypothesis testing. It assumes that the risk of the secret equals to one is higher than the case where it is zero. This assumption is aligned with Neyman-Pearson criterion which aims to maximize the true detection rate by putting a constrain on false alarm rate and is valid in many disease-related scenarios. However, it does not apply to the cases where both secret values have the same significance, such as protecting participants' political beliefs (being left or right). In contrast, our proposed approach treats both values of secret equally.

In [7], Hsu et al. propose a solution based on economics for setting ε. They consider the case, where sensitive datasets are associated to a given amount of budget. Participants are compensated from that budget in case of privacy leakages. By assessing the risks of participating and calculating the expected cost for each participants, they calculate the upper bound for ε given the available budget, the desired accuracy, and the number of participants.

[11] takes a different approach for monetizing privacy. Here, data analysts provide privacy as a premium service to data owners. Data owners pay the analysts for their desired level of privacy, and each individual specifies a desired privacy level. Considering users' preferences and the analyst's requested accuracy level, the proposed mechanism calculates the differentially private query answers.

4   Preliminaries

In this section, we present the foundations on DP.

Differential Privacy. Let D be a dataset with size $n \geq 1$ records, where each record represents an individual and every column is an attribute. Neighboring datasets are defined as two datasets D and D' that have the same attributes and differ in one record, i.e., $|D - D'| = 1$. Let $\mathcal{D}$ be the set of datasets. Formally, a query $Q : \mathcal{D} \rightarrow \mathbb{R}$ processes a dataset and outputs a real answer. $\mathcal{M}$ is a randomized function that obfuscates the result of Q. Formally, a mechanism $\mathcal{M}$ is ε-differentially private if the inequality:

$$P(\mathcal{M}(D) \in S) \leq e^{\varepsilon} \cdot P(\mathcal{M}(D') \in S) \tag{1}$$

holds for every $S \subseteq range(Q)$ and for every pair of neighboring datasets. ε provides the mean to quantify the imposed privacy.

Composition Theorem. The composition theorem states that if multiple differentially private mechanisms access a dataset, the union of the outputs of these mechanisms is differentially private, and the privacy guarantee is the summation of the ε's of the applied mechanisms. Formally, if there are n mechanisms $\mathcal{M}_1, \mathcal{M}_2, \ldots, \mathcal{M}_n$ with ε equal to $\varepsilon_1, \ldots, \varepsilon_n$ respectively, the set of all these mechanisms $\mathcal{M} = (\mathcal{M}_1, \ldots, \mathcal{M}_n)$ is $\sum_{i=1}^{n} \varepsilon_i$-differentially private.

Laplace Mechanism and Global Sensitivity. One common way to build a differentially private mechanism is to add random noise drawn from a Laplace distribution with parameter $\frac{\Delta Q}{\varepsilon}$ to the query's result [4]. ΔQ is the *global sensitivity* of the query Q and is defined as:

$$\Delta Q = \max_{\forall D, D' \in \mathcal{D}: |D - D'| = 1} |Q(D) - Q(D')|. \tag{2}$$

In this paper, we consider three different queries: *count*, *sum*, and *average* queries.

In *count queries*, e.g., Q_1^c in Sect. 2, ΔQ is 1 because adding (or removing) a record in (from) a dataset can change the result at most by one.

In *sum queries*, ΔQ is the maximum value of the attribute, provided that the range of such an attribute is known. Datasets usually have several numerical attributes, each with its own range. One can either calculate ΔQ for each attribute separately, or normalize the attribute values between zero and one and consider $\Delta Q = 1$. In the following, we consider the latter case without loss of generality. Applying DP to *sum* queries on normalized data is similar to the count query case: it adds random noise drawn from $lap(\frac{1}{\varepsilon})$ to the real query result.

To compute differentially-private *average queries*, one naive solution is to compute the ratio between noisy *sum* and noisy *count* values. According to composition theorem, for this solution, the allocated ε for *average* query needs to be divided between *sum* and *count* causing noisier result than adding noise once according to full allocated ε. Alternatively, Algorithm 2.3 in [14] introduces the division of noisy sum by true count as a differentially private *average* with higher accuracy compared to the former solution for the same level of privacy. As shown in Algorithm 2.3 in [14], this division is not differentially private unless the result is restricted to the range of the attribute $[a_{min}, a_{max}]$.

Adding noise according to the global sensitivity of *average* query is another solution to compute differentially private average. To determine the *average* global sensitivity, we need to investigate the impact of adding (or removing) a value to (or from) a dataset. Let m be the average of the list $(a_1, \ldots, a_k, \ldots, a_n)$ where $a_i \in [a_{min}, a_{max}]$. Adding a new element a_{n+1} (in the range $[a_{min}, a_{max}]$) or removing an element a_k, changes m by:

$$\frac{a_{n+1} - m}{n + 1} \quad (3) \qquad \qquad or \qquad \qquad -\frac{a_k - m}{n - 1} \quad (4)$$

respectively. The global sensitivity is the maximum of the Eq. 3 and Eq. 4 values. For these two equations, the denominator is smallest when either $n = 1$ or $n - 1 = 1$. As mentioned earlier, we assume that datasets contain at least one record, $n \geq 1$. The maximum value of Eq. 3 happens where $n = 1$ and $a_{n+1} = a_{max}$ and $m = a_{min}$. For Eq. 4, the maximum value happens when $n - 1 = 1$ and $a_k = a_{max}$ and $m = \frac{a_{max} + a_{min}}{2}$. Therefore, the global sensitivity of *average* is $\frac{a_{max} - a_{min}}{2}$. The noise drawn from $lap(\frac{a_{max} - a_{min}}{2\varepsilon})$ is excessive for the accuracy of average and unnecessarily large since when the dataset size is sufficiently large, the contribution of a value in the average is considerably smaller than $lap(\frac{a_{max}-a_{min}}{2})$. For instance, the size of the dataset introduced in Sect. 2 can be 100 to 1000 or even larger. Thus, in this paper, to compute differentially private average, we consider Algorithm 2.3 in [14].

5   Our Approach to Interpreting ε

An ideal value for ε should minimize the privacy risks whilst reducing the noise introduced into the results of queries to ensure as adequate as possible answers. In the case of differencing attacks, this happens when an adversary cannot make a guess about the individuals' binary secret better than a random guess, i.e., success probability equal to 0.5. Our goal is, therefore, to find the largest value of ε that restricts the success of a differencing attack to 0.5. In the following, we first discuss assumptions on the adversary's prior knowledge for initiating a differencing attack. Next, we define P_{SDA} as the success probability of such an attack and calculate the approximation of P_{SDA}. Finally, we use P_{SDA} to set ε.

5.1   The Adversary's Prior Knowledge

DP literature often considers the worst case when it comes to the adversary's knowledge about a dataset, i.e., s/he is aware of all the records and attributes in the dataset, except for the secret bit of a target person. This is not a realistic assumption in real-world datasets with hundreds of thousand of records. Although the attack defined in [13] highly depends on this worst case scenario, for the differencing attack in this paper, the adversary needs to be aware of enough auxiliary information to successfully formulating Q_1 and Q_2 as exemplified in Sect. 2. This information may be easily gathered from knowing the true result of only one histogram query over the dataset. This point is worth emphasizing as being focused on worst case scenario may mislead data owners about the safety of their datasets. If a data owner presumes none of the subsets of the dataset with full amounts of detail are publicly accessible, s/he may believe that the attacks introduced in [13,15] are ineffective. However, there can be other attacks relying on less knowledge than all of the records or every attribute of the dataset.

To conduct a successful attack, the adversary needs to compute d, which is the difference of the true values of Q_1 and Q_2, i.e., $Q_1 - Q_2$, when the target person's secret is not zero. According to the person's secret, $Q_1 - Q_2$ is either 0 or d. d varies according to the query type. For *count* queries, d is constant and equals to 1. In *sum* and *average* queries, d varies and depends on the data. Let a be the value of the attribute A of the target user. d equals a in the case of *sum* queries. For *average*, d is either $\frac{a-Q_2(D)}{n+1}$ or $\frac{a-Q_1(D)}{n-1}$ (as in Eq. 3 and Eq. 4).

Once the adversary defines Q_1 and Q_2 and calculates d, s/he interacts with the DP-protected dataset to receive noisy results of Q_1 and Q_2. For this interaction, the adversary is granted a fixed privacy budget ε. In this paper, we assume the adversary uses up the whole allocated privacy budget to perform a differencing attack. According to the composition theorem, the ε should be split between Q_1 and Q_2. We assume the ε is divided equally between the two queries.

Finally, we assume that the parameter b of the Laplace distribution employed by the DP mechanism is also public information. As shown in Sect. 4, b equals to $\frac{\Delta Q}{\varepsilon}$. There are many possibilities that this information becomes available for the adversary. To give insights on how to interpret the noisy results, DP based query systems often release the accuracy of the results, which are calculated according to the distribution used to generate the injected noise [4,5]. The reported accuracy along with the allocated ε can be used by the adversary to calculate $b = \frac{\Delta Q}{\varepsilon}$. Moreover, since most DP libraries and tools are open source, the mechanisms' implementations can be assumed to be publicly available.

5.2 Guessing the Secret

In this section, we discuss how to perform the differencing attack in a DP framework. In contrast to the attack described in Sect. 2, here the adversary receives $\mathcal{M}_1(D)$ and $\mathcal{M}_2(D)$, which are noisy versions of Q_1 and Q_2. S/he knows that:

$$Q_1(D) - Q_2(D) \in \{0, d\}. \tag{5}$$

As explained in Sect. 4, $\mathcal{M}_1(D) = Q_1(D) + \nu_1$ and $\mathcal{M}_2(D) = Q_2(D) + \nu_2$, where ν_1 and ν_2 are random samples drawn from $lap(\frac{2\Delta Q}{\varepsilon})$. The number two in the numerator comes from splitting the ε between the two queries. Hence, to infer the secret, the adversary takes the difference of the observations:

$$\mathcal{M}_1(D) - \mathcal{M}_2(D) = Q_1(D) + \nu_1 - (Q_2(D) + \nu_2). \tag{6}$$

By taking Eq. 5 into account, Eq. 6 simplifies to either Eq. 7 or Eq. 8.

$$\mathcal{M}_1(D) - \mathcal{M}_2(D) = \nu_1 - \nu_2 + 0 = \Delta\nu + 0 \tag{7}$$
$$\mathcal{M}_1(D) - \mathcal{M}_2(D) = \nu_1 - \nu_2 + d = \Delta\nu + d \tag{8}$$

The adversary knows $\mathcal{M}_1(D)$ and $\mathcal{M}_2(D)$, but not the values of ν_1, ν_2, or even $\Delta\nu$. However, s/he knows the probability density of $\Delta\nu$ as it is a linear combination of two Laplace distributions [10] with parameters $\frac{2\Delta f}{\varepsilon}$ and $\mu = 0$. Therefore, the adversary investigates which of the occurrences of Eq. 7 and Eq. 8 are more likely using the distribution of $\Delta\nu$. Let the $pdf_{\Delta\nu}$ be the probability density function of $\Delta\nu$. The adversary's guess for the secret bit of the target person is:

$$guess = \begin{cases} 1, \text{if } pdf_{\Delta\nu}(\mathcal{M}_1(D) - \mathcal{M}_2(D) - 0) < \\ \quad\quad pdf_{\Delta\nu}(\mathcal{M}_1(D) - \mathcal{M}_2(D) - d) \\ 0, \text{otherwise.} \end{cases} \tag{9}$$

The attack strategy explained above is applicable for *count* and *sum* queries but it requires slight changes for *average* queries. As mentioned in Sect. 5.1, to calculate d for the *average* query, in addition to the target person's attribute value a, the adversary requires some information about the dataset, e.g., the true result of either Q_1 or Q_2. As Q_1 is a more general query than Q_2, we assume without loss of generality Q_1 is public and known to the adversary.

Algorithm 1. Performs the differencing attack and guesses the target person's secret bit for given ε, DP results, and true result of either Q_1 or Q_2 if available

```
1: function GUESS_SECRET( M₁, M₂, ε, ΔQ, d,Q₁ₒᵣ₂ = 0, n = 0)
2:     guess ← 0
3:     if Q₁ₒᵣ₂! = 0 then
4:         compute the pdf_lap of lap(ΔQ/ε)
5:         if M₁! = 0 then
6:             ΔM ← M₁ − Q₁ₒᵣ₂
7:         else
8:             ΔM ← Q₁ₒᵣ₂ − M₂
9:         if n == 0 and pdf_lap(ΔM − d) ≥ pdf_lap(ΔM − 0) then
10:             guess ← 1
11:         if n! = 0 and pdf_lap((n − 1) × (ΔM − d)) ≥ pdf_lap(n × (ΔM − 0)) then
12:             guess ← 1
13:     else
14:         compute the pdf of Δν which is lap(2ΔQ/ε) − lap(2ΔQ/ε)
15:         ΔM ← M₁ − M₂
16:         if pdf_Δν(ΔM − d) ≥ pdf_Δν(ΔM − 0) then
17:             guess ← 1
18:     return guess
```

Therefore, s/he only queries for Q_2 without the need to divide the allocated ε. In this case, Eq. 7 and Eq. 8 become $Q_1(D) - \mathcal{M}_2(D) = 0 - \frac{\nu}{n}$ and $Q_1(D) - \mathcal{M}_2(D) = \frac{a - Q_1(D)}{n-1} - \frac{\nu}{n-1}$ respectively. Using pdf_ν, which is basically the pdf of a Laplace distribution, the adversary makes a guess for the secret bit of the target person by comparing

$$pdf_\nu(n \times (Q_1(D) - \mathcal{M}_2(D) - 0)) \tag{10}$$

and

$$pdf_\nu((n-1) \times (Q_1(D) - \mathcal{M}_2(D) - \frac{a - Q_1(D)}{n-1})). \tag{11}$$

If Q_1 equals to a, it is not possible to guess the secret bit with probability more than 0.5 (even in case of no noise addition) as adding or removing a value to the dataset equal to the average does not affect the average. The same happens when the noisy average falls out of $[a_{min}, a_{max}]$ and the mechanism used for average returns a_{min} or a_{max} (see Sect. 4). Without the trace of added noise, the adversary can only guess randomly.

Algorithm 1 shows *GUESS_SECRET*. When the adversary is aware of the true result of either Q_1 or Q_2, the input Q_{1or2} equals to that true result. Depending on the known query, the corresponding $\mathcal{M}$ is set to zero.

5.3   The Definition of P_{SDA}

In this section, we define P_{SDA}—a metric for the probability of a successful differencing attack. Let Z be a random variable:

$$Z = \alpha A + \beta B, \tag{12}$$

where α and β are real numbers and A and B are two random variables. When the attack bases on the difference between the two queries, A and B are sampled from $lap(\frac{2\Delta Q}{\varepsilon})$, and α and β are set to one and minus one, respectively. When Q_1's real value is known (e.g., for the average query), α becomes zero and B is a Laplace distribution with parameter $\frac{\Delta Q}{\varepsilon}$.

The probability density function of $\overset{\circ}{Z}$ is $pdf_Z(Z; \varepsilon, \Delta Q)$. pdf_Z is a function of Z defined based on ε and ΔQ. For an elaborate calculation of pdf_Z, we refer to Theorem 2 in [17]. Let g be a step function defined as:

$$g(y) = \begin{cases} 1, \text{if } y \geq 0 \\ 0, \text{if } y < 0 \end{cases} \tag{13}$$

The binary random variable X describes whether the *guess* from Eq. 9 is correct or not. X takes 1 if *guess = secret* and 0 otherwise. Using equations Eq. 7, Eq. 8, and Eq. 9, X is defined as the XNOR between *guess* and actual *secret*:

$$X = 1 - |g(pdf_Z(\Delta\mathcal{M}; \varepsilon, \Delta Q) - pdf_Z(\Delta\mathcal{M} - d; \varepsilon, \Delta Q)) - secret| \tag{14}$$

We define P_{SDA} as the probability parameter of the binary random variable X. As the probability parameter of any binary random variable with zero and one values is its expected value, it follows that $P_{SDA} = P(X = 1) = E[X]$.

When the adversary guesses the target person's secret, s/he knows that the guess is correct with probability P_{SDA}. Intuitively, this translates to a scenario where the adversary owns a biased coin with probability P_{SDA}. Given a guess, s/he tosses the coin and decides whether such a guess is correct based on the outcome. With a heavily unbiased coin, the adversary's becomes more confident about the guess. Therefore, the risk of target person's secret leakage increases.

5.4   The Estimation of P_{SDA}

The calculation of P_{SDA} is not trivial because X, defined in Eq. 14, is a random variable defined as a combination of other two random variables. Therefore, we provide a method to calculate the approximated P_{SDA} called $\widehat{P}_{SDA}$. Let us assume that *secret* is known. To estimate $\widehat{P}_{SDA}$ with a tight confidence interval, the adversary needs to sample X for a sufficiently large number of times. This means that the adversary has to resubmit the queries many times, which would require way more budget than the one that is usually allowed.

Therefore, we take a different approach and *simulate* the interaction with the DP mechanism: we run this simulation long enough to assess $\widehat{P}_{SDA}$. Since our attack is designed without dependencies on the underlying data, there are no direct interactions with the dataset D. Furthermore, in this work, it is assumed that the adversary has sufficient computational resources to run the simulation with enough iterations.

As shown in Algorithm 2, for each iteration, a random independent value is assigned as the secret bit *secret* and two random samples are drawn from $lap(\frac{2\Delta f}{\varepsilon})$ as ν_1 and ν_2 (or just a single sample from $lap(\frac{\Delta f}{\varepsilon})$ in case of non-zero Q_{1or2}). The adversary makes a guess *guess* based on this potential observation $\nu_1 - \nu_2 + secret \times d$. In real interaction with DP mechanism, the adversary's guess would be based

Algorithm 2. Estimates P_{SDA} with confidence interval no bigger than CI for α confidence level

```
1: function ESTIMATE_P_SDA(ε, ΔQ, d, Q_1or2 = 0, n = 0)
2:     initialize CI and α
3:     initialize Q_Idx based on Q_1or2          ▷ Q_Idx is 1 if Q_1 is provided and 2 otherwise
4:     itr ← 0
5:     successes ← 0
6:     while true do
7:         itr ← itr + 1
8:         secret ← faircoinflip          ▷ secret is 1 if coin flips Head and 0 otherwise
9:         if Q_Idx == 0 then
10:            ν_1 and ν_2 ← random samples from lap(2ΔQ/ε)
11:            M_1 ← ν_1 + secret × d
12:            M_2 ← ν_2
13:        if Q_Idx == 1 then
14:            ν_2 ← random sample from lap(ΔQ/ε)
15:            M_1 ← 0
16:            if n == 0 then
17:                M_2 ← Q_1or2 + ν_2 − secret × d
18:            else
19:                M_2 ← Q_1or2 + ν_2/(n−secret) − secret × d
20:        if Q_Idx == 2 then
21:            ν_1 ← random sample from lap(ΔQ/ε)
22:            if n == 0 then
23:                M_1 ← Q_1or2 + ν_1 + secret × d
24:            else
25:                M_1 ← Q_1or2 + ν_1/(n+secret) + secret × d
26:            M_2 ← 0
27:        guess ← GUESS_SECRET(M_1, M_1, ε, ΔQ, d, Q_1or2)
28:        if guess == secret then
29:            successes ← successes + 1
30:        P_SA, CI_a, CI_b ← binomial_fitting(itr, sucess, α)
31:        if CI_b − CI_a ≤ CI then
32:            return P_SDA
```

on $\mathcal{M}_1(D) - \mathcal{M}_2(D)$. In the simulation, it is not possible to interact with the dataset. Thus, as $\mathcal{M}_1(D) - \mathcal{M}_2(D)$ is equal to $\nu_1 - \nu_2 + secret \times d$, we use the latter. Finally, if $guess$ equals to $secret$, this iteration is counted as a success. We calculate $\widehat{P}_{SDA}$ by counting the successes and fit a binomial distribution to this number. The parameter of the fitted distribution is $\widehat{P}_{SDA}$.

For binomial fitting, we use the Clopper-Pearson method [2]. This method takes three inputs: the number of iterations, the number of successful guesses, and the confidence level for the fit as α. It outputs the binomial mean along with a lower bound CI_a and an upper bound CI_b. The estimated mean falls in the interval defined by CI_a and CI_b with probability of $1 - \alpha$. In Algorithm 2, the whole procedure iterates until the interval for the estimated binomial fit agrees with the defined CI which is the length of the interval $[CI_a, CI_b]$.

5.5 Setting ε

An ideal value for ε should not allow P_{SDA} to exceed 0.5. This can be formulated as Eq. 15. As we use an approximation for P_{SDA}, the equality in Eq. 15 turns to an inequality in Eq. 16 where δ is a sufficiently small number ensuring the closeness of the approximation of P_{SDA} to its true value.

Algorithm 3. Calculates the biggest possible ε for given P_{SDA} for the given dataset D, $query_type$, and upper bound for tolerable P_{SDA}

```
1: function SET_ε( D, query_type, target_P_SDA = 0.5)
2:      based on query_type, calculate ΔQ
3:      based on query_type and D, calculate d
4:      decide on Q_Idx, Q_1or2, and n
5:      ε_b ← upper bound on ε
6:      while ε_b > 0 do
7:          if  target_P_SDA −δ ≤ ESTIMATEP_P_SDA (ε_b, ΔQ, d, Q_Idx, Q_1or2, n) ≤ target_P_SDA
    +δ then
8:              return ε_b
9:          else
10:             ε_b ← decreaseε_b
```

$$maximize \ \varepsilon$$
$$subject \ to: \ P_{SDA} = 0.5 \tag{15}$$

$$maximize \ \varepsilon$$
$$subject \ to: \ |P_{SDA} - 0.5| \leq \delta \tag{16}$$

Algorithm 3 provides a method for setting ε for different query types. The function set_ε takes the most tolerable value for $\widehat{P}_{SDA}$ (in this paper 0.5) as $target\_P_{SDA}$, along with the dataset and query type. Given that the provided attack strategy aims at a specific individual, we need to identify and protect individuals that are at highest risk of exposure to protect the dataset. Therefore, at Line 3 of Algorithm 3, the calculation of d can be based on such an individual. One conservative way to initialize d is to set it to the maximum possible value ΔQ. At Line 4, the data owner needs to decide on whether adversary has access to the true result of Q_1 or Q_2. Finally, the algorithm starts with a sufficiently large ε. It explores for an upper bound by decreasing ε at every step and investigating whether the current ε provides the given P_{SDA} or not. The algorithm stops when the condition in Eq. 16 is met when $|\widehat{P}_{SDA}$- $target\_P_{SDA}| \leq \delta$.

6   Evaluations

In this Section, we illustrate the relation between P_{SDA} and ε for the case study described in Sect. 2. The dataset used for this section is from a real IPTV provider. A considerable number of individuals in this dataset are vulnerable to be isolated with two queries due to the wide range of features and viewership captured by the company. However, for privacy concerns, throughout this section, we focus on an imaginary case of Alice. The results elaborated in this section are generated based on the Algorithm 2 with ε in the range $[0.01, 20]$ with step 0.01. We set the inputs to the function $ESTIMATE\_P_{SDA}$ i.e., d, Q_{1or2} and n according to the query type. δ in Eq. 16 is set to 0.01. Finally, for the Clopper-Pearson method, we set $\alpha = 0.01$ and $CI = 0.02$ as in [2].

It is worth noting that the purpose of the IPTV case study is to contextualize the problem. Therefore, none of the evaluation in this section is anyway dependent on the IPTV dataset.

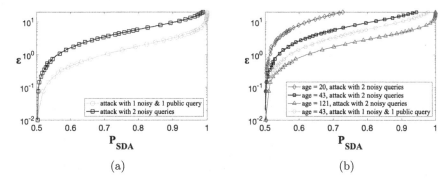

Fig. 1. P_{SDA} for (a) *count* and (b) *sum* queries for different values of ε (Color figure online)

Count Queries. To guess Alice's secret using a *count* query, Bob runs Q_1^c and Q_2^c as described in Sect. 2. Blue line in Fig. 1a represents how ε changes according to P_{SDA}. As ε grows, Bob can correctly guess the Alice's secret with higher probability. When the real value of Q_1^c is known (e.g., it is publicly available), the adversary has a higher chance in guessing the secret as shown by magenta line in Fig. 1a. To set ε for *count* query, once the data owner decides on publicity of Q_1^c or Q_2^c and tolerable P_{SDA}, ε can be selected.

Sum Queries. Figure 1b represents the case where the attacker is aware of the exact value of a queryable attribute of the target individual and exploits it to reveal a secret. The attacker decides to use a *sum* query for the attack. He submits the two queries Q_1^s and Q_2^s, as defined in Sect. 2. Differently from the count case, the attribute used in aggregations affects the leakage of the secret. The larger the attribute value, the more vulnerable the secret. Figure 1b, considers various hypothetical values of the age attribute. The red, blue, and green lines indicate the age of 20, 43 (Alice's real age), and 121^2 consecutively. It should be noted that the age of 121 is the maximum present in the dataset. Note that for normalized data (i.e., fitted between 0 and 1), the corresponding graph behaves exactly like the one shown for count query. Like in the count case, it can happen that the adversary knows the real value of one of the two queries. Magenta line in Fig. 1b depicts how the adversary success probability varies due to the auxiliary information.

An important question raises here: *what should the criteria for setting ε for sum query be?* Some may prefer to set ε based on the worst case, treating sum queries like count queries. However, this approach may add more noise than needed. For instance, in the dataset in Sect. 2, users with maximum age values are not at the risk of isolation with two queries. Hence, data owners may set the ε value based on those users' having the potential of being isolated.

---

[2] Many users tend to select the year 1900 as their birth year. Whilst this is unlikely to be the actual birth year of an user, we assume that this entry is still worthy of hiding, as it exposes an habit of the target person.

Average Queries. Let us assume that count and sum queries are not available. Hence, an adversary may exploit *average* queries, e.g., Bob wants to discover the secret of Alice through the following two queries Q_1^a and Q_2^a:

Q_1^a. SELECT AVG(Age) FROM dataset WHERE Gender = 'female' AND $Channel\_1$ = 1

Q_2^a. SELECT AVG(Age) FROM dataset WHERE Gender = 'female' AND $Channel\_1$ = 1 AND (Language <> 'English' OR Location <> 'Austria').

To perform the attack with *average* query, the adversary needs to know the value of the queryable attribute associated to the target individual (Alice's age), the size of the dataset (i.e., the real value of Q_1^c or Q_2^c as defined in Sect. 2), and the real value of Q_1^a or Q_2^a. Q_1^c and Q_1^a are both generic queries. It is possible for an adversary to collect the required information from the company reports or announcements. Therefore, we assume the adversary knows Q_1^a's true result.

Unlike the case of *sum* queries, where the magnitude of individual value (e.g. age) plays an important role in the secret leakage, here the distance between the individual value and the average value influences the leakage. The size of the dataset is another factor that may affect the secret disclosure. Figure 2a depicts P_{SDA} for three different ages and three different dataset sizes. We consider two hypothetical Alice's ages, 20 and 121, in addition to her true age, 43. As dataset sizes, we consider 13, 1320 and 16959 by limiting the *average* query to the number of users (including Alice) watched $Channel\_1$ in 1 h, 6 h, and 24 h consequentially. The average value of age is 50 in every case.

Figure 2a shows that the larger the distance of the true age from mean value, the higher the probability of a successful attack. As expected, due to the employed mechanism to release noisy *averages* in this paper, the size of dataset has a minor impact on the results. To simplify comparison of the P_{SDA} and ε for all three query types, Fig. 2b shows how Alice, 43 year old, is vulnerable to differencing attack in terms of P_{SDA} through her age. As shown in the figure, it is clear that privacy loss is different depending on the query type.

7   Comparison with Related Work

In this section, we qualitatively and quantitatively compare P_{SDA} with [13,15].

Comparing P_{SDA} with Lee et al., 2011. To compare P_{SDA} with Lee et al. [13], we shorty summarize the notions and assumptions taken in the latter. The dataset S includes two columns: the ID and a numerical attribute ($|S| = n$). S is fully known to the adversary. However, there is another dataset S', which is hidden from the adversary ($S' \subset S$ and $|S| = |S'| + 1$). The adversary's objective is to ascertain who is excluded in S'. Therefore, the absence from S' is the secret to be protected. The adversary assigns a uniform prior ($\frac{1}{n}$) to all the n possible subsets S_i' ($i = 1, ..., n$) of S such that $|S| = |S_i'| + 1$. Then, s/he submits an aggregate query over S' and receives a noisy result. Based on the observed result, s/he calculates the posterior belief distribution over the all S_i's. The S_i' with the highest posterior probability is selected as the potential S'.

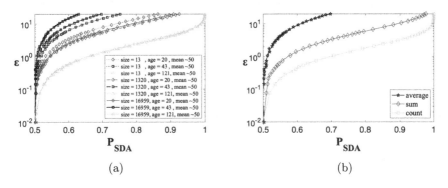

(a)   (b)

Fig. 2. (a) P_{SDA} for *average* query and different values of ε. (b) Alice's secret leakage in term of P_{SDA} by different queries and different values of ε.

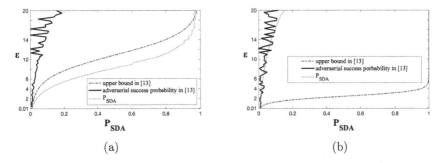

(a)   (b)

Fig. 3. Comparing two adversarial models for (a) *sum* and (b) *average* queries. (Color figure online)

Consequently, the missing person is revealed. [13] suggests ε shall be selected according to restricting the adversary's posterior belief when the missing person owns the maximum value among all the members.

The blue lines in Fig. 3 illustrate how the adversary's posterior belief of the S' depends on ε. The oscillations are due to the stochastic nature of the DP mechanism chosen by [13]. Resubmitting the query for the same value of ε results in a different posterior belief distribution. The green lines in Fig. 3 show the upper bound provided by [13]. The tightness of the upper bound depends to the distribution of data. Due to the different scenarios, we take few steps to properly compare P_{SDA} and [13]. First, we build a scenario where both methods can be used. Such a scenario is similar to the running example, with the additional constraint that Alice's secret is zero, i.e., she is the only female subscriber that did not watch *Channel_1*. We draw 120 random samples from the normal distribution $\mathcal{N}(74.5, 9)$, in the range $[0, 121]$ to serve as ages of individuals in S. The selected numbers and distribution are based on the real viewership of a randomly chosen channel for a randomly chosen period. We consider the maximum value from the sampled data as Alice's *age* since [13] suggests to set ε based on

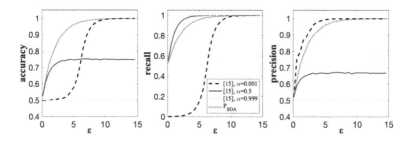

Fig. 4. Comparison with [15]: *accuracy*, *recall*, and *precision* for *count* queries.

protecting the secret of a participant with the maximum value. Second, we need incorporate the prior of [13] into the adversary model of P_{SDA}. P_{SDA} equals to $Pr(guess = secret)$ while the probability of adversarial success in [13] equals to $Pr(guess = secret|secret = 0)$ and $Pr(secret = 0) = \frac{1}{n}$, where n is the size of the dataset. One can calculate the former probability based on P_{SDA} by using a probability tree diagram. Third, the adversary in [13] knows the attributes of the users in the dataset, excluding the secret. This translates to the case where the actual value of Q_1^s or Q_1^a is known in the current study. Thus, both adversaries submit only one query to carry out the attack. As a consequence, we can construct an attack following our procedure for both *sum* and *average* queries based on the same assumptions as made by [13].

Figure 3a shows the comparison for the *sum* query. We plot both the posterior belief and the upper bound of [13] as described in their article. Our method outperforms [13] in gaining knowledge about the secret as it offers a higher probability of guessing the secret for any given ε. Note that in contrast to the previous plots, this plot starts close to 0, the prior probability is $\frac{1}{120} \approx 0.0083$.

For the *average* query, both adversaries perform similarly, as shown in Fig. 3b. Note that the shown upper bound does not indicate that the adversary of [13] outperforms the one of our model. [13] suggests using the adversary's posterior belief (blue lines in Fig. 3) to set ε when the upper bound is not tight, which occurs when the dataset does not contain outliers that significantly deviate from the average. The solution in [13] can not provide a value for ε in case of *count* queries as the size of S' is given.

Choosing ε based on the upper bound proposed in [13] may not protect against all adversarial models. As shown in Fig. 3a, our adversary may leak information from data protected by that mechanism. Also, the gaps between the blue and green lines in Fig. 3 indicate that the upper bound is not tight. Therefore, we may end up adding more noise than necessary.

Comparing P_{SDA} with Liu et al., 2019. Liu et al. [15] use hypothesis testing to guess the secret, i.e., a value that is either zero or one. To compare our method with [15], we implemented their attack model. Such a model requires the adversary to be aware of ε, ΔQ, Q_2, and a parameter $\alpha \in [0,1]$. α controls the false alarm rate in their hypothesis testing. For αs close to one, the attack model in [15] is more prone to guess the secret to be one than zero and vice-versa.

Figure 4 plots the *accuracy, recall*, and *precision* of the attack models of [15] and our approach for three values of α. We run both attack models for 10000 times to guess the randomly generated secret for the *count* query. For a fair comparison, both adversaries submit only one query, as [15] assumes that the true value of Q_2 is public. As illustrated in Fig. 4, the two approaches perform similarly in detecting where *secret* = 1 for $\alpha = 0.5$ (they have similar *recall*). However, our attack model achieves higher *accuracy* and *precision* than [15] in detecting the two values of secret for $\alpha = 0.5$. Note that in [15], one can tune αs to either slightly outperform our approach in terms of recall ($\alpha = 0.999$)) or perform similarly in terms of precision ($\alpha = 0.0001$). In those cases, however, our approach outperforms [15]'s approach in the two other metrics. This may be a consequence of [15]'s goal of "only" protecting the cases where the secret is 1.

8 Discussion

In this section we discuss the application of P_{SDA}, we elaborate on other possible attacks, and future works.

Application of P_{SDA}. The notion presented in this paper can be used in many interactive data analysis settings that provide DP guarantees [1,5,8,9,16,18,19]. These settings are mostly offered as a library or programming platform that facilitates data curators to build a private interface for interacting with the data without privacy violations (e.g., due to the wrong implementations). However, to benefit from the privacy preservation of these packages, the data curator still needs to determine a good value for ε. The discussion here relies on PINQ [16] a LINQ based platform designed for differentially private interactive analysis of a dataset, to exemplify the challenges arising from this choice and how our contribution can help address these.

PINQ supports major aggregation queries like *count, sum, average*, and *median*. It also contains differentially private implementations of operations like *select, where*, and *groupby*. The count and sum queries used in this paper follow the same algorithms. For average queries we use the algorithm from [14], as [14] shows that the PINQ *average* operator does not satisfy ε-differential privacy.

One of the access policy provided by PINQ is fixed budget access, which allows the data curator to decide on the value of ε as a fixed budget for the user. Then it is up to the user to distribute this budget among the aggregations and operations of his/her interest. PINQ follows the composition theorem and it does not allow the analyst to run a query with ε exceeding the allocated budget. In terms of P_{SDA}, a fixed budget setup of PINQ is as secure as its weakest aggregation, which, looking at the plots in Fig. 2b, is the *count* queries. As a result, the maximum budget should be allocated by focusing on the count query.

Other Threats. We discuss two other threats from the scenario in Sect. 2. We did not consider *differencing attacks with more than two queries*, as we focused on attacks aiming at isolating the target person with one or two queries. The cases with one or two queries are the ones where differencing attacks are the most successful. According to the composition theorem (Sect. 4), asking more queries results in noisier answers, as the available budget is shared among the queries. Also, the linear combination of two Laplace distributions (both centered at the same mean value) is flatter than the two distributions themselves [17]. As the number of distributions increases, the result becomes flatter and closer to the uniform distribution. This makes it hard to make a decision with higher success. Thus, if an adversary can isolate a person with multiple queries, it is better to merge these queries to only one query (or two queries, in case the dataset may have a restriction on querying minorities). Even though this query may require a complex condition, it has no effect on the privacy budget consumption [16]. As a consequence, setting ε based on differencing attacks with one or two queries protects also against differencing attacks with three or more queries.

Selecting ε with our proposed method is enough to protect the dataset against *linear reconstruction attacks*. A linear reconstruction attack is an attack for reconstructing a private dataset (fully or partially) by running several aggregate queries on the dataset. According to [3], a linear reconstruction attack's success depends on three parameters: 1) the number of participants in the dataset n, 2) the number of released noisy aggregates m, and 3) the error bound added to the aggregate queries E. This attack works in two settings: in one setting, m is exponential in n, and the error E is linear in n. In the second setting, m is polynomial in n, and the error E is on the order of $\sqrt{n}$.

In the DP setting, according to the composition theorem, the noise order depends only on m, and not n. If we equally distribute the budget among the queries, m and E are linearly related. For a fixed and sufficiently large n and a given ε, the adversary cannot achieve a successful reconstruction attack. As explained in Sect. 2 Footnote (See Footnote 1), we assume that the protected dataset does not allow querying over a subset smaller than some threshold. Hence, provided that such a threshold is large enough to mitigate a reconstruction attack, the differencing attack is a more relevant threat than the reconstruction attack.

Future Work. In the DP literature there is a huge misalignment between methods to set DP parameters and design of novel mechanisms and their application in different use cases [21]. To fill this gap, we started analysing base mechanisms, such as *count*, *sum*, and *average*. The next step of our research is to extend our framework to other widely used mechanisms such as median or histograms. Our final goal is to develop a general framework that covers a large amount of queries.

For the mechanisms which employ distributions beyond Laplace distribution, the introduced attack strategy in Sect. 5.2 can be adapted to any symmetric distribution for which the formula for a linear combination is calculable. Exploring the effect of different distributions on P_{SDA} is another direction for future work.

To mitigate the adversarial threat introduced in this paper, one possible solution is to add fake users with similar features to the users vulnerable to differencing attacks using techniques such as k-anonymity [12]. Investigating how such a method will impact P_{SDA} can be another direction to extend the current study.

9 Conclusions

For DP to be trusted, we need to investigate transparent approaches for setting ε. The P_{SDA} (the probability of successful differencing attack) approach presented in this paper—whilst limited to three query types and exhibiting certain underlying assumptions—presents an important step in this direction.

Our findings show that, for a given value for ε, the probability of a privacy leak varies depending on the query type and the target person's data. Furthermore, comparison of our method with the methods of [13,15] shows that the privacy loss of a given value of ε differs for different adversarial models. Our proposed adversary carries out equal or more successful attacks than the adversaries proposed in [13] and [15]. Moreover, our method is designed to work in more generic scenarios than the ones considered by [13]. Hence, to the best of our knowledge, our P_{SDA} provides a more general approach for choosing an appropriate ε than either of these related works.

Acknowledgements. We thank the Swiss National Science Foundation for their partial support under contract number #407550_167177.

References

1. Beck, M., Bhatotia, P., Chen, R., Fetzer, C., Strufe, T., et al.: PrivApprox: privacy-preserving stream analytics. In: 2017 USENIX Annual Technical Conference USENIX ATC 2017, pp. 659–672 (2017)
2. Clopper, C.J., Pearson, E.S.: The use of confidence or fiducial limits illustrated in the case of the binomial. Biometrika **26**(4), 404–413 (1934)
3. Dinur, I., Nissim, K.: Revealing information while preserving privacy. In: Proceedings of the Twenty-Second ACM SIGMOD-SIGACT-SIGART Symposium on Principles of Database Systems, pp. 202–210 (2003)
4. Dwork, C., Roth, A., et al.: The algorithmic foundations of differential privacy. Found. Trends Theor. Comput. Sci. **9**(3–4), 211–407 (2014)
5. Gaboardi, M., et al.: Psi (ψ): a private data sharing interface. arXiv preprint arXiv:1609.04340 (2016)
6. Garfinkel, S.L., Abowd, J.M., Powazek, S.: Issues encountered deploying differential privacy. In: Proceedings of the 2018 Workshop on Privacy in the Electronic Society, pp. 133–137 (2018)
7. Hsu, J., et al.: Differential privacy: an economic method for choosing epsilon. In: 2014 IEEE 27th Computer Security Foundations Symposium, pp. 398–410. IEEE (2014)
8. Johnson, N., Near, J.P., Hellerstein, J.M., Song, D.: Chorus: a programming framework for building scalable differential privacy mechanisms. In: 2020 IEEE European Symposium on Security and Privacy (EuroS&P), pp. 535–551. IEEE (2020)
9. Johnson, N., Near, J.P., Song, D.: Towards practical differential privacy for SQL queries. Proc. VLDB Endow. **11**(5), 526–539 (2018)
10. Kotz, S., Kozubowski, T., Podgorski, K.: The Laplace Distribution and Generalizations: A Revisit with Applications to Communications, Economics, Engineering, and Finance. Springer, Heidelberg (2012). https://doi.org/10.1007/978-1-4612-0173-1

11. Krehbiel, S.: Choosing epsilon for privacy as a service. Proc. Priv. Enhanc. Technol. **2019**(1), 192–205 (2019)
12. Latanya, S.: k-anonymity: A model for protecting privacy. Int. J. Uncertain. Fuzziness Knowl.-Based Syst. **10**(05), 557–570 (2002)
13. Lee, J., Clifton, C.: How much is enough? Choosing ε for differential privacy. In: Lai, X., Zhou, J., Li, H. (eds.) ISC 2011. LNCS, vol. 7001, pp. 325–340. Springer, Heidelberg (2011). https://doi.org/10.1007/978-3-642-24861-0_22
14. Li, N., Lyu, M., Su, D., Yang, W.: Differential privacy: from theory to practice. Synth. Lect. Inf. Secur. Priv. Trust **8**(4), 1–138 (2016)
15. Liu, C., He, X., Chanyaswad, T., Wang, S., Mittal, P.: Investigating statistical privacy frameworks from the perspective of hypothesis testing. Proc. Priv. Enhanc. Technol. **2019**(3), 233–254 (2019)
16. McSherry, F.D.: Privacy integrated queries: an extensible platform for privacy-preserving data analysis. In: Proceedings of the 2009 ACM SIGMOD International Conference on Management of Data, pp. 19–30. ACM (2009)
17. Nadarajah, S.: The linear combination, product and ratio of Laplace random variables. Statistics **41**(6), 535–545 (2007)
18. Proserpio, D., Goldberg, S., McSherry, F.: Calibrating data to sensitivity in private data analysis: a platform for differentially-private analysis of weighted datasets. Proc. VLDB Endow. **7**(8), 637–648 (2014)
19. Roy, I., Setty, S.T., Kilzer, A., Shmatikov, V., Witchel, E.: Airavat: security and privacy for mapreduce. In: NSDI, vol. 10, pp. 297–312 (2010)
20. Tao, Y., He, X., Machanavajjhala, A., Roy, S.: Computing local sensitivities of counting queries with joins. In: Proceedings of the 2020 ACM SIGMOD International Conference on Management of Data, pp. 479–494 (2020)
21. Wagner, I., Eckhoff, D.: Technical privacy metrics: a systematic survey. ACM Comput. Surv. (CSUR) **51**(3), 1–38 (2018)
22. Wood, A., et al.: Differential privacy: a primer for a non-technical audience. Vand. J. Ent. Tech. L. **21**, 209 (2018)

Explanation-Guided Diagnosis of Machine Learning Evasion Attacks

Abderrahmen Amich[(✉)] and Birhanu Eshete

University of Michigan, Dearborn, USA
{aamich,birhanu}@umich.edu

Abstract. Machine Learning (ML) models are susceptible to evasion attacks. Evasion accuracy is typically assessed using aggregate evasion rate, and it is an open question whether aggregate evasion rate enables feature-level diagnosis on the effect of adversarial perturbations on evasive predictions. In this paper, we introduce a novel framework that harnesses explainable ML methods to guide high-fidelity assessment of ML evasion attacks. Our framework enables explanation-guided correlation analysis between pre-evasion perturbations and post-evasion explanations. Towards systematic assessment of ML evasion attacks, we propose and evaluate a novel suite of model-agnostic metrics for sample-level and dataset-level correlation analysis. Using malware and image classifiers, we conduct comprehensive evaluations across diverse model architectures and complementary feature representations. Our explanation-guided correlation analysis reveals correlation gaps between adversarial samples and the corresponding perturbations performed on them. Using a case study on explanation-guided evasion, we show the broader usage of our methodology for assessing robustness of ML models.

Keywords: Machine learning evasion · Explainable machine learning

1 Introduction

The widespread usage of machine learning (ML) in a myriad of application domains has brought adversarial threats to ML models to the forefront of research towards dependable and secure ML systems. From image classification [29] to voice recognition [12], from precision medicine [18] to malware/intrusion detection [38] and autonomous vehicles [42], ML models have been shown to be vulnerable not only to training-time poisoning and evasion attacks, but also to model extraction and membership inference attacks [10]. In typical evasion attacks, an adversary perturbs a legitimate input to craft an *adversarial sample* that tricks a victim model into making an incorrect prediction.

Motivation: Prior work has demonstrated adversarial sample-based evasion of ML models across diverse domains such as image classifiers [11,20,30], malware classifiers [6,9,14,26,38], and other domains such as speech and text processing. In the current state-of-the-art, the effectiveness of evasion is typically assessed

J. Garcia-Alfaro et al. (Eds.): SecureComm 2021, LNICST 398, pp. 207–228, 2021.
https://doi.org/10.1007/978-3-030-90019-9_11

through *aggregate evasion rate* by computing the percentage of crafted adversarial samples that lead a model to make evasive predictions. For a ML model f that accepts a d-dimensional input $x = [x_1, ..., x_d]$ to predict $f(x) = y_{true}$, the adversary perturbs x to obtain $x' = [x_1 + \delta_1, ..., x_d + \delta_d]$, where $\delta = [\delta_1, ..., \delta_d]$ represents *pre-evasion perturbations* applied to each feature. When f is queried with x', it produces an evasive prediction $f(x') = y' \neq y_{true}$. The natural question then is whether there exists *correlation between pre-evasion perturbations and the evasive prediction*. Unfortunately, aggregate evasion rate is inadequate to offer fine-grained insights to answer this question. It does not show how much the evasion strategy, through adversarial perturbations, influences individual samples to result in an evasive prediction. We consequently argue that unless one "unpacks" aggregate evasion rate at the resolution of an adversarial sample, it could give false sense of evasion success for it lacks the fidelity at the level of individual features. Such a coarse-grained nature of the aggregate evasion metric can potentially misguide the evaluation of model robustness in the face of adversarial manipulations.

Approach: In this paper, we harness feature-based ML explanation methods and propose an explanation-guided correlation analysis framework for evasion attacks on ML models. Explainable ML techniques [23,33,39,44] interpret predictions returned by a ML model and attribute model's decision (e.g., predicted class label) to feature importance weights. In particular, for each evasive prediction $f(x') = y' \neq y_{true}$, explanation methods such as LIME [39] and SHAP [33] produce *post-evasion explanations* of the form $[x_1 : w_1, ..., x_d : w_d]$, where w_i is the weight of contribution of feature x_i to the evasive prediction y'. To address the lack of detailed insights from aggregate evasion rate, we leverage post-evasion explanations and empirically explore their feature-level correlations with pre-evasion perturbations performed by the adversary. Our key insight is that, since the perturbations are the only manipulations done on the feature-space of an input sample, when the model makes an evasive prediction on a perturbed variant of the input sample, there should exist some correlation between pre-evasion perturbations and post-evasion explanations. Towards systematic assessment of the link between adversarial perturbations and evasive predictions, we propose and evaluate a novel suite of metrics that allow (adversarial) sample-level and (evasion) dataset-level diagnosis of evasion attacks. Our suite of metrics is applicable to any ML model that predicts a class label given an input because, in the design of the metrics, we make no assumptions about the ML task and model architecture. The benefit of the fine-grained diagnosis for a defender is twofold. First, it enables systematic measurement of the strength of correlation between an evasive prediction and feature-level perturbations across diverse classification tasks, model architectures, and feature representations. Second, it allows zooming-in on limitations of feature perturbation strategies to inform pre-deployment adversarial robustness evaluation of ML models.

Note on Scope: This paper is not yet another adversarial sample crafting approach for which problem-space to feature-space mapping is crucial to maintain functional integrity of adversarial samples (e.g., in adversarial malware samples). Our approach rather relies on *feature-space perturbations* performed to craft an adversarial sample and model output explanations of the same sample. Our goal correlation analysis between perturbations and explanations.

Evaluation Highlights: We evaluate our framework across different classification tasks (image, malware), diverse model architectures (e.g., neural networks, multiple tree-based classifiers, logistic regression), and complementary feature representations (pixels for images, static and dynamic analysis-based features for malware). Our explanation-guided correlation analysis reveals an average of 45% per-model adversarial samples that have low correlation links with perturbations performed on them –indicating the inadequacy of aggregate evasion rate, but the utility of fine-grained correlation analysis, for reliable diagnosis of evasion accuracy. Our results additionally suggest that, although a perturbation strategy evades a target model, at the granularity of each feature perturbation, it can lead to a per-model average of 36% *negative* feature perturbations (i.e., perturbations that contribute to maintain the original true prediction $f_b(x') = y_{true}$). We further evaluate the utility of our framework in a case study on explanation-guided adversarial sample crafting.

Contributions: In summary, this paper makes the following contributions:

- *Explanation-guided diagnosis of evasion attacks.* To improve the sole reliance of evasion assessment on aggregate evasion rate, we propose an *explanation-guided correlation analysis* framework at the resolution of individual features. To that end, we introduce a novel *suite of correlation analysis metrics* and demonstrate their effectiveness at pinpointing adversarial examples that indeed evade a model yet exhibit loose correlation with perturbations performed to craft them.
- *Comprehensive evaluations.* In malware classification and image classification, we conduct extensive evaluations across diverse model architectures and feature representations, and synthesize interesting experimental insights that demonstrate the utility of explanation-guided correlation analysis.
- *Further case study.* We conduct a case study using *pre-perturbation feature direction analysis* to guide evasion strategies towards crafting more accurate adversarial samples *correlated* with their evasive predictions.

2   Background: ML Evasion and Explanation Methods

In this section, we introduce ML evasion attacks and ML explanation methods.

2.1   ML Evasion Attacks

Adversarial Sample Crafting. Given a deployed ML model (e.g., malware classifier, image classifier) with a decision function $f : X \rightarrow Y$ that maps an input sample $x \in X$ to a true class label $y_{true} \in Y$, then $x' = x + \delta$ is called an *adversarial sample* with an *adversarial perturbation* δ if: $f(x') = y' \neq y_{true}, ||\delta|| < \epsilon$, where $||.||$ is a distance metric (e.g., one of the L_p norms) and ϵ is the maximum allowable perturbation that results in misclassification while preserving semantic integrity of x. Semantic integrity is domain and/or task specific. For instance, in image classification, visual imperceptibility of x' from x is desired while in malware detection x and x' need to satisfy certain functional equivalence (e.g., if x was a malware pre-perturbation, x' is expected to exhibit maliciousness post-perturbation as well). In *untargeted* evasion, the goal is to make the model misclassify a sample to any different class (e.g., for a roadside sign detection model: misclassify red light as any other sign). When the evasion is *targeted*, the goal is to make the model to misclassify a sample to a specific target class (e.g., in malware detection: misclassify malware as benign).

Evasion attacks can be done in *white-box* or *black-box* setting. Most gradient-based evasion techniques [11,20,30,34] are white-box because the adversary typically has access to model architecture and parameters/weights, which allows to query the model directly to decide how to increase the model's loss function. In recent years, several white-box adversarial sample crafting methods have been proposed, specially for image classification tasks. Some of the most notable ones are: Fast Gradient Sign Method (FGSM) [20], Basic Iterative Method (BIM) [30], Projected Gradient Descent (PGD) method [34], and Carlini & Wagner (CW) method [11]. Black-box evasion techniques usually start from some initial perturbation δ_0, and subsequently probe f on a series of perturbations $f(x + \delta_i)$, to craft a variation of x that evades f (i.e., misclassified to a label different from its original). In malware classifiers, while *gradient-based* methods have been widely adopted both in white-box and black-box settings, two other strategies also standout for evasion in a black-box setting. The first one is called *additive* because it appends adversarial noise (e.g., no-op bytes) to the end of a sample (e.g., Windows PE) to preserve original behavior [21,28]. The second class of methods uses *targeted and constrained manipulations* after identifying regions in the PE that are unlikely to be mapped to memory [49].

One of the challenges for state-of-the-art adversarial sample crafting methods is the lack/impossibility of mapping of feature-space perturbations to the problem space. Such a mapping and reversibility between the two spaces is essential in domains where the functionality of an adversarial sample needs to be preserved post-perturbation [24]. A recent work by Pierazzi et al. [37] proposes formulations and shows promising experimental results towards the feasibility of crafting evasive malware samples with real-world consequences. As discussed in Sect. 1, problem space perturbations are out of this paper's scope.

2.2   ML Explanation Methods

ML models have long been perceived as black-box in their predictions until the advent of explainable ML [33,39,44], which attribute a decision of a model to features that contributed to the decision. This notion of attribution is based on quantifiable contribution of each feature to a model's decision.

ML explanation is usually accomplished by training a substitute model based on the input feature vectors and output predictions of the model, and then use the coefficients of that model to approximate the importance and *direction* (class label it leans to) of the feature. A typical substitute model for explanation is of the form: $s(x) = w_0 + \sum_{i=1}^{d} w_i x_i$, where d is the number of features, x is the sample, x_i is the ith feature for sample x, and w_i is the contribution/weight of feature x_i to the model's decision. While ML explanation methods exist for white-box [45,47] or black-box [23,33,39] access to the model, in this work we consider ML explanation methods that have black-box access to the ML model, among which the notable ones are LIME [39], SHAP [33] and LEMNA [23]. Next, we briefly introduce these explanation methods.

LIME and SHAP. Ribeiro et al. [39] introduce LIME as one of the first model-agnostic black-box methods for locally explaining model output. Lundberg and Lee further extended LIME by proposing SHAP [33]. Both methods approximate the decision function f_b by creating a series of l perturbations of a sample x, denoted as $x'_1, ..., x'_l$ by randomly setting feature values in the vector x to 0. The methods then proceed by predicting a label $f_b(x'_i) = y_i$ for each x'_i of the l perturbations. This sampling strategy enables the methods to approximate the local neighborhood of f_b at the point $f_b(x)$. LIME approximates the decision boundary by a weighted linear regression model as: $_{g \in G} \sum_{i=1}^{l} \pi_x(x'_i)(f_b(x'_i) - g(x'_i))^2$, where G is the set of all linear functions and π_x is a function indicating the difference between the input x and a perturbation x'. SHAP follows a similar approach but employs the SHAP kernel as weighting function π_x, which is computed using the *Shapley Values* [43] when solving the regression. Shapley Values are a concept from game theory where the features act as players under the objective of finding a fair contribution of the features to the payout –in this case the prediction of the model.

LEMNA. Another black-box explanation method designed work well for non-linear models is LEMNA [23] that uses a mixture regression model for approximation, i.e., a weighted sum of K linear models defined as: $f(x) = \sum_{j=1}^{K} \pi_j(\beta_j.x + \epsilon_j)$, where the parameter K specifies the number of models, the random variables $\epsilon = (\epsilon_1, ..., \epsilon_K)$ originate from a normal distribution $\epsilon_i \sim N(0, \sigma)$ and $\pi = (\pi_1, ..., \pi_K)$ holds the weights for each model. The variables $\beta_1, ..., \beta_K$ are the regression coefficients and can be interpreted as K linear approximations of the decision boundary near $f_b(x)$.

3 Explanation-Guided Evasion Diagnosis Framework

In this section, we present our explanation-guided correlation analysis methodology. Table 1 describes notations used here and in the rest of the paper.

3.1 Overview

As described in Sect. 1, the effectiveness of an evasion method is typically assessed using aggregate evasion accuracy. While aggregate evasion quantifies the overall success of an evasion strategy, it fails to offer sufficient insights. It does not show how the evasion mechanism influences individual samples to result in evasive predictions. We argue that, unless one examines evasion success at the resolution of each adversarial sample, aggregate evasion rate could give

Table 1. Notations.

Notation	Brief description
X_b	Training set of black-box model f_b
X_e	Evasion set disjoint with X_b
X'_e	Adversarial counterpart of X_e
X_s	Training set of explanation model f_s
$x \in X_e$	Sample in evasion set
$x' \in X'_e$	Adversarial variant of x
$Y = \{y_1, ..., y_k\}$	Set of classes (labels)
$x = [x_1, ..., x_d]$	d-dimensional feature vector of sample x
$W_{x,y_i} = \{w_1, ..., w_d\}$	Feature weights (explanations) of a sample x toward the class y_i
$pos(x, y_i)$	Number of features in x *positive* to the prediction $f_b(x) = y_i$
$neg(x, y_i)$	Number of features in x *negative* to the prediction $f_b(x) = y_i$
$neut(x, y_i)$	Number of features in x *neutral* to the prediction $f_b(x) = y_i$
$P(x')$	Number of perturbed features in x'
τ	Threshold to decide highly correlated adversarial samples

false sense of adversarial success for it lacks feature-level fidelity of perturbations that result in an adversarial sample. To address the stated lack of fidelity in aggregate evasion accuracy, we systematically explore how ML explanation methods are harnessed to assess feature-level correlations between pre-evasion adversarial perturbations and post-evasion explanations.

Figure 1 shows an overview of our explanation-guided correlation analysis framework. Given an evasion set X'_e of adversarial samples, our framework enables correlation analysis both at the sample-level (for each $x' \in X'_e$ at the granularity of each perturbed feature) and at the evasion dataset-level ($\forall x' \in X'_e$). Intuitively, given a decisive feature (obtained via ML explanations) of an evasive sample ($f_b(x') \neq y_{true}$), for such a feature to be considered the cause of (correlated to) the evasion, there needs to be a corresponding feature that was perturbed in the original sample x. By repeating the correlation of each decisive feature with its perturbed counterpart, our sample-level correlation analysis establishes empirical evidence that links an evasive prediction with its cause.

More precisely, our correlation analysis is performed by harnessing the *post-evasion features directions* ("2. Explanation" in Fig. 1) of adversarial samples ("1. Evasion" in Fig. 1). First, we explore the feature directions of the *pre-evasion perturbations* to obtain an assessment of the contribution of each feature perturbation to the attack (i.e., *feature-level assessment*). Second, we use those results to zoom-out to a *sample-level assessment* (Sect. 3.3). Finally, we move to the higher level of the whole evasion dataset to obtain an overall assessment of the evasion attack (Sect. 3.4).

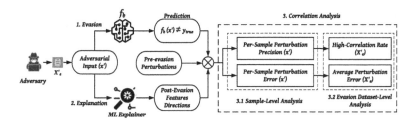

Fig. 1. Explanation-guided correlation analysis framework.

Conducting such fine-grained correlation analysis has two key benefits. Firstly, it verifies whether evasion can be attributed to the adversarial perturbations employed on the sample, and, in effect, performs diagnosis on aggregate evasion accuracy. Secondly, it provides visibility into how sensitive certain samples and/or features are to adversarial perturbations, which could inform robustness assessment of ML models in the face of evasion attacks.

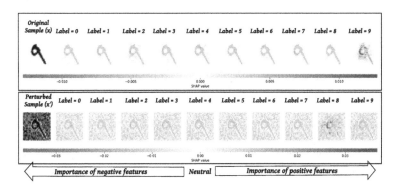

Fig. 2. A comparative illustration of pre-perturbation and post-perturbation explanations using SHAP [33] on a test sample from the MNIST [31] dataset.

3.2   Post-Evasion Feature Direction

In a typical classification task, for an input sample x, $f_b(x) = y_i \in Y = \{y_1, ..., y_k\}$, where Y is the set of k possible labels. For example, in the multiclass handwritten digit recognition model of the MNIST [31] dataset, the input is an image of a handwritten digit and the label is one of the 10 digits (i.e., $Y = \{0, .., 9\}$ where $k = 10$). In the malware detection domain, the typical model is a binary classifier (i.e., $Y = \{\texttt{Benign}, \texttt{Malware}\}$ where $k = 2$). Next, we use MNIST as an illustrative example to describe post-evasion feature direction.

Explanations returned from ML explanation methods reveal the *direction* of each feature. For each class $y_i \in Y$ and an adversarial sample x', a ML explanation method returns a set of *feature weights* $W_{x',y_i} = \{w_1, .., w_d\}$ where

w_j reflects the importance (as the magnitude of w_j) and the *direction* (as the sign of w_j) of the feature x'_j towards the prediction $f_b(x') = y_i$. Depending on the sign of w_j, feature x'_j can be *positive*, *negative*, or *neutral* with respect to the prediction $f_b(x') = y_i$. When $w_j > 0$, we say x'_j is positive to (directed towards) y_i. Conversely, when $w_j < 0$, x'_j is negative to (directed away from) y'_i. When $w_j = 0$, we say x'_j is neutral to y_i (does not have any impact on the prediction decision). In case of binary classification ($k = 2$), if x'_j is not directed to the label y_1 (**Benign** for malware detection) and is not neutral, then x'_j can only be directed to the other label y_2 (**Malware**) and vice versa. To illustrate how we leverage feature direction in our analysis, next we describe a concrete example from the MNIST [31] handwritten digit recognition model.

In Fig. 2, the upper box shows SHAP [33] pre-evasion feature explanations of a correct prediction on an image of "9"(i.e., $f_b(x) = 9$). The lower box shows post-evasion feature explanations of the misclassification $f_b(x') \neq 9$ using an adversarial variant $x' \leftarrow x + \delta$. Each column (i.e., "*Label* $= y_i$"; $y_i \in \{0, ..., 9\}$) represents the feature explanations for the possibility of a prediction $f_b(x) = y_i$ (upper box) and $f_b(x') = y_i$ (lower box). The color codes are interpreted as follows: given an explanation, pink corresponds to positive features while blue corresponds to negative features. The intensity of either color (pink or blue) is directly proportional to the feature weight towards the prediction. Neutral features are represented with white. For instance, focusing on the correct prediction label $y_{true} = 9$ in the upper-box, we notice a large concentration of pink features which positively contribute to the predicted label (9).

Our approach primarily relies on post-evasion explanations (lower box in Fig. 2) and we observe that feature importance weights vary for each studied label as a potential prediction $f_b(x') = y_i \in \{0, ..., 9\}$. When the prediction $f_b(x') = 8$ (image below 'Label $= 8$' in lower box), the explanations show that most features are *positive* (directed to label 8), which explains the change of the prediction label from 9 to 8. Examining the colors, we realize that most features that were directed to label 9 in the pre-perturbation explanations have become either neutral to the prediction $f_b(x') = 9$ or are positive towards $f_b(x') = 8$. It is noteworthy that some perturbed features are oriented to the original label 9 (notice pink pixels in the image below 'Label $= 9$' in lower box). Such observations suggest that even though the attack is successful (i.e., $f_b(x') = 8 \neq 9$), the effectiveness of each single feature perturbation is not guaranteed to result in an evasive prediction. Thus, the evasion success may not always be correlated with each feature perturbation the adversary performs on the original sample. We, therefore, argue that a perturbation strategy that produces many features that are uncorrelated with the misclassification might perform poorly on other feature representations (e.g., colored or not centered images in image classification) or other feature types (e.g., static vs. dynamic features in malware detection) which reflects a potential limitation of the stability of a perturbation method. Next, we introduce novel sample-level metrics that capture the fine-grained assessment that leverages post-evasion explanations. We refer to Table 1 for the feature direction-related notations. Our focus will be on the *post-perturbation feature directions* of an evasive sample x' and we suppose that its original prediction (pre-perturbation) is $f_b(x) = y_{true}$.

3.3   Sample-Level Analysis

Post-evasion explanations reveal the direction (*positive*, *negative*, or *neutral*) of each perturbed feature in an adversarial sample x'. Sample-level analysis is performed to empirically assess feature perturbations that positively contribute towards misclassification (*positive perturbations*) against the ones that contribute to maintain the true label as a prediction (*negative perturbations*). Next, we introduce two sample-level metrics which will later serve as foundations to conduct overall correlation analysis over the evasion dataset.

Definition 1: Per-Sample Perturbation Precision (PSPP). Out of all performed feature perturbations $(P(x'))$ to produce an adversarial sample x', PSPP enables us to compute the rate of perturbations that contribute to change the original prediction y_{true} to another label $y_i \in Y - \{y_{true}\}$. In other words, it measures the rate of perturbed features that are *"negative"* to the original prediction (y_{true}) and *"positive"* to other predictions $y_i \neq y_{true}$. We call such perturbations *positive perturbations* because they positively advance the evasion goal. More formally, the Per-Sample Perturbation Precision for an adversarial sample x' is computed as follows:

$$PSPP(x') = \frac{1}{2}(\frac{1}{k-1}(\sum_{y_i \in Y\, y_i \neq y_{true}} \frac{pos(x', y_i)}{P(x')}) + \frac{neg(x', y_{true})}{P(x')}) \qquad (1)$$

Equation 1 is the average of two ratios:

- $(\frac{1}{k-1}(\sum_{y_i \in Y\, y_i \neq y_{true}} \frac{pos(x', y_i)}{P(x')})$: The average rate of perturbed features that are directed to a class $y_i \neq y_{true}$, over all $k - 1$ possible false classes $y_i \in Y - \{y_{true}\}$.
- $(\frac{neg(x', y_{true})}{P(x')})$: The rate of perturbed features that are not directed to the original label y_{true} and not neutral.

Both ratios that are considered in Eq. 1 measure *Positive Perturbations* that contribute to a misclasssification. We note that $PSPP(x')$ falls in the range $[0, 1]$. The closer $PSPP(x')$ is to 1, the more the overall perturbations performed on the features of x' are precise (effective at feature level). More importantly, when x' evades the model, i.e., $f_b(x') \neq f_b(x)$, then the closer $PSPP(x')$ is to 1 the stronger the correlation between the evasion success and each performed feature perturbation that produced adversarial sample x'.

Definition 2: Per-Sample Perturbation Error (PSPE). Another per-sample measurement for our correlation analysis is the Per-Sample Perturbation Error, $PSPE(x')$, that computes the rate of perturbed features that are directed to the original class y_{true} (*positive* to the original prediction y_{true}). These features stand against the adversary's goal of misclassifying x'. Such features are considered *negative perturbations* with respect to the original class. More formally, $PSPE(x')$ is defined as follows:

$$PSPE(x') = \frac{pos(x', y_{true})}{P(x')} \qquad (2)$$

Given an adversarial sample x', $PSPE(x')$ returns the rate of perturbation errors over all perturbed features. We note that a perturbed feature that is *neutral* ($w_j = 0$) to the original prediction ($f_b(x') = y_{true}$) is considered neither as perturbation error nor an effective manipulation to advance the evasion goal. Thus, $PSPE(x')$ may not be directly computed from $PSPP(x')$ and vice versa. Moreover, in the case of a slightly different threat model in-which the evasion is *targeted* to change the original prediction y_{true} to a new target label $y_{target} \in Y - \{y_{true}\}$, then only the term $\frac{pos(x', y_{target})}{P(x')}$ would be considered to compute the perturbation precision $PSPP(x')$, and only the term $\frac{neg(x', y_{target})}{P(x')}$ suffices to compute the rate of committed perturbation errors, $PSPE(x')$.

3.4 Evasion Dataset-Level Analysis

Using $PSPP(x')$ and $PSPE(x')$ defined in Eqs. 1 and 2 as foundations, we now introduce novel correlation analysis metrics that operate at the level of the evasion dataset X'_e to empirically analyze correlation between perturbations and post-evasion explanations.

Definition 3: High-Correlation Rate (HCR). As explained in Sect. 3.3, $PSPP(x')$ quantifies the correlation of each single feature perturbation with the evasion $f_b(x') \neq y_{true}$. The closer $PSPP(x')$ is to 1, the higher is the correlation and vice-versa. We consider a threshold τ that indicates the "strength" of the correlation between positive perturbations on x that resulted in x' and the important features that "explain" $f_b(x') \neq y_{true}$. Based on an empirically estimated τ, we call an adversarial sample x' a *High-Correlated Sample* if $PSPP(x')$ falls in $[\tau, 1]$. In our evaluation, based on empirical observations, we use $\tau = 0.5$.

Based on the above definition, we compute *High-Correlation Rate (HCR)* as the percentage of *High-Correlated Samples* in the evasion set X'_e as follows:

$$HCR = \frac{|X'_e(PSPP > \tau)|}{|X'_e|} \tag{3}$$

where $X'_e(PSPP > \tau) = \{x' \in X'_e : PSPP(x') > \tau\} \cap \{f_b(x') \neq y_{true}\}$. We note that *HCR* quantifies the degree to which adversarial samples are both *evasive* and *correlated* to most feature perturbations performed on original samples.

Definition 4: Average Perturbation Error (APE). As shown in Eq. 2, $PSPE(x')$ computes the number of errors committed during the perturbation of each feature in x to produce the manipulated sample x' (which is the same as computing the number of *negative perturbations*). We leverage $PSPE(x')$ to compute the average of negative perturbations (APE) over all samples in X'_e. Formally, APE is given as follows:

$$APE = \sum_{x' \in X'_e} \frac{PSPE(x')}{|X'_e|} \tag{4}$$

As opposed to aggregate evasion rate that computes the percentage of *evasive samples* versus *non-evasive samples* without deeper insights about the effectiveness of each single feature perturbation, *APE* computes the rate of *"evasive features"* versus *"non-evasive features"* of each evasive sample, over all perturbed samples. Such in-depth investigations into evasion attacks provide a fine-grained assessment of any evasion strategy on ML models.

4   Evaluation

We now evaluate the utility of our suite of metrics for high-fidelity correlation analysis of ML evasion attacks. We describe our datasets and experimental setup in Sect. 4.1 and 4.2, respectively. We then validate our methodology in Sect. 4.3. Finally, we extend our evaluation with a case study in Sect. 4.4.

4.1   Datasets

We use three datasets from two domains. From the malware classification domain, we use two complementary datasets, one based on static analysis, and the other on dynamic (execution behavior) analysis. From image classification, we use a benchmark handwritten digits recognition dataset. We selected these two as representative domains because (*a*) malware detection is a naturally adversarial domain where adversarial robustness to evasion attacks is expected and (*b*) image recognition has been heavily explored for evasion attacks in recent adversarial ML literature. We describe these datasets next.

CuckooTrace (PE Malware). We collected 40K Windows PEs with 50% malware (from VirusShare [4]) and the rest 50% benign PEs (from a goodware site [1]). We use 60% of the dataset as a training set, 25% as a training for explanation substitute model, and the remaining 15% as evasion test. Each sample is represented as a binary feature vector. Each feature indicates the presence/absence of behavioral features captured up on execution of each PE in the Cuckoo Sandbox [2]. Behavioral analysis of 40K PEs resulted in 1549 features, of which 80 are API calls, 559 are I/O system files, and 910 are loaded DLLs.

EMBER (PE Malware). To assess our framework on complementary (static analysis-based) malware dataset, we use EMBER [7], a benchmark dataset of malware and benign PEs released with a trained LightGBM with 97.3% test accuracy. EMBER consists of 2351 features extracted from 1M PEs using a static binary analysis tool LIEF [3]. The training set contains 800K samples composed of 600K labeled samples with 50% split between benign and malicious PEs and 200K unlabeled samples, while the test set consists of 200K samples, again with the same ratio of label split. VirusTotal [5] was used to label all the samples. The feature groups include: PE metadata, header information, byte histogram, byte-entropy histogram, string information, section information, and imported/exported functions. We use 100K of the test set for substitute model training, and the remaining 100K as our evasion set against the LightGBM pretrained model and a DNN which we trained. We use version 2 of EMBER.

MNIST (Image). To further evaluate our framework on image classifiers, we use the MNIST [31] dataset, which comprises 60K training and 10K test images of handwritten digits. The classification task is to identify the digit corresponding to each image. Each 28×28 gray-scale sample is encoded as a vector of normalized pixel intensities in the interval [0, 1].

4.2   Models and Setup

Studied ML Models. Across CuckooTrace, EMBER and MNIST, we train 8 models: Multi-Layer Perceptron (MLP), Logistic Regression (LR), Random Forest (RF), Extra Trees (ET), Decision Trees (DT), Light Gradient Boosting decision tree Model (LGBM), a Deep Neural Network (DNN), and a 2D Convolutional Neural Network (CNN). As in prior work [35,36], we choose these models because they are representative of applications of ML across domains including image classification, malware/intrusion detection, and they also complement each other in terms of their architecture and susceptibility to evasion.

Employed Evasion Attacks. Using the evasion set of each dataset, we craft adversarial samples. For the evasion attack, we consider a threat model where the adversary has no knowledge about the target model, but knows features used to train the model (e.g., API calls for malware classifiers, pixels for image classifiers). More precisely, for CuckooTrace and EMBER we incrementally perturb features of a Malware sample until the model flips its label to Benign. Following previous adversarial sample crafting methods [26,49], we adopt only additive manipulations. For instance, for binary features of CuckooTrace (where 1 indicates presence and 0 indicates absence of an API call), we flip only a 0 to 1. Like prior work [46], we also respect the allowable range of perturbations for each static feature in EMBER (e.g., file size is always positive). For MNIST, we add a random noise to the background of the image to change the original gray-scale of each pixel without perturbing white pixels that characterize the handwritten digit. The outcome is an adversarial image that is still recognizable by humans but misclassified by the model. Table 2 shows the comparison between pre-evasion accuracy and post-evasion accuracy. All models exhibit significant drop in the test accuracy after the feature perturbations. We recall that the main purpose of our analysis is to explore the correlation between a perturbed feature and the misclassification result, regardless of the complexity of the evasion strategy. Thus, our choice of perturbation methods is governed by convenience (e.g., execution time) and effectiveness (i.e., results in evasion).

Table 2. Pre-evasion accuracy and post-evasion accuracy across studied models.

Dataset	Model	Pre-evasion accuracy	Post-evasion accuracy	Aggregate evasion accuracy
CuckooTrace	MLP	96%	6.05%	89.95%
CuckooTrace	LR	95%	21.75%	73.25%
CuckooTrace	RF	96%	18.61%	77.39%
CuckooTrace	DT	96%	7.8%	88.20%
CuckooTrace	ET	96%	16.27%	79.73%
EMBER	LGBM	97.3%	56.06%	40.94%
EMBER	DNN	93%	12.08%	80.92%
MNIST	CNN	99.4%	33.1%	66.30%

Table 3. High-correlation rate and average perturbation error for all models.

Dataset	Model	High-correlation rate	Average perturbation error
CuckooTrace	MLP	34.56%	32.96%
CuckooTrace	LR	34.96%	38.92%
CuckooTrace	RF	36.09%	60.73%
CuckooTrace	DT	66.85%	37.86%
CuckooTrace	ET	33.41%	54.62%
EMBER	LGBM	95.03%	7.47%
EMBER	DNN	96.72%	4.89%
MNIST	CNN	44.31%	49.40%

Employed ML Explanation Methods. Informed by recent studies [15,50] that compare the utility of ML explanation methods, we use LIME [39] on CuckooTrace and EMBER, and SHAP [33] on MNIST. More specifically, these studies perform comparative evaluations of black-box ML explanation methods (e.g., LIME [39], SHAP [33], and LEMNA [23]) in terms of effectiveness (e.g., accuracy), stability (i.e., similarity among results of different runs), efficiency (e.g., execution time), and robustness against small feature perturbations. On the one hand, these studies show that LIME performs best on security systems (e.g., Drebin+ [21], Mimicus+ [23]). Thus, we employ LIME on the two malware detection systems (i.e., CuckooTrace and EMBER). On the other hand, SHAP authors proposed a ML explainer called "Deep Explainer", designed for deep learning models, specifically for image classification. Thus, we use SHAP to explain predictions of a CNN on MNIST. We note that independent recent studies [15,50] suggested that both LIME and SHAP outperform LEMNA [23].

4.3   Correlation Analysis Results

Results Overview. Across all models and the three datasets, the evasion attack scores an average $HCR = 55\%$ and $APE = 36\%$. Linking back to what these metrics mean, an average $HCR = 55\%$ shows that for each model an average of only 55% of the adversarial samples have strong feature-level correlation with their respective perturbations. That entails an average of 45% adversarial samples per-model are loosely correlated with their perturbations. APE assesses the per-model average number of negative perturbations per sample. Results in Table 3 suggest a significant rate of negative perturbations are produced by the evasion attack. More precisely, on average across all models around 36% of the perturbations are negative (i.e., they lead the evasion strategy in the wrong direction, by increasing the likelihood of predicting the original label). Next, we expand on these highlights of our findings.

Correlation Between Perturbations and Explanations. Although an evasion attack can achieve a seemingly high aggregate evasion rate (e.g., as high as 94% accuracy drop on MLP on CuckooTrace), we notice that the correlation between each single feature perturbation and a misclassification is not guaranteed. In fact, averaged across models, 45% of the crafted adversarial samples have low-correlated perturbations more than high-correlated ones ($PSPP(x') < 0.5$), suggesting that almost 1 in 2 adversarial samples suffers from weak correlation between post-evasion explanations and pre-evasion perturbations. As a result, counting in such samples in the aggregate evasion rate would essentially give false sense of the effectiveness of an attack strategy at the granularity of each feature perturbation. We underscore that such insights would not have been possible to infer without the high-fidelity correlation analysis. In summary, these results confirm that *not all evasive predictions of an adversarial sample are correlated with the performed feature manipulations.*

Visualizing the Per-sample Perturbation Precision. Figure 3 shows the distribution of $PSPP$ values of all crafted malware samples of CuckooTrace across the 5 models. In the figure, we use the shorthand PP instead of $PSPP$ in the y-axis and we refer to the index of each sample in x-axis. The true prediction of each malware sample is $f_b(x') = 1$, while the evasive prediction is $f_b(x') = 0$ (i.e., adversarial malware sample is misclassified as benign). The red line in the middle represents the threshold τ that decides whether the adversarial sample has more positive perturbations or more negative ones. In almost all the plots, we notice the occurrence of a significant number of low-correlation adversarial malware samples ($PP(x') < \tau$) that evaded the classifier (purple circles below the red line). Once again, these findings suggest that the evasion attack results in a high number of negative perturbations. However, despite the low number of positive perturbations for these samples, the evasion is still successful. This result goes along with our previous finding that high evasion aggregate accuracy can have low correlation with performed perturbations. Thus, even for a successful evasion the perturbations at the feature-level can apparently be ineffective.

It is noteworthy that Fig. 3 exhibits an unusual behavior. Some crafted samples with a true prediction $f_b(x') = 1$ (yellow circles) appear to have high Perturbation Precision, $PP(x') > \tau$, despite the failure to flip the model's prediction from 1 to 0. This is especially true for models: LR, DT, ET and RF. On one hand, this observation suggests that even a small number of negative perturbations $(PP(x') < \tau)$ may affect the outcome of the evasion. On the other hand, it suggests potential limitations of Black-Box ML explanation methods in terms of accuracy and stability between different runs. More discussion is provided about this in Sect. 5.

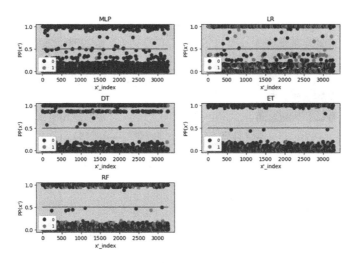

Fig. 3. Distribution of Perturbation Precision (PSPP) values of each adversarial sample across models on CuckooTrace. (Color figure online)

Correlation Analysis Across Domains and Model Architectures. While our results so far strongly suggest the importance of post-evasion correlation analysis for an in-depth assessment of an evasion attack strategy, we also observe that HCR and APE values vary across studied domains (malware, image), model architectures, and feature representations (static, dynamic). This variation speaks to the sensitivity of different domains, models, and feature values to adversarial feature perturbations with implications on robustness and dependability in the face of individual feature perturbation. In fact, ML models trained on EMBER (LGBM and DNN) showed acceptably low rate of negative perturbations (i.e., $APE = 6\%$ on average) and a high rate of samples with highly correlated perturbations (i.e., $HCR = 96\%$ on average). This suggests that static features of Windows PE malware are more sensitive to a feature perturbation considering the higher rate of negative perturbations on dynamic features in CuckooTrace. In terms of comparison between different domains and different ML models, despite the high evasion rate at sample-level, almost all ML models showed some robustness at the level of a single feature perturbation. Most importantly, RF on CuckooTrace showed the highest robustness since more than 60%

of the overall feature perturbations are negative which suggest that they did not contribute to the misclassification decision. ET on CuckooTrace ($APE = 54\%$) and CNN on MNIST ($APE = 49\%$) showed lower robustness than RF, but higher than the other models.

Summary. Our results suggest that aggregate evasion accuracy is inadequate to assess the efficacy of perturbation attack strategy. Our findings also validate that explanation-guided correlation analysis plays a crucial role in diagnosing aggregate evasion rates to winnow high-correlation adversarial samples from low-correlation ones for precise feature-level assessment of evasion accuracy.

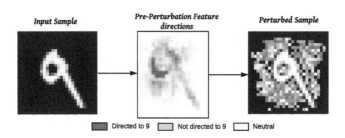

Input Sample   Pre-Perturbation Feature directions   Perturbed Sample

⬛ Directed to 9   ⬜ Not directed to 9   ☐ Neutral

Fig. 4. Example for explanation-guided feature perturbations on MNIST sample. (Color figure online)

4.4   Case Study

The correlation analysis results showed that, while an evasion strategy may result in an evasive adversarial sample, at the granularity of feature perturbations it may produce a considerable number of *negative perturbations*. In other words, the correlation analysis can be leveraged towards more accurate evasion strategy that significantly minimizes negative perturbations. In the following, we explore the potential of explanation methods to guide a more effective evasion strategy.

Explanation-Guided Evasion Strategy. In this case study, we demonstrate how a defender leverages ML explanation methods to examine pre-perturbation predictions before making feature manipulations. In particular, the *pre-perturbation feature directions* reveal *positive features* that significantly contribute to the true prediction (pink pixels in Fig. 4). Intuitively, positive features are strong candidates for perturbations, while *negative features* (blue pixels in Fig. 4) need not be perturbed since they are already directed away from the true label. *Neutral features* (white pixels in Fig. 4) are also not candidates for perturbations since they have no effect on the original label decision. We note that in this case study we consider all positive features (i.e., pink pixels) as candidates for perturbation regardless of the color intensity that represents its explanation weight. In Fig. 4, some positive pixels ($w_i > 0$) with a low explanation weight ($w_i \sim 0$) are almost neutral (i.e., closer to the white color) but still perturbed since they are directed to the true label. Using the same experimental setup, we enhance the evasion strategies used on the three datasets with *explanation-guided pre-perturbation feature selection*. Then, we measure changes to *post-evasion accuracy*, *HCR*, and *APE*.

Impact of Explanation-Guided Evasion. Table 4 suggests an overall improvement not only in aggregate evasion accuracy, but also in the correlation strength between evasion explanations and feature perturbations. Comparing the "Post-Evasion Accuracy" columns of Tables 2 and 4, using explanation-guided evasion strategy post-evasion accuracy drops for all studied models, with an average per-model drop of 13.4% (which translates to the same percentage of improvement in aggregate evasion accuracy). Interestingly, in 4 out of the 5 models in CuckooTrace, post-evasion accuracy drops to zero, with up to 21% drop in post-evasion accuracy for models such as LR. We note that the eventual complete evasion in almost all models in CuckooTrace is most likely attributed to the binary nature of the features, where the explanation-guided feature selection filters out negative features and leaves only positive features that are flipped with just one perturbation. Comparing the HCR columns of Tables 4 and 3, we notice an increase in HCR for all studied models. On average, HCR increased by 27% per-model, which shows the positive utility of the pre-perturbation explanations that guided the evasion strategy to perturb positive features instead of negative ones. Again, comparing the APE columns of Tables 4 and 3, we notice a significant drop in APE, with an average per-model decrease of 20%, which indicates a decrease in the number of *negative perturbations*. Better performance in terms of post-evasion accuracy is also observed for all studied target models.

Table 4. Post-evasion accuracy, HCR, and APE using explanation-guided evasion.

Dataset	Model	Post-evasion accuracy	HCR	APE
CuckooTrace	MLP	0%	92.03%	14.22%
CuckooTrace	LR	0%	96.25%	6%
CuckooTrace	RF	0%	48.53%	51.31%
CuckooTrace	DT	1.41%	98.84%	3.41%
CuckooTrace	ET	0%	48.11%	1.21%
EMBER	LGBM	27.16%	99.58%	2.69%
EMBER	DNN	11.7%	97.8%	2.71%
MNIST	CNN	24.67%	64.5%	43.4%

We note that although we perturb only *positive features*, in the APE column of Table 4 all values are still non-zero. Ideally, the explanation method would guide the perturbation strategy to perform only positive perturbations and make no mistaken perturbations. Nevertheless, we still observe a minimal percentage of *negative perturbations* due to the inherent limitations of the accuracy and stability of explanations by LIME and SHAP, which is also substantiated by recent studies [15,50] that evaluated LIME and SHAP among other ML explanation methods. We will expand on limitations of ML explainers in Sect. 5.

Summary. An explanation-guided feature selection strategy leads to more effective evasion results both in terms of aggregate evasion accuracy and effectiveness at the level of each feature manipulation.

5   Discussion and Limitations

Recent studies [15,50] have systematically compared the performance of ML explanation methods especially on security systems. In addition to general evaluation criteria (e.g., explanation accuracy and sparsity), Warnecke et al. [50] focused on other security-relevant evaluation metrics (e.g., stability, efficiency, and robustness). Fan et al. [15] also proposed a similar framework that led to the same evaluation results. Next, we highlight limitations of LIME [39] and SHAP [33] based on *accuracy* (degree to which relevant features are captured in an explanation), *stability* (how much explanations vary between runs), and *robustness* (the extent to which explanations and prediction are coupled).

Limitations of Explanation Methods. While LIME and SHAP produce more accurate results compared with other black-box explanation methods (e.g., DeepLIFT [44], LEMNA [23]), the *accuracy* of the explanation may vary across different ML model architectures (e.g., MLP, RF, DT, etc.), and across different ML tasks/datasets (e.g., CuckooTrace, EMBER, and MNIST). For instance, the inherent linearity of LIME's approximator could negatively influence its accuracy and stability in explaining predictions of complex models such as RF and ET. More importantly, like all learning-based methods, LIME and SHAP are sensitive to non-determinism (e.g., random initialization, stochastic optimization) which affect their *stability* between different runs. In other words, it is likely to observe a slight variation in the output of multiple runs performed by the same explanation method using the same input data. In fact, we observed that the average difference between Shapley values (i.e., feature importance weights) returned by SHAP is around 1% over 100 runs on the same MNIST sample. Such variation in ML explanation outputs might partly explain some of the unexpected results of our explanation-guided analysis that we noted in Sect. 4.3.

Vulnerability of Explanation Methods. Another issue worth considering is *robustness* of ML explanation methods against adversarial attacks. Studies [19,25,53] have demonstrated that the explanation results are sensitive to small systematic feature perturbations that preserve the predicted label. Such attacks can potentially alter the explanation results, which might in effect influence our explanation-guided analysis. Consequently, our analysis may produce less precise results for correlation metrics such as HCR and APE. Considering the utility of ML explanations we demonstrated in this work, we hope that our framework can be instantiated for adversarial perturbations performed in the problem-space. We note, however, that there needs to be careful consideration in mapping the units of adversarial perturbations in problem space manipulations (e.g., the organ transplant notions proposed in [37]) to the metrics we proposed in Sect. 3. Finally, vulnerability to adversarial attacks is a broader problem in ML, and progress in defense strategies will inspire defense for ML explanation methods.

6 Related Work

Comparing how evasion is assessed, our approach is complementary to prior work which rely on aggregate evasion accuracy. Next, we shed light on prior work focusing on evasion of image classification and malware/intrusion detection.

Image Classification. Several evasion methods have been proposed for image classification tasks. Some of the most notable ones are: Fast Gradient Sign Method (FGSM) [20], Basic Iterative Method (BIM) [30], Projected Gradient Descent (PGD) method [34], and Carlini & Wagner (CW) method [11].

Windows Malware. Kolosnjaji et al. [27] proposed a gradient-based attack against MalConv [38] by appending bytes (in the range 2KB-10KB) to the overlay of a PE. As a follow-up to [27], Demetrio et al. [13] extended the adversarial sample crafting method by demonstrating the feasibility of evasion by manipulating 58 bytes in the DOS header of PE. Suciu et al. [49] explored FGSM [20] to craft adversarial samples against MalConv [27] by padding adversarial payloads between sections in a PE if there is space to perform padding.

Hu and Tan [26] train a substitute model using a GAN to fit a black-box malware detector trained on API call traces. Other works utilize reinforcement learning (RL) to evade malware classifiers. For instance, Anderson et al. [8] aim to limit perturbations to a select set of transformations that are guaranteed to preserve semantic integrity of a sample using RL. Additionally, Apruzzese et al. [9] generate realistic attack samples that evade botnet detectors through deep RL. The generated samples can be used for adversarial learning. Rosenberg et al. [41] adopt the Jacobian-based feature augmentation method introduced in [36] to synthesize training examples to inject fake API calls to PEs at runt-time. Using the augmented dataset, they locally train a substitute model to evade a target RNN black-box malware detector based on API call features.

Android Malware. Like [26], Grosse et al. [21] demonstrate evasion by adding API calls to malicious Android APKs. Yang et al. [52] explore semantic analysis of malicious APKs with the goal of increasing resilience of Android malware detectors against evasion attacks. Recently, Pierazzi et al. [37] take a promising step towards formalization of the mapping between feature space and problem space on Android malware detector.

PDF Malware. Srndic et al. [48] demonstrate vulnerabilities of deployed PDF malware detectors using constrained manipulation with semantic preservation. Xu et al. [51] use genetic algorithms to manipulate ASTs of malicious PDFs to generate adversarial variants while preserving document structure (syntax).

Explanation Methods. In a black-box setting, LIME [39], Anchors [40], SHAP [33], and [22] are among black-box explanation methods that use local approximation. Other methods (e.g., [17,32]) use input perturbation by monitoring prediction deltas. DeepLIFT [44] explains feature importance with respect to a reference output, while white-box explanation techniques (e.g., [45–47]) use gradient-based feature importance estimation. Recent studies [15,19,25,50] explore the utility of explanation methods across criteria such as accuracy, stability, and robustness of explanations. A more recent interesting application is the use of SHAP signatures to detect adversarial examples in DNNs [16].

In summary, prior work typically rely on comparing pre-perturbation accuracy and post-perturbation accuracy to evaluate ML evasion attacks, which lacks deeper diagnosis of the attack's success. We propose complementary suite of metrics to map a single feature perturbation to its contribution to evasion.

7 Conclusion

We introduced the first explanation-guided methodology for the diagnosis of ML evasion attacks. To do so, we use feature importance-based ML explanation methods to enable high-fidelity correlation analysis between pre-evasion perturbations and post-evasion prediction explanations. To systematize the analysis, we proposed and evaluated a novel suite of metrics. Using image classification and malware detection as representative ML tasks, we demonstrated the utility of the methodology across diverse ML model architectures and feature representations. Through a case study we additionally confirm that our methodology enables evasion attack improvement via pre-evasion feature direction analysis.

Acknowledgements. We thank our shepherd Giovanni Apruzzese and the anonymous reviewers for their insightful feedback that immensely improved this paper.

References

1. CNET freeware site (2020). https://download.cnet.com/s/software/windows/?licenseType=Free
2. Cuckoo sandbox (2020). https://cuckoosandbox.org
3. LIEF project (2020). https://github.com/lief-project/LIEF
4. Virus share (2020). https://virusshare.com
5. Virus total (2020). https://www.virustotal.com/gui/home/upload
6. Ali, A., Eshete, B.: Best-effort adversarial approximation of black-box malware classifiers. In: Park, N., Sun, K., Foresti, S., Butler, K., Saxena, N. (eds.) SecureComm 2020. LNICST, vol. 335, pp. 318–338. Springer, Cham (2020). https://doi.org/10.1007/978-3-030-63086-7_18
7. Anderson, H.S., Roth, P.: EMBER: an open dataset for training static PE malware machine learning models. ArXiv e-prints (2018)
8. Anderson, H.S., Kharkar, A., Filar, B., Evans, D., Roth, P.: Learning to evade static PE machine learning malware models via reinforcement learning. CoRR arXiv:1801.08917 (2018)
9. Apruzzese, G., Andreolini, M., Marchetti, M., Venturi, A., Colajanni, M.: Deep reinforcement adversarial learning against botnet evasion attacks. IEEE Trans. Netw. Serv. Manage. **17**, 1975–1987 (2020)
10. Biggio, B., Roli, F.: Wild patterns: ten years after the rise of adversarial machine learning. Pattern Recogn. **84**, 317–331 (2018)
11. Carlini, N., Wagner, D.A.: Towards evaluating the robustness of neural networks. In: IEEE SP, pp. 39–57 (2017)

12. Dahl, G.E., Yu, D., Deng, L., Acero, A.: Context-dependent pre-trained deep neural networks for large-vocabulary speech recognition. IEEE Trans. Audio Speech Lang. Process. **20**(1), 30–42 (2012)
13. Demetrio, L., Biggio, B., Lagorio, G., Roli, F., Armando, A.: Explaining vulnerabilities of deep learning to adversarial malware binaries. In: Proceedings of the Third Italian Conference on Cyber Security (2019)
14. Demontis, A., et al.: Yes, machine learning can be more secure! A case study on android malware detection. IEEE TDSC **16**(4), 711–724 (2019)
15. Fan, M., Wei, W., Xie, X., Liu, Y., Guan, X., Liu, T.: Can we trust your explanations? Sanity checks for interpreters in android malware analysis. IEEE Trans. Inf. Forensics Secur. **16**, 838–853 (2021)
16. Fidel, G., Bitton, R., Shabtai, A.: When explainability meets adversarial learning: Detecting adversarial examples using SHAP signatures. In: IEEE IJCNN, pp. 1–8 (2020)
17. Fong, R.C., Vedaldi, A.: Interpretable explanations of black boxes by meaningful perturbation. In: IEEE ICCV, pp. 3449–3457 (2017)
18. Gao, F., et al.: DeepCC: a novel deep learning-based framework for cancer molecular subtype classification. Oncogenesis **8**(9), 1–12 (2019)
19. Ghorbani, A., Abid, A., Zou, J.: Interpretation of neural networks is fragile. In: AAAI, vol. 33 (2017)
20. Goodfellow, I.J., Shlens, J., Szegedy, C.: Explaining and harnessing adversarial examples. In: ICLR (2015)
21. Grosse, K., Papernot, N., Manoharan, P., Backes, M., McDaniel, P.: Adversarial examples for malware detection. In: Foley, S.N., Gollmann, D., Snekkenes, E. (eds.) ESORICS 2017. LNCS, vol. 10493, pp. 62–79. Springer, Cham (2017). https://doi.org/10.1007/978-3-319-66399-9_4
22. Guidotti, R., Monreale, A., Ruggieri, S., Pedreschi, D., Turini, F., Giannotti, F.: Local rule-based explanations of black box decision systems. CoRR arXiv:1805.10820 (2018)
23. Guo, W., Mu, D., Xu, J., Su, P., Wang, G., Xing, X.: LEMNA: explaining deep learning based security applications. In: ACM SIGSAC CCS, pp. 364–379 (2018)
24. Han, D., et al.: Practical traffic-space adversarial attacks on learning-based nidss. CoRR arXiv:2005.07519 (2020)
25. Heo, J., Joo, S., Moon, T.: Fooling neural network interpretations via adversarial model manipulation (2019)
26. Hu, W., Tan, Y.: Generating adversarial malware examples for black-box attacks based on GAN. CoRR arXiv:1702.05983 (2017)
27. Kolosnjaji, B., et al.: Adversarial malware binaries: evading deep learning for malware detection in executables. In: EUSIPCO, pp. 533–537 (2018)
28. Kreuk, F., Barak, A., Aviv-Reuven, S., Baruch, M., Pinkas, B., Keshet, J.: Deceiving end-to-end deep learning malware detectors using adversarial examples (2018)
29. Krizhevsky, A., Sutskever, I., Hinton, G.E.: ImageNet classification with deep convolutional neural networks. Commun. ACM **60**(6), 84–90 (2017)
30. Kurakin, A., Goodfellow, I.J., Bengio, S.: Adversarial machine learning at scale. CoRR arXiv:1611.01236 (2016)
31. LeCun, Y., Cortes, C., Burges, C.J.: The MNIST database of handwritten digits (2020). http://yann.lecun.com/exdb/mnist/
32. Li, J., Monroe, W., Jurafsky, D.: Understanding neural networks through representation erasure. CoRR arXiv:1612.08220 (2016)
33. Lundberg, S.M., Lee, S.: A unified approach to interpreting model predictions. In: NeurIPS, pp. 4765–4774 (2017)

34. Madry, A., Makelov, A., Schmidt, L., Tsipras, D., Vladu, A.: Towards deep learning models resistant to adversarial attacks. CoRR arXiv:1706.06083 (2017)
35. Papernot, N., McDaniel, P.D., Goodfellow, I.J.: Transferability in machine learning: from phenomena to black-box attacks using adversarial samples. CoRR arXiv:1605.07277 (2016)
36. Papernot, N., McDaniel, P.D., Goodfellow, I.J., Jha, S., Celik, Z.B., Swami, A.: Practical black-box attacks against deep learning systems using adversarial examples. CoRR arXiv:1602.02697 (2016)
37. Pierazzi, F., Pendlebury, F., Cortellazzi, J., Cavallaro, L.: Intriguing properties of adversarial ML attacks in the problem space. In: IEEE SP (2020)
38. Raff, E., Barker, J., Sylvester, J., Brandon, R., Catanzaro, B., Nicholas, C.K.: Malware detection by eating a whole EXE. In: AAAI Workshops, pp. 268–276 (2018)
39. Ribeiro, M.T., Singh, S., Guestrin, C.: "Why should I trust you?": explaining the predictions of any classifier. In: ACM SIGKDD, pp. 1135–1144 (2016)
40. Ribeiro, M.T., Singh, S., Guestrin, C.: Anchors: high-precision model-agnostic explanations. In: AAAI, pp. 1527–1535 (2018)
41. Rosenberg, I., Shabtai, A., Rokach, L., Elovici, Y.: Generic black-box end-to-end attack against state of the art API call based malware classifiers. In: Bailey, M., Holz, T., Stamatogiannakis, M., Ioannidis, S. (eds.) RAID 2018. LNCS, vol. 11050, pp. 490–510. Springer, Cham (2018). https://doi.org/10.1007/978-3-030-00470-5_23
42. Sallab, A.E., Abdou, M., Perot, E., Yogamani, S.K.: Deep reinforcement learning framework for autonomous driving. CoRR arXiv:1704.02532 (2017)
43. Shapley, L.: A value for n-person games (1953)
44. Shrikumar, A., Greenside, P., Kundaje, A.: Learning important features through propagating activation differences. In: ICML, pp. 3145–3153 (2017)
45. Simonyan, K., Vedaldi, A., Zisserman, A.: Deep inside convolutional networks: visualising image classification models and saliency maps. In: ICLR Workshop Track Proceedings (2014)
46. Smilkov, D., Thorat, N., Kim, B., Viégas, F.B., Wattenberg, M.: SmoothGrad: removing noise by adding noise. CoRR arXiv:1706.03825 (2017)
47. Springenberg, J.T., Dosovitskiy, A., Brox, T., Riedmiller, M.A.: Striving for simplicity: the all convolutional net. In: ICLR Workshop Track Proceedings (2015)
48. Srndic, N., Laskov, P.: Practical evasion of a learning-based classifier: a case study. In: IEEE SP, pp. 197–211 (2014)
49. Suciu, O., Coull, S.E., Johns, J.: Exploring adversarial examples in malware detection. In: IEEE SP Workshops, pp. 8–14 (2019)
50. Warnecke, A., Arp, D., Wressnegger, C., Rieck, K.: Evaluating explanation methods for deep learning in security. In: IEEE EuroSP, pp. 158–174 (2020)
51. Xu, W., Qi, Y., Evans, D.: Automatically evading classifiers: a case study on PDF malware classifiers. In: NDSS (2016)
52. Yang, W., Kong, D., Xie, T., Gunter, C.A.: Malware detection in adversarial settings: exploiting feature evolutions and confusions in android apps. In: ACSAC, pp. 288–302 (2017)
53. Zhang, X., Wang, N., Shen, H., Ji, S., Luo, X., Wang, T.: Interpretable deep learning under fire. In: USENIX Security, pp. 1659–1676 (2020)

ToFi: An Algorithm to Defend Against Byzantine Attacks in Federated Learning

Qi Xia$^{(\boxtimes)}$, Zeyi Tao, and Qun Li

Department of Computer Science, William and Mary, Williamsburg, VA 23185, USA
{qxia,ztao,liqun}@cs.wm.edu

Abstract. In distributed gradient descent based machine learning model training, workers periodically upload locally computed gradients or weights to the parameter server (PS). Byzantine attacks take place when some workers upload wrong gradients or weights, i.e., the information received by the PS is not always the true values computed by workers. Approaches such as score-based, median-based, and distance-based defense algorithms were proposed previously, but all of them made the asumptions: (1) the dataset on each worker is independent and identically distributed (i.i.d.), and (2) the majority of all participating workers are honest. These assumptions are not realistic in federated learning where each worker may keep its non-i.i.d. private dataset and malicious workers may take over the majority in some iterations. In this paper, we propose a novel reference dataset based algorithm along with a practical Two-Filter algorithm (ToFi) to defend against Byzantine attacks in federated learning. Our experiments highlight the effectiveness of our algorithm compared with previous algorithms in different settings.

Keywords: Byzantine attacks · Federated learning

1 Introduction

Federated learning [6,11] is a collaborative machine learning scheme in which the participating machines hold their local data without exchanging them. Combined with edge computing, it has the advantages of easy implementation [14], better privacy [18,19], and communication efficiency improvement [9,10,13]. The machines (or workers and nodes) performing the training task in federated learning upload intermediate computation results to the parameter server (PS) for the aggregation and model update. In addition, federated learning sometimes only randomly selects some of the nodes to perform the computation in one synchronization round, and meanwhile, each node usually performs self-update for several intervals for this synchronization round. This significantly reduces the communication cost between nodes and the PS. Therefore, federated learning attracts more interests in both academic research and industry application.

Because federated learning is a special kind of distributed machine learning, it is naturally subject to security attacks when multiple nodes communicate

J. Garcia-Alfaro et al. (Eds.): SecureComm 2021, LNICST 398, pp. 229–248, 2021.
https://doi.org/10.1007/978-3-030-90019-9_12

with each other. For example, in classic distributed machine learning, Byzantine problems exist when some nodes undergo attacks and do not perform honestly when uploading the computation results to the PS. Thus the training process will be dominated by dishonest nodes. This problem becomes even more severe in federated learning. In federated learning settings, nodes are from different resources, among which some are trusted and some can be untrusted. This is different from the classic distributed machine learning, where we assume all the nodes are in the laboratory environment and are under control. In this scenario, nodes in the federated learning system are more likely to be attacked or compromised intentionally or unintentionally. For example, many users collaborate to train an image recognition model, during which some users may upload a cat picture and mark it as a dog. This operation apparently affects the performance of the model training. When the number of such users or activities is large, the training process will lead to a wrong model.

Although there are some algorithms that work well toward solving Byzantine problems in traditional distributed machine learning, these algorithms do not perform well for federated learning due to the following two major problems:

- The distribution of the dataset on each node may be different. Data heterogeneity is an important feature of federated learning. It by design comes along with the local data isolation in each node. Because each node can keep its own private dataset, the data distribution between different nodes may be significantly different. Therefore the computational results of each node based on the local dataset can be very different such that it is difficult and sometimes impossible to distinguish between honest nodes and Byzantine nodes.
- Honest majority is not a reasonable assumption in federated learning. A typical assumption made in Byzantine machine learning problems for traditional distributed machine learning is that honest nodes are the majority, which means the number of honest nodes is more than half of the total nodes. Although we can assume the honest nodes are the majority in federated learning, in each synchronization round, we cannot assume that there are more honest nodes in the random selection. For example, we have 100 nodes in total, among which 20 nodes are malicious. In each synchronization, we randomly choose 10 nodes to do the computation. It is possible that more than 5 malicious nodes are selected. This will make all the previous algorithms ineffective because malicious nodes can take over the training. Moreover, it is hard for some of the previous algorithms to be implemented in federated learning. For example, Zeno [22] and FABA [16] need to estimate the ratio of Byzantine nodes, which is hard because the ratio changes in different synchronization rounds in federated learning.

In this paper, we carefully investigate these two challenges of Byzantine problems in federated learning and propose a naive algorithm and modify it to an efficient algorithm ToFi to defend against Byzantine attacks. In summary, our contributions are:

- We compare the major differences of Byzantine problems between federated learning and distributed learning and analyze why previous Byzantine-resilient algorithms do not work well in federated learning.
- We propose a naive algorithm to solve Byzantine problems in federated learning. More importantly, we modify it to an efficient two-filter reference dataset-based algorithm ToFi to efficiently defend against Byzantine attacks in practical implementations.
- We conduct several simulated experiments in various heterogeneous environments to compare ToFi and other existing algorithms to show our superior performance of defending against Byzantine attacks in federated learning.

2   Related Works

In order to resist Byzantine attacks in classic distributed machine learning, some algorithms have been proposed. Basically, there are three directions for defending against Byzantine attacks: score-based, median-based, and distance-based algorithms.

The idea of score-based algorithms is that there is a scoring system on the server side such that this system assigns corresponding scores for each uploaded gradient. This is the earliest idea to defend against Byzantine attacks in this area. Blanchard et al. first proposed an algorithm called Krum [2]. In Krum's design, each gradient's score is based on the summation of the distances to its nearest neighbors. Then the server simply chooses the gradient with the smallest score as the aggregation result. This gradient has the property that it is the closest one that nears its neighbors, so it should come from an honest node with high probability. However, because only one gradient is selected as the aggregation result, a lot of useful information from other uploaded gradients is missing. Therefore, the convergence speed of Krum is slow. After this, they also proposed another algorithm to resist asynchronous Byzantine attacks [4]. In addition, Xie et al. also proposed methods based on a reference dataset to give scores for each node to solve fault-tolerance problems in distributed machine learning [21,22]. Their scoring systems use the reference dataset to examine the loss of each uploaded gradient and the server finally chooses the gradients that result in smaller loss.

Later the idea of defending against Byzantine attacks has been moved to the geometric median-based algorithms. By definition, the geometric median of a discrete set of points in Euclidean space is a point that minimizes the sum of distances to the sample points. For example, Xie et al. proposed geometric median, marginal median, and median-around-median [20], Yin et al. proposed coordinate-wised median [24], Lili et al. proposed a batch normalized median [3], Alistarh et al. proposed a more complicated modification of median-based methods called ByzantineSGD [1]. The geometric median is an important estimator of location in statistics and it can preserve the majority location information of the sample points, which in Byzantine problems, represent more about the honest update information. Although median-based algorithms usually have better convergence performance than score-based algorithms, they also have one short-coming. The geometric median of several sample points usually needs an iterative method to solve and thus the computational time is considerable. On the server side, it takes a too long time for the aggregation, so the training speed will be slower.

Distance-bases algorithms conduct the distance information to remove the dishonest gradients. From the i.i.d. dataset and central limit theorem, the honest gradients should be close to each other. Therefore, in order to defend against Byzantine problems in this scenario, the problem is transformed to outlier gradient removal based on distance information. Xia et al. proposed an alternative method called FABA [16]. Instead of using median-based methods, they used Euclidean distance to remove outlier gradients. They adaptively remove outliers based on the distance between the current average gradient and the current remaining gradients. They later provided another Byzantine-resilient algorithm for large-scale distributed machine learning [17]. By using simple statistics of multi-dimensional mean and standard deviation, it can remove the outliers in $O(n)$ time. It has comparable performance with other algorithms while keeping a fast training speed.

3   Preliminary

3.1   Federated Learning

Here we give a brief introduction about federated learning, which is a special kind of the distributed learning. Figure 1 is the structure of one synchronization in federated learning at time t. It has one central server PS and n workers $worker_1, \cdots, worker_n$. In each iteration, the PS randomly selects m workers. The selected workers then fetch the global model from the PS and perform the computation on their local dataset. Without loss of generality, we assume $worker_1$ to $worker_m$ are selected. On the worker side, those participated workers then update their local model on their private dataset ξ_i. If we assume the loss function on the neural network is $f(\cdot)$, weight at time t is w_t and learning rate at time t is γ_t, stochastic gradient descent will update the local weight for $worker_i$ at time $t + 1$ as:

$$w_{t+1}^i = w_t - \gamma_t \cdot \left.\frac{\partial f(w|\xi_i)}{\partial w}\right|_{w_t} \qquad (i = 1, 2, \cdots, m) \qquad (1)$$

On the PS side, it receives the updated weights uploaded by all the participated workers. PS uses an aggregation function $A(\cdot)$ to aggregate the uploaded weights and update the global model.

$$w_{t+1} = A(w_{t+1}^1, w_{t+1}^2, \cdots, w_{t+1}^m) \qquad (2)$$

In practice, we usually simply use a weighted average function to aggregate the uploaded weights.

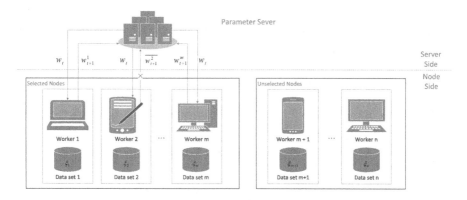

Fig. 1. Federated learning with Byzantine attackers at time t

3.2 Byzantine Problem

Byzantine problems exist when some workers are attacked or compromised and do not compute or upload weights correctly. In this scenario, the uploaded weights w_{t+1}^i in (2) may not be the real w_{t+1}^i computed by (1). Theoretically, the generalized Byzantine model that is defined in [2,20] is:

Definition 1 (Generalized Byzantine Model)

$$\overline{w_{t+1}^i} = \begin{cases} w_{t+1}^i & if\ i\text{-}th\ worker\ is\ honest \\ a_i \neq w_{t+1}^i & otherwise \end{cases} \tag{3}$$

Here we denote $\overline{w_{t+1}^i}$ as the actual weights received by PS from $worker_i$. In each iteration of the training phase, some workers may become Byzantine workers and upload attack weights a_i to the PS. As we can see in Fig. 1, $worker_2$ here is a Byzantine attacker. It uploads an alternative $\overline{w_{t+1}^2}$ rather than the actual w_{t+1}^2 to the PS. The PS, at the same time, does not know $worker_2$ is compromised. It aggregates all the uploaded weights and sends the incorrectly updated weights back to all workers. According to Theorem 1 in [16], when the aggregation function is an average function, one Byzantine attacker can take over the aggregation result and lead the whole training process to an incorrect phase.

3.3 Discussions About Byzantine Problems in Federated Learning

In the introduction, we have discussed two major differences between traditional distributed machine learning and federated learning. These two differences make it extremely difficult to solve Byzantine problems in federated learning. For example, if we assume the number of Byzantine nodes is equal to the number of honest nodes and let Byzantine nodes have the same data as honest nodes with different labels, the PS is not able to distinguish which training results are real.

Thus it is not able to solve Byzantine problems without other information. In addition, when the dataset is not i.i.d. and the computational results are totally different from each other, it is very hard for the PS to distinguish between honest results and Byzantine results.

Therefore, in order to solve Byzantine problems in federated learning, more conditions are needed. Here like [7] and [21,22], we assume that PS holds a small reference dataset to solve Byzantine problems in federated learning. Our theoretical assumptions are defined in Sect. 4.

4   Problem Definition

Let D and D_i respectively represent the distribution for the whole dataset and each worker. We first assume that the distributed environment is heterogeneous.

Assumption 1 (Heterogeneous environment). *Updated weights of each worker are computed based on their private non i.i.d. dataset, i.e.,*

$$w_{t+1}^i = w_t - \gamma_t \cdot \left. \frac{\partial f(w|\xi_i)}{\partial w} \right|_{w_t}, \quad \xi_i \sim D_i \quad (i = 1, 2, \cdots, m) \tag{4}$$

Here m is the number of selected workers in the federated learning system.

The second assumption is for the Byzantine environment. The Byzantine model is given by Definition 1.

Assumption 2 (Byzantine environment). *Denote $B_t = \{i | \overline{w_{t+1}^i} \neq w_{t+1}^i\}$. We have: (i) B_t can be different from each other; (ii) $0 \leq |B_t| \leq n$.*

Assumption 2 states two features of Byzantine attacks. First, Byzantine attacks can target any machine in the distributed system and can change target machines during the training process. This means that different sets of workers may be attacked during different iterations of the training. Second, there is no upper limit of the number that Byzantine attacks may happen in one iteration, i.e., in one iteration, it is possible that the majority of workers suffer Byzantine attacks.

Assumption 3 (Reference dataset). *PS holds a small reference dataset ξ_R such that $\xi_R \sim D$.*

Assumption 3 is reasonable because, in practice, PS is usually able to collect some data. The size of the reference dataset can be very small, for example, 100 to 500 is good enough, so we can assume PS has a reference dataset. We will talk about the existence of the reference dataset in Sect. 5.1.

With these three assumptions, the problem is finding an appropriate aggregation algorithm $A^*(\cdot)$ and using (2) to update weights until convergence point w_c such that

$$A^* = \arg\min_{A(\cdot)} f(w_c)$$

It is obvious that a simple average is not able to resist Byzantine attacks. Our goal is to find a Byzantine robust aggregation algorithm in federated learning.

5 Algorithm

5.1 Naive Algorithm

Because the PS has no other information about the dataset but only uploaded weights, it must have some extra information to filter and aggregate weights. The key of our algorithm is that PS holds a small reference dataset. As this reference dataset has the assumption that $\xi_R \sim D$, this guarantees that the reference dataset has the same distribution as the whole dataset and the most information about it. The whole dataset here is a pretty tricky definition. Since some workers are compromised, their subdatasets are inaccessible by the PS. This implies that the accessible dataset may only contain part of the whole dataset. However, we still take the whole dataset as the optimization goal, and the reference dataset is chosen from this distribution even though some data are hidden by Byzantine attackers. Because the PS collects reference dataset on its own and PS and all nodes share the same training goal, it is reasonable to assume there exists such reference dataset. We will use the reference dataset to examine the weights w_{t+1}^i uploaded by each worker and aggregate them to update the weights for each iteration.

The naive algorithm is described in Algorithm 1. Because we do not have access to each worker, our algorithm is only running on the PS side. In the PS, its inputs are the weights $\overline{w_{t+1}^1}, \overline{w_{t+1}^2}, \cdots, \overline{w_{t+1}^m}$ that are computed and uploaded by the selected workers. The output in one iteration should return the updated weights to all the workers.

Algorithm 1 Reference dataset based naive algorithm (PS Side)

Input:
 Weights computed from $worker_1$, $worker_2$, $\cdots$, $worker_m$: $G_w = \{w_{t+1}^1, w_{t+1}^2, \cdots, \overline{w_{t+1}^m}\}$;
 The reference dataset ξ_R.
Output:
 Weights at time $t+1$: w_{t+1}.

1: Solve α_i by minimizing α-weighted loss: $\alpha_i = \arg\min_{\sum \alpha_i = 1} f(\sum_{i=1}^m \alpha_i \overline{w_{t+1}^i}, \xi_R)$;
2: Aggregate weights by $w_{t+1} = \sum_i^m \alpha_i \overline{w_{t+1}^i}$;
3: Send back w_{t+1} to each worker.

Assume the weights at $t+1$ is w_{t+1}, it should be updated by w_t using the α-based weighted average. In each step, we minimize the loss on the reference dataset ξ_R to get the corresponding α_i. We have:

$$\arg\min f(w_{t+1}, \xi_R) = \arg\min_{\alpha_i} f(\sum_{i=1}^m \alpha_i \overline{w_{t+1}^i}, \xi_R) \qquad (5)$$

It should be noted that since $\xi_R \sim D$ while D stands for the distribution of the whole dataset, we can think that $f(\cdot, \xi_R)$ and $f(\cdot, \xi)$ are similar. Therefore our goal is going to minimize (5) to compute α_i.

Let us take a look at the (5). In fact, $\sum_{i=1}^{m} \alpha_i \overline{w_{t+1}^i}$ is a linear combination of $\overline{w_{t+1}^i}$. If we denote each $\overline{w_{t+1}^i}$ as a coordinate in a $(m-1)$-dimensional space $\mathbb{W}$, then solving α_i transforms to finding a point in the space $\mathbb{W}$ that minimizes a function $f(\cdot | w_t^i, \xi_R)$. We can use several existing techniques to find this minimal point. Grid method is an intuitive way with slow but effective performance. It divides the space into several grid points and tries to find a point with the lowest loss function value. However, its time complexity increases exponentially with the dimension. We can also use the classic gradient descent to find the optimization solution.

In addition, we can show the intuition of the correctness of this algorithm. In each iteration, we are going to choose the best updated direction of the weights on the reference dataset. Because this direction is an α-weighted average of all uploaded weights and it minimizes the loss function, assuming we have solved α_i, we have:

$$f(\sum_{i=1}^{m} \alpha_i \overline{w_{t+1}^i}, \xi_R) \leq f(\overline{w_{t+1}^k}, \xi_R) \tag{6}$$

This is because α_i is obtained by minimizing the loss function. We can get (6) by setting the α-weight of $w_t^{(k)}$ to be 1 and all the other α-weights to be 0. (6) shows that at least the performance of each iteration on the reference dataset is better than any worker, including honest workers and Byzantine workers. Mathematically, using the same idea, we can prove the following lemma:

Lemma 1. *The α-weights that we get from Algorithm 1 Step 1 introduce the smaller loss on the reference dataset than just ideally taking the average of all the honest weights in each iteration.*

Proof. Without loss of generality, denote the first p workers are honest and the rest are attack workers, i.e., $w_{t+1}^1, w_{t+1}^2, \cdots, w_{t+1}^p$ are true weights from honest workers and $w_{t+1}^{p+1}, w_{t+1}^{p+2}, \cdots, w_{t+1}^m$ are true gradients from dishonest workers. Then the loss of only taking the average of honest weights $loss_{honest}$ is:

$$loss_{honest} = f(\sum_{i=1}^{p} \frac{1}{p} w_{t+1}^i, \xi_R) \tag{7}$$

By the definition of α-weights, we have:

$$f(\sum_{i=1}^{m} \alpha_i \overline{w_{t+1}^i}, \xi_R) \leq loss_{honest} \tag{8}$$

This is because the right of (8) is obtained by letting $\alpha_i = \frac{1}{p}$ for $i = 1, 2, \cdots, p$ and all the other $\alpha_i = 0$. Since $\xi_R \sim D$, α-weighted average has smaller loss in each iteration.

We know that even if we only take the weights from one of the honest workers, the training can still converge to a reasonable model. When we have more workers, although there are some Byzantine workers, the loss function examination on the reference dataset and α-weighted average can help to get a reasonable model.

5.2 ToFi Algorithm

With the help of the reference dataset, the naive algorithm can defend against Byzantine attacks. However, this naive solution is hard to implement in practice. First of all, this method relies too much on the reference dataset. Therefore, it is more like searching minimal points on the space of the reference dataset using the computation weight projections from the local dataset to this space. Secondly, this naive method is lacking in solving the case that in some iterations, all of the participated nodes are attacked and become malicious. Thirdly, it is time-consuming to solve the optimization problem in each synchronization.

In order to mitigate these problems, we modify the naive algorithm to our reference dataset-based two-filter algorithm ToFi. The core ideas of ToFi are below. First, in order to approximate the α-weight in the naive algorithm, we adopt the softmax function of the examined loss on the reference dataset for each worker so that the worker with a smaller loss will get a larger α-weight. Second, in order to deal with the abnormal loss received by the PS, we adopt two filters based on the normalized loss and update similarity to remove outlier updates. The details of our enhanced algorithm are described in Algorithm 2.

Let us take a look at Algorithm 2. It is an adaptive way to compute the aggregated weight in a naive algorithm. In summary, there are two filters: reference dataset-based loss filter and update similarity-based filter. Those filters are designed to remove outlier weights. The detailed discussions are below.

Reference dataset-based loss filter. The reference dataset here is used to examine the performance of the uploaded weights computed by each node from their private dataset. Because of the heterogeneity of the data distribution, the uploaded weights may not be similar to each other. However, in the space of the whole dataset, the loss function should have a decreasing trend for those uploaded weights. Because the reference dataset is a subspace of the whole dataset, it can recognize this trend by examining the loss. Therefore, the reference dataset is an effective way to find how the uploaded weights perform and distinguish computational results between Byzantine nodes and honest nodes. In order to examine the performance of different nodes, the PS firstly computes the loss l_i based on the reference dataset. Then it normalizes l_i and filters out the weights with relatively larger loss using a loss filter parameter τ. The intuition behind this filter comes from Fig. 1 in [16] and Fig. 2 in [22], that is, Byzantine nodes must perform very badly in order to successfully attack the training process and therefore, the loss of the reference dataset must be much larger than those honest nodes. Through the normalization and filter process, it is easy to remove those outlier weights.

Algorithm 2 ToFi Algorithm (*PS* Side)

Input:

Weights computed from $worker_1$ to $worker_m$: $G_w = \{\overline{w_{t+1}^1}, \overline{w_{t+1}^2}, \cdots, \overline{w_{t+1}^m}\}$;

Weights at time $t, t-1$: w_t, w_{t-1};

Learning rate at time $t, t-1$: γ_t, γ_{t-1};

Reference dataset ξ_R;

Predefined loss filter parameter τ;

Predefined similarity filter parameter ζ.

Output:

Weights at time $t+1$: w_{t+1}.

1: Examine the loss for each worker with reference dataset $l_i = f(\overline{w_{t+1}^i}, \xi_R), i = 1, 2, \cdots, m$;

2: Compute the mean $\mu = \frac{1}{m} \sum_{i=0}^m l_i$ and standard deviation $\sigma = \sqrt{\frac{\sum_{i=0}^m (l_i - \mu)^2}{m}}$ for l_i;

3: Compute the normalized loss $L_i = \frac{l_i - \mu}{\sigma}$;

4: Filter the uploaded weights with the normalized loss $G_f = \{i | e^{-L_i} > \tau\}$;

5: Filter G_f with the similarity of the previous gradient direction $G_s = \{i | i \in G_f, SIM((w_t - \overline{w_{t+1}^i})/\gamma_t, (w_{t-1} - w_t)/\gamma_{t-1}) < \zeta\}$;

6: Derive the α-weight aggregation parameters by $\alpha_i = \frac{e^{-L_i}}{\sum_{i \in G_s} e^{-L_i}}, i \in G_s$;

7: Update the weights on time t: $w_{t+1} = \sum_{i \in G_s} \alpha_i \overline{w_{t+1}^i}$;

8: Send back the updated weights w_{t+1} to each worker.

Update similarity-based filter. After the reference dataset-based loss filter, we filtered out the uploaded weights who perform badly on the reference dataset. However, in some extreme scenarios such as all the uploaded weights are from Byzantine nodes in one synchronization, the normalized loss may have similar bad performance. Although this scenario may occur with a very low probability in the real world, for example, 30 out of 100 nodes are Byzantine nodes and in each iteration, only 10 nodes are selected, then the probability of all selected nodes are from Byzantine is around 10^{-6}, this still is a concern to pollute the training process. Therefore we propose an update similarity-based filter to filter out the weights that change much more than the update in the previous iteration. We compare the similarity of the update in this iteration and the previous iteration and filter out those who change too significantly. This is reasonable because the updates in the training process usually have momentum, and thus the update change is mild. This filter helps to deal with the extreme scenario that all participating nodes are Byzantine nodes or some Byzantine nodes are not examined by the reference dataset. Here we let $SIM(x, y) = \arccos \frac{x \cdot y}{||x|| ||y||} + b \cdot ||x - y||$. This guarantees the angle and distance change of weights in adjacent iterations are bounded. Even if there are still weights from Byzantine nodes, the influence on the current training process is not significant.

After these two filters, the weights that have extreme values are filtered out. Then we aggregate the rest weights using an α-weighted average. Here we use the normalized loss on the reference dataset to measure the contribution of different nodes and set softmax of them as the α-weight. This helps the training process learn more information from all the uploaded weights in the heterogeneous federated learning environment. In the next section, we also show ToFi performs well in experiments with practical conditions.

5.3 Remarks and Comparisons

The naive algorithm actually uses a lot of information provided by the reference dataset. Therefore the performance depends on how good the reference dataset is. In fact, this algorithm is like searching the minimum point of a function in a hyperplane whose coordinates are $\overline{w_{t+1}^i}$ and the objective function is the loss function on the reference dataset. Thus the discrepancy between the loss function on the reference dataset and the real whole dataset decides the performance. In a word, the naive algorithm uses the reference dataset to examine the performance of computation results from each node's local dataset and search for the best next move by the information from both the local dataset and the reference dataset.

Compared to the naive algorithm, the performance of ToFi does not fully depend on the quality of the reference dataset. ToFi adopts two filters. The first filter of ToFi is actually a practical modification of the naive algorithm. ToFi uses this filter to clean out the weights with abnormal loss on the reference dataset, it is a better and faster way to compute the optimization function in the naive algorithm. In addition, ToFi adds a second similarity filter to filter out the abnormal weights whose change is too significant than before. These two filters can cooperate to filter out those attack information. The reference dataset in ToFi is more like an examination dataset to remove the outlier weights rather than a decisive dataset to decide how to aggregate the weights in the naive algorithm.

6 Experiments

In this section, several experiments are conducted to show the effectiveness of our algorithm. Because the naive algorithm is slow and inefficient in practice, we focus our experiments on ToFi.

6.1 Experiment Environments Setting

In order to show how those two major differences (non-i.i.d. dataset and the possible minority of honest nodes) affect the Byzantine problems, we first compare different algorithms with those two assumptions in the federated learning environment with all node participation (i.e., all nodes are selected to perform the computation) and in the end, we show how different algorithms perform in the federated learning environment with partial node participation (i.e., some nodes are selected to perform the computation).

In this experiment, there are two challenges to set up experiment environments. One is how to simulate a heterogeneous non-i.i.d. environment for our experiment dataset. The other is how to simulate the Byzantine attacks. In order to simulate a heterogeneous non-i.i.d. distributed environment, we conduct two different level methods. The first method is a naive heterogeneous environment. It is simulated by evenly dividing the whole dataset into slices horizontally and each worker keeps one slice subdataset. Assume we have n workers and the whole dataset is $\xi = \{x_1, x_2, \cdots, x_p\}$, then each worker keeps their subdataset as $\xi_i = \{x_{p//n \cdot (i-1)+1}, \cdots x_{p//n \cdot i}\}$. The other method is an enhanced heterogeneous environment. Similar to the previous method, we first sort ξ by the label. In this case, each subdataset only keeps the data with a similar label. The difference between ξ_i should be very significant. As for Byzantine attacks, in our experiment, we conduct three different types of attacks. The first is the Gaussian attack. We simply generate Gaussian noise as attack weights. The second method is wrong labeled attack [12, 25]. We let the label of the Byzantine workers' data be randomly placed, then the Byzantine worker just normally computes the weights, and upload results with wrong labeled training results to the PS. The last method is one bit attack. For the uploaded weights, we only change one dimension of it with a random value. Although our algorithm is capable of defending Byzantine attacks in the bootstrap scenario, for simplicity, we fixed the Byzantine workers in the experiment. In fact, the bootstrap scenario should have a better performance because no subdataset is hidden by the Byzantine workers.

In our experiments, we use two most common datasets in Byzantine tolerant distributed machine learning area: MNIST dataset [23] and CIFAR-10 dataset [8]. Both datasets have 10 categories of labels. We use a server with 4 Nvidia GeForce GTX 1080Ti GPUs to simulate our experiments. For the federated learning environment with all node participation, we deploy 8 workers for the CIFAR dataset. Each GPU keeps 2 workers. For the federated learning environment, we deploy 100 workers, and 10 workers are randomly selected in each iteration. In our experiments, we will compare our α-weighted based algorithm with four other algorithms: (i) simply average aggregation with filtering out all Byzantine faults; (ii) score based algorithm Krum [2]; (iii) median-based algorithm GeoMedian [3]; (iv) distance-based algorithm FABA [16]. In the federated learning environment with partial node participation, we also compare with another reference dataset-based algorithm Zeno [22]. For ToFi, we set the loss filter parameter $\tau = 0.8$, similarity filter parameter $\zeta = 2, b = 1$ and randomly select 500 data from the test dataset as reference dataset and leave the rest as test dataset. We run all 5 algorithms with different Byzantine environments and Byzantine attacks described above.

6.2 Federated Learning with All Node Participation

We only show the results of CIFAR-10 here. The results of MNIST are presented in the Appendix.

Naive Heterogeneous Environment. We first compare ToFi with three classic methods and ground truth (filter out all Byzantine attacks, average aggregation) in the three Byzantine environments we described above. We choose ResNet-18 [5] as our neural network, 0.001 as the learning rate, and SGD with momentum and weight decay as optimizers. We use 10 as interval length to simulate a more general scenario. Because we just want to compare the effectiveness of defending against attacks, we do not optimize for the best accuracy. We first run experiments on naive heterogeneous environments along with no Byzantine environment, the results are in Fig. 2. As we can see from Fig. 2, Krum performs badly on defending against Byzantine attacks in naive heterogeneous environments. ToFi and FABA have good and stable performance on Gaussian attack and wrong label attack, but ToFi beats FABA on one bit attack. This is because in the naive heterogeneous environment, although the dataset is partitioned into slices, it is still randomly assigned. GeoMedian beats ground truth for some epochs, but the performance is really unstable in some epochs. As for no Byzantine environment, all methods perform well except Krum.

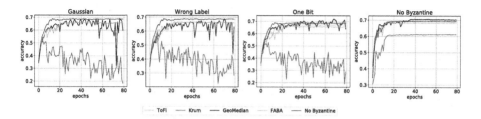

Fig. 2. Experiment results of different algorithms for Gaussian, wrong label, one bit Byzantine attacks and no Byzantine attack scenario on naive heterogeneous environment

Enhanced Heterogeneous Environment. We then compare different algorithms in the enhanced heterogeneous environment. Because the subdataset in each worker is very different and any complicated neural networks with batch normalization do not perform well in this environment, we use a LeNet [23] in this scenario. Using group normalization [15] to substitute batch normalization in complicated networks can be a good solution, but as we said that we only want to compare the performance of defending against attacks rather than chasing a good accuracy, we choose to use a simple neural network. The results are in Fig. 3. From Fig. 3, we can see that only ToFi and FABA are capable of defending against Byzantine attacks in this scenario, among which ToFi performs slightly better than FABA in the Byzantine environment and FABA is a little bit better than ToFi in no Byzantine environment. This is because that, in no Byzantine environment, the losses for all nodes are similar, so ToFi may filter out some useful information by both filters. Krum and GeoMedian have really

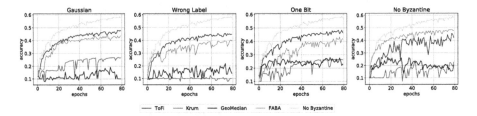

Fig. 3. Experiment results of different algorithms for Gaussian, wrong label, one bit Byzantine attacks and no Byzantine attack scenario on enhanced heterogeneous environment

bad performance in this environment. We can see that all algorithms do not perform very well compared to the ground truth, it is because, in this environment, a Byzantine attack may hide some labels of data such that the training data is missed and it will affect the performance.

Majority Attack. In order to simulate the majority attack, we choose 5 of 8 workers as Byzantine workers and use the same settings with the naive heterogeneous environment. Here we only examine the Gaussian attack because the other two types of attacks have similar performance. The results are in Fig. 4. It is obvious that Krum, GeoMedian, and FABA cannot defend against majority attacks. This is easy to understand because they only use information from uploaded weights. When the majority of workers are malicious, those methods will only take the malicious information as honest information and the whole training process will be dominated by Byzantine workers. ToFi uses the information from the reference dataset, so it is still able to defend against this kind of attack.

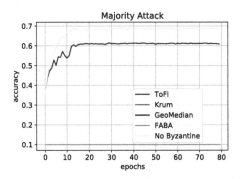

Fig. 4. Experiment results of majority Gaussian attack on naive heterogeneous environment

6.3   Federated Learning with Partial Node Participation

We compare Krum, GeoMedian, FABA, and Zeno with ToFi in the federated learning environment. In our setting, 30% of 100 nodes are Byzantine nodes and in each iteration, 10 nodes are randomly selected for computing. Here we use CIFAR-10 dataset, Gaussian attack, and enhanced heterogeneous environment. For other Byzantine attack types, the performance is similar. For FABA and Zeno that need to estimate the number of Byzantine nodes, we set it as $30\% \times 10 = 3$ in each iteration. The results are in Fig. 5. We can see that ToFi outperforms all other algorithms. It is because those algorithms are not designed to solve the two major differences in federated learning. When the distribution of each node's dataset is not i.i.d., Byzantine nodes may take the majority in some iterations, and the number of Byzantine nodes changes during the training, the performance downgrades a lot.

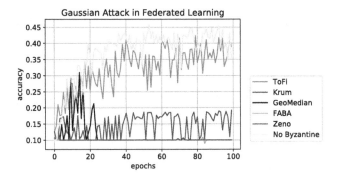

Fig. 5. Experiment results of Gaussian attack on enhanced heterogeneous environment in federated learning

7   Conclusion

In this paper, we address a practical issue of Byzantine attacks in federated learning. This is very different from Byzantine problems in classic distributed machine learning because, in federated learning, the distribution of the dataset in each worker is non-i.i.d., Byzantine workers can be the majority and the number of Byzantine nodes can change in different iterations. As far as we know, our paper is the first work to address this problem. We propose a naive algorithm and modify it to a reference dataset-based two-filter algorithm ToFi to adaptively filter out outlier computational results and take an α-weighted average based on the loss of all the uploaded weights from all involved workers as the aggregation results in each iteration. In our experiments, we compare ToFi with four existing algorithms in different environments with different kinds of Byzantine attacks and show the performance of our algorithm.

Acknowledgements. We thank all the reviewers for their constructive comments. This project was supported in part by US National Science Foundation grant CNS-1816399. This work was also supported in part by the Commonwealth Cyber Initiative, an investment in the advancement of cyber R&D, innovation and workforce development. For more information about CCI, visit cyberinitiative.org.

A   More Experiments on MNIST

All of the experiments in this section have the same setting as the main paper. We will mark any differences if there are. In this section, we supplement some results of experiments on the MNIST dataset and more workers [23]. The model we are using is LeNet-5 [23].

A.1   Federated Learning with All Node Participation

Naive Heterogeneous Environment. We compare our ToFi with three classic methods and ground truth (filter out all Byzantine attacks, average aggregation) in three Byzantine environments (Gaussian, wrong label, and one bit) we described in the main paper and no Byzantine environment. The distributed environment that we use here is the naive heterogeneous environment. We use 10 as interval length. The results are in Fig. 6. From this figure, we can see that the performance of Krum is not as good as ToFi, GeoMedian, and FABA, while these three methods have very similar performance in the naive heterogeneous environment for these three different types of attacks. As for the no Byzantine scenario, the performances are similar among ToFi, GeoMedian, and FABA, while Krum has a lower accuracy than those algorithms.

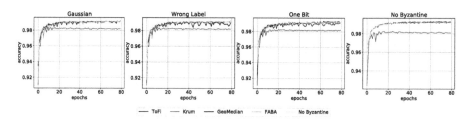

Fig. 6. Experiment results of different algorithms for Gaussian, wrong label, one bit Byzantine attacks and no Byzantine attack scenario on naive heterogeneous environment for MNIST dataset

Enhanced Heterogeneous Environment. In order to show the difference, we compare ToFi with three classic methods and ground truth (filter out all Byzantine attacks, average aggregation) in three Byzantine environments (Gaussian, wrong label, and one bit) and no Byzantine environment. This time we change the distributed environment to the enhanced heterogeneous environment. We use 10 as interval length. The results are in Fig. 7. From this figure, we can see that

ToFi has much better performance than Krum, FABA, and GeoMedian. GeoMedian has the second-best performance for Gaussian and one bit attacks. FABA has the second-best performance for wrong label attacks and no Byzantine scenario. But both of them have a significant accuracy decline than our algorithm. Krum has the worst performance in the enhanced heterogeneous environment.

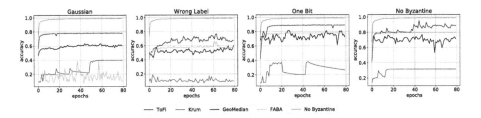

Fig. 7. Experiment results of different algorithms for Gaussian, wrong label, one bit Byzantine attacks and no Byzantine attack scenario on enhanced heterogeneous environment for MNIST dataset

More Workers Experiment. Because of the limitation of the hardware, we cannot make experiments for more workers than 8 on the CIFAR-10 dataset. Here we only examine the scenario with more workers on the MNIST dataset. In this experiment, we choose 32 workers, among which 8 out of 32 workers are Byzantine workers. To show the difference, we examine this setting in the enhanced heterogeneous environment. The results are in Fig. 8. From Fig. 8, it has a very similar performance with the 8-worker scenario. ToFi still outperforms other algorithms. For the Gaussian attack, ToFi has a similar performance with FABA and beats all other algorithms. For wrong label attack and one bit attack, ToFi performs much better than others. The best performance here is not as good as no Byzantine attack case. It is because in the experiment we fixed the workers who suffer Byzantine attacks. Since in this experiment we use the enhanced heterogeneous environment, the data with some labels may be hidden by the Byzantine workers. This will cause a decrease in the accuracy for the best performance.

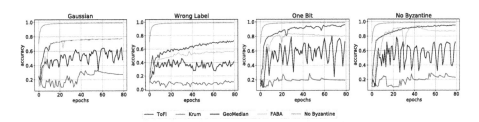

Fig. 8. Experiment results of different algorithms for Gaussian, wrong label and one bit Byzantine attacks on enhanced heterogeneous environment with 32 workers for MNIST dataset

A.2   Federated Learning with Partial Node Participation

We compare Krum, GeoMedian, FABA and Zeno with ToFi in the federated learning environment using similar setting with CIFAR-10 dataset. The results are in Fig. 9. We can see that ToFi outperforms all other algorithms. All the other algorithms are not designed for federated learning and thus have very bad performance.

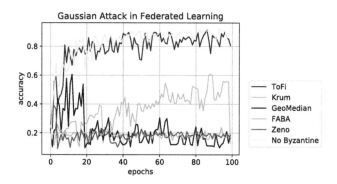

Fig. 9. Experiment results of Gaussian attack on enhanced heterogeneous environment in federated learning

References

1. Alistarh, D., Allen-Zhu, Z., Li, J.: Byzantine stochastic gradient descent. CoRR abs/1803.08917 (2018). http://arxiv.org/abs/1803.08917
2. Blanchard, P., El Mhamdi, E.M., Guerraoui, R., Stainer, J.: Machine learning with adversaries: byzantine tolerant gradient descent. In: Guyon, I., et al. (eds.) Advances in Neural Information Processing Systems, vol. 30, pp. 119–129. Curran Associates, Inc. (2017). http://papers.nips.cc/paper/6617-machine-learning-with-adversaries-byzantine-tolerant-gradient-descent.pdf
3. Chen, Y., Su, L., Xu, J.: Distributed statistical machine learning in adversarial settings: Byzantine gradient descent. Proc. ACM Meas. Anal. Comput. Syst. 1(2), 1–25 (2017). https://doi.org/10.1145/3154503
4. Damaskinos, G., El Mhamdi, E.M., Guerraoui, R., Patra, R., Taziki, M.: Asynchronous Byzantine machine learning (the case of SGD). In: Dy, J., Krause, A. (eds.) Proceedings of the 35th International Conference on Machine Learning. Proceedings of Machine Learning Research, vol. 80, pp. 1145–1154. PMLR, Stockholmsmässan, Stockholm Sweden (10–15 Jul 2018). http://proceedings.mlr.press/v80/damaskinos18a.html
5. He, K., Zhang, X., Ren, S., Sun, J.: Deep residual learning for image recognition. In: 2016 IEEE Conference on Computer Vision and Pattern Recognition (CVPR), pp. 770–778 (2016). https://doi.org/10.1109/CVPR.2016.90
6. Konecný, J., McMahan, H., Yu, F., Richtárik, P., Suresh, A., Bacon, D.: Federated learning: strategies for improving communication efficiency. CoRR abs/1610.05492 (2016)

7. Konstantinov, N., Lampert, C.: Robust learning from untrusted sources. CoRR abs/1901.10310 (2019). http://arxiv.org/abs/1901.10310

8. Krizhevsky, A.: Learning multiple layers of features from tiny images. Technical report, Google (2009)

9. Mao, Y., Hong, W., Wang, H., Li, Q., Zhong, S.: Privacy-preserving computation offloading for parallel deep neural networks training. IEEE Trans. Parallel Distrib. Syst. **32**(7), 1777–1788 (2021). https://doi.org/10.1109/TPDS.2020.3040734

10. Mao, Y., Yi, S., Li, Q., Feng, J., Xu, F., Zhong, S.: Learning from differentially private neural activations with edge computing. In: 2018 IEEE/ACM Symposium on Edge Computing (SEC), pp. 90–102 (2018). https://doi.org/10.1109/SEC.2018.00014

11. McMahan, H.B., Moore, E., Ramage, D., Hampson, S., Arcas, B.A.: Communication-efficient learning of deep networks from decentralized data. In: Proceedings of the 20th International Conference on Artificial Intelligence and Statistics (AISTATS) (2017). http://arxiv.org/abs/1602.05629

12. Paudice, A., Muñoz-González, L., Lupu, E.C.: Label sanitization against label flipping poisoning attacks. In: Alzate, C., et al. (eds.) ECML PKDD 2018 Workshops, pp. 5–15. Springer, Cham (2019). https://doi.org/10.1007/978-3-030-13453-2_1

13. Tao, Z., Li, Q.: eSGD: Communication efficient distributed deep learning on the edge. In: USENIX Workshop on Hot Topics in Edge Computing (HotEdge 18). USENIX Association, Boston, MA, July 2018

14. Tao, Z., et al.: A survey of virtual machine management in edge computing. Proc. IEEE **107**(8), 1482–1499 (2019). https://doi.org/10.1109/JPROC.2019.2927919

15. Wu, Y., He, K.: Group normalization. Int. J. Comput. Vis. **128**(3), 742–755 (2020). https://doi.org/10.1007/s11263-019-01198-w

16. Xia, Q., Tao, Z., Hao, Z., Li, Q.: FABA: an algorithm for fast aggregation against byzantine attacks in distributed neural networks. In: Proceedings of the Twenty-Eighth International Joint Conference on Artificial Intelligence, IJCAI-19, pp. 4824–4830. International Joint Conferences on Artificial Intelligence Organization (July 2019). https://doi.org/10.24963/ijcai.2019/670

17. Xia, Q., Tao, Z., Li, Q.: Defenses against byzantine attacks in distributed deep neural networks. IEEE Transactions on Network Science and Engineering (2020). https://doi.org/10.1109/TNSE.2020.3035112

18. Xia, Q., Tao, Z., Li, Q.: Privacy issues in edge computing. In: Chang, W., Wu, J. (eds.) Fog/Edge Computing For Security, Privacy, and Applications. AIS, vol. 83, pp. 147–169. Springer, Cham (2021). https://doi.org/10.1007/978-3-030-57328-7_6

19. Xia, Q., Ye, W., Tao, Z., Wu, J., Li, Q.: A survey of federated learning for edge computing: Research problems and solutions. High-Confidence Computing (2021). https://doi.org/10.1016/j.hcc.2021.100008

20. Xie, C., Koyejo, O., Gupta, I.: Generalized byzantine-tolerant SGD. CoRR abs/1802.10116 (2018). http://arxiv.org/abs/1802.10116

21. Xie, C., Koyejo, O., Gupta, I.: Zeno++: Robust fully asynchronous sgd (2020). https://openreview.net/forum?id=rygHe64FDS

22. Xie, C., Koyejo, S., Gupta, I.: Zeno: Distributed stochastic gradient descent with suspicion-based fault-tolerance. In: Chaudhuri, K., Salakhutdinov, R. (eds.) Proceedings of the 36th International Conference on Machine Learning. Proceedings of Machine Learning Research, vol. 97, pp. 6893–6901. PMLR, Long Beach, California, USA (09–15 Jun 2019). http://proceedings.mlr.press/v97/xie19b.html

23. Lecun, Y., Bottou, L., Bengio, Y., Haffner, P.: Gradient-based learning applied to document recognition. Proc. IEEE **86**(11), 2278–2324 (1998). https://doi.org/10.1109/5.726791

24. Yin, D., Chen, Y., Kannan, R., Bartlett, P.: Byzantine-robust distributed learning: towards optimal statistical rates. In: Dy, J., Krause, A. (eds.) Proceedings of the 35th International Conference on Machine Learning. Proceedings of Machine Learning Research, vol. 80, pp. 5650–5659. PMLR, Stockholmsmässan, Stockholm Sweden (10–15 Jul 2018). http://proceedings.mlr.press/v80/yin18a.html
25. Zhang, M., Hu, L., Shi, C., Wang, X.: Adversarial label-flipping attack and defense for graph neural networks. In: 2020 IEEE International Conference on Data Mining (ICDM), pp. 791–800 (2020). https://doi.org/10.1109/ICDM50108.2020.00088

TESLAC: Accelerating Lattice-Based Cryptography with AI Accelerator

Lipeng Wan[1,2,3], Fangyu Zheng[1,3(✉)], and Jingqiang Lin[4]

[1] State Key Laboratory of Information Security, Institute of Information Engineering, Chinese Academy of Sciences, Beijing, China
zhengfangyu@iie.ac.cn
[2] School of Cyber Security, University of Chinese Academy of Sciences, Beijing, China
[3] Data Assurance and Communication Security Research Center, Chinese Academy of Sciences, Beijing, China
[4] School of Cyber Security, University of Science and Technology of China, Hefei, China

Abstract. In this paper, we exploit AI accelerator to implement cryptographic algorithms. To the best of our knowledge, it is the first attempt to implement quantum-safe Lattice-Based Cryptography (LBC) with AI accelerator. However, AI accelerators are designed for machine learning workloads (e.g., convolution operation), and cannot directly deliver their strong power into the cryptographic computation. Noting that polynomial multiplication over rings is a kind of time-consuming computation in LBC, we utilize a straightforward approach to make the AI accelerator fit well for polynomial multiplication over rings. Additional non-trivial optimizations are also made to minimize the overhead of transformation, such as using low-latency shared memory, coalescing memory access. Moreover, based on NVIDIA AI accelerator, Tensor Core, we have implemented a prototype system named TESLAC and give a set of comprehensive experiments to evaluate its performance. The experimental results show TESLAC can reach tens of millions of operations per second, achieving a performance speedup of two orders of magnitude from the AVX2-accelerated reference implementation. Particularly, with some techniques, TESLAC can also be scaled to other LBC with larger modulo q.

Keywords: Lattice-based cryptosystems · Polynomial multiplication over rings · AI accelerator · Tensor Core · LAC

1 Introduction

Quantum computing has brought a huge security challenge to the widely-used conventional cryptosystems. If large-scale quantum computers are ever built,

This work was partially supported by National Key R&D Program of China under Award 2018YFB0804401 and National Natural Science Foundation of China under Award No. 61902392.

ⓒ ICST Institute for Computer Sciences, Social Informatics and Telecommunications Engineering 2021
Published by Springer Nature Switzerland AG 2021. All Rights Reserved
J. Garcia-Alfaro et al. (Eds.): SecureComm 2021, LNICST 398, pp. 249–269, 2021.
https://doi.org/10.1007/978-3-030-90019-9_13

they will be able to break many of the public-key cryptosystems currently in use, such as RSA and ECDSA [17], with Shor's algorithm [24]. That would seriously compromise the confidentiality and integrity of digital communications. In this situation, NIST has initiated a project [20] to solicit, evaluate, and standardize one or more quantum-safe public-key cryptographic algorithms (also called post-quantum cryptography, PQC [8]). The goal of PQC project is to develop cryptosystems that are secure against both quantum and classical computers and can be compatible with existing communication protocols and networks. Among the candidates, LBC, a kind of quantum-safe cryptographic algorithm that has been studied for several years, is considered to be the most promising public-key cryptographic standard scheme. The well-known LBC includes NTRU [12], NewHope [4], Kyber [5], Saber [11], etc.

On the other hand, high performance cryptographic computing has always been the pursuit of academia and industry. Since performance is also an important metric in the evaluation of NIST PQC project, researchers have tried to optimize the proposed schemes in both levels of algorithm design and hardware implementation, such as FPGA [6,19], ASIC [18], CPU supported by AVX2 or AVX-512 [1,23], and even GPU [2,3,10,14]. Compared with the basic implementation, these optimization solutions may have some improvement in performance. However, the performance is still difficult to meet the needs of practical applications.

Along with quantum computing and quantum-safe cryptography, AI (artificial intelligence) is another hot issue that attracts a lot of attention. At the same time, many processor vendors have designed their own dedicated AI processors or accelerators, including server products (e.g., NVIDIA Tensor Core[1], Google TPU), mobile terminals (e.g., Apple Neural Engine), and embedded devices (e.g., Intel neural network stick, and even Tesla self-driving car), to power AI applications. Because AI accelerators are designed for high-density machine learning workloads, they can deliver multiple times computing power than the general-purpose CPU or even GPU. Taking NVIDIA Tensor Core as an example, it can deliver up to 125 Tensor TFLOPS on Tesla V100 for training and inference applications [13], while typical CUDA cores can only provide up to 15 TFLOPS.

Such a huge performance advantage has inspired us to introduce AI accelerators to cryptographic implementation. However, little work has been done ever. In this paper, we have explored the feasibility of implementing LBC with AI accelerators. It is not easy to utilize AI accelerators to implement the cryptographic computation directly, since they are generally dedicated to specific operations and it is almost impossible for third-party developers to control AI accelerators in a more fine-grained way. As for Tensor Core, the 125 TFLOPS can only be achieved in its unique mixed-precision matrix-multiply-and-accumulate computing model which is designed for convolution operation. Specifically, the data precision is very small, the input multiplier of Tensor Core is half-precision floating-point format (abbreviated as FP16 or half) with only 11 bits of significance.

---

[1] NVIDIA has launched different generations of **Tensor Core**. If there is no additional explanation, **Tensor Core** in this paper refers to the one on the architecture of Volta.

Polynomial multiplication over rings is often the performance bottleneck of LBC. To demonstrate the application of AI accelerators in high performance cryptographic computing, we extend polynomials to matrices of a specific size to adapt it to the operating mode. Compared with other approaches, such as NTT, this method is straightforward and more suitable for Tensor Core. And we choose LAC [15], a kind of LBC, to be implemented with Tensor Core on Tesla V100, and name the prototype as TESLAC (**TEnS**or-core accelerated **LAC**).

Our Contributions. The highlight of TESLAC is to turn the machine learning workloads into cryptography workloads. To exploit the maximum potential of TESLAC, we have made the following contributions:

- Firstly, as far as we know, it is the first time to introduce AI accelerators into LBC acceleration, which can provide a new high-performance alternative platform for the development and application of cryptography.
- Secondly, we propose a framework to turn the machine learning workloads (more precisely, convolution operation) to polynomial multiplication over rings. For instance, we represent a method to expand the polynomial (or vector) into a matrix of a specific size to apply the calculation to the operating mode of Tensor Core.
- Thirdly, we have implemented the entire LAC prototype system TESLAC on NVIDIA Tesla V100. A series of optimizations have been made to bring the true power of Tensor Core into practice, such as making full use of low-latency shared memory to cache data, coalescing global memory accesses. Consequently, TESLAC can deliver tens of millions of LAC operations per second, which is two orders of magnitude faster than the LAC submission implementation running in CPU with AVX2, and outperforms other LBC schemes on CPU or GPU by a wide margin.

Organization. The rest of this paper is organized as follows. Section 2 presents background knowledge. Section 3 expounds the polynomial multiplication rule over rings, and explains the reason why we choose LAC. Section 4 demonstrates how to apply Tensor Core to the implementation of LAC and the details of TESLAC. Section 5 illustrates the environment configuration, shows the evaluation and analysis of experimental results, and compares with other implementations. Section 6 concludes our work.

2   Preliminaries

2.1   Lattice-Based Cryptography

A lattice $L \subset \mathbb{R}^n$ is the set of all integer linear combinations of basis vectors $v_1, v_2, \ldots, v_n \in \mathbb{R}^n$, i.e., $L := \{\sum a_i b_i | a_i \in \mathbb{Z}\}$. LBC (Lattice-Based cryptography) is the generic term for constructions of cryptographic primitives that involve lattices, either in the construction itself or in the security proof. Lattice-Based constructions are currently important candidates for PQC. Compared with more widely used and known public-key schemes such as RSA, DH, and ECC, LBC is believed to be secure against both classical and quantum computers.

Vectors and Matrices. Vectors are denoted by bold lower-case characters, such as $\boldsymbol{a}$. And matrices are denoted by uppercase characters, such as $\boldsymbol{A}$.

An m-dimensional vector $\boldsymbol{a} = (a_0, \ldots, a_{m-1})$, where the a_i is the component of $\boldsymbol{a}$ for $0 \leq i < m$.

Algebraic Structures. Let $\mathbb{R}$ be real numbers, $\mathbb{Q}$ be rational numbers, and $\mathbb{Z}$ be integers. For an integer $q \geq 1$, let $\mathbb{Z}_q$ be the residue class ring modulo q and $\mathbb{Z}_q = 0, \ldots, q-1$. Define the ring of integer polynomials modulo $x^n + 1$ as $R = \mathbb{Z}[x]/(x^n + 1)$ for an integer $n \geq 1$, and the ring $R_q = \mathbb{Z}_q[x]/(x^n + 1)$ denotes the polynomial ring modulo $x^n + 1$ where the coefficients are from $\mathbb{Z}_q$. The addition and multiplication of the elements in R_q are performed according to those of polynomials.

2.2   LAC

Currently, most lattice-based cryptosystems are based on learning with errors (LWE) assumption [22] and its variants. In case of Ring-LWE, the noisy equation is $(\boldsymbol{a}, \boldsymbol{b} = \boldsymbol{as} + \boldsymbol{e})$, where $\boldsymbol{a}, \boldsymbol{s}, \boldsymbol{e}$ are chosen from a ring. Usually, the integer polynomial ring $R_q = \mathbb{Z}_q[x]/(x^n + 1)$ for suitable ring dimension n is used. LAC, a proposal to the NIST PQC standardization that has advanced to round 2, is a kind of LBC based on Poly-LWE (a simplification version of Ring-LWE). The basic primitive comprises three algorithms: KG (key generation), Enc (encryption), Dec (decryption). The core of the whole cryptographic scheme is based on the above three algorithms.

Notations. Define the message space $\mathcal{M} \in \{0,1\}^{l_m}$ for a positive integer l_m, and the space of random seeds $\mathcal{S}$ be $\{0,1\}^{l_s}$ for a positive integer l_s. We use n independently identical distribution of Ψ_σ, namely Ψ_σ^n.

Subroutines. In the subroutines dealing with the encoding and decoding of the error correction, ECCEnc, ECCDec, the conversion between $m \in \{0,1\}^{l_m}$ and its encoding $\widehat{m} \in \{0,1\}^{l_v}$ is provided, wherein l_v is a positive integer denoting the length of the encoding and depending on the specific choice of the parameter settings. Key Generation randomly generates a pair of public key and secret key (pk, sk). Details are described in **Algorithm 1**.

The algorithm Encryption on the input pk and a message m, encrypts m with the randomness seed. In case that seed is not given, the process is randomized. Otherwise, the encryption is deterministic for the same seed. Details are described in **Algorithm 2**. The subroutine ECCEnc converts the message into a codeword $\widehat{m}$.

The Decryption on input sk and a ciphertext c, recovers the corresponding message m. The subroutine ECCDec inputs an encoding $\widehat{m}$, and decodes the codeword in it.

Algorithm 1. Key Generation

Ensure: A pair of public key and secret key (pk, sk).

1: $seed_a \xleftarrow{\$} \mathcal{S}$
2: $a \leftarrow \mathsf{Samp}(U(R_q; seed_a)) \in R_q$
3: $s \xleftarrow{\$} \Psi_\sigma^{n,h}$
4: $e \xleftarrow{\$} \Psi_\sigma^{n,h}$
5: $b \leftarrow as + e$
6: **return** $(pk := (seed_a, b), sk := s)$

Algorithm 2. Encryption

Require: $(pk, seed_a, b), m \in \mathcal{M}; seed \in \mathcal{S}$
Ensure: A ciphertext c.

1: $seed_a \xleftarrow{\$} \mathcal{S}$.
2: $a \leftarrow \mathsf{Samp}(U(R_q; seed_a)) \in R_q$
3: $\widehat{m} \leftarrow \mathsf{ECCEnc}(m) \in \{0, 1\}$
4: $(r, e_1, e_2) \leftarrow \mathsf{Samp}(\Psi_\sigma^{n,h}, \Psi_\sigma^{n,h}, \Psi_\sigma^{l_v})$
5: $c_1 \leftarrow ar + e_1 \in R_q$
6: $c_2 \leftarrow (br)_{l_v} + e_2 + \lfloor \frac{q}{2} \rceil \cdot \widehat{m} \in \mathbb{Z}_q^{l_v}$
7: **return** $c := (c_1, c_2) \in R_q \times \mathbb{Z}_q^{l_v}$

Algorithm 3. Decryption

Require: $sk = s, c = (c_1, c_2)$
Ensure: A plaintext m

1: $u \leftarrow c_1 s \in R_q$
2: $\widetilde{m} \leftarrow c_2 - (u_{l_v}) \in \mathbb{Z}_q^{l_v}$
3: **for** $i = 0$ to $l_v - 1$ **do**
4:    **if** $\frac{q}{4} \le \widetilde{m}_i < \frac{3q}{4}$ **then**
5:       $\widehat{m}_i \leftarrow 1$
6:    **else**
7:       $\widehat{m}_i \leftarrow 0$
8:    **end if**
9: **end for**
10: $m \leftarrow \mathsf{ECCDec}(\widehat{m})$
11: **return** m

2.3   Tensor Core

When we talk about NVIDIA GPU cores, it usually refers to CUDA Cores. From intelligent assistants to autonomous robots and beyond, the deep learning models are addressing challenges that are rapidly growing in complexity. But converging these models has become increasingly difficult and often leads to underperforming and inefficient training cycles. To mitigate these problems, NVIDIA adds

Tensor Core to their GPUs to accelerate AI training. Unlike CUDA Core, Tensor Core, available on Volta and subsequent architectures, is a kind of accelerator designed for computationally-intensive tasks such as fully-connected and convolutional layers in CNN. It consists of programmable matrix-multiply-and-accumulate units, and its associated data path is custom-crafted to dramatically increase floating-point computing throughput at only modest area and power costs.

The Convolution Operation. Taking Convolutional Neural Network (CNN) as an example, Fig. 1 shows the operating procedure of the convolutional layer when performing feature extraction on pictures. The input image (a 5×5 matrix) works with the convolution kernel (a 3×3 matrix).

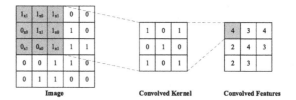

Fig. 1. Basic convolution operation.

The operating mode of Tensor Core is similar to this operation. Each Tensor Core of Tesla V100 provides a matrix processing array which performances the operation $D = A * B + C$, where D, A, B, C are 4×4 matrices.

Data Type and Precision. What Tensor Core really performs is Fused Multiply and Add (FMA) mixed-precision operation (FP16 as multipliers and FP32 as an accumulator, shown in Fig. 2).

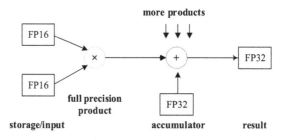

Fig. 2. Tesla V100 Tensor Core operation.

FP16, or half, is a binary floating-point computer number format that occupies 16 bits [9], shown in Fig. 3. In the IEEE 754–2008 standard, the 16-bit base-2 format is referred to as binary16. It is intended for the storage of floating-point values in the application where higher precision is not essential for performing arithmetic computations. The exponent is encoded using an offset-binary representation, with 11-bit (10 bits fraction and an implicit lead bit with value 1) significand precision. Therefore, the maximum value exactly represented is $2^{11} = 2048$.

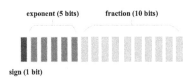

Fig. 3. IEEE 754 half-precision binary floating-point format.

2.4   CUDA Programming Model

CUDA is a general-purpose parallel computing platform launched by NVIDIA. Our proposed prototype is programmed based on this platform.

Thread Model. CUDA hardware can possess thousands of cores, which means thousands of threads can execute in parallel. In CUDA C++, it is allowed to define the function as kernel, executed by multiple threads simultaneously. CUDA threads are organized in three levels, grid, block, and thread.

A CUDA hardware contains several SMs (Streaming Multiprocessors), and a block is usually executed on an SM. However, SM schedules only one warp (usually 32 threads) of the block each time. These threads work in SIMT (Single-Instruction, Multiple-Thread) mode. And block is the basic unit of device resource (such as shared memory) allocation. Therefore, when setting the number of threads included in the block, it is better to set an integer multiple of the number of warp.

Memory Model. CUDA hardware has multiple available memory spaces, i.e., global, local, register, shared, constant, or texture memory, and they all have different scopes, lifetimes, and caches.

In general, registers are the fastest, but they are allocated and used by a single thread and are difficult to be used for data sharing and interaction between threads. Local memory is private to the thread and is automatically allocated by the compiler when all registers are used up. Shared memory is allocated according to a single block and visible to all threads in the block. Since shared memory is on-chip, it has much higher bandwidth and much lower latency than local and global memory.

Low-Level Programming of Tensor Cores. However, a single Tensor Core is the smallest execution unit, but not the smallest control unit. Multiple Tensor Cores are used concurrently by a full warp. A larger $16 \times 16 \times 16$ matrix operation (shown in Fig. 4), implicitly divided by multiple Tensor Cores, is conducted by the warp. In addition to using the cuBLAS and cuDNN libraries, developers can also program Tensor Core directly in CUDA C++ via a set of functions and types in the nvcuda::wmma namespace. These warp-level matrix operations are exposed in the CUDA warp matrix-multiply-and-accumulate (WMMA) API listed in the appendix.

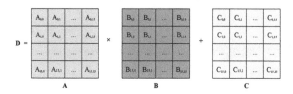

Fig. 4. A warp-level $16 \times 16 \times 16$ matrix operation

At first, the data need to be loaded or initialized to the specific format (fragment) required by Tensor Core, with load_matrix_sync or fill_fragment. In CUDA, fragment is an overloaded class containing a section of a matrix distributed across all threads in the warp. The mapping of matrix elements into fragment internal storage is unspecified. Only certain combinations of template arguments are allowed. The first template parameter specifies how the fragment will participate in the matrix operation. The namespace and class fragment are also shown in the appendix listing. Acceptable values for Use are: matrix_a (A), matrix_b (B), accumulator (C or D). The m, n, and k describe the shape of the warp-wide matrix tiles participating in the multiply-accumulate operation. The dimension of each tile depends on what value for Use. The data type, T, may be half, float on Tesla V100. After the MMA (matrix-multiply-and-accumulate) operation (mma_sync) is performed , the result needs to be stored into memory through the function store_matrix_sync.

Meanwhile, the parameter mptr in function load_matrix_sync and store_matrix_sync must be a 256-bit aligned pointer pointing to the first element of the matrix in memory. In addition, ldm describes the stride in elements between consecutive rows (for row-major layout) or columns (for column-major layout) and must be a multiple of 16 bytes.

Since CUDA does not provide more fine-grained APIs, these functions should be treated as atomic operations on the thread warp. And the focus of programming is how to divide matrix tiles, fill fragments, and achieve parallelism and synchronization.

3   Design

3.1   The Reason to Choose LAC

As mentioned previously, Tensor Cores have a special working mode that is based on dedicated matrix fragments, and the mapping of matrix elements into internal storage of fragment is unspecified. In addition to the warp matrix functions provided in CUDA, third-party developers cannot get more fine-grained programming interfaces.

On the other hand, polynomial multiplication over a ring in LBC is not the calculation of dot product, while the execution of Tensor Core is that of the multi-tuples dot product. It is impossible to utilize Tensor Core with LAC directly.

Compared with other NIST-PQC candidates, LAC is not well-known. However, LAC has unique design features: it uses a byte-wide modulus. Adopting error-correcting codes means that LAC can tolerate a higher decryption failure rate, which allows it to use a smaller modulus that leads to improved performance. The Table 1 lists some values for different LBC cryptosystems selected from NIST-PQC Round-2 [21]. In the table, pk stands for public key, sk for secret key, ct for cipher-text, n for dimension, and q for modulus. Since Kyber [5] is based on Module-LWE and Saber [11] is based on Module-LWR, k means the module rank.

Table 1. Comparison of Several LBC

Algorithm	pk(B)	sk(B)	ct(B)	n	q	k
KYBER512	800	1632	736	256	3329	2
LAC128	544	1056	712	512	251	–
NewHope512	928	869	1088	512	12289	–
NTRU443	611	701	611	443	2048	–
Saber(Light)	672	1568	736	256	2^{13}	2

Since the multiplier's data type of Tensor Core on Tesla V100 is FP16, only integers between 0 and 2048 can be exactly represented in a single data. In LAC, each coefficient is less than 251 (the modulus $q = 251$) and is very suitable to be directly represented in FP16. That is the main reason for choosing LAC. However, this is not to say that our scheme can only be utilized for LBC with a small modulus. For the modulus larger than 2048, taking additional processing and techs, such as multi-precision representation and KaraTsuba algorithm, this platform can also be applied to some other eligible algorithms. More details will be discussed later.

3.2   The Rule of Polynomial Multiplication Rule over Rings

Polynomial multiplication is the basic and most computationally intensive operation in Lattice-Based cryptosystems. There are some rules for polynomial multiplication over rings, which can be used for fast reduction.

Over ring $R_q = \mathbb{Z}_q[x]/(x^n + 1)$, since the modulus is $x^n + 1$, there is

$$x^n \equiv -1 \bmod (x^n + 1)$$

Assume a, b are n-dimensional vectors on the ring, define a, b as:

$$a = a_0 + a_1 x + a_2 x^2 + \cdots + a_{n-1} x^{n-1}$$

$$b = b_0 + b_1 x + b_2 x^2 + \cdots + b_{n-1} x^{n-1}$$

For $c = ab$, there is

$$
\begin{aligned}
c &= a_0 b_0 + (a_0 b_1 + a_1 b_0)x + \ldots + (a_0 b_{n-1} + \ldots + a_{n-1} b_0) \\
&\quad x^{n-1} + (a_1 b_{n-1} + \ldots + a_{n-1} b_1)x^n + \ldots + a_{n-1} b_{n-1} x^{2n-2} \\
&= a_0 b_0 + (a_0 b_1 + a_1 b_0)x + \ldots + (a_0 b_{n-1} + \ldots + a_{n-1} b_0) \\
&\quad x^{n-1} - (a_1 b_{n-1} + \ldots + a_{n-1} b_1) - \ldots - a_{n-1} b_{n-1} x^{n-2}
\end{aligned}
\tag{1}
$$

$c = (c_0, \cdots, c_{n-1})$, then

$$
\begin{aligned}
c_0 &= a_0 b_0 - (a_1 b_{n-1} + a_2 b_{n-2} + \cdots + a_{n-1} b_1) \\
c_1 &= a_0 b_1 + a_1 b_0 - (a_2 b_{n-1} + \cdots + a_{n-1} b_2) \\
&\cdots \\
c_{n-1} &= a_0 b_{n-1} + a_1 b_{n-2} + \cdots + a_{n-1} b_0
\end{aligned}
$$

$$\Rightarrow c_i = \sum_{j=0}^{i} a_j b_{i-j} - \sum_{j=i+1}^{n-1} a_j b_{n+i-j} \tag{2}$$

3.3   The Application of Tensor Core

We decide to apply Tensor Core to accelerate the polynomial multiplication and addition ($c = ab + e$) over the ring $R_q = \mathbb{Z}_q/(x^n + 1)$. However, the parameter vectors are generally one-dimensional and cannot be used directly on Tensor Core. In a thread warp, Tensor Cores operate on a 16×16 tile, while the dimension $n = 512$ is greater than the tile capacity, then all coefficients cannot be completely loaded into the tile at one time. What's more, the tile operates in rows and columns. For each intermediate result, that is, 16 pairs of coefficients are multiplied and then accumulated. If a vector (part) is placed in the 16 rows of one tile, shown in Fig. 5, it will make the process more complicated. For instance, the intermediate values are at the diagonal position of the **Tile C**, and need to be rearranged and sorted.

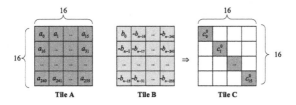

Fig. 5. Tensor Core operation on 1 vector

Some adjustments must be made. There are some idiosyncrasies of (2) and the matrix representation (3) can be inferred.

$$c = \begin{bmatrix} a_0 & a_1 & \ldots & a_{n-1} \end{bmatrix} \begin{bmatrix} b_0 & b_1 & \cdots & b_{n-1} \\ -b_{n-1} & b_0 & \cdots & b_{n-2} \\ \cdots & \cdots & \ddots & \cdots \\ -b_1 & -b_2 & \ldots & b_0 \end{bmatrix} \tag{3}$$

Therefore, we consider placing a vector (part) in a single row instead of 16 rows of the **Tile A**. In a round of calculation, Tensor Cores manipulate 16 different vectors and get 16 different rows of valid intermediate results, shown in Fig. 6. Further, the vector corresponding to **Tile B** is transformed into an $n \times n$ matrix.

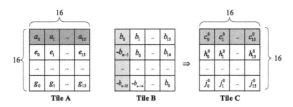

Fig. 6. Tensor Core operation on 16 vectors

In this way, the results of a vector are all in one row and can be directly stored in memory without filtering. What's more, this can also handle multiple (at least 16) vectors simultaneously, solving the applicability of Tensor Core. As for the final results, they can be obtained through the accumulation of these intermediate values and should look like (4), where a^i, c^i represent different vectors and b^* is the expanded form of vector.

$$\begin{bmatrix} a^0 \\ a^1 \\ a^2 \\ \ldots \end{bmatrix} b^* = \begin{bmatrix} c^0 \\ c^1 \\ c^2 \\ \ldots \end{bmatrix} \tag{4}$$

All multipliers on the right side of (2) (or (3)) are elements of a and b. The difference lies in the index of the elements, and the sign may also change. For each c_i, supposing the sequence a (b is equivalent here) is fixed, and then the relative position of the coefficient sequence of b has not been changed, while it is similar to a cycle, shown in Fig. 7.

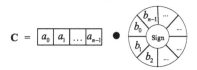

Fig. 7. $c = ab$

As for the matrix representation of b, only $[b_{n-1}, b_{n-1}, \cdots, b_0, -b_{n-1}, -b_{n-2}, \cdots, -b_1]$ needs to be stored, and the number of elements is $2n - 1$. On the other hand, the mptr in WMMA API must be a 256-bit aligned pointer pointing to the first element of the matrix in memory. 256-bit means 16 elements (half). For instance, when the pointer is pointing to b_0, if you need to execute a new line starting with b_1, you need to move to another row (stride of at least 16 FP16 elements or integral times of 16) instead of just adding 1 to the pointer. At the same time, the **Tile B** should contain 16 columns. Finally, to meet the alignment requirements of the Tensor Core, we expand a vector into a $2n \times 16$ matrix that is completely suitable, shown as Fig. 8. In addition, each column will be padded with 0.

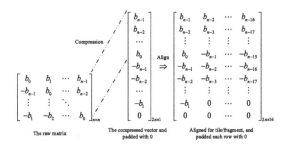

Fig. 8. Compression and expand for alignment

4   Implementation

4.1   Overview

The overview of the prototype system is shown in Fig. 9. Data is transmitted between the host and CUDA Hardware through the PCIe bus. Because the two are heterogeneous, the overall task needs to be split. The random number

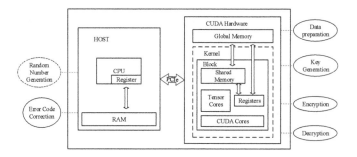

Fig. 9. The overview of the prototype system.

generation and error correction code are generally carried out by the host, while CUDA hardware, also called device, is mainly responsible for computing tasks involving polynomial multiplication. If the error correction code processing is assigned to the device, the control flow would become very complicated. As for random number generation, it can be considered as a portable module, and where it is generated doesn't need to be concerned if the security requirements are satisfied. In other words, the random numbers can be generated by the host, the device, or a third-party hardware module. For convenience, we arrange this task on the host.

The key generation, encryption, and decryption tasks are arranged for the device. However, there are specific requirements for the type and format of the data to be processed by Tensor Core, therefore, the data from the host need to go through a data preparation stage before they participate in the calculation.

4.2 Setting of LAC Parameters

Depending on different security strengths, the dimension n of the LAC can be 512 or 1024. Further, according to the length of plaintext, there are 3 categories of parameters, as Table 2.

Table 2. Parameter settings of LAC

Categories	n	q	Distribution	BCH$[n_e, l_e, d_e, t_e]$	Plaintext length l_m
LAC128	512	251	Ψ_1	[511, 264, 59, 29]	256
LAC192	1024	251	$\Psi_{\frac{1}{2}}$	[511, 392, 27, 13]	384
LAC256	1024	251	Ψ_1	[1023, 520, 111, 55]	512

4.3   Data Type Conversion

On Tesla V100, the data processed by Tensor Core is required to be half, while the parameters generated by the host are byte or int. That requires the use of some CUDA built-in functions, such as short2half, to perform data type conversion on the original parameters.

4.4   Memory Coalescing

Grouping of threads into warps is not only relevant to computation but also global memory accesses. The device coalesces global memory loads and stores issued by threads of a warp into as few transactions as possible to minimize DRAM bandwidth. If each thread holds a running instance, the memory access stride will be very large. That might lead to an increase in the number of memory requests. Therefore, we coalesce all the instances' memory and use the block as a computing unit to ensure that the memory accessed by threads in a block is as continuous as possible.

4.5   Iteration

Intermediate iterations need to be set according to the size of block. As mentioned earlier, the WMMA APIs are warp-wide functions and manipulate 16 elements for a single vector parameter. An approach is to set up enough threads, and each warp (32 threads) performs only one WMMA operation. Due to the limitation of hardware resources, this method is not feasible. The other method is to iterate in a multiplexed manner, that is, each warp calculates multiple tiles. The iterations should satisfy:

$$\frac{Total\ Tensor\ Core\ operations}{Warps} = \frac{(n/16) \times (n/16)}{block\_size/warp\_size}$$

Meanwhile, n of LAC128 is 512, and a total of $512/16 \times 512/16$ Tensor Core operations are performed. In TESLAC, the block size should be equal or less than n. We set the default block size as 512 and the warp size as 32. That is to say, each warp iterates 64 times. Considering that Tensor Core can automatically sum up, the calculation results, which is obtained by iterating on the matrix B in 16 columns as a round, are parts of the final results without the need for subsequent processing. This also means that the workload of a warp is two columns of tiles of matrix B. The partition of overall workload and iterations are shown in Fig. 10.

4.6   Exploiting Shared Memory and Optimization

For each load operation, data are read from global memory. This part of delay seriously affects the performance. When iterating, the matrix B takes the form of $n \times n$, and while storing, it is compressed into $2n \times 16$, which has been described

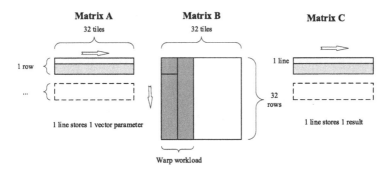

Fig. 10. Partition and iterations of $\mathbf{C} = \mathbf{AB}$

earlier. Even so, it is not a small piece of memory for the cache. Therefore, it is necessary to reduce the proportion of memory access time in the whole iteration. After comparing several memory spaces, we decide to use shared memory for caching, considering its low latency and relatively large capacity. On Tesla V100, each block can use up to 48 kB shared memory. However, as for matrix $\mathbf{B}$, its storage size is $2 \times 512 \times 16 \times sizeof(\text{half}) = 32$ kB. After being copied to shared memory, the data is loaded from shared memory rather than global memory. Moreover, if the data in shared memory does not need to be used later, the intermediate results can also be cached in that storage.

Although, this will also encounter another trouble—n might be 1024 or larger, the capacity of shared memory is not enough for caching two or more expanded matrices. Simply, the solution is to divide the matrix into parts and copy data several times. Whatever, a little more cost is acceptable.

5   Results and Analysis

5.1   Setup

Our TESLAC is implemented on a machine with CPU (Intel(R) Xeon(R) CPU E5-2620 v2, 2.10 GHz) and CUDA hardware (NVIDIA Tesla V100). The operating system is Ubuntu 16.04.6 LTS, the CUDA runtime version is 10.1 and the driver version is 460.56. More technical specifications of Tesla V100 are shown in Table 3.

5.2   Performance

The main purpose of our experiments is to demonstrate the feasibility of combining AI accelerator with LBC and understand the performance gain. Firstly, we test polynomial multiplication ($c = ab$) to get the performance of running equal instances under different configurations. Then, we have evaluated and compared the calculation part of TESLAC with the original implementation. Furthermore, we have also compared TESLAC with other PQC implementations.

Table 3. Some technical specifications of Tesla V100

Item	Spec	Item	Spec
CUDA Capability	7.0	Memory Bus Width	4096-bit
GPU Max Clock rate	1380 MHz	Memory Clock rate	877 Mhz
CUDA Cores	5120	SM	80
CUDA Cores/SM	64	Shared memory/block	49152 B
Total Global memory	16160 MB	Registers available/block	65536
Tensor Cores	640	Tensor Cores/SM	8
Max threads/SM	2048	Max threads/block	1024

Polynomial Multiplication. We randomly generate 81920 pairs (a, s) to test $b = as$. The grid size and block size is Configurable. And the test record is shown in Table 4.

Table 4. Test polynomial multiplication under different configurations

Grid size	80	80	160	160
Block size	128	256	128	256
Elapsed time (ms)	21.2664	25.4433	18.903	23.1496
Performance million pairs (a, s)/s	3.85208	3.21971	**4.33369**	3.53872

We have compared the performance of polynomial multiplication with the experimental results in [14], shown in Fig. 5. Lee et al. have performed polynomial multiplication using the Nussbaumer algorithm on RTX2060, 490,061 op/s, while our implementation result is 44,150,108 op/s. After scaled by GFLOPS (CUDA Cores×Boost Clock), our implementation is still about 4 times speedup, which mainly results from the utilization of Tensor Core.

Table 5. Comparison of polynomial multiplication implemented on different platform

	GPU Platform	Architecture	CUDA Cores	Boost Clock (MHz)	op/s	op/s (scaled)
[14]	RTX 2060	Turing	1920	1680	490,061	1,073,234
TESLAC	Tesla V100	Volta	5120	1380	4,333,690	4,333,690

Comparison with Original LAC Implementation. After modifying the CPU source code downloaded from the NIST PQC website [21], we compile and execute as the *readme* file, then evaluate the same calculation steps of LAC on Intel(R) Core(TM) i7-7700K CPU. Error correction coding and random number generation are not in the scope of our evaluation, because they are replaceable and not the core of the computation. The results are shown in Table 6. The original source code of LAC provides 3 implementation methods, including *Normal*, *Optimized*, and *AVX2*. We use the latter two to compare with TESLAC.

Table 6. Comparison with original work

	LAC128.KeyGen (op/s)	LAC128.Enc (op/s)	LAC128.Dec (op/s)
CPU Optimized [21]	55,488	28,615	61,118
AVX2 [21]	237,494	114,092	234,157
TESLAC	4,005,495	15,488,955	49,720,202

In terms of CPU implementations, the performance of the AVX2 implementation is about 4 times of the *Optimized*. In addition, the computing performance of LAC128.Enc is much lower than that of LAC128.KeyGen and LAC128.Dec. Because each round of encryption operation needs to perform polynomial multiplication and addition twice (c_1 and c_2). As for TESLAC, at least 16 sets of data were processed simultaneously with Tensor Core. So the computing performance has been greatly improved, which is about 16x, 135x, and 212x that of the *AVX2*, respectively.

However, these results mainly consider the calculation part of each algorithm. Developers will also encounter time-consuming operations such as data transmission. They can also use other techniques such as pipeline, multiple execution streams and preprocessing to circumvent these effects.

Comparison with Related Work. We have chosen the AVX2 implementation of Kyber512 [5], LightSaber [11] from NIST-PQC Round 2, and GPU implementation of NTRU443 from [2] to compare with TESLAC. The performance evaluation of Kyber512 and LightSaber in [5,11] is conducted by counting CPU cycles consumed. Here, we assume that the CPUs (Intel Core i7-4770K, Intel Core i7-6600U, respectively) are at the maximum frequency, and convert the results to operations per second. In addition, the implementation of NTRU443 is based on NVIDIA GTX1080. The details are shown as Table 7. TDP means the Thermal Design Power.

As far as we know, there is no solution to implement encryption algorithm on AI accelerator yet. Generally speaking, the results of GPU implementation are significantly better than CPU because of massively parallel computation. With the support of AI accelerator, TESLAC greatly exceeds pure GPU implementation. In particular, performance per watt of Tensor Core is far superior. It only needs to consume several times of power and gain hundreds of times of computing performance.

Table 7. Comparison with related work

Algorithm	Platform	Supported technology	Base frequency	Max frequency	TDP	KeyGen (op/s)	Enc (op/s)	Dec (op/s)
Kyber512 [5]	Intel i7-4770K	AVX2	3.50 GHz	3.90 GHz	84 W	116,669	79,294	96,144
LightSaber [11]	Intel i7-6600U	AVX2	2.60 Ghz	3.40 Ghz	15 W	54,973	46,773	48,155
NTRU443 [2]	GTX1080	CUDA Cores	–	–	180 W	–	508,541	–
TESLAC (LAC128)	Tesla V100	Tensor Core	–	–	250 W	4,005,495	15,488,955	49,720,202

Of course, these performance improvements might mainly come from the hardware revenue, while the characteristics of the algorithm itself can not be ignored, and how to make full use of the hardware resources to match the algorithm is the biggest challenge.

5.3   The Scalability for Larger Modulus

Certainly, the techniques used in TESLAC are not limited to LAC. In fact, it is very rare to use a small modulus like LAC, while the coefficients of most LBCs are greater than 2048. In this case, the modulus q exceeds the range represented by FP16. Then, multi-precision presentation can be used to deal with it. Now, suppose we need to calculate $Z = X \times Y$, where X, Y is greater than 2048. Then, we can represent X and Y in more than one FP16 data, for example, $X = X_h \cdot 2^{Base} + X_l$ and $Y = Y_h \cdot 2^{Base} + Y_l$, where X_h, X_l, Y_h, Y_l meets the requirements. The procedure in multi-precision presentation is shown in (5).

$$
\begin{aligned}
Z &= X \times Y \\
&= (X_h \cdot 2^{Base} + X_l) \times (Y_h \cdot 2^{Base} + Y_l) \\
&= X_h \times Y_h \cdot 2^{2Base} + (X_h \times Y_l + X_l \times Y_h) \cdot 2^{Base} + X_l \times Y_l
\end{aligned}
\tag{5}
$$

Besides, other technologies such as Montgomery reduction [16] or Barrett reduction [7] can also be combined. With the upgrade of hardware products, the significand precision of Tensor Core may be larger, then there will be less restrictions on the scalable application.

6   Conclusion

In this paper, we introduce AI accelerators to high performance cryptographic computing for the first time. Based on NVIDIA's Tensor Core, a kind of AI accelerator, we present a vector expanding method for polynomial multiplication over rings to adapt to the operating mode of Tensor Core. Considering the precision and simplicity of computation, we choose to implement LAC selected from NIST PQC with our techniques on Tesla V100. Consequently, the performance improvement is outstanding.

AI accelerator, which can be treated as an optional platform for high performance cryptographic computing, has great potentiality to be tapped. The performance gain mainly comes from the hardware revenue, but how to make full use of the hardware resources to match the algorithm is the biggest challenge. Meanwhile, these techniques can also be scalable to other LBCs of which the modulus is larger, with a method such as multi-precision representation.

A   Appendix

```
1 #include <mma.h>
2 using namespace nvcuda;
3
4 template<typename Use,int m,int n,int k,typename T,typename
    Layout=void> class fragment;
```

Listing 1.1. The namespace and class fragment

```
1 void load_matrix_sync(fragment<...> &a, const T* mptr,
    unsigned ldm);
2 void load_matrix_sync(fragment<...> &a, const T* mptr,
    unsigned ldm, layout_t layout);
3 void store_matrix_sync(T* mptr, const fragment<...> &a,
    unsigned ldm, layout_t layout);
4 void fill_fragment(fragment<...> &a, const T &v);
5 void mma_sync(fragment<...> &d, const fragment<...> &a,
    const fragment<...> &b, const fragment<...> &c, bool
    satf=false);
```

Listing 1.2. The WMMA functions

References

1. Aguilar-Melchor, C., Barrier, J., Guelton, S., Guinet, A., Killijian, M.-O., Lepoint, T.: NFLlib: NTT-based fast lattice library. In: Sako, K. (ed.) CT-RSA 2016. LNCS, vol. 9610, pp. 341–356. Springer, Cham (2016). https://doi.org/10.1007/978-3-319-29485-8_20

2. Akleylek, S., Goi, B., Yap, W., Wong, D.C., Lee, W.: Fast NTRU encryption in GPU for secure IoP communication in post-quantum era. In: 2018 IEEE SmartWorld, Ubiquitous Intelligence Computing, Advanced Trusted Computing, Scalable Computing Communications, Cloud Big Data Computing, Internet of People and Smart City Innovation (SmartWorld/SCALCOM/UIC/ATC/CBDCom/IOP/SCI), pp. 1923–1928 (2018)

3. Akleylek, S., Dağdelen, Ö., Yüce Tok, Z.: On the efficiency of polynomial multiplication for lattice-based cryptography on GPUs using CUDA. In: Pasalic, E., Knudsen, L.R. (eds.) BalkanCryptSec 2015. LNCS, vol. 9540, pp. 155–168. Springer, Cham (2016). https://doi.org/10.1007/978-3-319-29172-7_10

4. Alkim, E., Ducas, L., Pöppelmann, T., Schwabe, P.: Post-quantum key exchange—a new hope. In: 25th USENIX Security Symposium (USENIX Security 16), pp. 327–343 (2016)

5. Avanzi, R., et al.: CRYSTALS-KYBER: algorithm specifications and supporting documentation. https://pq-crystals.org/kyber/. Accessed 15 Sep 2020
6. Aysu, A., Patterson, C., Schaumont, P.: Low-cost and area-efficient FPGA implementations of lattice-based cryptography. In: 2013 IEEE International Symposium on Hardware-Oriented Security and Trust (HOST), pp. 81–86. IEEE (2013)
7. Barrett, P.: Implementing the Rivest Shamir and Adleman public key encryption algorithm on a standard digital signal processor. In: Odlyzko, A.M. (ed.) CRYPTO 1986. LNCS, vol. 263, pp. 311–323. Springer, Heidelberg (1987). https://doi.org/10.1007/3-540-47721-7_24
8. Bernstein, D.J.: Introduction to post-quantum cryptography. In: Post-Quantum Cryptography, pp. 1–14. Springer (2009). https://doi.org/10.1007/978-3-540-88702-7_1
9. Committee, I.S., et al.: 754–2008 IEEE standard for floating-point arithmetic. IEEE Comput. Soc. Std. **2008**, 517 (2008)
10. Dai, W., Sunar, B., Schanck, J., Whyte, W., Zhang, Z.: NTRU modular lattice signature scheme on CUDA GPUs. In: 2016 International Conference on High Performance Computing & Simulation (HPCS), pp. 501–508. IEEE (2016)
11. D'Anvers, J.P., Karmakar, A., Roy, S.S., Vercauteren, F.: Saber: Mlwr-based kem. https://www.esat.kuleuven.be/cosic/pqcrypto/saber/index.html. Accessed 15 Sep 2020
12. Hoffstein, J., Pipher, J., Silverman, J.H.: NTRU: a ring-based public key cryptosystem. In: Buhler, J.P. (ed.) ANTS 1998. LNCS, vol. 1423, pp. 267–288. Springer, Heidelberg (1998). https://doi.org/10.1007/BFb0054868
13. Jeremy Appleyard, S.Y.: Programming tensor cores in CUDA 9. https://devblogs.nvidia.com/programming-tensor-cores-cuda-9/. Accessed 5 Apr 2020
14. Lee, W.K., Akleylek, S., Wong, D.C.K., Yap, W.S., Goi, B.M., Hwang, S.O.: Parallel implementation of nussbaumer algorithm and number theoretic transform on a GPU platform: application to qTESLA. The Journal of Supercomputing, pp. 1–26 (2020)
15. Lu, X., et al.: LAC: practical Ring-LWE based public-key encryption with byte-level modulus. IACR Cryptology ePrint Archive 2018, 1009 (2018). https://eprint.iacr.org/2018/1009
16. Montgomery, P.L.: Modular multiplication without trial division. Math. Comput. **44**(170), 519–521 (1985)
17. Nist, F.: FIPS 186-4-Digital Signature Standard (DSS). National Institute of Standards and Technology (2013)
18. Oder, T., Güneysu, T., Valencia, F., Khalid, A., O'Neill, M., Regazzoni, F.: Lattice-based cryptography: From reconfigurable hardware to ASIC. In: 2016 International Symposium on Integrated Circuits (ISIC), pp. 1–4. IEEE (2016)
19. Pöppelmann, T., Güneysu, T.: Towards efficient arithmetic for lattice-based cryptography on reconfigurable hardware. In: Hevia, A., Neven, G. (eds.) LATIN-CRYPT 2012. LNCS, vol. 7533, pp. 139–158. Springer, Heidelberg (2012). https://doi.org/10.1007/978-3-642-33481-8_8
20. Post-quantum cryptography project, N.: Post-quantum cryptography. https://csrc.nist.gov/Projects/Post-Quantum-Cryptography. Accessed 23 Sep 2020
21. Post-quantum cryptography project, N.: Round 2 submissions. https://csrc.nist.gov/Projects/Post-Quantum-Cryptography/Round-2-Submissions. Accessed 4 Apr 2020
22. Regev, O.: On lattices, learning with errors, random linear codes, and cryptography. J. ACM (JACM) **56**(6), 1–40 (2009)

23. Seiler, G.: Faster AVX2 optimized NTT multiplication for Ring-LWE lattice cryptography. IACR Cryptology ePrint Archive 2018, vol. 39 (2018)
24. Shor, P.W.: Algorithms for quantum computation: discrete logarithms and factoring. In: Proceedings 35th Annual Symposium on Foundations of Computer Science, pp. 124–134. IEEE (1994)

Research of CPA Attack Methods Based on Ant Colony Algorithm

Xiaoyi Duan[1] , You Li[1] , Jianmin Tong[1] , Xiuying Li[1], Siman He[2(✉)],
and Peishu Zhang[1]

[1] Beijing Electronic Science and Technology Institute, Beijing, China
[2] Hunan National Secrecy Science and Technology Evaluation Center, Hunan, China

Abstract. The Power analysis attack is an effective method of attacking encryption devices for leakage of side-channel information. CPA (Correlation Power Analysis) is a common method. The traditional method of Power Analysis Attack, which is only one-byte key, is analyzed in one attack and repeats multiple operations to obtain the whole secret key. In this way, a successful attack needs more power curves. In this paper, a new attack method is proposed to select the optimal secret key group through the Ant Colony Algorithm and attack all the bytes of the secret key simultaneously. It can greatly eliminate the influence of the channel noise and improve the efficiency of the attack. To prove the effectiveness of this new method, the AES algorithm as an example is implemented on the MEGA16 microcontroller. The power consumption curve of the AES algorithm with a fixed secret key and random plaintext is collected, and the power consumption is analyzed separately by the original method and the new method. As a result, the success rate of the original method is only 10.981% when using 4000 power curves; however, the new one is up to 100%, which is increased by 89.019%. When the power curves do not exceed 3000, the success rate of the original method is zero. However, the success rate of the new method can reach 34.375% even if only 1500 power curves are used. The new method is more effective than the original one. Being affected by parameters, the attack time of the new method is not consistent but much less than the original method.

Keywords: Power analysis attack · CPA (Correlation Power Analysis) · AES algorithm · Ant Colony Algorithm

1 Introduction

Power analysis attack is a method of attacking encryption devices for leakage of side-channel information such as time consumption, power consumption, or electromagnetic radiation during these devices works [1]. This new type of attack is much more effective than the mathematical method of cryptanalysis, thus posing a serious threat to cryptographic devices. In recent years, with the popularization of varieties of cryptographic chips and embedded devices, power analysis attack brings more damage to system security. Thus power analysis attack and their corresponding countermeasure have become

J. Garcia-Alfaro et al. (Eds.): SecureComm 2021, LNICST 398, pp. 270–286, 2021.
https://doi.org/10.1007/978-3-030-90019-9_14

popular research fields in the world at present. CPA (Correlation Power Analysis) is less affected by the noise, and attackers using CPA do not need to know the detail about the attacked device. It has become one of the main methods of Power Analysis Attack for domestic and foreign scholars.

At present, the research of energy analysis attack focuses on the relationship between the energy change of a byte in the chip and the hypothesis model. In 2009, Massimo et al. [2] designed a general multi-bit power consumption model for a precharged circuit based on the characteristics of symmetric algorithm and the structure of the processor. This model has high accuracy for the precharged circuit. In 2013, Oswald research found that after linear transformation of power consumption curve, it can accurately quantify the impact of a linear filter on power analysis attack so as to effectively select the optimal linear filter to improve attack efficiency [3]. Satoh R et al. proposed a new power analysis attack method that can be used to improve the efficiency of the resistance evaluation of cryptographic LSI. The proposed method performs power analysis not in the conventional time-domain but the frequency domain [4]. In 2014, Kim et al. found that due to the existence of noise information in the power consumption curve, the attack efficiency will be reduced. They proposed a principal component analysis method based on the original data to raise the idea of correlation coefficient analysis. This method first sought the principal component of the original data and then selected the power consumption curve with good quality according to the principal component to attack the power consumption analysis. The efficiency of this method is higher than that of ordinary methods. The attack has been greatly improved [5]. In paper [6] explores the use of machine learning techniques to perform a power analysis attack and to deal with high dimensional feature vectors. In this paper [7] investigate the vulnerability of SIMON and LED lightweight block cyphers against Differential Power Analysis (DPA) attack. In 2015, Pozo Applied singular spectrum analysis (SSA) to power analysis attacks to improve the signal-to-noise ratio of signals and attack efficiency [8], aiming at the problem that low sampling rate will affect the signal analysis. L Guo et al. proposed a differential power analysis attack on dynamic password token based on the SM3 algorithm [9]. This paper [10] present a review of the power analysis attack and its techniques. Also, a brief detail on some of the power analysis attacks on smart card and FPGA has been presented. In 2016, L Guo et al. proposed a chosen-plaintext differential power analysis attack on HMAC-SM3 [11]. Masoumiet et al. proposed a practical smart card implementation of an advanced encryption standard (AES-128) algorithm combined with a simple yet effective masking scheme to protect it against first-order power analysis attacks in both time and frequency domain [12]. The paper [13] proposes a method for performing power analysis attacks against SIMECK. In 2017, Eleonora et al. Proposed an end-to-end attack method based on a convolutional neural network for the problem of power curve dislocation, which can effectively achieve the attack without realigning the power curve in advance [14], Chakraborty A et al. proposed a generic Correlation Power Analysis (CPA) attack strategy against STT-MRAM based cryptographic designs using a new power model [15]. In 2018, Wiemers A et al. based on a theoretical analysis on quantifying the remaining entropy, deriving a practical search algorithm. Which even in a setting with high noise or few available traces can either successfully recover the full AES key or reduce its entropy significantly [16]. In 2019, Kim et al. [17] introduced a method to analyze side channels using convolutional neural networks. The paper [18] used a Convolutional Neural Network (CNN) to attack the algorithm implementation on the single-chip computer with mask and interference defence. In 2020, Cai X et al. proposed an energy trace compression method for differential power analysis attack [19]. Xiaoyi Duan et al. proposed data enhancement to solve Hamming weight imbalance of Sbox output values in machine learning [20].

The traditional method of Power Analysis Attack, which is only one-byte key, is analyzed in one attack and repeats multiple operations to obtain the whole secret key. In this way, a successful attack needs more power curves. The new CPA attack method proposed in this paper is an innovative application of the Ant Colony Algorithm. This approach takes full advantage of the leaking of the whole 8 S-boxes, significantly reducing the number of power curves and increasing the success rate of attack. As a result, the success rate of the original method is only 10.981% when using 4000 power curves; however, the new one is up to 100%, which is increased by 89.019%. When the power curves do not exceed 3000, the success rate of the original method is zero. However, the success rate of the new method can reach 34.375% even if only 1500 power curves are used. When the power curves are limited in number or greatly impacted by noise, the original attack method may be difficult to succeed. The new method, however, can efficiently use the limited power curves to analyze and increase the possibility of obtaining the correct secret key.

The structure of this paper is as follows: In Sect. 2, relevant research at home and abroad is introduced in brief. In Sect. 3, some concepts are discussed, such as AES, CPA method, Ant Colony Algorithm and the new attack method proposed by us. In Sect. 4, an attack experiment is implemented separately by the original method and the new method. Also, the results of the experiment are analyzed. In Sect. 5, the new attack method and its efficiency are summarized.

2 Background Knowledge

2.1 Introduction of AES Algorithm

With the rapid development of computing power, the DES algorithm is not enough to ensure information security and is gradually replaced by the AES algorithm. AES algorithm is a symmetric encryption algorithm used by the American National Standards Institute and was officially adopted in business in 2001.

As shown in Table 1, the block size of the AES algorithm is 128 bits, and the key length can be 128, 192 or 256, which determines the number of encryption rounds. In this paper, the 128-bit AES algorithm is introduced briefly, and it is attacked to verify the effectiveness of the new attack method proposed by us.

AES algorithm is a block cypher algorithm based on iterative computation, in which the data stream is encrypted or decrypted with 128 bits as a block. AES uses a substitution/permutation network, called SP structure, to carry out round operation iteratively. Before data encryption, the input data was divided into blocks. Each block has four words (32 bits). Each word contains 4 bytes, and 8 bits consist of a bit.

In general, plain text is described in terms of square matrices in bytes, called state matrices. In each round of the algorithm, the contents of the state matrix continually

Table 1. AES key length and the number of Encryption rounds

	Key length (32 bit)	Block size (32 bit)	Encryption rounds
AES-128	4	4	10
AES-192	6	4	12
AES-256	8	4	14

transmit changes, and the result is output as ciphertext. Similarly, a 128-bit key is also a matrix represented in bytes, called the key matrix. The key matrix is expanded into a sequence of 44 words through the key scheduling program-$\omega[0]$, $\omega[1]$, $\cdots \omega[43]$, the first four elements of which are $\omega[0]$, $\omega[1]$, $\omega[2]$, $\omega[3]$ as the original key to plus the initial key; The last 40 words are divided into ten groups, each of 4 words (128 bit) respectively for ten rounds of round-keys plus computing.

AES does not use the Feistel network. The whole block is processed in each round instead of a half. So AES decryption process is not consistent with its encryption process.

During encryption, plaintext and original key are encrypted once before the first iteration of the AES algorithm. In the last round of iteration, no column mixed. The decryption operation is the inverse operation of the encryption operation. Therefore, the round key addition operation is performed once before the first round of decryption, and

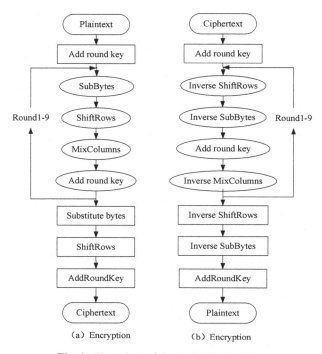

Fig. 1. Flow chart of the AES-128 algorithm

the reverse column mixing is not performed in the last round. The algorithm flow chart is shown in Fig. 1.

Before encryption and decryption, AES divides the plaintext and the key into several bytes and rearranges them to form a matrix. The basic processing steps include SubBytes, ShiftRows, MixColumns, and AddRoundKey. To increase the effectiveness of AES, the calculations are done in finite fields in SubBytes and MixColumns. AddRoundKey uses the operation of bitwise XOR. ShiftRows uses the operation of cyclic shift. Though SubBytes must perform the multiplicative inverse over finite fields, the operation can be simplified by using a look-up table. MixColumns reflects the validity of AES. It makes the bytes of plaintext and key fully mixed, which increases the difficulty of attacking. Combining with the operating characteristics of the 9-round transform of AES, our energy attack mainly focused on the first round, then extracted the voltage of the AES cryptographic chip and recorded 10,000 valid data.

2.2 Introduction of CPA

Unlike Simple Power Analysis (SPA), Differential Power Analysis (DPA) attack does not analyze the power consumption of the device along the time axis. However, it analyzes the linear dependence of the power consumption and the processed data at fixed times. DPA attack can analyze the key information from the small differential signal of the power curve. However, it needs to collect a large amount of information and collect multiple sets of the power curve and record the plaintexts and ciphertexts of each power curve. Usually, it needs Some SPA analysis experience and longer time to operation, and the high requirements of the platform equipment. Using the differential mathematical statistics method, PDA poses a severe challenge to the security of the cryptographic chip. It has become the focus of many researchers at home and abroad.

Correlation Power Analysis (CPA) is an extension of Kocher's classical differential power attacks, and it was proposed by Brier et al. in 2004. Selecting an unknown but constant reference state, CPA establishes a Hamming model and analyses the coefficient of correlation between power consumption sample and Hamming-weight of the processed data. The main idea is that when the attacker knows the plaintext, he can change the plaintext and collect the corresponding power curve. Specific steps are as follows:

1) The oscilloscope is used to collect the power consumption data of the encryption chip being performing encryption or decryption (In this paper, the output voltage value of S-box in the first round of AES is collected) to obtain a power consumption matrix T of $M \times N$.

$$T = \begin{bmatrix} t_{1,1} & t_{1,2} & \cdots & t_{1,M} \\ t_{2,1} & t_{2,2} & \cdots & t_{2,M} \\ \vdots & \vdots & \ddots & \vdots \\ t_{N,1} & t_{N,2} & \cdots & t_{N,M} \end{bmatrix} \tag{1}$$

Wherein, M rows of the matrix T represent M different sampling values of power curve, and N columns represent N power curves. Each power curve has the same key but different plaintext.

2) The attacker guesses the secret key of the encryption chip and uses plaintext and guess the key to calculate the hypothetical intermediate value matrix $X_{N \times 256}$ according to the formula (2).

$$\begin{cases} X = [X_{i,j}]_{N \times 256} \\ X_{i,j} = SBOX(m_i, k_j) \end{cases}$$

$$i = 1, 2, \ldots, N; j = 1, 2, \ldots, 256$$

(2)

Wherein, $k = (k_1, k_2, \ldots, k_{256})$ contains the entire guess key of one byte. $m = (m_1, m_2, \ldots, m_N)$ is the plaintext of the N power curves and $SBOX(m_i, k_j)$ is the operation function of SubBytes in AES.

3) Using the Hamming Weight model, the hypothetical intermediate value matrix is mapped to a hypothetical power matrix H.

Therein, HW is a function to calculate the Hamming Weight (the number of logic 1).

4) Use Eq. (3) to calculate the correlation coefficient between the hypothetical power matrix H and the measured power matrix T obtained from the collected power curves.

$$\begin{cases} \rho = [\rho_{i,j}]_{256 \times M} \\ \rho(H_i, T_j) = \dfrac{E(H \times T) - E(H) \times E(T)}{\sqrt{Var(H) \times Var(T)}} \end{cases}$$

$$i = 1, 2, \ldots, 256; j = 1, 2, \ldots, M$$

(3)

Therein, $E(H)$ and $E(T)$ are the mathematical expectation of the column vectors H_i and T_j. $Var(H)$ and $Var(T)$ are the covariance of H_i and T_j. i is the number of all possible key of one byte. M is the number of sampling points per power curve.

5) Find the highest point of the correlation coefficient, and regard the corresponding guess key as the correct key of this byte.

In the CPA attack, calculating the correlation coefficient is a very important part to be distinguished from the other side-channel attack methods. A correlation coefficient is also known as the Person correlation coefficient called ρ. It has no unit, and its value range is $[-1, 1]$. A positive value represents a positive correlation. A negative value represents a negative correlation. The absolute value of 1 means completely related, and one of 0 means irrelevant. CPA analyzes the correlation coefficient between Hamming Weight and power consumption of the intermediate variable and determines the linear relationship between column hi $(i = 1, 2, \ldots\ldots, K)$ and column tj $(j = 1, 2, \ldots\ldots, T)$ by the correlation coefficient. The result is the estimated correlation coefficient in matrix R. The highest correlation coefficient is corresponding to the correct key. Otherwise, the intermediate variable and power consumption have not the expected relationship of direct proportional due to the wrong key. The estimate for each ri, j is based on D elements of column hi and column tj.

The theoretical premise of the CPA is that the power consumption of the encryption chip with a precharge bus is proportional to the number of "1" been processed. However, there is usually no precharge bus in the encryption chip. According to the principle of CMOS (Complementary Metal-Oxide Semiconductor Transistor), the power consumption is proportional to the frequency of 0/1 conversions (Hamming Distance) instead of the number of "1" been processed (Hamming Weight). Therefore, existing CPA methods cannot obtain the correlation coefficient between the high-power consumption and the success key. In the case of large noise, the correlation coefficient between the correct key and the wrong one may be almost the same. Therefore, the correlation coefficient analysis methods still need to be improved.

2.3 Introduction of Ant Colony Algorithm

During the study of ant foraging, Italian scholar Dorigo et al. found that the ants can release chemical called pheromone in the path they passed through. The ants can walk along the path of higher concentration of pheromone, and every passing ant will leave pheromone on the road, which forms a positive feedback mechanism. After a period, the entire ant colony can reach the food source along the shortest path. Inspired by this behavior, Dorigo proposed an evolutionary algorithm called Ant Colony Algorithm. It is a new heuristic optimization algorithm and has distributed computation, information positive feedback and heuristic searchability. In essence, the ant colony algorithm is a new heuristic optimization method. Its flow chart is shown in Fig. 2.

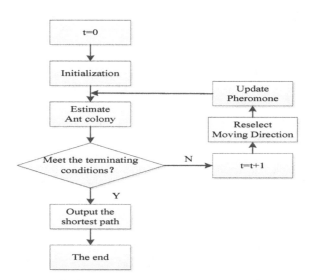

Fig. 2. Flow chart of Ant Colony Algorithm

Initially, the pheromone on each path is equal and it is set as $\tau ij(0) = C$ (C is a constant). During the movement, ant $k(k = 1, 2, \ldots\ldots, m)$ can decide the transfer direction according to the pheromone in the road. The rule of state transfer using by ant colony is called the random proportional rule. When located at a node i, an ant k uses the pheromone trail to compute the probability of choosing j as the next node. At time t, the probability $P_{ij}^k(t)$ is:

$$P_{ij}^k(t) = \begin{cases} \dfrac{\tau_{ij}^\alpha(t)\eta_{ij}^\beta(t)}{\sum\limits_{s \in allowed_k} \tau_{is}^\alpha(t)\eta_{is}^\beta(t)}, & j \in allowed_k \\ 0, & otherwise \end{cases} \tag{4}$$

Therein, $allowed_k = \{0, 1, \ldots, n-1\}$ means the next node that the ant k can choose. According to formula (4), the transfer probability $P_{ij}^k(t)$ is directly proportional to $\tau_{ij}^\alpha(t) \cdot \eta_{ij}^\beta(t)$. η_{ij} is the visibility factor. α and β are the two parameters respectively reflect the relative weights of accumulated information and heuristic information in the ants' path selection.

After the ant completes its tour, the pheromone amount on each path will be adjusted according to the formula (5) and formula (6).

$$\tau_{ij}(t+1) = \rho \cdot \tau_{ij}(t) + \Delta\tau_{ij}(t, t+1) \tag{5}$$

$$\Delta\tau_{ij}(t, t+1) = \sum_{k=1}^m \Delta\tau_{ij}^k(t, t+1) \tag{6}$$

Therein, $\Delta\tau_{ij}^k(t, t+1)$ is the amount of pheromone left in the path (i, j) by the ant k now of $(t, t+1)$. Its value depends on the performance of the ants. The shorter the path, the more pheromone is released. $\Delta\tau_{ij}(t, t+1)$ is the pheromone increment of path (i, j) in this cycle. $(1 - \rho)$ is the pheromone decay parameter. Usually, $\rho < 1$ is set to avoid the infinite accumulation of the pheromone amount on the path.

Ant colony algorithms can be applied to many optimization problems. Ant's walking path represents the feasible solution of the problem to be optimized, and all the paths of the ant colony form the solution space. In the optimal path, the ants release more pheromones, and in the inferior path, the ants release less. With time, the concentration of pheromone accumulated on the optimal path and the number of ants choosing this path is also increasing. In the end, the whole ant colony will concentrate on the optimal path, which is the optimal solution under the positive feedback. Energy Analysis Attack can also be considered as an optimization problem. A possible key can be regarded as a feasible solution, and the collection of all possible keys (2^{128} in total) constitutes the solution space of the optimization problem. The key with a higher correlation coefficient corresponds to a better path, and the one with a lower correlation coefficient corresponds to a poorer path. The final optimal solution is the correct key.

3 Introduction to the New Method

In order to generate the guessed key by Ant Colony Algorithm, Firstly, a map must be established between the guessed key and the ants' path. As shown in Fig. 3, each bit

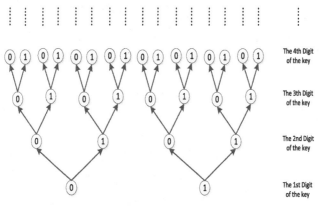

Fig. 3. The map between the guessed key and the ants' path

of the guessed key can be regarded as a node of the path, and each complete ant path corresponds to a guessed key.

After mapping between the guess key and the ants' path, it is necessary to initialize the ant colony algorithm. Specific parameters settings are shown in Experimental Data and Analysis.

After initialization, the evaluation way of ants' route needs to be modified. The ant colony algorithm was originally used to find the shortest path between two points, and the evaluation indicator of the pros and cons of the path is the length of it. If the ant colony algorithm is used in the CPA attack, it is necessary to replace the indicator by the probability of the guessed key being the real key. This can be judged by the correlation coefficient. The higher the correlation coefficient is, the better the path is, and the lower the correlation coefficient is, the worse the path is.

In each round of iteration of the ant colony algorithm, an optimal path will be found, that is, the guessed key with the largest correlation coefficient. It can generate the ant path of the next round iteration according to the best path in this round. The specific rules are as follows:

1) Using the correlation coefficient of this optimal path and the other paths of this round, the relative error value can be found respectively according to the formula (7). Therein, is the absolute error and is the true value (the correlation coefficient of the optimal path in this round).

$$\delta = \frac{\Delta}{L} \cdot 100\% \tag{7}$$

2) The relative error value can determine the search range of the ant colony in the next round of iteration. If the relative error value δ is less than 20%, then the iteration path of the next round will be generated in the vicinity of this path with a certain probability. If the relative error value δ is greater than or equal to 20%, then the iteration path of next round will be generated in the global scope with a certain probability. The probability of choosing which road at each branch depends on the

concentration of pheromones on that road. In other words, the concentration of pheromone will affect each value (0 or 1) of the guess key value.

3) Finally, the termination condition of the ant colony algorithm needs to be set. Since the solution space of the real key is too large, we cannot and do not need to successively verify all the solutions in the entire solution space. Therefore, we regard the number of iterations as the termination condition of the algorithm. When the pre-set iteration round is completed, the shortest path is output, and its corresponding guess key is the correct key calculated by the algorithm. The ant colony algorithm may tend to converge and achieve the correct key before the pre-set iteration round is accomplished. If the pre-set iteration round is too small, the ant colony algorithm may not converge, and the correct key achieved is not the true key. If the pre-set iteration round is too large, the ant colony algorithm tends to converge, but the correct key found in the optimal local solution rather than the optimal global solution. The calculated correct key is not the true key. As for the choice of iteration rounds, we will discuss in detail in Experimental Data and Analysis.

4 Experimental Data and Analysis

4.1 Experimental Environment

To obtain reliable experimental data, a power analysis platform is established, which consists of three parts, encryption equipment, data acquisition and data analysis. Atmel ATMEGA16A microcontroller is selected as an encryption device, and its clock frequency is set to 4 MHz. For the data acquisition part, the Tektronix DPO7104 oscilloscope was selected in this experiment, and its sampling frequency is set to 50 MHz. In order to ensure the validity of the experimental data, a total of eight sets of data are collected for repeated experiments in this experiment. Each group of data collects 10,000 fixed-key and random plaintext power consumption curves, and each curve has 25,000 power consumption sampling points. The fixed key of each group of data is different.We choose MATLAB to implement CPA, in which the guessed key is generated by the Ant Colony Algorithm, and the attack target is the output bytes of S-box in the first round of AES-128.

4.2 Analysis of Experimental Data

4.2.1 Experimental Performance

There are many indicators to measure the efficiency of attack, such as the success rate of attack, the number of power curves, the amount of computation, computation time and so on. Among them, the amount of computation is inconvenient for statistics and comparison, and the success rate of attack is strongly correlated with the number of power curves. Therefore, we choose the success rate of attack as the main indicator of attack efficiency. Also, computation time is related to many factors, and we will analyze and compare separately.

First of all, we keep the related parameters of the Ant Colony Algorithm unchanged and use different numbers of power curves for CPA attacks. The success rate of attack with the original method and the new method is separately recorded, as shown in Table 2 and Fig. 4.

Table 2. CPA attack success rates for different numbers of power curves

The number of power curves	Success rate	
	Original method (%)	New method (%)
1500	0	34.375
2000	0	57.031
2500	0	69.531
3000	0	86.719
3500	3.775	96.094
4000	10.981	100
4500	18.032	100
5000	89.213	100
5500	98.072	100
6000	100	100

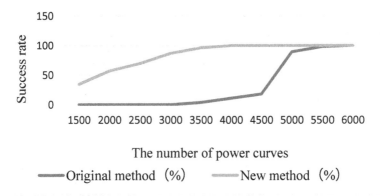

Fig. 4. CPA attack success rates for different numbers of power curves

Because the collected power curve is greatly disturbed by noise, and no denoising is performed, the noise interference in the analysis result is relatively large. It can be seen from Table 2 that the increase in the numbers of power curves has a positive effect on the improvement of attack success rate. CPA attacks using the original method have a success rate of 0 when the number of power curves is less than 3000. With the increase of the numbers of power curves, the success rate of CPA increases. When the number of power curves reaches 6000, the attack success rate of the original method reaches 100%. However, the success rate of the new method can reach 34.375% even if only 1500 power curves are used. When the number of power curves is up to 4000, the attack success rate of the original method can reach 100%. In order to ensure a successful attack, the power curves of the new method are about 33.33% less than those of the original method. We conclude that the new method can greatly reduce the number of power curves required for a successful attack. Also, when the number of power curves is less than 5000, the attack success rate of the new method is far greater than that of the original method. When the number reaches 4500, the success rate of the new method is still 81.968% higher than that of the original method. It can be inferred that the new method can achieve higher success rates with fewer power curves.

It is important to reduce the number of curves needed to successfully attack. For example, in some restricted situations, only a certain number of power curves can be collected. The original method maybe with a low success rate or even completely unsuccessful. However, the new method can efficiently use the limited power curves and analyze to increase the probability of obtaining the correct key. Another possibility is that the collected power curves may be of poor quality and greatly affected by noise, due to environmental constraints. Only enough power curves collected can reduce the effect of noise. As the number of power curves drastically increases, the entire analysis process of power attack can last if dozens of days and the data storage space occupied can become very large. If the data utilization can be improved, and the number of power curves can be substantially reduced, a considerable amount of analysis and processing time and data storage space will be saved.

When using the original method, it takes about one minute to verify each byte of a guess key, and completing the computation of all the 16 bytes may cost 16 min to 4096 min (68 h and 16 min) in theory. While using the new method of CPA attack, the same power curves of 4000 can accomplish the attack within 4 h. If you ignore the data loading time, it needs less than 2 h (The real-time depends on the specific parameters of the Ant Colony Algorithm, which will be discussed later) for computation itself, saving 97% of the computation time. As mentioned earlier, the number of power curves is positively related to the success rate, and more power curves are usually used to ensure a higher attack success rate. For the original method, the number of power curves has nothing to do with the computation time. Even if the number of power curves is increased, the computation time will not be increased. For the new method, with the increase of the numbers of power curves, the attack success rate gradually increases, but the time needed for the attack also increases. It can be seen from the experimental results that even though the time needed for the attack increases, the increase is not big, and the computation time is still far less than the time required by the original method; furthermore the attack success rate is always far higher than that of the original method. Therefore, the price is acceptable. Also, when the number of power curves reaches 4000, the success rate of attack can increase to 100%. So we can use no more than 4,000 curves to attack, which can maintain the success rate of 100% and avoid unnecessary time-consuming.

4.2.2 Analysis of Experimental Results

The traditional energy analysis attack method CPA only analyzes the problem of one byte key in one attack. This attack method only uses part of the collected energy curve, that is, the energy change caused by only one byte key, and does not make full use of the energy characteristics of the collected 16 bytes. This paper uses the characteristics of ant colony algorithm to propose a CPA attack method based on ant colony algorithm. This method can make full use of all 16 S-boxes of AES algorithm to leak information and maximize the utilization rate of leaked information. Through ant colony algorithm, the optimal key group in energy analysis attack can be selected and all key bytes can be attacked at the same time, and it can eliminate the influence of channel noise to a great extent. To sum up, as the experimental results show, the new method is far superior to the original method in attack success rate, the number of power consumption curves and operation time, which fully verifies the effectiveness of the new method.

4.2.3 Influencing Factors

Before using the CPA attack based on Ant Colony Algorithm, the parameters of the Ant Colony Algorithm need to be set, including the number of ants *ant*, the number of ants' movements *times*, pheromone volatile coefficient *rou*, transfer probability constant *P*0 and search range. In the experiment, using the characteristics of distributed computing of the Ant Colony Algorithm, we split the key of 128 bits into 16 bytes, each of which is 8 bits. The computation time is reduced because of parallel computing, so the search area is 0–255. Also, the pheromone volatility coefficient *rou* is set to 1 and the transition probability constant *P*0 is set to 0.1. The number of ants *ant* and the number of ants' movements *times* also affect the experimental results.

As mentioned above, one of the main application directions of the new method is to improve the attack success rate as much as possible under the premise of the limited number of power curves. Therefore, we limit the number of power curves to 3000 in discussing the success rate of different parameters in the Ant Colony Algorithm. Then we keep the other parameters unchanged and record the success rate of the CPA attack and the average computation time with different numbers of ants *ant* and ants' movements *times*. The experimental results are shown in Table 3, Table 4, Fig. 5 and Fig. 6.

There is a positive correlation between the number of ants and the success rate of CPA attacks. When the number of ants reaches 25, the increase of attack success rate becomes more slowly than before. When the number is up to 150, the success rate reaches a maximum of 84.375%.

Table 3. CPA attack success rate with different numbers of ants

Ant	Success rate(%)	Average computation time(s)
5	34.375	14.3312
10	57.031	19.0709
15	70.313	23.6315
20	72.656	28.8801
25	79.688	34.0064
30	80.469	38.3656
35	81.250	42.0212
40	81.250	45.8054
45	82.813	49.8914
50	83.594	60.7187
100	83.594	120.7354
150	84.375	205.3296

CPA attack success rate and average computation time
with different numbers of ants

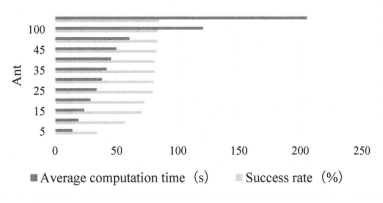

Fig. 5. CPA attack success rate with different numbers of ants

Simultaneously, there is a positive correlation between the number of ants and the average computation time. When the number of ants increases by 5, the average computation time averagely increases by 6.5862 s. Since the increase in the number of ants does not increase the cost of time much, it is a good choice to appropriately increase the number of ants, which can enhance the success rate of attack.

Table 4. CPA attack success rate with a different number of times

Times	Success rate (%)	Average computation time (s)
10	82.813	201.7058
20	74.219	233.8375
30	83.594	258.8970
40	83.594	289.9357
50	86.719	327.9992
60	83.594	354.6122
70	83.594	380.5585

CPA attack success rate average computation time
with different number of times

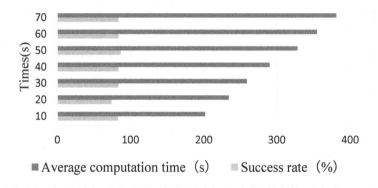

■ Average computation time（s）   ▪ Success rate（%）

Fig. 6. CPA attack success rate with a different number of times

As mentioned before, the relationship between the number of ants' movement (iteration rounds) and the success rate of attack is not linear. When the number of ants' movements is 50, the success rate of attack is the highest, reaching 86.719%. Using this as a benchmark, the success rate of attack will decrease no matter how ants' movement is increased or decreased. In this experiment, we can conclude that the optimal number of ants' movements of the Ant Colony Algorithm is 50.

To ensure that the experimental results are not affected by the number of ants, it is set to 200, leading to a longer average computation time. Also, the average computation time is positively related to the number of ants moving. While the number of ant movement increase by 10, the average computation time averagely increase by 25.5504 s. Since the increase in the number of ants' movement does not necessarily increase the success rate of attack, we do not recommend setting the ants number too large. It is more appropriate to repeat the experiments until the ant's number is adjusted to an optimal value.

5   Conclusion

In this paper, a new CPA attack method based on Ant Colony Algorithm is proposed. Based on the traditional CPA attack, this method combines the advantages of the Ant Colony Algorithm, including distributed computation, information positive feedback and heuristic searchability. It can fast search the optimal solution (the correct key) in the whole situation to improve the efficiency of the CPA attack. We believe the new method takes full advantage of all the eight S-boxes leakage and maximizes the utilization of leakage information. Thus, it significantly reduces the number of power curves needed for the attack and increases the success rate of the attack with limited power curves. To verify this, we compared the attack results of the new method and the original method by the attack experiment to the AES algorithm. The experimental results show that the new method far surpasses the original one in terms of the success rate of attack, the number of power curves required for attack, and computation time etc., which fully validates the validity of the new method. During the experiment, we found that some parameters of the ant colony algorithm, such as the number of ants and the number of ants' movements, will have an impact on the attack efficiency. We briefly discussed this and gave some suggestions on choosing the best parameters. The new CPA attack method proposed in this paper is universal, so it has a certain value for power analysis technology.

Acknowledgments. This research was supported by the High-tech discipline construction funds of China (No. 20210032Z0401, No. 20210033Z0402) and the open project of Key Laboratory of cryptography and information security in Guangxi, China (No. GCIS201912).

References

1. Kocher, P., Jaffe, J., Jun, B.: Differential power analysis. In: Wiener, M. (ed.) CRYPTO 1999. LNCS, vol. 1666, pp. 388–397. Springer, Heidelberg (1999). https://doi.org/10.1007/3-540-48405-1_25
2. Alioto, M., Poli, M., Rocchi, S.: Differential power analysis attacks to precharged buses: a general analysis for symmetric-key cryptographic algorithms. Dependab. Secure Comput. IEEE Trans. 7(3), 226–239 (2009)
3. Oswald, D., Paar, C.: Improving side-channel analysis with optimal linear transforms. In: Mangard, S. (ed.) CARDIS 2012. LNCS, vol. 7771, pp. 219–233. Springer, Heidelberg (2013). https://doi.org/10.1007/978-3-642-37288-9_15
4. Satoh, R., Matsushima, D., Shiozaki, M., et al.: Subkey driven hybrid power analysis attack in frequency domain against cryptographic LSIs and its evaluation. IEEJ Trans. Electron. Inf. Syst. 133(7), 1322–1330 (2013)
5. Kim, Y., Ko, H.: Using principal component analysis for practical biasing of power traces to improve power analysis attacks. In: Lee, H.-S., Han, D.-G. (eds.) ICISC 2013. LNCS, vol. 8565, pp. 109–120. Springer, Cham (2014). https://doi.org/10.1007/978-3-319-12160-4_7
6. Lerman, L., Bontempi, G., Markowitch, O.: Power analysis attack: an approach based on machine learning. Int. J. Appl. Cryptogr. 3(2), 97–115 (2014)
7. Shanmugam, D., Selvam, R., Annadurai, S.: Differential power analysis attack on SIMON and LED block ciphers. In: Chakraborty, R.S., Matyas, V., Schaumont, P. (eds.) SPACE 2014. LNCS, vol. 8804, pp. 110–125. Springer, Cham (2014). https://doi.org/10.1007/978-3-319-12060-7_8

8. Merino Del Pozo, S., Standaert, F.-X.: Blind source separation from single measurements using singular spectrum analysis. In: Güneysu, T., Handschuh, H. (eds.) CHES 2015. LNCS, vol. 9293, pp. 42–59. Springer, Heidelberg (2015). https://doi.org/10.1007/978-3-662-483 24-4_3

9. Guo, L., Li, Q., Wang, L., et al.: A differential power analysis attack on dynamic password token based on SM3 algorithm. International Conference on Information Science & Electronic Technology (2015)

10. Mahanta, H.J., Azad, A.K., Khan, A.K.: Power analysis attack: a vulnerability to smart card security. In: International Conference on Signal Processing & Communication Engineering Systems. IEEE (2015)

11. Guo, L., Wang, L., Liu, D., et al.: A chosen - plaintext differential power analysis attack on HMAC - SM3. In: 2015 11th International Conference on Computational Intelligence and Security (CIS). IEEE (2016)

12. Masoumi, M., Habibi, P., Dehghan, A., Jadidi, M., Yousefi, L.: Efficient implementation of power analysis attack resistant advanced encryption standard algorithm on side-channel attack standard evaluation board. Int. J. Internet Technol. Secur. Trans. **6**(3), 203 (2016). https://doi.org/10.1504/IJITST.2016.080392

13. Yoshikawa, M., Nozaki, Y., Asahi, K.: Multiple rounds aware power analysis attack for a lightweight cipher SIMECK. In: IEEE Second International Conference on Big Data Computing Service & Applications. IEEE (2016)

14. Cagli, E., Dumas, C., Prouff, E.: Convolutional neural networks with data augmentation against Jitter-based countermeasures. In: Fischer, W., Homma, N. (eds.) CHES 2017. LNCS, vol. 10529, pp. 45–68. Springer, Cham (2017). https://doi.org/10.1007/978-3-319-66787-4_3

15. Chakraborty, A., Mondal, A., Srivastava, A.: Correlation power analysis attack against STT-MRAM based cyptosystems. In: IEEE International Symposium on Hardware Oriented Security & Trust. IEEE (2017)

16. Wiemers, A., Klein, D.: Entropy reduction for the correlation-enhanced power analysis collision attack. In: Proceedings of the 13th International Workshop on Security, IWSEC 2018, Sendai, Japan, 3–5 Sep 2018 (2018)

17. Kim, J., Picek, S., Heuser, A., Bhasin, S., Hanjalic, A.: Make some noise unleashing the power of convolutional neural networks for profiled side-channel analysis. IACR Trans. Cryptogr. Hardw. Embed. Syst. **2019**(3), 148–179 (2019). 430

18. Benadjila, R., Prouff, E., Strullu, R., Cagli, E., Dumas, C.: Deep learning for side-channel analysis and introduction to ASCAD database. J. Cryptogr. Eng. **10**(2), 163–188 (2019)

19. Cai, X., Li, R., Kuang, S., Tan, J.: An energy trace compression method for differential power analysis attack. IEEE Access **8**, 89084–89092 (2020)

20. Duan, X., Chen, D., Fan, X., Li, X., Ding, D., Li, Y.: Research and implementation on power analysis attacks for unbalanced data. Secur. Commun. Netw. **2020**, 1–10 (2020)

Local Model Privacy-Preserving Study for Federated Learning

Kaiyun Pan[1], Daojing He[1(✉)], and Chuan Xu[2]

[1] Software Engineering Institute, East China Normal University, Shanghai, China
51184501038@stu.ecnu.edu.cn, djhe@sei.ecnu.edu.cn
[2] Inria Sophia Antipolis, Valbonne, France
chuan.xu@inria.fr

Abstract. In federated learning framework, data are kept locally by clients, which provides naturally a certain level of privacy. However, we show in this paper that a curious onlooker can still infer some sensitive information of clients by looking at the exchanged messages. More precisely, for the linear regression task, the onlooker can decode the exact local model of each client in a constant number of rounds under both cross-device and cross-silo federated learning settings. We improve one of the learning algorithms and experimentally show that it makes the onlooker harder to decode the local model of clients.

Keywords: Federated learning · Privacy-preserving · Distributed optimization · Differential privacy

1 Introduction

Nowadays, data privacy draws public attention in the approach of machine learning and statistics. Under the distributed network, many mobile devices can generate amounts of rich data and store them locally every day. With the improvement of computing and storage capabilities on these devices, it introduces the concern on the transmission of private sensitive data. Therefore, training statistical global models on remote devices rather than overpowered data server and making the storage of data locally become urgent problems to be solved. This is where the concept of federated learning (FL) comes from [1]. For privacy concerns, clients may not be willing to share their original data to data centers and keeping all private data on a central data processing server to train statistical models.

In conventional federated learning optimization algorithms, there is an assumption with a synchronous updating scheme running on entities communicating round by round in a distributed network. There is one server and fixed selected clients with fixed local dataset in this network, which the server sends the current global model parameters such as the model weight to selected clients for efficiency. In convex setting, each selected client calculates the updating

J. Garcia-Alfaro et al. (Eds.): SecureComm 2021, LNICST 398, pp. 287–307, 2021.
https://doi.org/10.1007/978-3-030-90019-9_15

gradient-descent step using the receiving model parameters from the server and sends the update to the server. The server averages on all receiving updates from selected clients and gets the updating global model parameter, and the process repeats. All selected clients and the server agree with a common optimal global model parameters.

The objective of the training is to solve the problem below:

$$\min_{w \in \mathbb{R}^d} l(w) \quad \text{where} \quad l(w) = \frac{1}{n} \sum_{i=1}^{n} l_i(w), \tag{1}$$

where n is the number of clients, w is the model parameters and $l_i(w)$ is the loss function of client i with respect to its local dataset. For a machine learning problem, the objective can be non-convex neural network and convex functions.

One primary advantage of federated learning is that the raw data are locally stored on the clients which can avoid the hidden onlooker to eavesdrop the personal raw data on the communication channels between clients and server. With the increasing attention of data privacy-preserving of personal information, data security and privacy-preserving analysis become important hotspots in myriad domains. Whereas FL has a prominent advantage on protecting personal information for clients, the sensitive information still could be deduced somehow by onlookers with analyzing the differences of the trained and uploaded relevant parameters sent by the clients. For example, paper [2] showed FL can disclose some important personal data from the parameter updates for distributed optimization and the transmission of gradients, the work in [3] demonstrated the client-level privacy leakage from federated learning by the attack from a malicious server.

In the literature, the traditional method to prevent privacy leakage is differential privacy (DP) [4]. Methods of DP based on FL were taken into account the trade-off between the convergence performance and privacy during the training process. The work in [6] proposed DP based FL algorithm focusing on the clients' privacy-preserving which utilized secure multiparty computation (SMC) for avoiding differential attacks. Whereas, the above works did not take into consideration the risk about local model privacy of clients from hidden onlookers during the uploading process. Motivated by this issue under the FL framework, we give an attempt to improve one FL algorithm and focus on how to protect the local model privacy for clients if there exists the onlooker based on our assumptions. There has been work done to show that sensitive information was hidden inside the model. The work in [7] introduced a model inversion attack for a linear classifier study, in which sensitive information of clients might be learned by the adversarial access to an ML model. Paper [8] proposed a novel class of model inversion attack, which showed how the adversarial queries recovered facial images only given the related names and access to ML model.

In our work, we consider two federated learning settings in paper [9]. Under the cross-device FL setting, a great deal of clients who are mobile or IOT devices can collaboratively train a model, the scale of clients is up to 10^{10}, which is massively parallel. The primary problems on the setting might be the communication efficiency. It's been applied in many domains, for example, Apple applied cross-device FL in IOS 13, applications like the voice recognition for "Hey Siri" [10], Google applied it extensively to features on Pixel phones [11] and the Gboard mobile keyboard [12]. Under cross-silo FL setting, clients train a model on siloed data who are different organizations, such as financial or medical data centers, while the scale of clients is normally 2–100 clients. The primary problem in the setting is about the communication or the computation. Cross-silo FL has been applied in rich domains like smart manufacturing [13] and reinsurance financial risk prediction [14]. For the data distribution under these settings, data are generated and stored locally on clients without the right to read data from others.

We give the counter-examples to show in both settings to show the known FL algorithms we studied can not protect the local model privacy when solving a simple linear regression task. Surprisingly, the onlooker can decode the exact local model in $O(1)$ time by just looking at exchanged messages. We improve one of the learning algorithms and experimentally show that it makes the onlooker harder to decode for the local model of clients.

The reminder of this paper is organized as follows: In Sect. 2, we introduce the preliminaries and background of FL. In Sect. 3, we introduce two kinds of FL settings, give the decoding process for the onlooker and propose our private method. In Sect. 4, we design a new onlooker to decode the model privacy and demonstrate our numerical experiments. In Sect. 5, we give our concluding remarks.

2   Preliminaries and Background

This section introduces some preliminaries and the related work about our study.

2.1   Graph Theory

Consider a network of N nodes represented by a directed graph $G = (V, E)$. Node set is $V = \{1, 2, ..., n\}$. Edge set is $E \subset V \times V$, whose elements are $(i, j) \in E$ if and only if there is a communication link from node j to node i, i.e., node j can send messages to node i. We assume no self-edges, i.e., $(i, i) \notin E$ for all $i \in V$. Parameter $p_{i,j} > 0$ represents the weight associated with each edge (i, j). The out-neighbor set of node i, i.e., the set of nodes that can receive messages from node i, denoted as $N_i^{out} = \{j \in V | (j, i) \in E\}, j \in N_i^{out}$. Similarly, the in-neighbor of node i which the set of nodes can send messages to node i, denoted as $N_i^{in} = \{j \in V | (i, j) \in E\}, j \in N_i^{in}$. Node i's out-degree is denoted as $D_i^{out} = |N_i^{out}|$ and its in-degree is denoted as $D_i^{in} = |N_i^{in}|$. Our work focuses on strongly connected graphs [15–17] which are defined as follows.

Definition 1. *A directed graph is strongly connected if for any $i, j \in V$, there is at least one directed path from i to j in G [18].*

2.2 Differential Privacy (DP)

The differential privacy was first proposed by Dwork et al. [19] in 2006 and has been widely studied, (ϵ, δ)–differential privacy was first addressed in [20].

Definition 2. *Differential privacy. A randomized algorithm $\mathcal{M}$ with domain $\mathbb{N}^{|x|}$ is (ϵ, δ)–differential private if for all $\mathcal{S} \subseteq \mathcal{M}$ and for all $x, y \in \mathbb{N}^{|x|}$ such that $\|x - y\|_1 \leq 1$:*

$$\Pr[\mathcal{M}(x) \in \mathcal{S}] \leq \exp(\epsilon) \Pr[\mathcal{M}(y) \in \mathcal{S}] + \delta,$$

where the probability space is over the coin flips of the mechanism $\mathcal{M}$, x is the dataset which we will query on, $\|x - y\|_1 \leq 1$ is a measure of how many records differ between x and y. If $\delta = 0$, we say that $\mathcal{M}$ is ϵ–differential private (DP).

2.3 Related Work

With the improvement of computing and storage capabilities of mobile devices, and the fact that the rich data which trained on data center is often private–sensitive, McMahan et al. [1] introduces the concept of *Federated learning*, in which keeping the trained local data on the mobile devices and learning a shared global machine learning model by collecting the updates locally calculated.

Achieving average consensus is an important problem in distributed computing and has been widely studied in distributed networks. Kempe et al. [21] and Bénézit et al. [22] introduced the conventional push–sum algorithm to achieve average consensus for nodes interacting on a directed graph. In the convex setting, Nedic et al. [23] proposed consensus–based gradient descent (CBGD) algorithm for distributed optimization. The work in [15] took efforts to study the converging rate to consensus. In this research direction, the relationship between consistency and convergence was worthy of attention [24]. Olshevsky et al. [25] proposed push–sum gradient descent (PSGD) algorithms while clients only sent partial model parameters to its neighbors for privacy which was the first setting on directed time–varying graphs. Paper [26,27,34] attached great importance to distributed optimization and estimation in machine learning. Paper [28,33,35] proposed a distributed subgradient optimization algorithm which was very close to the work done in [25].

During the federated learning process, even sensitive data held on the mobile devices, risks of privacy leakage are still available among the transmitted channels. One approach for privacy–preserving for sensitive data is adding noises on them. Differential privacy provides privacy guarantee, which ensures that the output from a query on the dataset does not change obviously whether one single data point for the inputting dataset is absent or not [4]. The work in [5] first gave an attempt to propose a novel DP algorithm which not only satisfied the privacy requirement but also kept the provable learning guarantees in convex settings. Nabi et al.[29] proposed an optimization algorithm applied a differential privacy mechanism into FL. Wei et al. [30] presented a novel approach by applying differential privacy before aggregating step, i.e., noising before model aggregation FL (NbAFL). DP could give the guarantees of privacy while sacrificing the accuracy, the trade–off between privacy and accuracy should be considered. In our work, we will show that our proposed algorithm could protect more privacy which means making the onlooker harder to decode the local model without sacrificing accuracy of results.

3   Model Privacy

In this section, we introduce the conception of local model privacy. We take into account the topology of a network as a distributed network with n clients. The communication channels are connected among n clients in a strongly connected directed graph $G = (V, E)$. Client i can send(receive) messages to (from) client $j, j \in N_i^{out}(N_i^{in})$. In this directed graph, every client i has a weight parameter vector $w_i \in \mathbb{R}^d$ related to the (global) model. Let $l_i(w) : \mathbb{R}^b \to \mathbb{R}$ be the local(loss) function of client i and w_i^* be the optimal local model, i.e., $w_i^* = \arg\min l_i(w)$. During the federated training process, clients can communicate with neighbors and update their w_i approximate to the optimal global parameter $w^* = \arg\min \sum_{i=1}^N l_i(w)$.

In our work, we assume that there is a strong onlooker who can eavesdrop all transmissions on channels during the training process, and know the training algorithm $\mathcal{A}$ and even the structure of the local (loss) function. Let $\mathcal{M}_i(\mathcal{A}, t)$ be the set of all the observations the onlooker collected by listening to the channels of the client i till round t when the algorithm is running on the network. Based on $\mathcal{M}_i(\mathcal{A}, t)$, the onlooker runs its decoding algorithm $\mathcal{D}$ to infer the client i's local model w_i^*. Let $w_i^{\mathcal{D}}(t)$ be the decoded model obtained by the onlooker, i.e., $w_i^{\mathcal{D}}(t) = \mathcal{D}(\mathcal{M}_i(\mathcal{A}, t))$. When the strong onlooker has the decoded model $w_i^{\mathcal{D}(t)}$ equaling to w_i^*, we say that the algorithm can not protect the local model privacy. In the following, we show that in both cross–device and cross–silo FL settings, the model privacy could not be protected when clients learn a linear regression model.

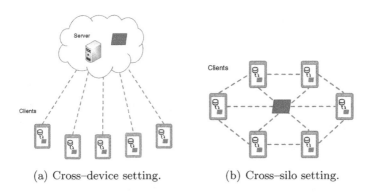

(a) Cross–device setting.   (b) Cross–silo setting.

Fig. 1. FL networks

3.1   Cross–Device Federated Learning

In order to achieve more efficient communication during the process of training global model, paper [1] proposed FederatedAveraging (FedAvg) algorithm shown in Algorithm 1. FedAvg is one of the cross–device FL algorithms controlled by three key parameters: C, the fraction of clients that perform calculation on each round; B, the local minibatch size used for clients at updating step; and E, the number of training passes (epochs) on local data of clients on each round. FedAvg calculates the updating gradient–descent step with E times instead only one time on selected clients at each round before averaging step. The server chooses C–fraction of clients on each round to do the SGD step over all data maintained on these clients [1]. At each round, the selected clients execute local SGD updates for E epochs before sending the updated model parameters back to the server, then the server averages all the model parameters sent by clients and sends back the updating parameters to clients, the process repeats at each round.

Note that the structure of cross–device FL distributed network is shown in Fig. 1(a) in which it has a server and clients, the communication among them is not peer–to–peer.

Algorithm 1. FederatedAveraging (FedAvg) algorithm.

//The K clients are indexed by k and η is the learning rate.
Server executes:
    initialize w_0
    for each round $t = 1, 2, \ldots$ **do**
        $m \leftarrow \max(C \cdot K, 1)$
        $S_t \leftarrow$ (random set of m clients)
        for each client $k \in S_t$ **in parallel do**
            $w_{t+1}^k \leftarrow$ ClientUpdate(k, w_t)
      $w_{t+1} \leftarrow \sum_{k=1}^{K} \frac{n_k}{n} w_{t+1}^k$

ClientUpdate(k, w): *// Run on client k*
    $\mathcal{B} \leftarrow$ (split $\mathcal{P}_k$ into batches of size B)
    for each local epoch i from 1 to E **do**
        for batch $b \in \mathcal{B}$ **do**
            $w \leftarrow w - \eta \nabla \ell(w; b)$
    return w to server

Observation 1. *When clients train a linear regression task using full local batch for gradient updates, FedAvg can not protect the local model privacy.*

Proof. Here, we give a simple instance to demonstrate Observation 1. We assume there is an onlooker who knows the structure of the loss function, the learning rate η, and how FedAvg works.

We consider a simple one–dimensional linear regression model ($d = 1$) and the loss function is least quadratic. Thus the loss function is shown as following:

$$l_i(w) = a_i(w - w_i^*)^2 + b_i \tag{2}$$

and

$$\nabla l_i(w) = 2a_i w - 2a_i w_i^*. \tag{3}$$

So at round t, the onlooker who listens on the channels between client i and server can collect the messages w_t and w_t^i, w_t represents the model parameter on server and w_t^i represents the updated model on client i.

We set the notation $e \in \{1, ..., E\}$ and $w_t^i(e)$ represents the model that updated of the eth local epoch on client i at round t, note that $w_t^i = w_t^i(E)$. At the phase of ClientUpdate in Algorithm 1, we get the following updating equation on client i at round t:

$$
\begin{aligned}
w_t^i(e) &= w_t^i(e-1) - \eta \nabla l_i(w_t^i(e-1)) \\
&= (1 - 2a_i\eta)^e w_t + 2\eta a_i w_i^* \sum_{j=0}^{e-1} (1 - 2a_i\eta)^j \\
&= x_i^e w_t + w_i^*(1 - x_i^e),
\end{aligned}
\tag{4}
$$

where $x_i = 1 - 2a_i\eta$ and only x_i and w_i^* are unknown.

The decoding algorithm $\mathcal{D}$ works as follows.

Once the onlooker gets the messages $w_t, w_t^i(E)$ at round t, he rebuilds the following linear equation in two unknowns:

$$w_t^i(E) = x_i^E w_t + w_i^*(1 - x_i^E), \tag{5}$$

where $w_t^i(E), w_t, E$ are known.

At round $t+1$, the onlooker rebuilds another linear equation in two unknowns if $i \in S_{t+1}$:

$$w_{t+1}^i(E) = x_i^E w_{t+1} + w_i^*(1 - x_i^E). \tag{6}$$

By solving the system of linear equations in two unknowns (5) and (6), at round $t + 1$, the onlooker gets:

$$x_i^E = \frac{d_{t+1}^i(E)}{d_{t+1}} \tag{7}$$

and

$$w_i^{\mathcal{D}} = w_i^* = \frac{w_t^i(E) - x_i^E w_t}{1 - x_i^E}, \tag{8}$$

where $d_{t+1}^i(E) = w_{t+1}^i(E) - w_t^i(E), d_{t+1} = w_{t+1} - w_t$.

The above analysis shows that the onlooker can succeed in decoding the sensitive local model of client i, i.e., w_i^*. Therefore, when clients train a linear regression task, FedAvg which is under cross–device FL setting can not protect the local model privacy.

3.2 Cross–Silo Federated Learning

Consensus–Based Gradient Descent Algorithm (CBGD). We first study the widely used CBGD algorithm[23] that was first proposed for decentralized optimization where no centralized node exists that can be easily applied in a cross–silo setting. This algorithm can avoid the communication bottleneck introduced in FedAvg, and can be highly adaptive to the communication network among silos. One feature of CBGD algorithm is that clients can interact and send (receive) their updating models to (from) their neighbors in an undirected graph. The algorithm can be realized synchronous distributed optimization based on consensus (but requiring convex and separable functions) [17,31].

The CBGD algorithms follow the following general procedures at round t, for each client i on a strongly connected graph shown in Fig. 1(b) seen as undirected.

Algorithm 2. Consensus–based gradient descent algorithm by client $i \in V$ at round t.

---

1. **for** $t \in \{0, ..., T\}$ **do**
2.   broadcasts model $w_i(t)$ to its neighbors in N_i and receives models $w_j(t)$ from every $j \in N_i$
3.   calculates a weighted average over all the received models and its own model $w_i(t)$: $z_i(t) = \sum_{j \in N_i \cup \{i\}} p_{i,j} w_j(t)$,
    notes that the weight matrix P is doubly stochastic
4.   updates its model: $w_i(t+1) = z_i(t) - \eta_t \nabla l_i(\tilde{w}(t))$,
    where $\tilde{w}(t)$ could be $w_i(t)$ or $z_i(t)$ depending on the algorithm

---

Observation 2. *When clients train a linear regression task, consensus–based gradient descent algorithm can not protect the local model privacy.*

Proof. We consider the same linear regression model as the former subsection and the knowledge of the local loss function is the form as (2) and (3). Therefore, the onlooker who listens for the channels of client i collects the data $\mathcal{M}_i(\mathcal{A}, t) = \mathcal{M}_i(\mathcal{A}, t-1) \cup \{w_j | j \in N_i \cup \{i\}\}$. Since the onlooker knows how the algorithm works including the consensus matrix P and learning rate η, he can obtain $z_i(t)$ and $\tilde{w}(t)$, then obtain $w_i(t+1)$.

The process of decoding algorithm $\mathcal{D}$ works as follows.

Once the onlooker gets the knowledge of $w_i(t+1)$ at round $t+1$, he can rebuild the following linear equation:

$$w_i(t+1) - z_i(t) = -2\eta_t(a_i \tilde{w}(t) - a_i w_i^*), \qquad (9)$$

where only a_i and w_i^* are unknown. At round $t+2$, doing the same as before, he can get another linear equation:

$$w_i(t+2) - z_i(t+1) = -2\eta_{t+1}(a_i \tilde{w}(t+1) - a_i w_i^*). \qquad (10)$$

Thus, the onlooker can get two unknown linear equations from (9) and (10), then recalculate the solutions as:

$$a_i = \left(\frac{d_i(t+2)}{2\eta_{t+1}} - \frac{d_i(t+1)}{2\eta_t} \right) \times \frac{1}{\tilde{w}(t) - \tilde{w}(t+1)}$$

and

$$w_i^{\mathcal{D}}(t+2) = w_i^* = \tilde{w}(t) + \frac{d_i(t+1)}{2a_i\eta_t},$$

where $d_i(t+1) = w_i(t+1) - z_i(t)$.

Therefore, starting from round 0, the onlooker under assumptions could succeed in decoding the local optimum w_i^* of client i at round 2, i.e., when clients train a linear regression task, the cross–silo FL algorithm can not protect local model privacy.

Push–Sum Gradient Descent Algorithm (PSGD). In CBGD algorithm, we observe that the entire model parameters sent by the clients to neighbors gave an important hint for the decoding process of the onlooker. In order to avoid the privacy leakage, we turn to study PSGD algorithm [25] in which clients only send partial models to their neighbors in directed graphs (also works in undirected graphs). PSGD algorithm aims to solve the minimize problem shown in (1) in a time–varying series of uniformly strongly connected directed graphs with a collection of n nodes, which have access to the local dataset to calculate the corresponding loss functions (convex functions). Each node knows its out–degree and the state of the algorithm by rounds, while unknown about the number of clients and the graph series as the condition to implement the algorithm. Paper [25] shows that this algorithm can achieve distributed optimization with the convergence rate as $O(\log t/\sqrt{t})$. Nevertheless, we find the privacy vulnerability risk during the communication among all nodes in the distributed networks.

We reference the knowledge of graph theory shown in Sect. 2.1, $p_{j,i}(t)$ represents the weight put on the client i's model when i sends its model parameters to its neighbor $j, j \in N_i^{out}(t)$ at round t, and $\sum_{j \in N_i^{out}(t) \cup \{i\}} p_{j,i}(t) = 1$, i.e., P is column–stochastic.

For initialization, client i has $x_i(0) = w_i(0) \in \mathbb{R}^d$, scalar variable $y_i(0) = 1$, weights $p_{j,i}(t), \forall j \in N_i^{out}(t) \cup \{i\}, t \in \{0, ..., T\}$. The algorithm works as follows at round t, for each client i.

Algorithm 3. Push–sum gradient descent (PSGD) algorithm by client $i \in V$ at round t.

---

1. **for** $t \in \{0, ..., T\}$ **do**
2.   computes $p_{j,i}(t)x_i(t)$ and $p_{j,i}(t)y_i(t)$, sends them to all client $j \in N_i^{out}(t)$
3.   receives $p_{i,j}(t)x_j(t)$ and $p_{i,j}(t)y_j(t)$ from every client $j \in N_i^{in}(t)$ and sums them as follows:

$$z_i(t+1) = \sum_{j \in N_i^{in}(t) \cup \{i\}} p_{i,j}(t)x_j(t), \quad y_i(t+1) = \sum_{j \in N_i^{in}(t) \cup \{i\}} p_{i,j}(t)y_j(t)$$

4.   updates local parameter: $w_i(t+1) \leftarrow \frac{z_i(t+1)}{y_i(t+1)}$
5.   executes one step of gradient descent: $x_i(t+1) \leftarrow z_i(t+1) - \eta_{t+1}\nabla l_i(w_i(t+1))$

Observation 3. *When clients train a linear regression task, push–sum gradient descent algorithm can not protect the local model privacy.*

Proof. With the assumptions that the onlooker knows how Algorithm 3 works, the learning rate $\eta(t)$, the structure of the loss function of clients and $y_i(0) = 1$, we give the decoding procedures for the onlooker to decode $x_i(t), z_i(t), w_i(t+1)$ during the execution of Algorithm 3.

We consider a simple one–dimension linear regression task ($d = 1$), and the knowledge of the local loss function is the form as (2) and (3).

At round 0, the onlooker who eavesdrops the channels of i collects messages such as $\mathcal{M}_x^{in}(0) = \{p_{i,j}(0)x_j(0), \forall j \in N_i^{in}(0)\}$, $\mathcal{M}_y^{in}(0) = \{p_{i,j}(0)y_j(0), \forall j \in N_i^{in}(0)\}$, $\mathcal{M}_x^{out}(0) = \{p_{j,i}(0)x_i(0), \forall j \in N_i^{out}(0)\}$, $\mathcal{M}_y^{out}(0) = \{p_{j,i}(0)y_i(0), \forall j \in N_i^{out}(0)\}$. Because he knows $y_i(0) = 1$, he can randomly pick one pair of corresponding data from $\mathcal{M}_x^{out}(0), \mathcal{M}_y^{out}(0)$ for calculating $x_i(0) = \frac{p_{j,i}(0)x_i(0)}{p_{j,i}(0)y_i(0)}y_i(0)$. Due to weight matrix P is column–stochastic, i.e., $\sum_{j \in N_i^{out}(t) \cup \{i\}} p_{j,i}(t) = 1$, he can obtain the values of $z_i(1), y_i(1)$:

$$
\begin{aligned}
z_i(1) &= \sum_{j \in N_i^{in}(0)} p_{i,j}(0)x_j(0) + p_{i,i}(0)x_i(0) \\
&= \sum_{j \in N_i^{in}(0)} p_{i,j}(0)x_j(0) + (1 - \sum_{j \in N_i^{out}(0)} p_{j,i}(0))x_i(0) \\
&= \sum_{m \in \mathcal{M}_x^{in}(0)} m - \sum_{m \in \mathcal{M}_x^{out}(0)} m + x_i(0)
\end{aligned}
\tag{11}
$$

and

$$
\begin{aligned}
y_i(1) &= \sum_{j \in N_i^{in}(0) \cup \{i\}} p_{i,j}(0)y_j(0) \\
&= \sum_{m \in \mathcal{M}_y^{in}(0)} m - \sum_{m \in \mathcal{M}_y^{out}(0)} m + y_i(0).
\end{aligned}
\tag{12}
$$

Therefore, the onlooker can decode the value of $w_i(1)$ from updating step in Algorithm 3:

$$
w_i(1) = \frac{z_i(1)}{y_i(1)}.
$$

Then the onlooker can rebuild the following linear equation according to the gradient–descent step in line 5 from Algorithm 3 and the structure of loss function:

$$
x_i(1) = z_i(1) - 2\eta_1 a_i(w_i(1) - w_i^*),
\tag{13}
$$

where $x_i(1)$ can be obtained by the onlooker at round 1 by doing the same process for decoding the value of $x_i(0)$ at round 0.

As the process repeats, the onlooker can obtain $z_i(2), y_i(2), w_i(2)$ by listening the channels of client i to rebuild the following linear equation:

$$
x_i(2) = z_i(2) - 2\eta_2 a_i(w_i(2) - w_i^*),
\tag{14}
$$

where the onlooker can obtain $x_i(2)$ by repeating the same procedures as before at round 2.

Thus the onlooker can get the two unknown linear equations from (13) and (14) to recalculate the solutions as:

$$a_i = (\frac{d_i(2)}{2\eta_2} - \frac{d_i(1)}{2\eta_1}) \times \frac{1}{w_i(1) - w_i(2)})$$

and

$$w_i^{\mathcal{D}} = w_i^* = \frac{d_i(1)}{2a_i\eta_1 + w_i(1)},$$

where $d_i(t) = x_i(t) - z_i(t)$.

Thus, the onlooker can obtain the local models of clients only by 3 rounds from round 0, i.e., the PSGD algorithm can not protect local model privacy.

3.3   Private Push–Sum Gradient Descent Algorithm (PPSGD)

Algorithm 4. Private push–sum gradient descent by client $i \in V$ at round t.

    // Client i has initial value $x_i(0) = w_i(0) \in \mathbb{R}^d$ and scalar value $0 < \beta < \alpha < \frac{1}{2}$.

1. randomly generates $y_i(0)$ from a distribution on a non–zero positive range
2. **for** $t \in \{0, ..., T\}$ **do**
3.   **if** $|N_i^{out}(t)| > 0$ **then**
4.   chooses $p_{i,i}$ from a distribution on range $[\beta, \alpha]$
5. $p_{j,i} \leftarrow \frac{1-p_{i,i}(t)}{|N_i^{out}(t)|}, \forall j \in N_i^{out}(t)$
6.   **else** $p_{i,i} \leftarrow 1$
7.   broadcasts $p_{j,i}(t)x_i(t), p_{j,i}(t)y_i(t)$ to clients $j \in N_i^{out}(t)$ and receives
     $p_{i,j}(t)x_j(t), p_{i,j}(t)y_j(t)$ from every client $j \in N_i^{in}(t)$ and sums them as follows:

$$z_i(t+1) = \sum_{j \in N_i^{in}(t) \cup \{i\}} p_{i,j}(t)x_j(t), \quad y_i(t+1) = \sum_{j \in N_i^{in}(t) \cup \{i\}} p_{i,j}(t)y_j(t)$$

8.   updates local parameter: $w_i(t+1) \leftarrow \frac{z_i(t+1)}{y_i(t+1)}$
9.   executes gradient descent step: $x_i(t+1) \leftarrow z_i(t+1) - \eta_{t+1}\nabla l_i(w_i(t+1))$

According to the analysis about the privacy leakage from the three observations, we focus on improving Algorithm 3 to make the onlooker harder to decode the local model privacy. Since the onlooker can deduce the local models by eavesdropping all the transmission without adding noises on channels under the three FL algorithms, we find the condition of $y_i(0) = 1$ in Algorithm 3 can give the onlooker very important information to decode local model privacy. In order to puzzle the onlooker, we propose our private method shown in Algorithm 4 by randomly generating $y_i(0)$ at the client side in line 1 and designing a new strategy for weight matrix P in line 3–6. The work in [25] showed the weight strategy in time–varying graphs that the weights put on the messages of client i were the same as $p_{j,i}(t) = \frac{1}{|N_i^{out}(t)|+1}, \forall j \in N_i^{out}(t) \cup \{i\}$. However, the design for the weight matrix P in [25] can be deduced easily for the onlooker who can listen the messages on the channels with the knowledge of the degree $|N_i^{out}(t)|$ of each client at each round, so that to help the onlooker to obtain the values of $x_i(t), y_i(t), z_i(t+1), w_i(t+1)$ at round t, then even decoding the local model. The weight strategy in our proposed private method can hardly make the onlooker to decode the value of $p_{j,i}(t)$ even he knows the degree $|N_i^{out}(t)|$ of client i, i.e., making the onlooker harder to decode the local privacy. We experimentally show the performance of PPSGD in the next section.

4 Experiments and Relevant Analysis

In this section, we implement on our distributed network shown in Fig. 2 to show the convergence of our PPSGD, the performance of the onlooker designed in Sect. 4.2 on decoding from the time–series data by listening the channels of client i, the classification accuracy for the onlooker from different distributions of $y_i(0)$ on our PPSGD and we also run our algorithm on a real dataset to see the corresponding results.

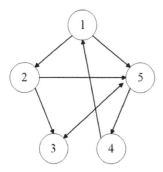

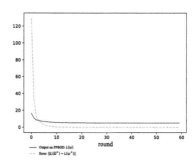

Fig. 2. A strongly connected directed graph with 5 nodes.

Fig. 3. Convergence on PPSGD.

We consider a network of 5 nodes whose goal is to distributively solve the following minimization problem which is the same idea with (1):

$$\min \quad L(w) \triangleq \sum_{i=1}^{n} l_i(w) \quad \text{over} \quad w \in \mathbb{R}^d, \tag{15}$$

where we assume node i has already trained its local model on the local dataset which is a convex function $l_i : \mathbb{R}^d \to \mathbb{R}^1$, i.e., the loss function. Under the assumption that the set of optimal solutions $w^* = \arg\min_{w \in \mathbb{R}^d} L(w)$ is not empty. We apply the PPSGD by which all clients maintain variables $w_i(t)$ converging to the same point in w^* over time.

Thus, our baseline is the original local models (loss functions) trained by the clients are shown in following:

$$\begin{cases} l_1(w) = w^2 - 4w + 4 \\ l_2(w) = w^2 - 9w + 9 \\ l_3(w) = w^2 - 4w + 7 \\ l_4(w) = w^2 - 4w + 4.75 \\ l_5(w) = w^2 + w + 0.25 \end{cases} \tag{16}$$

and

$$\min \quad L(w) \triangleq \sum_{i=1}^{5} l_i(w) = 5(w-2)^2 + 5. \tag{17}$$

Hence, we can see the optimum of the global model $L(w)$ is 5 when $w = 2$ which means each client converges to the optimal solution $w^* = 2$.

4.1   The Convergence of PPSGD Algorithm

We use the programming language Python to implement our PPSGD algorithm to see the convergence results based on the baseline. Figure 3 shows the evolution of $L(w)$ and the error between the real global optimum $L(w^*)$ and the output $L(\tilde{w}^*)$ from our PPSGD. We observe that the output converges to the exact optimal value 5 and the error is equal to 0 after around 20 rounds. Thus, our proposed algorithm can still guarantee the convergence without sacrificing the accuracy of the optimal solution and achieve distributed optimization. Actually the convergence of Algorithm 4 can be proven, but here we move the result to the future work.

4.2   New Design for Onlooker

Now we consider an onlooker with an easier task: is the local model different from our baseline when the onlooker only has the ability of listening to the transmitted messages on the channels of client i. Baseline represents the original setting of our distributed network such as the local dataset maintained by clients set in (16) and the structure of the network shown in Fig. 2. The task means if we do modification on one client's local dataset (local model) as a new case, could the onlooker notice that we did such modification according to all transmitted observations collected from our baseline and the new cases. This could be the same spirit of the differential privacy shown in Sect. 2.2.

Shortly, now we assume the onlooker can train a machine learning classifier model from the two datasets (one is collected from original network, i.e., our baseline with label 0, another dataset is collected from the case that we do a little change on one client's local model with label 1). If he uses the model he learned on these two datasets, we want to see that he still can't distinguish whether local model has been changed from the outputs of his learning model, which could confirm our method could make the onlooker harder to deduce the local model of clients.

We can see that all the observations collected by the onlooker have time–series property. Here, we let the training model trained by the onlooker be the inception model [32] by importing package fast–ai[1] in the implementation, then he can predict the data from which classes according to the output of the learning model.

The performance of the onlooker is related to how we define the training dataset and testing dataset collected by the onlooker. Moreover, we define the weak onlooker and the strong onlooker. The details are shown in the following experimental subsection.

4.3   Classification on Time–Series Data

As the new onlooker we designed in Sect. 4.2 under the above setting shown in (16) and (17), i.e., our baseline, we assume all time–series observations transmitted on the channels belonging to class 0, and all the observations transmitted on the channels belonging to class 1 under the case that we did change on the local model of client 5.

Then we change the local model of client 5 increasingly to see the classification results by weak onlooker and strong onlooker under Algorithm 3 and Algorithm 4. The change on the local model of client 5 is shown in Table 1 and Table 2.

Weak Onlooker. Table 1 shows the form of the testing dataset and training dataset for the weak onlooker's classification model. We generate new local models by changing the local model of client 5 from our baseline (Case 0). And it shows the variation on the optimal global model $L(w^*)$ and the optimal solution w^* by changing the local model $l_5(w)$.

For the training dataset, we respectively run 100 times of Algorithm 3 and Algorithm 4 with 100 rounds for our baseline (Case 0) to get 100 data with label 0, then we respectively run 20 times of these 2 algorithms with 100 rounds for Case 1–5 to get totally 100 data with label 1. For the testing dataset, we run 100 times of the 2 algorithms with 100 rounds for Case 0 to get 100 data with label 0, then we get another 100 data with label 1 for Case 6 with the same way. Therefore, we finish the collections of the dataset for the onlooker.

To visualize the classification, we use the UMAP[2] to do the dimensional reduction and the data point in the leftmost column of Fig. 4 represents all the observations from the channels got from one single execution(time) of the

---

[1] https://github.com/tcapelle/timeseries_fastai.

[2] UMAP is a general purpose manifold learning and dimension reduction algorithm: https://umap-learn.readthedocs.io/en/latest/basic_usage.html.

Table 1. Weak onlooker

Samples	Case	Local function of client 5	w^*	$L(w^*)$	Label
Training dataset (200 data)					
100	0 (baseline)	$w^2 + w + 0.25$	2	5	0
20	1	$w^2 + 0.4w + 1.75$	2.06	5.28	1
20	2	$w^2 - 0.2w + 3.25$	2.12	5.528	1
20	3	$w^2 - 0.8w + 4.75$	2.18	5.74	1
20	4	$w^2 - 1.4w + 6.25$	2.24	5.91	1
20	5	$w^2 - 2w + 7.75$	2.3	6.05	1
Testing dataset (200 data)					
100	0	$w^2 + w + 0.25$	2	5	0
100	6	$w + 0.5w + 1.2625$	2.05	5	1

Table 2. Strong onlooker

Samples	Case	Local function of client 5	w^*	$L(w^*)$	Label
Training dataset (200 data)					
100	0 (baseline)	$w^2 + w + 0.25$	2	5	0
100	6	$w^2 + 0.5w + 1.2625$	2.05	5	1
Testing dataset (200 data)					
100	0	$w^2 + w + 0.25$	2	5	0
100	6	$w + 0.5w + 1.2625$	2.05	5	1

algorithms we use, such as there are 200 data points which each of them has the length of 1600 values in our experiment due to there are 8 links in Fig. 2.

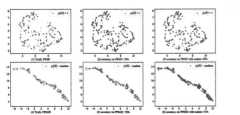

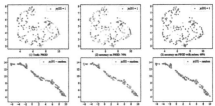

Fig. 4. Classification accuracy by weak onlooker.

Fig. 5. Classification accuracy by strong onlooker.

The ground truth of the classification is shown in Fig. 4(1) and (4) where the red points belong to class 0, violet points belong to class 1 on Algorithm 3 and Algorithm 4. From the horizontal direction in Fig. 4, the rightmost column plots (3) and (6) represent the classification accuracy results by adding the Gaussian noises on the transmitted observations with the accuracy as 66%, 51%, respectively. And the middle two column plots (2) and (5) represent the classification accuracy results under the two algorithms with the accuracy as 74%, 72%. From the vertical direction, the upper three plots (1), (2), (3) are the classification results under Algorithm 3, and the lower three plots (4), (5), (6) represent the classification results under Algorithm 4.

Thus, we observe that the classification accuracy under Algorithm 3 is higher than it under our proposed Algorithm 4, which means our private method can make the onlooker harder to decode the local model without harming the accuracy of the result from the cross–silo FL algorithms, i.e., the global optimum. Adding Gaussian noises can somehow protect privacy but also sacrifice the accuracy of the result.

Strong Onlooker. In the similar way, we define the dataset for the strong onlooker shown in Table 2, in which the training dataset and testing dataset are from the same two cases. Figure 5 shows the classification accuracy by the strong onlooker. We observe the similar conclusions with the weak onlooker, comparing to Fig. 4, it shows that the classification accuracy by the strong onlooker is higher than the results from the weak onlooker, i.e., the weak onlooker is harder to decode the local model privacy of clients.

4.4   The Influence on PPSGD from the Distribution of $y_i(0)$

Table 3. The distribution of $y_i(0)$

No.	Distribution of $y_i(0)$	Exp	Var	Algorithm
1	$y_i(0) = 1$	\	\	PSGD
2	$y_i(0) = 1$ Adding noises $\sim N(0, 0.065)$	\	\	PSGD
3	$y_i(0) \sim U(0.5, 1.5)$	1	0.083	PPSGD
4	$y_i(0) \sim U(0.3, 1.7)$	1	0.163	PPSGD
5	$y_i(0) \sim U(0.1, 1.9)$	1	0.27	PPSGD
6	$y_i(0) \sim Exp(1)$	1	1	PPSGD
7	$y_i(0) \sim Lognormal(-1, 2)$	1	6.39	PPSGD

To observe the influence of $y_i(0)$ for the classification accuracy from the strong onlooker's model on the test dataset, we choose to test 20000 data on a strong onlooker's model to do classification. Then we choose to randomly generate $y_i(0)$ from three kinds of distributions and add Gaussian noises to data when $y_i(0) = 1$ to see the corresponding classification results, the details are shown in Tab. 3.

Here, we only focus on the transmitted data on the channels related to client 1, and for one single execution only with 3 rounds which means the shape of the training and test dataset is (20000, 18), note that we set the number of epochs as 10 in the learning model.

Figure 6(a) and (b) show that the relation of the training loss and accuracy is inverse. The higher classification accuracy means the onlooker can decode better to more accurately distinguish two classes, instead easier to decode the local privacy. PPSGD can make the onlooker harder to decode more privacy of local model and can't harm the accuracy results from the algorithm than the traditional privacy–preserving way like adding noises (see the red dashed lines and green lines with square marker).

From the results under the cases we randomly generate $y_i(0)$ from different distributions, we observe that when the expectation of $y_i(0)$ is equal to 1, the larger the variance of $y_i(0)$ is, the smaller the classification accuracy is, instead the more secure to protect local privacy, and harder for the onlooker to distinguish two classes (see the lines except red lines).

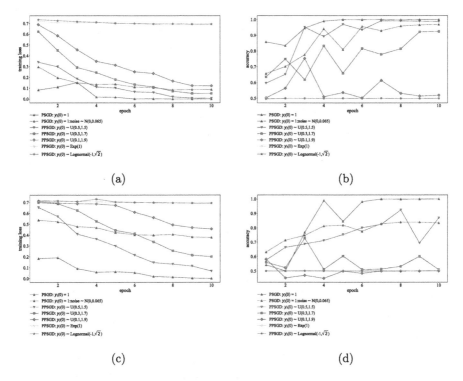

Fig. 6. (a), (b) represent the evolution of training loss and accuracy of the training model of the onlooker with 10 epochs, respectively; (c), (d) represent the evolution of training loss and accuracy of the training model of the onlooker with 10 epochs by removing $y_i(t)$, respectively. (Color figure online)

Then we do the same experiment but removing the information about $y_i(t)$ from the dataset, we want to see whether the onlooker considers the element

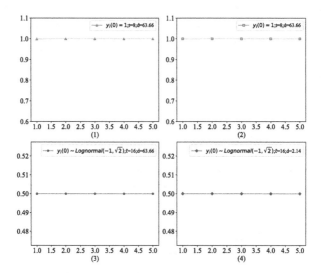

Fig. 7. Classification results on multivariate data.

about $y_i(t)$ for its decoding classifier algorithm in its learning process. The results are shown in Fig. 6(c) and (d). Comparing to Fig. 6(a) and (b), we infer that there is a relation between $x_i(t)$ and $y_i(t)$ in the learning model of the onlooker. And removing the information about $y_i(t)$ from the dataset makes the onlooker harder to do classification correctly. While it won't influence the results under the case $y_i(0) = 1$ (PSGD) (see the red lines with triangle marker in Fig. 6(b) and Fig. 6(d)) which shows the onlooker doesn't need to consider $y_i(t)$ in its learning algorithm and still could accurately distinguish the two classes.

4.5 Classification on Multivariate Data

To show the performance of the onlooker on multivariate data, we change the network as a ring with 10 nodes. We choose the Boston Housing Dataset[3] to simulate clients to do multi–feature linear regression on this dataset with 5 epochs. Shortly, in the same way, to see the performance of the model trained by the onlooker on multivariate data, we respectively do experiments under different cases.

Figure 7 shows that the classification results by the onlooker under PSGD and PPSGD, d represents the variation of the local optimum on one client's local model, t represents the number of rounds at each execution. Obviously, it shows that our private method makes the onlooker harder to decode the local model privacy of clients.

---

[3] Boston House Dataset:https://scikit-learn.org/stable/modules/generated/sklearn. datasets.load_bost-on.html.

5   Conclusion

In our work, we first focus on studying FL algorithms under cross–device and cross–silo FL settings, and we propose the concept of local model privacy. We demonstrate that these algorithms can not protect the local model privacy for clients when they train a linear regression task with the assumption of existing a curious onlooker. We improve one cross–silo FL algorithm, experimentally show the relevant performance of our private method and it makes the onlooker harder to decode the local model privacy of clients. In the future work, we will focus on study the performance on PPSGD in more complex ML problems, such as neural network.

Acknowledgment. Most of the work was finished during the master internship of the first author in Inria Sophia Antipolis, France. We would like to thank Prof. Giovanni Neglia and Dr. Chuan Xu for their ideas and suggestions. And this research is supported by the National Key R&D Program of China (2017YFB0801701 and 2017YFB0802805), the National Natural Science Foundation of China (Grants: U1936120, U1636216), Joint Fund of Ministry of Education of China for Equipment Preresearch (No. 6141A020333), the Fundamental Research Funds for the Central Universities, and the Basic Research Program of State Grid Shanghai Municipal Electric Power Company (52094019007F). Daojing He is the corresponding author of this article.

References

1. McMahan, B., Moore, E., Ramage, D., et al.: Communication-efficient learning of deep networks from decentralized data. In: Artificial Intelligence and Statistics. PMLR, pp. 1273–1282 (2017)
2. Ma, C., Li, J., Ding, M., Shu, F., et al.: On safeguarding privacy and security in the framework of federated learning. IEEE Network **34**(4), 242–248 (2020)
3. Wang, Z., Song, M., Zhang, Z., Song, Y., Qi, H.: Beyond inferring class representatives: user-level privacy leakage from federated learning. In: IEEE INFOCOM 2019 - IEEE Conference on Computer Communications, pp. 2512–2520. IEEE (2019)
4. Dwork, C., Roth, A.: The algorithmic foundations of differential privacy. Found. Trends Theor. Comput. Sci. **9**(3–4), 211–407 (2014)
5. Li, J., Khodak, M., Caldas, S., Talwalkar, A.: Differentially Private Meta-Learning. arXiv preprint arXiv:1909.05830 (2019)
6. Truex, S., Baracaldo, N., Anwar, A., Steinke, T., et al.: A hybrid approach to privacy-preserving federated learning. In: Proceedings of the 12th ACM Workshop on Artificial Intelligence and Security, pp. 1–11. ACM (2019)
7. Fredrikson, M., Lantz, E., Jha, S., et al.: Privacy in pharmacogenetics: an end-to-end case study of personalized warfarin dosing. In: 23rd USENIX Security Symposium (USENIX Security 2014), pp. 17–32. USENIX (2014)
8. Fredrikson, M., Jha, S., Ristenpart, T.: Model inversion attacks that exploit confidence information and basic countermeasures. In: Proceedings of the 22nd ACM SIGSAC Conference on Computer and Communications Security, pp. 1322–1333. ACM (2015)

9. Kairouz, P., McMahan, H.B., Avent, B., et al.: Advances and open problems in federated learning. arXiv preprint arXiv:1912.04977 (2019)
10. Apple: Designing for privacy (video and slide deck). Apple WWDC (2019). https://developer.apple.com/videos/play/wwdc2019/708
11. ai.google: Under the hood of the Pixel 2: How AI is supercharging hardware (2018). https://ai.google/stories/ai-in-hardware
12. Hard, A., Rao, K., Mathews, R., et al.: Federated learning for mobile keyboard prediction. arXiv preprint arXiv:1811.03604 (2018)
13. Musketeer: The MUSKETEER cross-domain platform will validate progress in the two industrial scenarios: SMART MANUFACTURING and HEALTH CARE (2019). http://musketeer.eu/project
14. WeBank: WeBank and Swiss resigned cooperation MOU (2019). https://finance.yahoo.com/news/webank-swiss-signed-cooperation-mou-112300218.html
15. Blondel, V.D., Hendrickx, J.M., Olshevsky, A., et al.: Convergence in multiagent coordination, consensus, and flocking. In: Proceedings of the 44th IEEE Conference on Decision and Control, pp. 2996–3000. IEEE (2005)
16. Jadbabaie, A., Lin, J., Morse, A.S.: Coordination of groups of mobile autonomous agents using nearest neighbor rules. IEEE Trans. Autom. Control **48**(6), 988–1001 (2003)
17. Tsitsiklis, J., Bertsekas, D., Athans, M.: Distributed asynchronous deterministic and stochastic gradient optimization algorithms. IEEE Trans. Autom. Control **31**(9), 803–812 (1986)
18. Gao, H., Wang, Y.: Dynamics Based Privacy Protection for Average Consensus on Directed Graphs. arXiv preprint arXiv:1812.02255 (2018)
19. Dwork, C.: Differential privacy. In: Bugliesi, M., Preneel, B., Sassone, V., Wegener, I. (eds.) ICALP 2006. LNCS, vol. 4052, pp. 1–12. Springer, Heidelberg (2006). https://doi.org/10.1007/11787006_1
20. Dwork, C., Kenthapadi, K., McSherry, F., Mironov, I., Naor, M.: Our data, ourselves: privacy via distributed noise generation. In: Vaudenay, S. (ed.) EUROCRYPT 2006. LNCS, vol. 4004, pp. 486–503. Springer, Heidelberg (2006). https://doi.org/10.1007/11761679_29
21. Kempe, D., Dobra, A., Gehrke, J.: Gossip-based computation of aggregate information. In: 44th Annual IEEE Symposium on Foundations of Computer Science, Proceedings, pp. 482–491. IEEE (2003)
22. Bénézit, F., Blondel, V., Thiran, P., Tsitsiklis, J., Vetterli, M.: Weighted gossip: distributed averaging using non-doubly stochastic matrices. In: 2010 IEEE International Symposium on Information Theory, pp. 1753–1757. IEEE (2010)
23. Nedic, A., Ozdaglar, A.: Distributed subgradient methods for multi-agent optimization. IEEE Trans. Autom. Control **54**(1), 48–61 (2009)
24. Boyd, S., Ghosh, A., Prabhakar, B., Shah, D.: Randomized gossip algorithms. IEEE Trans. Inf. Theory **52**(6), 2508–2530 (2006)
25. Nedić, A., Olshevsky, A.: Distributed optimization over time-varying directed graphs. IEEE Trans. Autom. Control **60**(3), 601–615 (2015)
26. Balcan, M.F., Blum, A., Fine, S., et al.: Distributed learning, communication complexity and privacy. In: Conference on Learning Theory. JMLR Workshop and Conference Proceedings, pp. 26-1 (2012)
27. Shamir, O., Srebro, N.: Distributed stochastic optimization and learning. In: 2014 52nd Annual Allerton Conference on Communication, Control, and Computing (Allerton), pp. 850–857. IEEE (2014)

28. Tsianos, K.I., Lawlor, S., Rabbat, M.G.: Push-sum distributed dual averaging for convex optimization. In: 2012 IEEE 51st IEEE Conference on Decision and Control (CDC), pp. 5453–5458. IEEE (2012)
29. Geyer, R.C., Klein, T., Nabi, M.: Differentially private federated learning: a client level perspective. arXiv preprint arXiv:1712.07557 (2017)
30. Wei, K., Li, J., Ding, M., et al.: Federated learning with differential privacy: algorithms and performance analysis. IEEE Trans. Inf. Forensics Secur. **15**, 3454–3469 (2020)
31. Nagumey, A.: Book review: parallel and distributed computation: numerical methods. Int. J. Supercomput. Appl. **3**(4), 73–74 (1989)
32. Fawaz, H.I., Lucas, B., Forestier, G., et al.: Inceptiontime: finding alexnet for time series classification. Data Min. Knowl. Disc. **34**(6), 1936–1962 (2020)
33. Tsianos, K.I.: The Role of the Network in Distributed Optimization Algorithms: Convergence Rates, Scalability, Communication/Computation Tradeoffs and Communication Delays. McGill University Libraries (2013)
34. Fercoq, O., Qu, Z., Richtárik, P., Takáč, M.: Fast distributed coordinate descent for non-strongly convex losses. In: 2014 IEEE International Workshop on Machine Learning for Signal Processing (MLSP), pp. 1–6. IEEE (2014)
35. Tsianos, K.I., Lawlor, S., Rabbat, M.G.: Consensus-based distributed optimization: practical issues and applications in large-scale machine learning. In: 2012 50th Annual Allerton Conference on Communication, Control, and Computing (allerton), pp. 1543–1550. IEEE (2012)

Applied Cryptography

Cryptonite: A Framework for Flexible Time-Series Secure Aggregation with Non-interactive Fault Recovery

Ryan Karl, Jonathan Takeshita, and Taeho Jung[✉]

University of Notre Dame, Notre Dame, IN 46556, USA
{rkarl,jtakeshi,tjung}@nd.edu

Abstract. Private stream aggregation (PSA) allows an untrusted data aggregator to compute statistics over a set of multiple participants' data while ensuring the data remains private. Existing works rely on a trusted third party to enable an aggregator to achieve fault tolerance, that requires *interactive recovery*, but in the real world this may not be practical or secure. We develop a new formal framework for PSA that accounts for user faults, and can support *non-interactive recovery*, while still supporting strong individual privacy guarantees. We first must define a new level of security in the presence of faults and malicious adversaries because the existing definitions do not account for faults and the security implications of the recovery. After this we develop the first protocol that provably reaches this level of security, i.e., individual inputs are private even after the aggregator's recovery, and reach new levels of scalability and communication efficiency over existing work seeking to support fault tolerance. The techniques we develop are general, and can be used to augment any PSA scheme to support non-interactive fault recovery.

Keywords: Fault tolerance · Trusted hardware · Secure aggregation

1 Introduction

Third-party analysis on private records is becoming more important due to widespread data collection for various analysis purposes in business, government, academia, etc. This can be observed in many real life applications, such as the Smart Grid, Social Network Services, Location Based Services, etc. [14]. Given the great abundance of user-generated data and the collection of it in modern times, data analysis frameworks must be capable of processing queries over millions and sometimes billions of devices with little to no latency. While existing service providers support this over unencrypted data, data in its plaintext form often contains private information about individuals, and the publication of such data may violate privacy laws such as HIPPA, FERPA, GDPR, etc.

Within the context of many applications that process large amounts of data, it is paramount that fresh results be available to consumers, despite the presence

© ICST Institute for Computer Sciences, Social Informatics and Telecommunications Engineering 2021
Published by Springer Nature Switzerland AG 2021. All Rights Reserved
J. Garcia-Alfaro et al. (Eds.): SecureComm 2021, LNICST 398, pp. 311–331, 2021.
https://doi.org/10.1007/978-3-030-90019-9_16

of frequent system faults [20]. For example, web companies such as Facebook and LinkedIn execute daily data mining queries to analyze their latest web logs, and online marketplace providers such as eBay and BetFair run fraud detection algorithms on real-time consumer trading activity [22]. Similarly, various types of failures are common in systems with user interactions, and the fault recovery must not affect performance adversely. Critically, due to the number of users participating in such protocols, the per-machine resource overhead of any fault tolerance mechanism should be low. Thus, such systems must be able to recover from failures without significantly impacting output accuracy, computation time expectations, or requiring interaction with unreliable/untrusted parties.

It is well known that existing work has proposed to support privacy preserving computation (secure multi-party computation (MPC), functional encryption (FE), perturbation, etc.) over multiple users' data. Of the existing techniques, Private Stream Aggregation (PSA) is very promising. PSA allows a third-party aggregator to receive encrypted values from multiple parties and compute an aggregate function without learning anything else, except what is learnable from the aggregate value. PSA is generally superior to other types of secure computation paradigms (e.g., MPC, FE) in large-scale applications involving time-series data because of its extremely low overhead and the ease of key management [13,23]. Notably, PSA is non-interactive (i.e., users send their time-series data in a "stream" and only one message is sent per time interval) and asynchronous (i.e., users can leave after submitting their inputs), making it more efficient in communication than most existing alternative techniques [26]. However, existing solutions fail to achieve tolerance against faults during the aggregation without placing trust in the aggregators. We distinguish between *non-interactive* fault tolerance, which is the ability to recover from faults dynamically and "on the fly" without requiring extra messages be sent from/to faulted users or some trusted party, and *interactive* fault tolerance, which requires additional messages be exchanged to support recovery.

In this paper, we present a novel framework, Cryptonite, that allows any PSA scheme to gain non-interactive fault tolerance without significant additional overhead. There are many existing works that build ad-hoc solutions for this purpose that generally focus on providing one or a few of the following goals: privacy, efficiency, practical benefits such as permitting a user to drop in and out, or some type of interactive fault recovery mechanism. In contrast, our framework generalizes data aggregation, while still achieving traditional levels of performance and security, but more importantly, it introduces non-interactive recovery against faults to existing secure aggregation primitives without requiring users to trust the aggregator or requiring extra interaction.

This is a challenging problem to solve efficiently and securely, as most existing solutions require communicating with a trusted third party key dealer, which requires sending additional messages (generally two) during the protocol, greatly increasing the total overhead. A better solution would be *non-interactive* and would allow the aggregator to recover from a fault locally without sending additional messages, or requiring additional computation on the user end. However, a non-interactive protocol would need to guarantee correct function output with only one communication round. As a result, such a protocol would be by its nature vulnerable to the residual function attack [15] in the standard model. In this attack, an adversary can repeatedly evaluate the function locally, while varying some inputs and fixing the inputs of others, to deduce the values entered by the participants. This vulnerability occurs because an aggregator that does not receive all of the users' encrypted inputs must be able to simulate acquiring such inputs, in order to complete the calculation. Existing work allows an aggregator to recover some partial data from the function they were to compute, but does so by sending a message to a trusted third party [8,11] or aggregator to provide sensitive information that could harm an individual user's privacy if released publicly [6,16]. Such existing work supports interactive fault tolerance simply by allowing the aggregator to evaluate an aggregation multiple times, which is essentially the residual function attack. This technique is insecure, and presents a serious privacy risk even if the data is protected with privacy preserving (e.g., differentially private) noise. We need a new, more rigorous notion of privacy that accounts for fault tolerance without sacrificing traditional security expectations.

In contrast, our scheme does not rely on any interaction with a third party, thus cutting down on communication, while also supporting partial aggregation among the surviving participants (thus achieving non-interactive fault tolerance), to maximize utility for the aggregator. Our simulations show that the fault recovery mechanism introduces negligible extra overhead to a PSA scheme when no faults occur. More importantly, when faults occur, our framework allows the PSA to recover from faults much more efficiently than other fault recovery mechanisms for PSA. We achieve all of this while providing security in the presence of stronger adversaries, and our scheme can be easily extended to support a wider variety of functions, such as max, average, etc. [11,24]. Our goals in designing this framework are to 1) devise a system that is able to recover from failures without significantly impacting processing result accuracy or computation/communication time expectations. 2) maximize user's trust in the protocol by requiring that any servers used to facilitate the aggregation not be trusted by the users, and 3) enable computations at aggregate levels while still protecting any individual level data. Any system seeking to support such goals should provide a formal privacy analysis to demonstrate that the mechanism achieves the above privacy goals. Our contributions are as follows:

1. We identify the trust issues of aggregators when fault tolerance needs to be achieved during secure aggregation without extra interactions, and define a new, stronger level of privacy in the presence of faults and malicious aggregators – *fault-tolerable aggregator obliviousness*.
2. We develop a new formal framework for PSA that accounts for user faults, and develop general techniques that can be used to augment any PSA scheme to support *non-interactive fault recovery*.
3. We develop the first protocol that provably reaches this level of privacy using a Trusted Execution Environment (TEE). Rather than compute everything in the TEE, we minimize the performance impact from the TEE by outsourcing

computationally intensive work to an untrusted domain for efficiency, while still allowing for strong privacy guarantees.

4. We demonstrate new levels of scalability and communication efficiency over existing work that supports interactive fault tolerance. Our code is available at: https://github.com/RyanKarl/CryptoniteDemo.

2 Related Work

Recently there has been interest in constructing PSA systems that allow for dynamic user groups or interactive fault tolerance, that are similar to fault-tolerant deterministic threshold signatures [21]. Fault tolerance in this context is the property that in the event that a user or group of users do not send data to the aggregator, either due to a natural failure or a malicious act, the aggregator can still recover a partial sum over the remaining users' messages that were successfully sent. There are primarily two existing paradigms for this.

(1) Recovery via trusted parties: In the first [1,2,11,16], the aggregator communicates with an independent third party to notify them of the fault, and the third party provides the inputs to the aggregator to allow for the successful completion of the protocol for each aggregation. Since the third party knows the secrets assigned to every node, if some nodes fail to submit data, the aggregator asks the dealer to submit synthetic data on behalf of those failed nodes. This method incurs a round trip communication overhead between the key dealer and the aggregator for each aggregation (i.e., interactive). Some researchers [16] used a circle based construction to improve efficiency, but had to interact with a third party to recover from faults, which can lead to high communication delay. Other work [1,2] explored using elliptic curves to improve the overhead of communication and computation, while still supporting interactive fault tolerance, but this requires that some trusted, independent third parties be communicated with each round for fault recovery. Similar work explored outsourcing expensive computations to the cloud [11] to support a wider variety of functions instead of just sum, such as min, average, etc., but they also require interactions with trusted third parties.

(2) Recovery via input buffering: In the second paradigm [3,7,8], users buffer their inputs that they send to the aggregator. Essentially, in this method users send a set of ciphertexts corresponding to several timestamps/inputs to the aggregator. Thus, if a user fails to communicate in the future, the aggregator can utilize these ciphertexts to complete the aggregation and cancel out the noise needed to recover the partial sum. This increases the overall message size by a factor of how many rounds the user buffers their input (to buffer for 2 rounds, the size of the message is twice as large, etc.). One of the first works explicitly interested in supporting interactive fault tolerance [6] used a novel approach based on a binary interval tree technique to reduce the communication cost for joins and leaves, via input buffering. However, their scheme has a high aggregation error, which leads to the poor utility of the aggregate. Another technique [30] for buffering future ciphertexts was developed to reduce communication overhead, and was later made more efficient and scalable [3,7]. A security-enhanced data aggregation scheme [8] with interactive fault tolerance based on Paillier's encryption scheme has been proposed. Unfortunately, internal attacks are not considered in the above data aggregation schemes thereby allowing internal attackers to access the consumers' data. This was later improved [19] by leveraging lifted El-Gamal encryption to improve performance, and authentication methods were added for message integrity, although the vulnerability to internal attackers was left as an open problem. Later work [9] investigated using techniques to make key generation non-interactive. There has been some work that tries to solve this problem by allowing users to communicate with each other if a fault is detected to restart the protocol [28,31], but we are interested in developing better approaches that do not require interaction among users, as this can lead to significant overhead and scalability issues.

Advantage of Our Work: The aforementioned schemes are either inefficient, fail to achieve non-interactive fault tolerance (i.e. extra messages must be sent to trusted parties), and/or are insecure against the residual function attack. In contrast, our scheme supports non-interactive fault tolerance, thus cutting down on communication, while also supporting partial aggregation among the surviving participants without introducing residual function attack vulnerabilities.

Orthogonal Work: Defending against users that lie about their values to pollute the final output is outside the scope of the paper, but one possible defense is for each user to use a non-interactive zero-knowledge proof to prove the encrypted input is either in a valid range or an already-committed value.

Common Misconceptions: Note that it is not possible to simply leverage historical data, or utilize machine learning techniques to estimate possible inputs of faulted users and use the inferred inputs to recover the final aggregation. This is because, to have provable security guarantees, the ciphertexts shared with the aggregator in the PSA are computationally indistinguishable from random numbers. Therefore, no inference approaches can gain meaningful information from the ciphertexts to predict and recover the missing inputs (e.g., due to faults).

3   Preliminaries: Private Stream Aggregation

The field of PSA seeks to solve the following problem. Suppose an aggregator wishes to calculate the sum of n users periodically. Let $x_i^{(t)}$ (where $x_i^{(t)} \in \{0, 1, \ldots, \Delta\}$) denote the data of user i in aggregation period t (where $t = 1, 2, 3, \ldots$). Then, the sum for time period t is $\sum_{i=1}^{n} x_i^{(t)}$. In some scenarios, in each time period t, each user i adds noise $r_i^{(t)}$ to their data $x_i^{(t)}$, encrypts the noisy data $\hat{x}_i^{(t)} = x_i^{(t)} + r_i^{(t)}$ with their key $k_i^{(t)}$ and sends the ciphertext to the aggregator. The aggregator can then use their own key, $k_0^{(t)}$ to decrypt the noisy sum $\sum_{i=1}^{n} \left(x_i^{(t)} + r_i^{(t)} \right)$. In this scenario, $k_i^{(t)}$ and $k_0^{(t)}$ change in every time period. Note that we focus on the aggregation scheme over the same time period and omit the t to save space when the context is clear. We also do not add noise $r_i^{(t)}$ for simplicity of presentation. We assume that every user communicates with the aggregator via a wireless connection, but note that in our setup there is no need for users to communicate with each other. We assume that time is synchronized among nodes. Generally speaking, for a private aggregation protocol to be secure, it must achieve three properties: 1) the aggregator cannot achieve any meaningful intermediate results (i.e. they learn the final noisy sum but nothing else), 2) the scheme is aggregator oblivious (a party without the aggregator learns nothing), and 3) the scheme achieves differential privacy. Note that requirement 3 is needed in some contexts where it is assumed the accurate sum may leak user privacy in presence of side information. Thus, the aggregator is only allowed to obtain a noisy sum (the accurate sum plus noise).

4   New Notion of Security

To achieve a meaningful level of security, current aggregation schemes strive to guarantee *aggregator obliviousness* which is informally defined as follows:

Definition 1 (Aggregator Obliviousness). *Assuming that each honest participant p_i only encrypts once in each time period, a secure aggregation scheme achieves aggregator obliviousness if: 1) the aggregator can only learn the final aggregate for each time period, 2) without knowing the aggregator key, no one can learn anything about the encrypted data, even if several users collude, and 3) if the aggregator colludes with a subset of the users, or if a subset of the encrypted data has been leaked, the aggregator learns no additional information about the honest participants' individual data, beyond what can be inferred by the final aggregation.*

While this definition is useful in schemes that do not consider fault tolerance, it becomes less useful once faults occur and need to be recovered without interactions. To recover from a fault without interactions, an aggregator must be able to generate synthetic input from any user to complete the calculation. This is because PSA schemes must encode data in such a way that no partial information can be gained unless every participant's key is used in the final aggregation (for the sake of aggregator obliviousness). However, this actually violates the aggregator obliviousness, since to recover from faults without interactions, an aggregator must be able to calculate any partial sums, which would allow the aggregator to deduce everyone's input by subtracting the partial sums (i.e., residual function attack). Introducing differential privacy is not sufficient as the noise must be significantly larger than that in the PSA schemes with computational differential privacy ($O(n)$ where n is the number of users rather than $O(1)$ in existing schemes [4,23]) to prevent such residual function attack. Many applications cannot afford to operate over results with excessive noise, as the significant loss in data accuracy prevents the subsequent data analysis from having any utility to analysts [10]. Therefore, we are primarily interested in investigating how to design a system where the residual function attack is not possible even without differentially private noise being introduced to the input.

Note that introducing computational differential privacy [4,23] on top of such a system is trivial. Users can locally add calibrated noise to their inputs before encryption for the sake of computational differential privacy. This is independent from the rest of the PSA and our framework, therefore we omit the description due to the space limit.

Issues with Existing Techniques: Existing works try to avoid this issue by introducing a trusted, independent third party that can assist the untrusted aggregator with completing the protocol. This is facilitated by allowing the aggregator to request the third party provide the keys or ciphertexts the user was supposed to send to the aggergator so that they can complete the calculation and determine the partial sum. While there may be scenarios where this adversary model is acceptable, in the real world, it may be difficult or even impossible to find such a trusted third party (arguably, if such a third party exists it may be easier for users to send their plaintexts directly to them to speed up processing). More specifically, we are interested in supporting privacy in a scenario where there are no independent third parties involved in fault recovery. In this setting, the two existing methods of achieving fault tolerance are ineffective, as they are vulnerable to the residual function attack. An aggregator can compute the same function over different inputs, compute the difference between the final outputs, to infer individual values inputted by different users.

Consider the first family of fault tolerant protocols, which allow the aggregator to ask an independent third party to provide the information needed to recover the output. If such an third party is not trusted, the aggregator can request all of the private information from this third party and recover every party's individual input via the residual function attack. We also note that even if this third party is trusted, in existing work, it is unclear how to prevent the untrusted aggregator from lying about users faulting, even if they complete their part of the protocol, to recover the synthetic inputs they need to launch the residual function attack. The second family of fault tolerant protocols, where users buffer future inputs to the aggregator is similarly vulnerable. If there is no trusted third party, the aggregator can simply request the buffered inputs, even if a user does not fault, to execute the residual function attack. Similarly, even if the third party that stores the buffer is trusted, the security guarantee is somewhat unclear, as the aggregator can lie about the fault status of users to recover the synthetic input needed to execute the residual function attack. Clearly, we need a new definition of aggregator obliviousness within the context of fault tolerant systems, that accounts for such scenarios. By extending the existing definitions [12,23], we define the *fault-tolerable aggregator obliviousness* as follows:

Definition 2 (Fault-Tolerable Aggregator Obliviousness). *Define a set of users $i \in N$, where $0 \leq i \leq |N|$, where the subset of users that fault is denoted U and the set of users that do not fault is denoted J, were $N = U \cup J$. A set of users N participating in a secure aggregation scheme β, with public*

parameters params, during timestep t, whose inputs and secret keys are denoted
x_i *and* sk_i *respectively, achieve aggregator obliviousness with fault tolerance if*
no probabilistic polynomial-time adversary has more than negligible advantage in
winning the below security game:

Setup: Challenger runs a Setup algorithm, and returns the public parameters
params to the adversary.

Queries: The adversary makes the following three types of queries:

1. Encrypt: The adversary may specify (i, t, x) and ask for the ciphertext. Challenger returns the ciphertext affiliated with $\text{Enc}(sk_i, t, x_i)$ to the adversary.

2. Compromise: The adversary specifies an integer $i \in \{0, \ldots, |N|\}$ If $i = 0$,
the challenger returns the aggregator key sk_0 to the adversary. If $i \neq 0$, the
challenger returns sk_i the secret key for the ith participant, to the adversary.

3. Challenge: This query can be made only once throughout the game. The
adversary specifies a set of participants Q and a time t^* Any $q \in Q$ must not
have been compromised at the end of the game. The adversary also specifies
a subset of Q denoted Y of users they *claim* faulted (i.e. a user in Y may not
have actually faulted). For each user $q \in Q$ the adversary chooses four plaintexts
$(x_q), (x'_q), (x_y), (x'_y)$. The challenger flips a random bit b. If $b = 0$, the challenger
computes $\forall q \in Q\backslash Y : \text{Enc}\,(sk_q, t^*, x_q), \forall y \in Y : \text{Enc}\,(sk_y, t^*, x_y)$ and returns the
ciphertexts to the adversary. If $b = 1$, the challenger computes and returns the
ciphertexts $\forall q \in Q\backslash Y : \text{Enc}\,(sk_q, t^*, x'_q), \forall y \in Y : \text{Enc}\,(sk_y, t^*, x'_y)$ instead.

Guess: The adversary outputs a guess of whether b is 0 or 1. We say that the
adversary wins the game if they correctly guess b and the following condition
holds. Let $K \subseteq N$ denote the set of compromised participants at the end of the
game. Let $M \subseteq N$ denote the set of participants for whom an Encrypt query
has been made on time t^* by the end of the game. Let $Q \subseteq N$ denote the set of
(uncompromised) participants specified in the Challenge phase. If $Q = \overline{K \cup M} :=$
$N\backslash(K \cup M)$, $J \cup Y \neq \emptyset$, and the adversary has compromised the aggregator key,
the following condition must be met: $\sum_{q \in Q} x_q + \sum_{y \in Y} x_y = \sum_{q \in Q} x'_q + \sum_{y \in Y} x'_y$.

Essentially we say that a secure aggregation scheme achieves fault-tolerable
aggregator obliviousness if: 1) the aggregator can only learn one sum for each
time period, even if a subset of users fault, 2) without knowing the aggregator
key, no one can learn anything about the encrypted data, even if several users
collude, and 3) if the aggregator colludes with a subset of the users, or if a
subset of the encrypted data has been leaked, the aggregator learns no additional
information about the honest participants' individual data. This better captures
the requirements needed to protect against the residual function attack, since
at least two separate function evaluations must be completed by an adversary
for the attack to be successful. In the previous definition, multiple sums could
still be calculated by an attacker, while still fulfilling the requirements of the
definition. Also, to be fault tolerant, multiple ciphertexts associated with one
user need to be available to the aggregator, so making an assumption that only

one ciphertext is associated with each user may limit the utility of the previous definition, as if a user faults, another ciphertext associated with the user, but generated independently from the user may be needed for recovery.

5   Cryptonite: A Novel Framework for Any PSA Scheme

5.1   The Framework Definition

To achieve the above notion of privacy, we design a new secure aggregation framework β in Fig. 1, that addresses fault tolerance. At a high level, our framework follows the same general procedure used by existing PSA schemes based on additive key homomorphism to distribute private keys to each participant during **Setup**. Following this, each user leverages their private key to encrypt their private data during **Enc**. After the aggregator receives all the users' ciphertexts, the aggregator can optionally invoke a fault recovery mechanism, **FaultRecover**, for a subset of users they claim faulted. This mechanism will verify that the aggregator's claim is accurate, and they did not claim a user faulted when they in fact received their ciphertext. If it is found the aggregator made a false claim the protocol aborts. After this, the aggregator can recover the final aggregation result of the data it successfully received from the users with **AggrDec**. We formalize

---

Framework β

Setup(1^λ) : Takes in a security parameter λ, and outputs public parameters $param$, a private key sk_i for each participant, as well as a aggregator key sk_0 needed for decryption of aggregate statistics in each time period. Each participant i obtains the private key sk_i, and the data aggregator obtains the key sk_0 at the end of this algorithm.

Enc($param, sk_i, t, x_i$) : During time step t, each participant calls the Enc algorithm to encode its data x_i via sk_i. The result is an encryption of x_i using the additive key homomorphism from the chosen PSA, denoted $ENC(x_i)$ or c_i.

FaultRecover(J, U, t): The fault recovery algorithm takes in the set of all the IDs of all the users that the aggregator reports as having faulted, denoted J, during time period t, along with the IDs of all of the users that successfully sent their encrypted data U. The algorithm then verifies that the two sets of users are disjoint. If the sets are not disjoint the algorithm outputs nothing and the protocol aborts. If the two sets are disjoint, the algorithm outputs for all $j \in J$ the ciphertexts corresponding to an encryption of 0 as c_j. This algorithm can only be called once for each time period.

AggrDec ($param, sk_0, t, c_u \forall u \in U, c_j \forall j \in J$) Takes in the public parameters $param$, a key sk_0, the ciphertexts for all users in the set of users that did not fault $u \in U$ as c_u, and the ciphertexts for all users in the set of users that did fault $j \in J$ as c_j, for the same time period t. For each $i \in N$ where N is the union of U and J let $c_i = Enc\,(sk_i, t, x_i)$. Let $\mathbf{x} := (x_1, \ldots, x_n)$. The decryption algorithm outputs $f(\mathbf{x})$.

Fig. 1. Our framework

the fault recovery mechanism so that we can better enforce that protocols will not be vulnerable to the residual function attack. This framework supports the same general functionality as the previous framework, but allows the aggregator to recover the needed information regarding users who fault to complete the protocol in a privacy preserving manner as described in Definition 2.

5.2   Framework Instantiation

To formally investigate the correctness and the security of our framework, we instantiate a precise protocol, θ, using Cryptonite. We first present our basic approach, and we later overcome performance limitations in our optimized version, which is presented in the following section. The greatest challenge we face when designing this protocol is how to guarantee that the aggregator cannot act maliciously and acquire the synthetic data it needs to execute a residual function attack. Since any actions taken by an aggregator must be tightly controlled to support non-interactive fault recovery, and previous work has shown achieving specific security guarantees in certain non-interactive protocols is impossible in the standard model without additional hardware assumptions [15], a natural choice to support this functionality is to leverage trusted hardware, such as a Trusted Execution Environment (TEE), combined with PSA based on additive key homomorphism. We summarize the requisite background below.

Trusted Hardware: One of the most prevalent forms of trusted hardware in modern computing is Intel SGX, a set of new CPU instructions that can be used by applications to set aside private regions of code and data. It allows developers to protect sensitive data from unauthorized access or modification by malicious software running at higher privilege levels. To support this, the CPU protects an isolated region of memory called Processor Reserved Memory (PRM) against other non-enclave memory accesses. Sensitive code and data is encrypted and stored as 4KB pages in the Enclave Page Cache (EPC), a region inside the PRM. Although EPC pages are allocated and mapped to frames by the OS kernel, page-level encryption guarantees confidentiality and integrity. To provide access protection to the EPC pages, the CPU maintains an Enclave Page Cache Map (EPCM) that stores security attributes and metadata associated with EPC pages. Note our framework can work with any TEE. To utilize Intel SGX, applications must be written in a two part model, where applications must be seperated into secure parts and non-secure parts. The application can then launch an enclave, that is placed in protected memory, to allow user-level code to define private segments of memory. The contents of these segments are protected and unable to be read or saved by any process outside the enclave. Enclave entry points are defined during compilation, such that the secure execution environment is part of the host process, and the application contains its own code, data, and the enclave, but the enclave contains its own code and data too [18].

Elliptic Curves: Note that our framework instantiation can work with any PSA that is based on additive key homomorphism [25], but we chose elliptic curve cryptography (ECC) for our concrete instantiation. ECC provides the same level of security as RSA, Paillier, or discrete logarithm systems over Z_p with considerably shorter operands (approximately 160–256 bit vs. 1024–3072 bit), which results in shorter ciphertexts and signatures. As a result, in many cases, ECC has performance advantages over other public-key algorithms [5].

Protocol θ: Note that [25] uses a key-homomorphic weak PRF to construct PSA, and uses the seminal PSA of Shi et al. [23] as an example. Thus we choose to instantiate our framework with theirs, so that our framework can be adapted to turn any PSA that is based on additive key homomorphism into a fault-tolerable version. When the context is clear, we sometimes use standard addition and multiplication operators, as done in previous PSA papers [6,23], when operating over ciphertexts, for simplicity of presentation. Let $\mathbb{G}$ denote a cyclic group of prime order p for which Decisional Diffie-Hellman is hard. Let $H : \mathbb{Z} \to \mathbb{G}$ denote a hash function modeled as a random oracle. We assume the aggregator is equipped with an Intel SGX, and model our system design in Fig. 2.

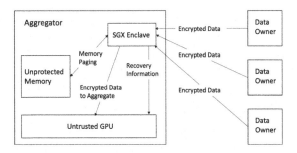

Fig. 2. System diagram

Setup(1^λ): Each user first performs attestation with the aggregator's Intel SGX, to verify it will faithfully execute the protocol (this is a one time process). The Intel SGX performs key generation, and chooses a random generator $g \in \mathbb{G}$, and $n + 1$ random secrets $s_0, s_1, \ldots, s_n \in \mathbb{Z}_p$ such that $s_0 + s_1 + s_2 + \ldots + s_n = 0$. The public parameters $param := g$. The aggregator obtains the key $sk_0 := s_0$ and participant i obtains the secret key $sk_i := s_i$. For practical purposes, we can use secret shares that sum to zero as secret keys.

Enc$(param, sk_i, t, x_i)$: For participant i to encrypt a value $x \in \mathbb{Z}_p$ for time step t, they compute the following ciphertext $c_i \longleftarrow g^{x_i} \cdot H(t)^{sk_i}$, where $H(t)$ denotes the hash of t that maps t to an elliptic curve. Note, after this the user sends its ciphertext and unique id to the aggregator's SGX.

FaultRecover(c_j, c_u, t): Here, after the time period has ended, within the Intel SGX, we check each ciphertext that was received against a hash table of all users who participated in the setup process, and record which users failed to respond within the time window. Note this process cannot be tampered with from outside the enclave. Then, since the Intel SGX has each user's secret key, it can compute

$c_i \longleftarrow g^0 \cdot H(t)^{sk_j}$ for all users $j \in J$. Notice that a nice property of this setup is that if a user is late and sends a ciphertext associated with time period t after that time period has passed, the Intel SGX can simply discard it and there is no danger of it being leaked to the aggregator.

AggrDec$(param, sk_0, t, c_j, c_u)$: Compute within the enclave (note $N = U \cup J$) $V \leftarrow H(t)^{sk_0} \prod_{i=1}^{n} c_i$. To decrypt the sum, we can leverage Pollard's lambda method, as done in previous works [23], to compute the discrete log of V base g. This method requires decryption time roughly square root in the plaintext space, although in general solving the discrete log is highly parallelizable and can be done efficiently in practice as long as the plaintext is small [6].

Note that this construction is secure under Definition 2, and we can prove this via a security game, using proof techniques from existing work [23]. We include the full proof in Appendix A, and sketch it here for completeness. Essentially, assuming that the Decisional Diffie-Hellman problem is hard in the group $\mathbb{G}$ and that the hash function H is a random oracle, we can prove that the above construction satisfies aggregator oblivious security with fault tolerance, by showing via reduction to a series of hybrid games that the game described above is hard to win for our scheme. More specifically, to prove the theorem, we will modify the aggregator oblivious security game as such. In the **Encrypt** queries, if the adversary submits a request for some tuple (q, x, t^*) where t^* is the time step specified in the **Challenge** phase, the challenger treats this as a **Compromise** query, and simply returns the sk_q to the adversary. Given sk_q, the adversary can compute the requested ciphertext. The adversary has access to a the functionality, **FaultRecover**, that can only be called once (since this is enforced via trusted hardware), which takes in a set of users that have not been compromised ($j \in J$), and returns the set of ciphertexts that correspond to those users encrypting 0. This modification actually gives more power to the adversary. Note that this protocol is not vulnerable to the residual function attack, as the adversary cannot access multiple ciphertexts associated with a user for a given timestamp. Here, the individual ciphertexts are sent into the enclave, which can independently handle the computations needed for fault recovery in an isolated environment that cannot be spoofed or tampered with by an attacker (unlike in the previously discussed techniques that provide fault tolerance that requires additional communication rounds). Thus, the fault recovery process can be performed in a secure, non-interactive way, that removes the opportunity for an attacker to spoof the fault recovery to obtain an encryption of 0 for a user, even when the user participates and does not fault, such that the attacker can perform the residual function attack by utilizing both ciphertexts to deduce the user's plaintext input. Achieving differential privacy is not the primary focus of this paper, but we can easily adapt the methods of existing works if needed [6,23].

A More Efficient Protocol. The above protocol achieves security according to Definition 2, but it incurs additional computational overhead since the aggregation is done inside the TEE. It would be better if we could outsource the aggregation computation to the untrusted aggregator to improve performance and avoid the MEE's overhead. We can accomplish this by following the same **Setup** procedure as before, but instead having users send two messages simultaneously. They can send their ciphertext (i.e. the result of **Enc**) to the untrusted aggregator, and also send one separate message to the Intel SGX to indicate they are participating in the protocol. Intuitively, the aggregator can simultaneously begin the partial summation of the ciphertexts of the users that did not fault outside the TEE (by calling **AggrDec**), while inside the SGX, **FaultRecover** is run to determine which users faulted and computes their synthetic ciphertexts which are sent out of the TEE to the aggregator. In this way, the somewhat expensive aggregation step can be done on more powerful, albeit untrusted hardware (e.g., GPU, FPGA), that has better access to parallel computing resources, without compromising security. We note that this scheme is not secure if the adversary can disrupt communication between the users and the Intel SGX, but we can solve this by simply having all users send their ciphertexts signed with a digital signature directly to the SGX first, instead of just the separate message. Then the SGX can output the users' ciphertexts who did not fault to the untrusted space controlled by the aggregator, along with the synthetic data used to overcome existing, verified faults, which can be more efficiently aggregated outside the enclave.

Outsourcing to Parallel-Friendly Processors. It may seem more efficient to simply send plaintext data to an SGX enclave to be aggregated, but it is known that Intel SGX has difficulties exploiting multi-threading due to the lack of common synchronization primitive support often found on traditional operating systems [18] (threading can also introduce security vulnerabilities [29]). Also, TEEs have been shown to run common functionalities over an order of magnitude slower than what can be achieved on comparable untrusted hardware, due to the overhead of computing within the enclave [18], and performing a large number of context switches to send each user's data into the TEE can add serious overhead, especially in a big data setting. Overall performance can be improved if we minimize the number of context switches and outsource the aggregation step (i.e., **AggrDec** over inputs without faults) to processors with high parallel computing ability (e.g., many-core CPUs, GPUs, or FPGAs), because the additions of **AggrDec** are perfectly parallelizable.

PSA Schemes Requiring Trusted Parties. In PSA schemes, the **Setup** is run only once and in a trusted manner [4,12,23]. This is typically accomplished through the use of an additional trusted third party key dealer or secure multiparty computation. However, with our framework, this can be replaced with the TEE, since the integrity of private key generation that is secure from eavesdropping will be guaranteed via remote attestation. Thus, our framework can remove the reliance on an external trusted third party in our PSA building block.

6   Experiments

To better understand the practical performance of our protocol we ran experiments using C++11 that simulated having thousands of users run our protocol, as is standard in the literature [6,16]. For these tests, we used a workstation running Ubuntu 16.04 LTS equipped with a Intel(R) Core(TM) i7-8700 CPU @ 3.20GHz (6 cores and 12 threads) with Intel SGX support. We did not leverage GPUs/FPGAs because we did not have access to computers equipped with both Intel SGX and GPUS/FPGAs. During tests we simulated the cryptosystem over Koblitz curve secp160k1, that offers 160 bits of security. We used time series data from the 3W dataset from the UCI machine learning data repository [27], and report the average time for 50 trials for each experiment.

Although there are space constraints associated with an Enclave, and a program that exceeds the allocated space incurs paging overhead, we found that in practice we could efficiently process aggregation over large numbers of users without major issues. Note the data footprint per user is roughly 100 bytes, and since in practice we can fit roughly 93 mb of data into an Enclave before triggering paging, we conservatively estimate that we can support about 900,000 users per Enclave, assuming we can fit the remaining program logic and metadata into roughly 3 mb. Since Intel plans to support Enclaves up to 1 terabyte in size in upcoming releases, we anticipate this being less of an issue in the future [17].

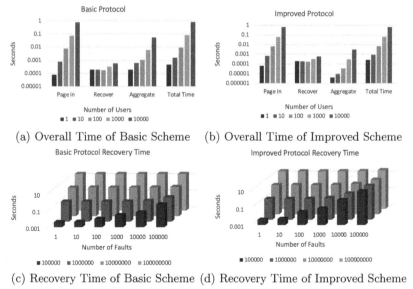

(a) Overall Time of Basic Scheme   (b) Overall Time of Improved Scheme

(c) Recovery Time of Basic Scheme (d) Recovery Time of Improved Scheme

Fig. 3. Experimental results

Basic Scheme: The results for our basic scheme, assuming no users fault, are shown in Fig. 3a. It is interesting to note that in all cases the overall time is dominated by the overhead of paging into and out of the enclave, and other important operations, such as performing the aggregation, only minimally contribute to the overall runtime. This makes sense, as it has been documented that these operations are comparatively expensive, due to the expensive cryptographic operations involved and the time needed to marshal the data. However, our results show that the overall time scales well in the presence of a large number of users. For instance our protocol takes about a second to finish when there are 10,000 users, assuming the setup step is precomputed. We report the additional time needed to recover from faults in Fig. 3c. We notice that since the dummy ciphertexts can be precomputed, the amount of time needed to recover is dominated by the time needed to traverse the hash table to determine which users faulted. As a result, the more users that are involved in the protocol, the longer this process takes. However, we note that even in the worst case, when many thousands of users fault, the additional recovery time is under 30 s. Unlike existing work that requires additional communication to support fault recovery, since we leverage a co-located TEE, we can remove the time needed for two communication rounds over existing works [8,11], while still supporting strong privacy guarantees, to improve communication complexity.

Improved Scheme: Since the amount of time needed to page into the enclave leads to significant overhead, we designed an improved protocol to try and minimize the performance impact by safely outsourcing more computations to the untrusted adversary. We report our results, assuming no users fault, in Fig. 3b. It is interesting to note that because we reduce the amount of enclave computation, we are able to improve our overall performance by approximately 26% in most cases. This makes sense, as we are able to reduce the amount of expensive enclave operations. We report the recovery time in Fig. 3d. We note that the amount of time needed to recover is comparatively more expensive than in the basic scheme, as we need to marshal out of the enclave the dummy ciphertexts needed to recover from faults to the untrusted aggregator. As a result, this can sometimes increase the overall runtime by several seconds in the worst case practical scenario when many users fault. This is tolerable for our applications, but it does illustrate a tradeoff that may inform which scheme should be used on a case by case basis.

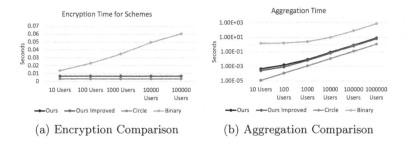

(a) Encryption Comparison   (b) Aggregation Comparison

Fig. 4. Experimental comparison results

Comparison to Existing Work: We experimentally evaluated our work when compared to baseline techniques, and ran simulations to compare our scheme to two state of the art secure aggregation schemes: 1) the Binary scheme [6] which has users buffer their inputs that they send to the aggregator, and 2) the Circle scheme [16], which has the aggregator communicate with a trusted party, to support fault tolerance. Our technique outperforms these schemes in scenarios where faults occur, often by several orders of magnitude. We compare times reported in Figs. 4 and 5.

We compare the encryption time and the aggregation time of the respective protocols, assuming no users fault, and vary the number of users. Note that the computational complexity of both of our schemes and the Circle Scheme is much less than that of the Binary scheme. This makes sense, as the Binary scheme requires that users compute $\lfloor (log_2(n)) \rfloor$ encryptions per round where n is the number of users, in order to support fault tolerance via their binary tree mechanism, which negatively impacts the run time. In contrast, our schemes and the Circle scheme only require one encryption per round, and thus support more efficient encryption. Note that the Circle scheme is slightly faster than our scheme, as they leverage a more efficient cryptographic primitive, the HMAC. The HMAC also contributes to the improved performance of the Circle scheme over our schemes and the Binary technique during aggregation. Thus we conclude that our encryption scheme scales well in the presence of large numbers of users, but is roughly 2–6x slower that the state of the art Circle scheme if no users fault.

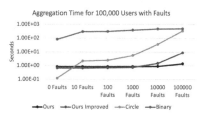

Fig. 5. Aggregation with faults comparison

We also compared the aggregation time of the respective protocols when there are 100,000 participants, and varied the number of user faults. We report results in Fig. 5. Note our schemes have the fastest overall run time when faults are introduced, sometimes by several orders of magnitude. This makes sense, as to recover from faults, we can efficiently interact with the on board TEE. In contrast the Circle Scheme incurs the roundtrip time of communicating with a trusted key dealer to collect the cryptographic keys needed to recover from the faults, and the Binary scheme must traverse the binary tree of ciphertexts it constructed to gather the ciphertexts it needs to cancel the appropriate randomness and recover the noisy plaintext. Unlike both of these schemes, we can recover from faults without either buffering ciphertexts, which causes increased communication overhead, or requiring additional rounds of communication, while supporting a stronger level of security overall, that does not require that we communicate with a trusted third party to recover from a fault.

7   Conclusion

We defined a new level of security for Private Stream Aggregation in the presence of faults and malicious adversaries. After describing a new framework for PSA that accounts for fault tolerance, we developed the first protocol that provably reaches this security level. Our simulations demonstrated our work reaches high levels of scalability and communication efficiency over existing work while supporting a higher level of security and better fault tolerance. Our techniques are general, and can extend any PSA scheme to support non-interactive fault recovery.

Acknowledgement. This work was supported by Facebook as a winner of the Role of Applied Cryptography in a Privacy-Focused Advertising Ecosystem Facebook RFP. Any opinions, findings and conclusions or recommendations expressed in this material are those of the authors and do not necessarily reflect those of the sponsor.

A   Proof of Fault Tolerable Aggregator Obliviousness

Theorem 1. *Assuming that the Decisional Diffie-Hellman problem is hard in the group G and that the hash function H is a random oracle, then the above construction satisfies aggregator oblivious security with fault tolerance, as described in Definition 2.*

Proof. First, we prove that the following intermediate game is difficult to win, given that Decisional Diffie-Hellman is hard. Let $\mathbb{G}$ be a group of prime order p.

Setup: The challenger picks random generators $g, h \in \mathbb{G}$, and random $\alpha_0, \alpha_1, \ldots, \alpha_n \in \mathbb{Z}_p$ such that $\sum_{i=0}^{n} \alpha_i = 0$. The challenger gives the adversary: $g, h, g^{\alpha_0}, g^{\alpha_2}, \ldots, g^{\alpha_n}$.

Queries: The adversary can compromise users adaptively and ask for the value of α_i. The challenger returns α_i to the adversary when queried.

Challenge: The adversary selects an uncompromised set $Q \subseteq \{0, \ldots, N\}$, and specifies a subset of Q denoted Y of users they claim faulted, where $J = Y$ for the duration of the game. The challenger flips a random bit b. If $b = 0$, the challenger returns to the adversary $\{h^{\alpha_q} \mid q \in Q \backslash Y\}, \{h^{\alpha_y} \mid y \in Y\}$. If $b = 1$, the challenger picks $|Q|/|Y|$ random elements h'_q, for $q \in Q/Y$ and $|Y|$ random elements h'_y, for $y \in Y$ from the group $\mathbb{G}$, such that $\sum_{q \in Q} h'_q + \sum_{y \in Y} h'_y = \sum_{q \in Q} h^{\alpha_q} + \sum_{y \in Y} h^{\alpha_y}$. The challenger returns h'_q, for $q \in Q/Y$ and h'_y, for $y \in Y$ to the adversary. The adversary can make additional compromise queries, as described in the above step as they see fit.

Guess: The adversary guesses either $b = 0$ or 1. The adversary wins if they have not asked for any α_q for $q \in Q$, $Y = J$, and if they successfully guess b.

Lemma 1. *The above game is difficult for computationally bounded adversaries assuming Decisional Diffie Hellman is hard for group* $\mathbb{G}$.

We define the following sequence of hybrid games, and assume that the set Q specified by the adversary in the challenge stage is $Q = \{q_1, q_2, \ldots, q_m\}$. For simplicity, we write $(\beta_1, \ldots, \beta_m) := (\alpha_{q_1}, \ldots, \alpha_{q_m})$, and include Y within Q to save space. In $Game_d$, the challenger sends the following to the adversary: $R_1, R_2, \ldots, R_d, h^{\beta_{d+1}}, \ldots, h^{\beta_m}$. Here, each $R_q (q \in [d])$ means an independent fresh random number, and the following condition holds: $\prod_{1 \leq q \leq d} R_q = \prod_{1 \leq q \leq d} h^{\beta_q}$. Clearly $Game_1$ is equivalent to the case when $b = 0$, and $Game_{m-1}$ is equivalent to the case when $b = 1$. With the hybrid argument we can show that games $Game_{d-1}$ and $Game_d$ are computationally indistinguishable. To demonstrate this, we show that if, for some d, there exists a polynomial-time adversary $\mathcal{A}$ who can distinguish between $Game_{d-1}$ and $Game_d$, we can then construct an algorithm $\mathcal{B}$ which can solve the DDH problem.

Suppose $\mathcal{B}$ obtains a DDH tuple (g, g^x, g^l, T). $\mathcal{B}$'s task is to decide whether $T = g^{xl}$ or whether T is a random element from $\mathbb{G}$. Now $\mathcal{B}$ randomly guesses two indices e and b to be the dth and the $(d+1)^{\text{th}}$ values of the set Q specified by the adversary in the challenge phase. The guess is correct with probability $\frac{1}{N^2}$, and in case the guess is wrong, the algorithm $\mathcal{B}$ aborts. Now $\mathcal{B}$ picks random exponents $\{\alpha_q\}_{q \neq e, q \neq b}$ and sets $\alpha_b = x$ and $\alpha_e = -\sum_{q \neq e} \alpha_q$. Notice that $\mathcal{B}$ does not know the values of α_e and α_b, however, it can compute the values of $g^{\alpha_b} = g^x$ and $g^{\alpha_e} = \left(\prod_{q \neq e} g^{\alpha_q}\right)^{-1} = (g^x)^{-1} \cdot \prod_{q \neq e, q \neq b} g^{\alpha_q}$. $\mathcal{B}$ gives $\mathcal{A}$ the tuple $(g, h = g^l, g^{\alpha_1}, \ldots, g^{\alpha_n})$. If $\mathcal{A}$ asks for any exponent except α_e and α_b, $\mathcal{B}$ returns the corresponding α_q value to $\mathcal{A}$; if $\mathcal{A}$ asks for α_e or α_b, the algorithm $\mathcal{B}$ aborts.

In the challenge phase, $\mathcal{A}$ submits a set $Q = \{q_1, q_2, \ldots q_m\}$. If e and b are not the dth and the $(d+1)^{\text{th}}$ values of the set Q, i.e., if $q_d \neq e$ or $q_{d+1} \neq b$, the algorithm $\mathcal{B}$ aborts. If $q_d = e$ and $q_{d+1} = b$, then $\mathcal{B}$ returns to $\mathcal{A}$: $R_1, R_2, \ldots, R_{d-1}$, $(\prod_{q \notin \{q_1, \ldots, q_{d+1}\}} (g^l)^{\alpha_q} \cdot \prod_{q=1}^{d-1} R_q \cdot T)^{-1}$, T, and $(g^l)^{\alpha_{q_{d+2}}, \ldots, (g^l)^{\alpha_{q_m}}}$. Clearly if $T = g^{xl}$, then the above game is equivalent to $Game_{d-1}$. Otherwise, if $T \in_R \mathbb{G}$, then the above game is equivalent to $Game_d$. Thus, if $\mathcal{A}$ has a non-negligible advantage in guessing whether it is playing $Game_{d-1}$ or $Game_d$ and $\mathcal{B}$ could solve the DDH problem with non-negligible advantage.

Now to prove the theorem, we will modify the aggregator oblivious security game. In the **Encrypt** queries, if the adversary submits a request for some tuple (q, x, t^*) where t^* is the time step specified in the **Challenge** phase, the challenger treats this as a **Compromise** query, and simply returns the sk_q to the adversary. Given sk_q, the adversary can compute the requested ciphertext. The adversary has access to a the functionality, **FaultRecover**, that can only be called once (since this is enforced via trusted hardware), which takes in a set of users that have not been compromised ($j \in J$), and returns the set of ciphertexts that correspond to those users encrypting 0. Note that this modification actually gives more power to the adversary. From now on, we will assume that the adversary does not make any **Encrypt** queries for the time t^*.

Let $K \subseteq N$ denote the set of compromised participants. Let $\bar{K} := N \backslash K$ denote the set of uncompromised participants. Since we assume the aggregator is untrusted, we are interested in the case where $Q = \bar{K}$ or the aggregator key has been compromised. We must show that the adversary cannot distinguish whether the challenger returns a true encryption of the plaintext submitted in the challenge stage, or a random tuple with the same aggregation.

Given an adversary $\mathcal{A}$ who can break the PSA game with non-negligible probability, we construct an algorithm $\mathcal{B}$ that can solve the above intermediate problem with non-negligible probability. $\mathcal{B}$ obtains from the challenger $\mathcal{C}$ the tuple $g, h, g^{\alpha_0}, g^{\alpha_1}, \ldots, g^{\alpha_n}$. $\mathcal{B}$ sets α_0 to be the aggregator's key, and $\alpha_1, \ldots, \alpha_n$ to be the secret keys of participants 1 through n respectively. Note $param$ is g.

Let q_H denote the total number of oracle queries made by the adversary $\mathcal{A}$ and by the algorithm $\mathcal{B}$ itself. $\mathcal{B}$ guesses at random an index $b \in [q_H]$. Suppose the input to the bth random oracle query is t^*. The algorithm $\mathcal{B}$ assumes that t^* will be the challenge time step. If the guess is found to be wrong later, $\mathcal{B}$ aborts.

Hash Function Simulation: The adversary submits a hash query for the integer t. $\mathcal{B}$ first checks the list $\mathcal{L}$ to see if t has appeared in any entry (t, z). If so, $\mathcal{B}$ returns g^z to the adversary. Otherwise, if this is not the bth query, $\mathcal{B}$ picks a random exponent z and returns g^z to the adversary, and saves (t, z) to a list $\mathcal{L}$. For the bth query, $\mathcal{B}$ returns h.

Then the following **Queries** can take place:

- **Encrypt**: The adversary $\mathcal{A}$ submits an **Encrypt** query for the tuple (q, x, t). In the modified version of the game, we ensure that $t \neq t^*$, as otherwise, we simply treat it as a **Compromise** query. $\mathcal{B}$ checks if a hash query has been made on t, and if not, $\mathcal{B}$ makes a hash oracle query on t. Thus, $\mathcal{B}$ learns the discrete log of $H(t)$. Now $H(t) = g^z$, so $\mathcal{B}$ knows z, and since $\mathcal{B}$ also knows g^{α_q}, $\mathcal{B}$ can compute the ciphertext $g^x \cdot (g^z)^{\alpha_q}$ as $g^x \cdot (g^{\alpha_q})^z$.
- **Compromise**: $\mathcal{B}$ forwards $\mathcal{A}$'s query to its own challenger $\mathcal{C}$, and forwards the answer α_q to $\mathcal{A}$.
- **FaultRecover**: $\mathcal{B}$ forwards $\mathcal{A}$'s query to its own challenger $\mathcal{C}$, and forwards the set of ciphertexts (i.e. $\forall j \in J, c \longleftarrow g^0 \cdot H(t)^{sk_j}$)) to $\mathcal{A}$.

Challenge: The adversary $\mathcal{A}$ submits a set $N = J \cup Q$ and a time t^*, as well as plaintexts $\{x_q \mid q \in N\}$. If t^* does not agree with the value submitted in the bth hash query, then $\mathcal{B}$ aborts. $\mathcal{B}$ submits the set Q in a **Challenge** query to its own challenger, and it obtains a tuple $\{T_q\}_{q \in N}$. The challenger returns the following ciphertexts to the adversary: $\forall q \in Q : g^{x_q} \cdot T_q$ (i.e. $c \longleftarrow g^{x_q} \cdot H(t)^{sk_q} \cdot T_q$).

More Queries: Same as the **Query** stage.

Guess: If the adversary $\mathcal{A}$ guesses that $\mathcal{B}$ has returned a random tuple then $\mathcal{B}$ guesses $b' = 1$. Otherwise, $\mathcal{B}$ guesses that $b' = 0$

If the challenger $\mathcal{C}$ returns $\mathcal{B}$ a faithful Diffie-Hellman tuple $\forall q \in Q : T_q = h^{\alpha_q}$, then the ciphertext returned to the adversary $\mathcal{A}$ is a true encryption of the plaintext submitted by the adversary. Otherwise, if the challenger returns to $\mathcal{B}$

a random tuple, then the ciphertext returned to $\mathcal{A}$ is random under the product constraint.

References

1. Bao, H., Lu, R.: DDPFT: secure data aggregation scheme with differential privacy and fault tolerance. In: IEEE ICC 2015, pp. 7240–7245. IEEE (2015)
2. Bao, H., Lu, R.: A new differentially private data aggregation with fault tolerance for smart grid communications. IEEE IoT-J **2**(3), 248–258 (2015)
3. Bao, H., Lu, R.: A lightweight data aggregation scheme achieving privacy preservation and data integrity with differential privacy and fault tolerance. Peer Peer Netw. Appl. **10**(1), 106–121 (2017)
4. Becker, D., Guajardo, J., Zimmermann, K.H.: Revisiting private stream aggregation: lattice-based PSA. In: NDSS (2018)
5. Boneh, D., Goh, E.-J., Nissim, K.: Evaluating 2-DNF formulas on ciphertexts. In: Kilian, J. (ed.) TCC 2005. LNCS, vol. 3378, pp. 325–341. Springer, Heidelberg (2005). https://doi.org/10.1007/978-3-540-30576-7_18
6. Chan, T.-H.H., Shi, E., Song, D.: Privacy-preserving stream aggregation with fault tolerance. In: Keromytis, A.D. (ed.) FC 2012. LNCS, vol. 7397, pp. 200–214. Springer, Heidelberg (2012). https://doi.org/10.1007/978-3-642-32946-3_15
7. Chen, J., Ma, H., Zhao, D.: Private data aggregation with integrity assurance and fault tolerance for mobile crowd-sensing. Wireless Netw. **23**(1), 131–144 (2017)
8. Chen, L., Lu, R., Cao, Z.: PDAFT: a privacy-preserving data aggregation scheme with fault tolerance for smart grid communications. Peer Peer Netw. Appl. **8**(6), 1122–1132 (2015)
9. Chotard, J., Dufour Sans, E., Gay, R., Phan, D.H., Pointcheval, D.: Decentralized multi-client functional encryption for inner product. In: Peyrin, T., Galbraith, S. (eds.) ASIACRYPT 2018. LNCS, vol. 11273, pp. 703–732. Springer, Cham (2018). https://doi.org/10.1007/978-3-030-03329-3_24
10. Gillin, D.: The federal trade commission and internet privacy. Mark. Res. **12**(3), 39 (2000)
11. Han, S., Zhao, S., Li, Q., Ju, C.H., Zhou, W.: PPM-HDA: privacy-preserving and multifunctional health data aggregation with fault tolerance. IEEE Trans. Inf. Forensics Secur. **11**(9), 1940–1955 (2015)
12. Joye, M., Libert, B.: A scalable scheme for privacy-preserving aggregation of time-series data. In: Sadeghi, A.-R. (ed.) FC 2013. LNCS, vol. 7859, pp. 111–125. Springer, Heidelberg (2013). https://doi.org/10.1007/978-3-642-39884-1_10
13. Jung, T., Mao, X., Li, X., Tang, S., Gong, W., Zhang, L.: Privacy-preserving data aggregation without secure channel: multivariate polynomial evaluation. In: IEEE INFOCOM (2013)
14. Jung, T., Han, J., Li, X.Y.: PDA: semantically secure time-series data analytics with dynamic subgroups. TDSC **15**(2), 260–274 (2016)
15. Karl, R., Burchfield, T., Takeshita, J., Jung, T.: Non-interactive MPC with trusted hardware secure against residual function attacks. In: Chen, S., Choo, K.-K.R., Fu, X., Lou, W., Mohaisen, A. (eds.) SecureComm 2019. LNICST, vol. 305, pp. 425–439. Springer, Cham (2019). https://doi.org/10.1007/978-3-030-37231-6_25
16. Li, Q., Cao, G.: Efficient privacy-preserving stream aggregation in mobile sensing with low aggregation error. In: De Cristofaro, E., Wright, M. (eds.) PETS 2013. LNCS, vol. 7981, pp. 60–81. Springer, Heidelberg (2013). https://doi.org/10.1007/978-3-642-39077-7_4

17. Martin, D.: Intel Xeon ice lake CPUs to get SGX with expanded security features (2020)
18. Mofrad, S., Zhang, F., Lu, S., Shi, W.: A comparison study of intel SGX and AMD memory encryption technology. In: ACM HASP, pp. 1–8 (2018)
19. Ni, J., Zhang, K., Alharbi, K., Lin, X., Zhang, N., Shen, X.S.: Differentially private smart metering with fault tolerance and range-based filtering. IEEE Trans. Smart Grid 8(5), 2483–2493 (2017)
20. Parikh, N., Sundaresan, N.: Scalable and near real-time burst detection from ecommerce queries. In: ACM SIGKDD, KDD 2008, pp. 972–980. ACM (2008)
21. Rabin, T.: A simplified approach to threshold and proactive RSA. In: Krawczyk, H. (ed.) CRYPTO 1998. LNCS, vol. 1462, pp. 89–104. Springer, Heidelberg (1998). https://doi.org/10.1007/BFb0055722
22. Russell, M.A.: Mining the Social Web. O'Reilly Media, Inc., Sebastopol (2011)
23. Shi, E., Chan, T.H., Rieffel, E., Chow, R., Song, D.: Privacy-preserving aggregation of time-series data. In: Proceedings of NDSS, vol. 2, pp. 1–17. Citeseer (2011)
24. Shi, J., Zhang, R., Liu, Y., Zhang, Y.: Prisense: privacy-preserving data aggregation in people-centric urban sensing systems. In: INFOCOM, pp. 1–9. IEEE (2010)
25. Valovich, F.: Aggregation of time-series data under differential privacy. In: Lange, T., Dunkelman, O. (eds.) LATINCRYPT 2017. LNCS, vol. 11368, pp. 249–270. Springer, Cham (2019). https://doi.org/10.1007/978-3-030-25283-0_14
26. Valovich, F., Aldà, F.: Computational differential privacy from lattice-based cryptography. In: Kaczorowski, J., Pieprzyk, J., Pomykała, J. (eds.) NuTMiC 2017. LNCS, vol. 10737, pp. 121–141. Springer, Cham (2018). https://doi.org/10.1007/978-3-319-76620-1_8
27. Vargas, R.E.V., et al.: A realistic and public dataset with rare undesirable real events in oil wells. J. Pet. Sci. Eng. 181, 106223 (2019)
28. Wang, X., Liu, Y., Choo, K.: Fault tolerant, multi-subset aggregation scheme for smart grid. IEEE Trans. Ind. Inform. 17(6), 4065–4072 (2020)
29. Weichbrodt, N., Kurmus, A., Pietzuch, P., Kapitza, R.: AsyncShock: exploiting synchronisation bugs in intel SGX enclaves. In: Askoxylakis, I., Ioannidis, S., Katsikas, S., Meadows, C. (eds.) ESORICS 2016. LNCS, vol. 9878, pp. 440–457. Springer, Cham (2016). https://doi.org/10.1007/978-3-319-45744-4_22
30. Won, J., Ma, C.Y., Yau, D.K., Rao, N.S.: Proactive fault-tolerant aggregation protocol for private smart metering. In: INFOCOM, pp. 2804–2812. IEEE (2014)
31. Xue, K., Yang, Q., Li, S., Wei, D.S., Peng, M., Memon, I., Hong, P.: PPSO: a privacy-preserving service outsourcing scheme for real-time pricing demand response in smart grid. IEEE Internet Things J. 6(2), 2486–2496 (2018)

Cryptonomial: A Framework for Private Time-Series Polynomial Calculations

Ryan Karl, Jonathan Takeshita, Alamin Mohammed, Aaron Striegel,
and Taeho Jung$^{(\boxtimes)}$

University of Notre Dame, Notre Dame, IN 46556, USA
{rkarl,jtakeshi,amohamm2,striegel,tjung}@nd.edu

Abstract. In modern times, data collected from multi-user distributed applications must be analyzed on a massive scale to support critical business objectives. While analytics often requires the use of personal data, it may compromise user privacy expectations if this analysis is conducted over plaintext data. Private Stream Aggregation (PSA) allows for the aggregation of time-series data, while still providing strong privacy guarantees, and is significantly more efficient over a network than related techniques (e.g. homomorphic encryption, secure multiparty computation, etc.) due to its asynchronous and efficient protocols. However, PSA protocols face limitations and can only compute basic functions, such as sum, average, etc.. We present Cryptonomial, a framework for converting any PSA scheme amenable to a complex canonical embedding into a secure computation protocol that can compute any function over time-series data that can be written as a multivariate polynomial, by combining PSA and a Trusted Execution Environment. This design allows us to compute the parallelizable sections of our protocol outside the TEE using advanced hardware, that can take better advantage of parallelism. We show that Cryptonomial inherits the security requirements of PSA, and supports fully malicious security. We simulate our scheme, and show that our techniques enable performance that is orders of magnitude faster than similar work supporting polynomial calculations.

Keywords: Private multivariate polynomial evaluation · Trusted execution environment · Secure aggregation

1 Introduction

Third-party analysis on personal records is becoming increasingly important due to widespread data collection in the modern world. However, this data often contains private information about users such that its publication could seriously compromise their privacy, and a number of studies have shown that significant precautions must be taken to protect such data from malicious actors [5]. Accordingly, it would be beneficial to have a technology that allows a third-party aggregator to learn the result of the analysis performed on users' private

J. Garcia-Alfaro et al. (Eds.): SecureComm 2021, LNICST 398, pp. 332–351, 2021.
https://doi.org/10.1007/978-3-030-90019-9_17

datasets over a network, but nothing else. Many such distributed analyses can be done by or approximated by multivariate polynomial calculations. Common machine learning (ML) tasks such as linear regression, support vector machines (SVMs), activation functions, etc., can be formulated as a multivariate polynomial function over users' private inputs. In recent times, the COVID-19 crisis has led to a renewed interest in applying ML to disease detection and diagnosis, and a number of highly successful techniques [8,29] have been developed to assist medical researchers in combating the virus. For such pressing demands, we consider the problem of allowing a set of users in S to privately compute a polynomial function over their collected time-series data such that an untrusted aggregator only learns the final result, and no individual honest user's data is revealed. More formally, we aim at supporting polynomial evaluation over users' time-series input data in the following format of a *general multivariate polynomial*: $f(\{x_{i,j}\}_{i \in S, j=1,\dots,z}) = \sum_{j=1}^{z} c_j (\prod_{i \in S} \mathbf{m}_{i,j,ts}^{e_{i,j}})$, where z is the number of product terms in the polynomial, c_j and $e_{i,j}$ are public parameters, and $\mathbf{m}_{i,j,ts}$ are secret data from the i-th user at time stamp ts.

There are relatively few practical techniques that can be utilized in this setting, where maintaining the privacy of patients' medical data is of critical (and due to HIPAA, legal) importance. Fully Homomorphic Encryption (FHE), Differential Privacy (DP), Secure Multiparty Computation (MPC), or Oblivious Polynomial Evaluation (OPE) might be used individually as black boxes to solve this problem, but each have significant constraints that negatively impact their practical deployment in the real world. FHE's high computational overhead leads to significant slowdown that makes it impractical in large-scale settings. DP adds noise to the final output of the function, and the resulting accuracy loss can greatly harm the predictive power of any ML analysis. MPC requires participants to send multiple messages during protocol execution, which can seriously degrade overall runtime. OPE also requires multiple messages to be sent, and is focused on the two party setting, which limits its applicability in large scale data analysis.

Private Stream Aggregation (PSA) is a form of distributed secure computing that is promising for achieving this functionality. With this technique, users independently encrypt their input data and send it to an aggregator in a way that allows the aggregator to efficiently learn the aggregation results of time-series data without being able to infer individual data. PSA is generally superior to other types of secure computation paradigms (e.g., MPC, FHE) in large-scale applications involving time-series data because of its extremely low overhead and the ease of key management [16,30]. Notably, PSA is non-interactive (i.e., users send their time-series data in a "stream" and only one message is sent per time interval) and asynchronous (i.e., users can leave after submitting their inputs), making it more efficient in communication than most existing alternative techniques [36]. Although PSA is a mature field of study, prior work in this field is mostly limited to simple aggregation (sum, average, etc.). Due to these limitations, it is challenging for even the most advanced PSA protocols to be deployed in real-world applications for computing stream polynomial evaluation over users' time-series data.

To overcome this limitation with existing works, we developed the Cryptonomial framework, which can convert any PSA scheme amenable to a complex canonical embedding (CCE) [7], an isometric ring homomorphism between complex numbers and integral polynomials, into a privacy-preserving stream polynomial evaluation scheme, that supports additional functionality beyond an additive sum, up to general stream polynomial evaluation. With the use of a Trusted Execution Environment (TEE), we avoid sacrificing security or performance, and can build a highly scalable protocol that is capable of computing richer statistics with high efficiency and throughput. Our framework intelligently combines/tweaks traditional quantum-secure PSA, the CCE, and a TEE to efficiently support stream polynomial evaluation without incurring the drawbacks of simply using a TEE alone or a PSA scheme alone to directly do so. Although it may seem more efficient to simply send plaintext data to an SGX enclave to be computed over, it is known that some TEEs (e.g., Intel SGX) have difficulties exploiting multi-threading [35] due to the lack of common synchronization primitives often found on traditional operating systems, and leveraging threading within TEEs can introduce security vulnerabilities [37] which compromise data privacy. Overall performance can be improved by outsourcing the computationally expensive steps to an untrusted space in an encrypted form, so we can leverage more robust forms of parallel computing especially on high performance hardware such as GPUs, which is not possible with the approaches entirely based on TEEs.

Cryptonomial combines additive PSA with a complex canonical embedding to develop a multivariate polynomial PSA, where single product terms are leaked to the aggregator in a basic design. This leakage is prevented by integrating a TEE into the design, where only a small constant amount of computations are outsourced due to the nature of our design. These techniques allow for significant performance improvements over the current state-of-the-art protocols for privacy-preserving polynomial calculations by multiple orders of magnitude. It is noteworthy that our framework is compatible with state-of-the-art techniques in computational differential privacy [2,31,36] which prevent adversarial inference from the outcomes of aggregation. Cryptonomial contributes to the development of secure ecosystems of collection and analysis involving user-generated datasets, by increasing the utility of the data gathered for data aggregators, while still ensuring the privacy of users with a strong set of guarantees. Note that tolerance of online/offline faults and input poisoning (when malicious users send false inputs to poison the final function output) are orthogonal problems to our work, and this paper focuses on expanding the versatility of PSA. Existing solutions towards these problems [17,19] can be incrementally deployed on top of ours if either of these properties are needed.

In summary, our contributions are as follows:

- We present a new framework to support for the first time PSA-based general stream polynomial evaluation.
- We demonstrate the strong provable privacy guarantees of our instantiated protocol by presenting a formal proof of security.

– We provide an experiments in order to evaluate the performance when compared to existing work and verify the improved efficiency over existing work by multiple orders of magnitude. Our code is open source and available at https://github.com/RyanKarl/CryptonomialDemo.

2   Potential Applications of Cryptonomial

Regression Analysis: Regression analysis (i.e. polynomial regression and ridge regression) is a statistical process for estimating the relationship among multiple variables, with numerous applications in finance, medical research, and a number of other domains [28]. In this type of data analysis each user i 's data record is described as a feature vector $\mathbf{x}$ and a dependent variable y_i, and training a regression model is to find $\mathbf{p}$ which minimizes $MSE(\mathbf{p}) = \sum_i (y_i - \mathbf{px}_i)^2$, i.e., the linear predictor who predicts users' dependent variable vector $\mathbf{y}$ using their feature matrix $\mathbf{X}$ with minimum mean squared error. Since $MSE(\mathbf{p})$ is convex, it is minimized if and only if $\mathbf{Ap} = \mathbf{b}$ where $\mathbf{A} = \mathbf{X}^T\mathbf{X}$ and $\mathbf{b} = \mathbf{X}^T\mathbf{y}$, such that $\mathbf{A} = \sum_i \mathbf{x}_i \mathbf{x}_i^T$ and $\mathbf{b} = \sum_i y_i \mathbf{x}_i$. By using our technique, the aggregator can obliviously evaluate any polynomial regression model.

Support Vector Machines: This protocol can be useful for modeling/predicting diseases in individuals, by supporting a variety of privacy-preserving ML techniques, such as support vector machines (SVM). Supervised machine learning methods have high performance in solving classification problems in many biomedical fields, particularly the SVM [38]. Because the SVM approach is data-driven and model-free, it has discriminative power for classification, especially in cases where sample sizes are small and there are large numbers of variables. This technique has recently been used to develop automated classification and detection of diseases in the clinical setting [24,33], but in all of these cases, participants' privacy was not preserved, and participants either forfeited their data or signed legal agreements that their data would not be shared. In many instances this level of privacy protection may not be sufficient, and we seek to design a system that protects the privacy of each individual data point from public health authorities.

3   Related Work

There are six primary techniques that can be leveraged to achieve traditional secure aggregation or secure polynomial evaluation: 1) FHE, which suffers from high computational overhead, 2) DP, which introduces noise that negatively impacts accuracy, 3) MPC, which increases the communication complexity (number of communication rounds) compared to other techniques, 4) PSA, which overcomes most of the communication and computational overhead constraints of the previous approaches, but is limited to computing simple functions, 5) OPE which supports polynomials but suffers from high communication complexity and is primarily focused on the two party setting, and 6) Secure/Privacy-preserving

Polynomial Evaluation, which also suffers from high communication complexity and scalability issues. We discuss these in more detail below:

Fully Homomorphic Encryption: FHE [7] can be applied to evaluate a multivariate polynomial securely. However, the key management is nontrivial. The aggregator must be trusted to not decrypt ciphertexts pre-aggregation, or the duties of aggregation and decryption should be separated between two servers. Furthermore, there can be significant computational overhead when using FHE. For instance, existing work leveraging FHE [21] to construct secure protocols for aggregation reports an overall computation time of approximately 15 min when computing over only 40 thousand data points. As a result, FHE is often impractical in large-scale aggregations.

Differential Privacy: Modified DP has been used in existing works [27,30] to achieve $O(1)$ error, while using generic differential privacy techniques alone would result in at least $\Omega(N)$ error. Note, [27] also considers periodic aggregation of the sum statistic in the presence of an untrusted aggregator. Their work does not present a formal security definition and requires that the aggregator engage in an extra round of interaction with the participants to decrypt the sum for every time interval. While these techniques can be useful, we are interested in better techniques that do not seriously impact the final accuracy of the aggregation. High amounts of noise or accuracy loss in the secure aggregation can greatly harm the predictive power of future data analysis, and we are primarily focused on the case where users do not apply differentially private noise to their inputs.

Secure Multiparty Computation: MPC protocols allow a set of parties to securely compute an arbitrary function over their inputs [3]. While it is feasible to evaluate a polynomial with MPC, MPC protocols require multiple messages be sent each time interval (round) between users, limiting scalability. All users must wait on the slowest user, and the runtime of each round is determined by that of the slowest user. In cases when MPC is conducted over the Internet, communication round complexity is often the primary bottleneck [3,18], since network latency slows the delivery of packets necessary for continuing to execute the protocol. This problem becomes significantly worse when parties are geographically distant and the communication latency of each message is high.

Private Stream Aggregation: PSA was first studied by Rastogi et al. [27] and Shi et al. [30]. There have been many papers that build on these works, but the vast majority focus on sum aggregation, and not on more complicated functions, such as those based on polynomials. The most extensively studied domain is the pre-quantum PSA based on the Decisional Diffie-Hellman (DDH) assumption and/or the Decisional Composite Residuosity (DCR) assumption [15]. These PSA schemes are vulnerable against quantum computers. Some post-quantum PSA schemes are superior to pre-quantum PSA schemes in overall throughput due to the smaller parameters enabled by the quantum-secure constructions and the various algorithmic optimizations available in quantum-proof cryptography. Early work in quantum-secure PSA [2] employed existing lattice-based encryption schemes as black-box building blocks and was disadvantaged in performance due to complex designs. More recent work in quantum-secure PSA [31] has used a white-box approach to reduce the complexity and overhead in both computation and communication, but is still limited to a single additive aggregation.

Paper	Supports Polynom.	Computation Complexity	Comm. Complexity	Comm. Rounds	Users	Tools and Techniques	Security Remarks
[2]	No	$\mathcal{O}(n)$	$\mathcal{O}(n)$	1	n	PSA, FHE	Q, AO
[16]	No	$\mathcal{O}(n)$	$\mathcal{O}(n)$	1	n	ECC, PSA	AO
[26]	No	$\mathcal{O}(n)$	$\mathcal{O}(n)$	1	n	ECC, PSA	DP
[30]	No	$\mathcal{O}(n + \sqrt{n}\Delta)$	$\mathcal{O}(n)$	1	n	ECC, PSA	AO
[4]	Yes	$\mathcal{O}(l \cdot n)$	$\mathcal{O}(l \log l)$	Multiple	n	MPC	SH
[13]	Yes	$\mathcal{O}(\lambda(l + x))$	$\mathcal{O}((\lambda + dn^{1/d})n^2)$	Multiple	n	MPC	FM
[18]	Yes	$\mathcal{O}(n)$	$\mathcal{O}(kn^2\chi + xk)$	Multiple	n	ECC, PSA	Sem
[10]	Yes	$\mathcal{O}(n)$	$\mathcal{O}(n)$	Multiple	n	MPC	SH
[25]	Yes	$\mathcal{O}((\lambda d + 1)on)$	$\mathcal{O}((\lambda d + 1)n)$	Multiple	n	OPE, MPC	SH
[24]	Yes	$\mathcal{O}((\lambda d + 1)o)$	$\mathcal{O}(\lambda d + 1)$	Multiple	2	OPE	FM
[34]	Yes	$\mathcal{O}((\lambda d + 1)o)$	$\mathcal{O}(\lambda d + 1)$	Multiple	2	OPE	FM
[14]	Yes	$\mathcal{O}(|X| + |Y|\log|X|)$	$\mathcal{O}(|X| + |Y|)$	Multiple	2	OPE	FM
[7]	Yes	$\mathcal{O}(dl + \lambda)$	$\mathcal{O}(dl(dl + \lambda))$	Multiple	2	OPE	FM
[39]	Yes	$\mathcal{O}((\lambda d + 1)o)$	$\mathcal{O}(\lambda d + 1)$	Multiple	2	OPE	FM
[12]	Yes	$\mathcal{O}(dDrn)$	$\mathcal{O}(d(10D + 1)(\sum_{j=1}^{n} \sum_{i=1}^{b_j} \log \alpha_{j,i} + 1))$	Multiple	2	OPE	FM
Ours	Yes	$\mathcal{O}(n)$	$\mathcal{O}(n)$	1	n	PSA,TEE	Q, AO

Fig. 1. Comparison of Existing Work and Cryptonomial; s is the number of secret shares, n is the number of users, w is the plaintext modulus, Δ is the range of inputs, l is the bit length of the inputs, λ is the security parameter, d is the degree of the polynomial, x is the number of terms in the polynomial, χ is the bitlength of the safe prime numbers, t is the minimum threshold of participants in the aggregation, o is the number of points defined on the polynomial, a is the length of the RSA modulus, X and Y are sets of elements, D is the sum of the logarithms of the variable degrees for polynomials consisting of r monomials, b is the number of inputs for each user, α is the degree of the inputs, and k is a parameter where $k \leq n$. Q indicates quantum security, AO indicates aggregator obliviousness, SH/FM indicates security against semi-honest and fully malicious adversaries respectively, Sem indicates semantic security, DP indicates differential privacy and TA indicates a trusted aggregator is required.

Oblivious Polynomial Evaluation: OPE is a protocol involving two parties, a sender whose input is a polynomial $\mathcal{P}$, and a receiver whose input is a value α. At the end of the protocol the receiver learns $\mathcal{P}(\alpha)$ and the sender learns nothing [25]. There are many interesting applications of this idea, including private comparison of data, mutually authenticated key exchange, and anonymous coupons. Many have built on top of this idea, to support operations over floating point numbers for use training neural networks [6], to allow verifiable outsourcing of polynomial calculations to enable secure set intersection [13], to have tighter bounds on computational and/or communication efficiency [34,39]. These techniques can be powerful, but a major drawback is that they only consider the two party setting and generally require multiple rounds of communication (i.e. multiple messages must be sent each time-interval).

Secure/Privacy-Preserving Stream Polynomial Evaluation: There is existing work that supports private polynomial calculations [16,17]. However, individual product terms are disclosed to the aggregator in some work [16], and they generally rely on the DDH assumption and are not quantum secure. Also, existing works have limited scalability, and their polynomial degree is limited to a constant [12], otherwise the communication overhead is prohibitively large. Some approaches also suffer from high communication round complexity and low scalability [9,11,26]. A more general approach exists [4], however it is also an interactive protocol with high communication round complexity.

Our work is more general than standard PSA, and can be used to compute any function that can be written as a polynomial. It avoids the drawbacks of the previous approaches by combining PSA and a TEE, to maximize efficiency while supporting polynomial evaluation. We summarize our findings in Fig. 1.

4   Preliminaries

PSA Adversary Model: In general, PSA schemes are designed to allow an untrusted third party (the aggregator) to perform aggregation computation while providing semantic security to data sent by users. We consider a slightly different adversary model than what is standard in PSA. The users have the same role as before, and send ciphertexts to an aggregator, but in our work the aggregator is equipped with a TEE. We assume that all users may collude with each other and/or the aggregator, although the TEE is trusted according to its specification. We want to guarantee that the aggregator cannot learn any individual input from any honest user (this implies if an aggregator corrupts or colludes with a user to learn their input, this does not impact the privacy of the honest users). All the aggregator can learn is the output of the function. Standard aggregator obliviousness [2,15,17,30], which states the aggregator and colluders learn only the final aggregation outcome and what can be inferred from their inputs, is guaranteed. More specifically, we consider the case of a set of n users and a single aggregator A. Each user $u_i \in S$ where $0 < i \leq n-1$ possesses a piece of data $x_{i,ts}$, corresponding to some timestamp ts. The users wish to calculate an aggregation function f over the private values they send. PSA is formalized as the following 3 algorithms:

- $Setup(\lambda, \cdots)$: Takes a security parameter λ as input, along with any other required parameters, e.g. the number of users n and the range of their data. Returns a set of parameters $parms$, users' secret keys $s_i, i \in [0, n-1]$, and the aggregation key s'.
- $Enc(parms, x_{i,ts}, s_i, ts, \cdots)$: Takes the scheme's parameters, and a user's secret key s_i and time-series input $x_{i,ts}$, along with a timestamp ts. Returns an encryption c_i of the user's noisy input under their secret key.
- $Agg(parms, s', ts, c_{0,ts}, \cdots c_{n-1,ts})$: Takes the scheme's parameters, the aggregation key, a timestamp ts, and the n time-series ciphertexts from the users (with timestamp ts). Returns $y_{ts} = f(x_{0,ts}, x_{1,ts}, \cdots, x_{n-1,ts})$, where f is the aggregation function.

Users will run *Enc* on their data, and send their results $c_{i,ts}$ to the aggregator. Then the aggregator calls *Agg* on the ciphertexts $c_{0,ts}, \cdots c_{n-1,ts}$ it has collected to learn the aggregation result y_{ts}. Note we sometimes omit the timestamp notation moving forward for clarity when the context is clear. In PSA schemes, the algorithm *Setup* is run in a trusted manner [2], via the use of an additional trusted third party, secure hardware, or secure multiparty computation. Informally, we wish to require that an adversary able to compromise the aggregator and any number of other users is unable to learn any new information about uncompromised users' data. This idea is known as *aggregator obliviousness*, and the standard definition [2,30] is summarized below:

Definition 1. *Suppose we have a set of n users, who wish to compute an aggregation at a time point specified by the timestamp ts. An aggregation scheme π is aggregator oblivious [2,30] if no polynomially bounded adversary has an advantage greater than negligible in the security parameter λ in winning the following game:*

The challenger runs the Setup algorithm which returns the public parameters parms to the adversary. Then the adversary will guess which of two unknown inputs was a users' data, by performing the following queries:

Encrypt: *The adversary argues $(i, x_{i,ts}, r_{i,ts})$ to the challenger and receives back $Enc(parms, sk_i, ts, x_{i,ts}, r_{i,ts})$ from the challenger.*

Compromise: *The adversary argues $i \in [0,n) \cup \{\zeta\}$. If $i = \zeta$, the challenger gives the aggregator's decryption key s' to the adversary. Otherwise, the challenger returns the ith user's secret key s_i to the adversary.*

Challenge: *The adversary may only make this query once. The adversary argues a set of participants $S \subset [0,n)$, with $i \in S$ not previously compromised. For each user $i \in S$, the adversary chooses two plaintext-noise pairs $(x_{i,ts}, r_{i,ts}), (\tilde{x}_{i,ts}, \tilde{r}_{i,ts})$ and sends them to the challenger. The challenger then chooses a random bit b. If $b = 0$, the challenger computes $c_{i,ts} = Enc(parms, s_i, ts, x_{i,ts}, r_{i,ts})$ for every $i \in S$. If $b = 1$, the challenger computes $c_{i,ts} = Enc(parms, s_i, ts, \tilde{x}_{i,ts}, \tilde{r}_{i,ts})$ for every $i \in S$. The challenger returns the ciphertexts $\{c_{i,ts}\}_{i \in S}$ to the adversary. The adversary wins if they can correctly guess bit b chosen during the Challenge.*

Trusted Execution Environment: Note that our framework can work with any form of Trusted Execution Environment (TEE), but we chose the Intel SGX for our concrete instantiation.

Intel SGX is a set of new CPU instructions that can be used by applications to set aside private regions of code and data. It allows developers to (among other things) protect sensitive data from unauthorized access or modification by malicious software that may be running at superior privilege levels. To do this, the CPU protects an isolated region of memory called Processor Reserved Memory (PRM) against other non-enclave memory accesses, including the kernel, hypervisor, etc. Sensitive code and data is encrypted and stored as 4KB pages in the

Enclave Page Cache (EPC), a region inside the PRM. Even though EPC pages are allocated and mapped to frames by the OS kernel, page-level encryption guarantees confidentiality and integrity. In addition, to provide access protection to the EPC pages, the CPU maintains an Enclave Page Cache Map (EPCM) that stores security attributes and metadata associated with EPC pages. This allows for strong privacy and integrity guarantees if applications can be written in a two part model [10,19].

Applications must be split into a secure part and a non-secure part. The application can then launch an enclave, which is placed in protected memory, that allows user-level code to define private segments of memory, whose contents are protected and unable to be read or saved by any process outside the enclave. Enclave entry points are defined during compilation. The secure execution environment is part of the host process, and the application contains its own code, data, and the enclave, but the enclave contains its own code and data too. An enclave can access its application's memory, but not vice versa, due to a combination of software and hardware cryptographic primitives. Only the code within the enclave can access its data, and external accesses are always denied. The enclave is decrypted "on the fly" only within the CPU itself, and only for code and data running from within the enclave itself. This is supported by an autonomous piece of hardware called the Memory Encryption Engine (MEE) that protects the confidentiality and integrity of the CPU-DRAM traffic over a specified memory range. Code running within the enclave is therefore protected from being "spied on" by other code. Although the enclave is trusted, no process outside it needs to be trusted, including the operating system [10,19]. Before performing computation on a remote platform, a user can verify the authenticity of the trusted environment. By using the attestation mechanism, users can establish that software is running on an Intel SGX enabled device inside an enclave.

Lattice-Based Cryptography: Our framework utilizes the complex canonical embedding (CCE) [7], to support privacy-preserving polynomial evaluation on floating-point data. The CCE and the inverse of it allows one to map a polynomial ring element to a vector of complex numbers and vice versa, and this mapping is an isometric ring homomorphism, making it possible to encode complex numbers into a quotient ring of polynomials. Thus, it is frequently used in the lattice-based cryptography using polynomial rings, as complex-number inputs can be encrypted with the CCE. As such, we anticipate our framework will be most useful in conjunction with lattice-based PSA schemes. In general, lattice-based cryptography has recently generated significant interest among cryptography researchers, as it is quantum secure and generally faster than more traditional approaches (RSA, etc.) due to its shorter operands and other recent optimizations. With large coefficients, Residue Number System (RNS) representations can be used to break large numbers down into smaller components. Using Single Instruction Multiple Data (SIMD) optimizations allows multiple plaintexts to be encoded into a single ciphertext. Large polynomial degrees can make polynomial multiplication very expensive, and to mitigate this the Number-

Theoretic Transform (NTT) can be used to decrease the theoretical complexity [7,31]. Full-RNS variants of lattice-based cryptosystems reduce the complexity of the cryptosystems' most expensive operations to the complexity of the NTT [7]. The Ring Learning with Errors (RLWE) problem is frequently used as a hardness assumption when designing lattice-based cryptosystems, and we give an overview of it below. Note that we use boldface lowercase letters to denote elements of rings. Consider two coprime numbers q, p, with $q \gg p$, and let $\mathbf{s}$ be a random element of R_q with coefficients bounded by b (b is often 1), where R is the quotient ring of $\mathbb{Z}[X]/\Phi(X)$, and $\Phi(X)$ is the $M = 2N$-th cyclotomic polynomial with degree $N = 2^d$ for some positive integer d, such that $R_t = \mathbb{Z}_t[X]/\Phi(X)$, is the ring with all coefficients in $\mathbb{Z}_t$. We let $[x]_t$ be the centered modular reduction of $x \mod t$, such that $[x]_t = x - \lfloor \frac{x}{t} \rceil \cdot t \in \mathbb{Z}_t$, where $\mathbb{Z}_t = [\frac{-t}{2}, \frac{t}{2}) \cap \mathbb{Z}$; when centered modular reduction is applied coefficientwise to ring elements we write $[\mathbf{a}]_t \in R_t$. Let $\mathbf{a}_i, \mathbf{e}_i$ be a polynomially bounded number of elements of R_q, with $\mathbf{a}_i$ chosen randomly and $\mathbf{e}_i$ random and also b-bounded.

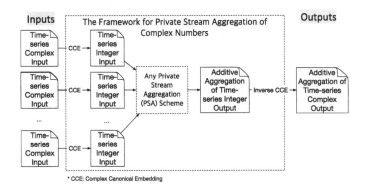

Fig. 2. The framework for complex-number PSA

An adversary is given the set of pairs $(\mathbf{a}_i, \mathbf{b}_i) \in R_q^2$. Unknown to the adversary is whether $(\mathbf{a}_i, \mathbf{b}_i)$ are *RLWE terms*, i.e. $\mathbf{b}_i = [\mathbf{a}_i \cdot \mathbf{s}_i + p' \mathbf{e}_i]_q$ with $p' \in \{1, p\}$, or if $\mathbf{b}_i$ was randomly chosen from R_q. The decisional RLWE problem is then to determine whether the terms $\mathbf{b}_i$ are RLWE terms or random elements of R_q, without any knowledge of $\mathbf{s}_i$ or $\mathbf{e}_i$. The RLWE problem is believed to be intractable for quantum computers; its difficulty comes from reduction to the Shortest Vector Problem [22]. The difficulty of the RLWE problem is parameterized by q and N. Larger values of q provide more utility for RLWE-based cryptosystems, but decreases the difficulty of the RLWE problem. Note increasing N also increases the difficulty of the RLWE problem and thus the overall security.

5 Our Framework

We enable the stream polynomial evaluation via a composition of additive PSA and CCE, and address its partial leakages with a TEE. It is extremely challenging to apply an approach that uses RLWE terms as the computationally indistinguishable random elements to design multiplicative PSA with exact aggregation [2,31]. One reason among others is that the RLWE term is inherently additive, i.e., the error term $\mathbf{e}_{i,ts}$ is added instead of multiplied in the term $\mathbf{a}_{ts}\mathbf{s}_i + \mathbf{e}_{i,ts}$, making it challenging to cancel out the random terms if the ciphertexts are multiplied together at the aggregator's side. It should be said that traditional PSA schemes are defined over integers, but by leveraging the CCE [7] we can transform any PSA taking quotient rings of polynomials as the plaintext space (e.g. any lattice-based PSA schemes based on the RLWE problem [2,23,31]) into PSA defined over floating point numbers. We summarize our framework for transforming any PSA scheme operating over integers to operate over floating point numbers in Fig. 2.

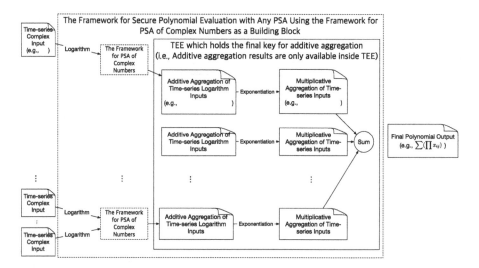

Fig. 3. The Framework of Polynomial Evaluation with Complex-Number PSA (using the Framework for PSA of Complex Numbers, Fig. 2, as a building block)

The nature of PSA makes it possible to execute only a small constant amount of computations inside a TEE, which minimizes the performance impact. We achieve PSA for the multivariate polynomial f by composing the additive PSA with a TEE so that each user i provides a ciphertext corresponding to their private data $\{\mathbf{m}_{i,j,ts}^{e_{i,j}}\}_{j=1}^{z}$ and the aggregator can multiply each product term $\prod_{i \in S} \mathbf{m}_{i,j,ts}^{e_{i,j}}$ for $j = 1$ to z. Note that, due to the SIMD technique, each user can pack all z input values for the z product terms into one plaintext polynomial, and the aggregator only needs to perform one multiplicative aggregation to get the outcome of z individual products. More specifically, we rely on the following technique to build our multiplicative PSA: For each input $\mathbf{m}_{i,j,ts} \in \mathbb{C}$ of i-th user, let the user calculate the natural logarithm of the input and encode it into a polynomial as $\mathbf{m}'_{i,ts} = \mathbf{CCE}(\ln(\mathbf{m}_{i,j,ts}))$ using the complex canonical embedding [7]. Then, the nearly-exact additive PSA is leveraged to let the aggregator compute $\sum_{i \in S} \mathbf{m}'_{i,ts}$ with negligible error terms. We then undo the complex canonical embedding to recover $\sum_{i \in S} \ln(\mathbf{m}_{i,j,ts}) = \ln(\prod_{i \in S} \mathbf{m}_{i,j,ts})$, and a natural exponential function can be computed to get $\prod_{i \in S} \mathbf{m}_{i,j,ts}$. Due to the limitation of the multiplicative PSA, we are limited to nearly-exact aggregation only, i.e., the outcome is exact up to the pre-defined precision only. Then, the aggregator can locally calculate $f(\{\mathbf{m}_{i,j,ts}\}_{i \in S, j=1,\ldots,z})$ using the public parameters c_j, where S is the set of users whose ciphertexts are received by the aggregator. Such an approach guarantees correct aggregation up to the precision of the outcome, however, the aggregator learns all individual product terms which may not be acceptable especially when the product terms are correlated.

Although such additional knowledge does not always lead to complete disclosure of individuals' inputs, the search space can be reduced by leveraging such knowledge. Thus, the proposed PSA above fails to achieve the *aggregator obliviousness* [2,30] that states the aggregator should learn only the final output. To address this, we adopt the idea of a *one-time program* [14] that leverages trusted hardware implementations to prevent the leakages similar to the one above. Namely, we let the aggregator deploy a TEE, e.g., Intel SGX and leverage its secure functionality to prevent the aggregator from receiving more information than the final result. The memory encryption and isolation of the TEE guarantees that operating systems cannot view or change the program/data within the TEE. A naïve way to prevent the aforementioned leakages is to let the aggregator perform the aggregation within the TEE. Then, even though the multiple aggregation results are calculated for many different subsets, the final outcome resides inside the TEE only, and the program running in it (which is verified by all users through remote attestation) can decide to output the appropriate result(s) to the outside of the TEE, i.e., the aggregator. In the case of stream polynomial evaluation, the outcome of the multiplicative aggregation, i.e., the individual product terms, resides in the TEE, and the remotely verified program running in the TEE computes and returns only the sum of the product terms to the aggregator. Though being secure, such a method is more complicated. One can simply let users set up secure communication channels with the aggregator's TEE (by exchanging the keys) and let users send their input data to the TEE who performs arbitrary aggregation within the TEE securely.

We design a method to integrate the TEE into the PSA such that users benefit from the security guarantees of TEE while the overhead at the aggregator's end is much smaller than the overhead of the entire raw data being sent to the TEE and aggregated inside the TEE. Note that if only one or a few constant number of user ciphertexts are sent to the TEE and the rest, which are sent to the aggregator, are aggregated outside the TEE, the aggregator only observes the incomplete aggregation results which are indistinguishable from random elements due to the security of the PSA (e.g., randomness of the RLWE terms [2,31]). After the aggregation of the ciphertexts outside the TEE is finished, the aggregator can send the aggregated incomplete results into the TEE who continues the aggregation inside the TEE, at which point only a constant number of operations need to be performed since only a few operations are needed inside the TEE. Considering that the TEE introduces the extra overhead of memory encryption for every communication between the CPU and the DRAM, the PSA with our optimization has higher throughput than the plain aggregation performed entirely within the TEE especially when the scale of the aggregation is large. Recall it is known that some TEEs (e.g., Intel SGX) have difficulties exploiting multi-threading [35] due to the lack of common synchronization primitives, and leveraging threading within TEEs can introduce security vulnerabilities [37]. Also, TEEs have been shown to run common functionalities over an order of magnitude slower than what can be achieved on comparable untrusted hardware, due to the overhead of computing within the enclave [35], and performing a large number of context switches to send each user's data into the TEE can add serious overhead, especially in a big data setting. Overall performance can be improved if we minimize the number of context switches and outsource computationally expensive steps to an untrusted space that can better leverage parallel computing. More specifically, we aggregate all of the users' ciphertexts outside the enclave, and only perform a single context switch to send this intermediate result into the enclave, where we add the aggregator's secret key to recover the product terms of the polynomial. We later calculate the sum of the calculated products, so we learn the final output inside the TEE. We summarize the data flow in our framework for transforming any PSA scheme into a secure stream polynomial evaluation scheme in Fig. 3, and we formalize it with the following 3 algorithms:

- $Cryptonomial.Setup(\lambda, \cdots)$: All users perform attestation on the aggregator's TEE, and input to the TEE a security parameter λ as input, along with any other required parameters, e.g. the number of users n and the range of their data. The TEE returns a set of parameters $parms$, users' secret keys $k_i, i \in [0, n)$ (over a secure channel), and the aggregation key k'.

- $Cryptonomial.Enc(parms, \mathbf{m}_{i,ts}, k_i, ts, \cdots)$: Takes the scheme's parameters, and a user's secret key k_i and vector of time-series input $\mathbf{m}_{i,j,ts}$, along with a timestamp ts. Returns $\mathbf{c}_{i,ts}$, an additively homomorphic encryption of $\mathbf{CCE}(\ln(\mathbf{m}_{i,j,ts}))$, the natural logarithm of the user's vector of noisy inputs encrypted under their secret key, where the natural log is taken componentwise over the vector, and $\mathbf{CCE}$ is the complex canonical embedding function.

- $Cryptonomial.Agg(parms, k', ts, \mathbf{c}_{0,ts}, \cdots \mathbf{c}_{n-1,ts})$: Takes the scheme's parameters, the aggregation key, a timestamp, and the n time-series ciphertexts from the users (with timestamp ts). In the untrusted space compute $\mathbf{y}_{ts} = \sum_{i=0}^{n-1} \mathbf{c}_{i,ts}$ via homomorphic addition. Then send $\mathbf{y}_{ts}$ into the TEE and add in the aggregation key k' as appropriate based on the underlying PSA scheme. Then within the TEE take the inverse of the $\mathbf{CCE}$ of this as $\sum_{i=0}^{n-1} \mathbf{CCE}^{-1}(\mathbf{CCE}(\ln(\mathbf{m}_{i,j,ts}))) = \sum_{i=0}^{n-1} \ln(\mathbf{m}_{i,j,ts}) =$

$\ln(\prod_{i=0}^{n-1} \mathbf{m}_{i,j,ts})$. They then take the exponential to recover $\prod_{i=0}^{n-1} \mathbf{m}_{i,j,ts}$ and recover $\sum_{j=1}^{z} c_j (\prod_{i=0}^{n-1} \mathbf{m}_{i,j,ts}^{e_{i,j}})$, where z is the number of product terms in the polynomial, and c_j's and $e_{i,j}$'s are public parameters.

6 Framework Instantiation with Existing PSA

PSA Chosen for Instantiation: Our scheme can leverage any PSA amenable to a complex canonical embedding as a building block. There are several such schemes [1,2], but we chose the noise-scaled variant of SLAP (i.e. $SLAP_{NS}$, [31]) as a building block for its simplicity and open-source implementation. Before describing our protocol, we review the SLAP protocol below. Note, in the scheme operands are ring elements, not matrices or vectors. We denote the plaintext domain as the ring R_t and the ciphertext domain as the ring R_q, with $q \gg t$ and an appropriate value of the polynomial modulus degree N to allow for the necessary security. Secret keys and error terms are drawn from distributions χ, ζ (1-bounded in practice) on R_q. The scheme is defined as follows:

- $SLAP_{NS}.Setup(\lambda, t, n)$: Takes in the security parameter λ, the plaintext modulus t, and the number of users n. Choose q such that $\log_2(3) + \log_2(n) + \log_2(t) < \log_2(q)$ and q, t are coprime. Choose the polynomial modulus N such that λ bits of security are provided for the RLWE problem with ring polynomial coefficients in $\mathbb{Z}_q$. Choose a set of public keys $\{\mathbf{a}_{ts}\}$ uniformly at random, or a method of generating keys indistinguishable from such. Choose users' secret keys $\mathbf{s}_0 \cdots \mathbf{s}_{n-1}$ from χ. Construct the aggregator's key as $\mathbf{s}' = -[\sum_{i=0}^{n-1} \mathbf{s}_i]_q$. Return $parms = (R_q, t, n, \{\mathbf{a}_{ts}\})$, the users' secret keys $\mathbf{s}_i$, and the aggregation key $\mathbf{s}'$.
- $SLAP_{NS}.Enc(parms, \mathbf{s}_i, \mathbf{m}_{i,ts} \in R_t, ts)$: Choose the user's error $\mathbf{e}_{i,ts}$ from ζ. Return the user's ciphertext $\mathbf{c}_{i,ts} = [\mathbf{a}_{ts} \cdot \mathbf{s}_i + t\mathbf{e}_{i,ts} + \mathbf{m}_{i,ts}]_q$ (based upon the secret key, the user's input, a small random error, and the timestamp ts).
- $SLAP_{NS}.Agg(parms, \mathbf{s}', ts, \mathbf{c}_{0,ts} \cdots \mathbf{c}_{n-1,ts})$: If any of $\mathbf{c}_{0,ts} \cdots \mathbf{c}_{n-1,ts}$ are absent or not well-formed (i.e., an element of R_q), then abort. Otherwise, compute and return $\mathbf{y}_{ts} = [[\mathbf{a}_{ts} \cdot \mathbf{s}' + \sum_{i=0}^{n-1} \mathbf{c}_{i,ts}]_q]_t$

Our Instantiated Protocol (τ): We now present the concrete instantiation of our scheme. Let **CCE** be the complex canonical embedding described in [7], which is an isometric ring homomorphism that preserves the magnitude of the elements, to encode complex numbers into polynomials. We assume the set of users u_i perform remote attestation with the aggregator A's TEE, and the polynomial function is agreed upon beforehand. We model our system in Fig. 3. The protocol instantiated with our framework and the building block SLAP is denoted as τ and defined as follows:

- $\tau_{Setup}(\lambda, t, n)$: Inside the TEE, call $SLAP_{NS}.Setup(\lambda, t, n)$. The secret keys $\mathbf{k}_0 \cdots \mathbf{k}_{n-1}$ and the relevant parameters are then distributed to their owners over secure channels, and the aggregator's key $\mathbf{k}'$ remains inside the TEE.

- $\tau_{Enc}(parms, \mathbf{k}_i, \mathbf{m}_{i,j,ts}, ts)$: Note in this functionality each user determines their private values $\mathbf{m}_{i,j,ts} \in R_t$ they wish to send for a given time stamp ts, and encrypt it as follows: First, take the natural logarithm of their inputs as $\ln(\mathbf{m}_{i,j,ts})$, and apply the complex canonical embedding over this as $\mathbf{m}'_{i,ts} = \mathbf{CCE}(\ln(\mathbf{m}_{i,j,ts}))$. Finally they encrypt this as $\mathbf{c}_{i,ts} = SLAP_{NS}.Enc(parms, \mathbf{s}_i, \mathbf{m}'_{i,ts}, ts)$. Then each u_i sends their $\mathbf{c}_{i,ts}$ to A.

- $\tau_{Agg}(parms, \mathbf{k}', ts, \mathbf{c}_{i,ts} \cdots \mathbf{c}_{n-1,ts})$: In the untrusted space A computes $\mathbf{y}_{ts} = [\sum_{i=0}^{n-1} \mathbf{c}_{i,ts}]_q$. Then they send $\mathbf{y}_{ts}$ into the TEE, and inside they compute $[[\mathbf{y}_{ts} + \mathbf{a}_{ts} \cdot \mathbf{k}']_q]_t = \sum_{i=0}^{n-1} \mathbf{CCE}(\ln(\mathbf{m}_{i,j,ts}))$. Then within the TEE they take the inverse of the $\mathbf{CCE}$ of this as $\sum_{i=0}^{n-1} \mathbf{CCE}^{-1}(\mathbf{CCE}(\ln(\mathbf{m}_{i,j,ts}))) = \sum_{i=0}^{n-1} \ln(\mathbf{m}_{i,j,ts}) = \ln(\prod_{i=0}^{n-1} \mathbf{m}_{i,j,ts})$. They then take the exponential to recover $\prod_{i=0}^{n-1} \mathbf{m}_{i,j,ts}$ and compute $\sum_{j=1}^{z} c_j(\prod_{i=0}^{n-1} \mathbf{m}_{i,j,ts}^{e_{i,j}})$, where z is the number of product terms in the polynomial, and c_j's and $e_{i,j}$'s are public parameters.

Correctness: This protocol is correct, since we know that when adding n ciphertexts $\mathbf{c}_{i,ts}$, we find $[\mathbf{a}_{ts} \cdot \mathbf{k}' + \sum_{i=0}^{n-1} \mathbf{c}_{i,ts}]_q = [\sum_{i=0}^{n-1}(t\mathbf{e}_{i,ts} + \mathbf{CCE}(\ln(\mathbf{m}_{i,j,ts})))]_q$. The magnitude of the sum of the errors is bounded by $n \cdot t$, and the magnitude of the sum of the inputs is bounded by $n \cdot \frac{t}{2}$. Then as long as $\frac{3 \cdot n \cdot t}{2} < \frac{q}{2}$, $\sum_{i=0}^{n-1}(t\mathbf{e}_{i,ts} + \mathbf{CCE}(\ln(\mathbf{m}_{i,j,ts})))$ does not overflow modulo q, guaranteeing correctness. Then reducing $\sum_{i=0}^{n-1}(t\mathbf{e}_{i,ts} + \mathbf{m}_{i,j,ts})$ modulo t removes the error terms, leaving us with the sum of the users' inputs modulo t. Note $\sum_{i=0}^{n-1} \ln(\mathbf{m}_{i,j,ts}) = \ln(\prod_{i=0}^{n-1} \mathbf{m}_{i,j,ts})$, so exponentiating recovers $\prod_{i=0}^{n-1} \mathbf{m}_{i,j,ts}$.

Security: Although a formal proof of aggregator obliviousness is in the full version for completeness [20], note by the underlying security of SLAP [31], the RLWE problem [22], and the TEE, the protocol is secure. Even if the untrusted aggregator colludes with some malicious users, although they can learn the individual inputs of the malicious users, since they only receive the aggregated function output as a final result, they cannot learn which honest user inputted which value, provided there is more than one honest user. Similarly, since each term in the polynomial is calculated inside the TEE, there is no partial leakage. Security follows from SLAP [31], and from the underlying security of AES encryption [10], which is used by the Intel SGX to encrypt data in the enclave. We can easily guarantee differential privacy for our protocol using existing techniques if necessary [2,31].

Parallel-Friendliness: Note that the computation of the product terms is perfectly parallelizable (except for one operation, adding the aggregator's secret key, which must be done inside the enclave) and thus can be outsourced to many-core hardware. Existing work [32] notes the DDR4 specification gives a peak data transfer rate of 25,600 MB/s, which gives 70 μs seconds per ciphertext transfer time from DRAM to the hardware used for parallelization. In practice, the overhead from data transfer can be significantly less, due to pipelining and interleaving of execution and data transfer. They estimate 21.2 μs seconds per ciphertext transfer time from DRAM to the hardware after observing the time difference between operating upon ciphertexts that were/were not resident in cache memory [32].

7   Experimental Evaluation

To better understand the improvements gained in performance we simulated our scheme using C++11, and version 2.10 of the Intel SGX SDK and present our results below. For our PSA backend we used the open-source implementation of SLAP's noise-scaled variant [31], which uses optimizations including RNS, SIMD batching, and NTT, which are discussed in Sect. 4. We used SLAP's default parameters; security parameter $\lambda = 128$, polynomial modulus degree $N = 1024$, and ciphertext modulus q with 56 bits. Our experiments were run on a computer running Ubuntu 18.04 with an Intel(R) Xeon(R) W-1290P 3.70GHz CPU with 10 cores, 20 threads, 128 GB of memory, and Intel SGX support. We did not leverage GPUs/FPGAs because we did not have access to computers equipped with both Intel SGX and GPUS/FPGAs. Our tests took average runtimes of 5 trials.

Benchmarks: To benchmark our protocol, we computed polynomials of the form $\sum_{j=1}^{2} \prod_{i=1-j+1}^{n-j+1} \mathbf{m}_{i,j,ts}$ and report the time for each step below. Achieving accurate timings for operations within the enclave is difficult, because the SGX primitive sgx_get_trusted_time only supports second level precision, but many operations can be computed at millisecond precision (Intel is committed to providing better timing support in future releases). To measure benchmarks, we used C++ std::chrono, which supports microsecond precision, and timed the overall time to compute ECALLs within the untrusted component of the program. We report how these times scale as we increase the number of users in Fig. 4. In general, we find that preprocessing time is linear in the number of users, and is ≤ 1 ms for 100,000 users (excluding network latency). Also, encryption and decryption time is linear in the number of users, and is approximately 1 ms per user. Aggregation time is logarithmic in the number of users, but is still practical in large scale computation.

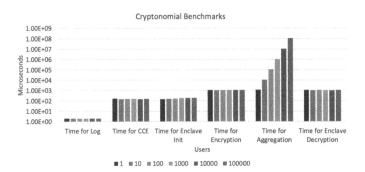

Fig. 4. Benchmarks of cryptonomial using SLAP as the PSA

Case Study: To better understand how our technique performs in a real world setting, we simulated multiple linear regression analysis using Cryptonomial, and compared it to the performance reported by the current state-of-the-art privacy-preserving polynomial evaluation technique known as PDA [17]. The linear regression model consists of one equation of linearly increasing variables (also called parameters or features) along with a coefficient estimation algorithm called least squares, which attempts to determine the best possible coefficient given a variable. Multiple linear regression is a model that can capture the linear relationship between multiple variables and features, assuming that there is one. The multiple linear regression formula is $y = \beta_0 + \beta_1 x_1 + \beta_2 x_2 + \ldots + \beta_i x_i + \varepsilon$, where β_0 is known as the intercept, β_1 to β_i are known as coefficients, x_1 to x_i are the features of the dataset, and ε are the residual terms.

We can also represent the formula for linear regression in vector notation. Linear least squares (LLS) is the main algorithm for estimating coefficients of the formula just shown. We use the most popular variant called ordinary least squares (OLS). The OLS algorithm minimizes the sum of squares of residuals. The following formula ensures that the resulting coefficients define a minimum for the normal equation, which means that the result is the minimized total sum of squared residual: $\hat{\beta} = \left(\mathbf{X}^\mathrm{T}\mathbf{X}\right)^{-1}\mathbf{X}^\mathrm{T}\mathbf{y}$. Here $\hat{\beta}$ is a vector containing all of the coefficients that can be used to make predictions by using the formula presented in the beginning for multiple linear regression. We simulated training a linear regression model over the datasets in a privacy-preserving manner using our scheme (Sect. 6) with data from the UCI Machine Learning Database as done in PDA [17]. We measured the time to complete the training in a local computer and our times are reported in Table 1. By utilizing batching and other optimizations in SLAP, data for all features was encoded into a single ciphertext, significantly reducing computation and communication overhead.

Table 1. Cryptonomial OLS performance on UCI dataset

Datasets	Records	Features	Our time	PDA time	Speedup
Census	48,842	14	2.85 s	355 s	125x
Bank	45,211	17	2.75 s	341 s	124x
Insurance	9,822	14	0.64 s	74 s	115x
White wine	4,898	11	0.35 s	33 s	94x
Red wine	1,599	11	0.17 s	12 s	71x

We note that our technique is always the fastest by at least an order of magnitude. This makes sense as our lattice-based PSA cryptographic primitive combined with a TEE as discussed in our framework is considerably less computationally expensive than the ECC-based techniques of PDA. Also, PDA makes use of an interesting but expensive ECC-based encoding procedure that allows for a form of fault tolerance, where users can be dynamically added or dropped from the system. This encoding negatively impacts the overall run time, and this trend continues as we increase the number of records in the final aggregation calculation. We note that although this paper does not consider fault tolerance, there are preexisting techniques that leverage a TEE to transform any traditional PSA scheme into a fault tolerant PSA scheme [19], and such techniques can be incrementally deployed on our solution. Thus, we can conclude that in secure polynomial evaluation scenarios where aggregation times greatly impact the overall performance, our method offers the best efficiency.

8   Conclusion

We presented Cryptonomial, a framework for converting any PSA scheme amenable to a CCE into a secure computation protocol that can compute any function that can be written as a polynomial, by combining PSA and a TEE. We showed that Cryptonomial meets the security and privacy requirements of PSA, and supports strong security guarantees. Simulations show our scheme's performance is orders of magnitude faster than similar work supporting polynomial calculations.

Acknowledgement. This work was supported by the Office of the Director of National Intelligence (ODNI), Intelligence Advanced Research Projects Activity (IARPA) via contract #2020-20082700002. Any opinions, findings and conclusions or recommendations expressed in this material are those of the authors and do not necessarily reflect those of the sponsor.

References

1. Abdallah, A., Shen, X.S.: A lightweight lattice-based homomorphic privacy-preserving data aggregation scheme for smart grid. IEEE Trans. Smart Grid **9**(1), 396–405 (2016)
2. Becker, D., Guajardo, J., Zimmermann, K.H.: Revisiting private stream aggregation: lattice-based PSA. In: NDSS (2018)
3. Ben-Efraim, A., Lindell, Y., Omri, E.: Optimizing semi-honest secure multiparty computation for the internet. In: CCS, pp. 578–590. ACM (2016)
4. Blanton, M.: Achieving full security in privacy-preserving data mining. In: Social-Com, pp. 925–934. IEEE (2011)
5. Bonneau, J.: The science of guessing: analyzing an anonymized corpus of 70 million passwords. In: IEEE Symposium on Security and Privacy, pp. 538–552. IEEE (2012)
6. Chang, Y.-C., Lu, C.-J.: Oblivious polynomial evaluation and oblivious neural learning. In: Boyd, C. (ed.) ASIACRYPT 2001. LNCS, vol. 2248, pp. 369–384. Springer, Heidelberg (2001). https://doi.org/10.1007/3-540-45682-1_22
7. Cheon, J.H., Kim, A., Kim, M., Song, Y.S.: Floating-point homomorphic encryption. IACR Cryptology ePrint Archive 2016/421 (2016)
8. Chowdhury, M.E., et al.: Can AI help in screening viral and COVID-19 pneumonia? IEEE Access **8**, 132665–132676 (2020)

9. Cianciullo, L., Ghodosi, H.: Efficient information theoretic multi-party computation from oblivious linear evaluation. In: Blazy, O., Yeun, C.Y. (eds.) WISTP 2018. LNCS, vol. 11469, pp. 78–90. Springer, Cham (2019). https://doi.org/10.1007/978-3-030-20074-9_7

10. Costan, V., Devadas, S.: Intel SGX explained. IACR Cryptology ePrint Archive **2016**(086), 1–118 (2016)

11. Dachman-Soled, D., Malkin, T., Raykova, M., Yung, M.: Secure efficient multiparty computing of multivariate polynomials and applications. In: Lopez, J., Tsudik, G. (eds.) ACNS 2011. LNCS, vol. 6715, pp. 130–146. Springer, Heidelberg (2011). https://doi.org/10.1007/978-3-642-21554-4_8

12. Franklin, M., Mohassel, P.: Efficient and secure evaluation of multivariate polynomials and applications. In: Zhou, J., Yung, M. (eds.) ACNS 2010. LNCS, vol. 6123, pp. 236–254. Springer, Heidelberg (2010). https://doi.org/10.1007/978-3-642-13708-2_15

13. Hazay, C.: Oblivious polynomial evaluation and secure set-intersection from algebraic PRFs. J. Cryptol. **31**(2), 537–586 (2018)

14. Järvinen, K., Kolesnikov, V., Sadeghi, A.-R., Schneider, T.: Garbled circuits for leakage-resilience: hardware implementation and evaluation of one-time programs. In: Mangard, S., Standaert, F.-X. (eds.) CHES 2010. LNCS, vol. 6225, pp. 383–397. Springer, Heidelberg (2010). https://doi.org/10.1007/978-3-642-15031-9_26

15. Joye, M., Libert, B.: A scalable scheme for privacy-preserving aggregation of time-series data. In: Sadeghi, A.-R. (ed.) FC 2013. LNCS, vol. 7859, pp. 111–125. Springer, Heidelberg (2013). https://doi.org/10.1007/978-3-642-39884-1_10

16. Jung, T., Mao, X., Li, X., Tang, S., Gong, W., Zhang, L.: Privacy-preserving data aggregation without secure channel: multivariate polynomial evaluation. In: IEEE INFOCOM (2013)

17. Jung, T., Han, J., Li, X.Y.: PDA: semantically secure time-series data analytics with dynamic user groups. TDSC **15**(2), 260–274 (2018)

18. Karl, R., Burchfield, T., Takeshita, J., Jung, T.: Non-interactive MPC with trusted hardware secure against residual function attacks. In: Chen, S., Choo, K.-K.R., Fu, X., Lou, W., Mohaisen, A. (eds.) SecureComm 2019. LNICST, vol. 305, pp. 425–439. Springer, Cham (2019). https://doi.org/10.1007/978-3-030-37231-6_25

19. Karl, R., Takeshita, J., Jung, T.: Cryptonite: a framework for flexible time-series secure aggregation with online fault tolerance. IACR Cryptology ePrint Archive 2020/1561 (2020)

20. Karl, R., Takeshita, J., Mohammed, A., Striegel, A., Jung, T.: Cryptonomial: a framework for private time-series polynomial calculations. Cryptology ePrint Archive, Report 2021/473 (2021). https://eprint.iacr.org/2021/473

21. Lu, W., Kawasaki, S., Sakuma, J.: Using fully homomorphic encryption for statistical analysis of categorical, ordinal and numerical data. IACR Cryptology ePrint Archive 2016/1163 (2016)

22. Lyubashevsky, V., Peikert, C., Regev, O.: On ideal lattices and learning with errors over rings. J. ACM (JACM) **60**(6), 1–35 (2013)

23. Lyubashevsky, V., Peikert, C., Regev, O.: A toolkit for ring-LWE cryptography. In: Johansson, T., Nguyen, P.Q. (eds.) EUROCRYPT 2013. LNCS, vol. 7881, pp. 35–54. Springer, Heidelberg (2013). https://doi.org/10.1007/978-3-642-38348-9_3

24. Maglogiannis, I., Loukis, E., Zafiropoulos, E., Stasis, A.: Support vectors machine-based identification of heart valve diseases using heart sounds. Comput. Methods Programs Biomed. **95**(1), 47–61 (2009)

25. Naor, M., Pinkas, B.: Oblivious polynomial evaluation. SIAM J. Comput. **35**(5), 1254–1281 (2006)

26. Özarar, M., Özgit, A.: Secure multiparty computation via oblivious polynomial evaluation. In: Theory and Practice of Cryptography Solutions for Secure Information Systems, pp. 253–278. IGI Global (2013)

27. Rastogi, V., Nath, S.: Differentially private aggregation of distributed time-series with transformation and encryption. In: ACM SIGMOD ICM, pp. 735–746 (2010)

28. Sen, A., Srivastava, M.: Regression Analysis: Theory, Methods, and Applications. Springer, New York (2012). https://doi.org/10.1007/978-1-4612-4470-7

29. Sethy, P.K., Behera, S.K., Ratha, P.K., Biswas, P.: Detection of coronavirus disease (COVID-19) based on deep features and support vector machine. arXiv Preprint (2020)

30. Shi, E., Chan, T.H., Rieffel, E., Chow, R., Song, D.: Privacy-preserving aggregation of time-series data. In: Proceedings of NDSS, vol. 2, pp. 1–17. Citeseer (2011)

31. Takeshita, J., Karl, R., Gong, T., Jung, T.: Slap: simple lattice-based private stream aggregation protocol. arXiv Preprint (2020)

32. Takeshita, J., Reis, D., Gong, T., Niemier, M., Hu, X.S., Jung, T.: Algorithmic acceleration of B/FV-like somewhat homomorphic encryption for compute-enabled RAM. In: Dunkelman, O., Jacobson, Jr., M.J., O'Flynn, C. (eds.) SAC 2020. LNCS, vol. 12804, pp. 66–89. Springer, Cham (2021). https://doi.org/10.1007/978-3-030-81652-0_3

33. Thurston, R.C., Matthews, K.A., Hernandez, J., De La Torre, F.: Improving the performance of physiologic hot flash measures with support vector machines. Psychophysiology **46**(2), 285–292 (2009)

34. Tonicelli, R., et al.: Information-theoretically secure oblivious polynomial evaluation in the commodity-based model. IJIS **14**(1), 73–84 (2015)

35. Tramer, F., Boneh, D.: Slalom: fast, verifiable and private execution of neural networks in trusted hardware. ICLR (2018)

36. Valovich, F., Aldà, F.: Computational differential privacy from lattice-based cryptography. In: Kaczorowski, J., Pieprzyk, J., Pomykała, J. (eds.) NuTMiC 2017. LNCS, vol. 10737, pp. 121–141. Springer, Cham (2018). https://doi.org/10.1007/978-3-319-76620-1_8

37. Weichbrodt, N., Kurmus, A., Pietzuch, P., Kapitza, R.: Asyncshock: exploiting synchronisation bugs in intel SGX enclaves (2016)

38. Yu, W., Liu, T., Valdez, R., Gwinn, M., Khoury, M.J.: Application of support vector machine modeling for prediction of common diseases: the case of diabetes and pre-diabetes. BMC Med. Inform. Decis. Mak. **10**(1), 16 (2010)

39. Zhu, H., Bao, F.: Augmented oblivious polynomial evaluation protocol and its applications. In: di Vimercati, S.C., Syverson, P., Gollmann, D. (eds.) ESORICS 2005. LNCS, vol. 3679, pp. 222–230. Springer, Heidelberg (2005). https://doi.org/10.1007/11555827_13

Provably Secure Contact Tracing
with Conditional Private Set Intersection

Jonathan Takeshita, Ryan Karl, Alamin Mohammed, Aaron Striegel,
and Taeho Jung$^{(\boxtimes)}$

University of Notre Dame, 46556 Notre Dame IN, USA
{jtakeshi,rkarl,amohamm2,striegel,tjung}@nd.edu

Abstract. The novel coronavirus COVID-19 spreads easily through personal contact, requiring the use of contact tracing to track the spread of the disease. Many existing approaches either trust a public health authority with private data, or publish patients' data, leading to privacy breaches. Private Set Intersection based on Homomorphic Encryption is a promising solution, but it is limited because the management of keys is challenging and further filtering of contacts is not included. We present a protocol for secure and private conditional contact tracing, allowing the tracking of users' contacts subject to extra conditions. We construct and apply our new primitive of Conditional Private Set Intersection and combine it with a Trusted Execution Environment (TEE) to construct a protocol with provable security and a high degree of functionality. Our approach moves the memory- and computation-intensive portions of contact tracing out of the TEE to a cloud server. We also present how multi-hop contact tracing can be done with minimal user communication. Our proof-of-concept implementation with Microsoft SEAL allows users to perform their computation in less than 9 min, and the cloud's per-user computation can be as little as 11 min for a population of 50,000 users with 500 infected (assuming 40 contacts/user) in a day. With other HE libraries/schemes that allows customized parameter sets, our protocol will show much higher scalability.

Keywords: Contact tracing · Lattice-based cryptography · Private set intersection · Trusted execution environment

1 Introduction

The disease COVID-19 is highly contagious and spreads easily through personal contact. Contact tracing is used to determine a person's past personal contacts to aid in tracking the spread of the disease, in particular to find which individuals are sources of or are at risk for infection. Human-based contact tracing by public health authorities is inherently invasive to one's privacy and individuals may be reluctant to participate. Users' smartphones can automatically trace their movements and contacts, which can be useful for accurate contact tracing, but disclosing such information poses a significant threat to individual

© ICST Institute for Computer Sciences, Social Informatics and Telecommunications Engineering 2021
Published by Springer Nature Switzerland AG 2021. All Rights Reserved
J. Garcia-Alfaro et al. (Eds.): SecureComm 2021, LNICST 398, pp. 352–373, 2021.
https://doi.org/10.1007/978-3-030-90019-9_18

privacy. Such concerns can discourage participation in contact tracing, and to incentivize participation in contact tracing, it is desirable to construct a contact tracing protocol that guarantees a high degree of individual privacy.

Various privacy-sensitive smartphone-based contact tracing protocols have weaknesses in privacy and accuracy [3,4,24,26,33,41]. Further, these protocols are generally rigid, and not easily extensible to calculations beyond basic tracing of contacts. There are many different additional conditions that a Public Health Authority (PHA) might wish to apply to the contact tracing (i.e., *conditional contact tracing*). For example, a PHA may only wish to deem users who have had exposure of 10 min as at risk for elderly people while the threshold could be higher for younger people (e.g., 15 min per CDC guidelines [16]). Many other conditions may be needed similarly (e.g., degree of infectiousness, vaccinated or not). Other cryptographic approaches require significant amounts of repeated network communication and/or computation to achieve this [34,37]. Cryptographic protocols such as Private Set Intersection (PSI) can be useful in such problems, but key management makes it challenging to apply it in scenarios with multiple users. Trusted Execution Environments (TEEs) support isolated and secure program execution, but they face difficulties with scalability, parallelism, and latency from memory access at scale [25,38], which leads us to the strategy of combining TEEs and cryptography for scalability.

To address such limitations, we let users provide encrypted lists of contacts and enable more sophisticated contact tracing that meets the needs of privacy and versatility. We combine TEE and homomorphic cryptography to create a protocol that allows a PHA to obliviously perform contact tracing without harming individual privacy. We also extend existing PSI based on HE to devise our novel *Conditional Private Set Intersection (CPSI)* protocol which can enforce additional conditions for PSI , and combine it with TEE to construct protocols for secure contact tracing with minimal privacy loss and conditional contact tracing. We use cryptographic approaches to maintain semantic security of messages to completely protect users' data with provable security, and combine this with the use of the TEE to solve issues such as key management that would otherwise make a straightforward application of HE difficult with multiple users. By performing homomorphic computation outside the TEE, we allow for parallel computation and avoid the overhead incurred by the TEE [38].

Our contact tracing protocol improves upon previous work by guaranteeing provable security and privacy for all users including the infected ones, which is not possible in existing decentralized approaches based on smartphones [2]. The computation and network communication are minimized for all users and parties, and more functionality in filtering out contacts is enabled without violating individual privacy. We selectively use a TEE to avoid excessive overhead caused by large-scale data processing within a capacity-limited TEE. Finally, we present further extensions useful for COVID contact tracing such as multi-hop tracing, while minimizing extra network communication from this. This paper has following contributions:

- A new notion of CPSI is presented, which returns only the intersection of elements that satisfies certain conditions, and it is constructed based on HE. We also present two novel optimization techniques for CPSI to (1) prevent false positive cases and (2) address the trade-off between efficiency of condition calculation and admissible set sizes.
- A protocol combining CPSI and TEE to conditionally trace personal contacts with provable data security is presented, with variants that differ in which party receives the final result. Further, an extension of the contact tracing protocol allowing timestamp-based multi-hop tracing with backward/forward tracking is presented, with no additional communication needed for unexposed users even with multi-hop tracing.
- An open-source proof-of-concept implementation for continued research and reproducibility is provided via anonymized source code repository (URL available in Sect. 6).
- We use real-world bluetooth datasets to perform experiment, and show that our protocol's preprocessing and decryption times are negligible and that both user-side and cloud-side computation are acceptable.

2 Related Work in Contact Tracing

The Google/Apple Exposure Notification (GAEN) from Google and Apple [24] uses daily Temporary Exposure Keys (TEKs) to generate 15-minute rolling Pseudo-IDs. These IDs are broadcast via Bluetooth and are collected by users who come into contact with one another. In the event of an infection, the infected user's TEKs are made public and used to retrieve all past Pseudo-IDs that they have broadcast. This protocol has the large weakness of not lending privacy to infected users: once an infected users' TEKs have been released, their movements can be retroactively tracked through the Pseudo-IDs. Practical attacks on this protocol have been demonstrated in [3] which showed that the weaknesses in GAEN are *protocol-level*, not implementation-level. The weakness in GAEN is that a user ID is publicly broadcast on a list of infected users, which can allow retroactive tracing of an infected user by passive collection of Bluetooth beacons and cross-referencing with the released TEKs. In our work, we repair this vulnerability by not publicly revealing users' ID strings. We also note that GAEN is not capable of easily allowing computation on users' data with private parameters, while our protocol allows such computation.

The BlueTrace protocol (Singapore) [4] is heavily dependent on human intervention; it is not designed to be solely automated. In BlueTrace, Pseudo-IDs and searches on that data are all performed in plaintext, leading to the weakness of a Public Health Authority (PHA) being able to easily track users through their persistent IDs [10,41]. A similar issue is present with the EPIC protocol [1].

Protocols such as Covid Watch [26], Hamagen (Israel) [29], and TrackCOVID [45] have users perform the computation for contact tracing. We aim to not follow this path, but instead aim to remove as much of a computational burden from users as possible, shifting computation to cloud computing and greatly reducing the amount of data that users must download.

The SafePaths (MIT) [32,33] project, along with Hamagen [29], uses GPS-based tracing instead of Bluetooth tracking, which may be less precise at detecting contacts. SafePaths uses the cryptographic protocol of PSI, but has other weaknesses in security and privacy. Namely, infected users lose any privacy under SafePaths because they must release their past location traces to allow contact searching by other users. A contact tracing method based on Secure Multi-party Computation (MPC) [34] that uses imprecise location-based tracking may improve its precision by using bluetooth signals, but such solutions face serious scalability issues [41] and do not provide any privacy to infected users. The PPContactTracing protocol [37] takes a similar approach to SafePaths in combining PSI and locality-sensitive hashing. The Epione [42] system also uses a PSI construction, though their Diffie-Hellman-based construction lacks the quantum security and extensibility to other computations that modern FHE-based computation provides.

The TraceSecure protocol [5] provides a high level of security for users, even preventing any central authority from learning if users are exposed. However, TraceSecure requires frequent communications throughout the day between users and a central server, uses wasteful flooding to mask meaningful messages informing users of exposure, and its design (based on additive HE) is not easily extensible to further functionality.

3   Preliminaries

Mathematical Notation: The set $\mathbb{Z}_t$ is the set of integers modulo t. We use R to denote the quotient ring of $\mathbb{Z}[X]/\Phi(X)$, where $\Phi(X)$ is a properly chosen cyclotomic polynomial of degree N, a power of two. We define $R_t = \mathbb{Z}_t[X]/\Phi(X)$, the subring of R with all coefficients in $\mathbb{Z}_t$. The bitsize of a number t is $bit(t) = \lfloor log_2(t) \rfloor + 1$. A number $a \in \mathbb{Z}_t$ is a quadratic residue (QR) if there is a $b \in \mathbb{Z}_t$ such that $b^2 \equiv a \pmod{t}$ and a non-quadratic residue (non-QR) otherwise.

Trusted Execution Environment: TEEs [12] can provide trusted computing on a platform where other applications or even the host operating systems are untrusted. Secured memory contents are encrypted and not visible to untrusted processes and execution cannot be tampered with externally. TEEs can also perform remote attestation to prove to other parties that they are running a certain program, so that users will know that TEEs are performing the correct computation on users' data. TEEs do have pitfalls including expensive paging, and limitations with memory space and parallel computing [38], making a purely TEE-based approach undesirable.

Fully/Somewhat Homomorphic Encryption: HE schemes allow for computation to be done on encrypted operands. Modern HE schemes derive their post-quantum security from the Ring-Learning With Errors (RLWE) problem, and deal with operands in polynomial rings [6,8,15]. Schemes that allow for arbitrarily-sized arithmetic circuits to be computed are called Fully Homomorphic Encryption (FHE) schemes. In practice, most modern FHE schemes are implemented as Somewhat Homomorphic Encryption (SHE) schemes to avoid the complex and intensive operation of bootstrapping. Arithmetic circuits in SHE are limited by pre-determined multiplicative depths. This work and related PSI work [8,9] use the B/FV scheme [15] that is parameterized by (N, q, t), where R_t is the plaintext space and R_q is the ciphertext space.

Private Set Intersection (PSI): PSI protocols allow two users to securely compute the intersection of their sets of elements, without revealing any information to eavesdroppers, or any elements not in the intersection to the other party. State-of-the-art PSI protocols have been constructed using HE [8,9]. These constructions are well-suited for a scenario where one user (the *sender*) is much more powerful than the other user (the *receiver*). This makes PSI particularly useful for our use case of contact tracing, where the PHA uses cloud servers and users use COTS phones/computers for contact tracing. Other PSI schemes also exist, but they are not suitable for our scenario. The protocols of De Cristofaro et al. [14] and Ion et al. [20] are insecure against quantum-capable adversaries. The PSI schemes based on MPC [11,30] have poor scalability due to multiple rounds of communication required. Our work is the first to formulate and construct CPSI for the needs of real-world applications.

Bluetooth Message Exchange: Bluetooth Low Energy (BLE) is a technology used for constructing short-range wireless mobile ad-hoc networks. BLE was specifically designed to facilitate low-cost and power-efficient implementations. BLE has been used to detect contact events by most contact-tracing apps [2,28,46] with which smartphones periodically broadcast Bluetooth beacon advertisements. When a smartphone in close proximity detects such advertisements, the underlying operating system notifies the observing application. Furthermore, the app can leverage the Received Signal Strength Indicator (RSSI) to gauge the distance between the two phones [22]. In a typical approach for Bluetooth-based contact tracing, Pseudo-IDs are woven into the Bluetooth advertisement which in turn is leveraged for contact tracing. In this work, we do not consider weaknesses of or attacks against Bluetooth [23,44], as it is not in the scope of the problem we consider.

4   Conditional Private Set Intersection

In this section, we introduce our new cryptographic primitive of CPSI, and show an FHE-based construction of CPSI. In Sect. 5, we deconstruct our CPSI protocol and distribute it among different parties to protect the privacy of both infected and at-risk users during contact tracing.

4.1   Definitions

Ideal Functionality: PSI between parties with sets X and Y computes the intersection $X \cap Y$ [8]. We may wish to subject the result to a further condition, calculating $X \cap_P Y = \{z \in X \cap Y | P\}$ for some predicate P where the parameters

Inputs: The sender and receiver input their secret finite sets X and Y, respectively. The receiver also inputs a secret set Y' of metadata associated with elements of Y. The cardinality of X and Y, as well as the sizes in bits of the elements of X, Y and Y', respectively, are publicly known. A predicate P operating on elements of Y' is computable by the sender, though its parameters may be kept secret from the sender.
Output: The receiver learns $X \cap_P Y = \{z \in X \cap Y | P(z')\}$, where $z' \in Y'$ is the metadata element corresponding to z. The sender does not learn anything. No additional information is learned by either party or any eavesdropper.

Fig. 1. Ideal functionality δ of CPSI.

of P may be kept private from both parties. Formally, we define a CPSI protocol as follows: consider a sender and receiver with respective sets X, Y, where the number of the elements in each set is known, and the domain size (in bits) of the elements is known. The predicate P is known to the sender. A CPSI protocol returns the result $X \cap_P Y$ to the receiver, and nothing to the sender. Neither party learns anything about the other party's held elements not in $X \cap_P Y$. The predicate P may be a predicate on the encrypted elements of X or Y, on attached metadata (encrypted or plain), or something else. We require in the formal definition of CPSI, given in Fig. 1, that P operate on metadata strictly correlated to the elements of the parties and kept private, though these requirements may be relaxed in some applications. It is common in many applications (e.g., machine learning) to wish to allow computation with hidden parameters, which is possible when P is computed homomorphically or otherwise privately. In practice, P might also be a function of a parameter s of the sender, i.e., $P = P_s$. Constructions where P is a function of multiple-valued data from both the sender and receiver are possible, but would require $\mathcal{O}(|X| \cdot |Y|)$ separate calculations, so we do not consider those in this work.

Adversary Model: In this scenario, we consider the parties to be honest-but-curious, i.e., they will follow the protocol accurately. Communication between the parties is through authenticated and non-malleable channels. An adversary may be an eavesdropper, or either party.

Security Model: A CPSI protocol is secure if the execution of the protocol is computationally indistinguishable from the execution of the ideal functionality of CPSI given in Fig. 1. This is formalized in Definition 1.

Definition 1. *A CPSI protocol Γ securely computes the ideal CPSI functionality δ if for every probabilistic polynomial-time (PPT) adversary A against Γ, there exists a PPT adversary S (the "simulator") against δ such that for every possible combination of input sets X, Y, Y' (with $|Y| = |Y'|$) with sizes polynomial in the security parameter λ, the views of $S_\delta(\lambda, X, Y, Y')$ and $A_\Gamma(\lambda, X, Y, Y')$ are computationally indistinguishable w.r.t. the security parameter λ. The view generated by S from the execution of δ is $S_\delta(\lambda, X, Y, Y')$, and similarly the view generated by A from the execution of Γ is $A_\Gamma(\lambda, X, Y, Y')$.*

4.2 Novel CPSI Construction Without False Positives

Our novel CPSI is shown in Fig. 2. Let the FHE plaintext modulus t be a prime number, so there are $\frac{t-1}{2}$ elements of $\mathbb{Z}_t$ that are not quadratic residues modulo t. In Chen et al.'s FHE-based PSI protocol [8], a decrypted result of the protocol is zero if and only if the corresponding element is in the set intersection, and is a random nonzero number otherwise. We construct our CPSI protocol to maintain that property by adding a nonzero predicate value to the PSI circuit result to force a result of zero to be nonzero when the condition is not met.

Unfortunately, this naïve approach may result in a false positive when a result is zero by coincidence even though the corresponding element is not in the intersection. We prevent this with a novel technique: we force the sum of the PSI and predicate values to be zero if and only if an element is in the intersection and the predicate is fulfilled. This is achieved by squaring the PSI result to force it to be a QR, and having the nonzero predicate value added be a non-QR, so that the sum of those values can never be zero modulo t unless both values are zero. More specifically, we let $t - k$ with $k \in [1, t)$ be a non-QR modulo t. We then require that the predicate $P(\cdot)$ be zero when the element being tested should be included in the PSI result (so that the computation is unaffected), and that $P(\cdot) = k$ when the element should be excluded from the intersection. Because no element of $\mathbb{Z}_t$ squared results in $t - k \pmod{t}$, $P(c_i') + (\prod_{x \in X}(c_i - x))^2$ will only be zero modulo t exactly when both P and $\prod_{x \in X}(c_i - x)$ are zero modulo t. Because $t - k$ is a non-QR, adding k to any squared element of $\mathbb{Z}_t$ will never result in zero modulo t, preventing false positives caused by adding in a predicate value.

Input: The sender's set X, the receiver's set Y and the metadata set Y' associated with X, and the sender's predicate P operating on Y' are private inputs. The cardinalities of X, Y, and Y' are public inputs.

Output: The receiver learns $X \cap_P Y = \{z \in X \cap Y | P\}$.

1. **Setup:** The sender and receiver agree on appropriate parameters for a FHE scheme. The receiver generates a public-private key pair (pk, sk), and retains the secret key privately.

2. **Set Encryption:** The receiver encrypts its elements as $c_i = FHE.Enc_{pk}(y_i)$ for $y_i \in Y$, $c_i' = FHE.Enc_{pk}(y_i')$ for $y_i' \in Y'$, and sends the ciphertexts c_i, c_i' to the sender.

3. **Computing the Intersection:** For each c_i, the sender samples a random nonzero plaintext element r, and homomorphically computes

$$d_i = r \cdot (P(c_i') + (\prod_{x \in X}(c_i - x))^2) \qquad (1)$$

   The values d_i are returned to the receiver.

4. **Intersection Decryption:** The receiver outputs the conditioned intersection $X \cap_P Y = \{y_i | FHE.Dec_{sk}(d_i) = 0\}$

Fig. 2. Conditional private set intersection (CPSI) protocol Γ.

When computing the predicate P over metadata that should be kept private (e.g. times or durations of contact), we can homomorphically encrypt the metadata, and use the homomorphic polynomial interpolation function calculation [40] described in Sect. 5.2 to compute the predicate. Correctness is easy to see: if the predicate is zero, then the result is the same as the ordinary PSI circuit. If the predicate is nonzero, then adding it to a zero-valued PSI result results in k, which is nonzero. If the PSI result is nonzero, then adding a nonzero predicate to it will never result in a value that is zero modulo t, as shown above. This CPSI construction allows the filtering of elements based on arbitrary predicates, with no additional work required for decryption. Like related work in PSI, this basic protocol may have a high multiplicative depth (linear in $|X|$), which should be mitigated through the optimizations presented in Sect. 4.4.

4.3   Proof of Security

Theorem 1. *The CPSI protocol Γ ((Fig. 2) is secure under Definition 1.*

Proof. The views of the sender, receiver, and an external eavesdropper in the real and ideal protocols are computationally indistinguishable, so that a simulator operating in the ideal world can generate a view indistinguishable from that of the view a party or eavesdropper would see in the real world [21].

Sender: In both the real and ideal views, the sender sees the sets X and X', and knows $|Y|$ (and $|Y|'$). In the real view, the sender also sees the ciphertexts c_i, c_i'. A simulator S simulating the execution to an adversary $\mathcal{A}$ acting as a sender in the ideal case can easily provide HE ciphertexts. Due to the semantic security of the underlying HE scheme [15], these views are computationally indistinguishable w.r.t. the security parameter λ.

Receiver: In both the real and ideal views, the receiver sees the sets Y and Y', and learns $X \cap_P Y$. In the real view, the receiver also sees the decrypted results d_i, which are zero if $y_i \in X \cap_P Y$ and a random nonzero element otherwise. A simulator S in the ideal model can generate an identical view to that of the real model for the adversary $\mathcal{A}$ acting as a receiver by constructing the set $D = \{\tilde{d}_i\}$, where $\tilde{d}_i$ encrypts zero if $y_i \in X \cap_P Y$ and a random nonzero value otherwise. Thus the receiver's view of a real execution is indistinguishable from a view that a simulator can generate in the ideal execution.

Eavesdropper: In the ideal and real views, an eavesdropping adversary $\mathcal{A}$ knows $|X|, |Y|, |X'|, |Y'|$, and the bit-sizes of their elements. In the real view they additionally see the ciphertexts c_i, c_i', d_i. Similarly to the case of the sender, semantically secure ciphertexts add nothing to the view generated, as the sizes of X, Y, Y' are already known. Indeed, a simulator S can easily generate ciphertexts c_i, c_i', d_i, thus simulating the real view to S.   □

4.4   Compatibility with Standard Optimizations

Standard optimizations in FHE and FHE-based PSI can be applied to our protocol with little modification needed as we discuss below. Our contact tracing implementation presented in Sect. 6 uses the most important optimizations of windowing, batching, and partitioning.

Windowing: With windowing, by precomputing powers and polynomial coefficients the original PSI protocol can be reduced to have a depth as low as one through precomputation of some terms and some additional communication [8]. Our CPSI protocol requires only one additional homomorphic multiplication and one homomorphic addition, after the original PSI circuit and predicate have been calculated. The circuit depth incurred is only two more than the original PSI protocol, though calculation of P may incur additional depth and computation.

Batching: A well-known optimization in lattice-based cryptography is batching, which encodes vectors of up to N elements of $\mathbb{Z}_t$ into a single plaintext element of R_t [18]. Homomorphic operations on data encoded in this manner can be carried out with parallelism (i.e., batching). As previously shown in previous PSI work [8], batching can be applied to reduce the network communication and computation by a factor of N. The only modification to the original PSI protocol is to sample random elements to be a batched vector instead of singleton elements. Our CPSI protocol can use the batching in the same way.

Hashing and Partitioning: The computation and depth of the protocol depend on the size of the sender's set. Hashing and partitioning are applied in previous PSI work to divide the sender's set into smaller, more manageable subsets [8,31]. With partitioning, the sender's set is simply partitioned into α subsets of approximately equal size, which reduces network communication and computation by a factor of α. Hashing similarly divides elements into hash buckets, and the parties only need to compare elements in the same bucket. Both can be applied to our CPSI protocol.

Modulus Switching: This technique reduces a ciphertext in R_q to one in $R_{q'}$, with $q' < q$, such that the switched-down ciphertext decrypts to the same value [6]. This can be performed in our CPSI protocol after the sender's computation to reduce the size of the response to the receiver by $\frac{log(q)}{log(q')}$, which is observed empirically by [8] to be a reduction of up to 20%.

4.5   Novel Optimization with Dual Plaintext Space

When a predicate P is homomorphically calculated on the receiver's private metadata, the two goals of our protocol come into conflict. To make the homomorphic calculation of P via polynomial interpolation as efficient as possible, the plaintext space of our HE scheme should be held as small as possible [40]. On the other hand, to express many distinct set elements, it is desirable to have larger plaintext spaces.

With batching, both these goals are possible. Let c be an integer factor, and suppose that we have a plaintext space of $\mathbb{Z}_t$. Recall that the batching allows encoding up to N values into a single ciphertext. We can then encode elements from $\mathbb{Z}_{t^c}$ to $\mathbb{Z}_t^c$ by placing each base-t "digit" of the element into a separate slot. The corresponding metadata value in $\mathbb{Z}_t$ can then be duplicated across all c corresponding slots in the metadata plaintext polynomial. By doing so, we can deal with the randomly generated IDs in the space $\mathbb{Z}_{t^c}$ with the smaller actual message space $\mathbb{Z}_t$. This allows a CPSI protocol to be run with a large set of possible elements and a smaller predicate metadata domain, while maintaining a smaller and more efficient plaintext space for interpolation.

Using this strategy requires the receiver to check that all c slots that a value is decomposed into before concluding that an element is in the intersection, as two values are equal if and only if their t-digit decompositions are equal. This method of representing and packing elements thus does not affect correctness of CPSI. Using this dual plaintext space is most useful when a large plaintext space is desired to handle many distinct set elements (e.g., Pseudo-IDs) but the space of the metadata can be smaller.

5   Protocol for Conditional Contact Tracing

In this section, we present a CPSI-based contact tracing system that can filter contacts to be recorded only when some additional predicate is satisfied. Our system has a high degree of functionality and privacy guarantees, with the tradeoff of more complexity and computation. The core idea behind our protocol is computing a CPSI of users' encountered and broadcast Pseudo-IDs, so that a nonempty intersection indicates exposure. We take the strategy of using the TEE to handle some trusted computation such as key distribution, preprocessing, and result distillation, while still outsourcing the heavy homomorphic computations to a cloud server. By encrypting all data sent to the cloud, we fix the weakness in the GAEN [2] which discloses unencrypted Pseudo-IDs of infected users. While it is possible to use a TEE for all private outsourced computation, doing so may severely limit the ability to scale and compute concurrently over large workloads, due to both a bottleneck at the TEE's memory transfer and vulnerabilities in TEE multithreading [25]. Further, large workloads may incur extremely high overhead due to the TEE's overhead in paging and memory encryption [38]. For these reasons, we aim to use the TEE as little as possible, and shift as much work as possible to scalable and parallel cloud computation. Communications are assumed to be authenticated and nonmalleable, with authorized access controls.

Our protocol has two variations, determining which of the user and public health authority gets the final results. Some countries with more libertine policies may prefer the former approach, while countries with more centralized governmental authority may prefer the latter.

5.1   Scenario of Conditional Contact Tracing

System Model: Our formulation considers three types of parties: (1) *Ordinary users*, who participate through a smartphone application. The users' smartphones can receive and record information from nearby users' smartphones via Bluetooth. During nights, a user's smartphone can sync while charging with their laptop or desktop computer, which is then able to perform operations such as encryption on the phone's behalf, making the overhead of homomorphic encryption less of an issue for users. We aim to minimize the amount of data that users must download to participate, and only send a constant and small amount of data to users. (2) The *computation server C* (possibly untrusted), which performs the computation of CPSI, acting in the modified role of sender in a CPSI protocol (C does not have access to plaintext data, but carries out the computation of the sender). (3) The PHA's *key management server (PHA_M)*, who distributes keys and manages interaction between the parties. This entity has access to a TEE. We assume the PHA knows the IDs of the participating users but nothing else. They receive the final result identifying exposed users, and will choose if and how to inform those users. Any party can perform remote attestation to verify the integrity of the code running inside the TEE.

Condition to be Used: As described in Sect. 1, there are many possible additional conditions that the PHA might wish to apply to contact tracing. In our proof-of-concept system, we use thresholding with a private bound as the condition in the predicate P (e.g., if $x \geq h$, $P = 0$; $P = k$ otherwise), as such conditions are likely useful in real-world contact tracing (e.g., age, degree of infectiousness, number of contacts) and other applications.

Adversary Model: Adversaries in this scenario may be any of the three parties above, an external eavesdropping adversary, or any collusion thereof. We assume communications between users and both the TEE and cloud server are authenticated and nonmalleable. We assume that participants in this protocol are honest-but-curious, meaning that they may carry out arbitrary computation to try to learn other users' private data, but will otherwise participate honestly in the protocol. As noted in other work in secure computation, honest-but-curious parties are a reasonable assumption, as even participation in this protocol requires some level of trust between participants [43].

---

* Users periodically broadcast randomly-rotating Pseudo-IDs.

Inputs: Infected users input their previously broadcast Pseudo-IDs from the past 14 days (or other interval). Uninfected users input their previously encountered Pseudo-IDs from the past 14 days (or other interval), along with any corresponding metadata used to filter contacts conditionally. A PHA does not give any input.

Output: The PHA learns which users have both been in contact with infected users and satisfy the conditions.

Fig. 3. Ideal functionality of conditional contact tracing.

Ideal Functionality and Informal Security Model: Our ideal functionality, shown in Fig. 3, is for users to input their data, and for each uninfected user to learn only if they are exposed. Informally, security of a protocol is maintained if the view of an adversary or collusion of adversaries is indistinguishable from the view of an execution of the ideal protocol.

5.2   Strategy in Constructing Our Protocol

A user can be said to be at risk if the set of people they have encountered intersects the set of infected persons, and the PHA can set conditions for further filtering. However, naively using the CPSI protocol has security and privacy issues. In particular, the sender would need to know the entire unencrypted set of infected persons, and the receiver could learn when and from whom they were exposed by noting which elements in the intersection are held in common. We thus apply the ability of HE to separate knowledge and computation, and deconstruct the role of sender in a CPSI protocol into that of a sender and computer. In this formulation, the sender is a party much like the receiver, who sends their encrypted data, and the computer is tasked with the actual CPSI computation. Due to the need for preprocessing of the sender's data (for windowing and partitioning), the sender is further split into data holders and a party who collects the aggregate data and performs the preprocessing. The role of the receiver is also split - one party will receive and decrypt the CPSI result from the computing party, and will send a final distilled result indicating exposure or non-exposure to users. CPSI is used to allow for further filtering, though if no additional condition on the intersection is required then regular PSI can be used. Though CPSI requires that the sizes of users' sets be publicly known, for contact tracing we want to conceal the number of contacts a user has had; batching masks this information. The number of batching slots can be increased as needed (at the cost of extra computation), allowing such masking.

Conditional statements such as "if $x \geq h$, $P = 0$; $P = k$ otherwise" are not directly supported in FHE schemes. Therefore, we use Lagrange Interpolation to formulate a polynomial function that allows for *homomorphic thresholding*, i.e., comparison and equality over ciphertexts, at the cost of extra multiplicative depth [40]. For any function $f : \mathbb{Z}_t \to \mathbb{Z}_t$ with prime t (or a prime power), there is a polynomial expression of f, defined as $F : \mathbb{Z}_t \to \mathbb{Z}_t$ and constructed as $F(x) = \sum_{x_i \in \mathbb{Z}_t} f(x) \cdot (\prod_{x_a \in \mathbb{Z}_t, x_a \neq x_i} \frac{x - x_a}{x_i - x_a})$, which is well-defined if all of the denominators and t are coprime (i.e., the denominators are multiplicatively invertible). The degree of this polynomial is at most $t - 1$, and its multiplicative depth is logarithmic in t. Precomputing powers of an argument x makes computing this function a simple, single-depth dot product.

Integrating CPSI into our protocol to allow for conditional contact tracing does not require any additional computation on the TEE's part during decryption; nor is there any difference to the TEE's preprocessing computations. Users do have the extra overhead of additional preprocessing (computing and encrypting powers of their metadata), and the cloud server now has to homomorphically compute the predicate P. However, this tradeoff allows the inclusion of private conditional contact tracing by the PHA and its TEE.

Conditional Contact Tracing

Parties: The parties here are users U, the PHA PHA_M with a TEE, and a cloud computation server C.

Setup: PHA_M uses its TEE to generate a public/private key pair for use in FHE. The TEE retains the private (decryption) key. PHA_M distributes the public (encryption) key and any other public parameters. Additionally, the PHA may pass a set of parameters for predicate calculation pr (e.g., a threshold value) to C, either as a cleartext or a homomorphic ciphertext.

ID Collection: Throughout the day (or another specified interval), users collect randomly-chosen Pseudo-IDs broadcast through Bluetooth. These Pseudo-IDs are changed every 15 minutes to protect privacy. (Alternately, they can be changed for every contact, as in [5].)

Encryption and Upload: Each user U formulates a set Y of Pseudo-IDs encountered since its last upload and more recent than 14 days (or another interval), along with any associated metadata (Y'). The Pseudo-IDs and metadata are homomorphically encrypted, and uploaded to C. If a user is confirmed to be infected with COVID-19, then their broadcast Pseudo-IDs are uploaded to the TEE of PHA_M for preprocessing, and thereafter forwarded to C as the homomorphically encrypted set X. The set X can be partitioned by daily or two-day intervals, to reduce the required size of the plaintext space.

Compute Intersection of Contacts:

1. The cloud server C has a set of ciphertexts S of Pseudo-IDs from infected users. The cloud server can also (homomorphically) compute $P_{pr}(\cdot)$.
2. For each user U with a set Y sent to C as ciphertexts c_i and associated metadata Y' sent as ciphertexts c_i', C will homomorphically compute the PSI circuit of Y and X as $d_i' = \prod_{x \in X}(y_i - x)$ for $y_i \in Y$.
3. The predicate value is calculated as $p_i = P_{pr}(c_i') \in \{k, 0\}$, where $t - k$ is not a QR mod t. The calculation of p_i can be homomorphically calculated through polynomial interpolation [40].
4. The CPSI result is $d_i = r_i \cdot (p_i + (d_i')^2)$, for a random nonzero value r_i. (Alternately, if no condition is used, then $d_i = r_i \cdot d_i'$.) This encrypted result is forwarded to the TEE of PHA_M.
5. The TEE will decrypt the result, and determine whether the user is at risk of infection. If the conditioned intersection is nonempty, then there was some contact between a user and an infected individual which puts that user at risk of infection. The TEE can then forward each users' result to the user (first variant) or the PHA (second variant).

Fig. 4. A CPSI-based protocol for conditional contact tracing.

5.3 Protocol Description

Our protocol is detailed in Fig. 4. The key management server PHA_M uses its TEE to derive public-private key pairs for HE, along with any other parameters used in the CPSI protocol. Public (encryption) keys are distributed to users, and the secret (decryption) key is held by the TEE of PHA_M and not distributed.

Table 1. Network communication/computation overhead for TEE

Operation	Plain intersection in TEE	Our protocol (Colocated TEE)	Our protocol (No Colocation)
Input received	$\mathcal{O}(N_x \cdot N_{pid} + N_y \cdot N_c)$	$\mathcal{O}(N_x \cdot N_{pid})$	$\mathcal{O}(N_x \cdot N_{pid})$
Processing	$\mathcal{O}(N_x \cdot N_{pid} \cdot N_y \cdot N_c)$	$\mathcal{O}(N_x \cdot N_{pid} + N_y \cdot N_c)$	$\mathcal{O}(N_x \cdot N_{pid} + N_y \cdot N_c)$
Output sent	$\mathcal{O}(N_y)$	$\mathcal{O}(N_y)$	$\mathcal{O}(N_y + N_x \cdot N_{pid})$

Throughout the day, each users' phone will broadcast randomly changing Pseudo-ID strings to other nearby phones. At the end of each day (or other interval), users will have an list of IDs of contacts. Users who are infected with COVID-19 will (not necessarily homomorphically) encrypt their list, and upload their encrypted Pseudo-IDs to PHA_M, whose TEE will preprocess those values (partition and precompute windowing coefficients) and send the homomorphically encrypted results to C as the set S (with partitioning and other preprocessing performed).

Each uninfected user U will then send their encrypted set Y of encountered Pseudo-IDs with accompanying encrypted metadata Y' to C. Then for each user U, C will run the computation of CPSI on Y, Y', and S, and send the result to PHA_M. The TEE of PHA_M will then be able to decrypt the result, and return only an indication of exposure or nonexposure for each user. The result may be returned to either users (the first variant) or the PHA (the second variant) - this can be easily configured, and users can verify the security of decryption through remote attestation of the TEE. In practice, the precomputation and encryption of uninfected users can be done overnight via a synced laptop or desktop computer, and this computation is "offline", so the time and energy of encryption is not an issue.

5.4 Performance and Optimizations

This scheme aims to shift the greatest burdens of PSI computation away from users or a TEE and onto cloud servers with scalable resources. A system simply using the TEE to compute contacts would be heavily burdened by the amount of communication, computation, and memory used. Let N_x be the number of infected users with N_{pid} IDs each, and N_y be the number of uninfected users with up to N_c collected Pseudo-IDs each. Then the TEE needs to receive and operate upon $N_x \cdot N_{pid} + N_y \cdot N_c$ operands. In our protocol, the TEE only needs to take in $N_x \cdot N_{pid}$ operands and forward $\mathcal{O}(N_x \cdot N_{pid})$ preprocessed ciphertexts, then decrypt and forward N_y results. This represents a significant savings in communication, memory, and computation for the TEE. When the TEE, PHA, and cloud are colocated (in the same machine), the network savings are even greater. This is shown in Table 1. The runtime of comparison in the TEE can be reduced to loglinear with a binary search tree or even linear with a hash table, but this will incur a higher memory overhead. Seeing as the TEE is memory-limited, these strategies may not be advisable.

Most of the optimizations from Sect. 4.4 can be applied directly to our CPSI-based protocol. *Batching, hashing,* and *modulus switching* can be applied "out-of-the-box" to reduce computation and communication. *Windowing* and *partitioning* can also be applied to decrease the depth of the homomorphic computations. However, the preprocessing for these optimizations requires knowledge of the entire set of the infected users' broadcast Pseudo-IDs, which is why they are sent to the TEE for preprocessing. The data of infected and uninfected users can be partitioned by sorting IDs based on the 1-day or 2-day interval in which they are broadcast, making it easier to update and deprecate datasets. The dual plaintext space of Sect. 4.5 can also be applied to allow for a larger pool of random Pseudo-IDs to reduce the probability of collisions, while keeping predicate calculation runtimes tolerable. In general, a high degree of parallelism is applicable to our scheme. The cloud server can calculate each users' PSI in parallel, and that computation can be further parallelized across the partitions of the set of infected IDs.

5.5   Security

We informally discuss the security of our protocol, as the security comes from the security of CPSI proved in Theorem 1. This protocol is essentially deconstructing the CPSI protocol of Sect. 4.2 to aggregate all infected users' data in a secure environment for preprocessing as a single set, and to allow the decrypted result to be privately distilled to a binary result. There may be some privacy leakage in practice: for example, a person only in contact with one other person who receives an indication of exposure can conclude that their contact poses a health risk to them. However, such leakage is unavoidable, as it also occurs in an execution of the ideal protocol of Fig. 3.

The amount of ciphertexts sent may give upper and lower bounds to how many personal contacts a user has had, which may breach privacy. However, it is a generally reasonable assumption that a user will have much fewer than N contacts in a day, so that they only need to send one ciphertext. With this assumption, the exact number of a user's contacts is not leaked in this protocol, and privacy is maintained. For high-density populations, N can be increased as needed. If batching is not used, then padding sets of Pseudo-IDs with encryptions of a dummy element guaranteed to never be chosen as a Pseudo-ID can protect the number of a user's observed contacts.

Uninfected users only see Pseudo-IDs of other users, which rotate every 15 min or upon a contact, so that a user's movement cannot be easily tracked for longer intervals. They do not see anything else throughout the protocol. The cloud server never sees any unencrypted user data. The cloud server sees encrypted Pseudo-IDs from uninfected users, but due to batching, only a single ciphertext is sent to the cloud. Uninfected users learn that they came into contact with an infected user, but are not provided any other information. In extreme cases (e.g. a user only seeing one other person), the user may be able to learn if other people are infected. However, this is an unavoidable leakage as aforementioned. The PHA (sans TEE) learns which users have come into contact with infected people only, as the TEE only returns the final result for each user to the PHA. It is assumed that the PHA knows which users are infected.

Table 2. Performance on Real-world dataset

Operations by different entities	Time (seconds)
User Pseudo-ID Preprocessing & Encryption (for each user on average)	0.03
User Metadata Preprocessing & Encryption (for each user on average)	519.57
User Time for each contact tracing (for each user on average)	**519.60**
One-time Infected Pseudo-ID Preprocessing & Encryption for 27 Pseudo-IDs	0.19
Cloud Predicate (per user on average)	352.01
Cloud CPSI Circuit (per user on average)	0.45
Cloud Time for each contact tracing (per user on average)	**352.46**
Decryption total (for 20 users)	0.78
Total TEE time for each contact tracing (for 20 users)	**0.97**

6   Evaluation with Real-World and Synthetic Datasets

Our proof-of-concept implementation consists of four core programs performing the functionalities described in Sect. 5. These programs are written in standard C++ (no actual TEE was used for the proof-of-concept implementation), with the sole external dependency of Microsoft SEAL [36]. Our code is available at https://gitlab.com/jtakeshi/contact-tracing. We chose to use B/FV [15] and SEAL [36] due to their successful use in previous related work [8,9]. We included the optimizations of batching, windowing, and partitioning.

Our tests were run on a computer with an Intel Xeon 20-core CPU operating at 3.7 GHz with Intel SGX support, 128 GB of RAM, and Ubuntu 18.04. We used parameters of $t = 114,689$, $bit(t) = 17$, $N = 8,192$. We chose a partition size of 5 for the infected users' Pseudo-IDs. These parameters are the smallest that can be chosen in Microsoft SEAL to allow all the computations needed for CPSI.

The real-world dataset we use is an anonymized set of collected users' beacon contacts from real-world users. It is obtained via request from Project Tesserae [17], a multi-university research involving the collection, instrumentation and analysis of data from hundreds of smartphones and wearables over several years of continuous data streaming. The dataset includes one-month interactions of 20 users in an office building in 2018. The 20 users averaged about 228 contacts, allowing the use of only a single batched plaintext for all of a user's inputs. There were 27 Bluetooth beacons interpreted as infected Pseudo-IDs broadcast, so with a partition size of 5, 6 partitions were used for infected users' data. The CPSI metadata used was signal strength.

We first tested the performance of our implementation on the real-world dataset (Table 2). Reported figures are an average across all 20 users' computations for the user and cloud computations. Our results show that our protocol is effective and reasonably efficient for a small pool of users. The most intensive steps were the users' and cloud's work in predicate preprocessing and calculation, which is expected as the runtime of interpolation is linear in $t = 114,689$. When not using a condition, both cloud and user computations can be performed in less than a second; health authorities with less powerful servers and more constituents may thus wish to consider this alternative. These results show a benchmark for execution time on a (small) real-world dataset, and give an estimate of calculation of predicate runtimes.

To test our scheme's scalability, we generated synthetic data with increasing amounts of infected users' Pseudo-IDs broadcast, using 200, 1000, 2000, and 20,000 Pseudo-IDs. Each user in this dataset observes $N = 8192$ Pseudo-IDs including the non-infected users', and 10 users' data was generated, so numbers reported are the average across 10 trials. The real-world dataset already shows the per-user predicate calculation time and user preprocessing time (which are independent of the number of users, infected or unexposed), so our main goal in this experiment is to see how the number of infected users affects the per-user performance of the cloud server. TEE preprocessing and decryption scaled well (as expected); Fig. 5(b) shows these operations taking less than 118 s and 2.1 s/user, respectively, with 20,000 infected users' Pseudo-IDs used. As shown in Fig. 5(a), the cloud's computation also increases linearly (as expected) with the number of infected users' Pseudo-IDs used. The cloud CPSI computations take 616.24 s/user, with 20,000 infected users' Pseudo-IDs used.

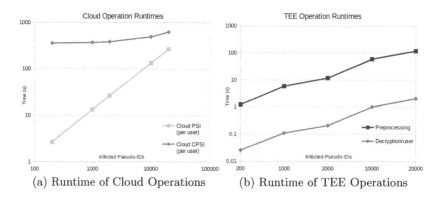

(a) Runtime of Cloud Operations   (b) Runtime of TEE Operations

Fig. 5. Experimental results

We judged our efficiency in three areas. First, it is desirable that the computational load on the TEE-based computations be small; this goal is easily fulfilled, as shown with both real-world and synthetic datasets. Second, we want users' computation to be doable during overnight charging of devices; our results show that a user's computation can be performed in approximately 10 min or less (considerably less without metadata processing), easily achieving this goal. Third, we want the cloud to be able to perform its computation efficiently. Suppose that the Pseudo-IDs are rotated upon a new contact, as in [5]. Empirical observation at our university shows that an average of 20 contacts are revealed in contact tracing, so it is reasonable to assume that 20,000 infected users' Pseudo-IDs being broadcast represents 500 infected users (40 contacts per user). Assuming that 1% of the population are infected users, this gives us a total population of about 50,000. With these conditions, a user's CPSI calculation can be performed by the cloud in about 10 min. Then the entire population's contact tracing can be computed in 12 h with 24 24-core machines (or 12 48-core machines), though this is a slightly optimistic estimate.

We conclude that our CPSI-based protocol can compute overnight contact tracing for a population of thousands of people (e.g., a neighborhood, college, or small city). This scale is useful for contact tracing on small populations, e.g., college communities [7,27], small cities. Our implementation has such a limited scalability due to the rigidity of the B/FV scheme [15] and Microsoft SEAL [36] that we used for ease of prototype system development. In SEAL's B/FV parameter selection, users are forced to use a large plaintext space, which made predicate precomputation/calculation slow. This does not indicate the design of our protocol has low scalability. Other schemes and libraries (e.g. BGV [6] and PALISADE [13]) allow the use of smaller plaintext spaces. If such schemes/libraries are combined with our novel dual plaintext space technique (see Sect. 4.5), our CPSI can be much more efficient and thus scalable. Also note that our implementation is only a proof-of-concept; a fully optimized implementation will be much more efficient. Real-life use of this protocol can achieve much greater scalability by utilizing strategies such as parallelization, cloud computing, and hardware acceleration to improve homomorphic computation [35,39]. Due to the lack of other works' experimental runtime data and the relatively high degree of security and functionality of our scheme, a direct experimental comparison to other work cannot be made.

7 Extensions for More Sophisticated Applications

7.1 Duration-Based Conditioning

Recent CDC guidelines state that people are at risk if they are in contact with infected people for over 15 min in any 24-h windows [16]. Conditions like this can be accounted for by using CPSI.

The homomorphically encrypted intermediate values d'_i can be saved and reduced to a Boolean value as $b_{d'_i} = 0$ when $d_i = 0$ and $b_{d'_i} = 1$ otherwise, using the interpolation discussed in Sect. 5.2 [40]. The duration of each contact can be recorded by a user's phone as dur_i. We can then homomorphically compute $S = \sum_i b_{d'_i} \cdot dur_i$, an encryption of the total duration of a person's exposure. With batching, computing this may require the use of ciphertext rotation [19]. The cloud server can then use the threshold predicate $p = p_{pr}(S)$ to test if $S \geq 15$ in CPSI. The calculation of S requires a multiplicative depth of 2 with windowing, and the calculation of p may require a depth of up to $log_2(t)$. The other parts of CPSI can be calculated with a depth as small as 3, with the final multiplication taking place after the predicate's inclusion, so the first two levels of depth are not dominating terms in the total depth for reasonable t larger than 4. Thus the total required depth is $log_2(t) + 1$.

7.2   Multi-hop Tracing

Consider the scenario of multi-hop contact tracing: if an infected person Charlie was found to have a contact with a person Bob, then it is desirable to detect contacts of Bob before and after that contact to find multi-hop contacts. In existing approaches, entirely rerunning new iterations of the protocol is required for multi-hop tracing. We aim to support the multi-hop tracing, in not forcing uninfected users to participate in multiple rounds of the protocol until and unless they are identified as a contact, while identifying the contacts from backward and forward tracing separately. We can accomplish this by modifying the second variant of our protocol, so that additional rounds of contact tracing can be performed without needing additional participation from unexposed users.

Conditional Contact Tracing with Multi-Hops

Let $N_h \geq 2$ be the number of hops from confirmed infected users that we wish to trace. Then the number of additional rounds N_r is $N_h - 1$.

Parties, Setup, ID Collection, Initial Encryption and Upload: These phases are as originally formulated in Figure 4, with the modification of timestamps being encrypted (not necessarily homomorphically) and attached to all Pseudo-IDs.

Initial Intersection: C performs the CPSI computation as in Figure 2, and returns the result with corresponding encrypted timestamp to the TEE of PHA_M. The result and timestamp are decrypted internally, and infected users as well as the time of contacts are revealed to the TEE.

Multi-Hop Tracing: For $i = 1$ to N_r:

1. The TEE collects broadcast Pseudo-IDs from each previously identified user for preprocessing. The IDs are grouped into sets PRE_i and $POST_i$, based on whether the ID was broadcast before or after the contact of the identified user. (In case of multiple contacts, Pseudo-IDs can be included in both sets.) The TEE then homomorphically encrypts these sets, and sends them to C.

2. For each user U, C will homomorphically compute the CPSI of U's contacts with both PRE_i and $POST_i$, and forward the results to the TEE of PHA_M.

3. The TEE will decrypt the results. From this, the TEE learns who has been in contact with an indirect contact of a COVID-positive individual, and whether that contact occurred before or after the contact with an infected person. The contacts from PRE_i and $POST_i$ will be used as the individuals whose broadcast Pseudo-IDs comprise PRE_{i+1} and $POST_{i+1}$, and those individuals can be notified to upload their broadcast Pseudo-IDs.

Final Results: After completing all N_r rounds, the TEE of PHA_M returns the result of exposure for all participants not notified in a previous round.

Fig. 6. A CPSI-based protocol for multi-hop contact tracing.

The TEE is already utilized for preprocessing. With minimal extra overhead, it can be used to selectively choose which data is used for different CPSI computations. Consider the earlier example, where Bob would be identified as a close contact of the infected Charlie. When Bob sends his data to the TEE for preprocessing, he can also upload timestamps as metadata. Suppose Bob and Charlie met at $ts_{b,c}$. Then the TEE can sort Bob's broadcast Pseudo-IDs into a set PRE_2 or $POST_2$, depending on if they happened before or after $ts_{b,c}$. (PRE_i is the set of contacts i hops away from the initial set.) After the sets PRE_2 and $POST_2$ have been aggregated from all users who were in contact with those individuals confirmed to be infected, they are preprocessed, homomorphically encrypted, and sent (separately) to C. Then C can rerun the CPSI computation against these two sets, and return the results to the TEE. This shows the TEE who was in contact with Bob (and others like him who contacted an infected individual) before and after they contacted an infected individual. By having uninfected users also attach timestamps, the TEE will additionally learn when that secondary contact happened. The above process can then be repeated to form sets PRE_3, $POST_3$, PRE_4, $POST_4$, etc. In practice, only a few rounds would be necessary. The above process is detailed in Fig. 6. Unlike some existing approaches [24], our multi-hop tracing does not require uninfected and uncontacted users to perform any additional computation or communication.

8 Conclusion

We present a secure protocol for COVID contact tracing based on the use of our novel CPSI protocol and TEE. Our contact tracing protocol is extended beyond basic conditioned contact tracing to filtering by duration with CPSI, and is also expanded to forward/backward multi-hop tracing. With our implementation, a users' required computations can be completed in as little as 9 min, and the cloud's per-user computation can be as little as 11 min for 20,000 total Pseudo-IDs broadcast by all infected users, with negligible overhead for TEE preprocessing and decryption.

Acknowledgement. This work was supported by the Office of the Director of National Intelligence (ODNI), Intelligence Advanced Research Projects Activity (IARPA) via contract #2020–20082700002. Any opinions, findings and conclusions or recommendations expressed in this material are those of the authors and do not necessarily reflect those of the sponsor. The authors also thank Dr. Alex Perkins (Department of Biological Sciences, University of Notre Dame) for his helpful comments.

References

1. Altuwaiyan, T., et al.: Epic: efficient privacy-preserving contact tracing for infection detection. In: IEEE ICC, pp. 1–6 (2018)
2. Apple and Google. Privacy-Preserving Contact Tracing (2020). apple.co/3bFFWzp
3. Baumgärtner, L., et al.: Mind the GAP: security and privacy risks of contact tracing apps. arXiv preprint (2020). arXiv:2006.05914
4. Bay, J., et al.: BlueTrace: a privacy-preserving protocol for community-driven contact tracing across borders. Tech. Rep. GovTech-Singapore (2020)
5. Bell, J., et al.: Tracesecure: towards privacy preserving contact tracing. arXiv preprint arXiv:2004.04059 (2020)
6. Brakerski, Z., Gentry, C., Vaikuntanathan, V.: (Leveled) fully homomorphic encryption without bootstrapping. ACM TOCT **6**(3), 1–36 (2014)
7. Burke, L.:. New variant meets its first university (2021)
8. Chen, H., et al.: Fast private set intersection from homomorphic encryption. In: ACM CCS, pp. 1243–1255 (2017)
9. Chen, H., et al.: Labeled PSI from fully homomorphic encryption with malicious security. In: ACM CCS, pp. 1223–1237 (2018)

10. Cho, H., Ippolito, D., Yu, Y.W.:. Contact tracing mobile apps for covid-19: Privacy considerations and related trade-offs. arXiv preprint arXiv:2003.11511 (2020)

11. Ciampi, M., Orlandi, C.: Combining private set-intersection with secure two-party computation. In: Catalano, D., De Prisco, R. (eds) Security and Cryptography for Networks. SCN 2018. Lecture Notes in Computer Science, vol. 11035. Springer, Cham (2018). https://doi.org/10.1007/978-3-319-98113-0_25

12. Costan, V., Devadas, S.: Intel SGX explained. IACR Cryptol. ePrint Arch. **86**, 1–118 (2016)

13. Dave C., Kurt R., Yuriy P., Ryan, G.:. The PALISADE lattice cryptography library (2020). bit.ly/35Bthtz

14. De Cristofaro, E., Gasti, P., Tsudik, G.: Fast and private computation of cardinality of set Intersection and Union. In: Pieprzyk, J., Sadeghi, A., Manulis, M. (eds.) CANS 2012. LNCS, vol. 7712, pp. 218–231. Springer, Heidelberg (2012). https://doi.org/10.1007/978-3-642-35404-5_17

15. Junfeng Fan, J., Vercauteren, F.: Somewhat practical fully homomorphic encryption. IACR Cryptol. ePrint Arch., 144 (2012)

16. Centers for Disease Control and Prevention. Appendix A - Glossary of Key Terms (2020). bit.ly/2LljkK0

17. Garmin. Project Tesserae powered by Garmin (2018). bit.ly/3nI2yBC

18. Gentry, C., Halevi, S., Smart, N.P.: Homomorphic evaluation of the AES Circuit. In: Safavi-Naini, R., Canetti, R. (eds.) CRYPTO 2012. LNCS, vol. 7417, pp. 850–867. Springer, Heidelberg (2012). https://doi.org/10.1007/978-3-642-32009-5_49

19. Halevi, S., Shoup, V.: Design and implementation of a homomorphic-encryption library. IBM Research (Manuscript) **6**, 12–15 (2013)

20. Ion, M., et al.: Private intersection-sum protocol with applications to attributing aggregate ad conversions. IACR Cryptol. ePrint Arch. 738 (2017)

21. Lindell, Y.: How to simulate it-a tutorial on the simulation proof technique. Tutorials on the Foundations of Cryptography, pp. 277–346 (2017)

22. Liu, S., Jiang, Y., Striegel, A.: Face-to-face proximity estimationusing bluetooth on smartphones. IEEE Trans. Mobile Comput. **13**(4), 811–823 (2014)

23. Lounis, K., Zulkernine, M.: Attacks and defenses in short-range wireless technologies for iot. IEEE Access **8**, 88892–88932 (2020)

24. Michael, K., Abbas, R.: Behind covid-19 contact trace apps: the Google-Apple partnership. IEEE Consumer Electronics Magazine **9**(5), 71–76 (2020)

25. Mofrad, S., Zhang, F., Lu, S., Shi, W.: A comparison study of intel sgx and amd memory encryption technology. In: HASP, pp. 1–8 (2018)

26. Morgan, A.U., et al.: Remote monitoring of patients with covid-19: design, implementation, and outcomes of the first 3,000 patients in COVID Watch. NEJM Catalyst Innovations in Care Delivery, **1**(4) (2020)

27. Nietzel, M.: Duke University suddenly imposes week-long stay-at-home order on all undergraduates (2021)

28. Government of Singapore. TraceTogether (2020). www.tracetogether.gov.sg

29. Benny, P., Eyal, R.: Hashomer-a proposal for a privacy-preserving bluetooth based contact tracing scheme for Hamagen (2020)

30. Benny, P., Thomas, S., Christian, W., Udi, W.:. Efficient circuit-based PSI via cuckoo hashing. In: EUROCRYPT, pp. 125–157 (2018)

31. Benny, P., Thomas, S., Michael, Z.: Faster private set intersection based on {OT} extension. In: Usenix Security, pp. 797–812 (2014)

32. Ramesh, R., et al.: Apps gone rogue: maintaining personal privacy in an epidemic. arXiv preprint arXiv:2003.08567 (2020)

33. Raskar, R., Pahwa, D., Beaudry, R.: Contact tracing: holistic solution beyond bluetooth. IEEE Data Eng. Bull **43**(2), 67–70 (2020)
34. Reichert, L., Brack, S., Scheuermann, B.:. Privacy-preserving contact tracing of covid-19 patients. IACR Cryptol. ePrint Arch. 375 (2020)
35. Riazi, M.S., et al.: HEAX: an architecture for computing on encrypted data. In: ACM ASPLOS, pp. 1295–1309 (2020)
36. Microsoft SEAL (release 3.6) (2020). bit.ly/3qgKCjd
37. Singh, P., et al.: Ppcontacttracing: a privacy-preserving contact tracing protocol for covid-19 pandemic. arXiv preprint arXiv:2008.06648 (2020)
38. Taassori, M., et al.: Vault: reducing paging overheads in SGX with efficient integrity verification structures. In: ASPLOS, pp. 665–678 (2018)
39. Takeshita, J., et al.: Algorithmic acceleration of B/FV-Like somewhat homomorphic encryption for compute-enabled RAM. In: Dunkelman, O., Jacobson, Jr., M.J., O'Flynn, C. (eds.) SAC 2020. LNCS, vol. 12804, pp. 66–89. Springer, Cham (2021). https://doi.org/10.1007/978-3-030-81652-0_3
40. Tan, B.H.M., et al.: Efficient private comparison queries over encrypted databases using fully homomorphic encryption with finite fields. IEEE TDSC (2020)
41. Tang, Q.: Privacy-preserving contact tracing: current solutions and open questions. arXiv preprint arXiv:2004.06818 (2020)
42. Trieu, N., et al.: Epione: lightweight contact tracing with strong privacy. arXiv preprint arXiv:2004.13293 (2020)
43. Wang, X.S., et al.: Efficient genome-wide, privacy-preserving similar patient query based on private edit distance. In: ACM CCS, pp. 492–503 (2015)
44. Wu, J., et al.: {BLESA}: spoofing attacks against reconnections in Bluetooth low energy. In: 14th {USENIX} Workshop on Offensive Technologies ({WOOT} 20) (2020)
45. Yasaka, T.M., Lehrich, B.M., Sahyouni, R.:. Peer-to-peer contact tracing: development of a privacy-preserving smartphone app. JMIR Mhealth Uhealth, **8**(4), e18936 (2020)
46. Yoneki, E.: Fluphone study: virtual disease spread using haggle. In: CHANTS, pp. 65–66 (2011)

Origin Attribution of RSA Public Keys

Enrico Branca, Farzaneh Abazari, Ronald Rivera Carranza,
and Natalia Stakhanova[(✉)]

Department of Computer Science, University of Saskatchewan, SK, Canada
{enb733,faa851,rer655,natalia}@usask.ca

Abstract. In spite of strong mathematical foundations of cryptographic algorithms, the practical implementations of cryptographic protocols continue to fail. Insufficient entropy, faulty library implementation, API misuse do not only jeopardize the security of cryptographic keys, but also lead to distinct patterns that can result in keys' origin attribution. In this work, we examined attribution of cryptographic keys based on their moduli. We analyzed over 6.5 million keys generated by 43 cryptographic libraries versions on 20 Linux OS versions released over the past 8 years. We showed that with only a few moduli characteristics, we can accurately (with 75% accuracy) attribute an individual key to the originating library. Depending on the library, our approach is sensitive enough to pinpoint the corresponding major, minor, and build release of several libraries that generated an individual key with an accuracy of 81%–98%. We further explore attribution of SSH keys collected from publicly facing IPv4 addresses showing that our approach is able to differentiate individual libraries of RSA keys with 95% accuracy.

Keywords: RSA security · Cryptographic libraries · Attribution

1 Introduction

Secure communication on the Internet is becoming a norm. Nowadays, nearly 90% of all Internet communication is encrypted. While in theory, cryptographic solutions are provably secure, in practice, the security of communication depends on the correctness of implementation of the existing tools that support encryption standards. Over the past decade, numerous studies pointed out weaknesses of cryptographic security of various protocols (TLS/SSL [18], SSH [16], HTTPS [2,10,17]). The majority of these studies investigated insufficient security of generated keys as a main root cause of the problem. Some studies traced the problem to weak random key generators and the lack of entropy [8,13,18], while others noted the improper implementation of cryptographic libraries [11,26,29,37], and pure misuse of cryptographic algorithms, e.g., keys embedded in binary files [12].

As a consequence, the number of studies developed techniques to identify insecure and vulnerable keys. The vast majority of these approaches focus on analysis of binaries that contain vulnerable keys [26,27,33,35], or crypto libraries and APIs that produce those keys [31,37].

J. Garcia-Alfaro et al. (Eds.): SecureComm 2021, LNICST 398, pp. 374–396, 2021.
https://doi.org/10.1007/978-3-030-90019-9_19

Misconfigurations of cryptographic algorithms and cryptographic operations can potentially lead to distinct patterns in the generated keys and can be leveraged in identifying their origins. This observation was first explored in the study by Svenda et al. [37] that noted that combination of implementation decision made in software libraries in a presence of certain hardware is sufficient to identify a probable origin of a key. Their work was further improved by Nemec et al. [31]. Both approaches in their attribution analysis relied on a set of rules defined through a preliminary analysis of biases of the known libraries. In spite of higher accuracy of attribution obtained by [31], none of these approaches were able to attribute an individual key to a specific library, focusing on attribution to groups of similar libraries.

The question that remains is whether *it is feasible to identify an exact origin of an individual cryptographic key*. Addressing this question has direct practical implications. In cryptographic theory, the attribution of keys should not be possible, an accurate tracing of a key to its specific library version allows for fine-grained fingerprinting of cryptographic libraries, which has a number of practical uses from undermining anonymity of Internet users by allowing more accurate profiling of their activities to direct attacks on libraries and protocols [25]. The attribution of keys also implies that these identifiable library implementations embed predictable patterns in the generated keys, thus reducing key space, and allowing for faster key factorization [14].

In this work, we propose a source attribution approach based on the characteristics of RSA key modulus. We analyze the characteristics of RSA public key modulus to understand how much information one needs to trace an individual key to its originating library. The underlying assumption of the source attribution of cryptographic keys is the presence of distinct bit patterns in keys that allows to predict where this key was generated. To quantify these patterns, we derive spatial characteristics of each key moduli to estimate its position in the numerical spectrum and the likelihood that such key may have been generated by a particular library.

To validate our approach, we tested over 6.5 million keys generated by 43 cryptographic libraries versions on 20 Linux OS versions released over the past 8 years. Our experiments show that we can accurately attribute an individual key to the originating library with 75% accuracy with only a few modulus characteristics regardless of its patch level, and its release date. We are further able to produce a fine-grained attribution of a key to the corresponding major, minor, build and in some cases patch releases for several libraries achieving accuracy in the range of 81%–98%.

Our findings suggests that code changes applied to some library implementation between versions leave significant traces in the generated keys, consequently, allowing for accurate origin attribution.

We compare our approach to the most recent study by Nemec et al. [31]. Their previous work was able to accurately (94% accuracy) attribute the keys to the groups of similar libraries. We show that our approach outperforms their technique providing a more granular attribution to an individual library and its version.

We further explore origin attribution of almost 200,000 RSA keys collected from publicly facing IPv4 addresses. Our analysis of these collected keys shows that they generally come from homogeneous pool of libraries. We are able to differentiate individual libraries of RSA collected keys with 95% accuracy. For individual versions we obtained 68% to 100% accuracy for most libraries that had a sufficient number of keys. More importantly, we have been able to do this without any prior knowledge on the system, hardware platform or the library that generated them. To summarize, we

1. Propose a source attribution approach that can link an individual cryptographic key to the originating library and its specific version. Our approach does not rely on previous knowledge of cryptographic library's weaknesses.
2. We evaluate and select the top distinctive moduli characteristics that contribute the most in discriminating individual keys.
3. We test the performance of our attribution on a set of keys collected from publicly facing IPv4 addresses. Both sets of generated keys and collected keys are available at https://cyberlab.usask.ca/attributionRSAkeys.html.

This paper is organized as follows: Sect. 2 gives an overview of related work in the field. We briefly introduce the RSA cryptosystem in Sect. 3 and explain our proposed approach in Sect. 4. In Sect. 5, we demonstrate the results of key attribution. Section 6 applies our attribution approach to a real-world keys collected on the Internet.

2   Related Work

In spite of strong mathematical foundations of cryptographic algorithms, the practical implementations of cryptographic protocols continue to fail. The study of real-life spread of vulnerable keys across the Internet by Heninger et al. [18] showed that out of 6.2 million SSH keys collected in the wild 0.03% can be factored within 2 h. Similar results were obtained by Lenstra et al. [24] on the analysis of TLS certificates.

These cryptographic failures rarely occur due to shortcomings of an algorithm's theoretic design or technological advances. Predominantly the compromise of cryptographic protocols happens due to errors in their implementation or due to human oversight in proper configuration or selection of parameters. Lazar et al. [23] examined 269 cryptographic vulnerabilities showing that 83% of bugs were related to misuses of cryptographic libraries, while 17% were bugs in libraries' implementation. Several studies showed that application programming interfaces (APIs) themselves, their complexity and improper default parameters, contribute to the cryptographic misuse [1,30].

A significant number of vulnerabilities in cryptographic keys are stemming from problems of random numbers generators (RNGs). The 2012 study by Heninger et al. [18] attributed the majority of factored RSA keys to memory constrained devices (such as routers, smart cards, firewalls) that have limited sources for generating appropriate randomness. Indeed, RSA prime factorization arithmetic can be computationally expensive for resource constrained devices. This often leads to various practises that shortcut appropriate key generation and consequently leads to weak public keys that allow an attacker to calculate the private key from a public key.

Yilek et al. [39] examined the spread of keys affected by the highly publicized bug discovered in 2008 in OpenSSL library that generated predictable random numbers. They noted that even after six months of disclosure, weak keys resulting from the buggy implementation were still being issued and widely used. Slow response was also noted by Hastings et al. [17] in their follow-up study that factored 313,000 RSA keys.

Several studies developed techniques to identify insecure and vulnerable keys. The vast majority of these approaches focus on analysis of binaries that contain vulnerable keys [26,27,33,35]. Insufficient entropy, faulty library implementation, API misuse do not only jeopardize the security of cryptographic keys, but also lead to distinct patterns that can result to keys' origin attribution.

Svenda et al. [37] tested if cryptographic hardware cards and libraries comply with the quality and security expectations regarding randomness and resistance against well-known RSA attacks. Within this study they identified seven implementation decisions tied to specific hardware cards and libraries. Cumulatively, these implementation patterns allow to attribute the origin of RSA keys based on the moduli. Their analysis of 60 million generated RSA keys showed the viability of the approach. They were able to correctly label the origin of 40% due to software and hardware differences in their design, implementation choices and faulty RNGs.

Nemec et al. [31] applied the approach developed by Svenda et al. [37] to examine popularity of cryptographic libraries on the Internet. They identified that efficiency improvements, implementation choices and bugs are the main sources of biases when selecting primes p and q, and since these biases can sometimes be observable from the moduli, it is possible to group libraries based on their similarities. The authors showed that it possible to attribute individual keys (with over 94% accuracy) to groups of similar libraries.

Both approaches (i.e., [37] and [31]) in their classification analysis relied on a set of rules defined through preliminary analysis of key misuses of known libraries. Among other things, both approaches required an estimation of prior probabilities for domain where the key to be attributed is coming from. The studies showed that the better this estimate, the better the accuracy of their approaches. Yet, in spite of high accuracy of attribution, none of these approaches were able to attribute keys to individual libraries within groups.

Muslukhov et al. [29] also noted that the improper implementation of cryptographic libraries can leak the origin of a key. Their approach, BinSight, performed a static analysis of Android applications detecting calls to crypto APIs. Similarly to [37] and [31], it was identifying misuses against a set of crypto rules. In this

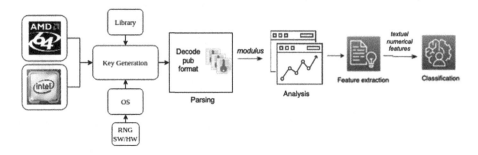

Fig. 1. The flow of the proposed approach

research, we attribute individual keys to the corresponding libraries without a prior knowledge of specific library weaknesses.

3   Background

In this work, we focus on the RSA (Rivest–Shamir–Adleman) algorithm as this is arguably the most popular cryptographic system utilized on the Internet today. RSA is an asymmetric cryptographic algorithm that leverages the fact that while multiplication of large prime numbers is not computationally intensive, factorization of large prime numbers is significantly more complex.

As such an RSA public key is theoretically generated based on two large prime numbers p and q used to calculate the modulus n. Specifically, an RSA key can be generated as follows:

1. Pick two primes p and q to calculate the modulus n, $n = p * q$. Both primes should be large (i.e., $size \geq 1024$), random and $p \neq q$.
2. Calculate $\phi(n) = (p - 1)(q - 1)$,
3. Select exponent e, $\phi(n) - 1$ will serve as an upper limit when selecting a value for e which should be large (i.e., $size \geq 1024$) and random. The value for e should be restricted to $e \in 1, 2, ..., \phi(n) - 1$. In addition, the $GCD(e, \phi(n))$ must be equal to 1 so that we know that they are relatively prime.
4. Calculate private key component d: $de \equiv 1(\mathrm{mod}\phi(n))$.

As a result, an RSA public key $Pub_k = (e, n)$ is represented by an exponent e and a modulus n, while an RSA private key $Priv_k$ is usually a pair (d, n).

The RSA algorithm is implemented in a variety of the cryptographic libraries. For our analysis, we use the most common open-source libraries: OpenSSH, OpenSSL, GnuTLS, and GPG.

4   Analysis Methodology

Several previous studies [31,37] showed that various implementation decisions and shortcuts of cryptographic libraries propagate to RSA keys creating a bias.

In this work, we analyze the characteristics of RSA public key to understand how much information one needs to trace an individual key to its originating library.

The underlying assumption of the source attribution of cryptographic keys is the presence of distinct bit patterns in a single key that allows to predict where this key was generated. Source attribution of the keys does not consider factorizing the modulus n and relies on the numerical and textual features of the modulus, such as a longest repeated substring and a percentage of bits equal to one.

The overview of the attribution approach is illustrated in Fig. 1. The generated cryptographic keys are decoded and parsed to derive a key modulus. As the first step in our analysis, we examine the characteristics of keys' moduli generated from known libraries, estimate the randomness of moduli, establish and analyze the distinctive bit patterns. We use the retrieved patterns in classification analysis to attribute keys to their origin library.

We further analyze contribution of individual patterns to the accuracy of attribution. In our attribution analysis, we employ six classifiers with different logic to understand their effectiveness in discriminating keys originated from different libraries.

4.1   RSA Keys Generation and Parsing

To establish 'ground truth', we generated 6.5 million RSA keys using 4 cryptographic libraries on 9 most widely used Linux distributions released over the past 8 years. We made the design choice to use the cryptographic library version that was shipped with the OS, assuming that this version would have been officially tested and certified by each Linux distribution security teams. Overall, we tested 43 cryptographic libraries versions on 20 versions of Linux distributions. To ensure sufficient entropy for key generation, we enabled software-level random number generator Haveged [36] and used two hardware random number generators: TrueRNG [38] and NeuG [40].

The details of the generated keys are given in Table 2. All keys were generated 2048 bit long as this is the minimum key size recommended by NIST to be used in an RSA algorithm. We verified that all generated keys are valid and NIST standard-compliant, i.e., all moduli are unique, exactly 2048 bits long, and have prime components. To test for primality, we used the Miller-Rabin primality test. To understand the potential randomness of generated keys, we performed the following NIST statistical tests [5]:

Discrete Fourier Transform (DFT) test that detects periodic features (i.e., repetitive patterns that are near each other) in the tested sequence that would indicate a deviation from the assumption of randomness.

Monibit test that checks the proportion of zeroes and ones for the sequence. The purpose of this test is to determine whether the number of ones and zeros in a sequence are approximately the same as would be expected for a truly random sequence.

While a number of studies acknowledged weaknesses of some NIST statistical tests (e.g., Marsaglia's Diehard, and TestU01 [20]), they still serve as one of generic instruments in assessing key randomness.

The results of these tests are given in Table 1. The overwhelming majority of the keys passed both tests. In other words, the produced bit sequences are considered random.

Table 1. The results of NIST statistical tests on the set of generated keys

Test	Number of keys that passed the test	Number of keys that failed the test
Monobit test	6,700,705 (99%)	66,373 (1%)
DFT test	6,674,844 (98%)	92,234 (2%)

4.2 Key Analysis and Representation

Previous study by Nemec et al. [31] identified several rules that cumulatively form a fingerprint allowing to identify a key source (i.e., a group of similar libraries). The rules are specific to the analyzed libraries and are derived from the identified in advance bias of cryptographic libraries. We take a different approach and extract features that are independent of knowledge of the originating library, underlying platform, and operation system.

The intuition of our approach is simple. A bounded numerical space determines a pool of available keys for each library. If any specific rule exists in the key generation process, the generated keys will contain a pattern that reflects the reduced numerical space.

For each key, we consider numerical and textual representation of a modulus and derive features that quantify its randomness and its spatial characteristics.

Numerical Representation. The following types of features are derived:

- *Modulus characteristics*: size, primality of components, entropy.
- *The cutoff value characteristics*: most algorithms for generating RSA modulus set bits in certain positions (usually first two bits are set to 1, and last is set to 1)[1] which defines/reduces a numerical space for selecting potential modulus. For example, for an explanation of how OpenSSL library sets the bits refer to [32]. The *cutoff value* represents the minimum value that can be ever generated for a modulus in such space. We calculate a cutoff value and check its position against an actual integer value of the generated modulus (we refer to it as offset position).
- *Bin position*: helps us determine the preference of the library in choosing a modulus within a specific range. Given the fact that the numerical space available for each key is defined by the size in bits, to compare keys of different sizes, we divide the numerical space into 100 sections and assign a positional

---

[1] For example, setting last bit to 1 ensures that the number is odd.

Table 2. The summary of the generated keys

OS	OS Version	Year	OpenSSH library	GnuTLS library	GPG library	OpenSSL library
Ubuntu	20.04	2020	8.2p1	3.6.13	2.2.19	1.1.1d
Ubuntu	18.04	2018	7.6p1	3.5.18	2.2.4	1.1.1
Ubuntu	16.04	2016	7.2p2	3.4.10	2.1.11	1.0.2g
Ubuntu	14.04	2014	6.6	*	2.0.22	1.0.1f
Ubuntu	12.04	2012	5.9	*	*	*
Mint	20	2020	8.2p1	3.6.13	2.2.19	1.1.1f
Mint	19	2020	7.6p1	3.5.18	2.2.4	1.1.1h
Fedora	30	2019	8.0p1	3.6.10	2.2.13	1.1.1b
Fedora	23	2015	7.1p1	3.4.5	2.1.7	1.0.2d
Fedora	20	2014	6.3	3.1.16	*	1.0.1e
Fedora	17	2012	5.9	*	*	1.0.0i
Fedora	14	2010	5.5	*	*	1.0.0a
CentOS	8.2.2004	2019	8.0p1	3.6.8	*	1.1.1c
Manjaro	20	2020	8.3p1	3.6.15	2.2.23	1.1.1g
Swift	4.19.0	2018	7.9p1	*	*	1.1.1d
Endeavour	5.8	2020	8.3p1	3.6.15	2.2.23	1.1.1g
Kali	2020.3	2020	8.3p1	3.6.15	2.2.20	1.1.1g
Oracle	R8	2019	8.0p1	3.6.8	*	1.1.1c
Oracle	R7	2017	7.4p1	*	*	1.0.2k
Oracle	R6	2013	5.3p1	*	*	1.0.1e
Total generated keys			3,084,936	1,165,984	616,159	1,899,999

Asterisks (*) indicate cases when certain libraries or their dependencies are no longer available for specific Linux distributions.

value to each key depending on where it falls with respect to its relative section. An analysis of the spatial characteristics of a key moduli (Bin value together with cutoff and its position) can allow us to identify, not only the size of the theoretical numerical space used by the library, but also compare the relative position of each key with the position of all other keys that share same characteristics and belong to the same numerical space.

– As an estimator of string randomness, we employ *Brotli* [21] and *Lempel–Ziv–Markov chain (LZMA) compression* [34] algorithms. The 'degree of randomness' can be expressed as 'ratio of compressed file to uncompressed file', where the compression ratio provides a quick way to visualize the randomness used by a library when generating a key.

Textual Representation. To identify and derive all possible bit patterns, we convert the binary representation of a key into a textual format. To exhaustively search for all possible patterns, we employ an overlapping sliding window technique with windows of size $n = 8$ to 256. We derive the following types of textual features for all window sizes:

- *Longest repeated substring (LRS) characteristics*: we estimate the presence and the corresponding characteristics of longest repeated substring patterns within a modulus.
- *0's & 1's characteristics*: we determine and profile a maximum length of continuous zeroes or ones within the string representation of a modulus.
- *Characteristics of mirror patterns.* The modulus' binary string is represented as two halves of equal size, we then perform a comparative analysis of the n bit patterns found in the first half vs the n bit patterns in the second half. This produces features such as *Most significant bits (MSB) - Least significant bit (LSB) pattern* of length n, *mirror pattern*, i.e., n bits of the first half of the modulus found on the second half of the modulus, position and frequency of mirror patterns, etc.

4.3   Classification

We explored performance of 6 classification algorithms: Gaussian Naïve Bayes, Neural Networks, Decision Trees, Discriminant Analysis, Random Forest, and Logistic Regression analysis.

Gaussian Naïve Bayes is based on Bayes' theorem that assumes an independence between features [6]. Even though feature independence assumption rarely holds true, NB models perform surprisingly well in practice [3]. The Gaussian Naïve Bayes classifier is one of its versions that follows a Gaussian distribution and assumes the presence of data with continuous values which is the case in our datasets.

Neural Networks (NN) [28] are a series of algorithms that mimic the operations of a human brain to detect relationships between high volumes of data. Since neural networks can have many layers and parameters with non-linearities, they are very effective at modelling highly complex non-linear relationships. Neural networks operate well with large amounts of training data.

Decision Trees (DT) [7] produces a sequence of rules that can be used to classify the data when a data of features together with its target are given. The decision tree classifier can be unstable because small variations in the data might result in a completely different tree being generated.

Discriminant Analysis model is composed of discriminant functions based on linear combinations of the features that provide the best discrimination between the classes [22]. This model assumes that different classes generate data based on different Gaussian distributions. Linear Discriminant Analysis (LDA) provides multi-class classification which is suitable for our analysis.

Random forest (RF) [19] classifier is an ensemble that fits a number of decision trees on various sub-samples of datasets and uses the average to improve the predictive accuracy of the model.

Logistic Regression(LR) [9] is a linear classifier that predicts probabilities rather than classes. We use multinomial logistic regression classification to calculate the probability of key modulus x belonging to a target class.

Our approach was implemented using the Python language (v 3.8.5) with the scikit-learn library (v 0.23.2). A summary of the classification algorithms' parameters is given in Table 3. 5-fold cross-validation was employed to measure the accuracy of the machine learning models.

Table 3. Machine learning model parameters

Name	Parameter	Kernel
Gaussian Naive Bayes	var_smoothing = 1e-9	Non-linear
Neural Network	max_iter=10000, learning_rate='adaptive', solver='adam', alpha=1	Non-linear
Decision Trees	max_depth=100	Non-linear
Linear Discriminant Analysis	solver = 'svd', shrinkage = None	Linear
Random Forest	n_estimators = 100, min_samples_split = 2, min_samples_leaf = 1, max_features="log2", criterion = 'entropy'	Non-linear
Logistic Regression	penalty="l2", max_iter=100000, solver="lbfgs", multi_class="multinomial"	Linear

5 Attribution Results

The results of attributing 6,767,078 keys to the individual libraries are shown in Fig. 2(a). The best average classification accuracy (75% accuracy) is obtained with Random Forest, Logistic Regression, and Neural Network algorithms. The average accuracy is computed based on the accuracy for each class and the number of keys in that class. 5-fold cross-validation was employed to measure the accuracy of the models with 75% of data for training purposes and 25% for testing.

Features. As we anticipated, not all the characteristics extracted from the key material equally contribute to the classification accuracy. To ensure that we keep only features with a measurable impact on the overall accuracy, we have retained features which have an 'Information Gain' (IG) of at least 0.005.

Compared to the overall set of features, we have been able to maintain the same accuracy by selecting the 14 most contributing features (see Appendix). The further analysis of the most significant features shows that while different features are ranked differently for different libraries, the core features remain the same. The core features across various libraries are Brotli compression, LRS pattern, LRS position, Zeroes position, Ones position, Mirror all positions, Mirror position, Mirror all patterns and Bin. Note that only features with windows size $n = 8$ proved to be most significant across all libraries.

One of the challenges that previous studies faced is the necessity to define crypto rules, i.e., weak implementation decisions that effectively lead to bias in the produced keys. The selected characteristics mentioned before are generic and independent from the underlying library.

Attribution Across Library Versions. While the performance of classifiers remain somewhat stable for different amount of keys, we found that the accuracy varies depending on the individual characteristics of the source library.

To further understand the granularity of our approach to discriminate keys, we have evaluated attribution across library versions. Figure 2(b) shows the average accuracy of attributing the individual keys to the libraries' versions. The best average accuracy of 85% is obtained with Random Forest (RF) classification algorithm. Since both experiments showed that RF performs the best in our setting, we further use this classifier in the analysis.

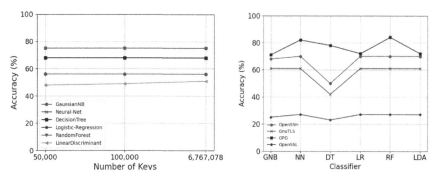

(a) Attribution of keys to their source li- (b) Inter-Library attribution of keys to
braries   the corresponding library version

Fig. 2. The accuracy of attributing generated keys to the originating library and library versions

Table 4 presents more granular results of attributing keys by major and minor release versions with its corresponding libraries[2]. Since we do not have enough key material from GnuTLS, GPG, and OpenSSL libraries to discriminate between major versions, their corresponding experiments were performed for major and minor releases.

We can observe that certain libraries have clearly distinguishable patterns (e.g., GPG, OpenSSH 8.x).

Theoretically, code changes applied to a library that occurred within a major version should not have any significant impact on the generated keys, while major changes that culminate with the release of a new version should equate to marked differences. Despite our assumptions, our results seem to suggest that, regardless of the library type or version, it is possible to attribute a cryptographic key not only to the library type but more specifically to its specific major and minor version.

---

[2] We refer to library version using a conventional notation of software versioning where each version is represented by major.minor[.build[.patch]].

Table 4. Attribution accuracy for library versions (Random Forest)

Library	Version	Accuracy	Number of keys
OpenSSH	5.x	100%	391,928
OpenSSH	6.x	0%	193,009
OpenSSH	7.x	24%	700,000
OpenSSH	8.x	63%	1,799,999
GnuTLS	3.1.x	0%	100,000
GnuTLS	3.4.x	0%	200,000
GnuTLS	3.5.x	0%	154,142
GnuTLS	3.6.x	61%	711,842
GPG	2.0.x	76%	28,657
GPG	2.1.x	98%	149,010
GPG	2.2.x	82%	438,492
OpenSSL	1.0.x	53%	800,000
OpenSSL	1.1.x	63%	1,099,999

The most difference among versions is produced by GPG library, where it is possible to attribute the key to a specific version with an accuracy ranging from a minimum of 76% for 2.0.x version to a maximum of 98% for 2.1.x version.

The accuracy for other types of libraries varies depending on the library version. For example, we were only able to attribute keys to 3.6 version of GnuTLS library (61%). Our current assumption is that such variability may stem from the changes in the logic or structure of cryptographic primitives implemented in a library.

Fine-grained Origin Attribution. To further understand this phenomenon, we analyzed the release notes for each library[3]. We aggregated the library versions available in our generated set to reflect the modifications in libraries that involve any changes (i.e., improvements) related to random number generation process. As a side note, the GPG release notes did not provide sufficient level of details on what was changed and when, therefore we were not able to derive further groupings for this library.

The results presented in Table 5 give an insight into the variability in attribution of keys, where only major and minor versions are taken into consideration. For example, OpenSSH 5.9/5.9p1 release switched to obtaining random numbers directly from OpenSSL or from a PRNGd/EGD instance specified at configuration time. This caused a structural change in produced keys resulting in distinctive patterns in keys generated before 5.9 release. Hence, we were able to distinguish keys generated with earlier versions with 81% accuracy.

---

[3] GnuTLS: https://gitlab.com/gnutls/gnutls/blob/master/news.
OpenSSH: https://www.openssh.com/releasenotes.html.
GPG: https://gnupg.org/download/release_notes.html.
OpenSSL: https://www.openssl.org/news/changelog.html.

Table 5. Attribution accuracy of generated keys by minor build version groupings (Random Forest)

Library	Release groupings**	Accuracy	Number of keys
OpenSSH	[5.3p1–5.9]*	**81%**	191,928
OpenSSH	[6.3]	50%	293,009
OpenSSH	[6.6]	0%	100,000
OpenSSH	[7.1p1–7.2]	0%	200,000
OpenSSH	(7.2–7.6]	0%	300,000
OpenSSH	(7.9+]	**69%**	199,999
GnuTLS	[3.1.16]	0%	100,000
GnuTLS	[3.4.5–3.4.10]	0%	200,000
GnuTLS	[3.5.18]	0%	154,142
GnuTLS	[3.6.8+]	**61%**	711,842
GPG	2.0.x	**76%**	28,657
GPG	2.1.x	**98%**	149,010
GPG	2.2.x	**82%**	438,492
OpenSSL	(1.0.0a–1.0.1f]	13%	200,000
OpenSSL	(1.0.1f–1.0.2k]	20%	300,000
OpenSSL	(1.0.2k–1.1.0]	20%	300,000
OpenSSL	[1.1.1]	34%	299,999
OpenSSL	[1.1.1b]	8%	100,000
OpenSSL	[1.1.1c]	13%	200,000
OpenSSL	[1.1.1d]	**93%**	200,000
OpenSSL	(1.1.1d–1.1.1h]	34%	300,000

* An inclusive bound is represented by '[', an exclusive bound is represented by '('.
** Based on the available data in Table 2.

It should be also noted that in some cases such drastic changes to underlying libraries happen between even within build releases. For example, OpenSSL library version 1.1.1d came out with a completely rewritten random number generator which in turn resulted in 93% of the produced keys to be positively linked to this specific version of OpenSSL.

In some cases, such as GnuTLS before version 3.5.19, or OpenSSH between version 6.8 and 7.8, our approach was unsuccessful in attributing keys to the corresponding library (0% accuracy), which in fact is a general expectation of cryptographic keys. The produced key should not bear any signs of the originating library.

We speculate that changes involving the memory usage of the randomness pools, and the decision of leaving to the OS the responsibility to ensure a proper initialization during early boot time, negatively impacts the entropy distillation process that leads to the presence of discernable patterns in the resulting cryptographic key.

Comparative Analysis. To better estimate the accuracy and efficacy of our solution, we have decided to compare the performance of our source attribution approach to the performance of the model developed by Nemec et al. [31]. We have therefore implemented and applied their approach on the set of our generated keys. The results are given in Table 6.

Nemec et al. approach showed a feasibility of attributing keys to groups of similar libraries (with over 94% accuracy), yet it fails to trace individual keys to their corresponding libraries achieving at most only 42% accuracy. Since the accuracy of their approach is low, we have not evaluated a more granular attribution to specific library versions.

Table 6. Classification accuracy of Nemec et al. [31] approach on the generated keys

Model	Accuracy	Model	Accuracy
GaussianNB	35%	Logistic Regression	42%
Neural-Net	42%	Linear Discriminant	42%
Decision Tree	23%	Random Forest	40%

6   Internet Scan of IPv4 Hosts

To explore the origins of RSA keys on the Internet, we have performed an attribution of RSA public keys collected from openly available and publicly reachable Internet servers.

6.1   Collected Data

For our analysis, we contacted 220,837 systems over IPv4, with each system geo-located within the Canadian cyber-space and that would accept connections on ports 22 and/or 2222. We collected the keys during 83 d from August to November 2019, collecting keys using the Secure Shell Host (SSH) protocol, by making a single connection to each host and requesting their public SSH-RSA key. Over this period of time we collected 191,976 SSH keys. Among our collected keys, the majority (191,005) were received through SSH v2.0 protocol (Table 7).

The majority of keys (155,107) were generated using the *OpenSSH* library, which is known to be one of the most widely used SSH libraries on the Internet. Among the collected keys, part of them was generated using older versions of the library (e.g., OpenSSH 1.x and OpenSSH 3.x were released in 2000 and 2001, respectively). It is worth noting that we did not find any key having been generated with OpenSSH 2.x. Furthermore, we also noticed the existence of 89 keys apparently generated by an OpenSSH library version 12.x that seems to be invalid as the most recent version of OpenSSH at the time of this writing is 8.x.

We then proceeded to extract keys components (i.e., modulus and exponent) from the SSH-RSA public keys and compiled a set of 110,798 unique moduli associated with 7 unique exponents. We then organized the SSH-RSA keys according to their size in bits (i.e., the moduli size) and identified 24,400 keys with a *legacy* or *deprecated* status. Currently, NIST compliant RSA keys are required to have a lengths greater or equal to 2048-bits [4], and in our set 167,576 keys were found to have at least 2048 bits.

In addition to the cryptographic material from RSA keys, we have recorded key collection date, IP address and TCP port, SSH protocol version and SSH banner. When a banner was present, we have parsed such banner to infer the name of the SSH library that answered our connection request, the SSH version of such library, and the presence or absence of High-Performance SSH/SCP patches. Finally, from the key material we computed SSH-MD5 and SSH-SHA256 of each key to use as fingerprints. We refer to these data points as protocol-related features.

Table 7. General statistics of the retrieved keys

Total distinct IPv4 hosts scanned	220,837	Key with moduli size <2048 bits	24,400
Distinct SSH RSA keys	191,976	SSH version 1.99	971
Distinct SSH RSA moduli	110,798	SSH version 2.0	191,005
Distinct SSH RSA exponents	7	OpenSSH library	155,107
Keys with moduli size ≥2048 bits	167,576	Other library	36869

6.2   Source Attribution

To analyze the performances of our key attribution approach, we designed a set of experiments to analyze the effect of the key size on the accuracy of different types of classifiers. In order to analyze the importance of dataset size, we randomly selected 7 subsets of 191,976 keys collected from the Internet and created sub-samples with a size of 100, 1000, 5000, 10000, 50000, 100,000 and 191,975 keys each. For each of the subsets we allocated 75% of data for training purposes and 25% for testing, using a random sampling technique that makes use of stratified k-folding to reduce bias and increase the likelihood of balanced samples.

Subsequently, we performed two experiments, one to identify the type of library regardless of major or minor versions of each library, and another series of tests where we tried to positively associate each key with a major and minor version of each library. We performed such experiments with different combinations of feature sets in order to understand what type of features may provide a better source attribution.

Figure 3 shows the ability of six distinct types of classifiers to attribute a key to a specific library, according to different combinations of feature sets.

Most classifiers have a comparable performance with the exception of Gaussian Naive Bayes. With our approach, we are able to reach a significant level of accuracy (over 90% with RF) across all sets of features for 191,976 keys. The best accuracy (95%) was obtained with all, textual alone, and protocol-related together with textual features with RF classifier (Fig. 3 (a), (c) and (f)).

Table 8. The list of top features (Random Forest)

Features	Description	Accuracy
Top 1	Mirror all patterns	62%
Top 2	Bin, Offset	65%
Top 5	Bin, LZMA compression, Offset, Brotli compression, Mirror all patterns	78%

While it is not surprising to see the effect of protocol-related features on attribution, it should be noted that textual features that only retain internal characteristics of a modulus provide the same accuracy. This finding supports our earlier assumption that *the logic or structure of cryptographic primitives implemented in a library leaves distinct traces on the generated key modulus.*

Table 8 clarifies the impact that certain features may have on the accuracy. We are able to reduce the features set of the top 14 features selected in Sect. 5 even further to six characteristics retaining a significant portion of our original accuracy (78% with only 5 modulus characteristics). The description of the top features are provided in Table 8.

If we focus our attention on the size of the data set being used, our analysis reveals that most classifiers perform consistently well across different sample sizes that have at least with 1000 keys (Fig. 3), but seems to perform poorly with sample sizes that have less then 1000 keys, resulting in significant loss of accuracy that is proportional to the size of the sample.

The results of more granular experiments, i.e., attribution to a source library and its version are given in Table 9. In most cases, we are able to attribute keys to their originating library and its version. The performances ranges between 68% to 100% attribution accuracy. The performance is generally lower for libraries/versions with fewer keys which is expected due to lack of sufficient data. For example, in cases of FTP server and Reflection, we were not able to produce any attribution due to very small amount of collected keys (3 and 1, respectively).

It is interesting that although we were not able to obtain any information for 'Unknown' libraries or versions, they seem to clearly represent homogeneous groups with distinct patterns. For example, we achieved 89% accuracy in classifying 'Unknown' library with 'Unknown' version. Similarly, non-existent 12.x version of OpenSSH library can be very accurately traced (100% accuracy) to individual keys.

Note that this attribution is based solely on the key's modulus technical characteristics that are independent of library version, patch level, type of kernel used, or hardware platform.

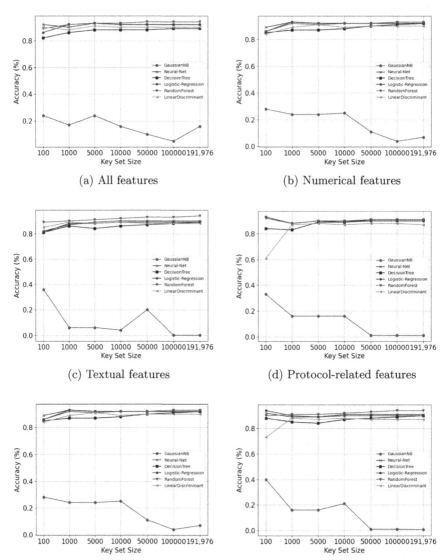

(a) All features

(b) Numerical features

(c) Textual features

(d) Protocol-related features

(e) Protocol-related and numerical features (f) Protocol-related and textual features

Fig. 3. Attribution accuracy of collected keys by individual library

7   Discussion

Fine-grained attribution of keys to their specific library versions has direct practical implications. Tracing an individual key to an exact version of the cryptographic library that produced it extends our ability to accurately fingerprint cryptographic libraries employed by remote parties, which in turn, undermines security of these systems. Knowledge of a specific library version can

Table 9. Attribution results for the collected SSH keys by the individual library and its version (Random Forest)

Library*	Version	Accuracy	Number of keys	Library*	Version	Accuracy	Number of keys
Dropbear	0.x	100%	83	NetVanta	4.x	0%	2
Dropbear	2011.x	100%	222	OpenSSH	3.x	78%	503
Dropbear	2012.x	87%	16,521	OpenSSH	4.x	99%	4,484
Dropbear	2013.x	100%	220	OpenSSH	5.x	91%	23,279
Dropbear	2014.x	98%	1,212	OpenSSH	6.x	98%	25,564
Dropbear	2015.x	98%	538	OpenSSH	7.x	79%	99,564
Dropbear	2016.x	98%	2,854	OpenSSH	8.x	82%	1,535
Dropbear	2017.x	100%	236	OpenSSH	12.x	100%	89
Dropbear	2018.x	91%	143	OpenSSH	Unknown	100%	89
Dropbear	2019.x	100%	146	Reflection	7.x	0%	1
Dropbear	Unknown	68%	5,776	iLO	0.x	100%	34
FTP Server	3.x	0%	3	Unknown	Unknown	89%	8,787

* As announced in the the SSH banners.

simplify targeted and library-specific attacks. For example, such detailed knowledge would also disclose the technical capabilities of a library in terms of key validation and signing. With this information, an attacker can craft a certificate with characteristics that would result in the acceptance of such certificate as valid instead of it be recognized as forged or malicious (e.g., prefix-collision attacks [25]).

Similarly, an attacker could provide certificate details that would trigger specific bugs in the library parsing routines. Such attack would potentially result in the execution of arbitrary code and in privilege escalation and pivoting attacks, where the cryptographic library is effectively executing code on behalf of a malicious attacker.

The presence of predictable patterns in keys can be also leveraged to expedite the factorization process, effectively undermining the security of this key. Several studies offered heuristics for key factorization in situation when certain bits are set [14]. Another application of this research is finding more information about the type of ransomware [15]

Mitigation of key attribution is challenging at this point. Our results seem to point out that the logic or structure of cryptographic primitives implemented in the libraries are the main cause of the distinct bit patterns in keys. As a result, all keys produced by an identifiable library version will be bound to the same distinct patterns and only modification of library's code can help address them. One potential solution is analysis of quality generated keys. Typically, the output of cryptographic applications is judged by their ability to produce random or pseudo random sequences. As we showed in this work, these tests do not necessarily recognize the presence of unique patterns, and thus do not fully address the quality of a generated key.

8   Conclusion

Assessing the characteristics of the cryptographic key material in RSA keys through the use of machine learning techniques has allowed us to identify a series of potentially significant aspects of RSA key that are directly linked to the level of security of RSA keys.

The general expectation of cryptographic keys requires the produced key not bear any signs of the originating library. Yet, we have been able to positively associate a percentage of the collected RSA keys not only to a specific library but more worryingly to a specific version of such library.

We generated 6,767,078 keys with different cryptographic libraries, different versions and on different platform. We were able to attribute the keys moduli to the library with an average of 75% accuracy and its version with an average accuracy of 85%. We have been able to find features that can discriminate between keys generated by different libraries, between keys with different major, minor, build and in some case patch versions. For example, we obtained 76% for GPG 2.0.x version and 98% for GPG 2.1.x version.

In the second round of experiments, we collected 191,976 SSH keys from the Internet. We used six classifiers to analyze the collected keys. Results show that, our approach can attribute individual keys to specific library versions with 68% to 100% accuracy, without any prior knowledge on the system or the library that generated them.

The significance of our work lies in the fact that we can accurately perform attribution of a number of valid, standard-compliant cryptographic keys, both generated and collected from random sources from the Internet. We have evaluated a large number of libraries that span more than a decade, and we found recognizable patterns in every library, regardless of which year the library was published, its patch level, and what is important, its release date. We have been able to perform attribution based solely on the key's modulus technical characteristics that are independent of version, patch level, version of OS, type of kernel used, or class of Linux distribution used for the tests or hardware platform.

9   Appendix

See Table 10.

Table 10. The top 14 features extracted for attribution of generated and collected keys

Feature	Feature type	Description
Shannon entropy	Numerical	The Shannon Entropy of a RSA modulus
Brotli compression	Numerical	Percentage of compression using the Brotli algorithm for text compression
LZMA compression	Numerical	Percentage of compression using the LZMA algorithm for text compression
Offset	Numerical	Cutoff value for moduli of keys that are generated with standard logic
Bin	Numerical	Which bin, between the range of 1 and 100, the value of n falls in
Longest repeated substring (LRS)	String	Longest repeated substring pattern within each string representation of a modulus
LRS position	String	Index positions in which LRS pattern is present within each string representation of a modulus
Zeroes position	String	Index positions in which the continuous zeroes are present within each string representation of a modulus (list)
Ones position	String	Index positions in which the continuous ones are present within each string representation of a modulus
MSB - LSB pattern	String	The first n bits found in the first half of the modulus string are equal to the last n bits in the second half of the string
Mirror pattern	String	The n bits found in the first half of the modulus string are equal to n bits in the second half of the string (regardless of their position)
Mirror position	String	Index positions of mirror pattern
Mirror all patterns	String	The first MSB n bits found in the remaining string of the modulus (regardless of their position)
Mirror all positions	String	Index positions of mirror all patterns

References

1. Acar, Y., et al.: Comparing the usability of cryptographic apis. In: 2017 IEEE Symposium on Security and Privacy (SP), pp. 154–171 (2017)
2. Acer, M.E., et al.: Where the wild warnings are: Root causes of chrome https certificate errors. In: Proceedings of the 2017 ACM SIGSAC Conference on Computer and Communications Security, CCS 2017, pp. 1407–1420. ACM, New York (2017)
3. Aly, M.: Survey on multiclass classification methods. Neural Netw. **19**, 1–9 (2005)

4. Barker, E., Chen, L., Roginsky, A., Vassilev, A., Davis, R., Simon, S.: Recommendation for pair-wise key establishment using integer factorization cryptography. Tech. rep., National Institute of Standards and Technology, Gaithersburg (2019). DOI: https://doi.org/10.6028/NIST.SP.800-56Br2,https://nvlpubs.nist.gov/nistpubs/SpecialPublications/NIST.SP.800-56Br2.pdf
5. Bassham, L.E., et al.: Sp 800-22 rev. 1a. a statistical test suite for random and pseudorandom number generators for cryptographic applications. Tech. rep., Gaithersburg (2010)
6. Bayes, T.: LII. an essay towards solving a problem in the doctrine of chances. by the late rev. Mr. Bayes, FRS communicated by Mr. price, in a letter to john canton, AMFR S. Philos. Trans. R. Soc. Lond. **53**, 370–418 (1763)
7. Breiman, L., Friedman, J.H., Stone, C.J., Olshen, R.A.: Classification and Regression Trees. Wadsworth International Group, Franklin (1984)
8. Costin, A., Zaddach, J., Francillon, A., Balzarotti, D.: A large-scale analysis of the security of embedded firmwares. In: Proceedings of the 23rd USENIX Conference on Security Symposium, SEC 2014, pp. 95–110. USENIX Association, Berkeley (2014)
9. Cox, D.R., Snell, E.J.: Analysis of Binary Data, vol. 32. CRC Press, Boca Raton (1989)
10. Durumeric, Z., Kasten, J., Bailey, M., Halderman, J.A.: Analysis of the https certificate ecosystem. In: Proceedings of the 2013 Conference on Internet Measurement Conference, IMC 2013, pp. 291–304. ACM, New York (2013)
11. Durumeric, Z., et al.: The matter of heartbleed. In: Proceedings of the 2014 Conference on Internet Measurement Conference, IMC 2014, pp. 475–488. ACM, New York (2014)
12. Egele, M., Brumley, D., Fratantonio, Y., Kruegel, C.: An empirical study of cryptographic misuse in android applications. In: Proceedings of the 2013 ACM SIGSAC Conference on Computer & Communications Security, CCS 2013, pp. 73–84. Association for Computing Machinery, New York (2013)
13. Everspaugh, A., Zhai, Y., Jellinek, R., Ristenpart, T., Swift, M.: Not-so-random numbers in virtualized linux and the whirlwind rng. In: 2014 IEEE Symposium on Security and Privacy, pp. 559–574, May 2014
14. Faugère, J.-C., Marinier, R., Renault, G.: Implicit factoring with shared most significant and middle bits. In: Nguyen, P.Q., Pointcheval, D. (eds.) PKC 2010. LNCS, vol. 6056, pp. 70–87. Springer, Heidelberg (2010). https://doi.org/10.1007/978-3-642-13013-7_5
15. Fernando, D.W., Komninos, N., Chen, T.: A study on the evolution of ransomware detection using machine learning and deep learning techniques. IoT **1**(2), 551–604 (2020)
16. Gasser, O., Holz, R., Carle, G.: A deeper understanding of SSH: Results from internet-wide scans. In: 2014 IEEE Network Operations and Management Symposium (NOMS), pp. 1–9, May 2014
17. Hastings, M., Fried, J., Heninger, N.: Weak keys remain widespread in network devices. In: Proceedings of the 2016 Internet Measurement Conference, IMC 2016, pp. 49–63. ACM, New York (2016)
18. Heninger, N., Durumeric, Z., Wustrow, E., Halderman, J.A.: Mining your PS and QS: detection of widespread weak keys in network devices. In: Proceedings of 21st USENIX Security Symposium (USENIX Security 12), pp. 205–220. USENIX, Bellevue (2012)
19. Ho, T.K.: Random decision forests. In: Proceedings of 3rd International Conference on Document Analysis and Recognition, vol. 1, pp. 278–282. IEEE (1995)

20. Hurley-Smith, D., Hernandez-Castro, J.: Great expectations: a critique of current approaches to random number generation testing & certification. In: Cremers, C., Lehmann, A. (eds.) Sec. Standardisation Res., pp. 143–163. Springer International Publishing, Cham (2018)
21. IETF: Brotli compressed data format. https://tools.ietf.org/html/rfc7932
22. Lachenbruch, P.A., Goldstein, M.: Discriminant analysis. Biometrics 69–85 (1979)
23. Lazar, D., Chen, H., Wang, X., Zeldovich, N.: Why does cryptographic software fail? a case study and open problems. In: Proceedings of 5th Asia-Pacific Workshop on Systems, APSys 2014. Association for Computing Machinery, New York (2014)
24. Lenstra, A.K., Hughes, J.P., Augier, M., Bos, J.W., Kleinjung, T., Wachter, C.: Ron was wrong, whit is right. IACR Cryptol. ePrint Arch. 2012, 64 (2012)
25. Leurent, G., Peyrin, T.: Sha-1 is a shambles: First chosen-prefix collision on sha-1 and application to the PGP web of trust. In: 29th USENIX Security Symposium (USENIX Security 20), pp. 1839–1856. USENIX Association, August 2020. https://www.usenix.org/conference/usenixsecurity20/presentation/leurent
26. Li, J., Lin, Z., Caballero, J., Zhang, Y., Gu, D.: K-hunt: pinpointing insecure cryptographic keys from execution traces. In: Proceedings of the 2018 ACM SIGSAC Conference on Computer and Communications Security, CCS 2018, pp. 412–425. ACM, New York (2018)
27. Li, Y., Zhang, Y., Li, J., Gu, D.: iCryptoTracer: dynamic analysis on misuse of cryptography functions in iOS applications. In: Au, M.H., Carminati, B., Kuo, C.-C.J. (eds.) NSS 2014. LNCS, vol. 8792, pp. 349–362. Springer, Cham (2014). https://doi.org/10.1007/978-3-319-11698-3_27
28. McCulloch, W.S., Pitts, W.: A logical calculus of the ideas immanent in nervous activity. Bull. Math. Biophys. 5(4), 115–133 (1943)
29. Muslukhov, I., Boshmaf, Y., Beznosov, K.: Source attribution of cryptographic api misuse in android applications. In: Proceedings of the 2018 on Asia Conference on Computer and Communications Security, ASIACCS 2018, pp. 133–146. Association for Computing Machinery, New York (2018)
30. Nadi, S., Krüger, S., Mezini, M., Bodden, E.: Jumping through hoops: why do java developers struggle with cryptography apis? In: Proceedings of the 38th International Conference on Software Engineering, ICSE 2016, pp. 935–946. Association for Computing Machinery, New York (2016)
31. Nemec, M., Klinec, D., Svenda, P., Sekan, P., Matyas, V.: Measuring popularity of cryptographic libraries in internet-wide scans. In: Proceedings of the 33rd Annual Computer Security Applications Conference, ACSAC 2017, pp. 162–175. ACM, New York (2017)
32. OpenSSL: Bn_generate_prime (2021). https://www.openssl.org/docs/man1.1.1/man3/BN_generate_prime.html
33. Piccolboni, L., Di Guglielmo, G., Carloni, L.P., Sethumadhavan, S.: Crylogger: Detecting crypto misuses dynamically. In: Proceedings of the IEEE Symposium on Security and Privacy (S&P). IEEE (2021)
34. Python: The Lempel–Ziv–Markov chain (LZMA) compression algorithm. https://docs.python.org/3/library/lzma.html
35. Rahaman, S., et al.: Cryptoguard: high precision detection of cryptographic vulnerabilities in massive-sized java projects. In: Proceedings of the 2019 ACM SIGSAC Conference on Computer and Communications Security, CCS 2019, pp. 2455–2472. Association for Computing Machinery, New York (2019)
36. Seznec, A., Sendrier, N.: Havege: a user-level software heuristic for generating empirically strong random numbers. ACM Trans. Model. Comput. Simul. 13(4), 334–346 (2003)

37. Svenda, P., et al.: The million-key question—investigating the origins of RSA public keys. In: Proceedings of 25th USENIX Security Symposium (USENIX Security 16), pp. 893–910. USENIX Association, Austin, August 2016

38. ubld.it: TrueRNG. https://hackaday.io/project/630-truerng

39. Yilek, S., Rescorla, E., Shacham, H., Enright, B., Savage, S.: When private keys are public: results from the 2008 debian openssl vulnerability. In: Proceedings of the 9th ACM SIGCOMM Conference on Internet Measurement, IMC 2009, pp. 15–27. Association for Computing Machinery, New York (2009)

40. Yutaka, N.: NeuG: a true random number generator implementation. Tech. rep. (2015)

Network Security

Fine-Grained Intra-domain Bandwidth Allocation Against DDoS Attack

Lijia Xie[1,2,3], Shuang Zhao[4], Xiao Zhang[1,2,3(✉)], Yiming Shi[1,2,3], Xin Xiao[1,2,3], and Zhiming Zheng[1,2,3]

[1] LMIB and School of Mathematical Sciences, Beihang University, Beijing, China
{xielijia,xiao.zh,ymshi,xinxiao}@buaa.edu.cn, zzheng@pku.edu.cn
[2] Peng Cheng Laboratory, Shenzhen, China
[3] Beijing Advanced Innovation Center for Big Data and Brain Computing, Beihang University, Beijing, China
[4] China Academy of Information and Communications Technology, Beijing, China
zhaoshuang@caict.ac.cn

Abstract. Multiple bandwidth reservation mechanisms based on network capability have been proposed to resolve Distributed Denial of Service (DDoS) attacks towards the transit-link. However, previous capability-based techniques are insufficient to provide accurate protection towards legitimate users of contaminated domains. In this paper, we present FIBA, an intra-domain bandwidth allocation mechanism with fine-grained accessing control granularity. FIBA enables source domains to locally differentiate the capability requests by state measuring according to two attributing factors. Moreover, FIBA can establish hierarchical channels for capability requesting packets to realize the isolation of traffic from the same source domain. Our scheme is integrated with existing methods and can be optionally deployed by source domains. Finally, through network experiments, we evaluate FIBA can realize user-level DDoS protection even in 90%-contaminated domain.

Keywords: DDoS attack · Network capability · Fine-grained · Intra-domain · Bandwidth allocation

1 Introduction

A recent Neustar report (2020) [5] pointedly indicates that Distributed Denial of Service (DDoS) attacks, as a menace of network availability, are becoming increasingly intense and sophisticated. As the rapidly rising of attacking volume (up to 2.3 Tbps [4]) of transit-link flooding attack (e.g., coremelt and cross-fire attack [14,24]), how to avoid target network infrastructure collapsing has been a significant challenge. To mitigate a large-scale volumetric DDoS attack, researchers are actively exploring capability-based resource reservation mechanisms [7,28–32] to manage an effective admission control of transit-link.

An important issue is to select the *allocating granularity*. The *network capability*, which is constituted of a series of authentication tokens, enables legitimate

© ICST Institute for Computer Sciences, Social Informatics and Telecommunications Engineering 2021
Published by Springer Nature Switzerland AG 2021. All Rights Reserved
J. Garcia-Alfaro et al. (Eds.): SecureComm 2021, LNICST 398, pp. 399–417, 2021.
https://doi.org/10.1007/978-3-030-90019-9_20

pairs of end hosts to acquire a guaranteed accessing admission of prioritized bandwidth. In this way, DDoS prevention is realized through capability-based bandwidth allocation by degrading the malicious flows. However, massive attackers may send traffic to flood the capability-setup channel to prevent the legitimate pairs from obtaining capability, namely Denial of Capability (DoC) attacks. Fair resource allocation using granularity such as per-flow [28], per-user [29] is inadvisable, resulting in tragedy of the network-link commons [7]. Thus, recent approaches adopt Autonomous System (AS) as the allocating granularity to confine attacking effects in the source domain.

Several fine-grained inter-domain allocating techniques [30–32] aim to priovide differential bandwidth guarantees among heterogeneous ASes by domain characterizing. Tumbler [31] considers utilization and reputation to compute the allocation. D4 [32] employs a state-defined reservation by adding popularity and locality aspects. STBA [30] introduces the spreader metric to protect influential ASes. Nonetheless, the above domain-level bandwidth gurantee is necessary to protect legitimate ASes, but are insufficient to protect legitimate users within contaminated source ASes. Moreover, uncontaminated source ASes also needs differential accessing control to the internal users. To explain in more detail, if a source AS locally allocate resources to their internal end hosts by simple per-client fair sharing, it will lead to:

- inadequate protection to *legitimate users* (complying with the allocation) located in the same source AS with *attackers* (over-requesting/over-using) in an attacking scenario;
- unreasonable allocation between *active users* (with high bandwidth demand) and *ordinary users* (with medium bandwidth demand) in a normal scenario.

In this paper, we present FIBA, a fine-grained intra-domain bandwidth allocation mechanism with user-level DDoS resistance. The key insight of FIBA is to manage differential accessing control of network capability to intra-domain users by *state measurement* and *hierarchical channels*. Upon the domain-level allocation, source ASes locally perform the traffic control to their internal bandwidth-requesting entities. First, FIBA leverages the *allocating index* to quantitatively measure the state of each capability request to determine the accessing priority. Thus, we combine two key attributing factors to enforce the computation the allocating index according to the topological effects and traffic features, namely (1) centrality factor, and (2) legitimacy factor. The legitimate request from an active user tends to obtain a larger allocating index and vice versa. Based on the attributing factors, the source ASes maintain the periodical renewal of allocating index for each request. Then, FIBA enables transit ASes to build hierarchical channels for the multi-state capability requests by unspoofable accessing priority tag and weight-customized hierarchical queue. The bandwidth guarantees of legitimate users/attackers and active users/ordinary users can be differentiated due to their diverse allocating indexes. Futhermore, the user-level DDoS protection is realized by intra-domain traffic isolation.

Hereby, we list the main contributions of FIBA as follows.

- We propose FIBA, a novel capability-based DDoS protection that realizes intra-domain state measurement and fine-grained accessing control of capability. By measuring state, FIBA enables each user to obtain reasonable capability accessing priority (Sect. 3.2–3.4).
- Our scheme is built with hierarchical channel to separate multi-state capability requests. Through intra-domain traffic isolation, FIBA is able to provide user-level DDoS resistance upon the domain-level DDoS protection (Sect. 3.5–3.7).
- FIBA is established with existing network methods, protocols and cryptographic algorithms. We demonstrate the effectiveness of FIBA through multiple simulations (Sect. 4).

2   Problem Definition

2.1   Network and Threat Model

In this paper, our aim is to protect legitimate flows against the volumentric transit-link DDoS attack, in which the victim link is traversed by legitimate pairs (source-to-destination) and malicious pairs (bot-to-bot (e.g. Coremelt [24]) or bot-to-server (e.g. Crossfire [14])). Our DDoS prevention is established upon inter-domain capability-based bandwidth allocation [18,30–32], which is another active, but orthogonal problem to this paper.

Compling with the current network architectures, each user is managed by a certain domain (i.e., AS). The distribution of botnets is unlimited to launch the transit-link DDoS attack. In other words, any AS may be contaminated with an arbitrary proportion of malicious bots by sending large amounts of traffic (network capability requests and data packets) to congest the link and prevent legitimate pairs from acquiring bandwidth resource. And the attackers can flood the capability-setup channel or data-transmit channel, which corresponds to DoC attack and DDoS attack, respectively. However, the attack that misbehaving routers intentionally delay/drop packets is out of our scope. Note that the network links may fail, resulting in naturally loss of capability request packets or data packets.

2.2   Assumptions

We make the following assumptions. First, the bandwidth-requesting sources are able to acquire the AS-path to include the inter-domain path in the packet headers, which is feasible by several routing protocols (e.g. BGP [21] and Pathlet routing [11]). Second, every flow can be assigned a unique flow identifier and AS identifier (e.g., IP address [25] and Autonomous System Number (ASN) [1], respectively). Third, multiple approaches can be leveraged to make the flow identifier further non-hijackable [6,12] and the AS identifier further unforgettable [15,27]. In addition, the source AS can utilize traffic features to detect the attacking flows originated from malicious entities [16,26].

2.3 Desired Goals

Under the defined threat model, we specify the desired goals of fine-grained bandwidth reservation mechanism as follows.

- **User-level DDoS resistance.** The scheme should establish hierarchical channels for capability requesting packets to realize the traffic isolation between benign users and misbehaving users, even when they are from the same source AS.
- **Allocating reasonability.** Source domains are able to realize differential local intra-domain bandwidth allocation. Namely, the mechanism should be able to provide differential bandwidth guarantees for active users/ordinary users from a certain source domain.
- **Deployability.** The mechanism is able to be integrated with existing network protocols and cryptographic algorithms.

3 The Design of FIBA

In this section, we first give a overview to introduce the key insight of FIBA. Then we describe FIBA' s design of state measurement in detail. Finally, we present how FIBA processes with allocating index to achieve fine-grained accessing control by establishing hierarchical channels.

3.1 Overview

The overall goal of FIBA is to enforce fine-grained accessing control of network capability. The capability enables legitimate user pairs to acquire a guaranteed accessing admission of prioritized bandwidth. *Fine-grained* means that the source domain can differentially control the accessing priority of capability to its internal users. More specifically, FIBA manages differential accessing control by **state measurement** (in source ASes) and **hierarchical channels** (in transit ASes). Source ASes leverage state measuring to determine the accessing priority and tramit the information to transit ASes. Then thansit ASes can accordingly establish hierarchical channels for multi-state capability requests.

First, to quantitatively measure the state of capability request, source ASes calculate **allocating indexes** for the internal users by making use of two attributing factors: (1) **centrality** factor and (2) **legitimacy** factor. The allocating index describes the priority of accessing the target link. The two factors are related to normal scenario and attacking scenario. In normal scenario, FIBA employs the centrality factor to differentiate active users and ordinary users (Sect. 3.3). In attacking scenario, FIBA employs the legitimacy factor to differentiate legitimate users and attackers (Sect. 3.4). The centrality factor describes the spreading influence of an end host from the aspect of topological effects. The legitimacy factor describes whether the capability requesting flows is malicious from the aspect of traffic features. After the two-factor integration, source ASes are able to compute allocating indexes for every capability requests. Moreover, requests from the users that behave inactively or illegally will obtain low accessing priority with low allocated indexes. Then, the request packet is attached with an *accessing priority tag* (Sect. 3.5), which indicates the state of capability requests. By carrying the tag, source ASes are able to transmit the preference information to transit ASes.

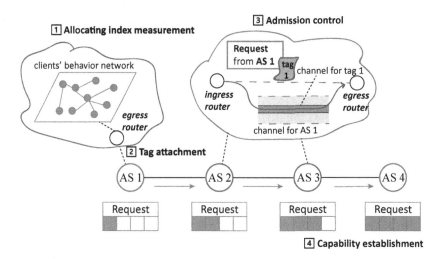

Fig. 1. The overview of FIBA. First, source ASes enforce the allocating index measurement by considering two attributing factors. Second, source ASes (blue) attach a suitable tag for each capability request. Third, transit ASes (green) leverage the hierarchical queue to execute the admission control for capability request. Finally, the capability initiated by bandwidth-requesting client is established hop-by-hop. (Color online figure)

Then, transit ASes establish hierarchical channels for multi-state capability requests. Specifically, transit ASes fair-queue the capability requests from multiple source ASes. Furthermore, according to the accessing priority tag, transit ASes will accordingly fair-queue the capability requests from the same source AS in sub-queues via the tags. The capability requests in different sub-queues are differentially processed. For instance, the sub-queue of requests possessing higher allocating indexes acquires a higher weight. Therefore, the accessing priority of diverse end hosts can be distinguished, even from the same source AS. In this way, transit ASes do not need to maintain allocating index information for every end host, which can greatly reduce storage costs.

Intuitively, the overall process of FIBA is shown as in Fig. 1. Based on aforementioned ideas, the fine-grained accessing control of network capability can be achieved: For each source AS, FIBA aims to establish hierarchical channels during capability establishment to differ the accessing priority for its internal users. Thanks to the state measurement for each capability request, the reasonable allocation is realized from two aspects. On the one hand, each benign user is able to be guaranteed with deserved accessing priority according to its centrality factor. Namely, the accessing priority of ordinary users is no more than active users from the same source AS. On the other hand, the attacking effects will be confined in the low-priority channel. With low legitimacy factor, attackers cannot compress the accessing priority of active legitimate users possessing high allocating indexes, even from the same source AS. Futhermore, if attackers flood the given link with low-rate attacking flows, FIBA can also confine the attacking effects through low centrality factor. Therefore, fine-grained accessing control of network capability is achieved.

Note that if a user is not satisfied with its accessing priority, the user can send a purchase request of premium service to its AS manager. The additional charge motivates source ASes to deploy FIBA. However, the premium service can only work for the centrality factor, not the legitimacy factor. Besides, if the source AS is weakly supervised and unable to deploy FIBA, transit ASes can also confine the attacking effects in the domain-level channel by deploying inter-domain allocation, not influencing other source ASes.

3.2 State Measurement by Allocating Index

To fine-grained reasonable bandwidth allocation, FIBA leverages the allocating index to numerically measure the state of each capability request. The allocating index is a one-byte parameter with a value between 0 and 255 (which can be extended). Users with a larger allocating index can get better accessing priority of capability.

Specifically, the allocating index (A) is constituted of centrality factor (C) and legitimacy factor (L).

- Centrality factor (C) is an attribute collected from the normal state of the request to represent activeness of the user. We define C as a one-byte parameter between 0 and 255.
- Legitimacy factor (L) is an attribute collected from the attacked state of the request to represent compliance of the user. We define L as a one-byte parameter between 0 and 255.

The combination of the two factors represents the state of capability-requesting packets. Source ASes locally calculate the user-level data packet allocating index for their internal clients based on topological effects from the user and traffic features from the data packet sent by the user. We denote $req_{i,j}$ as the jth capability-requesting packet sent by the user i. The allocating index of $req_{i,j}$ is calculated and updated by the egress router of the source AS where the user is located.

The allocating index reflects the state of each capability request. And the allocating index is utilized to determine the accessing priority levels. We now define the computation of allocating index $A_{i,j}$ of $req_{i,j}$ as:

$$A_{i,j} = \lceil xC_{i,j}^{\alpha} \cdot L_{i,j}^{1-\alpha} + (1-x)A_{i,j-1} \rceil, \tag{1}$$

where $C_{i,j}$ and $L_{i,j}$ are the centrality factor and legitimacy factor of $req_{i,j}$, $A_{i,j-1}$ is allocating index of last request packet $req_{i,j-1}$, and x $(0 < x < 1)$ is a constant smoothing factor. And α is an adjustable coefficient between 0 and 1. When the centrality and legitimacy factor become smaller, the corresponding allocating index will accordingly become smaller.

Note that users' state is dynamic, resulting in changeable centrality factor and legitimacy factor. Thus, source ASes can periodically update two attributing factors and allocating index. For example, the update period can be set to 30 s by default. According to the allocating index, the state of request packets is quantitatively measured in each source AS. On the basis of allocating index, how to differ the accessing priority of capability request is described with detail in Sect. 3.5 and Sect. 3.6.

3.3   Centrality Factor Calculation

We determine the users' centrality factor according to the *spreading influence* collected from the normal state of the users. The end hosts utilize bandwidth to process information dissemination with each other. The remove of structural nodes (called spreaders) will have a strong impact on information spreading capability in the behavioral network [19]. Thereby, in order to perform reasonable bandwidth allocation, FIBA leverages the thought of spreading influence to estimate the activeness of end hosts. Users with strong spreading influence deserve a greater bandwidth demand, and users with weak spreading influence deserve a smaller bandwidth demand. In FIBA, the allocated bandwidth is proportional to the spreading influence.

Then, the problem is how to efficiently evaluate the spreading influence of end hosts with acceptable computational costs. In information network, multiple centrality approaches are used for topological effects measurement and spreader identification. Inspired by this, we employ the topological characteristics of users to measure the spreading influence. The topological characteristics of users within the AS are different, resulting in different spreading influence of users. Intuitively, users with higher topological centrality will be connected to more users or routers. For the measurement of node users' spreading influence, academia has proposed multiple calculation methods (e.g., degree centrality [9], k-shell centrality [17], betweenness centrality [10]). Among those, several centrality methods are easy-to-compute, yet effective and local, which are suitable for FIBA state measurement. In our simulation, we simply select degree centrality as a measure of the spreading influence (SI_i) of user node i.

To obtain the centrality factor $C_{i,j}$ of $req_{i,j}$, we specify the calculation as:

$$C_{i,j} = \lceil 255 \cdot \frac{SI_i}{max(SI_i)} \rceil, \tag{2}$$

where $max(SI_i)$ is the maximum value SC_i of the users in the source AS where the user is located. Note that the centrality factor computed for the capability-requesting packet sent by the same user i is consistent. Moreover, considering the connections of end hosts in the network can be disconnected and reconnected, the network topology is dynamic and changeable. Source ASes periodically update the centrality factors of users based on the dynamic topology.

Consequently, in FIBA, active users with strong spreading influence can get more bandwidth guarantee than ordinary users, maximizing the information dissemination of behavioral network and ensuring reasonable bandwidth allocation.

3.4   Legitimacy Factor Calculation

We determine the legitimacy factor according to the malicious behavior information collected from the the users. The distribution of bot hosts within the AS is uneven. Previous mechanisms enable the transit ASes to isolate the traffic from uncontaminated ASes and contaminated ASes. Likewise, it is necessary to classify the benign users and attackers within a contaminated AS to guarantee the bandwidth allocation of legitimate users. The goal of legitimacy factor is to control the traffic flooding by limiting the bandwidth allocation of malicious bots. To do this, the packets flow of end hosts are evaluated to determine maliciousness of users. Therefore, FIBA defines the legitimacy factor as a one-byte number to reflect whether the user over-requests or over-uses, namely compliance.

Several detections are proposed to employ traffic features to distinguish the attacking flows from the normal flows [13,16,18,26]. In FIBA, the traffic features of packets are used to observe the abnormality of the data packets and estimate the legitimacy factor. According to those attacking flow identification methods, FIBA extracts five features, namely *packetCount*, *byteCount*, *durationSeconds*, *ipv4_src*, *ipv4_dst*, to distinguish legal packets and malicious packets. Based on these features, the scoring of data packets is achieved [13,16]. And we use $m_{i,j}$ to denote the attacking score obtained by $req_{i,j}$, which is a number between 0 and 1. Misbehaving flows will obtain higher attacking scores than legitimate flows. During a period of time, when data packets pass through the egress router, the egress router will extract the attributes of the data packets to perform statistical analysis. Then the legitimacy factor $L_{i,j}$ of $req_{i,j}$ is calculated according to the score as the following.

$$L_{i,j} = \lceil 255 \cdot \frac{1}{m_{i,j}} \rceil. \tag{3}$$

However, the above method may misidentify slight legitimate requests as attacking requests, which is acceptable. Once the users of those flows decreases the request rate, the mistake can be eliminated. Note that statistical analysis is an optional technique here. Source AS can use additional techniques to improve the accuracy of malicious flow identification and we leave it as a future work.

3.5   Accessing Priority Tags

To distinguish the accessing priority of network capability, source ASes attach adaptable tags for the capability requests originated from the internal users. First, according to the allocating indexes, the source AS determines how many types of tags to be set. Note that the distribution of allocating index is non-uniform. Temporally, the internal users of the source ASes maintains dynamic allocating index. Spatially, even in a same source AS, the disparity of centrality factor and legitimacy factor leads to the heterogeneous allocating index. Hence, FIBA involves the definition of network heterogeneity [23] to termly measure the heterogeneity of allocating index.

$$H(\{A_{i,j}\}) = \frac{\sqrt{Variance(A_{i,j})}}{Average(A_{i,j})}, \tag{4}$$

where $A_{i,j}$ is an array of set $\{A_{i,j}\}$ containing the allocating indexes of capability-requesting flows in the source AS. If the source AS obtains a higher heterogeneity, the number of tags' types will be greater to explicitly differentiate the capability request from various user entities.

Next, the source AS adds a tag t for every capability request to indicate the state according to its allocating index (e.g., $t = 1/2/3$ for low/medium/high accessing priority). The source AS can optionally transform the threshold determination for multi-state tags into an optimization problem[1]. Upon receipt of the tags, how the transit AS differs the accessing priority will be demonstrated in Sect. 3.6. Besides, if the heterogeneity of allocating index is small or the number of capability requests is relatively slight, the source AS can simplify the tag as $t = 0$ for all request flows. And when transit AS receives overmuch capability requests from a source AS, the transit AS will send a *tag-request* to request the source AS for multi-state tags. However, if the source AS refuses to deploy multi-tag, transit ASes can also confine the attacking effects in the domain-level channel by deploying inter-domain allocation, not influencing other source ASes. However, attackers may attempt to modify/replay the accessing priority tags on the path from source AS to transit AS. And we will specify how to prevent the modification/replay attacks in Sect. 3.7.

3.6   Hierarchical Queueing

End hosts initiate capability request to access the guaranteed link. However, attackers can over-request to overwhelm the requests from benign users. In order to prevent attackers from overwhelming legitimate requests, transit ASes establish isolated channel for each source AS. Each capability request is placed into a separate queue whose weight could be adjusted by the transit AS according to its preference. Nonetheless, the attackers can still overwhelm the legitimate requests from the attackers' source AS. The reason is that the benign requests and attacking requests from a certain source AS will share a same queue.

In this way, the source ASes are motivated to control the outgoing traffic to enforce local management. However, rate limiting simply on the egress router of source AS is not advisable. In FIBA, we leverage hierarchical fair-queue [8] to isolate the traffic. We demonstrate the queue management in Fig. 2. Transit ASes queue the packets according to the AS identifier and tag after receiving the

---

[1] For example, 2-state tag problem is to find an interger number a to minimize $H(\{A_{i,j}|A_{i,j} \le a\}) + H(\{A_{i,j}|A_{i,j} > a\})$. Also, the source AS can determine by itself.

capability request. The AS identifier and tag are used to identify the first-level queue and second-level queue, respectively. Therefore, if the attackers launch a DoC attack by sending a large number of requests, the misbehaving requests will be put into the sub-queue with low priority due to their low legitimacy factor. While the requests from active benign users are put into sub-queue with high priority, the accessing priority of legitimate users will not be influenced. Based on the hierarchical channel, transit ASes can filter unwanted requests flow according to its capacity. Moreover, transit ASes can adjust the weights of first-level queues and second-level queues and reallocate the unoccupied sub-queues.

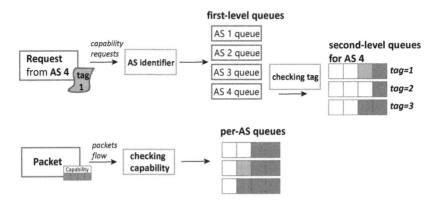

Fig. 2. Queue management at a ingress router of transit ASes. The blue block is occupied by precious packets. The orange block represents the newly added packet. The request from AS 4 with $t = 1$ is added in subqueue of tag 1 for AS 4 for AS 4. Regular packets with associated capabilities receive preferential forwarding through prioritized per-AS queue. Legacy traffic competes for best-effort bandwidth.

3.7 Capability Requesting

As described in Sect. 3.5, the egress router of a request packet's source AS adds its accessing priority tag into the packet header. Hence, the capability request can be comprised of five components:

$$req = bw \parallel exp \parallel AS\_ID \parallel flow\_id \parallel t. \tag{5}$$

Thereinto, bw is requested bandwidth amount of the user. And exp is expiration time of the requested capability. Then, AS_ID and $flow\_id$, as our assumptions, are the AS identifier and flow identifier, respectively. Besides, t is accessing priority tag of the request according to its allocating index.

However, the basic capability request may be modified or replayed by on-path attackers as in Fig. 3. To solve this problem, the source AS can simply add a digital signature to authenticate the tag. Nonetheless, the per-packet digital signature will incur significant computational overhead. Instead, to counter these attacks, FIBA leverages Message Authentication Code (MAC) as authentication of the requests' tags.

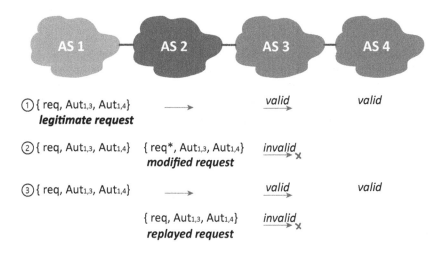

Fig. 3. The authentication process of priority access tags. The clients from AS 1 initiates a capability request. AS 2 is compromised by attackers, which is able to modify the tag of request or replay a request with high-priority tag. AS 3 can authenticate that the initial request from AS 1 is valid and the modified/replayed request is invalid.

To construct a unspoofable accessing priority tag, the source AS and the deployed transit AS first establish a shared secret key, which is viable by Diffie-Hellman algorithm. In FIBA, we assume each AS could obtain and authenticate the public keys of other ASes from a trusted certificate authority (e.g., ICANN [22]). In this way, AS i can generate a public/private key pair as (a_i, b_i). AS i and AS j can calculate their shared secret key as $k_{i,j} = a_i^{b_j} = a_j^{b_i}$.

When the source AS sends the request packet, the authentication MAC will be attached in the packet header. And the authentication MAC can be computed with the following equation.

$$Aut_{i,j} = MAC_{k_{i,j}}(req). \tag{6}$$

After receiving the request, transit AS verifies the authentication MAC using the authentication key. Moreover, the generation of authentication MAC includes the expiration time exp to prevent the replay attack. Therefore, the transit AS is able to acquire a unspoofable tag to accurately queue for capability requests.

If the request is approved, the transit AS and the destination AS will compute a cryptographic token to compose the final network capability (similar to [7,30,31]).

$$tok_j = MAC_{k_j}(tok_{j-1} \parallel req), \tag{7}$$

where k_j is the secret key of the AS j, and Tok_{j-1} is cryptographic token generated by the last-hop AS $j-1$ of AS j. The established capability is forwarded back to the end host in source AS. By carrying the capability, the subsequent flows from the client receive preferential forwarding via prioritized bandwidth channel.

4   Evaluation

We evaluate the performance of FIBA using Bene [2] in this section. And we mainly consider two scenarios: (1) both benign clients and attackers compete for bandwidth requesting (attacking); and (2) only legitimate users compete for bandwidth requesting (normal). The attacking scenario is set to verify user-level DDoS resistance. The normal scenario is set to verify allocating reasonability.

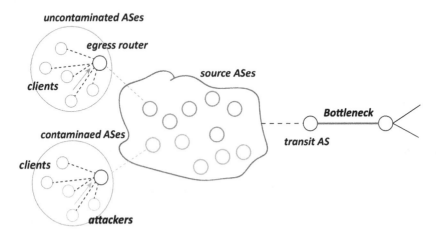

Fig. 4. The network topology of two scenarios.

Without loss of generality, we first demonstrate the network topology of two scenarios as in Fig. 4. We employ a real domain-level network topology from CAIDA AS-relationship dataset [3]. From the constructed topology, we select a link between two high-degree transit ASes as the bottleneck and we randomly select several leaf ASes as the source ASes. The capability request is originated from a certain source AS to request the link access of the bottleneck link. And we consider all source ASes can be deployed with FIBA mechanism. Namely, every source AS is able to measure the allocating index and attach a corresponding tag for the request. The uncontaminated ASes and contaminated ASes are randomly selected from leaf ASes. The end hosts in uncontaminated ASes are all benign users, while the contaminated ASes can include benign clients and attackers simultaneously. And there are 220 end hosts in every source AS.

Besides, we set the coefficient α as 0.2 for each source AS. And the egress routers of source ASes attach *high* tag for packets with allocating index over 128, *low* tag for packets with allocating index less than 108, and *medium* tag for the remaining. In the transit AS, the types of sub-queues is accordingly set as 3: high, medium and low. The weights of three sub-queues is set as 60% for *high* tag queue, 30% for *medium* tag queue and 10% for *low* tag queue. Note that all the aforementioned parameters can be adaptively adjusted. In our experiment, the capacity of bottleneck is set as 9.6 Gbps. Thereinto, 5% of the bandwidth (480

Mbps) is used for capability request. The size of each request packet is fixed as 1 KB. Moreover, in the domain-level, we simply set same share of per-AS bandwidth reservation for multiple source ASes.

4.1 Domain-Level DDoS Resistance

First, we consider the scenario that attackers flood the capability-setup channel by over-requesting the capability. The goal of this experiment is to mainly evaluate the impact of legitimacy factor. In the 10-min simulation, 100 legitimate ASes and 500 contaminated ASes send the bandwidth-requesting packets. And inside the contaminated ASes, there are benign end hosts and attacking end hosts. The number of attackers in each contaminated AS is increasing from 20 to 200. On average, benign users approximately send 1 request per minute, while attackers send 10 requests per second.

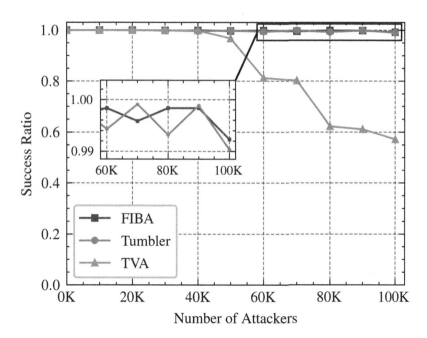

Fig. 5. Comparative simulation results (the average successful ratio of legitimate ASes) for Tumbler, TVA, and FIBA against DoC attack.

According to the above settings, we compare the successful ratio of capability requests from the legitimate ASes with two representative schemes (Tumbler [31] and TVA [29]). Figure 5 presents the change of successful ratio of three approaches. As the number of bots increases, FIBA and Tumbler can maintain the bandwidth guarantee of bottleneck link for legitimate ASes while the curve of TVA witnesses a descent. The slight fluctuation of FIBA and Tumbler is resulted from naturally loss of packets. Due to a per-AS share strategy, FIBA and Tumbler can establish isolated requesting channels for legitimate ASes. Therefore, even with the explosively increasing of requests from contaminated AS, the requests from the legitimate ASes can be processed by the transit AS.

However, the performance of TVA decreases because of the fair queueing approach based on the path-identifier during the capability establishment. The distances of source ASes are diverse in our simulation. When the path length rises, the requests from remote source ASes will be put into high-level queue. Hence, the link share of remote legitimate ASes is influenced when abundant requests flood the bottleneck. In consequence, FIBA is able to hold the domain-level DDoS resistance.

4.2   User-Level DDoS Resistance

Next, we evaluate the performance of FIBA in user-level DDoS resistance and we focus on the internal allocation in a contaminated AS in FIBA. According to aforementioned experimental settings, we compare the success ratios of legitimate users and attackers in the contaminated ASes and success ratios of uncontaminated ASes.

As observed from Fig. 7, only the success ratio of attackers are decreasing. The dash line indicates the success ratio of legitimate users from contaminated AS in simple per-client fair sharing scheme. Hence, in simple per-client fair sharing scheme, legitimate users from contaminated AS are influenced by attackers. However, FIBA, the curves of legitimate users from both contaminated ASes and uncontaminated ASes are almost 1, while the curve of legitimate users from contaminated AS is marginally lower than uncontaminated AS. The benign users in uncontaminated AS can establish capability with the help of isolated channel for its source AS. And FIBA hierarchical channels contributes to independent channels for benign users in contaminated AS, confining the attacking effects in the *low* tag channel.

To give an intuitive demonstration, we present the distribution of end hosts of source ASes in Fig. 6. The histogram represents the number of different allocating index of users. The curve indicates the Cumulative Distribution Function (CDF) of allocating index in uncontaminated ASes and contaminated ASes. From the Fig. 6, we can observe the dynamic change of clients' distribution as the proportion of attackers increases. Besides, due to the legitimacy factor, almost all of requests from attackers are attached with *low* tags.

Thereby, even in a 90%-contaminated AS, the legitimate users can be identified and guaranteed with deserved bandwidth. Meanwhile, the misbehaving users are controlled by limiting the success ratio (down to about 50%) of over-requesting packets. In a nutshell, FIBA performs the user-level DDoS resistance upon domain-level DDoS resistance by achieving the traffic isolation between legitimate users and attackers from a source AS.

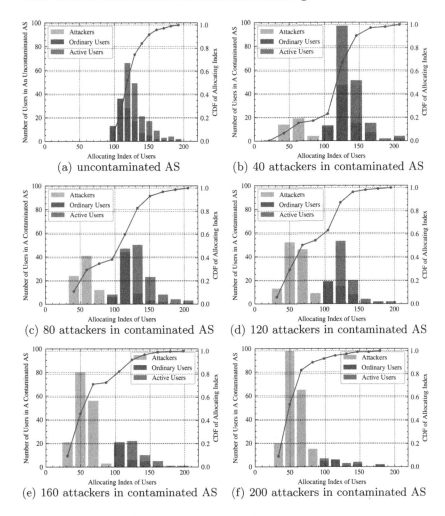

Fig. 6. The allocating index distribution of end hosts in source ASes. The blue and green histogram represents for benign users (ordinary users and active users), and the orange histogram represents for attackers. (Color figure online)

4.3 Allocating Reasonability

In this experiment, we then evaluate that FIBA can allocate different share for diverse legitimate users to realize reasonable bandwidth guarantee. We randomly select 1000 leaf ASes as the source ASes to send the capability request. According to above settings, the source AS divide the legitimate users into *high* tag (active users) and *medium* tag (ordinary users). Per-user sending rate of capability request ranges from 2 packet/s to 10 packet/s. We observe the average successful ratio of capability requesting in 10-min experiment.

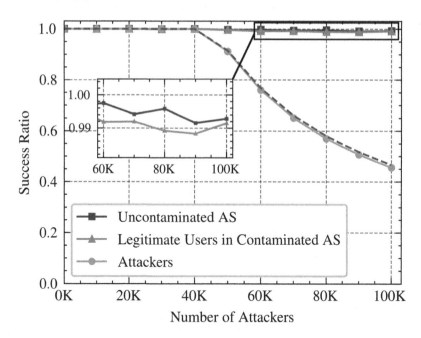

Fig. 7. The average successful ratio of the end hosts from source ASes of FIBA in an attacking scenario.

In Fig. 8, as with the increasing of number of the capability request packets, the successful ratios of both tags' requests witness a decline trend. The dash line is the average successful ratio in per-client fair sharing scheme. The curve of high-tag is consistently higher than the curve of medium-tag, which indicates the requests in high-queue obtain more bandwidth guarantee. Thus, if the end hosts from a legitimate AS maintain prioritized bandwidth demand for capability, the transit AS tends to preferentially process the request from active users with high centrality factor. In addition, as in Fig. 6 (blue and green histogram), the contaminated AS can also perform differential accessing control for legitimate users. Thereby, FIBA can achieve reasonable allocation by providing differential local intra-domain bandwidth guarantees for active users and ordinary users.

5   Related Work

To mitigate DDoS attack, the concept of network capability was proposed, which is an access authentication token related to the access authority. The packets with associated capabilities can transmit data with high priority. With this method, capability-based mechanisms can protect the normal access of legitimate traffic.

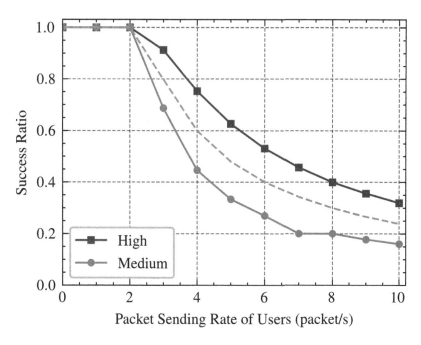

Fig. 8. The average successful ratio of the legitimate end hosts in a normal scenario.

An important part of the capability-based DDoS defense scheme is the research from the perspective of granularity (per-user [29], per-flow [28], per-computation [20], and per-AS [7,18,30,31]). SIFF [28] issues capability in per-flow granularity, and monitors the status of each flow to block or allow issuance. TVA [29] uses WF²Q+ to process the queues hierarchically, and uses specific routers on the ingress interface to receive and forward traffic with different priority traffic. Portcullis [20] employs proof-of-work to achieve per-computation granularity allocation. Floc [18] differentiates between legitimate and attack flows for a target link. However, Floc is too coarse-grained to differentiate low-rate attacking flows and DoC attack is not considered. SIBRA [7] prioritizes bandwidth to achieve fair bandwidth allocation. SIBRA achieves botnet-size independence together with the scalability of inter-domain resources. Tumbler [31] regards each AS as a unit to allocate bandwidth in its domain on demand, calculates the competition factor considering domain characteristics, and then uses the inter-domain queue to control the packet sending speed. STBA [30] proposes a spatio-temporal heterogeneous bandwidth allocation mechanism, which introduces superspreaders sub-metrics to discriminate the influence of ASes to ensure the bandwidth connection capability of influential ASes.

In addition, several approaches aim to identify and detect DDoS traffic. PacketScore [16] performs statistical analysis to score data packets based on the characteristics of data packets. To distinguish the data packets, PacketScore sets a baseline for data packets to classify the malicious traffic. ScoreforCore[13] proposes a dynamic selection attribute model for different attack types on the basis of PacketScore. However, the false positives are unavoidable in detection mechanisms. Thus, FIBA provides the malevolent-looking packets with low priority queue rather than simply filtering them.

6   Conclusion

We have proposed FIBA, a capability-based DDoS mitigation that realizes fine-grained intra-domain bandwidth allocation. According to the topological effects and traffic features, FIBA measures the state of request packets among diverse clients during capability establishment. FIBA is built with hierarchical channel to achieve differential accessing control of capability and traffic isolation. Upon the domain-level DDoS resistance, FIBA is able to provide a fine-grained protection and user-level DDoS resistance. Through comprehensive network experiments, we verify the performance of FIBA in terms of reasonable bandwidth reservation and user-level DDoS resistance.

Acknowledgement. This work is supported by National Key Research and Development Program of China (2020YFB1005702).

References

1. Autonomous system numbers (2016). http://www.iana.org/assignments/as-numbers/as-numbers.xhtml
2. Bene: A python network simulator (2017). https://github.com/zappala/bene
3. AS relationships (2020). https://www.caida.org/data/as-relationships/
4. AWS said it mitigated a 2.3 Tbps DDoS attack, the largest ever, June 2020. https://www.zdnet.com/article/aws-said-it-mitigated-a-2-3-tbps-ddos-attack-the-largest-ever/
5. DDoS attacks rise in intensity, sophistication and volume, September 2020. https://www.helpnetsecurity.com/2020/09/17/ddos-attacks-rise-in-intensity-sophistication-and-volume/
6. Andersen, D.G., Balakrishnan, H., Feamster, N., Koponen, T., Shenker, S.: Accountable internet protocol (aip). In: Proceedings of the ACM SIGCOMM 2008 Conference on Applications, Technologies, Architectures, and Protocols for Computer Communications, Seattle, 17–22, August 2008
7. Basescu, C., et al.: SIBRA: scalable internet bandwidth reservation architecture. In: Proceedings NDSS, San Diego, February 2016
8. Bennett, J.C.R., Zhang, H.: Hierarchical packet fair queueing algorithms. IEEE/ACM Trans. Netw. 5(5), 675–689 (2002)
9. Bonacich, P.: Factoring and weighting approaches to status scores and clique identification. J. Math. Soc. 2(1), 113–120 (1972)
10. Estrada, E., Rodriguez-Velazquez, J.A.: Subgraph centrality in complex networks. Phys. Rev. E Stat. Nonlin. Soft Matter Phys. 71(5), 056103 (2005)
11. Godfrey, P., Ganichev, I., Shenker, S., Stoica, I.: Pathlet routing. ACM SIGCOMM Comput. Commun. Rev. 39(4), 111–122 (2009)

12. Heer, H.: Host identity protocol certificates draft-ietf-hip-cert-12. Technology (2011)
13. Kalkan, K., Alagöz, F.: A distributed filtering mechanism against DDoS attacks. Comput. Netw. **108**, 199–209 (2016). https://doi.org/10.1016/j.comnet.2016.08.023
14. Kang, M.S., Lee, S.B., Gligor, V.D.: The crossfire attack. In: Proceedings IEEE S&P, pp. 127–141, Berkeley, May 2013
15. Kim, T.H.J., Basescu, C., Jia, L., Lee, S.B., Hu, Y.C., Perrig, A.: Lightweight source authentication and path validation. In: Proceedings ACM SIGCOMM, pp. 271–282, Chicago, August 2014
16. Kim, Y., Lau, W.C., Chuah, M.C., Chao, H.J.: Packetscore: a statistics-based packet filtering scheme against distributed denial-of-service attacks. IEEE Trans. Dependable Secure Comput. **3**(2), 141–155 (2006)
17. Kitsak, M., et al.: Identification of influential spreaders in complex networks. Nat. Phys. **6**, 888–893 (2010)
18. Lee, S.B., Gligor, V.D.: Floc : dependable link access for legitimate traffic in flooding attacks. In: IEEE International Conference on Distributed Computing Systems (2010)
19. Morone, F., Makse, H.A.: Influence maximization in complex networks through optimal percolation. Nature **524**(7563), 65 (2015)
20. Parno, B., Wendlandt, D., Shi, E., Perrig, A., Maggs, B., Hu, Y.C.: Portcullis: protecting connection setup from denial-of-capability attacks. ACM SIGCOMM Comput. Commun. Rev. **37**(4), 289–300 (2007). https://doi.org/10.1145/1282427.1282413
21. Rekhter, Y., Li, T.: A border gateway protocol 4 (BGP-4). RFC 1771, March 1995
22. Rouse, M.: ICANN (Internet Corporation for Assigned Names and Numbers) (2016). http://searchsoa.techtarget.com/definition/ICANN
23. Steve, H., Jun, D.: Understanding network concepts in modules. BMC Syst. Biol. **1**(1), 24 (2007)
24. Studer, A., Perrig, A.: The coremelt attack. In: Backes, M., Ning, P. (eds.) ESORICS 2009. LNCS, vol. 5789, pp. 37–52. Springer, Heidelberg (2009). https://doi.org/10.1007/978-3-642-04444-1_3
25. Touch, J.: Updated specification of the IPv4 ID field. RFC 6864, February 2013
26. Xiao, P., Li, Z., Qi, H., Qu, W., Yu, H.: An efficient DDoS detection with bloom filter in SDN. In: 2016 IEEE Trustcom/BigDataSE/ISPA, pp. 1–6. IEEE (2016)
27. Xie, L., Zhang, Y., Zheng, Z., Zhang, X.: TRIP: a tussle-resistant internet pricing mechanism. IEEE Commun. Lett. **21**(2), 270–273 (2017)
28. Yaar, A., Perrig, A., Song, D.: SIFF: a stateless internet flow filter to mitigate DDoS flooding attacks. In: IEEE Symposium on Security and Privacy, 2004. Proceedings, 2004, pp. 130–143 (2004)
29. Yang, X., Wetherall, D., Anderson, T.: Tva: a dos-limiting network architecture. IEEE ACM Trans. Netw. **16**(6), 1267–1280 (2008)
30. Zhang, X., Xie, L., Yao, W.: Spatio-temporal heterogeneous bandwidth allocation mechanism against DDoS attack. J. Netw. Comput. Appl. **162**, 102658 (2020)
31. Zhang, Y., Wang, X., Perrig, A., Zheng, Z.: Tumbler: adaptable link access in the bots-infested internet. Comput. Netw. **105**, 180–193 (2016)
32. Zhang, Y., Xie, L., Zhang, D., Liu, G., Wang, Q.: Scalable bandwidth allocation based on domain attributes: towards a DDoS-resistant data center. In: Proceedings IEEE GLOBECOM, pp. 1–6, Singapore, December 2017

TMT-RF: Tunnel Mixed Traffic Classification Based on Random Forest

Panpan Zhao[1,2], Gaopeng Gou[1,2], Chang Liu[1,2], Yangyang Guan[1,2], Mingxin Cui[1,2], and Gang Xiong[1,2(✉)]

[1] Institute of Information Engineering, Chinese Academy of Sciences, Beijing, China
{zhaopanpan,gougaopeng,liuchang,guanyangyang,cuimingxin,
xionggang}@iie.ac.cn
[2] School of Cyber Security, University of Chinese Academy of Sciences, Bejing, China

Abstract. With the explosive growth of the use of tunnels, network anomaly detection and security management are facing huge challenges, of which the first and an important step is tunnel traffic classification. Previous research on the classification of encrypted traffic is mainly based on machine learning methods using statistical features and deep learning methods using packet arrival time and packet length sequence. However, these works mainly focus on the identification of single application traffic. In a real scenario where a single user uses a tunnel, the traffic within a time may contain multiple applications. Due to the tunnel traffic has the same five-tuple, we can't get the start and end times of each application. Compared with encrypted application traffic classification, it is more difficult to identify applications in tunnels. In this paper, firstly we propose a TMT-RF framework to identify two mixed applications in IPSec tunnels. Then we introduce the first use of NoiseSplit module to split the traffic and then use a CombineBurst module for the second split. Finally, we collected four mixed traffic data sets of three types to evaluate our proposed method. Experimental results demonstrate that TMT-RF not only achieves a splitting accuracy of 93% in positive-time separation applications, but also outperforms other state-of-the-art methods on the data sets for zero-time separation applications and negative-time separation applications.

Keywords: Traffic classification · IPSec tunnel · Machine learning

1 Introduction

With the development of the Internet, the volume of encrypted network traffic is growing rapidly. Due to the encapsulation and encryption characteristics of tunnel traffic, it occupies a large part of the encrypted traffic [18]. More and more users use tunnel technology to protect the security of communication [4,12]. While the tunnel technology guarantees communication security, it also brings challenges to network management. According to Gartner's 2020 report

© ICST Institute for Computer Sciences, Social Informatics and Telecommunications Engineering 2021
Published by Springer Nature Switzerland AG 2021. All Rights Reserved
J. Garcia-Alfaro et al. (Eds.): SecureComm 2021, LNICST 398, pp. 418–437, 2021.
https://doi.org/10.1007/978-3-030-90019-9_21

[26], 70% of malicious network services bypass firewalls and intrusion detection systems through encryption and tunneling technology. Therefore, tunnel traffic identification is important in the network security and network management domain [1,2,5,15,16,24].

Prior studies have proposed some methods of encrypted traffic identification which is mainly divided into methods based on machine learning [8,14,17] and deep learning [11,28]. The machine learning method mainly extracts the following traffic features from the encrypted traffic, such as the first n packet length sequence with direction [17], packet length statistical characteristics [8] and statistical characteristics of packet arrival time interval [14]. Deep learning methods such as convolutional auto-encoding and convolutional neural networks are used for encrypted traffic classification [11].

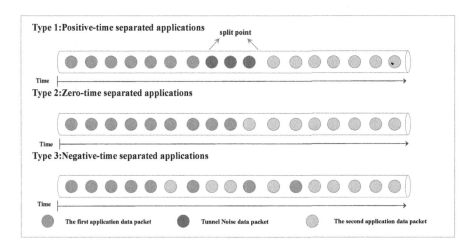

Fig. 1. Three types of mixed traffic in a tunnel

Mixed encrypted application traffic can be identified by flow classification because each application traffic has a different five-tuple (source IP, destination IP, source port, destination port, IP version). However, it is a challenging task to identify tunnel traffic accurately and efficiently. Firstly, the application traffic is encapsulated and encrypted in tunnels, and great improvements have been made to the original feature details [21]. Moreover, the application traffic in a tunnel has the same five-tuple [9], it is difficult to find the start and end time of the application. The encrypted traffic classification methods cannot be directly used to classify tunnel traffic. Secondly, there is a great difference in the mixture of tunnel traffic. The outcome of the classification is influenced by the form and overlap rate of the mixture.

Recently, researchers have proposed some methods for the classification of mixed websites on Tor which first split the mixed flow into a single flow, and then use the existing encrypted traffic classification model to classify the single flow. Splitting the mixed stream is mainly to find the split point. These methods propose to use data packet arrival time interval [29] and packet direction [6] characteristics, and feed these characteristics into KNN, Hidden Markov Model to identify split points [30]. The recognition result of the split points are affected by the mixed format and mixed rate of the applications.

In this paper, we propose a traffic classification method in a scenario where a single user using lots of different applications in an IPSec tunnel, relaxing the single application assumption. Figure 1 illustrates the terminology and scenario of this paper. For the first type of traffic, we try to find the split point and then classify the application traffic. We no longer seek to find the split point for the second and third forms of traffic but we split the mixed flow into many segments according to certain laws to classify the application traffic. To develop a successful tunnel traffic classification method, we make the following novel contributions:

- We innovatively propose a **framework** for identifying mixed traffic in IPSec tunnels, which can realize the classification of mixed traffic in a single user using many different applications scenarios. The framework specifically includes two split modules and a classification module. This is the first study to achieve the classification of mixed applications traffic in IPSec tunnels.
- A **module** to identify positive-time separated applications (Type 1). We propose a splitting algorithm based on the combination of packet length threshold and classifier. The results show that the splitting accuracy reaches 93%. Compared with processing without this module, our classification accuracy has been improved by 30%.
- A **module** to identify applications with zero-time separated (Type 2) and negative-time separated (Type 3). We propose a classification algorithm which uses a splitting algorithm to split the network data stream into several segments, and then predicts each segment, ignoring the impact of overlapping parts on application identification. Experiments show that the module achieves the best performance on overlapping data sets and is better than the most advanced methods (Sectioning).
- A **playback** method for labeling of mixed traffic in IPSec tunnels. Using this method, three types of mixed traffic in the tunnel are generated: positive-time separation applications traffic, zero-time separation applications traffic, and negative-time separation applications traffic.

The remaining of the paper are organized as follows. Section 2 reviews the related works. Then, Sect. 3 presents the two proposed algorithm models in detail. Section 4 describes the data collection process. Section 5 displays the experimental result. Finally, the paper is concluded in Sect. 6.

2   Related Work

Many researchers have proposed a wealth of encrypted traffic analysis methods, such as, based on machine learning and deep learning. Recent researchers have also proposed many methods for identifying mixed traffic on Tor. Next, we will introduce these three parts in detail.

2.1 Machine-Learning-Based Methods

In 2014, based on the burst feature and Haar feature, Shi et al. [22] used Bayesian networks to achieve 96.7% of dynamic pages and 97.8% of static pages. Faiz et al. [14] employed a set of Flow Spatio-Temporal Features (FSTF) to six well-known classifiers and the boosting technique consistently performed the best on all the given datasets using the FSTF. The results show that the classification accuracy of VoIP traffic is above 98.5%.

Meng et al.[17] selected 8 consecutive data packets after the tcp connection is established as the feature, such as packet length, packet time interval and packet direction, to describe network traffic using five algorithms: svm, c4.5, k-means, bayes and EM. They achieved an accuracy of 94.5% and described three types of traffic including http over ssh, ftp over ssh, scp and sftp using k-means. Alice et al. [8] used svm and gmm algorithms to select the first n directional packet length sequences of each ssh flow, and the accuracy of the two classification methods was 71.5% for seven types of traffic. Ding et al. [7] used 20-dimensional packet length and packet time statistical characteristics to describe network traffic using the c4.5 algorithm, which achieved an accuracy rate of 95.3%. The described http traffic includes http, smtp over http, and p2p over http.

2.2 Deep-Learning-Based Methods

He et al. [13] converted the payload of the data packet into a grayscale image and then classified it through a convolutional neural network. The classification accuracy of the five applications reached 98.5%. Vu et al. [27] developed a novel time-series feature extraction technique. The proposed method consists of two main steps. First, A feature engineering technique to extract significant attributes of the encrypted network traffic behavior through analyzing the time series of receiving packets. In the second step, a deep learning technique is developed to exploit the advantage of time series data samples in providing a strong representation of the encrypted network applications. Guo et al. [11] preprocessed the network traffic of six applications into conversation pictures, and then used convolutional auto-encoding and convolutional neural network algorithms. The accuracy rate of the algorithm classification based on cnn was 92.92%.

Zhou et al. [32] classified vpn and non-vpn traffic by using entropy estimation, and then used convolutional neural networks for further classification. The input of the convolutional neural network was packet length, packet time interval, and packet direction. Ali et al. [20] presented an end-to-end traffic classification method, using a multilayer perceptron and a recurrent neural network algorithm. Lu et al. [27] proposed a method of using time series to classify encrypted traffic. The first step was to extract time-series information, and the second step was to use the LSTM algorithm for classification.

2.3   Mixed Traffic Classification Methods

Gu et al. [10] first proposed a study on the classification of mixed traffic on Tor. They proposed to use the thinking time between two web pages to identify the first-page using fine-grained features and the second page using coarse-grained features. Wang et al. [29] presented a mixed website traffic identification framework on Tor. The framework used the splitting decision algorithm to judge whether the time threshold split was successful, and used the splitting finding algorithm to further split the traffic that failed to pre-split. This method has a poor splitting effect on overlapping traffic.

Cui et al. [6] proposed a splitting method of continuous websites based on the hidden markov model and classification algorithm of overlapping websites based on Sectioning. The algorithm based on the hidden markov model is too complicated, and the state transition probability within each website needs to be calculated every time. There are certain problems with the use of Sectioning algorithms. One of these is that there is a bad classification result for the mixed situation of short and long streams.

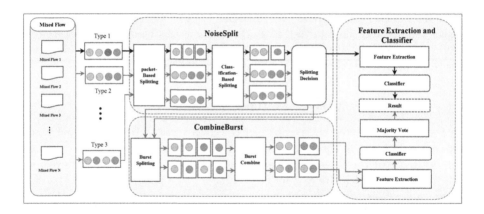

Fig. 2. The TMT-RF framework

3   Methodology

In this section, Fig. 2 presents the TMT-RF framework for the tunnel traffic classification. The upper middle part of Fig. 2 demonstrates the process in which type 1 traffic is split through NoiseSplit module. The lower middle part of Fig. 2 shows the CombineBurst module's traffic splitting for type 2 and type 3. The right part of Fig. 2 demonstrates the process in which the features are acquired through the feature extraction and classification results are acquired through the classifier.

The tunnel mentioned in this paper specifically refers to the IPSec tunnel. Internet Protocol Security (IPSec) is a secure network protocol suite that authenticates and encrypts the packets of data to provide secure encrypted communication between two computers over an Internet protocol network. IPSec mainly includes Authentication Headers (AH), Encapsulating Security Payloads (ESP) and Internet Security Association and Key Management Protocol (ISAKMP).

The traffic types (type 1, type 2, type 3) appearing in Fig. 2 are the same as those in Fig. 1. The three types of traffic represent three scenarios for using applications in IPSec tunnels. The type 1 traffic is generated in a scenario where there is a period of time between the first application and the second. The type 2 traffic is generated when there is no time gap between the first application and the second application. When there is overlap between the first application and the second application, the type 3 traffic is generated.

3.1 NoiseSplit

There are three steps in NoiseSplit module, as shown in Fig. 2. The positive time of the two applications is accompanied by tunnel noise which is the heartbeat packets in IPSec tunnels. Therefore, the split of mixed traffic is based on a rule that if multiple consecutive packets are identified as tunnel noise, mixed tunnel traffic will be split up into two segments. Since the packet length of tunnel noise traffic is extremely distinguishable, to make it efficient and fast, this module uses the packet length threshold method for preliminary splitting.

Based on the split of the packet length threshold, some application packets below the threshold may also be identified as tunnel noise, resulting in multiple cuts. We use machine learning technology to identify the noise filtered out in the first part and decide whether to split. After packet-based splitting and classifier-based splitting produce multiple different results, split decision selects different processing for different results. Three types of results will be generated from packet-based splitting, including that mixed traffic is split correctly, single application traffic is split, and multi-applications mixed traffic is not split.

Packet-Based Splitting. The first type of mixed traffic can be split by tunnel noise. As shown in Fig. 3, it can be seen that the packet length distribution of tunnel noise is quite different from the applied packet length distribution. The packet length of tunnel noise is distributed in a small value range. Therefore, the tunnel noise can be identified through the packet length feature, and then the mixed traffic can be split. L_{split} is the packet length threshold for identifying tunnel noise. Our choice of L_{split} seeks to maximize the chance of tunnel noise identification accuracy. If the value of L_{split} is inappropriate, it may cause multiple splits and non-splits of the mixed flow. We hope that any source of error is impossible. Therefore, an appropriate value must be selected. We will show how to choose L_{split} and how it affects the accuracy of splitting in the experiment.

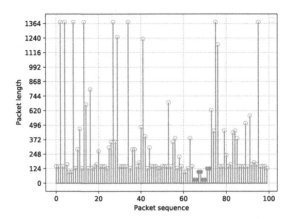

Fig. 3. Packet length distribution of positive-time separation applications

Classification-Based Splitting. The split method based on the packet length threshold may have three results. The first result is that mixed traffic is split correctly. This result does not need to be further processed and can be directly inputted into the classifier for classification. The second result is that single application traffic is split. This happens when the packet length threshold is inappropriate. There is a high probability that mixed traffic will be split into multiple parts. The classification-based method is to reduce the occurrence of this result. The third result is that multi-applications mixed traffic is not split. This happens when there is overlap between two applications. The classifier-based approach does not try to solve this problem, and the failure of the split will be further processed in the CombineBurst Module.

The idea of splitting based on the classifier is aimed to not only further improve the accuracy of tunnel noise identification but also greatly enhance the accuracy of splitting through the classifier. Random forest is an ensemble learning algorithm that is composed of decision trees [19]. It is an extended variant of bagging. The randomness of random forest is mainly reflected in the random training samples of each tree, and the selection of attributes is random. Random forest is simple and efficient, with low overhead.

For the split based on the classifier, we choose the random forest classifier, using the 54-dimensional statistical features of the packet-length sequence. The accuracy of split is measured by the following formula.

$$diff(P,Q) = \begin{cases} 1 & Q - R \leq P \leq Q + R \\ 0 & else \end{cases} \tag{1}$$

where P is the predicted value, Q is the actual value, R is the error range.

$$SA = \frac{1}{N} \sum_{i=1}^{N} diff(P_{predict}(i), P_{true}(i)) \tag{2}$$

where $P_{true}(i)$ is the packet sequence number of the real split point of the i-th sample, $P_{predict}(i)$ is the packet sequence number of the predict split point of the i-th sample, N is the total number of samples.

Splitting Decision. After the first two splits, there may be the three results mentioned above. It is necessary to identify different results for further processing. In the splitting decision, we use the knn classifier, which is an supervised learning algorithm [23]. KNN obtains k nearest neighbors based on the distance measurement method of formula (3). In knn classification, the output is a class membership. An object is classified by a majority vote of its neighbors, with the object being assigned to the class most common among its k nearest neighbors.

$$L(x_i, x_j) = (\sum_{l=1}^{n} |x_i^{(l)} - x_j^{(l)}|^2)^{\frac{1}{2}} \tag{3}$$

The splitting decision takes single application traffic and multi-applications traffic as input, and uses knn for binary classification. If the input is multi-applications mixed traffic, the prediction is true. Otherwise, the output is false. If the output result is true, it needs to be further processed by the combineBurst module and then be sent to the classifier. If the output result is false, it can be directly sent to the classifier for classification.

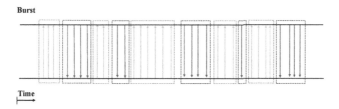

Fig. 4. Visualisation of burst.

3.2 CombineBurst

The NoiseSplit module can split the first type of mixed traffic well, but it cannot split the second and third types of mixed traffic. The combineBurst module is used to solve these types of traffic. There is overlap in the third type of mixed traffic. The overlap rate is the ratio of the total number of packets in the overlapping part to the total number of packets in the entire data stream, which is expressed as follows.

$$OR(T) = \frac{T_{overlap}}{T} \tag{4}$$

where $T_{overlap}$ is the overlapping part of the traffic, and T is the entire traffic. The overlapping part does not help the identification of applications. The previous idea is to spend time finding the split point, and then inputs the classifier to classify. The combineBurst module no longer spends most of the time searching for split points, but splits overlapping traffic into lots of segments and makes predictions for each segment.

A burst is the group of all network packets occurring together that satisfiesthe condition that the most recent packets with the same direction, the burst direction, of the previous packet [25,31]. Data packets from the client to the server are marked with a positive sign. Data packets from the server to the client are marked with a negative sign. This is visually depicted in the traffic burstification section of Fig. 4, where we can see the burst is separated by the packet direction.

Burst Splitting. The granularity of the data packet is too fine, while the granularity of the data stream is too coarse. The data stream can be split up into bursts according to specific tasks. A burst is composed of several consecutive data packets in the same direction. Overlapping traffic is split up into several parts according to burst. The length of overlapping streams of different applications is different, and the number of bursts generated may also be different. A burst may contain one, two, or multiple data packets.

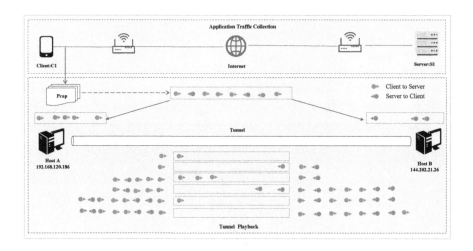

Fig. 5. Play back application data in a tunnel

Burst Combine. After overlapping traffic is split according to bursts, multiple bursts will be generated. If we simply split according to burst and then identify, there are the following two problems:

– Limited representation ability. The data packets contained in the burst are too few, and the ability to describe the application is limited.

– Increased delay time. If we split according to burst, a lot of data will be generated. Each burst needs to be classified, which will increase the delay time of the classifier.

To solve the above two problems caused by burst splitting, we propose to combine several continuous bursts into a segment to split. If a segment contains too many bursts, it will reduce the delay time. Meanwhile, the segment may contain more than two application data packets, it also will cause a drop in split accuracy. If a segment contains too few bursts, it will not reduce the delay time and increase the burden of the classifier. Therefore, we hope to choose a suitable value $N_{combine}$ that satisfies the following conditions as much as possible:

– Each segment should contain as few applications as possible. Ideally, each segment contains only a single application.
– Each segment should be as long as possible to contain as much information as possible for the corresponding application, while reducing the burden of the classifier.

It is easy to see that the above two conditions are contradictory: the shorter the segment, the less information it contains. The longer the segment, the easier it is to include multiple applications. We will show how to choose $N_{combine}$ and how it affects the accuracy of classification in the experiment.

3.3   Feature Extraction and Classifier

Feature Extraction. Feature extraction involves extracting 54 statistical features from each segment (using the features in Appscanner). For each segment, three series of packets are considered, including incoming packets only, outgoing packets only, and two-way traffic. Two-way traffic consists of incoming and outgoing packets. For each series (3 in total), we calculate the following values, including minimum, maximum, average, median absolute deviation, standard deviation, variance, skewness, kurtosis, percentile (from 10% to 90%), and the number of elements in the series (18 in total) [25].

Classifier. We use the Random Forest model as the classifier. The specific introduction of the random forest model is in the classifier-based module. The difference between the random forest model and the previous one is: the random forest model based on the classifier module is mainly used to identify whether it is tunnel noise through binary classifications, and the random forest model of this module is mainly multi-classification to identify the applications.

Majority Vote. KNN obtains the classification result through majority voting of k nearest neighbors. Majority voting is also used in our framework. The classifier will output the results for multiple segments of a stream, and through majority voting, to determine which applications constitute the data stream.

4 Data Collection

In this section, we introduce the data collection framework, mainly including application traffic collection and tunnel playback. Next, we will introduce each part in detail.

4.1 Application Traffic Collection

Since mobile traffic involves user private data, public mobile traffic data sets are currently not available. Therefore, existing work uses self-collected data sets to validate the proposed method. Firstly, we use black domain software to turn off irrelevant applications in the background (Black domain is a free super practical optimization tool for android rogue apps. It does not require root permission to perfectly prevent app from starting, running in the background, and waking up in the background).

Then the adb-monkey [3] is used to randomly click on the app, using tcp-dump to capture application traffic. We collected traffic of 30 applications in seven types. These seven types are mainly instant messaging applications, file transfer applications, email client applications, email web applications, media applications, social applications, and VoIP applications. These data will be used in tunnel playback module.

4.2 Tunnel Playback

Existing tunnel traffic collection methods have some shortcomings and poor scalability. Firstly, the existing tunnel traffic collection methods are difficult to solve the labeling problem of tunnel mixed traffic. Secondly, the traffic in the tunnel has the same five-tuple, so it is difficult to filter out the background traffic. There is a lot of background traffic in the application traffic, which will make it difficult for the application to get the accurate ground truth. Besides, when collecting mobile applications traffic, it is necessary to obtain the root permission of the mobile device, resulting in poor scalability.

To overcome the above shortcomings, we propose a method to generate tunnel traffic using tunnel playback. Tunnel playback is to simulate the client and server of the application at both ends of the host that establishes the tunnel to send packets. Figure 5 details the process of tunnel playback. During playback, the wait-stop mechanism and the timeout retransmission mechanism are used to ensure orderly packet sending and reduce packet loss.

The tunnel playback process is as follows. Firstly, a tunnel is established between host A and host B. Host A simulates the client of the application, and host B simulates the server of the application. Then, host A reads the data packets in the c2s (client to server) direction of the pcap file in order and sends them to host B through the tunnel. Next, host B reads the pcap file in order, and when it receives the previous data packet in the c2s direction, it sends data packets in the s2c (server to client) direction to host A. The two hosts read and send packets in sequence. Finally, the packets in pcap are completely sent to the tunnel. During tunnel playback, we use tcpdump to capture tunnel traffic on the host A.

The generation of tunnel mixed traffic depends on the application traffic collected by the application traffic collection module. In the experiment, we collected single-application label traffic and multi-applications label traffic in IPSec tunnels. For single-label applications, we collected 7 types of tunnel traffic for 30 applications through tunnel playback, and each class contains 100 instances. For the Multi-applications label dataset, we collected four three types of tunnel traffic. Through pcap splitting, random (different applications traffic) and orderly (same applications traffic) mixing, pcap merging, tunnel playback and other operations, three types of mixed traffic in the tunnel are generated. We generated three types of mixed traffic using 30 applications traffic collected by the application traffic collection module.

- **Positive-time separation applications traffic.** From 30 applications, we arbitrarily select two applications to mix, and collect mixed traffic containing 60 classes, each class includes 100 instances.
- **Zero-time separation applications traffic.** This data set contains 60 classes, and each class contains 100 instances.
- **Negative-time separation applications traffic.** The application traffic with negative time separation includes two types of data sets, 5% and 10%. Each type of data set includes 60 classes, and each class includes 100 instances.

5   Experimental Evaluation

In this section, we first introduce the experiment setup. Then, we analyzed the impact of three factors (data packet length threshold, measurement range and number of burst combinations) on the classification results. Finally we analyzed the classification results of traffic in three scenarios, and the result of the comparison experiment.

5.1   Experiment Setup

Comparison Methods. Some of the most advanced methods as a comparison method are summarized as follows.

- Sectioning (Packet-based) [6] uses data packets to split the mixed stream evenly into several sections, predicts each section, and gets the classification result.
- Sectioning (Time-based) uses time information to split the mixed stream evenly into several sections, and each section is predicted to obtain the classification result.

The classifier used by the sectioning algorithm is knn. In the comparative experiment, we find that random forest is better than knn for classification, so we choose random forest.

Setting of NoiseSplit Module. The selection of L_{split} will be introduced in the experiments. The noise classifier takes 54-dimensional statistical features of the packet-length sequence as input, and the classifier uses the random forest model. Splitting decision uses the knn model.

Setting of CombineBurst Module. The selection of $N_{combine}$ will be introduced in the experiments. The classifier takes 54-dimensional statistical features of the packet-length sequence as input, and the classifier uses a random forest model.

Cross-Validation. Our first step is to split each application instance into the training and test sets under 10-fold cross-validation. 10% of the instances are in the test set and the rest are in the training set. We replay the mixed 90% of the collected application instances into the tunnel to generate training sets, and replay the mixed 10% of the traffic into the tunnel to generate test sets.

Assessment Criteria. We analyze the accuracy of the split point. Formula 2 specifically introduces the measurement index of the result of finding the split point-splitting accuracy. For the classification of applications, we use the following metrics to measure.

- Precision: Precision is calculated using Eq. (5).

$$Precision = \frac{TP}{TP + FP} \tag{5}$$

- Recall: Recall is calculated according to Eq. (6).

$$Recall = \frac{TP}{TP + FN} \tag{6}$$

- F1-score: F1 is calculated according to Eq. (7), and it's the harmonic mean of precision and recall.

$$F1 = \frac{2 * Precision * Recall}{Precision + Recall} \tag{7}$$

- Accuracy: Accuracy is calculated according to Eq. (8).

$$Accuracy = \frac{TP + TN}{TP + FP + TN + FN} \tag{8}$$

where TP refers to the number of true positives, FP refers to the number of false positives, FN refers to the number of false negatives, and TN refers to the number of true negatives.

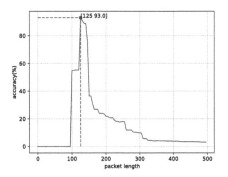
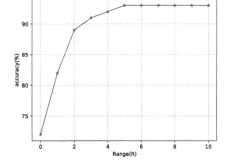

Fig. 6. The accuracy of the split varies with the packet length threshold (L_{split})

Fig. 7. Prediction accuracy of split with varying measure range (R)

5.2 Impact of Packet Length Threshold

In order to analyze the impact of packet length threshold on splitting accuracy, we conducted experiments to split mixed traffic by packet length threshold. In the experiment, L_{split} takes a value from 5 to 500.

Figure 6 shows the accuracy that results from correctly splitting mixed flow, when using different packet length thresholds. When the packet length threshold is 100 or 145, the classification result immediately changes greatly. If the packet length is in the range of 100–145, the accuracy is greater than 50%. When the packet length is 125, the splitting accuracy reaches the highest value, which is 93%. The results show that when the packet length threshold is between 100 and 145, it helps to improve the accuracy of the split.

It can be seen that the packet length threshold has a great influence on the accuracy of the split. As the packet length threshold increases, the accuracy of splitting first increases and then presents a downward trend. If L_{split} is selected too small, it will be lower than the noise packet length, and it is difficult to identify tunnel noise, which reduces the accuracy of the split. When L_{split} is selected too large, the packet length higher than the tunnel noise will filter out some applications traffic and reduce the accuracy of the split.

5.3 Impact of Measure Range

To analyze the changes of splitting accuracy under different measurement ranges, we conducted an experiment, and the results of the experiment are shown in Fig. 7.

The R in formula (1) means the R packets within the error range of the split point are all correct split points. As shown in Fig. 7, the prediction accuracy of split has varying measure ranges. With the increase of R from 0 to 10, the splitting accuracy of the mixed stream has been increased from 71% to 93%.

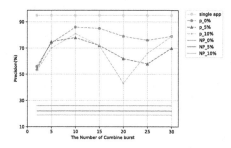
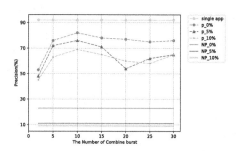

Fig. 8. Prediction accuracy of the first app with varying number of combine burst ($N_{combine}$) and overlap %

Fig. 9. Prediction accuracy of the second app with varying number of combine burst ($N_{combine}$) and overlap %

When the value of R reaches 5, the accuracy of classification no longer increases. The result shows that the split deviation of the split point is maintained within 5 packets before and after.

Figure 7 shows that with the increase of R, the accuracy of recognition just started to increase and then stabilized. When the R setting is small, the accuracy will be very low. Therefore, the R setting should be as large as possible within the error tolerance range in the experiment.

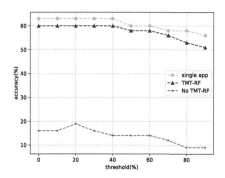
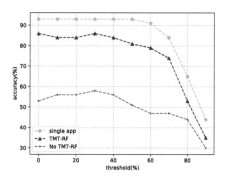

Fig. 10. Prediction accuracy of first app with varying possibility threshold

Fig. 11. Prediction accuracy of second app with varying possibility threshold

5.4   Impact of the Number of Burst Combinations

We conducted an experiment to explore the effect of the number of combined bursts on the classification results. The experimental results are shown in Figs. 8 and 9. In the results, P represents the classification result processed by the TMT-RF framework, and NP represents the classification result not processed by the TMT-RF framework.

Figures 8 and 9 show the precision of the first and the second application classification respectively. Under different overlap rates, the classification results of the applications vary greatly. Figures 8 and 9 present that the classification precision of mixed traffic has increased by 50% after processing by the CombineBurst module. As the combined burst value is different, the precision of the classification also changes. Experiments show that if the number of bursts combined is 10 or 15, it will help improve the classification results.

The experimental results show that the overall trend of rising first and then falling. Too small $N_{combine}$ selection may result in too little applications information included, which makes it difficult to identify effectively, and reduces the precision of identification. Too large selection of $N_{combine}$ may result in the inclusion of multiple applications information and reduce the precision of recognition.

5.5   Applications Classification of Positive-Time Separation

Through the above analysis of the impact of the packet length threshold and measurement range on the splitting accuracy, in the experiment, we set L_{split} as 125 and R as 6. As shown in Figs. 10 and 11, after processing by the TMT-RF framework, the recognition result of the first application in the mixed traffic is very close to the recognition result of a single application.

Compared with those not processed by the TMT-RF framework, the classification result is increased by 30%. Compared with the second application, the first application is closer to the classification result of a single application. Overall, it can be seen that the mixed flow has a greater impact on the second application than the first. It indicates that the first few packets have a greater impact on the accuracy of tunnel traffic identification.

Table 1. The precision of the applications under different overlap rates

R(%)	0 overlp					5 overlap					10 overlap				
P(%)	0	20	40	60	80	0	20	40	60	80	0	20	40	60	80
First	0.87	0.87	0.85	0.87	0.84	0.83	0.75	0.61	0.83	0.71	0.78	0.78	0.70	0.76	0.71
Second	0.84	0.84	0.84	0.74	0.71	0.76	0.76	0.65	0.58	0.56	0.69	0.69	0.67	0.62	0.57

Table 2. Experimental result on precision, recall and F1 (The Best result are in bold)

Algorithm	0% overlap						5% overlap						10% overlap					
	First APP			Second APP			First APP			Second APP			First APP			Second APP		
	P	R	F1	P	R	F1	P	R	F1	P	R	F1	P	R	F1	P	R	F1
CombineBurst	**0.87**	**0.71**	**0.76**	**0.74**	**0.45**	**0.56**	**0.83**	**0.69**	**0.73**	**0.58**	**0.40**	**0.47**	**0.76**	**0.69**	**0.72**	**0.62**	0.17	**0.27**
Sectioning(Packet-based)	0.83	0.18	0.22	0.45	0.33	0.34	0.61	0.11	0.13	**0.58**	0.29	0.38	0.59	0.09	0.11	0.52	0.17	0.22
Sectioning(Time-based)	0.78	0.45	0.51	0.64	0.25	0.26	0.76	0.26	0.28	0.47	0.29	0.27	0.72	0.26	0.30	0.32	**0.23**	0.21

5.6   Applications Classification of Zero-Time Separation

By analyzing the impact of the number of burst Combinations on application classification, we set $N_{combine}$ to 10. In this scenario, there is no overlap between the two applications, and all three methods have achieved good results. In Table 1, R represents the overlap rate of application traffic, and P represents the probability threshold. Table 1 shows that the classification results of our method do not change much, under different output probability thresholds. The classification result of the first application is better than the classification result of the second application

Table 2 shows that the CombineBurst method shows a very good performance than other methods on this data set. The CombineBurst gets 87% precision and 76% f1 value. Overall, combineBurst has achieved good performance, because it uses information between data streams in the same direction. The results demonstrate that CombineBurst method is very helpful to improve the identification precision of tunnel traffic.

5.7   Applications Classification of Negative-Time Separation

We set $N_{combine}$ to 10 as shown above. As shown in Table 1, there are classification results with different overlap rates in this scenario. Table 1 shows that overlap rate has a great impact on application identification, the higher the overlap rate, the greater the impact. Table 1 also shows that the output threshold also have a certain impact on the accuracy of recognition.

As shown in Table 2, as the overlap rate increases, the gap between the CombineBurst method and other methods gradually increases. Compared with the most advanced methods, CombineBurst shows the best performance at different overlap rates. The precision of the combineBurst method is slightly greater than the other two methods, and the recall rate and f1 value are much larger than these two comparison methods, mainly due to the combinationBurst method using the direction information between packets. With the increase of the overlap rate, the combineBurst method has the least decrease in precision, recall, and f1 value, showing strong robustness in the comparison method.

6   Conclusion

In this paper, we propose a classification framework for mixed traffic in a single user usage scenario in IPSec tunnels. In this scenario, each flow is classified according to the application visited by the user in the flow. To achieve the identification of three types of traffic in IPSec tunnels, we propose the NoiseSplit module to segment and classify the first type of traffic, and the CombineBurst module handles the second and third types of traffic. We collected four mixed traffic data sets of three types to evaluate our proposed method. Experimental results show that TMT-RF not only achieves the best performance of 93% on the data set for positive-time separation applications, but also outperforms other state-of-the-art methods on the data sets for zero-time separation applications and negative-time separation applications. Future research needs to further explore the classification of applications used in multi-person scenarios in IPSec tunnels.

Acknowledgement. This work is supported by The National Key Research and Development Program of China (No. 2020YFE0200500, No. 2018YFB1800200 and No.2020YFB1006100) and Key research and Development Program for Guangdong Province under grant No. 2019B010137003.

References

1. Aceto, G., Ciuonzo, D., Montieri, A., Pescapé, A.: Mobile encrypted traffic classification using deep learning. In: 2018 Network Traffic Measurement and Analysis Conference (TMA), pp. 1–8. IEEE (2018)
2. Aceto, G., Ciuonzo, D., Montieri, A., Pescapè, A.: Mimetic: mobile encrypted traffic classification using multimodal deep learning. Comput. Netw. **165**, 106944 (2019)
3. Alam, M.S., Vuong, S.T.: Random forest classification for detecting android malware. In: 2013 IEEE International Conference on Green Computing and Communications and IEEE Internet of Things and IEEE Cyber, Physical and Social Computing, pp. 663–669. IEEE (2013)
4. Booth III, E.H., Lingafelt, C.S., Nguyen, P.T., Temoshenko, L., Wang, X.: System and method to monitor and determine if an active ipsec tunnel has become disabled. US Patent 6,668,282, 23 Dec 2003
5. Cao, Z., Xiong, G., Zhao, Y., Li, Z., Guo, L.: A survey on encrypted traffic classification. In: Batten, L., Li, G., Niu, W., Warren, M. (eds.) ATIS 2014. CCIS, vol. 490, pp. 73–81. Springer, Heidelberg (2014). https://doi.org/10.1007/978-3-662-45670-5_8
6. Cui, W., Chen, T., Fields, C., Chen, J., Sierra, A., Chan-Tin, E.: Revisiting assumptions for website fingerprinting attacks. In: Proceedings of the 2019 ACM Asia Conference on Computer and Communications Security, pp. 328–339 (2019)
7. Ding, Y.j., Cai, W.d.: A method for http-tunnel detection based on statistical features of traffic. In: 2011 IEEE 3rd International Conference on Communication Software and Networks, pp. 247–250. IEEE (2011)
8. Dusi, M., Este, A., Gringoli, F., Salgarelli, L.: Identifying the traffic of ssh-encrypted applications (2014)
9. Freier, A., Karlton, P., Kocher, P.: The secure sockets layer (SSL) protocol version 3.0. Tech. rep., RFC 6101 **11** (2011)
10. Gu, X., Yang, M., Luo, J.: A novel website fingerprinting attack against multi-tab browsing behavior. In: 2015 IEEE 19th International Conference on Computer Supported Cooperative Work in Design (CSCWD), pp. 234–239. IEEE (2015)
11. Guo, L., Wu, Q., Liu, S., Duan, M., Li, H., Sun, J.: Deep learning-based real-time VPN encrypted traffic identification methods. J. Real Time Image Process. **17**(1), 103–114 (2020)
12. Hamed, H., Al-Shaer, E., Marrero, W.: Modeling and verification of IPSEC and VPN security policies. In: 13th IEEE International Conference on Network Protocols (ICNP 2005), pp. 10-pp. IEEE (2005)
13. He, L., Shi, Y.: Identification of SSH applications based on convolutional neural network. In: Proceedings of the 2018 International Conference on Internet and e-Business, pp. 198–201 (2018)

14. Islam, F.U., Liu, G., Liu, W.: Identifying voip traffic in VPN tunnel via flow spatio-temporal features. Math. Biosci. Eng. **17**(5), 4747–4772 (2020)
15. Korczyński, M., Duda, A.: Markov chain fingerprinting to classify encrypted traffic. In: IEEE INFOCOM 2014-IEEE Conference on Computer Communications, pp. 781–789. IEEE (2014)
16. Lotfollahi, M., Siavoshani, M.J., Zade, R.S.H., Saberian, M.: Deep packet: a novel approach for encrypted traffic classification using deep learning. Soft Comput. **24**(3), 1999–2012 (2020)
17. Meng, J., Wang, L., Xiong, G., Yao, Y.: Study on SSH application classification based on machine learning. Comput. Res. Dev. **2** (2012)
18. MontazeriShatoori, M., Davidson, L., Kaur, G., Lashkari, A.H.: Detection of doh tunnels using time-series classification of encrypted traffic. In: 2020 IEEE International Conference on Dependable, Autonomic and Secure Computing, International Conference on Pervasive Intelligence and Computing, International Conference on Cloud and Big Data Computing, International Conference on Cyber Science and Technology Congress (DASC/PiCom/CBDCom/CyberSciTech), pp. 63–70. IEEE (2020)
19. Pal, M.: Random forest classifier for remote sensing classification. Int. J. Remote Sens. **26**(1), 217–222 (2005)
20. Parchekani, A., Naghadeh, S.N., Shah-Mansouri, V.: Classification of traffic using neural networks by rejecting: a novel approach in classifying vpn traffic. arXiv preprint arXiv:2001.03665 (2020)
21. Pfeiffer, M., Girlich, F., Rossberg, M., Schaefer, G.: Vector packet encapsulation: the case for a scalable ipsec encryption protocol. In: Proceedings of the 15th International Conference on Availability, Reliability and Security, pp. 1–10 (2020)
22. Shi, Y., Biswas, S.: Website fingerprinting using traffic analysis of dynamic webpages. In: 2014 IEEE Global Communications Conference, pp. 557–563. IEEE (2014)
23. Su, M.Y.: Using clustering to improve the knn-based classifiers for online anomaly network traffic identification. J. Netw. Comput. Appl. **34**(2), 722–730 (2011)
24. Sun, G., Liang, L., Chen, T., Xiao, F., Lang, F.: Network traffic classification based on transfer learning. Comput. Electr. Eng. **69**, 920–927 (2018)
25. Taylor, V.F., Spolaor, R., Conti, M., Martinovic, I.: Appscanner: Automatic fingerprinting of smartphone apps from encrypted network traffic. In: 2016 IEEE European Symposium on Security and Privacy (EuroS&P), pp. 439–454. IEEE (2016)
26. Top, G.: Strategic technology trends for 2020 (2020)
27. Vu, L., Thuy, H.V., Nguyen, Q.U., Ngoc, T.N., Nguyen, D.N., Hoang, D.T., Dutkiewicz, E.: Time series analysis for encrypted traffic classification: a deep learning approach. In: 2018 18th International Symposium on Communications and Information Technologies (ISCIT), pp. 121–126. IEEE (2018)
28. Wang, P., Li, S., Ye, F., Wang, Z., Zhang, M.: Packetcgan: Exploratory study of class imbalance for encrypted traffic classification using cgan. In: ICC 2020–2020 IEEE International Conference on Communications (ICC), pp. 1–7. IEEE (2020)
29. Wang, T., Goldberg, I.: On realistically attacking tor with website fingerprinting. Proc. Priv. Enhancing Technol. **2016**(4), 21–36 (2016)
30. Xu, Y., Wang, T., Li, Q., Gong, Q., Chen, Y., Jiang, Y.: A multi-tab website fingerprinting attack. In: Proceedings of the 34th Annual Computer Security Applications Conference, pp. 327–341 (2018)

31. Yan, F., Xu, M., Qiao, T., Wu, T., Yang, X., Zheng, N., Choo, K.K.R.: Identifying wechat red packets and fund transfers via analyzing encrypted network traffic. In: 2018 17th IEEE International Conference on Trust, Security and Privacy in Computing and Communications/12th IEEE International Conference on Big Data Science and Engineering (TrustCom/BigDataSE), pp. 1426–1432. IEEE (2018)
32. Zhou, K., Wang, W., Wu, C., Hu, T.: Practical evaluation of encrypted traffic classification based on a combined method of entropy estimation and neural networks. ETRI J. **42**(3), 311–323 (2020)

CROCUS: An Objective Approach for SDN Controllers Security Assessment

Carlos Silva[1]([✉]), Bruno Sousa[1], and João P. Vilela[2]

[1] University of Coimbra, CISUC, DEI, Coimbra, Portugal
`carlosfelix@student.dei.uc.pt`, `bmsousa@dei.uc.pt`
[2] CRACS/INESCTEC, CISUC and Department of Computer Science,
Faculty of Sciences, University of Porto, Porto, Portugal
`jvilela@fc.up.pt`

Abstract. Software Defined Networking (SDN) facilitates the orchestration and configuration of network resources in a flexible and scalable form, where policies are managed by controller components that interact with network elements through multiple interfaces. The ubiquitous adoption of SDN leads to the availability of multiple SDN controllers, which have different characteristics in terms of performance and security support. SDN controllers are a common target in network attacks since their compromise leads to the capability of impairing the entire network. Thus, the choice of a SDN controller must be a meticulous process from early phases (design to production). CROCUS, herein proposed, provides a mechanism to enable an objective assessment of the security support of SDN controllers. CROCUS relies on the information provided by the Common Vulnerability Scoring System (CVSS) and considers security features derived from scenarios with stringent security requirements. Considering a vehicular communication scenario supported by multiple technologies, we narrow the selection of SDN controllers to OpenDayLight and ONOS choices. The results put in evidence that both controllers have security features relevant for demanding scenarios with ONOS excelling in some aspects.

Keywords: SDN · Security · ONOS · OpenDayLight · DoS · MADM

1 Introduction

Cloud computing has transformed the way computing resources are provisioned. The consolidation of the paradigm provided a significant increase in the number of services available on the Internet and, consequently, in the number of users connected to the network. According to some researches [1], it is estimated that the number of devices connected to the Internet will be one trillion by the year 2025. Multiple technologies can be employed to enable the connection of heterogeneous devices (e.g. vehicles, smart lamps), and IoT objects in scenarios with stringent performance and security requirements (e.g. low latency, data encryption) [2].

© ICST Institute for Computer Sciences, Social Informatics and Telecommunications Engineering 2021
Published by Springer Nature Switzerland AG 2021. All Rights Reserved
J. Garcia-Alfaro et al. (Eds.): SecureComm 2021, LNICST 398, pp. 438–455, 2021.
https://doi.org/10.1007/978-3-030-90019-9_22

The Software Defined Networking (SDN) paradigm facilitates the orchestration and configuration of network resources that can be placed at the edge and cloud side to fulfil scenarios' requirements. SDN Controllers are able to manage policies regarding network access, regarding services (to enable the chaining of service functions) in a flexible and scalable way. For such management the controllers have NorthBound interfaces to allow the connection from applications, SouthBound interfaces to allow the connection with network equipments using protocols like OpenFlow and NetConf. The East-West interfaces are employed for clustering purposes. SDN controllers like ONOS and OpenDayLight support features that are crucial to reduce security risks and to increase availability levels, such as the support of clustering to avoid Single Point of Failure (SPoF) [3–6]. Apart from these criteria, other aspects such as the scale of deployments and modularity also play a key role in the selection of suitable SDN controllers. For instance, controllers like Ryu or Pox, which are tailored for research purposes and are not seen as suitable choices for scenarios with stringent security requirements [7].

The ubiquitous adoption of SDN leads to the availability of multiple SDN controllers (e.g. ONOS, OpenDayLight, FloodLight, Ryu and Pox), which have different characteristics in terms of performance and security support. However, the increase in the number of aspects to be considered also generates an increase in the decision process complexity for choosing suitable controllers. The Multiple Attribute Decision Making (MADM) [8,9] is a multidisciplinary methodology that assists in the decision process when it is necessary to consider multiple attributes that should be maximized or minimized according to their degree of influence in the decision. In this regard, authors [10] propose feature based selection approaches to select SDN controllers, employing MADM mechanisms to compare diverse SDN controllers and enable an informed selection of SDN controllers, nonetheless the proposed approach does not includes security information and omits recent controllers like ONOS.

SDN controllers are a common target in network attacks since their compromise leads to the capability of impairing the entire network. Thus, the choice of a SDN controller must be a meticulous process from early phases, from design to production/deployment, without neglecting security aspects. Indeed, threat modelling and risk determination techniques are relevant to analyse different choices [11]. In spite of the availability of security analysis for SDN controllers [12], the employed threat modelling approaches like STRIDE [13] rely on subjective classifications, which may lead to biased or ineffective results. In addition, the modelling in such approaches is limited to the security features supported in SouthBound and NorthBound interfaces, taking out East-West interfaces required for clustering purposes.

The CROCUS methodology herein proposed provides a mechanism for objective assessment of the security support of SDN controllers. CROCUS relies on the information provided by the Common Vulnerability Scoring System (CVSS) [14], and also includes security features derived from scenarios with stringent security requirements and considered as mandatory in security studies [3,4].

CROCUS assesses the security support of SDN controllers in an objective fashion by considering: i) the vulnerability information (CVSSv3), updated frequently and supporting the activities of Chief Information Security Officer (CISO); ii) the information of risk assessment approaches that enable the determination of the severity levels and probability of occurrence [11]; iii) the information of security features deemed as necessary for SDN controllers [3,4], considering the application, control and data planes in SDN. CROCUS establishes a multi-step approach to consider the complexity of the multiple aspects in the decision process, through Methodical - a MADM approach which is available online[1], and has been employed by us in previous studies for an objective selection of choices for content migration and to enhance resilience support in cloud [15,16] In this work, considering a vehicular communication scenario supported by multiple technologies as case-study, we employ the proposed CROCUS methodology to narrow the selection of SDN controllers to OpenDayLight and ONOS. The obtained results put in evidence that both controllers have security features relevant for demanding scenarios, with ONOS standing out in some of the criteria.

This article is organised as follows: Sect. 2 discusses works that already exist in the literature, while Sect. 3 presents the background with the main topics of the paper. The CROCUS mechanism is described in Sect. 4, while Sect. 5 describes the employment of CROCUS to enable the selection of SDN controllers in scenarios with multiple technologies. The final conclusions are presented in Sect. 6.

2   Related Work

The choice of SDN controllers is commonly based on performance criteria [17]. As an example, authors [10] employ MADM mechanisms to compare OpenDayLight, FloodLight, Ryu and Pox controllers in order to select the one with the most appropriate feature set. The study does not includes security information and omits recent controllers like ONOS.

Apart from the performance concerns, there is an increasing focus on security aspects of SDN controllers. In particular, authors [18] reveal that the advantages of SDN also brings security concerns due to the split between the control and data plane, and due to the higher exposure of attacks, since one entity manages all the roles for traffic forwarding in the network.

Security analysis of controllers, employing threat modelling approaches [12], consider the selection of SDN controllers mainly based on the information of SouthBound and NorthBound interfaces, disregarding East-West interfaces that are required for clustering purposes. The threats are considered as per the STRIDE threat modelling approach [13] which tends to be subjective regarding the classification of threats.

Authors also propose an analysis of the security in SDN controllers, focusing on the implemented functionalities [3,4] and on threat models associated

---

[1] https://github.com/bmsousa/MeTHODICAL.

with Denial of Service attacks [19]. Authors specify the metrics that SDN controllers must support to mitigate such attacks. For instance, to avoid false master nodes to control other SDN controllers, the messages exchanged between controllers must have security mechanisms (e.g., integrity, encryption) associated. Notwithstanding, no methodology is provided to enable an objective selection of controllers in such studies. The work of these authors is, however, employed in CROCUS to help define the "standard security features" that SDN controllers must support.

The main objective of this work is to propose a selection strategy for SDN controllers that, unlike previous works, considers security aspects from design to production phases using MADM methodology. With the possibility of customising the factors considered in the process, as well as its impact on the decision, the MADM methodology allows for the flexibility of the proposed strategies to encompass different security requirements.

3 Background

3.1 Software Defined Networks

The Software Defined Networks (SDN) paradigm allows the dynamic programming of the network infrastructure, due to the split of the data plane and the control plane. The latter has the role of managing the logic regarding the forwarding of data through all the devices in the network (e.g. hosts, switches, routers, etc.). The SDN architecture considers three distinct planes, as suggested by the Open Network Foundation [20].

- **Application Plane** contains the applications that are responsible for the network management in real time. This plane includes applications that are responsible for the policies for traffic steering, load balancing, and security (e.g. Deep Packet Inspection). Such applications communicate with the SDN controller though specific APIs, available at the NorthBound Interface (NBI).
- **Control Plane** is responsible for the network management and sends to the controller requests to configure the behaviour of the data plane. For instance, data flows associated with a specific service (e.g. using as destination a certain port, 80 for HTTP service) are forwarded in a specific switch port, or also mirrored in another switch port for security analysis. This plane allows to manage the behaviour of the SDN controller, in particular on how the controller manages the flow policies. Another example is the usage of Intents, to express the desired behaviour regarding traffic steering, so that the controller is able to infer the necessary flow rules that are required for two entities to communicate [21].
- **Data Plane** abstracts the physical network components like switches that receive traffic and forward the traffic, firewalls which perform security functionalities. This plane is mainly concerned the forwarding process of data packets, which considers the information in the packets (e.g. MAC, IP addresses, etc.) to forward traffic. When no rules exist for a given flow, the

SDN controller is queried regarding the intended behaviour for that specific flow, if it should be discarded or forwarded.

3.2 Common Vulnerability Scoring System

The Common Vulnerability Scoring System (CVSS) [14] is an open framework to communicate the characteristics and severities of software. CVSS combines different categories of metrics into a score that varies in a $[0, 10]$ scale, where the first is classified as informative and the last as critical. The diverse categories of metrics include:

- **Base** contains information regarding the vulnerabilities that do not change with time, as happens with the temporal vulnerability categories.
- **Temporal** contains information regarding vulnerabilities that change over time due to events external to each vulnerability.
- **Environment** refer to the environment where the vulnerability can occur, thus including information regarding the required privileges to exploit a vulnerability.

The CVSS score is determined considering the metrics in the base category, which is required to determine the severity associated with a vulnerability. In addition, the base category considers two sub-types of metrics: the exploitability and impact, with the first related with the availability and easiness of exploring the vulnerabilities, while the impact is associated with the extent achieved with the successful exploitation of the vulnerability. Table 1 summarises the diverse metrics of the base category.

Table 1. CVSS Base metrics and values

Sub-type	Metric	Values	Description
Exploitability	Attack Vector #AV	{1,2,3,4}	Value 4 refers to physical access to the vulnerable component, 1-refers to remote access
	Attack Complexity #AC	{1,2}	Value 2 refers to high complexity while 1 refers to low complexity
	Privileges Required #PR	{0,1,2}	Value 2 refers to high privilege (e.g. root), 1 to low and 0 for none
	User Interaction #UI	{0,1}	0-No interaction, 1-Requires user interaction
	Scope #S	{0,1}	0-If only impacts the component, 1-If impacts other components beyond the security scope
Impact	Confidentiality #C	{0,1,2}	0-No loss of confidentiality, 2-Total loss of confidentiality
	Availability #A	{0,1,2}	0-Availability is not affected, 2-Successful denial of service
	Integrity #I	{0,1,2}	0-No impact on the integrity, 2- Total integrity loss
CVSS score **CVSS3**		[0, 10]	Score that combines the metrics of the base category.

The base metrics are required to establish the base score of CVSS. In addition, the scope metric allows to identify if a metric has impact on other component, for instance in Cross Site Scripting (XSS) vulnerabilities, the security of the Web servers needs to be compromised but it also impacts applications (e.g. browsers) running on end-user devices. The CVSS score is formulated according to the version of the CVSS. The most recent version is v3.1, but it does not introduces new metrics or metric values and changes in formulas when compared to v3.0 [22].

3.3   Multiple Attribute Decision Mechanism

Multiple Attribute Decision Mechanisms (MADM) have been employed in distinct domains as an approach to rank alternatives. For instance the Methodical algorithm [8] has been employed in scenarios for resource migration, path selection, QoS decision. In order to rank alternatives considering the MADM algorithms, the first step is to classify alternatives into two main categories/groups:

- **Benefits** includes all the metrics whose value should be maximised. For instance, values of #AV must be higher (physical access) in order to allow the full exploitation of vulnerability.
- **Costs** considers the metrics whose values must be minimised. For instance, values of the CVSS score must be close to zero, as they present lower probability of exploitation and reduced impact in the system and services.

The MADM also provides flexibility to specify the importance of one criterium over another, through weights. In addition, categories can also be weighted, for example to give preference to the benefits category over the costs category. MADM algorithms are performed in several steps, including normalisation of values to apply weights, determination of ideal values in terms of benefits and costs, the distance of each alternative to the ideal values, and an aggregation of the distances in a score to allow the ranking of alternatives. A score close to zero represents that an alternative is closer to the ideal values, thus holds best values. A more detailed description can be found in [8].

4   CROCUS: SDN Controllers' Security Assessment Approach

This section describes the CROCUS approach which aims to enable the assessment of SDN controllers at design and production phases. The approach relies on well established security methodologies, like the Common Vulnerability Scoring System (CVSS) and on MADM to rank the vulnerabilities, and aims to be employed as a tool to those who require SDN mechanisms. CROCUS works in multiple steps in a closed loop and include: 1) Identification of SDN Controllers; 2) Information of vulnerabilities; 3) Rank vulnerabilities; 4) and finally perform selection of SDN controller. Such steps are further documented in the following subsections.

4.1   Step #1 - Identification of SDN Controllers

Besides the flexibility and management of the diverse SDN data planes, as described in Sect. 3.1, the choice of SDN controllers can be related with the scenario, or with a specific purpose. From a security perspective, the choice can rely on controllers that can act in a cluster to avoid Single Point of Failures (SPoF) [23,24]. The scale of deployments and the modularity also play a key role in the selection step, where SDN controllers like Ryu or Pox are more focused on research, and thus not identified as suitable choices [7]. The output of this step is the identification of possible SDN controllers - set of SDN controllers to deploy in a specific scenario.

4.2   Step #2 - Information of Vulnerabilities

Considering the input of the first step on the set of SDN controllers, the information of vulnerabilities can be queried using available information, like the one present in CVSS, as presented in Sect. 3.2. The threat model can impact the collection of the vulnerabilities information, CROCUS does not instantiate to a particular threat model (e.g. DoS), as these are associated with the specificity of the scenario. As such, CROCUS proposes to include all the vulnerabilities, that may require physical access to be exploitable, or that map to insider threats (e.g., malicious administrators).

The CVSS version considered in CROCUS is CVSS v3, since the differences from v3.1 mainly rely on clarification aspects, and the vulnerabilities information conducted in the study case for SDN controllers mainly includes version v3. CVSS allows to determine the CVSS score, nonetheless, relevant information, such as the state of resolution, the update date, as well as the impact in the diverse SDN planes (application, control, and data) needs to be considered for a complete and informed decision process. In this aspect, CROCUS proposes a set of additional metrics to fulfil this gap, as summarised in Table 2.

Table 2. CROCUS added metrics and values

Metric	Values	Description
Status #Stat	{0,1}	1-If solved, or 0- yet without a fix
Update days #UptDay	[0, ∞]	Number of days since identification and publishing of vulnerability and its resolution
Actives at App plane #AppPlane	{0,1}	1- If affects actives at the application plane
Actives at Control plane #CtrlPlane	{0,1}	1- If affects actives at the control plane
Actives at Data plane #DataPlane	{0,1}	1- If affects actives at the data plane
Severity Level #SevLevel	[1, 6]	6- stands for extreme, while 1- is for negligible levels
Probability of Occurrence #Prob	[1, 6]	6- stands for maximum, while 1- is for negligible probability
Mitigation Measures #MitMea	{0,1,2}	0- no measures, while 2- if for more than one measure

The status and update days metrics, which provide information regarding the correction of the vulnerability (in the form of software patches, new software versions) can be collected using the available information of vulnerabilities in the National Vulnerabilities Databases (NVD) [14]. It should be noticed that the update days does not necessarily mean that the vulnerability is solved, as it may include updates regarding available information, for instance to apply temporary configuration fixes in order to reduce the impact. Such metrics are also relevant to highlight the support of the community to correct and enhance features in a given SDN controller. For instance, SDN controllers without modifications in a period of one year might indicate low support from the community to add new functionalities to a SDN controller (e.g. add support for P4), or to correct identified vulnerabilities.

The severity level and probability of occurrence are introduced, considering the combination of vulnerability assessment and risk determination logic for enterprise scenarios and services [11]. Such reasoning allows one to assess the real impact of the vulnerabilities in enterprise scenarios or services relying on SDN controllers. In such context, the metrics regarding the actives of the diverse planes highlight which components are affected considering the SDN planes, as described in Sect. 3.1. For instance, if a vulnerability only affects applications running on top of the controller, using the NBI interface, or affect either the control and data planes, either at the controller and/or switching equipments communicating through the SBI interface.

In a generic perspective, additional metrics like the number of mitigation measures are relevant, in particular when the vulnerability is not totally fixed. This mitigation measure accounts for configurations, documentation, procedures that can be performed to mitigate the impact of vulnerabilities. This metric has some similarities with the Remediation Level (RL) of the temporal metrics from CVSS. Nonetheless, CROCUS, considers the number of measures that can mitigate the impact of the vulnerability, while the RL metric only distinguishes if there are workarounds, temporary or official fixes. In addition, CROCUS does not consider Environmental Metrics, since they rely on customised CVSS scores, which are based on the subjective importance of users in organisations.

4.3   Step #3 - Rank Vulnerabilities

CROCUS ranks vulnerabilities using the Methodical algorithm [8], as outlined in Sect. 3.3. Figure 1 pictures the CROCUS metrics into the benefits and costs criteria categories for ranking. It also highlights the metrics proposed by CROCUS, extending the ones already provided by CVSS standards.

The output of the rank step is an ordered score $VSco$, where lower values are the most favourable, as they are close to the ideal solutions that Methodical internally considers. The list of vulnerabilities identified in the previous steps are ranked considering the multiple attributes, which derived from CVSS and introduced in CROCUS.

In CROCUS, each vulnerability of an SDN controller represents an alternative (in the terminology of MADM), and through the application of the ranking

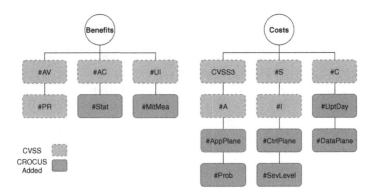

Fig. 1. CROCUS benefits and costs metrics from Tables 1 and 2 in ranking step.

step, an ordered list of vulnerabilities is obtained, requiring a final step to filter/select the SDN controller.

4.4   Step #4 - Selection of SDN Controller

The final selection of the SDN controller relies on a heuristic approach that combines the vulnerabilities of the diverse SDN controllers (VSo), the solvability ratio ($rCri$), and other relevant security features ($SeSo$) that are considered in three categories: Design, Interface and Security Services, as summarised in Table 3. The security features are evaluated in a three-level scale, where 0-no support, 1-partial support and 2-full support. Such classifications rely on the official and available documentation of the controllers. The provided features rely on the features that are reported in the literature as being mandatory or highly recommended for SDN controllers in enterprise environments [3–6]. Such features are then ranked using the Methodical algorithm.

The solvability ratio - $rCri$ corresponds to a composite metric assessing the reaction that the community/entity responsible for a SDN controller has to solve critical vulnerabilities, in a time period. $rCri_c$, regarding controller c, is determined as per Eq. 1 and considers the average of days to solve critical vulnerabilities - $uptDayCri_c$, which has a certain number of critical vulnerabilities - $nVulCri_c$. A critical vulnerability has a CVSS score above 4 (i.e. CVSS3 $\geq$ 4). The $TOTuptDayCri$ corresponds to the sum of the averages days to solve critical vulnerabilities in all N controllers.

$$rCri_c = \frac{\frac{\sum uptDayCri_c}{nVulCri_c}}{TOTuptDayCri}, with\ c \in [1, N] \tag{1}$$

Lower values of $rCri$ are more interesting, since they represent that a vulnerability takes less time to be solved/addressed.

The $CROCUS_c$, for controller c, corresponds to the result of the heuristic enabling the objective selection of the SDN controller. As per Eq. 2, $CROCUS_c$

Table 3. CROCUS functional metrics per category with values {0,1,2}

C.	Metric	Description
Design	Security Resources #**RS**	Mechanisms to protect networks resources
	Policy Conflicts resolution #**IRP**	Schemes to ensure that policies to not introduce opposite behaviours
	Multiple instances #**IMC**	Clustering support to avoid SPoF
	Protection of Inter-cluster msgs #**PIC**	In cluster mode ensure that the information of master is verified [5]
	Secure Storage #**AS**	Information is stored in a secure way and with integrity verification schemes
Interface	Secure communication interface #**CCS**	Communications with the SDN controller are secured (i.e. TLS)
	GUI/REST API security #**API**	Interfaces exposing the SDN controller, in particular the NBI are secured (e.g. TLS)
Services	IDPS integration #**IDPS**	Integration with Intrusion Detection Prevention Systems is performed in a seamless mode
	AAA support #**AAA**	Resources' usage requires authentication
	Resource Monitoring #**MR**	Resources are monitored (topology changes)
	Logs and audit #**AuD**	Information of SDN planes is logged

combines the solvability ratio - $rCri$, the vulnerabilities score - VSo, and the score of the security functions - $SeSo$ employing a utility function with a weighted sum of these metrics. The average of vulnerabilities score - VSo considers the number of vulnerabilities identified nV_c, while the average of the score of security functionalities - $SeSo$ is determined considering the number of secure functionalities nS_c. Weights for the solvability metric wR, for the score of the vulnerabilities wV and for the score of security functionalities wS are configurable to allow modelling user preferences, with $wR + wV + wS = 1$.

$$CROCUS_c = rCri_c * wR + \frac{\sum VSo_c}{nV_c} * wV + \frac{\sum SeSo_c}{nS_c} * wS \qquad (2)$$

The goal is to achieve lower values of $CROCUS_c$, as they represent more efficient solvability ratios and scores close to the ideal values.

5   A Case Study: SDN Controller for 5G Networks

This section describes a use case with the selection of a SDN controller in heterogeneous networks.

5.1   Scenario

A scenario consisting of heterogeneous technologies can be considered as a study use case [2]. Such technologies are employed to allow vehicles to communicate with the infrastructure. The mmWave or fiber can be employed to allow the connection between infrastructure nodes (e.g. Road Side Units - RSUs), while vehicles can communicate with the infrastructure (e.g. RSU) using 5G radio. The infrastructure can also support other services, like multimedia services with caching mechanisms or served through content delivery networks, to enhance the quality of video. In both scenarios, SDN is employed to facilitate the management of network policies, to enable the chaining of service functions (SFCs) and to facilitate the interconnection with orchestration platforms for VNFs.

In such scenario, performance metrics like Round-Trip-Time (RTT), throughput, bandwidth and burst rate are considered by the literature [25]. Nonetheless, the security features summarised in Table 3 are also relevant. For instance, the support of clustering, the support of secure resources (i.e. validate and enforce use of privileges of applications), the support for resource monitoring and the support for policy conflicts resolution are features that enhance the security in aforementioned scenarios. Given such security constraints, the choice of SDN controllers narrows to ONOS and OpenDayLight [4, 25]. SDN controllers like Ryu or Pox are not considered as feasible controllers [7, 24] since they lack support for clustering or do not have support for demanding scenarios.

5.2   SDN Controllers

The SDN controllers considered in the study case include ONOS and OpenDayLight for the study period between the years 2014 and 2020.

Table 4. OpenDayLight vulnerabilities

CVE-id	#Stat	Pub.Date	Upd.Date	#uptDay	CVSS3	#AV	#AC	#PR	#S	#UI	#C	#I	#A	#MitMea	#AppPlane	#CtrlPlane	#DataPlane	#SevLevel	#Prob
CVE-2018-10898	1	30/07/18	09/10/19	436	3	2	1	0	1	0	2	2	2	1	0	1	0	3	3
CVE-2018-1132	1	20/06/18	09/10/19	476	4	1	1	0	1	0	2	2	2	1	0	1	0	3	3
CVE-2018-1078	1	16/03/18	09/10/19	572	4	1	1	0	1	0	2	2	2	2	0	1	0	3	3
CVE-2017-1000411	1	31/01/18	03/10/19	610	3	1	1	0	1	0	0	0	2	1	0	0	0	2	3
CVE-2017-1000406	1	30/11/17	20/12/17	20	3	1	1	0	1	0	0	2	0	1	0	0	0	2	3
CVE-2015-1778	1	27/06/17	05/07/17	8	4	1	1	0	1	0	2	2	2	2	1	1	0	3	3
CVE-2014-8149	1	27/06/17	03/07/17	6	3	1	1	1	1	0	2	2	2	2	1	1	0	3	3
CVE-2017-1000361	1	24/04/17	03/10/19	892	3	1	1	0	1	0	0	0	2	1	0	1	0	2	3
CVE-2017-1000357	1	24/04/17	02/10/19	891	3	1	1	0	1	0	0	0	2	1	0	1	0	2	3
CVE-2016-4970	1	13/04/17	14/02/21	1403	3	1	1	0	1	0	0	0	2	1	0	1	0	2	3
CVE-2015-1612	1	04/04/17	11/04/17	7	3	1	1	0	1	0	0	2	0	2	0	1	1	2	3
CVE-2015-1611	1	04/04/17	11/04/17	7	3	1	1	0	1	0	0	2	0	2	0	1	1	2	3

$$uptDayCri_{ODL} = 1056/3 = 352 \ rCri_{ODL} = \frac{352}{352+155.54} \approx 69.35\%$$

Table 4 summarises the vulnerabilities of ODL in the study period, illustrating a total of 12 vulnerabilities with high and critical risk. The ODL vulnerabilities are reported considering the VSS and CROCUS proposed metrics (recall Tables 1 and 2).

Table 5. ONOS vulnerabilities

CVE-id	#Stat	Pub.Date	Upd.Date	#uptDay	CVSS3	#AV	#AC	#PR	#S	#UI	#C	#I	#A	#MitMea	#AppPlane	#CtrlPlane	#DataPlane	#SevLevel	#Prob
CVE-2020–35604	1	21/12/20	25/12/20	4	4	1	1	0	1	0	2	2	2	1	1	1	0	3	3
CVE-2019–16302	0	20/02/20	25/02/20	5	3	1	1	0	1	0	0	0	2	0	1	1	0	2	2
CVE-2019–16301	0	20/02/20	25/02/20	5	3	1	1	0	1	0	0	0	2	0	1	1	0	2	2
CVE-2019–16300	0	20/02/20	25/02/20	5	3	1	1	0	1	0	0	0	2	0	1	1	0	2	2
CVE-2019–16299	0	20/02/20	25/02/20	5	3	1	1	0	1	0	0	0	2	0	1	1	0	2	2
CVE-2019–16298	0	20/02/20	25/02/20	5	3	1	1	0	1	0	0	0	2	0	1	1	0	2	2
CVE-2019–16297	0	20/02/20	25/02/20	5	3	1	1	0	1	0	0	0	2	0	1	1	0	2	2
CVE-2019–11189	0	20/02/20	28/02/20	8	3	1	1	0	1	0	0	2	0	0	0	1	1	2	3
CVE-2020–8495	1	30/01/20	06/02/20	7	3	1	2	1	1	0	2	2	2	1	1	1	1	3	2
CVE-2020–8494	1	30/01/20	06/02/20	7	3	1	1	1	1	0	2	2	2	1	1	1	1	3	2
CVE-2019–18418	1	24/10/19	29/10/19	5	4	1	1	0	1	0	2	2	2	0	1	1	0	3	2
CVE-2019–12587	1	04/09/19	24/08/20	355	3	2	1	0	1	0	2	2	0	1	0	1	1	2	3
CVE-2019–15571	1	26/08/19	03/09/19	8	4	1	1	0	1	0	2	2	2	1	1	1	0	3	3
CVE-2019–1010234	1	22/07/19	25/07/19	3	4	1	1	0	1	0	2	2	2	1	1	1	0	3	3
CVE-2019–1010245	1	19/07/19	25/07/19	6	4	1	1	0	1	0	2	2	2	2	1	1	0	3	2
CVE-2019–13624	1	16/07/19	19/07/19	3	4	1	1	0	1	0	2	2	2	1	1	1	0	3	2
CVE-2018–15868	1	21/06/19	24/06/19	3	4	1	1	0	1	0	2	2	2	1	1	1	0	3	2
CVE-2018–1000616	1	09/07/18	04/09/18	57	4	1	1	0	1	0	2	2	2	2	0	1	0	3	2
CVE-2018–1000614	1	09/07/18	04/09/18	57	4	1	1	0	1	0	2	2	2	2	0	1	0	3	2
CVE-2018–11316	1	03/07/18	11/09/18	70	4	1	1	0	2	1	2	2	2	1	0	1	1	3	4
CVE-2018–11314	1	03/07/18	11/09/18	70	4	1	1	0	2	1	2	2	2	1	0	1	1	3	4
CVE-2018–1000155	1	24/05/18	03/10/19	497	4	1	1	0	1	0	2	2	2	2	0	1	1	3	3
CVE-2014–8129	1	01/03/18	06/04/18	36	3	1	1	0	1	1	2	2	2	1	0	1	0	3	2
CVE-2018–5452	1	07/03/17	18/09/20	926	3	1	1	0	1	0	0	0	2	1	0	1	1	3	2
CVE-2017–13763	1	29/08/17	03/10/18	765	3	1	1	0	1	0	0	0	2	2	0	1	1	2	2
CVE-2017–7516	1	24/08/14	30/08/17	1102	3	1	1	0	1	0	0	0	2	2	0	1	0	3	2
CVE-2017–1000081	1	17/07/17	07/12/20	1239	4	1	1	0	1	0	2	2	2	2	1	1	0	3	2
CVE-2017–1000080	1	17/07/17	07/12/20	1239	3	1	1	0	1	0	0	2	0	2	1	1	0	3	3
CVE-2017–1000079	1	17/07/17	07/12/20	1239	3	1	1	0	1	0	0	0	2	2	1	1	0	3	3

$$uptDayCri_{ONOS} = 2022/13 \approx 155.54 \quad rCri_{ONOS} = \frac{155.54}{352+155.54} \approx 30.65\%$$

It should be noticed that vulnerabilities below CVSS3 exist for the study period, but they have even omitted in the CROCUS evaluation, as they are not relevant for a final decision, and also to avoid introducing more bias in the selection process. The average update time for the critical vulnerabilities relies $\approx 352 days$, which is high when compared with the average update time of ONOS. Indeed, one can observe that the vulnerabilities of ODL are lower when compared to ONOS, but the solvability ratio is higher $rCri_{ODL} \approx 69.35\%$. In addition, ODL has also the vulnerability with high risk that took more time to be solved, when compared to ONOS. The average resolution time for the vulnerabilities of ODL relies ≈ 444 days and none of the vulnerabilities found in the study period are in the status open or without information.

Table 5 depicts 30 security vulnerabilities for the study period with $\approx 26.67\%$ with the status to be solved or without additional information. For instance, the CVE-2019–16302 has not yet available a solution, only mitigation measures [26]. ONOS has a total of 13 critical vulnerabilities, and in the same line of ODL, vulnerabilities with risk below high exist but are not included in the evaluation of CROCUS. The average time for vulnerability resolution relies in values $\approx 266.76 \, days$ which is lower than the one observed in ODL. Indeed the solvability ratio is lower in ONOS $rCri_{ONOS} \approx 30.65\%$, which means that ONOS has an active development process and that new features are being incorporated, since the vulnerabilities more recent when compared to ODL (after the year 2019). OpenDayLight does not disclose vulnerabilities information publicly since the end of 2018.

Another aspect refers to the type of vulnerabilities, which are reported as medium risk, and they result from events and interactions between components (e.g. bugs) of the ONOS controller. The main issue, is that these kind of vulnerabilities are harder to detect, since they require a deep knowledge of the controller and its internals. But on another perspective such kind of vulnerabilities are more interesting to attackers as they exploit is difficult but is also harder to detect. As stated, the identification of the vulnerabilities, the possible mitigation measures, through the analysis of available documentation, is one the contributions of this paper, since the results of such analysis are included in formulation of the $CROCUS_c$ objective selection.

5.3 Ranking Vulnerabilities

This section presents the results of applying the Methodical algorithm with different weights sets. To enable the comparison of the proposed approaches a set of weights has been considered, as summarised in Table 6. The *uniform* set considers the same relevance for the criteria within the respective category, while the *SDN* puts more emphasis on the set of SDN priorities the metrics related with SDN (e.g. #AppPlane, #CtrlPlane and #DataPlane) and the resolution of vulnerabilities (i.e. #Stat and #MitMea metrics). The *CVSS* and *CROCUS* sets aim to intensify the associated metrics, with the former putting emphasis on the CVSS standards (e.g. CVSS3 score), while the later mainly considered the metrics introduced in the CROCUS approach.

Table 6. Sets of metrics weights

Weight Set in (%)	Benefits						Costs										
	# UI	# AV	# PR	# AC	# Stat	# MitMea	# S	# C	# I	# A	CVSS3	# SevLevel	# Prob	# AppPlane	# CtrlPlane	# DataPlane	# UptDays
Uniform	16,67	16,67	16,67	16,67	16,67	16,67	9,09	9,09	9,09	9,09	9,09	9,09	9,09	9,09	9,09	9,09	9,09
SDN	5,00	10,00	10,00	25,00	25,00	25,00	5,00	5,00	5,00	5,00	5,00	5,00	5,00	20,00	20,00	20,00	5,00
CVSS	20,00	20,00	20,00	20,00	10,00	10,00	15,00	15,00	15,00	15,00	20,00	5,00	5,00	2,50	2,50	2,50	2,50
CROCUS	5,00	5,00	5,00	5,00	40,00	40,00	2,50	2,50	2,50	2,50	2,50	15,00	15,00	15,00	15,00	15,00	12,50

CROCUS also considers the possibility of establishing more preference to the benefits or costs metrics categories/groups. The *equalGrp* establishes the same importance (50%) for benefits and costs categories, while the *benefGrp* puts emphasis on the benefits category with 75% for benefits. The *costsGrp* places 75% of relevance in costs metric category.

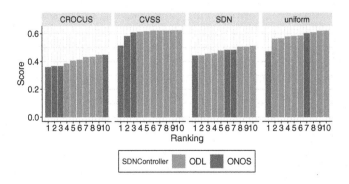

Fig. 2. TopTen per weight set and *equalGrp* weight category

Figure 2 depicts the topTen ranking of the vulnerabilities per the set of metrics weights. The vulnerabilities associated with ONOS for all the weight sets are always placed in the first place. All the weight sets rank the *CVE-2014-8129* in first place, due its low probability and reduced impact in diverse SDN planes. Although not pictured, the weight category/group does not affect the ranking in terms of placing the vulnerabilities of ONOS in first place.

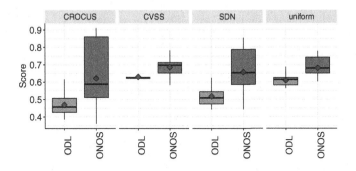

Fig. 3. Variation of vulnerability score per controller and weight set

Figure 3 depicts the variation of vulnerability scores per controller and per set of metrics weight. The scores associated with ONOS tend to haver a higher variation, in particular in the cases with the weight set defining extreme values in the relevance of some criteria. The *CROCUS* weight set introduces higher variation, where ONOS has vulnerabilities close to the ideal (values near zero) but also more distant from the ideal solution (close to one). The difference between ONOS and ODL is also patent in such case, with the an higher variation in the mean values (represented as diamond points), with values above 0.1. The variation in ONOS is also associated with the number of vulnerabilities which is more than the double when compared to ODL.

Such results also put in evidence, that the weights to rank vulnerabilities of SDN controllers must be set to put emphasis on the metrics that are associated with the CVSS score (#AV, #I, #A, etc.).

5.4   Selection of SDN Controller

Table 7 contains the values of the functional metrics for ODL and ONOS controllers that were determined considering Table 3 and available documentation.

Table 7. Values of functional metrics for ODL and ONOS controllers

Controller	Design					Interface		Service			
	#RS	#RP	#MC	#PIC	#AS	#CCS	#API	#IDS	#AAA	#MR	AuD
ODL	2	2	2	1	2	2	1	2	2	1	2
ONOS	1	2	2	0	1	2	2	1	1	2	2

ODL has a framework to support AAA, thus leading to the maximum classification in #RS, #AAA and #AS metrics. ONOS includes security features like the security mode, but some of these features are not well documented, being unclear the support for secure storage #AS. The Defense4All project of ODL facilitates the integration with IDPS, while ONOS does not provide documentation to perform such integration, thus the value 0 in the #IDS metric. On the other hand, ONOS provides support for multiple monitoring and audit solutions, while ODL only documents one approach. All the security functionalities are considered as belonging to the benefits category/group, since they provide a clear advantage in terms of security.

Table 8. Weights of functional metrics for ODL and ONOS controllers

Weight Set (%)	Design					Interface		Service			
	#RS	#RP	#MC	#PIC	#AS	#CCS	#API	#IDS	#AAA	#MR	AuD
Uniform	9,09	9,09	9,09	9,09	9,09	9,09	9,09	9,09	9,09	9,09	9,09
Design	17,50	17,50	17,50	17,50	15,00	2,50	2,50	2,50	2,50	2,50	2,50
Interface	5,00	5,00	5,00	5,00	2,50	30,00	30,00	5,00	5,00	5,00	5,00
Service	5,00	2,50	2,50	2,50	2,50	2,50	2,50	20,00	20,00	20,00	20,00

The weights of the security functionalities are also considered in diverse sets, as summarised in Table 8, where the *Design* puts emphasis on the design metrics, the *Interface* gives more preference to the security metrics in the controller interfaces, and the *Service* prioritises the security metrics associated with monitoring and audit support. Figure 4 outlines the best performance of ODL regarding the security functionalities, in the majority of the weight sets. ONOS only surpasses ODL in the *Interface* weight set due to stronger security mechanisms for REST APIs.

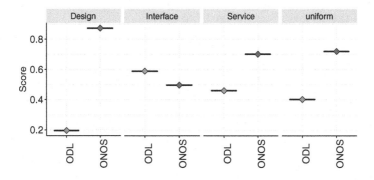

Fig. 4. Variation of score per controller and weight set

The results discussed so far only focus on particular scores or metrics, considering the different sets of weights. The CROCUS aggregation score, as per

Eq. 2 aggregates the solvability ratio of critical vulnerabilities - $rCric$, the average vulnerabilities score - VSo and the average score of security functionalities - $SeSo$. Figure 5 illustrates the CROCUS score for the ODL and ONOS controllers. CROCUS highlights that both controllers have the same security performance, if considering the mean values, represented as blue diamonds, the minimum values and the third quartile (75th percentile). The values for ODL and ONOS controllers are similar with low differences between them. The ONOS controller has higher values for CROCUS ($\approx$1.5), while ODL has around ≈ 1.4 (with some outliers). Nonetheless, the variation between the minimum value and the first quartile (25 th percentile) is lower for ONOS (≈ 0.45, while ODL has ≈ 0.65), which holds the tendency of ONOS to have values near zero. Thus, the best values for CROCUS metric, herein proposed. CROCUS assesses ONOS as the most suitable choice the SDN controller.

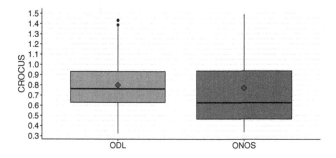

Fig. 5. CROCUS

6 Conclusions

CROCUS has been employed in a scenario considering multiple technologies and stringent requirements in terms of performance and security, to enable an objective selection of SDN controllers. CROCUS can also assist CISO and other security managers in the decision process of selecting the most suitable SDN controllers, focusing on security aspects, without disregarding performance constraints. CROCUS is simple to be applied in design, production phases and aggregates information publicly available. In particular, information regarding the vulnerabilities affecting controllers, as well their mitigation measures.

Our next steps include the integration of CROCUS in SDN controllers to enhance security support in real-time by enabling the configuration of multiple instances in the clustering process and the deployment of security policies to mitigate such kind of attacks.

Acknowledgements. This work was funded by the European Regional Development Fund (FEDER), through the Regional Operational Programme of Centre (CENTRO 2020) of the Portugal 2020 framework and FCT under the MIT Portugal Program [Project SNOB-5G with Nr. 045929 (CENTRO-01-0247-FEDER-045929)].

References

1. Taneja, M., Davy, A.: Resource aware placement of IoT application modules in fog-cloud computing paradigm. In: IFIP/IEEE IM. IEEE (2017)
2. Cohen, A., et al.: Bringing network coding into SDN: a case-study for highly meshed heterogeneous communications. CoRR, vol. abs/2010.00343 (2020)
3. Scott-Hayward, S.: Design and deployment of secure, robust, and resilient SDN controllers. In: IEEE NetSoft (2015)
4. Singh, M.P., Bhandari, A.: New-flow based DDoS attacks in SDN: taxonomy, rationales, and research challenges. Comput. Comm. **154**, 509–527 (2020)
5. Abdou, A.R., van Oorschot, C., Wan, T.: A framework and comparative analysis of control plane security of SDN and conventional networks. arXiv (2017)
6. Yoon, S., et al.: A security-mode for carrier-grade SDN controllers. In: ACM ACSAC. ACM, December 2017
7. Mamushiane, L., Lysko, A., Dlamini, S.: A comparative evaluation of the performance of popular SDN controllers. IFIP Wireless Days, April 2018
8. Sousa, B., Pentikousis, K., Curado, M.: Methodical: towards the next generation of multihomed applications. Comput. Netw. **65**, 21–40 (2014)
9. Baghla, S., Bansal, S.: VIKOR MADM based optimization method for vertical handover in heterogeneous networks. Adv. Syst. Sci. Appl. **18**(3), 90–110 (2018)
10. Khondoker, R., Zaalouk, A., Marx, R., Bayarou, K.: Feature-based comparison and selection of software defined networking controllers. In: WCCAIS 2014
11. Schumacher, M., Fernandez-Buglioni, E., Hybertson, D., Buschmann, F., Sommerlad, P.: Security Patterns: Integrating Security and Systems Engineering. Wiley, Hoboken (2005)
12. Arbettu, R.K., Khondoker, R., Bayarou, K., Weber, F.: Security analysis of Open-Daylight, ONOS, Rosemary and Ryu SDN controllers. In: 17th Networks Symposium (2016)
13. Microsoft: The STRIDE Threat Model (2009)
14. NIST Itl National Vulnerability Database: Common vulnerability scoring system calculator. https://nvd.nist.gov/vuln-metrics/cvss/v3-calculator
15. Araújo, M.C., Sousa, B., Curado, M., Bittencourt, L.F.: CMFog: proactive content migration using markov Chain and MADM in fog computing. In: 2020 IEEE/ACM UCC (2020)
16. Sousa, B., Pentikousis, K., Curado, M.: Optimizing quality of resilience in the cloud. In: 2014 IEEE Global Communications Conference (2014)
17. Zhu, L., et al.: Sdn controllers: a comprehensive analysis and performance evaluation study. ACM Comput. Surv. **53**(6), 1–40 (2020)
18. Schehlmann, L., Abt, S., Baier, H.: Blessing or curse? Revisiting security aspects of software-defined networking. In: CNSM (2014)
19. Xu, Y., Liu, Y.: DDoS attack detection under SDN context. In: IEEE INFOCOM 2016. IEEE Press (2016)
20. O.N.F. (ONF): SDN Architecture 1.0 Overview, November 2014

21. Sanvito, D., Moro, D., Gulli, M., Filippini, I., Capone, A., Campanella, A.: ONOS intent monitor and reroute service: enabling plug&play routing logic. In: 2018 4th IEEE NetSoft. IEEE, June 2018

22. FIRST: Common vulnerability scoring system version 3.1: user guide (2021). https://www.first.org/cvss/user-guide,

23. Martini, B., Gharbaoui, M., Adami, D., Castoldi, P., Giordano, S.: Experimenting SDN and cloud orchestration in virtualized testing facilities: performance results and comparison. IEEE TNSM **16**(3), 965–979 (2019)

24. Hamid, S., Zakaria, N., Ahmed, J.: ReCSDN: resilient controller for software defined networks. Int. J. Adv. Comput. Sci. Appl. **8**(8), 202–208 (2017)

25. Badotra, S., Panda, S.N.: Evaluation and comparison of OpenDayLight and open networking operating system in software-defined networking. Cluster Comput. **23**(2), 1281–1291 (2019). https://doi.org/10.1007/s10586-019-02996-0

26. Ujcich. B.E., et al.: Automated discovery of cross-plane event-based vulnerabilities in software-defined networking. In: NDSS Symposium. Internet Society, February 2020

Controlling Network Traffic Microstructures for Machine-Learning Model Probing

Henry Clausen[1]([⊠]) [iD], Robert Flood[1], and David Aspinall[1,2] [iD]

[1] School of Informatics, Edinburgh University, Edinburgh EH8 9AB, UK
{henry.clausen,s1784464,david.aspinall}@ed.ac.uk
[2] The Alan Turing Institute, London NW1 2DB, UK

Abstract. Network intrusion detection (NID) models increasingly rely on learning traffic microstructures that consist of pattern sequences in features such as interarrival time, size, or packet flags. We argue that precise and reproducible control over traffic microstructures is crucial to understand and improve NID-model behaviour. We demonstrate that probing a traffic classifier with appropriately generated microstructures reveals links between misclassifications and traffic characteristics, and correspondingly lets us improve the false positive rate by more than 500%. We examine how specific factors such as network congestion, load, conducted activity, or protocol implementation impact traffic microstructures, and how well their influence can be isolated in a controlled and near-deterministic traffic generation process. We then introduce DetGen, a traffic generation tool that provides precise microstructure control, and demonstrate how to generate traffic suitable to probe pre-trained NID-models.

Keywords: Data generation · Network intrusion detection · Machine learning · Model development · Containerisation

1 Introduction

Scientific machine learning model development requires both **model evaluation**, in which the overall predictive quality of a model is assessed to identify the best model, as well as model validation, in which the behaviour and limitations of a model is assessed through targeted **model probing**, as depicted in Fig. 1. Model validation is essential to understand how particular data structures are processed, and enables researchers to develop their models accordingly. Data generation tools for rapid model probing such as the *What-If tool* [32] underline the importance of model validation, but are not suitable for providing probing data that resembles the complex structures found in network packet streams.

Machine-learning breakthroughs in many fields have been reliant on a precise understanding of data structure and corresponding descriptive labelling to develop more suitable models. In *automatic speech recognition (ASR)*, tone and

© ICST Institute for Computer Sciences, Social Informatics and Telecommunications Engineering 2021
Published by Springer Nature Switzerland AG 2021. All Rights Reserved
J. Garcia-Alfaro et al. (Eds.): SecureComm 2021, LNICST 398, pp. 456–475, 2021.
https://doi.org/10.1007/978-3-030-90019-9_23

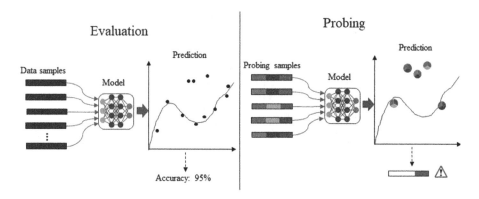

Fig. 1. Model evaluation and model probing with controlled data characteristics.

emotions can alter the meaning of a sentence significantly. The huge automatically gathered speech datasets however only contain speech snippets and if possible their plain transcripts. While modern speech models are in principle able to learn implicit structures such as emotions without explicit labels, it is impossible to determine the cause for systematic error when they are not. Datasets that contain labelled specialised speech characteristics such as the Ryerson Database of Emotional Speech and Song (RAVDESS) [15] not only allow researchers to identify if their model is susceptible to structural misclassification through targeted probing, but also inspire new methods to capture and understand these implicit structures [7], which in turn leads to design improvements of general speech recognition models [11].

Prominent network intrusion detection methods as Kitsune [19] or DeepCorr [21] learn structures in the sizes, flags, or interarrival times (IATs) of packet sequences for decision-making. These structures reveal information about attack behaviour, but are also influenced by a number of other factors such as network congestion or the transmitted data. We define **traffic microstructures** either as reoccurring patterns in the metadata of packet sequences within a connection, such as the packet sizes of a Diffie-Hellman exchange or typical IATs of video streaming, or as patterns within the summary statistics of individual connections or short sequences observed on a host such as the pattern of port 53 (DNS) connections being followed by port 80 or 443 connections (HTTP/S). No effort has been made so far to monitor or control these factors to probe models for specific microstructures, with the current quasi-benchmark NID-datasets paying more attention to the inclusion of specific attacks and topologies rather than the documentation of the generated traffic. This situation has so far led researchers to often simply evaluate a variety of ML-models on these datasets in the hope of edging out competitors, without understanding model flaws and corresponding data structures through targeted probing.

We demonstrate how to produce traffic effectively to probe a state-of-the-art traffic classifier, and why a certain degree of generative **determinism** is required for this to isolate the influence of traffic microstructures. The model insights

and corresponding performance improvements achieved through probing motivate our experimental examination of various influence factors over microstructures and how to control them during traffic generation. Finally, we present
DetGen, a traffic generation tool that provides near-deterministic control over
microstructure-shaping factors such as conducted activity, communication failures or network congestion to generate reproducible traffic samples along with
corresponding ground-truth labels.

This work provides the following contributions:

1. We demonstrate why model probing with controllable traffic microstructure
   is a crucial step to understand and ultimately improve model behaviour by
   probing a state-of-the-art LSTM traffic classifier and lowering its false positives five-fold.
2. We discuss requirements for traffic data suitable to probe models pre-trained
   on a given NIDS-dataset, and demonstrate how to generate probing traffic
   effectively through DetGen-IDS, a dedicated probing dataset.
3. We examine experimentally how different factors affect traffic microstructures, and how well they can be controlled in a more effective manner when
   compared to common VM-based traffic generation setups.
4. We propose DetGen, a container-based traffic generation paradigm that provides accurate control and labels over traffic microstructures, and experimentally demonstrate the level of provided generative determinism compared to
   traditional generation set-ups.

DetGen and the DetGen-IDS data are openly accessible for researchers on
GitHub.

1.1 Outline

The remainder of the paper is organized as follows: Sect. 2 discusses the need for
generating probing data with sufficient microstructure control before presenting
the probing and corresponding improvement of a state-of-the-art intrusion detection model as a motivating example. Section 3 proceeds to examine over which
traffic characteristics DetGen exerts control and the corresponding control level.
Section 4 provides details over the design paradigm of DetGen and the resulting
advantages over traditional setups, while Sect. 5 discusses the level of control
DetGen provides when compared to traditional setups. Section 6 discusses how
to generate probing data appropriately for pretained models, and provides an
overview over the DetGen-IDS data. Section 7 concludes our work.

1.2 Existing Datasets and Corresponding Ground-Truth
Information

Real-world NID-datasets such as those from the Los Alamos National Laboratory [12] (LANL) or the University of Grenada [16] provide large amounts of
data from a particular network in the form of flow records. Due to the lack of
monitoring and traffic anonymisation, it is impossible for researchers to extract

detailed information about the specific computational activity associated with a particular traffic sample. Synthetic NID-datasets such as the CICIDS-17 and 18 [26] or the UNSW-NB-15 [20] aim to provide traffic from a wide range of attacks as well as an enterprise-like topology in the form of pcap-files and flow-statistics. The CICIDS-17 data for example contains 5 days of network traffic from 12 host that include different Windows, Ubuntu, and Web-Server versions, and covers attacks from probing and DoS to smaller SQL-injections and infiltrations. While some effort is put in the generation of benign activities using activity scripting or traffic generators, we have seen no attention being spent at monitoring these activities accordingly, which leaves researchers with the limited information available through packet inspection. Furthermore, synthetic datasets can be criticised for their limited activity range, such as the CICIDS-17 dataset where more than 95% of FTP-transfers consist downloading the Wikipedia page for 'Encryption' [24], which leads to insufficient structural nuances for effective probing.

1.3   Scope of DetGen

The scope of DetGen is to generate traffic with near-deterministic control over factors that influence microscopic packet- and flow-level structures. DetGen separates program executions and traffic capture into distinct containerised environments to exclude any background traffic events, and simulates influence factors such as network congestion, communication failures, data transfer size, content caching, or application implementation.

2   Methodology and Example

Assume the following problem: You are designing a packet-level traffic classifier which is generating a significant number of false positives, something that is still a common problem for the state-of-the-art [22]. The false positives turn out to be caused by a particular characteristic such as unsuccessful logins or frequent connection restarts. However, existing real-world or synthetic datasets do not contain the necessary information to associate traffic events with these characteristics, which prevents you from identifying the misclassification cause effectively. To address this problem, we need a way to controllably generate and label traffic microstructures driven by these characteristics.

To provide an example, we look at a *Long-Short-Term Memory* (LSTM) network, a deep learning design for sequential data, by Hwang et al. [9], which is designed to classify attacks in web traffic and has achieved some of the highest detection rates of packet-based classifiers in a recent survey [29]. Through probing we will learn that retransmissions in a packet sequence dramatically deplete the model's classification accuracy. We take the following steps:

Step 1: Determine model performance and feed it suitable probing traffic.
Step 2: Examine the correlation between traffic misclassification scores and the generated traffic microstructure labels to find a likely cause.

Step 3: Examine at which latency levels specific connections are misclassified.

Step 4: Generate two similar connections, with one exposed to strong packet latency.

Step 5: Show that by removing retransmission sequences in the pre-processing, misclassification is significantly reduced.

We now explain these steps in more detail:

Step 1: To detect SQL injections, we train the model on the CICIDS-17 dataset [26] (85% of connections). For the evaluation, we also include a set of HTTP-activities generated by DetGen (7.5%) that mirror the characteristics in the training data, as explained in Sect. 6. In total, we use 30,000 connections for training and for evaluating the model, or slightly under 2 million packets. The initially trained model performs relatively well, with an *Area under curve* (AUC)-score of **0.981**, or a detection/false positive rate[1] of **96%** and **2.7%**. However, to enable operational deployment the false positive rate would need to be several magnitudes lower [18].

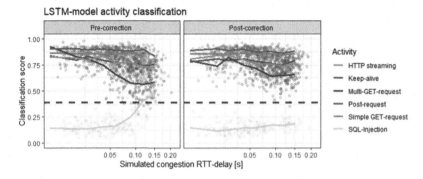

Fig. 2. Scores for the LSTM-traffic model before and after the model correction.

Step 2: Now suppose we want to improve these rates to both detect more SQL-injections and retain a lower false positive rate. To start, we explore which type of connections are misclassified most often. We retrieve the classification scores for all connections and measure their linear correlation to the microstructure labels available for the probing data. The highest misclassification ratio was measured for one of the three SQL injection scenarios (19% correlation) and connections with multiple GET-requests (11% correlation). When not distinguishing activities, we measured a high misclassification correlation with simulated packet latency (12%), which we now examine. More details on this exact procedure can be found in [3].

Step 3: Figure 2 depicts classification scores of connections in the probing data in dependence of the emulated network latency. The left panel depicts the scores

---

[1] Tuned for the geometric mean.

for the initially trained model, while the right panel depicts scores after the model correction that we introduce further down. The left panel shows that classification scores are well separated for lower congestion, but increased latency in a connection leads to a narrowing of the classification scores, especially for SQL-injection traffic. Since there are no classification scores that reach far in the opposing area, we conclude that congestion simply makes the model lose predictive certainty. Increased latency can both increase variation in observed packet interarrival times (IATs), and lead to packet out-of-order arrivals and corresponding retransmission attempts. Both of these factors can decrease the overall sequential coherence for the model, i.e. that the LSTM-model loses context too quickly either due to increased IAT variation or during retransmission sequences.

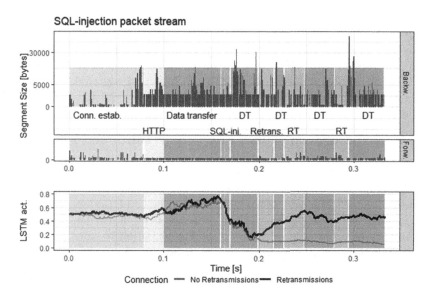

Fig. 3. LSTM-classification output in dependence of connection phases. (Color figure online)

Step 4: We use DetGen to generate two similar connections, where one connection is subject to moderate packet latency and corresponding reordering while the other is not. DetGen's ability to shape traffic in a controlled and deterministic manner allows us to examine the effect of retransmission sequences on the model output and isolate it from other potential influence factors. Figure 3 depicts the evolution of the LSTM-output layer activation in dependence of difference connection phases for the connection subject to retransmissions. Depicted are packet segment streams and their respective sizes in the forward and backward direction, with different phases in the connection coloured and labelled. Below is the LSTM-output activation while processing the packet streams. The red line shows the output for the connection without retransmissions[2] as a comparison. Initially the model begins to view the connection as benign when processing regular traffic, until the SQL-injection is performed. The model then quickly adjusts and provides a malicious classification score after processing the injection phase and the subsequent data transfer, just as it is supposed to.

The correct output activation is however quickly depleted once the model processes a retransmission phase and is afterwards not able to relate the still ongoing data transfer to the injection phase and return to the correct output activation. When we compare this to the connection without retransmissions, depicted as the red line in Fig. 3, we do not encounter this depletion effect. Instead, the negative activation persists after the injection phase.

Step 5: Based on this analysis, we try to correct the existing model with a simple fix by excluding retransmission sequences at the pre-processing stage. This leads to significantly better classification results during network latency, as visible in the right panel of Fig. 2. SQL-injection scores are now far-less affected by congestion while scores for benign traffic are also less affected, albeit to a smaller degree. The overall AUC-score for the model improves to **0.997** while tuned detection rates improved to **99.1%** and false positives to **0.345%**, a five-fold improvement from the previous false positive rate of 2.7%.

3   Traffic Microstructures and Their Influence Factors

As shown above, traffic microstructures and corresponding model predictions can be significantly influenced by external factors. The biggest and most obvious influence on traffic microstructures is the choice of the application layer protocols. For this reason, the range of protocols is often used as a measure for the diversity of a dataset. However, while the attention to microstructures in current NID-datasets stops here, computer communication involves a myriad of other different computational aspects that shape observable traffic microstructures. Here, we highlight and quantify the most dominant ones, which will act as a justification for the design choices we outline in Sect. 4.4. We look at both findings from previous work as well as our own experimental results.

1. Performed task and application. The conducted computational task as well as the corresponding application ultimately drives the communication between computers, and thus hugely influences characteristics such as the direction of data transfer, the duration and packet rate, as well as the number of connections established. These features are correspondingly used extensively in application fingerprinting, such as by Yen et al. [33] or Stober et al. [28].

2. Application layer implementations. Different implementations for TLS, HTTP, etc. can yield different computational performance and can perform handshakes differently and differ in multiplexing channel prioritisation, which

---

[2] Scaled temporally to the same connection phases.

can significantly impact IAT times and the overall duration of the transfer, as shown in a study by Marx et al. [17] for the QUIC/HTTP3 protocol[3].

3. LAN and WAN congestion. Low available bandwidth, long RTTs, or packet loss can have a significant effect on TCP congestion control mechanisms that influence frame-sizes, IATs, window sizes, and the overall temporal characteristic of the sequence, which in turn can influence detection performance significantly as shown in Sect. 2.

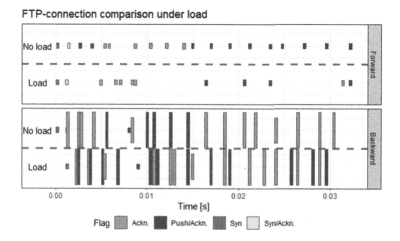

Fig. 4. Packet-sequence similarity comparison under different load.

4. Host level load. In a similar manner, other applications exhibiting significant computational load (CPU, memory, I/O) on the host machine can affect the processing speed of incoming and outgoing traffic, which can again alter IATs and the overall duration of a connection. An example of this is visible in Fig. 4, where a FTP-client sends significantly fewer PUSH-packets when under heavy computational load. Colours indicate packet flags while the height of the packets indicates their size. This effect is dependent on the application layer protocol, where at a load number of 3.5 we see about 60% less upstream data-packets while the downstream is only reduced by 10%, compared to HTTP where both downstream and upstream packet rates are throttled by about 40%.

5. Caching/Repetition effects. Tools like cookies, website caching, DNS caching, known hosts in SSH, etc. remove one or more information retrieval requests from the communication, which can lead to altered packet sequences and less connections being established. For caching, this can result in less than 10% of packets being transferred, as shown by Fricker et al. [5].

---

[3] Figure 2 in [17] illustrates these differences in a nice way.

6. User and background activities. The choice and usage frequency of an application and task by a user, sometimes called *Pattern-of-Life*, governs the larger-scale temporal characteristic of a traffic capture, but also influences the rate and type of connections observed in a particular time-window [1]. The mixing of different activities in a particular time-window can severely impact detection results of recent sequential connection-models, such as by Radford et al. [23] or by Clausen et al. [4]. To quantify this effect, we look at FTP-traffic in the CICIDS-17 dataset. As explained in Sect. 1.2, the FTP-traffic overwhelmingly corresponds to the exact same isolated task, and should therefore spawn the same number of connections in a particular time window. However, we observe additional connections from other activities within a 5-second window for 68% of all FTP-connections, such as depicted in Table 1, which contains FTP-, HTTPS- and DNS-, as well as additional unknown activity.

Table 1. 5-second window for host 192.168.10.9 in the CICIDS-17 dataset.

Time	Source-IP	Destination-IP	Dest. Port
13:45:56.8	192.168.10.9	192.168.10.50	21
13:45:56.9	192.168.10.9	192.168.10.50	10602
13:45:57.5	192.168.10.9	69.168.97.166	443
13:45:59.1	192.168.10.9	192.168.10.3	53
13:46:00.1	192.168.10.9	205.174.165.73	8080

Other prominent factors that we found had less effect on traffic microstructures include:

7. Networking stack load. TCP or IP queue filling of the kernel networking stack can increase packet waiting times and therefore IATs of the traffic trace, as shown by [25]. In practice, this effect seems to be constrained to large WAN-servers and routers. When varying the stack load in otherwise constant settings on an Ubuntu-host, we did not find any notable effect on packet sequences when comparing the corresponding traffic with a set of three similarity metrics. More details on this setting and the metrics can be found in Sect. 5.

8. Network configurations. Network settings such as the MTU or the enabling of TCP Segment Reassembly Offloading have effects on the captured packet sizes, and have been exploited in IP fragmentation attacks. However, these settings have been standardised for most networks, as documented in the CAIDA traffic traces [31].

We designed DetGen to control and monitor factors 1–6 to let researchers explore their impact on their traffic models, while omitting factors 7 and 8 for the stated reasons.

4   DetGen: Precisely Controlled Data Generation

4.1   Design Overview

Detgen is a container-based network traffic generation framework that distinguishes itself by providing precise control over various traffic characteristics and providing extensive ground-truth information about the traffic origin. In contrast to the pool of programs running in a VM-setup, such as used in the generation of the CICIDS-17 and 18 [26], or UGR-16 [16], DetGen separates program executions and traffic capture into distinct containerised environments in order to shield the generated traffic from external influences. Traffic is generated from a set of scripted *scenarios* that define the involved devices and applications and strictly control corresponding influence factors. Figure 5 provides a comparison of the DetGen-setup and traditional VM-based setups and highlights how control and monitoring is exerted.

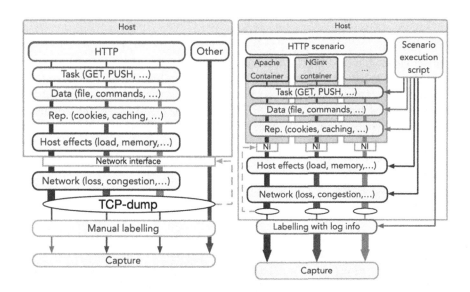

Fig. 5. Traditional traffic-generation-setups (left), and DetGen (right).

4.2   Containerization and Activity Isolation

As we will demonstrate in Sect. 5, containers provide significantly more isolation of programs from external effects than regular OS-level execution. This isolation enables us to monitor processes better and create more accurate links between traffic events and individual activities than on a virtual machine were multiple processes run in parallel and generate traffic. The corresponding one-to-one correlation between processes and network traces allows us to capture traffic directly from the process and produce labelled datasets with granular ground truth information.

Additionally, containers are specified in an image-layer, which is unaffected during the container execution. This allows containers to be run repeatedly whilst always starting from an identical state, allowing a certain level of **determinism** and reproducibility in the data generation.

4.3 Activity Generation

Scenario. We define a *scenario* as a composition of containers conducting a specific interaction. Each scenario produces traffic from a setting with two (client/server) or more containers, with traffic being captured from each container's perspective. This constructs network datasets with total interaction capture, as described by Shiravi et al. [27]. Examples may include an FTP interaction, an online login form paired with an SQL database, or a C&C server communicating with an open backdoor. Our framework is modular, so that individual scenarios are configured, stored, and launched independently. We provide a complete list of implemented scenarios in Table 3 in the Appendix.

Task. To provide a finer grain of control over the traffic to be generated, we create a catalogue of different tasks that allow the user to specify the manner in which a scenario should develop. To explore the breadth of the corresponding traffic structures efficiently, we prioritise tasks that cover aspects such as the direction of file transfers (e.g. GET vs POST for HTTP), the amount of data transferred (e.g. HEAD/DELETE vs GET/PUT), or the duration of the interaction (e.g. persistent vs non-persistent tasks) as much as possible. For each task, we furthermore add different failure options for the interaction to not be successful (e.g. wrong password or file directory).

4.4 Simulation of External Influence

Caching/Cookies/Known Server. Since we always launch containers from the same state, we shield traffic impact from **repetition effects** such as caching or known hosts. If an application provides caching possibilities, we implement this as an option to be specified before the traffic generation process.

Network Effects. Communication between containers takes place over a virtual bridge network, which provides far higher and more reliable throughput than in real-world networks [6]. To retard and control the network reliability and congestion to a realistic level, we rely on *NetEm*, an enhancement of the Linux traffic control facilities for emulating properties of wide area networks from a selected network interface [8].

We apply NetEm to the network interface of a given container, providing us with the flexibility to set each container's network settings uniquely. Packet delays are drawn from a Paretonormal-distribution while packet loss and corruption are drawn from a binomial distribution, which has been found to emulate real-world settings well [10]. Distribution parameters such as mean or correlation as well as available bandwidth can either be manually specified or drawn randomly before the traffic generation process.

Host Load. We simulate excessive computational load on the host with the tool *stress-ng*, a Linux workload generator. Currently, we only stress the CPU of the host, which is controlled by the number of workers spawned. Future work will also include stressing the memory of a system. We have investigated how stress on the network sockets affects the traffic we capture without any visible effect, which is why we omit this variable here.

4.5 Data Generation

Execution Script. DetGen generates traffic through executing script that are specific to the scenario. The script creates the virtual network and populates it with the corresponding containers. The container network interfaces of the containers are then subjected to the chosen NetEm settings and the host is assigned the respective load before the inputs for the chosen task are prepared and mounted to the containers.

Labelling and Traffic Separation. Each container network interface is hooked to a *tcpdump*-container that records the packets that arrive or leave on this interface. Combined with the described process isolation, this setting allows us to exclusively capture traffic that corresponds to the conducted activity and exclude any background events. The execution script then stores all parameters (conducted task, mean packet delay, ...) and descriptive values (input file size, communication failure, ...) for the chosen settings.

5 Traffic Control and Generative Determinism of DetGen

We now assess the claim that DetGen controls the outlined traffic influence factors sufficiently, and how similar traffic generated with the same settings looks like. We also demonstrate that this level of control is not achievable on regular VM-based NIDS-traffic-generation setup.

To do so, we generate traffic from three traffic types, namely HTTP, file-synchronisation, and botnet-C&C, each in four configurations that varied in terms of conducted activity, data/credentials as well as the applied load and congestion. Within each configuration all controllable factors are held constant to test the experimental determinism and reproducibility of DetGen's generative abilities. As a comparison, we use a regular VM-based setup, were applications are hosted directly on two VMs that communicate over a virtual network bridge that is subject to the same NetEm effects as DetGen, such as depicted in Fig. 5. Such a setup is for example used in the generation of the UGR-16 data [16].

To measure how similar two traffic samples are, we devise a set of similarity metrics that measure dissimilarity of overall connection characteristics, connection sequence characteristics, and packet sequence characteristics:

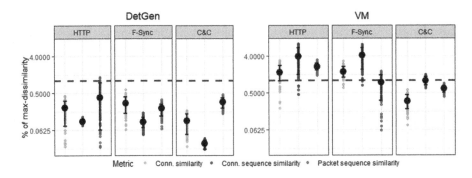

Fig. 6. Dissimilarity scores for DetGen and a regular VM-setup, on a log-scale.

- **Overall connection similarity.** We use the 82 flow summary statistics (IAT and packet size, TCP window sizes, flag occurrences, burst and idle periods) provided by CICFlowMeter [13], and measure the cosine similarity between connections, which is also used in general traffic classification [2].
- **Connection sequence similarity.** To quantify the similarity of a sequence of connections in a retrieval window, we use the following features to describe the window, as used by Yen et al. [33] for application classification: The number of connections, average and max/min flow duration and size, number of distinct IP and ports addresses contacted. We then again measure the cosine similarity based on these features between different windows.
- **Packet sequence similarity.** To quantify the similarity of packet sequences in handshakes etc., we use a Markovian probability matrix for packet flags, IATs, sizes, and direction conditional on the previous packet. We do this for sequences of 15 packets and use the average sequence likelihood as this accommodates better for marginal shifts in the sequence.

We normalise all dissimilarity scores by dividing them by the maximum dissimilarity score measured for each traffic type to put the scores into context. For each configuration, we generate 100 traffic samples and apply the described dissimilarity measures to 100 randomly drawn sample pairs. Figure 6 depicts the resulting dissimilarity scores on a log-scale.

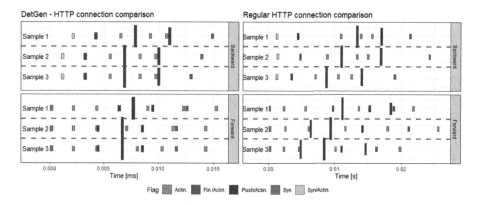

Fig. 7. Packet-sequence similarity comparison for HTTP-activity for DetGen and a regular setting.

The DetGen-scores yield consistently less than 1% of the dissimilarity observed on average for each activity. Scores are especially low when compared to traffic groups collected in the VM setting, which are consistently more dissimilar, in particular for connection-sequence metrics, where the average dissimilarity is more than 30 times higher than for the DetGen setting. Manual inspection of the VM-capture showed that high dissimilarity is caused by additional flow events from background activity (OS and application HTTP, NTP, DNS, device discovery) being present in about 24% of all captures. While sequential dissimilarity is roughly the same for the DetGen- and the VM-settings, overall connection similarity for the VM-setting sees significantly more spread in the dissimilarity scores when computational load is introduced.

Figure 7 depicts an exemplary comparison between HTTP-samples generated using DetGen versus generation using the VM-setup. Colours indicate packet flags while the height of the packets indicates their size. Even though samples from DetGen are not perfectly similar, packets from the VM-setup are subject to more timing perturbations and reordering as well as containing additional packets. Additionally, the packet sizes vary more in the regular setting.

These results confirm that DetGen exerts a high level of control over traffic shaping factors while providing sufficient determinism to guarantee ground-truth traffic information.

6   Reconstructing an IDS-Dataset for Efficient Probing

Moving towards a more general dataset constructed to apply the probing methodology discussed in Sect. 2, we constructed *DetGen-IDS*. This dataset is suitable to quickly probe ML-model behaviour that were trained on the CICIDS-17 dataset [26]. The dataset mirrors properties of the CICIDS-17 data to allow pre-trained models to be probed without retraining. The *DetGen-IDS* data therefore serves as complementary probing data that provides microstructure labels and a sufficient and controlled diversity of several traffic characteristics that is not found in the CICIDS-17 data.

We focus on mirroring the following properties from the CICIDS-17 data:

1. **Application layer protocols (ALP)**
2. **ALP implementations**
3. **Typical data volume for specific ALPs**
4. **Conducted attack types**

Extracting more information on characteristics such as conducted activities of current NID-datasets is difficult for the reasons explained in Sect. 1.2. However, our examination shows that aligning these high-level features with the original training data helps to significantly reduce the validation error of a model on the probing data, as discussed further down in this section and depicted in Fig. 8.

We then took the following steps to extract the necessary information from the CICIDS-17 data and implement the traffic-generation process accordingly:

1. The primary ALPs in the dataset can be identified using their corresponding network ports. We ordered connections by the frequency of their respective port, and excluded connections that do not transmit more than 15 packets per connection as these do not provide enough structure to create probing data from it. This leaves us with the ALPs *HTTP/SSL, SMTP, FTP, SSH, SQL, SMB, LDAP, and NTP*. We had already implemented traffic scenarios for each of them except SMB and LDAP, which we then added to the catalogue described in Sect. 4.3. Table 2 displays the frequency of the most common ALPs in the CICIDS-17 along with their average size and packet number per connection and how we adopted them in the DetGen-IDS data.
2. Most of the used ALP implementations, such as *Apache* and *Ubuntu Web-server* for HTTP, could be gathered from the description of the CICIDS-17 dataset. When this was not the case, it is mostly possible to gather this information by inspecting a few negotiation packets for the corresponding ALP with Wireshark to identify the TLS version or the *OpenSSH*-client. The correct ALP implementation can then be included in the traffic generation process by simply identifying and including a Docker-container that matches the requirements, which is explained more in Sect. 4.3.
3. Since the total size of a connection is one of the most significant features for its classification, we restrict connections in the DetGen-IDS data to cover the same range as their counterparts in the CICIDS-17 data. For this, we extracted the maximum and minimum connection size for each ALP in the benign data and use it as a cut-off to remove all connections from the DetGen-IDS data that do not meet this requirement.
4. Included attacks are well documented in the CICIDS-17 description. These include *SQL-injections, SSH-brute-force, XSS, Botnet, Heartbleed, Golden-Eye, and SlowLoris*. We aim to cover as many of these attack types in the DetGen-IDS data as well as adding them to the overall DetGen-attack-catalogue. We were not able to cover all attacks though as DetGen either did not provide the necessary network topology to conduct the attack, such as for port-scanning, or the attack types are not implemented in the catalogue of scenarios yet.

Table 2. ALPs in CICIDS-17 data and their adoption in DetGen-IDS.

ALP	Port	CICIDS-17			DetGen-IDS	
		Av. Conn. Size	Av. Packets /Conn.	# Packets	# Packets	# Activities
HTTP	80	131626.4	120.4	26631853	724032	7
HTTPS	443	24637.5	36.7	18531661	432104	7
DNS	53	286.2	3.6	3515510	–	–
SSH	22	4699.6	40.9	430380	379421	13
LDAP	389	5429.2	22.3	133471	94587	3
FTP	21	311.3	41.7	121472	183587	9
NetBIOS	137	773.6	14.3	111341	–	–
SMB	445	12941.5	61.9	88175	47945	3
NTP	123	157.0	3.2	73057	1243	1
SMTP	465	2663.5	21.5	77650	104967	3
Kerberos	88	2687.7	6.9	38262	–	–
mDNS	5353	3685.5	35.5	24592	–	–

In addition to the pcap-files, we used the *CICFlowMeter* to generate the same 83 flow-features as included in the CICIDs-17 data. Table 2 displays the content and statistics of the DetGen-IDS data.

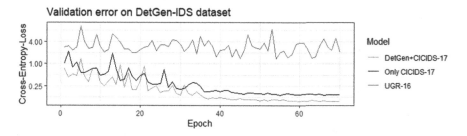

Fig. 8. Validation errors of LSTM-model [4] on DetGen-IDS data. (Color figure online)

In Fig. 8, we compare the validation error of a recent LSTM-model for network intrusion detection by Clausen et al. [4] on the DetGen-IDS data to demonstrate that a model trained on the CICIDS-17 data is able to perform well without retraining. We distinguish models when trained exclusively on the CICIDS data (green), and when also trained on the probing data (red). Even though the validation error is slightly higher when only trained on the CICIDS data, the difference is almost negligible compared to the error resulting from a model trained on a completely different dataset (UGR-16 [16], blue). These results do not fully prove that every model is able to transfer observed structures between the original CICIDS-17 and our DetGen-IDS dataset, but it gives an indicator that DetGen-IDS mirrors the characteristics of CICIDS-17.

7   Conclusions

In this paper, we described and examined a tool for generating traffic with controllable and extensively labelled traffic microstructures with the purpose of probing machine-learning-based traffic models. For this, we demonstrated the impact that probing with carefully crafted traffic microstructures can have for improving a model with a state-of-the-art LSTM-traffic-classifier with a detection rate that improved by more than 3% after understanding how the model processes excessive network congestion.

To verify DetGen's ability to control and monitor traffic microstructures, we performed experiments in which we quantified the experimental determinism of DetGen and compared it to traditional VM-based capture setups. Our similarity metrics indicate that traffic generated by DetGen is on average 10 times, and for connection sequences up to 30 times more consistent.

Alongside this work, we are releasing DetGen-IDS, a substantial dataset suitable for probing models trained on the CICIDS-17 dataset. This data should make it easier for researchers to understand where their model fails and what traffic characteristics are responsible to subsequently improve their design accordingly.

Difficulties and Limitations: While the control of traffic microstructures helps to understand packet- or connection-level models, it does not replicate realistic network-wide temporal structures. Other datasets such as UGR-16 [16] or LANL-15 [30] are currently better suited to examine models of large-scale traffic structures.

While controlling traffic shaping factors artificially helps at identifying the limits and weak points of a model, it can exaggerate some characteristics in unrealistic ways and thus alter the actual detection performance of a model.

The artificial randomisation of traffic shaping factors can currently not completely generate real-world traffic diversity. This problem is however more pronounced in commonly used synthetic datasets such as CICIDS-17, where for example most FTP-transfers consist of a client downloading the same text file.

Discussions about the implications of the model correction proposed in Sect. 2 are above the scope of this paper, and there likely exist more complex and suitable solutions.

Future Work: DetGen is currently only offering insufficient control over underlying **application-layer implementations** such as TLS 1.3 vs 1.2. In theory, it should be unproblematic to provide containers with different implementations, and we are currently investigating how to compile containers in a suitable manner.

We are currently investigating how to better simulate causality in connection spawning and other **medium-term temporal dependencies**, such as by importing externally generated activity timelines from tools such as Doppelganger [14].

A   Existing Scenarios

DetGen contains 31 scenarios, each simulating a different benign or malicious interaction. The protocols underlying benign scenarios were chosen based on their prevalence in existing network traffic datasets. According to our evaluation, our scenarios can generate datasets containing the protocols that make up at least 87.8% (MAWI), 98.3% (CICIDS 2017), 65.6% (UNSW NB15), and 94.5% (ISCX Botnet) of network flows in the respective dataset. Our evaluation shows that some protocols that make up a substantial amount of real-world traffic are glaringly omitted by current synthetic datasets, such as BitTorrent or video streaming protocols, which we decided to include.

Table 3. Currently implemented traffic scenarios along with the number of implemented subscenarios

Name	Description	#Ssc.	Name	Description	#Ssc.
Ping	Client pinging DNS server	1	SSH B.force	Bruteforcing a password over SSH	3
Nginx	Client accessing Nginx server	2			
Apache	Client accessing Apache server	2	URL Fuzz	Bruteforcing URL	1
SSH	Client communicating with SSHD server	9	Basic B.force	Bruteforcing Basic Authentication	2
VSFTPD	Client communicating with VSFTPD server	12	Goldeneye	DoS attack on Web Server	1
			Slowhttptest	DoS attack on Web Server	4
Wordpress	Client accessing Wordpress site	5	Mirai	Mirai botnet DDoS	3
Syncthing	Clients synchronize files via Syncthing	7	Heartbleed	Heartbleed exploit	1
			Ares	Backdoored Server	3
mailx	Mailx instance sending emails over SMTP	5	Cryptojacking	Cryptomining malware	1
			XXE	External XML Entity	3
IRC	Clients communicate via IRCd	4	SQLi	SQL injection attack	2
BitTorrent	Download and seed torrents	3	Stepstone	Relayed traffic using SSH-tunnels	2
SQL	Apache with MySQL	4			
NTP	NTP client	2			
Mopidy	Music Streaming	5			
RTMP	Video Streaming Server	3			
WAN Wget	Download websites	5			
SMB	File-sharing	3			
LDAP	Access directory services	3			

In total, we produced 19 benign scenarios, each related to a specific protocol or application. Further scenarios can be added in the future, and we do not claim that the current list exhaustive. Most of these benign scenarios also contain many subscenarios where applicable.

The remaining 12 scenarios generate traffic caused by malicious behaviour. These scenarios cover a wide variety of major attack classes including DoS, Botnet, Bruteforcing, Data Exfiltration, Web Attacks, Remote Code Execution, Stepping Stones, and Cryptojacking. Scenarios such as Stepping Stone behaviour or Cryptojacking previously had no available datasets for study despite need from academic and industrial researchers.

References

1. Aparicio-Navarro, F.J., Chambers, J.A., Kyriakopoulos, K., Gong, Y., Parish, D.: Using the pattern-of-life in networks to improve the effectiveness of intrusion detection systems. In: 2017 IEEE International Conference on Communications (ICC), pp. 1–7. IEEE (2017)
2. Aun, Y., Manickam, S., Karuppayah, S.: A review on features' robustness in high diversity mobile traffic classifications. Int. J. Commun. Netw. Inf. Secur. 9(2), 294 (2017)
3. Clausen, H., Aspinall, D.: Examining traffic micro-structures to improve model development. In: 2021 WTMC at IEEE Security and Privacy Workshops (SPW). IEEE (2021)
4. Clausen, H., Grov, G., Sabate, M., Aspinall, D.: Better anomaly detection for access attacks using deep bidirectional LSTMs. In: Renault, É., Boumerdassi, S., Mühlethaler, P. (eds.) MLN 2020. LNCS, vol. 12629, pp. 1–18. Springer, Cham (2021). https://doi.org/10.1007/978-3-030-70866-5_1
5. Fricker, C., Robert, P., Roberts, J., Sbihi, N.: Impact of traffic mix on caching performance in a content-centric network. In: 2012 Proceedings IEEE INFOCOM Workshops, pp. 310–315. IEEE (2012)
6. Gates, M., Warshavsky, A.: Iperf Man Page. https://linux.die.net/man/1/iperf. Accessed 11 Aug 2019
7. Haque, A., Guo, M., Verma, P., Fei-Fei, L.: Audio-linguistic embeddings for spoken sentences. In: ICASSP 2019–2019 IEEE International Conference on Acoustics, Speech and Signal Processing (ICASSP), pp. 7355–7359. IEEE (2019)
8. Hemminger, S., et al.: Network emulation with NetEm. In: Linux conf au, pp. 18–23 (2005)
9. Hwang, R.-H., Peng, M.-C., Nguyen, V.-L., Chang, Y.-L.: An LSTM-based deep learning approach for classifying malicious traffic at the packet level. Appl. Sci. 9(16), 3414 (2019)
10. Jurgelionis, A., Laulajainen, J.-P., Hirvonen, M., Wang, A.I.: An empirical study of NetEm network emulation functionalities. In: 2011 Proceedings of 20th International Conference on Computer Communications and Networks (ICCCN), pp. 1–6. IEEE (2011)
11. Kamper, H., Matusevych, Y., Goldwater, S.: Multilingual acoustic word embedding models for processing zero-resource languages. In: ICASSP 2020–2020 IEEE International Conference on Acoustics, Speech and Signal Processing (ICASSP), pp. 6414–6418. IEEE (2020)
12. Kent, A.D.: Comprehensive, Multi-Source Cyber-Security Events. Los Alamos National Laboratory (2015)
13. Lashkari, A.H., Draper-Gil, G., Mamun, M.S.I., Ghorbani, A.A.: Characterization of tor traffic using time based features. In: ICISSp, pp. 253–262 (2017)
14. Lin, Z., Jain, A., Wang, C., Fanti, G., Sekar, V.: Generating high-fidelity, synthetic time series datasets with doppelganger. arXiv preprint arXiv:1909.13403 (2019)
15. Livingstone, S.R., Russo, F.A.: The ryerson audio-visual database of emotional speech and song (RAVDESS): a dynamic, multimodal set of facial and vocal expressions in north American English. PLoS ONE 13(5), e0196391 (2018)
16. Maciá-Fernández, G., Camacho, J., Magán-Carrión, R., García-Teodoro, P., Therón, R.: UGR 16: a new dataset for the evaluation of cyclostationarity-based network IDSs. Comput. Secur. 73, 411–424 (2018)

17. Marx, R., Herbots, J., Lamotte, W., Quax, P.: Same standards, different decisions: a study of QUIC and HTTP/3 implementation diversity. In: Proceedings of the Workshop on the Evolution, Performance, and Interoperability of QUIC, pp. 14–20 (2020)
18. Mell, P., Hu, V., Lippmann, R., Haines, J., Zissman, M.: An overview of issues in testing intrusion detection systems (2003)
19. Mirsky, Y., Doitshman, T., Elovici, Y., Shabtai, A.: Kitsune: an ensemble of autoencoders for online network intrusion detection. arXiv preprint arXiv:1802.09089 (2018)
20. Moustafa, N., Slay, J.: UNSW-NB15: a comprehensive data set for network intrusion detection systems. In: 2015 Military Communications and Information Systems Conference (MilCIS), pp. 1–6. IEEE (2015)
21. Nasr, M., Bahramali, A., Houmansadr, A.: Deepcorr: strong flow correlation attacks on tor using deep learning. In: Proceedings of the 2018 ACM SIGSAC Conference on Computer and Communications Security, pp. 1962–1976 (2018)
22. Nisioti, A., Mylonas, A., Yoo, P.D., Katos, V.: From intrusion detection to attacker attribution: a comprehensive survey of unsupervised methods. IEEE Commun. Surv. Tutor. **20**(4), 3369–3388 (2018)
23. Radford, B.J., Apolonio, L.M., Trias, A.J., Simpson, J.A.: Network traffic anomaly detection using recurrent neural networks. arXiv preprint arXiv:1803.10769 (2018)
24. Ring, M., Wunderlich, S., Scheuring, D., Landes, D., Hotho, A.: A survey of network-based intrusion detection data sets. Comput. Secur. **86**, 147–167 (2019)
25. Sequeira, L., Fernández-Navajas, J., Casadesus, L., Saldana, J., Quintana, I., Ruiz-Mas, J.: The influence of the buffer size in packet loss for competing multimedia and bursty traffic. In: 2013 International Symposium on Performance Evaluation of Computer and Telecommunication Systems (SPECTS), pp. 134–141. IEEE (2013)
26. Sharafaldin, I., Lashkari, A.H., Ghorbani, A.A.: Toward generating a new intrusion detection dataset and intrusion traffic characterization. In: ICISSP, pp. 108–116 (2018)
27. Shiravi, A., Shiravi, H., Tavallaee, M., Ghorbani, A.A.: Toward developing a systematic approach to generate benchmark datasets for intrusion detection. Comput. Secur. **31**(3), 357–374 (2012)
28. Stöber, T., Frank, M., Schmitt, J., Martinovic, I.: Who do you sync you are? Smartphone fingerprinting via application behaviour. In: Proceedings of the Sixth ACM Conference on Security and Privacy in Wireless and Mobile Networks, pp. 7–12 (2013)
29. Tahaei, H., Afifi, F., Asemi, A., Zaki, F., Anuar, N.B.: The rise of traffic classification in IoT networks: a survey. J. Netw. Comput. Appl. **154**, 102538 (2020)
30. Turcotte, M.J., Kent, A.D., Hash, C.: Unified Host and Network Data Set. arXiv e-prints, August 2017
31. Walsworth, C., Aben, E., Claffy, K., Andersen, D.: The CAIDA UCSD anonymized internet traces 2018 (2018)
32. Wexler, J., Pushkarna, M., Bolukbasi, T., Wattenberg, M., Viégas, F., Wilson, J.: The what-if tool: interactive probing of machine learning models. IEEE Trans. Visual Comput. Graphics **26**(1), 56–65 (2019)
33. Yen, T.-F., Huang, X., Monrose, F., Reiter, M.K.: Browser fingerprinting from coarse traffic summaries: techniques and implications. In: Flegel, U., Bruschi, D. (eds.) DIMVA 2009. LNCS, vol. 5587, pp. 157–175. Springer, Heidelberg (2009). https://doi.org/10.1007/978-3-642-02918-9_10

Using NetFlow to Measure the Impact of Deploying DNS-based Blacklists

Martin Fejrskov[1(✉)], Jens Myrup Pedersen[2], and Emmanouil Vasilomanolakis[2]

[1] Telenor A/S, Aalborg, Denmark
mfea@telenor.dk
[2] Cyber Security Group, Aalborg University, Copenhagen, Denmark
{jens,emv}@es.aau.dk

Abstract. To prevent user exposure to a wide range of cyber security threats, organizations and companies often resort to deploying blacklists in DNS resolvers or DNS firewalls. The impact of such a deployment is often measured by comparing the coverage of individual blacklists, by counting the number of blocked DNS requests, or by counting the number of flows redirected to a benign web page that contains a warning to the user. This paper suggests an alternative to this by using NetFlow data to measure the effect of a DNS-based blacklist deployment. Our findings suggest that only 38–40% of blacklisted flows are web traffic. Furthermore, the paper analyzes the flows blacklisted by IP address, and it is shown that the majority of these are potentially benign, such as flows towards a web server hosting both benign and malicious sites. Finally, the flows blacklisted by domain name are categorized as either spam or malware, and it is shown that less than 6% are considered malicious.

Keywords: Blacklist · DNS · Netflow · Ipfix · ISP · RBL · Threat intelligence

1 Introduction

Threat Intelligence (TI) in the form of reputation-based blacklists of IP addresses and domain names have been made available by non-profit and commercial organisations for decades [19], and has later been the subject of academic research as well [9]. Improving the accuracy and completeness of the blacklists by the careful selection of entries to maximize the amount of true positives and minimize the amount of false negatives remains a continuous struggle. These metrics describe the blacklist itself, however they do not describe the actual impact of deploying a blacklist in practice. If there is not impact, the time and money spent by the user deploying the blacklist can be considered wasted. Therefore, we argue that the impact is an important metric from a practical perspective.

Funded by Telenor A/S and Innovation Fund Denmark, 2021.

J. Garcia-Alfaro et al. (Eds.): SecureComm 2021, LNICST 398, pp. 476–496, 2021.
https://doi.org/10.1007/978-3-030-90019-9_24

How to describe and measure the impact will naturally depend on the specific use case in which the blacklist is applied[1]. The most prevalent use cases for blacklists fall in two categories, offering protection to either the originating end of a connection (in antivirus software, in a web browser plugin, in a company firewall, in an Internet Service Providers (ISPs) DNS server, etc.) or the terminating end of a connection (a mail server, at a firewall protecting a web site, etc.). This paper focuses on the impact of deploying blacklists in DNS resolvers at ISPs. Deploying blacklists at ISPs is attractive as it can increase the security posture of all devices that default to use the ISP's DNS resolvers.

Informal conversations with blacklist vendors suggest that a common method for assessing the impact is to let the DNS resolver count the number of performed DNS queries that match an entry on a blacklist. Some ISPs and DNS security vendors even refer to this number directly as the number of blocked threats[3,21]. This is similar to counting the number of emails flagged as phishing by an email server, or counting the number of requests towards a web server originating from an IP address known to be malicious. However a DNS request in itself is only a threat indicator. In order for a user to be at risk, an IP connection towards the malicious host is a minimum precondition, and we therefore consider an IP connection as a stronger threat indicator than a DNS resolution. In this paper, we propose a method based on NetFlow/IPFIX measurements to evaluate the impact of deploying blacklists at an ISP DNS resolver.

Assessing the network-level impact of applying a blacklist at a DNS server will, however, not in itself tell anything about the user-level impact perceived by the user. For instance, blocking a user's connection attempt towards a shared web hosting environment that incidentally also hosts a known spam sender, is likely to be perceived as a nuisance rather than as protection against a threat. On the other hand, connecting to a web server known to solely host malicious payloads represents a high risk to the user. To supplement the measured network-level impact, it is necessary both to identify the cause for the entry to be blacklisted in order to assess the risk level of connecting to the blacklisted entity, and to assess the risk that a connection is in fact made towards the malicious entity.

The contributions of this paper are twofold:

- We show how existing methods for measuring the impact of deploying domain and IP address blacklists in DNS resolvers can be improved by including NetFlow measurements.
- Using the NetFlow method, we quantify the number of malicious and non-malicious flows, and we quantify the number of flows blacklisted by IP address that may be benign.

The paper is organised in 7 sections: Sect. 2 gives an overview of related work. Section 3 describes the concept of blacklisted flows and the method for merging DNS, NetFlow and blacklist data to identify blacklisted flows. Section 4 describes the 3 data sources used in the paper and the application of the previously described merging method. Section 5 categorizes the blacklisted flows by

---

[1] The elaborated definition of impact used in this paper is presented in Sect. 4.3.

the type of maliciousness and Sect. 6 identifies IP addresses that may contain multiple (and possibly both malicious and benign) endpoints. Section 7 combines the results from the previous sections to describe the network-level and user-level impact. Lastly, Sect. 8 summarizes and concludes the paper.

2   Related Work

As outlined in the introduction, the contribution of this paper is to show that existing measurement methods that *measure the impact* of implementing domain and IP address *blacklisting in DNS resolvers* can be improved by including *Net-Flow data* based measurements in addition to *DNS data* based measurements. We use the proposed measurement method together with information about the *type of maliciousness* and knowledge about the *type of endpoint* to identify if the endpoint may host both benign and malicious sites simultaneously. The columns of Table 1 represent each of the aspects highlighted in the above paragraph, and this section elaborates how related works cover some, but not all, of the aspects.

Many papers such as [23] focus on the creation, quality, accuracy or comparison of blacklists. Bouwman et al. focus on the differences between paid and free lists, and investigate the reasons (price, coverage, false positive rate, etc.) provided by operators/enterprises for choosing specific lists [2]. These topics are considered complementary to this paper, and such efforts will therefore not be the topic of this section. Similarly, papers such as [13,16] focusing on using blacklists for spam filtering in mail servers are also considered complementary.

Table 1. Related work and their focus areas

Author	Year	Focus area					
		Impact	Resolver BL	DNS data	NetFlow data	Endpoint	Maliciousness
Sheng et al. [15]	2009		✓	✓			✓
Bermudez et al. [1]	2012			✓	✓		
Connery [4]	2012	✓	✓	✓			
Zhang et al. [22]	2013	✓			✓	✓	✓
Kührer et al. [10]	2014		✓	✓		✓	✓
Foremski et al. [7]	2014			✓	✓		
Satoh et al. [14]	2019	✓					
Spacek et al. [17]	2019	✓	✓	✓			
Wilde et al. [20]	2019	✓	✓	✓			
Li et al. [11]	2019				✓	✓	✓
Telenor Norway [18]	2020	✓	✓	✓			
Griffioen et al. [8]	2020	✓		✓	✓	✓	✓

2.1   Network-Level Impact of Blacklisting

Although not focusing on malware and blacklists, the authors of [1] observe that around 50% of DNS responses have an associated flow. This suggests that a flow cannot be assumed to be associated with all *blacklisted* DNS responses either. This forms a motivation for focusing on flows rather than DNS responses.

Zhang et al. measure the impact of applying several (IP address) blacklists on NetFlow records obtained from the routers of a large regional ISP [22]. The paper differentiates between different types of maliciousness and endpoints, and concludes that up to 17% of the traffic measured by volume could be considered tainted. Although this work blacklists NetFlow entries rather than DNS entries, we consider it to be one of the works that are most closely related to our paper.

Sheng et al. evaluate blacklists in browser plugins to protect against phishing websites [15]. This approach represents several advantages to DNS-based filtering, as lists of URLs rather than lists of domain names or IP addresses can be used. The approach is, however, by nature very application and browser specific, thus representing a disadvantage in relation to a DNS-based approach.

Li et al. use telescopes of scanning activities to determine list coverage, thus including some flow level data [11]. Furthermore, the paper uses IP ranges of known CDNs as a source to determine list accuracy. However, the focus is still on assessing the quality of the lists, rather than on the impact of applying them.

Spacek et al. describe many practical considerations in deploying DNS based blacklisting, and elaborates on some of the consequences to the user [17]. These consequences focus on feedback about the blocked site, difficulties in relation to the use of TLS, etc., and does not quantify the impact of the blacklist itself.

Deploying blacklists at an ISP or company DNS server is becoming a common security measure. Public statements such as [18] and [4] with limited descriptions of the impact of such measures exist. Both of these statements measure the impact in terms of visits to a website, to which a user is redirected instead of being blocked. Similarly, DNS firewall/resolver vendors, TI providers, etc. provide use case descriptions focusing on DNS-level measurements only. Furthermore, Wilde et al. examine the blocking behaviour of several publicly available resolvers and conclude that none of them block for security purposes [20]. They also use lists of URLs to quantify to which extent an RPZ enabled DNS resolver would block the list entries. However, no real world traffic is used in the quantification.

Academic papers describe the impact of blacklisting at the router and browser level, and to a certain extent at the DNS level, as outlined above. However, we are not aware of any work that quantifies the impact at the NetFlow level.

2.2 User-Level Impact of Blacklisting

Kuhrer et al. categorize both commercial and public blacklists entries to identify if an endpoint is a sinkhole or a parked domain [10]. The purpose of performing the categorization therefore relates more to the validity of a blacklist entry than to the impact experienced by the user. Furthermore, the paper evaluates the ability of blacklists deployed at a DNS server to detect known botnets.

Using DNS and flow information to determine the used application is the topic of [7]. The application of named flows (flows to which a DNS response can be associated) such as HTTP, Roblox and Skype is identified. This classification, however, focuses solely on the application rather than the type of endpoint.

Determining the type of maliciousness is the main focus of [14]. The authors use Word2Vec to group 388 malicious queries into three clusters, each comprising queries with a common cause. The study focus solely on DNS TXT records, which does not extend well to the majority of queries that do not have TXT records.

Some blacklist vendors and tools such as [12] provide the cause for an entry to be listed. This is in many cases directly related to the type of maliciousness.

Griffioen et al. present several aspects related to our paper [8]. Their main emphasis is to compare open source blacklists, including the impact metric. NetFlow information from a Tier 1 provider is used to assess the timeliness of entries on the lists, but is not used to assess the impact of deploying the lists, which is the main topic of our paper. Instead, information from authoritative DNS servers is used to evaluate the impact of deploying the lists, by analyzing how many domain names were pointing to a particular IP address on the day it was marked as malicious. We will extend this by including other aspects, beyond a high domain name to IP address ratio, and by analysing the domain names and IP addresses to identify different scenarios like shared web hosting.

Both [22] and [8] consider blacklisting on the IP level, for example in firewalls. In our paper, the focus is on invoking the blacklisting in a DNS server, thus considering both domain name and IP address based blacklists. Despite this conceptual difference, we consider these the most closely related to our paper.

2.3 Summary

Although related work exists, the idea of using NetFlow measurements for evaluating a DNS-based blacklist deployment seems to be unexplored, and this will therefore be the topic of Sects. 3 and 4. Categorizing existing blacklist entries by type of maliciousness does not seem to be receiving a lot of academic attention, maybe because the categorization can be available as a supplement to the blacklists. Using knowledge about the type of maliciousness and endpoint to provide a risk based view of the blacklisted flows will be the topic of Sects. 5 and 6.

3 Method for Identifying Blacklisted Flows

The concept of blacklisted flows is central to the flow based measurement method proposed in this paper. The method to identify blacklisted flows requires three data sources and is comprised of several steps, as illustrated in Fig. 1. The three data sources are NetFlow data, DNS data and blacklists containing domain names and IP addresses. The first steps, relating to the practical collection and pre-processing of the three individual data sources are illustrated in blue in Fig. 1 and elaborated in Sect. 4. Combining the three data sources involves two additional processing steps, elaborated in the following subsections. First, all blacklisted DNS records are identified (green in Fig. 1). Then, all flows relating to the blacklisted DNS records are identified (red in Fig. 1).

3.1 Blacklisted DNS Data

All DNS records associated with a specific DNS response are considered black-listed if *any* of these conditions are satisfied for any of the records:

- The Qname or Rname of the DNS record matches a blacklisted domain name
- The Rdata of the DNS record matches a blacklisted IP address or a blacklisted IP prefix

The result of this is that D_{black} blacklisted DNS responses are identified.

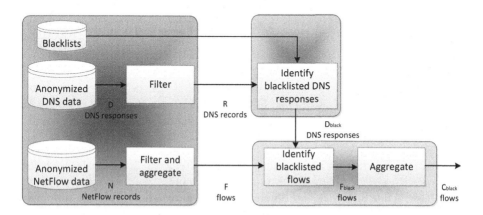

Fig. 1. The overall dataflow to identify blacklisted flows. (Color figure online)

3.2 Blacklisted Flows

A flow is considered blacklisted by a specific, blacklisted DNS record if *all* of the following conditions are satisfied:

- The DNS record has $rtype = A$
- The DNS record and flow timestamps are less than 30 min apart (as elaborated below), $t_{DNS} \leq t_{NetFlow} < t_{DNS} + 30m$
- The blacklisted DNS record is the temporally closest DNS record where the two conditions below are satisfied
- The blacklisted DNS record client IP matches the flow source IP
- The blacklisted DNS record rdata matches the flow destination IP

This yields a number of blacklisted flows, F_{black}.

Both the use of temporal correlation and anonymized IP addresses can cause a number of false positives and false negatives that are not immediately quantifiable as no ground truth exists for verification. The limit of 30 min is based on an analysis of the time difference between the DNS record and the flow. This analysis suggests that the number of matched DNS records and flows converge

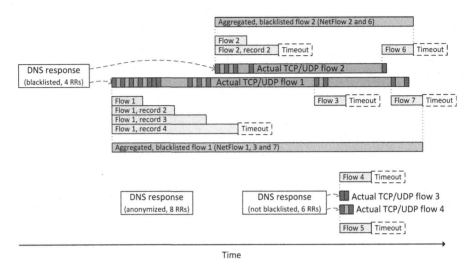

Fig. 2. Flow aggregation illustration. In this example, $D=3$, $R=10$, $D_{black}=1$, $N=11$, $F=7$, $F_{black}=5$, $C_{black}=2$ and $C_{black,DNS}=1$ (Color figure online)

towards 0 as a function of the time difference between the records, with few matches with a time difference of more than 15 min.

In case a flow matches two different DNS records where the only difference is the TTL, the DNS record with the highest TTL is considered a match.

The merging of NetFlow records into flows is described in Sect. 4.1. However, a NetFlow emitter may view a single, actual flow as two or more flows due to the use of aggressive timeouts for detection of flow end, especially for UDP traffic. Often this is referred to as flow splitting in related works. The effect is illustrated in Fig. 2, where light blue represents the lifespan of actual flows and dark blue represents packets transmitted in the flow. Green represents the lifespan of flows as perceived and reported by the NetFlow emitter in successive flow records. Due to timeouts, the NetFlow emitter perceives the two actual flows as 5 different flows. Therefore, a further aggregation of flows is desirable.

We choose to aggregate all blacklisted flows that are blacklisted by the same DNS record (considered unique by the qname, timestamp and clientip) and that have the same 5-tuple into a single flow, producing C_{black} flows. This aggregated entity is named an aggregated flow to distinguish it from the flow defined by the NetFlow emitter. The aggregated flows are represented in red in Fig. 2, where two aggregated, blacklisted flows (red) related to 5 different NetFlows (green), related to 2 actual flows (blue), and related to the same (blacklisted) DNS response (white) are depicted. The aggregated flow record has a cumulative bytes/packet count and the flow start timestamp that is the earliest timestamp found in the related flows.

4   Data Sources and Processing

This section will provide details on the selection and pre-processing of the three data sources illustrated in blue in Fig. 1 using data from Telenor Denmark's network (Sects. 4.1 to 4.3). Furthermore, the section will describe the results of performing the steps described in Sect. 3 on the data (Sects. 4.4 to 4.6).

Table 2. DNS and NetFlow data metrics

Metric	Symbol	Week 1	Week 2
Total DNS responses	D	$2,15 \cdot 10^{10}$	$2,25 \cdot 10^{10}$
Total relevant DNS records	R	$1,85 \cdot 10^{10}$	$1,88 \cdot 10^{10}$
Blacklisted DNS responses	D_{black}	$6,81 \cdot 10^{6}$	$4,56 \cdot 10^{6}$
Total NetFlow records	N	$4,63 \cdot 10^{9}$	$4,60 \cdot 10^{9}$
Total relevant flows	F	$3,92 \cdot 10^{8}$	$3,94 \cdot 10^{8}$
Blacklisted flows	F_{black}	185460	191923
Blacklisted, aggregated flows	C_{black}	90796	86854
Unique DNS responses in C_{black}	$C_{black,DNS}$	78312	70134
Blacklisted DNS response ratio	$\frac{D_{black}}{D}$	0,000317	0,000203
Entries in C_{black} matched by IP	C_{ip}	68045	62683
Entries in C_{black} matched by domain	C_{dom}	22842	24486

The three data sources are all collected during two separate weeks for the 1,5M mobile and 100k broadband subscriptions of Telenor Denmark. Notice that multiple users can use the same subscription, such as a household where all members are the users of a single broadband subscription. The data set for week 1 represent 7 full days from 2020–10–29 to 2020–11–04, and the data set for week 2 represent 7 full days of from 2020–11–26 to 2020–12–02. Table 2 lists the key properties for data in these time periods and the following sections will elaborate on these numbers. The following sections will for readability refer to the data from week 1, unless explicitly stated otherwise.

4.1   NetFlow Data

NetFlow data is collected at Telenor Denmark's Border Gateway Protocol (BGP) Autonomous System (AS) border routers, representing all Internet traffic entering and exiting Telenor's network, as depicted in Fig. 3. As indicated in the figure, two primary types of internal traffic not crossing the border routers exist:

– User-to-user traffic: The amount of user-to-user traffic is considered negligible compared to the amount of traffic crossing the border router and is therefore similarly considered negligible for the purpose of this paper.

– User-to-CDN traffic: A number of Content Delivery Network (CDN) nodes are deployed internally, and these serve a significant volume of traffic. However the types of data hosted on these nodes (Netflix/Youtube videos and similar static content etc.) are considered irrelevant to this paper from a user threat and blacklist perspective.

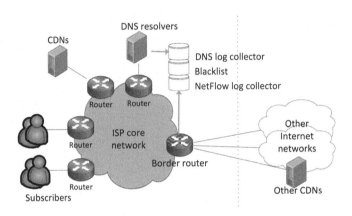

Fig. 3. A conceptual view of the Telenor network indicating the sources of DNS and NetFlow data.

A (unidirectional) NetFlow record is created by the border routers at least every 60 s for each active 5-tuple flow in each flow direction. A sample rate of $Q=512$ is used, therefore NetFlow records represent data from $\frac{1}{Q}$ packets. The collected data contains $N = 4,63 \cdot 10^9$ NetFlow records.

For the purpose of this paper, only connections initiated by users as a result of a DNS lookup are relevant. Therefore, only NetFlow records with an internal source address are considered, and for TCP connections only flows in which a SYN packet is seen are considered, as this will make sure that the flow start time actually represents the beginning of the flow. Multiple NetFlow records belonging to the same flow (defined by similar start-time and 5-tuple) are aggregated. As a result of this data reduction, $F = 3,92 \cdot 10^8$ flows are available for comparison with blacklisted DNS records. No application layer proxies are deployed.

NetFlow data is anonymized for legal reasons by truncating the internal (user) IP address to a /24 prefix for non-NAT'ed users (or truncating the port for NAT'ed users), truncating the external IP address to a /16 prefix, reverse truncating the timestamp, as well as a number of other measures less relevant to this paper. The anonymization policy applied follows the guidelines of [6]. Table 3 contains a number of example NetFlow records.

Table 3. Example NetFlow records. Timestamps are omitted for brevity.

srcip	srcport	dstip	dstport	proto	packets	bytes
129.142.227.0	56065	2.17.0.0	443	TCP	512	32768
83.73.228.0	49906	193.28.147.0	443	TCP	512	32768
85.80.228.0	45820	8.8.0.0	53	TCP	512	30720

4.2   DNS Data

DNS data is collected at Telenor Denmark's DNS resolvers, as depicted in Fig. 3. As the queried domain name is also a part of the DNS response packet, and as this study only focuses on syntactically valid DNS requests for which a response is always issued, only the response packets are collected (including for example NXDOMAIN responses). The resolvers are only accessible from Telenor Denmarks network, and are the default choice for all users. The collected data contains $D = 215 \cdot 10^8$ DNS responses. As a response can contain many Resource Records (RRs), the data is stored such that one record represents a unique RR augmented with the information common to all RRs in the same response.

There are no mechanisms preventing the use of 3rd party DNS resolvers residing outside the Telenor network, and therefore it is relevant to assess the prevalence of that type of traffic. NetFlow data contains $N_{DNS} = 5,92 \cdot 10^6$ records for traffic from users towards port 53 (DNS) and 853 (DNS-over-TLS) ($5,78 \cdot 10^6$ and $1,3 \cdot 10^5$ records respectively). It is not legally possible to inspect this traffic further to quantify how many and which queries this traffic represents. Assuming that one NetFlow record represents one DNS query (yielding the worst-case flow sample likelihood of 1:Q), the 3rd party DNS traffic represents only $\frac{QN_{DNS}}{(QN_{DNS}+D)} = 10,8\%$ of all queries. The traffic towards the Telenor DNS resolvers is therefore considered sufficiently representative of the total DNS traffic, and given the lack of legal basis for inspecting the 3rd party DNS resolver traffic, the 3rd party DNS traffic is disregarded for the purpose of this paper. Some anonymity services like TOR use private top level domains like '.onion'. These top level domains are not registered in the public DNS hierarchy. Therefore, such services are not considered relevant to this paper.

Only 0,1% of the DNS records, R, have an *rdata* field referring to a non-CDN IP address within the Telenor Denmark network. This supports the statement made in the NetFlow section that internal network traffic (both user-to-user and user-to-CDN) can be considered negligible to this paper.

DNS data is anonymized for legal reasons by truncating the client (user) IP address to a /24 prefix for non-NAT'ed users (or truncating the port for NAT'ed users), reverse truncating the timestamp, removing the domain name for the 15 most popular domains, and a number of other measures less relevant to this paper. The anonymization policy applied follows the guidelines of [6]. Discounting the anonymized records, $R = 185 \cdot 10^8$ records are therefore available for comparison with blacklists. Table 4 contains a number of example records.

Table 4. Example DNS records. The timestamp is omitted for brevity.

clientip	qname	rtype	rname	rdata	ttl
85.83.74.0	a.config.skype.com	A	l-0014.l-msedge.net	13.107.42.23	100–299
85.83.65.0	log.tiktokv.com	A	a2047.r.akamai.net	77.214.51.34	1–99
85.83.65.0	log.tiktokv.com	A	a2047.r.akamai.net	77.214.51.27	1–99

4.3 Blacklists

Blacklists that are available for a fee generally outperform free lists [10]. There-fore, blacklists provided by two well-known, commercial DNS blacklist vendors are used for this paper. After a review of the paper, the vendors opted to stay anonymous. The vendors will therefore be referenced as A and B, and the individual lists provided by each vendor as A_1, A_2, etc. The lists contain both IP addresses, IP prefixes and domains. Some of the lists are updated every minute, and the most realistic result would therefore be produced by doing a real-time correlation of DNS data and blacklists. However, as the DNS data is collected independently of the blacklists for operational and privacy reasons, this has not been possible in practice. Instead, the lists are collected at 23:00 CEST each day and the aggregated list is used for comparison for the whole period. In week 1, the aggregated lists contain 11878657 unique IP addresses, 3389 unique prefixes and 989490 unique domains. In week 2, the aggregated lists contain 16286208 unique IP addresses, 3320 unique prefixes and 1002913 unique domains.

For this paper, the impact of a blacklist describes the effect derived from a specific blacklist deployment. The impact of a blacklist with perfect accuracy and perfect completeness will be zero if a user never visits a malicious website. Conversely, if the completeness of a list is low, but deploying the list in practice would block the majority of traffic anyways, the impact will be high.

4.4 Blacklisted DNS Data

The result of the operation described in Sect. 3.1 is that $D_{black} = 6,81 \cdot 10^6$ blacklisted DNS responses are identified. This represents $\frac{D_{black}}{D} = 0,000317$ of the total number of DNS responses. The impact of applying DNS based blacklisting is often measured by the magnitude of this number, with the interpretation that user were protected by $6,81 \cdot 10^6$ threats.

4.5 Blacklisted Flows

The result of the operation described in Sect. 3.2 is that $F_{black} = 185460$ black-listed flows are identified. After performing aggregation, a total of $C_{black} = 90796$ blacklisted, aggregated flows are identified. Table 5 contains a number of examples of blacklisted, aggregated flows. C_{black} represents the number of flows found in the sampled NetFlows that would have been blocked in the sample week, if DNS based blacklists had been activated for all users.

Table 5. Example of the most relevant columns from blacklisted communication records.

qname	list	srcip	dstip	dstport	proto	timediff
www-pf-dk.filesusr.com	A_2	94.145.224.0	34.102.0.0	443	TCP	0
collection.decibelinsight.net	A_2	94.145.230.0	35.180.0.0	1789	UDP	434
collection.decibelinsight.net	A_2	94.145.230.0	35.180.0.0	0	ICMP	768
wahoofitness.com	A_2	2.130.11.0	151.101.0.0	443	TCP	93

4.6   Discussion

The $C_{black}=90796$ blacklisted, aggregated flows contain $C_{black,DNS}=78312$ unique DNS responses (defined by DNS timestamp, clientip, qname and ipprotocol). This represents $\frac{C_{black,DNS}}{D_{black}} = 1,1\%$ of all blacklisted DNS responses. However, as packet sampling is employed, this only accounts for the number of observed flows, not the actual number of flows. Techniques exist for estimating the actual number of flows based on the observed number of flows [5]. However, this does not imply that $\frac{C_{black,DNS}}{D_{black}}$ can be scaled by the same techniques, as the non-observed flows could in theory all be related to the DNS responses already found in $C_{black,DNS}$. Therefore, the data available in this study does not allow any further conclusions on the magnitude of $\frac{C_{black,DNS}}{D_{black}}$.

The data sets from week 1 and 2 show that the amount of blacklisted DNS responses in each week differ significantly from $D_{black} = 6,81 \cdot 10^6$ to $4,56 \cdot 10^6$, a drop of 33%. The collected data cannot offer an explanation for this difference, which may simply be attributed to varying activity levels of the malicious actors. As a consequence of this, the fraction $\frac{D_{black}}{D}$ differ proportionately.

It is, however, interesting to note that although D_{black} differ by 33%, the amount of observed flows blocked, C_{black}, only show a drop of 4%, from 90796 to 86854. The estimated ratio of blacklisted DNS requests that result in a TCP flow, $\frac{C_{black,DNS}}{D_{black}}$, does not vary much between the weeks either. This could indicate that the amount of blacklisted flows may be a temporally less variable metric than the amount of blacklisted DNS responses.

For readability, this paper will refer to the set of aggregated flows that are considered blacklisted because of an IP address entry on the blacklist as C_{ip} (68045 entries), the set of aggregated flows that are considered blacklisted because of a domain name entry on the blacklist as C_{dom} (22842 entries), and the set of aggregated flows that are considered blacklisted because of both a domain name and IP address entry on the blacklist as C_{both} (91 entries), where $C_{ip} \cup C_{dom} = C_{black}$ and $C_{ip} \cap C_{dom} = C_{both}$. As C_{both} contains an insignificant number of entries, this category will not be analysed separately in this paper.

5   Type of Maliciousness

Two sets of blacklisted flows, C_{ip} and C_{domain}, were identified in the previous section. These are the flows that would have been blocked if DNS based blacklists had been deployed, thus representing a network-level impact of black-list deployment (subject to scaling due to NetFlow sampling). However, as out-lined in the introduction, some blocked flows do not represent a threat to the user due to different types of maliciousness, and these may be seen as a nuisance instead. To quantify this user-level impact of blacklist deployment, this section will categorize the flows by the type of maliciousness.

Different types of malicious behaviour can cause a domain name or IP address to be blacklisted, but only some of the types should be considered a threat to the user connecting to the blacklist entry. The observations turn out to be different for C_{ip} and C_{domain}, therefore the observations will be described separately.

5.1   Flows Blacklisted by Domain Name

Both the A and B lists provide categories for phishing/malware/botnet related domains, as well as a more general spam category . The latter category includes for example domains in unsolicited mails promoting pills, counterfeits, dating sites etc., and is therefore in terms of badness distinct from malware/phishing domains. Although the sites and goods promoted in the spam category may not be desired to most users, they do not represent a cyber security threat. On the other hand, the phishing and malware related domains in what we will define as the malicious category clearly represent a cyber security threat to the user. In C_{dom}, 3% of the flows are in the malicious category, and the remaining 97% of the flows are in the spam category.

5.2   Flows Blacklisted by IP Address

Determining the type of maliciousness for entries in C_{ip}, requires different approaches for each list used.

The B lists provide a cause for an IP address to be blacklisted, and 99% of all IP address entries in the B lists are in the malicious category. However, only 5 entries in C_{ip} are blacklisted by B list entries (109 entries in the week 2 data set). As this is an insignificant amount compared to the total amount of entries in C_{ip}, no further analysis of the type of maliciousness of these entries is made.

Two A lists contain IP addresses: The A_1 and A_2 lists. The A_1 registers only spam emitters, and the 18292 flows blacklisted only by the A_1 list (and not also the A_2 list) are therefore considered in the spam category.

The type of maliciousness is not immediately available for the A_2 list. Two distinct groups of A_2 related flows (including flows that relate to both A_2 and A_1) are therefore categorized by other means:

- A subset of A_2, called A_3 is available as a separate list. 3179 entries in C_{ip} are marked by the A_3 (5%) and are therefore in the malicious category.
- A substantial amount of entries (13634, 20% of C_{ip}) relate to a single IP address owned by a laundry company. A manual lookup reveals that this IP address is in the spam category [12].

An informal conversation with list A representatives concluded that the vast majority of A_2 related flows not accounted for above are likely to be in the spam category as well. However, as we cannot quantify this, we will categorize the remaining flows as having unknown type of maliciousness.

5.3   Discussion

The type of maliciousness for the C_{ip} and C_{domain} flow sets are listed in Table 6. An important note is that if Telenor Denmark had only deployed domain name based blacklists, and only blocked the flows that are considered malicious to the user, a total of 1360 observed flows would have been blocked during week 2. The unknown C_{ip} entries are expected to mostly be in the spam category, with an informed guess setting the fraction of malicious flows in C_{ip} to less than 10%.

Table 6. Type of maliciousness for blacklisted flow sets.

Type	C_{ip}		C_{dom}	
	Week 1	Week 2	Week 1	Week 2
Spam	31926 (47%)	46918 (75%)	22061 (97%)	23126 (94%)
Malicious	3184 (5%)	1151 (2%)	781 (3%)	1360 (6%)
Unknown	32935 (48%)	14614 (23%)	0	0

Table 7. Port 80/443 (HTTP/HTTPS) fraction of flows. In the group of flows that are blacklisted by IP address (is in C_{ip}) in the week 2 data set, 13% of the spam-related flows in the group use port 80/443, and 18% of all flows in the group use port 80/443.

Type	C_{ip}		C_{dom}	
	Week 1	Week 2	Week 1	Week 2
Spam	20%	13%	40%	37%
Malicious	11%	47%	72%	61%
Entire data group	39%	18%	40%	38%

Some DNS based blocking implementations redirect the user to a web page warning the user that he has been blocked for security reasons. Web traffic, defined as traffic towards port 80 and 443, accounts for 40% of the entries in C_{dom}, and 72% of malware/phishing entries in C_{dom}. Further numbers are available in Table 7. Measuring the impact of the DNS based blocking by the number of visits to the warning web site will therefore underestimate the efficiency.

6   Misaligned Endpoints

In some scenarios where a user connects to a blacklisted IP address, there is a chance that the user does not in fact connect to the entity that caused the IP address to be blacklisted. A popular example is when a user connects to a web site hosted in a shared web hosting environment. The IP address of the shared hosting environment may be on the blacklist, but it may be included on the blacklist even though only one of the hosted sites serves malicious content. In this case, it is not possible to determine from either NetFlow or DNS data if the web site actually accessed by the user is benign or malicious. From a user perspective, this will likely be perceived as a nuisance, as the blacklist will then prevent access to benign sites not representing any risk. To assess the user-level impact of deploying DNS based blacklisting, it is therefore relevant to quantify the fraction of flows in C_{ip} where the endpoint of the flow and the endpoint causing the IP address to be blacklisted can differ. We shall refer to these flows as potentially having misaligned endpoints.

An analysis of each individual endpoint IP prefix would be impractical. In order to identify the most prominent groups of C_{ip} flows, we choose to focus the analysis on the groups of flows where:

- Many domain names are associated with a single destination IP prefix (high *qname/dstip* ratio).
- Many destination IP prefixes are associated with a single domain name (high *dstip/qname* ratio).
- A popular destination IP prefix is used (high *dstip* count).
- A popular domain name is used (high *qname* count).

Based on this analysis, three different scenarios that can cause misaligned endpoints has been identified in the C_{ip} data set, and these three scenarios are elaborated in the following three subsections.

6.1   Shared Content Providers

The entries in C_{ip} with a high *qname/dstip* ratio all have a *dstip* owned by a CDN, shared web hosting or similar cloud content provider like Amazon, Microsoft Azure, Google Cloud, DigitalOcean or Tencent. A total of 29556 entries (43% of C_{ip}) are related to such servers and we consider these flows to potentially having misaligned endpoints.

An number of *dstips* are owned by Virtual Private Server (VPS) service providers and regular ISP customers. 516 entries are considered ISP customers as well, as they relate to a server with a dynamic IP address, identified by the use of a .duckdns.org domain name, a service used for assigning a permanent domain name to a dynamic IP address. These will not be considered as potentially misaligned endpoints.

It could be argued that all destination IP addresses could easily be enumerated by the use of BGP AS numbers. In practice, however, this turns out not to be viable for a number of reasons. First, only the /16 prefix address is available due to anonymization, and such a prefix may cover several AS numbers. Second, some providers share the AS number between the ISP and hosting part of the company (like OVH). Third, some providers reserve smaller prefixes for specific customers (like Amazon). Fourth, some providers use IP space assigned to other entities (like Tencent using ChinaUnicom owned IP prefixes).

6.2 VPN Service Providers

VPN service provider (PrivateInternetAccess, Hula, NorthGhost etc.) traffic identified by the *qname* accounts for 12469 (18%) of all entries in C_{ip}. The specific implementations by the different providers is not known. However, it seems unlikely that a user creating a connection towards such an IP address will be relayed to a host residing behind the VPN service. A connection towards such a server seems more likely to be an attempt to use the service. The VPN provider IP addresses are likely to have been blacklisted because hosts using the service generated traffic that triggered a blacklisting. We shall therefore consider the VPN provider IP addresses as potentially having misaligned endpoints.

6.3 NTP Pool

Traffic towards hosts registered in the ntppool project[2] is identified by the *qname* containing .pool.ntp.org. This traffic accounts for 4006 (6%) of all entries in C_{ip}. A DNS request for a .pool.ntp.org domain will return a number of IP addresses, where each IP address belongs to a pool member. If the IP address of one of the pool members in the DNS response is blacklisted, the entire DNS response is considered blacklisted. Therefore, a connection towards a different pool member will be considered part of C_{ip}. This is not considered a flaw in the data analysis, as it reflects how DNS based blacklisting is implemented in practice. Blacklisting relates to the entire DNS request/response pair, not just to single response resource records. It is therefore likely that these flows have misaligned endpoints.

6.4 Discussion

Table 8 summarizes the amount of flows that may have misaligned endpoints and lists the 3 identified scenarios causing the potential misalignment. As seen in the table, we consider at least 45698 of 68045 C_{ip} entries (67%) as potentially having misaligned endpoints. Blocking these flows involves a risk of blocking benign sites. Although the specific IP address on the blacklist may be correct by reflecting a malicious endpoint using that IP address (a true positive), the user may perceive it as a false positive. When a provider considers deploying DNS based blacklists that includes IP addresses, the willingness of both operators and users to accept this risk should therefore be carefully considered up front.

---

[2] https://www.ntppool.org/.

Table 8. Amount of entries in C_{ip} with different causes for potential endpoint misalignment. Note that the total is less than the sum, as for example an NTP pool entry may also be a shared content provider entry, and this only counts as 1 in the total.

Cause	Week 1	Week 2
Shared content providers	29556 (43%)	19370 (31%)
VPN service providers	12469 (18%)	13710 (22%)
NTP pool	4006 (6%)	3505 (6%)
Total	45698 (67%)	36336 (58%)

Of the 45698 entries, only 5 are tagged by the B lists, while the rest is tagged by A lists. This highlights that the choice of blacklists represent an important limitation to the results presented in this section. The numbers presented are unlikely to be representative of other blacklists. However, looking outside the scope of this paper, this also suggests that when considering deploying DNS based blacklisting, the concept of IP address blacklists should not necessarily be deselected upfront. The risk of blocking benign sites due to endpoint misalignment can be decreased significantly by the careful selection of IP address blacklists.

As outlined in Sect. 2, we are only aware of one other paper that evaluates the risk of misaligned endpoints for the individual blacklist entries [8]. However, it is important to notice that the results presented in this section would not be directly comparable, as they relate to the blacklisted flows (C_{black}), not the blacklisted DNS responses (D_{black}) or the individual entries on a blacklist (the latter being the focus of [8]). The primary purpose of our work is to present the method of using NetFlow to measure the impact of deploying blacklists using a specific set of blacklists as examples, and not to compare blacklists. Hence, we consider evaluating a larger number of blacklists as an extension to this paper.

7   Impact

Sections 3, 4, 5 and 6 identify blacklisted flows, identify the type of maliciousness and assess the risk of endpoint misalignment. This section combines the result of the previous sections to quantify impact of deploying DNS-based blacklists seen from the network perspective and from the user perspective. Furthermore, this section describes interesting future works.

7.1   Network-Level Impact

The network-level impact of DNS based blocking is usually practically measured by counting the number of blocked DNS requests or by counting the number of visits to a warning page to which a user has been redirected. In this paper, the impact is instead measured using the number of blocked flows instead, and this reveals the fraction of web related flows.

- Approximately 0,02–0,03% of all DNS responses match a blacklist entry, and 1,1–1,5% of these blacklisted DNS responses can be associated with an observed flow, denoted a blacklisted flow. The use of sampled flow data was found to hinder the estimation of the actual fraction of blacklisted DNS responses that can be associated with a flow. Researchers or ISPs with access to non-sampled NetFlow and DNS data should assess the fraction of blacklisted DNS responses that can be associated with a flow. Given a known amount of blacklisted DNS responses, this would make it possible to more accurately assess impact of doing DNS based blocking.
- Some DNS based blocking implementations redirect the user to a website containing a message warning the user that he has been blocked for security reasons. Therefore, such implementations measure only the part of the traffic that is web traffic. Of the flows blacklisted by domain name, 38–40% are web traffic. Of the flows blacklisted by domain name *and* considered having a high threat level, 61–72% are web traffic. Therefore, this paper shows that measuring the impact of blacklisting by the number of visits to the warning web site underestimates the impact. ISPs and company system administrators should implement measures to also count non-web related connections, in order to get a more correct assessment of the blacklist impact.

These results are specific to a particular week, use particular blacklist vendors, and a particular ISP. Despite the listed limitations, we find the results significant enough to suggest that the method of using NetFlow to measure the impact of applying DNS based blacklists represents an improvement to existing methods.

7.2   User-Level Impact

Approximately 25% of the blacklisted flows relate to a blacklisted domain name, whereas the remaining 75% of the blacklisted flows relate to a blacklisted IP address.

- The flows blacklisted by domain name are, using the threat type categories provided by the blacklist vendors, divided into two groups. First, a group relating to general spam, considered a nuisance rather than a cyber security threat, accounts for 94–97% of the flows. Second, a group relating to phishing, malware and botnet accounts for the remaining 3–6%. When deploying DNS based blacklisting, it is therefore important to consider if both or only one of these types of traffic should be blocked, as this will have a significant impact on the amount of blocked connections experienced by the user.
- Of the flows blacklisted by IP address, this paper shows that 58–67% may be flows towards benign sites, primarily due to the prevalence of shared web hosting, whereby multiple web sites/domain share the same IP address. From a user and operator perspective, the willingness to risk blocking benign sites must be considered before deploying IP address based blacklists. This study shows that carefully selecting the IP address blacklist vendor can be a significant contribution to minimizing this risk.

These results are also specific to particular blacklist vendors and a particular ISP. Here, however, we show that the specific measurements depend a lot on the particular blacklist used, and therefore it is a clear limitation that these results cannot be generalized to different blacklists.

8 Conclusion

In this paper, we propose a method to measure the impact of deploying blacklists by combining NetFlow and DNS data. We evaluate the method on real data, containing anonymised NetFlow and DNS records collected by Telenor Denmark for two weeks, and combine these with blacklists containing IP addresses and domain names provided by two commercial vendors.

The measurements show that 0,02–0,03% of all DNS responses match a blacklist entry, however only 1,1–1,5% of these blacklisted DNS responses can be associated with an observed flow. Furthermore, only 38–40% of the blacklisted flows are web traffic. These observations suggest that the use of flow data can be used to make a more precise impact assessment than counting the amount of DNS responses matching a blacklist entry or counting the amount of visits to a warning web page.

For flows blacklisted by domain name, 3–6% of the flows related to phishing, malware and botnet domains, while the remaining flows relate to spam domains. For the flows blacklisted by IP address, 58–67% may be flows towards benign sites. These observations show that it the careful consideration of the choice of blacklist type (domain name or IP address) and category (spam, malware etc.) before deployment is essential to avoid undesired impact seen from a user perspective when deploying DNS-based blacklists.

References

1. Bermudez, I.N., Mellia, M., Munafò, M.M., Keralapura, R., Nucci, A.: DNS to the rescue: discerning content and services in a tangled web. In: IMC: Internet Measurement Conference (2012). https://doi.org/10.1145/2398776.2398819
2. Bouwman, X., Griffioen, H., Egbers, J., Doerr, C., Klievink, B., van Eeten, M.: A different cup of TI? The added value of commercial threat intelligence. In: USENIX Security Symposium (2020). https://www.usenix.org/system/files/sec20-bouwman.pdf
3. Cisco umbrella: better intelligence drives better security (2020). https://umbrella.cisco.com/solutions/reduce-security-infections
4. Connery, H.: DNS: response policy zone (2012). https://dnsrpz.info/spamhaus-rpz-case-study.pdf
5. Duffield, N., Lund, C., Thorup, M.: Properties and prediction of flow statistics from sampled packet streams. In: IMW: ACM SIGCOMM Internet Measurement Workshop (2002). https://doi.org/10.1145/637201.637225

6. Fejrskov, M., Pedersen, J.M., Vasilomanolakis, E.: Cyber-security research by ISPs: a NetFlow and DNS anonymization policy. In: International Conference on Cyber Security And Protection Of Digital Services (2020). https://doi.org/10.1109/CyberSecurity49315.2020.9138869

7. Foremski, P., Callegari, C., Pagano, M.: DNS-class: immediate classification of IP flows using DNS. In: ACM Int. J. Netw. Manage. (2014). https://doi.org/10.1002/nem.1864

8. Griffioen, H., Booij, T., Doerr, C.: Quality Evaluation of Cyber Threat Intelligence Feeds. In: Conti, M., Zhou, J., Casalicchio, E., Spognardi, A. (eds.) ACNS 2020. LNCS, vol. 12147, pp. 277–296. Springer, Cham (2020). https://doi.org/10.1007/978-3-030-57878-7_14

9. Jung, J., Sit, E.: An empirical study of spam traffic and the use of DNS black lists. In: IMC: Internet Measurement Conference (2004). https://doi.org/10.1145/1028788.1028838

10. Kührer, M., Rossow, C., Holz, T.: Paint it black: evaluating the effectiveness of malware blacklists. In: RAID: Research in Attacks Intrusions and Defenses (2014). https://doi.org/10.1007/978-3-319-11379-1_1

11. Li, V.G., Dunn, M., Pearce, P., McCoy, D., Voelker, G.M., Savage, S., Levchenko, K.: Reading the tea leaves: a comparative analysis of threat intelligence. In: USENIX Security Symposium (2019). https://www.usenix.org/system/files/sec19-li-vector_guo.pdf

12. MXToolbox: blacklist check (2021). https://mxtoolbox.com/blacklists.aspx

13. Ramachandran, A., Feamster, N.: Understanding the network-level behavior of spammers. In: ACM SIGCOMM Computer Communication Review (2006). https://doi.org/10.1145/1159913.1159947

14. Satoh, A., Nakamura, Y., Fukuda, Y., Sasai, K., Kitagata, G.: A cause-based classification approach for malicious DNS queries detected through blacklists. IEEE Access (2019). https://doi.org/10.1109/ACCESS.2019.2944203

15. Sheng, S., Wardman, B., Warner, G., Cranor, L., Hong, J., Zhang, C.: An empirical analysis of phishing blacklists. In: CEAS: Conference on Email and Anti-Spam (2009). https://doi.org/10.1184/R1/6469805.V1

16. Sinha, S., Bailey, M., Jahanian, F.: Shades of grey: On the effectiveness of reputation-based "blacklists". MALWARE: International Conference on Malicious and Unwanted Software (2008), https://doi.org/10.1109/MALWARE.2008.4690858

17. Spacek, S., Lastovicka, M., Horak, M., Plesnik, T.: Current Issues of Malicious Domains Blocking. IFIP/IEEE International Symposium on Integrated Network Management (2019), https://ieeexplore.ieee.org/document/8717891

18. Telenor Norway: Stanset over 80.000 besøk på falske nettsider på én måned (2020), https://www.mynewsdesk.com/no/telenor/pressreleases/stanset-over-80-dot-000-besoek-paa-falske-nettsider-paa-en-maaned-2986773

19. Wikipedia: Domain Name System-based Blackhole List (2020), https://en.wikipedia.org/wiki/Domain_Name_System-based_Blackhole_List

20. Wilde, N., Jones, L., Lopez, R., Vaughn, T.: A DNS RPZ Firewall and Current American DNS Practice. In: Kim, K.J., Baek, N. (eds.) ICISA 2018. LNEE, vol. 514, pp. 259–265. Springer, Singapore (2019). https://doi.org/10.1007/978-981-13-1056-0_27

21. Williamson, R.: What do Canada and New Zealand have in common? (2020), https://internetnz.nz/blog/dns-firewall-what-do-canada-and-new-zealand-have-in-common/

22. Zhang, J., Chivukula, A., Bailey, M., Karir, M., Liu, M.: Characterization of Blacklists and Tainted Network Traffic. In: Roughan, M., Chang, R. (eds.) PAM 2013. LNCS, vol. 7799, pp. 218–228. Springer, Heidelberg (2013). https://doi.org/10. 1007/978-3-642-36516-4_22
23. Zhauniarovich, Y., Khalil, I., Yu, T., Dacier, M.: A survey on malicious domains detection through DNS data analysis. ACM Computing Surveys (2018), https:// doi.org/10.1145/3191329

Digital Forensics

A Forensic Tool to Acquire Radio Signals Using Software Defined Radio

M. A. Hannan Bin Azhar[(⊠)] and German Abadia

School of Engineering, Technology and Design, Canterbury Christ Church University,
Canterbury, UK
{hannan.azhar,g.abadia173}@canterbury.ac.uk

Abstract. The adoption of radio technologies and wireless devices in our society
has been increasing with the time. A wide range of devices use radio communications for sending and receiving data. The increasing number of attack vectors
used in the radio field, and wireless technology's use in recent terrorist incidents,
make spectrum forensics essential to gathering intelligence, especially while the
crime is still unfolding, and the attackers remain at large. When most of the wireless acquisition tools on the market work either on Wi-Fi or Bluetooth protocols,
using software defined radio technology or SDR can allow us to capture signals
regardless of the protocol or modulation. This paper describes the development
of a forensically valid extension to the HackRF toolset which includes a SDR
module capable of logging details of files for penetration testing. The tools and
methods presented in this paper provide the specification and experimental validation of the SDR technology for forensic investigation of potentially vulnerable
wireless devices. The two case studies reported here use radio controls to simulate intruder attacks and walkie-talkies to simulate intelligence gathering during
a terrorist attack.

Keywords: SDR · HackRF · Network forensics · Spectrum forensics ·
Live-forensics · Cybersecurity

1 Introduction

Wireless data communications have evolved rapidly over the last few decades and have
become widely used worldwide. The growth of wireless communication devices has led
to an increase in misuse of these devices and their security vulnerabilities. It has been
reported that everyday wireless devices, such as a garage door with a fixed code, can be
brute forced in seconds using a cheap transceiver chip [1]. In a relay attack against Passive
Keyless Entry (PKE), attackers can steal high-priced cars using devices built for just 22
dollars [2]. The exploitation of Software Defined Radio (SDR) has been reported as signal
disruption, spoofing against the GPS protocol, and record and replay attacks [3]. Even as
attackers' techniques continue to evolve, law enforcement and forensic examiners lack
the tools and programs necessary to acquire radio spectrum. There has been a great deal of
research and guidelines developed regarding the forensic capture and analysis of wireless

© ICST Institute for Computer Sciences, Social Informatics and Telecommunications Engineering 2021
Published by Springer Nature Switzerland AG 2021. All Rights Reserved
J. Garcia-Alfaro et al. (Eds.): SecureComm 2021, LNICST 398, pp. 499–512, 2021.
https://doi.org/10.1007/978-3-030-90019-9_25

traffic in wireless local area networks. Several researchers have addressed technical and legal issues related to wireless forensics [4, 5]. Other researchers have developed forensic models for this type of wireless data acquisition [6]. Applications such as Kismet allow GPS logging in addition to performing passive network monitoring and logging, thus provide forensic examiners and law enforcement agencies the capability of intercepting traffic [7]. The increased attack vectors in the radio field [3] and the lack of security in Internet of Things (IoT) devices have forced the law enforcement and forensics community to find low-cost, flexible, and easy-to-operate spectrum forensics tools.

Software Defined Radio is a low-cost and flexible way to acquire radio signals. With SDR technology, investigators can record and save live samples without knowing the modulation or protocol being used. With the same tool and hardware, an investigator can record the signal from a key-fob, a GPS spoofing attack, a jamming attack, a walkie-talkie transmission, and any other radio transmission within the range and capabilities of SDR. It is possible to use Open-Source programs to monitor, demodulate, and save spectral data, such as the Linux based program GQRX [8]. Universal Radio Hacker (URH) [9] is another open-source program that records the radio spectrum from a variety of SDR devices and saves the data in multiple formats. Despite the fact that different SDR programs have the ability to record radio signals, they all lack forensic capabilities and logging features, making them insufficient for providing actionable evidence.

The remainder of the paper will be organised as follows: Sect. 2 will introduce legal and forensic procedural soundness of spectrum forensics, equipment used in the experiment will be detailed in Sect. 3, Sect. 4 will discuss the developed program, Sect. 5 will report the results in two simulated case studies and finally, Sect. 6 will conclude the paper and mention possible future work.

2   Spectrum Forensics

A sub-discipline of network forensics, wireless forensics involves employing methodologies and tools to intercept and analyse wireless traffic that can be presented as valid digital evidence. Since the data is volatile, special consideration should be given to the ACPO Principal [10], since conducting live forensics requires access to the original evidence. It is imperative that anyone taking part in such activities be competent and aware of the potential consequences. Following are the forensic minimum requirements for a wireless forensic tool to potentially produce a legal result:

- Minimal interaction - the forensic tool should have a minimal interaction with the potential sources of evidence, and if such an interaction is required, its effects must be understood and justified. Passive scanning is more suitable for forensic purposes, since no interaction is needed to collect evidence. This feature is linked with the forensic principle of the Locard's Exchange [11], relating also to Pollitt's work on Digital Forensics Models [12].
- Accuracy and repeatability - implying that the system will produce the same results when used in the same environment. It is also important to know the technical limitations of the procedure. This feature is linked to the scientific principle of ensuring repeatability in experimentation.

- The operation of the tool must comply with all legal requirements. The Wireless Telegraphy Act 2006 [13] and the Communications Act 2003 [14] govern radio use in the UK. UK's Office of Communications (OFCOM) is the government-approved body for spectrum management and regulation. It specifies the services that can be listened to without a license in its guidance on the use of radio scanners [15]. These services are licensed broadcasting stations, amateur and citizens band radio transmissions, weather, and navigation transmissions. The UK Frequency Allocation Table is available on the OFCON page [16]. Spectrum acquisition activities must be accomplished after receiving proper authorisation unless the radio band being utilised is an amateur radio band or other devices operated at short ranges and low power and exempted by regulations made by Ofcom [17]. The Investigatory Powers Act 2016 defines lawful authority for carrying out an interception, as well as the necessary warrant for a targeted or bulk interception [14]. These legislation acts must be followed by investigators in order to ensure that the data interception is legal.

3   Equipment for Experiment

In order to perform forensic acquisition of radio signals, the following hardware devices were used for the experiments:

- HackRF One: SDR half-duplex transceiver capable of receiving and transmitting from 1 MHz to 6 GHz with a maximum bandwidth of 20 MHz and an 8-bit resolution.
- RTL-SDR: Nooelec NESDR SMART v4 capable of receiving from 25 MHz to 1750 MHz, with an internal TCXO and an aluminium enclosure to reduce noise.
- Antenna: ANT500, is a 50 Ω telescopic antenna that covers a frequency range from 75 MHz to 1 GHz. Also, included is a Fixed frequency 433 MHz (ISM) antenna mast from Nooelec [18].
- Aluminium enclosure: Aluminium enclosure for the HackRF to prevent unwanted electromagnetic interferences [19].
- TCXO [20]: A 0.5 PPM external Temperature Compensated Crystal Oscillator for the HackRF One to improve noise performance and avoid frequency drifting.
- USB cable: A shielded USB to MicroUSB cable from HackRF was used along with three ferrite beads.
- GPS receiver: VFAN UG-353 GPS receiver was used to capture the GPS location and UTC timestamps.
- Faraday box: RF shielded environment to avoid legal issues and ensure that the transmitted radio signals are contained and do not interfere with any devices operating in the same frequency band.

4   Radio Signal Acquisition Tool

The tool aims to provide a forensically sound application for acquiring radio signals, allowing a uniform method of configuring different SDR devices. Python 3.8 was used to develop the tool. Interfacing with the SDR devices is done through the open-source library SoapySDR [21]. The library is used to instantiate, configure, and stream the samples of different SDR devices.

4.1 Generated Files

The following files are generated by the application:

- Report file: A detailed report file of the acquisition containing the following

  - Local and UTC time of start of the capture.
  - Session log filename.
  - GPS log filename, when GPS logging is enabled.
  - GPS coordinates, and GPS UTC timestamps of start when a receiver is available.
  - Hardware information of the device such as name, label, serial number or version.
  - The configuration used to capture the samples: Frequency, sample rate, bandwidth, gain of elements and stream format.
  - MD5 and SHA256 hashes of generated samples files. The filenames include the file index, the device name and serial identifier, a time stamp, and with and appendix corresponding to its stream format.
  - Total number of saved samples.
  - Total time of capture.
  - Local and UTC time of the end of the capture.

- Sample files: The captured signal has two components, I (In phase) and Q (Quadrature). I/Q samples are the real and imaginary parts of the digital complex baseband signal. The filenames of the captured files indicate the number of the file, the device id, the date and time, and the stream format used to store the samples. Due to the large amount of data generated when the samples are produced, the files are split and it prevents hashing one big file at the end of the capture.
- GPS file: Timestamped GPS log file indicating the UTC time, latitude, longitude and altitude when available.
- Log file: A timestamp log file contains the date, time, and information level of all logs generated by the GPS, the SoapySDR, and the application itself. The file structure of the capture includes first the log file of the capture, with logs from the GPS connection or the SoapySDR library. The capture report is located in the timestamped directory. Additionally, the directory contains the GPS log file. Inside the output directory are the captured I/Q samples files, and the appendix of each file indicates the stream format of the samples.

4.2 Libraries Used in the Tool

The program makes use of the following libraries:

- soapySDR: is used for interfacing with the SDR devices, instantiating, configuring and streaming the samples from the devices.
- gpsd: is used to get GPS coordinates and UTC timestamps when available.
- logging: is used to log the activity to an external file.
- datetime: is used to get date and time.
- time: is used for the sleep command.

- threading: for the use of threads when hashing the samples files or saving the IQ samples.
- hashlib: is a library for creating MD5 and SHA256 hashes.
- numpy: is a scientific computing library used for special data type arrays of complex numbers for the samples buffers.
- sys: is used to send errors to stderr.
- os: is used to interact with directory structure.
- readline: input line editing, tab completion and command history.
- signal: is used for detecting SIGINT signal and prevent from closing the application.

4.3 Program Console

The program provides a console where the devices can be configured. The different available commands will be described below:

- list: provides a list of the connected devices showing the device identifier and the driver being used.
- info: provides a detailed list of information about the device such as the name, the serial number, label or version. And also, information such as the frequency range, bandwidth rate, possible sample rates, stream formats or configuration specific to the device.
- status: indicates the status of the connected devices and the tuned frequency. If the device is recording samples, it indicates the elapsed time, the number of saved samples, and the total size of the recorded samples.
- configure [id]: is used to enter the configuration menu of a specific device to configure its attributes.
- show [id]: is used to show the current state of the different possible configurable attributes from a device.
- set [setting] [value]: command is used to set the different attributes of the devices.
- start [id]: command starts the radio acquisition once the necessary attributes are set.
- stop [id]: command to stop the radio acquisition of a specific device.

5 Experimental Scenarios and Findings

Two different scenarios were used for acquiring radio signals using the developed tool. Depending on the scenario, radio signals operated at different frequencies and modulation methods. Details of the scenarios and findings are given below:

5.1 Test Case 1 – Walkie Talkie in a Terror Attack

This scenario was based on a simulated case study in which members of a terrorist group were identified during an operation. Due to this, the terrorist group has been confined inside a warehouse with workers of the warehouse being held hostage. Intelligence reports that they are using PMR walkie-talkies to communicate with an external agent in the area. The PMR band covers 460.0–446.2 MHz. Therefore, no further information would be required to capture the signal.

To avoid legal issues in this test scenario, an equivalent FM transmission from a local station was used instead of the PMR446 band. Since the chosen station uses the same modulation to transmit the data, the data capture and analysis would be the same. In this case, the signal was captured from FM radio SER+MADRID, which transmits at 104.30 MHz.

Fig. 1. SDR capture hardware setup.

The hardware setup for the experiment is shown in Fig. 1. The hardware used were HackRF One, Antenna ANT500, GPS receiver, Aluminium enclosure, TCXO and a USB 2.0 shielded cable with ferrite beads. Initially, GQRX [8] was used to locate and identify the signal, providing details of the modulation used and the radio activity. Then, using the developed program, the radio signal was captured in a forensically sound manner.

5.2   Findings in Test Case 1 – Walkie Talkie in a Terror Attack

Figure 2 shows the radio spectrum analyser, showing the tuned FM SER+MADRID radio signal at 104.30 MHz, surrounded by different radio station signals.

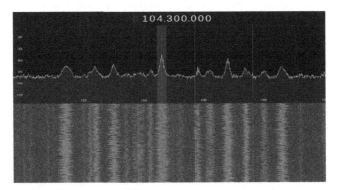

Fig. 2.   104.30 MHz captured by GQRX.

Once the signal was identified, the developed program was used to capture the signal. The sample rate was set to 20 MSPS and the frequency was set to the local FM frequency of 104.30 MHz. To ensure that the surrounding radio transmissions were captured, the bandwidth was set to 2.5 MHz. GPS logging was enabled to log position data to be able to estimate the transmitter location based on the output power. After setting the configuration for the capture (Fig. 3), the start command was executed in the tool to start the acquisition of the samples.

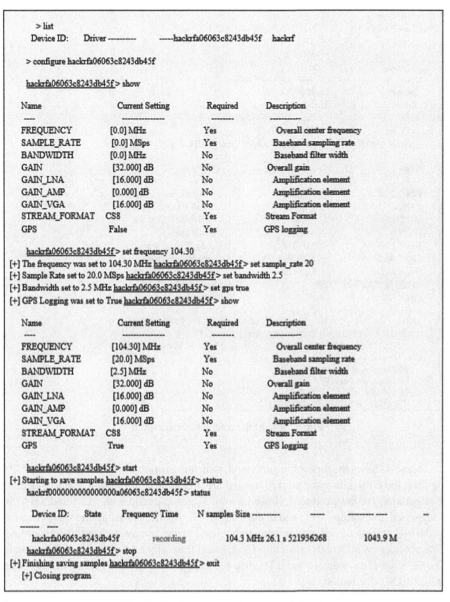

Fig. 3. Configuration and capture of signal.

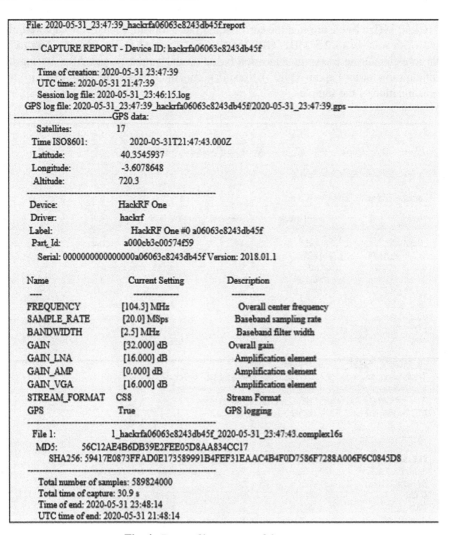

Fig. 4. Report file contents of the capture.

Figure 4 shows the report file generated, indicating timestamps, the session and GPS log files, the GPS data at the start of the capture, hardware information of the device, its configuration for the capture, followed by the IQ samples file with MD5 and SHA256 hashes, and timestamps at the end of the capture. The log file of the capture was generated by the tool indicating different information related to the capture such as settings applied, GPS connection information, stream format, and time of start and finish of the capture. The GPS log file contained the UTC time received by the GPS, the latitude, longitude, and altitude information.

Universal Radio Hacker [9] was used to analyse the complex IQ file in the format CS8 (complex 8-bit signed integer samples). The IQ file was converted into frequency domain data in this experiment. The captured signal was the FM modulated transmission from

SER+MADRID, surrounded by signals from other local stations. Open-Source tools like Gnu-Radio [22], GQRX [8] or SDR# [23] can be used to process the signal and demodulate it.

5.3   Test Case 2 – Intruder Attack of Garage Door

Reference [1] demonstrated how easy it was to brute-force any fixed-code garage door. The codes sent by the key-fob to the garage are usually modulated using ASK(OOK) modulation. An ASK(OOK) modulated 10-bit garage signal code is shown in Fig. 5.

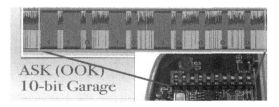

Fig. 5. Garage 10-bit code signal [1].

Reference [1] explained how shift registers decode received codes by sequentially loading each bit into the register, and then pushing the previous bits out as the new bits arrive. The De Brujin Sequence [24] interlaces multiple codes into one sequence to reduce the number of codes needed for transmission. Using the De Brujin Sequence and removing the wait periods between sending each code, for every 8 to 12-bit garage code the brute-force time is 8.2 s. This experiment simulates a real attack by generating and transmitting a De Brujin Sequence of 10 bits in the 433.92 MHz band and capturing the transmission.

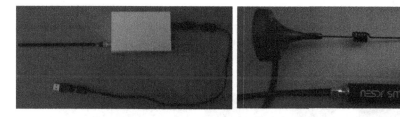

Fig. 6. SDR transmitter setup (left) and SDR capture setup (right).

To perform the experiment, two SDRs were used, one for transmitting the signal and another one for capturing. The hardware used for this experiment were: The HackRF One transmitter to transmit the generated De Brujin Sequence, the RTL-SDR to capture the signals transmitted from the HackRF using the developed program and a fixed frequency antenna for 433 attached to the RTL-SDR using an antenna base. Figure 6 shows the hardware setup for transmitting the data, as well as the RTL-SDR device and a 433 MHz antenna for capturing the data.

For the garage attack experiment to be reproduced legally, it was conducted within an RF shielded environment, using a very low power SDR without the airborne ability [17]. Thus, the transmitted radio signal would be contained within a very short range and not interfere with any other devices operating on the same frequency band. As a result of the RF shielded environment, GPS reception was not possible and therefore, the GPS receiver was not used. The experiment was performed by first generating a 10-bit Brujin Sequence with the 'rfpwnon' tool [25]. ASK (Amplitude Shift Key) modulation is needed to transmit this bit sequence. This was accomplished using the tool HackRF_OOK [26]. This program enables the modulation and transmission of OOK modulated data using the HackRF.

```
hackrf_ook -s 0 -b 1700 -0 1284 -1 416 -f 433920000 -r 1 -m 0001...
```

Fig. 7. Command to modulate and transmit OOK data.

Figure 7 shows the command used to modulate and transmit the bit sequence. The '−s' option sets the preamble duration to 0, '−b' option sets the overall bit duration in microseconds, and '−0' and '−1' indicate the gap widths for the 0 and 1 bits, respectively. The '−f' sets the frequency to 433.92 MHz. The '−r' indicates the number of repeated transmissions, and '-m' sets the bits sequence to transmit.

5.4   Findings in Test Case 2 – Intruder Attack of Garage Door

The procedure for acquiring the signal is similar to the previous experiment. Initially, the GQRX program was used to identify the signal. The transmitted sequence was captured with the RTL-SDR using the developed software tool, setting the frequency to 433.92 MHz, and using a sample rate of 2.048 MSPS. The device was unstable and dropped samples with a higher sample rate. Due to the RF shielded environment, GPS reception was not possible. The ASK radio signal transmitted by the HackRF is shown in Fig. 8. Figure 9 shows the configuration of the tool and the signal capture. The generated report of the capture is shown in Fig. 10. Figure 11 shows the content of the captured log file.

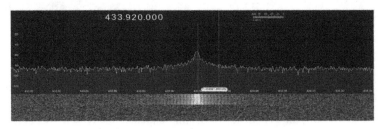

Fig. 8. Signal transmitted detected by GQRX.

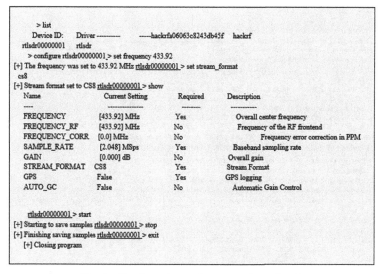

```
    > list
      Device ID:    Driver ----------    ------hackrfa06063c8243db45f    hackrf
rtlsdr00000001    rtlsdr
      > configure rtlsdr00000001 > set frequency 433.92
[+] The frequency was set to 433.92 MHz rtlsdr00000001 > set stream_format
cs8
[+] Stream format set to CS8 rtlsdr00000001 > show
      Name                    Current Setting        Required        Description
      ----                    ---------------        --------        -----------

      FREQUENCY               [433.92] MHz           Yes                Overall center frequency
      FREQUENCY_RF            [433.92] MHz           No                 Frequency of the RF frontend
      FREQUENCY_CORR          [0.0] MHz              No                 Frequency error correction in PPM
      SAMPLE_RATE             [2.048] MSps           Yes                Baseband sampling rate
      GAIN                    [0.000] dB             No                 Overall gain
      STREAM_FORMAT           CS8                    Yes                Stream Format
      GPS                     False                  Yes                GPS logging
      AUTO_GC                 False                  No                 Automatic Gain Control


      rtlsdr00000001 > start
[+] Starting to save samples rtlsdr00000001 > stop
[+] Finishing saving samples rtlsdr00000001 > exit
      [+] Closing program
```

Fig. 9. Configuration and capture of the signal.

```
File: 2020-06-03_19:21:06_rtlsdr00000001.report
-----------------------------------------------------
---- CAPTURE REPORT - Device ID: rtlsdr00000001
-----------------------------------------------------
   Time of creation: 2020-06-03 19:21:06
   UTC time: 2020-06-03 17:21:06
   Session log file: 2020-06-03_19:20:06.log

      Available:          Yes
      Driver:             rtlsdr
      Label:                 Generic RTL2832U OEM :: 00000001
      Manufacturer:       Realtek
      Product:            RTL2838UHIDIR
      Rtl:                0
      Serial:             00000001
      Tuner:                 Rafael Micro R820T

      Name                Current Setting       Description
      ----                ---------------       -----------

      FREQUENCY           [433.92] MHz          Overall center frequency
      FREQUENCY_RF        [433.92] MHz          Frequency of the RF frontend
      FREQUENCY_CORR      [0.0] MHz             Frequency error correction in PPM
      SAMPLE_RATE         [2.048] MSps          Baseband sampling rate
      GAIN                [0.000] dB            Overall gain
      STREAM_FORMAT       CS8                   Stream Format
      AUTO_GC             False                 Automatic Gain Control
      GPS                 False                 GPS logging
------------------------------------------------------
   File 1:          1_rtlsdr00000001_2020-06-03_19:21:06.complex16s
   MD5:          3685C794FD11E64470163485DF6B1BCC
                 SHA256: 002C4C28C5C2EC874C8851074FF5C872D1299C430AF73F153F27C54668726A2F
------------------------------------------------------
Total number of samples: 65536000
Total time of capture: 28.7 s
Time of end: 2020-06-03 19:21:34
UTC time of end: 2020-06-03 17:21:34
```

Fig. 10. Capture report.

```
File: 2020-06-03_19:20:06.log
-------------------------------------------------------------------------
2020-06-03 19:20:06,856 - DEBUG - [SOAPY_SDR_DEBUG] RTL-SDR Devices: 1
2020-06-03 19:20:06,858 - DEBUG - [SOAPY_SDR_DEBUG] Device #0: Generic RTL2832U OEM
2020-06-03 19:20:06,871 - DEBUG - [SOAPY_SDR_DEBUG]                Manufacturer: Realtek,
 ↪ Product Name: RTL2838UHIDIR, Serial: 00000001
2020-06-03 19:20:07,277 - DEBUG - [SOAPY_SDR_DEBUG]                Tuner type: Rafael
 ↪ Micro R820T
2020-06-03 19:20:07,344 - DEBUG - [SOAPY_SDR_DEBUG] Found device by index 0
2020-06-03 19:20:07,345 - DEBUG - [SOAPY_SDR_DEBUG] Found RTL-SDR Device using
 ↪ device index parameter 'rtl' = 0
2020-06-03 19:20:07,345 - DEBUG - [SOAPY_SDR_DEBUG] RTL-SDR Tuner type: Rafael Micro
 ↪ R820T
2020-06-03 19:20:07,346 - DEBUG - [SOAPY_SDR_DEBUG] RTL-SDR opening device 0
2020-06-03 19:20:21,421 - DEBUG - [SOAPY_SDR_DEBUG] Setting center freq: 433920000
2020-06-03 19:20:21,475 - INFO - [ID: rtlsdr00000001] [+] The frequency was set to
↪ 433.92 MHz
2020-06-03 19:20:30,440 - INFO - [ID: rtlsdr00000001] [+] Stream format set to CS8
2020-06-03 19:21:06,008 - DEBUG - Connecting to gpsd socket at 127.0.0.1:2947
2020-06-03 19:21:06,008 - INFO - [GPS] No device found 2020-06-03 19:21:06,010 - INFO - [SOAPY_SDR_INFO] Using format
CS8.
2020-06-03 19:21:06,011 - DEBUG - [SOAPY_SDR_DEBUG] RTL-SDR Using buffer length
↪ 262144
2020-06-03 19:21:06,011 - DEBUG - [SOAPY_SDR_DEBUG] RTL-SDR Using 15 buffers
2020-06-03 19:21:06,163 - INFO - [ID: rtlsdr00000001] Starting to receive and save
↪ samples
2020-06-03 19:21:34,819 - INFO - [ID: rtlsdr00000001] Finished receiving samples
2020-06-03 20:01:45,938 - INFO - Program closed
```

Fig. 11. Content of the log file.

Fig. 12. Matching binary sequence.

The open source program Universal Radio Hacker [9] was used to analyse and decode the signal of the captured IQ samples file. Figure 10 generated by the program shows the analogue representation of the OOK pulses of the transmission, representing the start of the binary sequence presented previously. The captured file was analysed and decoded and the decoded data from URH matched the binary sequence transmitted (Fig. 12). As a result of the forensic capture of the signal as shown in this scenario, information such as signal logging, GPS location, UTC time, etc. can be compiled to prove an event. Also, the signal can be reproduced with the original device in the future and compared with the forensic capture to prove that it is the same signal.

6   Conclusion

This paper reports the development of a forensic tool for acquiring radio spectrum in a forensically sound way with the necessary logging capabilities for examinations by investigators. Using the tool, two experiments were conducted involving the acquisition of radio signals. The main limitations of the acquisition are in the SDR receiver used, but there are also limitations in the software. During sampling at the highest sample rate supported by the HackRF (20 MHz) and using a complex 32-bit float stream format (CF32), an overflow was reported and logged to the log file (Fig. 13). The error did not occur when using the 8-bit integer complex sample (CS8) native format used by RTL-SDR and HackRF, but it would be a problem in high end SDR devices with higher bit resolution.

```
2020-06-04 12:28:18,388 - INFO - [SOAPY_SDR_SSI] O
2020-06-04 12:28:18,404 - INFO - [SOAPY_SDR_SSI] O
2020-06-04 12:28:18,417 - INFO - [SOAPY_SDR_SSI] O
```

Fig. 13. Log messages of stream status indicating overflow and lost samples.

The streaming implementation should be done using a low-level language rather than Python in order to increase the speed of the samples and avoid stream overflows. Currently, GPS logging consists of a file containing different information separated by colons. GPX is a standard format that can easily be processed and converted to other formats, so future implementations should record GPS data in this format. A visual display of the spectrum should be added to the tool in the future to allow live monitoring of radio activity for a selected band by investigators. While capturing samples, file compression techniques should also be examined to reduce file sizes.

References

1. Kamkar, S.: Drive It Like You Hacked It (DEF CON 23) (2015). https://samy.pl/defcon2015/. Accessed 10 June 2021
2. Keyless Entry System Attacks (2017). https://conference.hitb.org/hitbsecconf2017ams/ses sions/chasing-cars-keyless-entry-system-attacks/. Accessed 10 June 2021
3. Ballantyne, S.N.T.: Wireless Communication Security: Software Defined Radio-Based Threat Assessment, MSC by Research Thesis, Coventry University (2016)
4. Achi, H., Hellany, A., Nagrial, M.: Digital forensics of wireless systems and devices technical and legal challenges. In: 6th International Symposium on High Capacity Optical Networks and Enabling Technologies (HONET), pp. 43–46 (2009). https://doi.org/10.1109/HONET. 2009.5423057
5. Turnbull, B., Osborne, G., Simon, M.: Legal and technical implications of collecting wireless data as an evidence source. In: Sorell, M. (ed.) e-Forensics 2009. LNICSSITE, vol. 8, pp. 36–41. Springer, Heidelberg (2009). https://doi.org/10.1007/978-3-642-02312-5_5
6. Ngobeni, S., Venter, H., Burke, I.: A forensic readiness model for wireless networks. In: Chow, K.-P., Shenoi, S. (eds.) DigitalForensics 2010. IAICT, vol. 337, pp. 107–117. Springer, Heidelberg (2010). https://doi.org/10.1007/978-3-642-15506-2_8

7. Kismet (2020). https://www.kismetwireless.net/. Accessed 10 June 2021
8. Csete, A.: Gqrx SDR – Open Source Software Defined Radio by Alexandru Csete OZ9AEC (2021). https://gqrx.dk. Accessed 10 June 2021
9. Universal Radio Hacker (2021). https://github.com/jopohl/urh. Accessed 10 June 2021
10. ACPO Good Practice Guide for Digital Evidence (2012). https://www.digital-detective.net/digital-forensics-documents/ACPO_Good_Practice_Guide_for_Digital_Evidence_v5.pdf. Accessed 10 June 2021
11. Kirk, P.L.: Crime investigation: physical evidence and the police laboratory. Science 118(3061), 256–257 (1953). https://doi.org/10.1126/science.118.3061.256
12. Pollitt, M.: An ad hoc review of digital forensic models. In: Second International Workshop on Systematic Approaches to Digital Forensic Engineering, IEEE (2007). https://doi.org/10.1109/SADFE.2007.3
13. Wireless Telegraphy Act 2006. https://www.legislation.gov.uk/ukpga/2006/36/section/48. Accessed 10 June 2021
14. Communications Act (2003). https://www.legislation.gov.uk/ukpga/2003/21/contents. Accessed 10 June 2021
15. Office of Communications (OFCOM). Guidance on Receive-Only Radio Scanners. https://www.ofcom.org.uk/spectrum/interference-enforcement/radio-interception. Accessed 10 June 2021
16. Ofcom UK Frequency Allocation Table (UKFAT) (2017). https://www.ofcom.org.uk/__data/assets/pdf_file/0016/103309/uk-fat-2017.pdf. Accessed 10 June 2021
17. IR 2030 – UK Interface Requirements 2030 by Ofcom. https://www.ofcom.org.uk/__data/assets/pdf_file/0028/84970/ir-2030.pdf. Accessed 10 June 2021
18. Nooelec NESDR SMArt v4 & 3 Antennas (2021). https://www.nooelec.com/store/nesdr-smart.html. Accessed 10 June 2021
19. Nooelec - Extruded Aluminum Enclosure for HackRF One (2021). https://www.nooelec.com/store/sdr/sdr-addons/hackrf-enclosure.html. Accessed 10 June 2021
20. TCXO Nooelec for HackRF (2021). https://www.passion-radio.com/sdr-accessory/tiny-tcxo-719.html. Accessed 10 June 2021
21. Python Library, Pothosware/SoapySDR (2020). https://github.com/pothosware/SoapySDR. Accessed 10 June 2021
22. GNU Radio - The Free & Open Source Radio Ecosystem · GNU Radio (2021). https://www.gnuradio.org/. Accessed 10 June 2021
23. SDR# - airspy.com (2021). https://airspy.com/download/. Accessed 10 June 2021
24. De Bruijn Sequence (2021). https://en.wikipedia.org/wiki/De_Bruijn_sequence. Accessed 10 June 2021
25. Harding, C.: Exploitagency/Github-Rfpwnon (2016). https://github.com/exploitagency/github-rfpwnon. Accessed 10 June 2021
26. Bodor, D.: 0xDRRB/hackrf_ook (2019). https://github.com/0xDRRB/hackrf_ook. Accessed 10 June 2021

SEMFLOW: Accurate Semantic Identification from Low-Level System Data

Mohammad Kavousi[1]([✉]), Runqing Yang[2], Shiqing Ma[3], and Yan Chen[1]

[1] Northwestern University, Evanston, USA
kavousi@u.northwestern.edu, ychen@northwestern.edu
[2] Zhejiang University, Hangzhou, China
rainkin1993@zju.edu.cn
[3] Rutgers University, Piscataway, USA
shiqing.ma@rutgers.edu

Abstract. Forensic analysis, nowadays, is a crucial part of attack investigation in end-user and enterprise systems. Log collection and analysis enable investigators to rebuild the attack chain, find the attack source and possibly rollback the damage made to the system.

However, building the full attack chain is often time-consuming and error-prone. The reason is that existing audit systems cannot provide high-level semantics for low-level system events. To address this issue, we propose SEMFLOW, to accurately identify semantics for system events. Specifically, we generate signatures to link low-level system events to a particular high-level application behavior during an offline training phase. Then, during the labeling phase, our realtime data collector matches the generated signatures against audit logs and labels individual system-level events with high-level semantics.

Our evaluations show that in at set of 16 selected popular applications, our system can effectively identify semantics of certain system-level data while maintaining less than 4% of overhead on the CPU and memory.

Keywords: Security · System security · Semantic detection · Provenance graph · Living-off-the-land

1 Introduction

Large enterprises are increasingly being targeted by Advanced Persistent Threats (APTs). One of the main goals of APTs is obtaining and exfiltrating highly confidential information, e.g., APT1 [4] stole hundreds of terabytes of sensitive data (including business plans, technology blueprints, and test results) from at least 141 organizations across a diverse set of industries. By avoiding actions that would immediately arouse suspicion, security analysts can achieve dwell investigation times that range from weeks to months. Alternatively, Living-off-the-Land (LotL) tactics take advantage of native tools existent on a system in order to

© ICST Institute for Computer Sciences, Social Informatics and Telecommunications Engineering 2021
Published by Springer Nature Switzerland AG 2021. All Rights Reserved
J. Garcia-Alfaro et al. (Eds.): SecureComm 2021, LNICST 398, pp. 513–535, 2021.
https://doi.org/10.1007/978-3-030-90019-9_26

perform lateral movement and gain persistence of APT threats in operating systems. During Q3 2018 to Q3 2019, Symantec saw a 184% increase in blocked Windows PowerShell scripts. 87% of such attacks executed the PowerShell script through cmd.exe or Windows Management Infrastructure (WMI) [5].

To combat such threats, the notion of data provenance has been applied to traditional system event audit systems and have proven invaluable in detection and investigation. Highly confidential information is usually represented as file objects and any operations related to such file objects are recorded in system event audit logs. Data provenance analysis systems parse individual system events into provenance graphs that encode the history of a system's execution sequence. Such provenance graphs allow investigators to trace the data flow of highly confidential file objects. By leveraging such capability, security systems can identify attack steps and the involved objects, when the content of confidential files is read and is finally sent out to the opposition. Essentially, provenance graphs can help identify the whole attack chain of an adversary; beginning from the initial compromise up until their lateral movement and business damage. In this paper, we focus on attack types which use benign software to perform some of, or the whole attack.

Unfortunately, existing system event audit systems cannot provide application-level semantics for file events, which leads to inaccurate results on almost all existing data provenance based systems. For instance, WinSCP, a popular file transfer software on Windows, might read the confidential private key file for two different purposes: authentication, and upload. However, existing audit systems provide two totally equivalent events (i.e., two ReadFile events referring to the same file object) for such two scenarios. Without application-level semantics of ReadFile events in this example, a normal user logging onto the SSH server using WinSCP by reading the key file for authentication would be mistakenly considered as a data exfiltration attack. This would lead to the problem that provenance-based systems would lack such kind of information due to the semantic gap between low-level system events and high-level application operations.

Some prior works have been able to provide high-level application semantics for system events [13,22,28]. Although they demonstrated great potential, they suffer from several limitations:

1) **Requiring invasive instrumentation.** Some use instrumentation techniques [23] to intercept application-level APIs and correlate such semantics to system events. Such systems introduce notable performance degradation and instability, which is not applicable in enterprise environments.

2) **Inaccuracy.** Some works rely on heuristics (e.g., timestamp-based correlation [40]) to correlate application-level logs to system events without instrumentation. However, such heuristics cannot work in complex scenarios (e.g., logs generated by multiple individual behaviors occur in parallel in the background), which leads to inaccurate results.

3) **Post-processing.** Existing data provenance based works [15,29] consume system events and detect attacks in realtime, which requires the collector to

provide the semantics of system events in realtime to enhance those works, resulting in the need for labeling before the data is consumed. However, existing works [22] rely on complex behavior models (e.g., behavior graph model whose vertexes are system call and edges are causal relationships between system calls) to provide high-level semantics accurately, which makes them non-realtime.

Problem Statement. *The main problem tackled in this paper is providing application-level semantics for file and process/thread related events under user interactive scenarios without instrumentation accurately in realtime.*

In this work, we argue that existing system event-based works can be dramatically improved through identifying high-level application semantics of individual system events. To achieve that goal, we present SEMFLOW, an instrumentation-free framework that takes advantage of the native Windows audit system for identifying high-level application semantics of systems in realtime, with no need for post-processing of system data. Our methodology is inspired by analyzing the program callstack which reveals its API call chain, and observing that parts of the chain are designated to perform a specific task. The main secret that we can provide such semantics without complex binary instrumentation, is the return address of each frame in the application callstack, which we can refer to as the line of code. In other words, the execution sequence that caused the system-level event to be emitted. We argue that in most cases, the sequence of function calls leading to emitting a specific event are unique to each behavior and can accurately identify it.

For our approach, we will perform training on different sets of behaviors in various applications, generate signatures and after that, define a set of user interactions that can produce the same behavior; so that it can be done automatically for the later versions of the same program.

The training does not need to be done on the user end. Hence, it can be done on high-end servers as demanded, reducing the time of signature generation for each behavior on a specific program binary.

To implement and evaluate our approach, we have collected about 150 datasets from different application executables performing different behaviors. Part of which will be used to train and the rest for evaluation purposes.

Our evaluations show that we result in a very small percentage of false positives labeling individual events. In addition, since we use set matching and all of program behavior signatures can be loaded into memory, the overhead of performing such labeling is negligible, compared to collecting unlabeled events. We also show that our method can be applied to systems already using an existing intrusion detection system (IDS); as our system labels individual data/control flow events and performs such labeling in realtime.

In summary, this paper makes the following contributions:

- We recognize the gaps of existing event identification systems and try to fill by identifying high-level application semantics of events.
- We propose a novel behavior model based on callstacks to identify high-level semantics of individual events accurately and efficiently.

- We propose an instrumentation-free audit system, SEMFLOW, which provides the semantics of popular security-related file and control-flow events in real-time, and we evaluate SEMFLOW by providing cases of potential real-world attacks.

2   Background and Motivation

In this section, we discuss the concept of forensic analysis and building the attack chain, and the significance of labeling events as certain activities.

2.1   Motivating Example

A startup company purchased a virtual public server (VPS) to host its public website using Apache web server. Because of budget limitations, the purchased service only allows one communication token to the server. Thus, the whole web team shared the same public and private key files generated by the RSA algorithm (pub.rsa, pri.rsa) to communicate (via SSH) with the remote server whose IP address is x.x.x.x. Due to the importance and secrecy of these keys, the company forbids its usage in other scenarios. A daily routine for the team was to log onto the server using the communication keys via WinSCP program and update the files hosted under the root HTTP folder, www.

The company receives an alert from the VPS company about a possible data leakage. Specifically, a few files were hosted publicly under the folder www, and they verified that one of them was the private key pri.rsa used to communicate with the VPS machine. By checking the server communication log, they also confirmed that the only SSH connections were from the company machines. To investigate how the key got leaked, the startup company started to perform forensics on machines used by the web team.

2.2   Existing Audit Systems and Forensic Systems

Figure 1 (I) shows a typical provenance graph generated for different team members belonging to the web team in the motivating story. Note that in this figure (and the rest of the paper), we use *diamonds* to denote *sockets*, *boxes* to denote *processes*, and *ovals* to denote *files*. As we can see, all members seem to be suspicious, because all of them have an information flow from the private key file to the remote server. A deeper investigation shows that the reason is because the private key will be used for authentication purposes when using WinSCP to update files on the server.

This raises the problem that two totally different behaviors (i.e., authentication and uploading private key files to the server) can generate identical provenance graphs, which interferes with the investigation process and prevents us from effectively and efficiently identifying the attacker machine. The root reason is we do not know what the files are used for when the same operations happen (i.e., read in this case, for authentication, and uploading). We refer to this as the **semantic gap** problem, meaning that low-level provenance data lack semantic information (i.e., what the files are used for) from applications. This is a common issue for existing provenance graph-based forensic systems, leading to inaccurate results [12,20,26].

2.3 Our System

In this paper, we propose a provenance graph edge tagging technique SEMFLOW, which solves the semantic gap problem by leveraging the (user space) callstack information provided by Event Tracing for Windows (ETW) system to tag the provenance graphs generated by using low-level information. SEMFLOW first analyzes the callstack information of each ETW event and generates a "signature" for these events based on the callstack, which represents the high-level semantics (e.g., uploading or authentication). When a system event is produced, SEMFLOW will tag individual edges in the provenance graph based on generated signatures, so that events with the same event type can be distinguished.

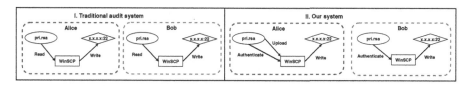

Fig. 1. Attack scenario in Sect. 2.1 without (left) and with (right) semantic identification

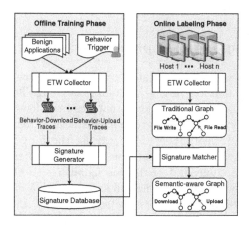

Fig. 2. Overview of SEMFLOW

Figure 1 (II) shows the graph generated by SEMFLOW for the aforementioned example. In the figure, we use blue and red colored texts to represent high-level semantic behaviors labeled by SEMFLOW for the benign scenario and the malicious scenario, respectively. Based on the tag, administrators can easily see the private key is uploaded using Alice's computer.

2.4 Threat Model

In this paper, we consider the OS kernel and auditing system (i.e., ETW) as part of the trusted computing base (TCB). We assume that the OS kernel is well protected by existing techniques [1,3]. Thus, the audit logs cannot be modified by attackers. Our threat model is as reasonable and practical as the models of previous forensic works [8,9,12]. This paper targets attacks involving benign applications, including insider attacks leveraging benign applications' functionalities to perform malicious behaviors and attacks injecting malware onto the machine to hide malicious behaviors under normal behaviors to bypass the Intrusion Detection Systems (IDS).

(1)

ProcessId	ThreadId	EventName
7068	716	ThreadCreate

(2)

Frame	Binary	Location
...		
3	ntdll.dll	NtCreateThread + 0x54
...		
16	xul.dll	BackgroundFileSaver::Init + 0xe8
...		
30	xul.dll	nsHttpChannel::ProcessResponse + 0x34
31	xul.dll	nsHttpChannel::OnStartRequest + 0x2c
...		
38	xul.dll	MessageLoop::RunHandler + 0x28

Fig. 3. An example of a low-level event log with its callstack

3 System Design and Implementation

Figure 2 illustrates our system architecture—the workflow of our system proceeds in two phases: offline training and online labeling. The goal of the offline training phase is to generate behavior signatures from low-level events. Specifically, we analyze why and how we leverage callstacks to represent the high-level semantics of low-level events (Sect. 3.1), and use the ETW collector (Sect. 3.2) to collect low-level system events and use *Signature Generator* to analyze the collected information to generate behavior signatures (Sect. 3.3). In the online labeling phase, our system utilizes the collector on each Windows host for audit logging. When a low-level event is generated, *Signature Matcher* will decide to label events based on generated behavior signatures (Sect. 3.4), which can help investigators distinguish between benign behaviors and malicious ones.

3.1 Assumptions and Observations

In this subsection, we first provide an example of a system log along with its callstack, and then discuss why callstack is important for semantics identification.

SemFlow configures a native low-level data collection tool on Windows to collect the callstack for each low-level event, which is essential to represent high-level semantics for low-level events.

An Example of Logs Along with Event Callstack. Figure 3 shows an example of a low-level event collected by SemFlow. The first block (1) includes the basic information of the event, including the process identifier (ProcessId), thread identifier (ThreadId), and the event name (EventName) (other fields are omitted). The second block (2) shows the above event's callstack, which is a function callstack with top ones (e.g., *Frame* 31) being callers and lower ones (e.g., *Frame* 30) being callees. Each entry has three fields, a frame number, a *Binary* field representing which binary file (e.g., Dynamic Linking Library on Windows) the function is in, and the *Location* fields denoting the resolved symbolic names and offset values. The data format of the *Location* field is *Class::Function + Offset*. The *Class* shows the C++ class in which the *Function* is defined, and the *Offset* represents the offset relative to the *Function* in which the lower function is invoked. Taking *Frame* 31 as an example, `OnStartRequest` is defined at the class `nsHttpChannel`, and the lower function `ProcessResponse` in *Frame* 30 is invoked at the offset 0x2c relative to `OnStartRequest`.

Table 1. Part of firefox file download signature

	Event Class	File Paths (only used for verification)	Signature type	Callstack
1	Create Thread	-	init	Hash values of callstacks
2	Write File	`C:\10MB.zip.part`; *Temp*`\VQkG8r+z.zip.part`	during	
3	Rename File	*Temp*`\VQkG8r+z.zip.part`	init	
4	Write File	`C:\10MB.zip:Zone.Identifier`	during	
5	Write File	*AppData*`\...\cache2\...\cachefilename`	during	
6	Write File	*AppData*`\...\places.sqlite-wal`	finalize, contextual	

The Essence of CallStack. Existing provenance-based systems only leverage event information (i.e., block 1 in Fig. 3). However, different behaviors might generate the same event information; causing the semantic gap issue. The fundamental reason is that system events are too low-level and general to capture the semantics of high-level application behaviors. Thus, looking for logs that contain more semantics than system events is necessary. We observe that *the combination of callstack with their system event effectively reflects the implementation logic of a high-level application behavior*, which is useful to solve this problem. Take the event in Fig. 3 as an example. The event is generated by Firefox initiating a file download from the Internet. In frame 16, the `BackgroundFileSaver::Init` function shows that this event is created to save a file in the background. Frames 30 and 31 show that the file saving operation is invoked via an HTTP channel. Intuitively, we come up with the idea to leverage callstack to recover high-level semantics of low-level events. Table 1 shows part of the Firefox file download signature. First row creating the thread to download the file, second one assigning a temporary file name, third one renaming the temporary file name after the user assigns a file name, fourth and fifth filesystem-related and caching operations, lastly, adding the downloaded file to the downloads library.

Based on our analysis of the programs and empirical results, we get the conclusion that a single event along with its callstack can be used to recover semantics for most behaviors. Based on such conclusion, we propose our semantic labeling system for low-level events.

3.2   ETW Collector

We build SEMFLOW upon ETW, a lightweight auditing system on the Windows platform, which has been widely adopted by many academic papers and industry products. In addition to the events pointed out in Sect. 2, SEMFLOW configures ETW to collect the callstack for each low-level event. Then, we iterate through the callstack and record the addresses we observe for each frame. Hence, at the end, we would be left with the basic event information, along with its execution callstack (as shown in Fig. 3).

3.3   Signature Generator

The signature generator module takes traces collected from different behaviors of different applications when triggered, and generates signatures for selected behaviors. We use two terms to describe different types of traces extracted from applications:

- *Matching Traces:* Execution traces that contain all or partial events (represented by logged events) related to the behavior.
- *Non-Matching Traces:* Execution traces that do not contain the operations related to the behavior.

The signature generator acts as a training module which goal is to identify unique events related to an operation, by removing out the events that are also happening when the target operation is not taking place. It then generates a unique hash for each unique event it finds in the matching traces. The final signature related to a behavior, will be a set of hashes representing each event's application-level callstack; which will be passed to the *Signature Matcher* for labeling.

Algorithm 1. Signature Generation Algorithm

Input: Matching and Non-Matching Trace Sets for an Operation Within a Process, and Path to the Process– $S_{matching}$, $S_{non-matching}$, $path$
Output: Signature added to $ProcessSet$
Initialize: $B_{Matching} \leftarrow \emptyset$, $B_{NonMatching} \leftarrow \emptyset$
Entrypoint: The Get-Signature Function

1: **function** FIND-NON-MATCHING(S_{input})
2:     **for** each Trace $T_i \in S_{input}$ **do**
3:         **for** each Event $U_i \in T_i$ **do**
4:             $B_{NonMatching}.add(U_i)$
5: **function** FIND-MATCHING(S_{input})
6:     **for** each Trace $T_i \in S_{input}$ **do**
7:         **for** each Event $U_i \in T_i$ **do**
8:             $B_{Matching}.add(U_i)$
9: **function** GET-SIGNATURE
10:     Find-Non-Matching($S_{non-matching}$)
11:     Find-Matching($S_{matching}$)
12:     $Signature \leftarrow B_{Matching}.removeAll(B_{NonMatching})$
13:     $ProcessSet.put(SHA256(path), Signature)$

Algorithm 2. Matching Algorithm for Signatures

Input: Event Stream– e and Process Creation Events– p
Output: Event Set Labeling $B_{EventList}$
Initialize: $SigList \leftarrow \emptyset$, $ProcessSet \leftarrow$ all processes with signatures

1: **function** ON-PROCESS(p)
2:     /* Find the executable location */
3:     $path \leftarrow find\_path(p)$
4:     /* Calculate the hash of executable */
5:     $hash \leftarrow SHA256(path)$
6:     **if** $ProcessSet.contains(hash)$ **then**
7:         $Siglist.add(ProcessSet.get(hash))$
8: **function** ON-EVENT(e)
9:     **if** $SigList.contains(e.callstack)$ **then**
10:         $Label(e)$

3.4 Signature Matcher

After building signatures for different behaviors in different applications, the *Signature Matcher* matches the signatures against each callstacks in the log stream. As for the process for matching signatures with the incoming events from ETW, upon creating a process, we see whether the signatures for the same binary exist in our signature database. If they do, then for upcoming events for the process, we search in the process-specific signature to see if we can find the same callstack hash in the event set in the signature. If we do find the event with similar callstack, we then label the event according to the signature. Each event in the signature is associated to a behavior which we have extracted from training. As the events enter the signature matcher, the set matching helps us to label (or not to label) each individual event.

Table 2. List of intercepted operations in SEMFLOW

Application	Operations
VLC Media Player	Video Playing
FileZilla	File Upload/Download
WinSCP	File Upload/Download/Copy
Notepad, Sublime Text	File Save
Skype	File Upload/Download
WinRAR	File Compression
Firefox, Chrome, Edge	File Upload/Download
Cobiansoft Cobian Backup	Routine Backup
Outlook	File Upload
Windows Explorer	File Copy/Move
Microsoft Word	Type and Save
TeamViewer	File Upload/Download
Adobe Reader DC	PDF Open and Fill

4   Implementation

In this section, we discuss how we implement each module discussed in Sect. 3.

4.1   Signature Generator

Algorithm 1 illustrates how signatures are generated for a certain behavior. Taking the matching and non-matching traces, we start running Algorithm 1 by triggering the `Get-Signature` function as entrypoint (line 9) to extract signatures for an activity. It starts by finding all events related to non-matching behaviors inside the `Find-Non-Matching` function (line 10), and all events related to the behavior in the `Find-Matching` function (line 11). The algorithm finds events that occur in matching traces but not the accumulated non-matching events; and finally extracts the unique set of events related to the operation extracted from matching traces, excluding events from the traces when the operation was not happening.

For example, for Firefox file download signature, we run the algorithm from a simulation of different file downloads as matching behaviors. Browsing, changing settings, and playing other functionalities are considered as non-matching behaviors. The algorithm starts by accumulating all non-matching events (line 4), collectively putting them in $B_{NonMatching}$. From three traces collected from matching behavior as $S_{matching}$ and five traces collected from non-matching scenarios as $S_{non-matching}$, line 8 then adds matching events using the same procedure. In the end, in line 12, we remove all the events that also happen in non-matching scenarios, allowing us to be left with unique events related to the certain behavior. We use the hash of the process to be able to later identify

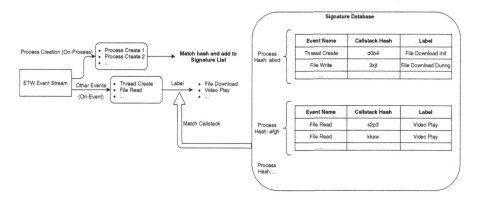

Fig. 4. Signature matching mechanism according to Algorithm 2

the binary (described in the next section). We will also propose a method for verifying signatures in Sect. 5.

4.2   Signature Matcher

Algorithm 2 shows how the matching takes place. Upon starting a process, the program finds the executable path (line 3) and generates a hash from the binary (line 5). Then, we see if we have any training data based on the process (line 6), then we load the signatures for that process into memory.

Upon receiving an event (line 8), the program determines if it maps to any behavior (line 9) that we have signatures on. Then finally, the labeling takes place, and the event can move forward in the stream (line 10). Figure 4 shows an example of signature database and its usage in the ETW event stream, as well as the mapping between Algorithm 2 and the diagram. Hashes from process executables are generated after receiving each *Process Start* event. If it matches any of the recorded hashes in the signatures, then the PID is recorded and the corresponding signature is loaded into the memory. Then if events emitted by any of the recorded processes would match any of the events in signatures, then the event is labeled.

5   Experiments and Evaluation Results

For evaluating our approach and measuring the effectiveness on an example collected dataset, we answer two questions:

- **Q1:** How effective is SEMFLOW in detecting benign activities and dealing with non-related ones?
- **Q2:** What is the performance cost of SEMFLOW?

To answer these questions, we first need to generate signatures for each behavior in each application (Table 2). Then, we compare with the ground truth which are trace files containing the information about when an operation was taking place in a sample trace file. Afterwards, we compare the labeled events to finally extract the coverage of event labeling as well as the false positives.

5.1 Experiment Setup

Collecting Matching Behavior: For selected behaviors, we first collect traces from behaviors that we *can* identify (from a user point of view), and we initially set to collect three datasets having different durations and interacting with different files (i.e., downloading file A then downloading file B). This ensures that we are not dependent on the objects involved. Instead, it confirms that we can detect the activity no matter the duration nor the involved objects might be. These three datasets are used to extract unique callstacks that may represent a certain activity, ensuring the uniqueness of events that are related to it. (We later discuss in **Accuracy** section about this number).

Collecting Non-matching Behavior: The non-matching behavior is intended for filtering out non-unique events that we obtained from the previous step. In this step, we do anything but the selected activity to finally find out unique events that we believe are related only and only for performing our selected activities. Since non-matching traces may result from more activities, we collect more number of traces than the previous step; namely, five traces. This is because programs have lots of more functionalities than what we usually expect from them (i.e., their main functionality). For example, almost any program would have a "setting" menu that would generate events not related to our intended activity set. Although the mentioned behaviors usually do not generate too many events, they can help filter out the ones that would happen in different contexts, leading to a reduction in our signature size, as well as decreasing false positives.

Test Sets: After collecting unique events for activities, we generate mixed traces, meaning the traces that are collected from a normal user interaction with the program, not restricted to any specific behavior. For collecting ground truth (i.e., the parts of the trace that we are supposed to *know* what the user is doing, versus the rest of the program execution), we ask the users to trigger a button and specify the activity they will be doing from the list of our detected activities in Table 2. Then we record the timestamp ranges where the specified operations were done. Hence, the rest of the trace would be the part that we have done anything *but* the said operations. The purpose of timestamp recording is to verify that none of the events that we have identified their operation, appear in the parts that we are not doing any of those that we have detected in Table 2. In test sets, we try to cover more activities and more running time than the mentioned ones in Table 3, since they were already used to generate the non-matching traces. But the actual activity might not be high-level enough to be put in Table 3, because some activities (such as background ones) overlap the ones put in the mentioned table. For example, in MS Word, we collect changing layout to a certain size and double-column the page, while in test sets, we also perform a change of indentation and more available actions in the layout tab.

Evaluation Methodology. Our system has been evaluated both in terms of accuracy and performance. In this section, we discuss how the generated signatures perform in a real-world system, and how we assess the overhead it suffers in labeling events.

Accuracy: For evaluating our signatures, one general consideration is why we chose numbers of three for matching and five for non-matching behavior to generate signatures. The reason is, based on experiment results, if we choose the minimum of having one matching and one non-matching trace, we would have more false positives since we cannot accurately filter unrelated events. This is considered to be a general concept in any learning-based solution; if one has more training data, the more accurate their results would be. Future researchers may choose to use more or less numbers, according to their performance/accuracy requirements.

- **False Positives:** Denote percentage of events that we *do* label, but are outside the timestamps of which the user claims performing a known activity (i.e., we mislabel them).
- **True Positives:** This rating will indicate the percentage of events that are solely related to an activity, which are labeled as they should be. Evaluating related events would require ground truth about the program implementation, which is often difficult to denote since most programs are closed-source, and even the open-source ones are often too complicated to analyze. Hence, we manually extract events that we are confident to be related to a particular activity and check how many of them we were able to identify. In order for that, we manually analyze signatures and the activity we are monitoring and extract events in the traces that correspond to the files involved in that activity. An example of such system knowledge would be in extracting events from a WinSCP file transfer. A little system knowledge can show us that when transferring files, the WinSCP program would not load the whole file at once in memory when sending it out. Hence, we expect the `ReadFile` event reading the source file to be one of the most frequent events in our traces. Then we see if we have included the callstack signature for that event in our traces. We can also perform a backward check by recording the objects involved in behaviors. As an example, for the Firefox file download signature, we also record the file paths of downloaded files, and we ensure that event callstacks in our signatures match the filename as the same object because we expect no other event in the trace to have the same filename and callstack in the trace, except the ones that were associated with the file download behavior.

Performance: Signature generation uses the simple filtering technique described in Algorithm 1, and the overhead essentially depends on the size of the trace files being collected. For deployment of the embedded collector and matcher, we used the normal ETW collector to perform collection of unlabeled events, then the comparison is done by adding the callstack parsing and event labeling part. Our system needs to iterate through each frame in the callstack, ranging between 10–69 frames in our datasets; then, for each frame, we find the related library according to the address we receive. This information is extracted from the *LoadLibrary* events (which are normally collected by ETW), providing the library load address for each loaded library on the system. We then determine if the library is under *C:/Windows* (except for MS-developed apps), then we find if the detected library is a user-level library. At last, we extract a hash out of the recorded addresses in the callstack for each event, adding it as an additional parameter in the event, which will be later compared to the signatures (if any) extracted from each activity.

5.2   Results

Table 3 shows the results for FPs and TPs. For some, we do have some FP since the same event would be used in a different context as well, such as in MS word where the complexity of the application would result in some non-deterministic events that would randomly occur in matching traces whereas, in the final test set, they would also appear in parts where the behavior was not taking place.

False Positives: In some cases, we have a few events that are considered to be unique as given in the matching traces and would not appear in the non-matching traces too. But, in test sets, we still see them occurring in the non-matching parts of the test trace. Hence, they are considered to be false positives. Analyzing the reason of why we have these FPs is a bit challenging since we do not have the source code for most applications, and for the ones we do, analysis of the code and following the code structure by a human is rather frustrating. One case for our false positive analysis is the false positive scenarios for Microsoft word. After analyzing the false positives, we look into the file paths of the files being read. It turns out two of the false positives read a file related to proofing data, the other four, read an `index.dat` which is also used by other Microsoft titles. There is no official documentation about the purpose of this file, but seemingly, this file is used to maintain file links in Microsoft applications and is read for multiple purposes. Hence, we can get the conclusion that some complex applications, perform different tasks in different scenarios and they decide how to perform the task in realtime, and it might not be deterministic for the application to behave the same in two different situations, while it is seen by the user to be performing the same task; as in MS word, typing and saving. Table 4 also shows some of the FP rates for having different numbers of matching and non-matching traces. The results show the lowest FPR obtained among the possible choices of the listed numbers of traces. As a general learning concept, the more training data, results in the observation of more accuracy rates.

Table 3. List of mixed operations used for testing SemFlow

Application	Operations	Duration (m)	Event size	FPR	TPR
VLC	Video Playing, Theme Change, Check for Updates	50	4250	0%	100%
FileZilla	File Upload & Download	20	90K	0%	100%
WinSCP	File Upload/Download/Copy (local), File Browsing, Adding Key, Changing Storage	20	50K	0%	100%
Notepad	File Save, Change Font, Print, Change Page Setup	15	14K	0%	100%
Sublime Text	File Save, Sorting, Setup Developer Commands, Change Color Scheme	15	25K	0%	100%
Skype	File Upload/Download, Upload Profile Photo, Change Settings, Add Contacts	25	120K	0%	100%
WinRAR	File Compression, Browsing, Test/Repair Archives, Licensing, Check for Updates	10	230K	0%	100%
Firefox	File Upload/Download, Install Extension, Change Settings, Browse History, Use Developer Tools	15	3M	5.6e−6%	85.67%
Chrome			7M	0.1e−3%	91.2%
MS Edge			4.5M	0.0013%	100%
Cobiansoft Cobian Backup	Routine Backup, Check Logs, Enc/Decrypt, Set Permissions, Edit Tasks	40	713K	0%	100%
Outlook	File Upload, Email w/o Attachments, Change Panes, Browse Folders	15	80K	0.1e−4%	100%
Windows Explorer	File Copy/Move, Browse, Search, Edit Taskbar, Create/Delete Objects, Change Properties	15	220K	0%	100%
Microsoft Word	Change Page Layout, Settings, Type and Save, Open New Doc	30	190K	0.078%	100%
TeamViewer	Connect, Remote Control, File Transfer, Local Settings	20	195K	0%	100%
Adobe Reader DC	Open and Fill Forms, Print, Change Window Layout	10	20K	0.0015%	100%

True Positives: For true positives, as mentioned in Sect. 5.1, we identify events that we expect to happen in a sample behavior. Results show that have included almost all related events from a user point of view, in the signatures. The only event that we had expected to see and we did not, was the final file rename of the *.part* file to the actual file name in Firefox. Our analysis shows that Firefox performs the file rename in a JavaScript submodule. And as we discuss in Sect. 7, interpreted languages' callstacks cannot be used to identify an activity as the code path will be determined by the interpreter at runtime.

Performance Overhead: The performance overhead of collecting callstacks in different applications, is measured by recording the percentage of the CPU utilization, compared to when we are only recording events and not collecting callstacks not labeling them. Our analysis show that in the most complicated application which generates the most events (file download in Firefox), the overhead remains less than 3.5%; showing much lower overheads for less complicated applications.

As for signature generation, since it does not need to be done on the user endpoint, we just show that it is also even feasible in a common machine. We used a desktop Intel Core i7 @3.60 GHz machine to generate signatures. The duration essentially is connected to how many events we have in our matching and non-matching traces, and how many traces we collect from each activity, and it increases linearly according to our implementation of Algorithm 1. The results in the sample of Firefox download signature show 6 min of generation time. Whereas, in the simple case of VLC, it only takes 8 s and in the average of MS word file manipulation, it takes 1:30 min.

5.3   Signature Verification

Upon collecting signatures from different activities, it is worthy to check if the extracted signatures represent the behavior that they were extracted from. It mainly remains a challenging task to perform the given task; given that most of the analysed programs are closed-source, and the open-source ones may be difficult to be analysed by human in order to verify the callstacks that appear in our signatures. In order to provide a general methodology for security analysts to verify the signatures, we provide a guideline on how we evaluate the accuracy of the signatures. The operations we have analysed, often have multiple objects involved within. For each application, we check whether the callstack of the related object does appear in the signature. Such as in Table 1, we can see the downloaded file name, the temporary file used during the operation, and the SQLite operation which adds the downloaded file to downloads library in Firefox.

Table 4. FP rate for different number of training sets

Activity	# Matching	# Non-matching	FPR
VLC Video Play	1	1	0.1e−4%
	1	3	0%
	2	3	0%
MS Word file manipulation	1	1	18.6%
	1	3	4.44%
	2	3	0.08%
Firefox download	1	1	1.8%
	1	3	0.004%
	2	3	0.1e−3%
Explorer file copy	1	1	1.8%
	1	3	0.03%
	2	3	0.1e−5%

Hence, we are able to verify signatures similar to how we calculate TPs mentioned in Sect. 5.1, so that security analysts would be able to refine the signatures generated from SEMFLOW; and revise them, according to their findings.

The need for manual involvement cannot be ignored, as at least the first time of signature generation from a software needs supervision to see if the signature and the involved objects in the event can actually represent the behavior and not just irrelevant events. The expectation is that minor updates to programs will not affect the sequence a program follows to generate the signature. Hence, after detecting the type of the behavior and verifying if the events in the signature are reasonable, the generation can happen automatically for future versions of the same program by replicating the same user behavior used to generate signatures from the original software version.

6 Case Study

In this section, we analyse a Living-off-the-Land attack, in which parts of the attack use existing tools on the system to finally perform a malicious DLL injection onto the system [6]. Figure 5 shows the attack example with the right graph being labeled by our system. An initial email contains a LNK file that uses wmic.exe to download XSL files. The downloaded file contains scripts for BitsAdmin.exe to download an encoded file. Also, the encoded file is a malicious DLL which is finally injected onto the system using the RegSvr32 tool. As seen, our system can label the LotL operations being performed during the attack for lateral movement. Tools such as wmic.exe are also used for LotL purposes and we can easily identify the operations done by such pre-installed applications by generating signatures from specific operations.

7 Limitations

While being effective, our system has certain limitations. Our signatures rely on program implementation, which leads to a few problems. Firstly, if the code of a program changes, the signature also needs to be updated. We can easily overcome this limitation by recording the activities once and performing them again

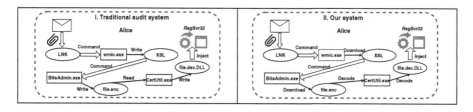

Fig. 5. Attack scenario in Sect. 6 without (left) and with (right) semantic identification

automatically using automation tools, collecting matching and non-matching behaviors from updated versions of applications.

Secondly, we cannot deal with cases where interpreters are used (e.g., Python), because in this case, the code path is decided by the interpreter at runtime, changing the callstack according to the interpreter's decisions. However, since the code is visible to interpreters, it would also be visible to a system trying to extract semantics from the code, or in Java, from the bytecode; making efforts possible for performing static analysis, which can be a future direction for researchers.

Another limitation is receiving accurate callstacks for network events. In our experiments, all network-related events have the same callstack, all frames pointing out to the kernel libraries. Hence, in addition to control flow operations, only file-related data flow operations can be labeled, so we completely ignore the labeling of network-related events as ETW cannot provide application-level callstacks for these types of events.

Lastly, our current implementation does not consider the connection of traces that represent the execution of a behavior and its dependencies. For example, the Spotify music playing application first caches a few songs when it starts and reads the cached songs from memory if the user decides to play them. In this case, SEMFLOW fails to get to know the caching behavior because it happens in the starting phase and is not unique for playing. And most importantly, it cannot be triggered by the user in order to collect traces specific to that operation.

8 Related Work

Callstack. SEMFLOW uses callstack information in order to extract semantic information from low-level system events. Using callstack information is used in other contexts as well. IntroPerf [19] uses such information to rank performance bugs using ETW. PerfGuard [18] also uses callstacks to apply performance assertions on application transactions.

Detection. There have been works on provenance analysis and attack reconstruction [12,26,29], which have proven to be accurate and efficient. However, not using callstack information from events may mislead those works as insider attacks tend to use similar events in benign scenarios. Our work was able to label individual events using callstack. We believe that even without semantic extraction, this data can be largely used to distinguish between events, resulting in a more accurate attack graph, as our semantics labels can be integrated to and improve those works.

Some works also focus on detecting system call sequences and marking attack sequences [14,25]. While the system call data has been shown to be more fine-grained, they would generate more events with less to be extracted from, compared to event-level work. [31] uses system call arguments to mitigate this problem, but ETW does not provide arguments for individual system calls, yet it can provide the arguments for system-level events instead.

Machine-learning work tend to train data based on previous attack and benign scenarios [16, 36], but they have been shown to have many false-positives and a huge reliance on having enormous training data for accuracy increment [10], in addition to being hard-to-verify.

CONAN [37] is a general framework to detect APT attacks through correlating multiple alerts or behaviors. Our work is complementary since we can use callstack to generate semantic information for labels or alerts, which is an input to CONAN.

Data Reduction. There also have been efforts to reduce the amount of data [24, 32, 38], which will be stored into permanent storage for future analysis. These works focus on maintaining provenance information between objects; so that the security analysts would be able to analyze the attack, even with reduced number of events. By using semantic information, in some cases, provenance information can be ignored or aggregated to save more space; if we completely are certain that an event cannot play any role in an attack scenario. Hence, we claim that by using semantic information, some events and their related objects can be ignored and the dependency information is not even needed in "harmlessly-labeled" events. Such an example would be the semantics of "VLC Video Play".

Provenance Tracking. Execution partitioning works such as [23, 35] require invasive training and instrumentation tools to perform provenance tracking, while our methodology uses the same data collected on the user machine to perform event labeling.

SEMFLOW generally is not an independent provenance constructor, and it only performs event labeling for future graph extraction using existing methods. Some use *semantic detection* [21, 22, 28] along with binary analysis for causality inference. But, binary analysis tends to be expensive while our approach is quite simple, and it uses the same type of data collected from the user machine to label the realtime event flow, making the process more clear to security analysts in each step. Some other use *tainting* [2, 7, 17, 27, 30], which generally is an expensive task and hence cannot be performed in realtime. There have been works towards optimizing it using hardware modifications [33, 34] but this is impractical, especially when using built-in data collectors in mostly common user systems which use Windows as their main operating system without any hardware modification or kernel access.

High-Level Semantic Identification. Table 5 shows an overview of the existing semantic identification works. Works such as [13, 22, 28, 40] are focused on extracting higher-level representations of low-level system data in order to make intrusion analysis easier for security experts. However, each suffers from multiple flaws. MPI [28] requires annotating high-level structures in source code. However, requiring source code is impractical on the Windows platform as most Windows internal and third-party applications are closed-sourced. Authors of MCI [22] use LDX [21] to extract causality information from system calls. However, in Windows, system calls do not provide their arguments individually, and only for some of them, we can extract the corresponding parameter by leveraging

Table 5. Comparison of semantic identification works

Work	Training overhead	Accuracy	Detection overhead	Dependency on source code
OmegaLog	High (instrumentation)	High	Low	Highly-Dependent
MPI	Low	High	Low	Highly-Dependent
MCI	High (instrumentation)	High	Low	None
UIScope	Low	Low	Low	None
SemFlow	Low	High	Low	None

system events. Also, it requires cumbersome training, and in comparison, it has higher false positives. Besides, model matching is not done at runtime as events arrive into the stream, and is performed after an attack is detected. It is also worth mentioning that system calls occur many times more than system-level events since they provide a lower-level abstraction of the system. It also faces the same limitation of needing to regenerate models upon receiving a newer version of the same program binary. Some works provide high-level contexts by leveraging application logs. OmegaLog [13] analyzes program binaries to identify and model application-layer logging behaviors, enabling accurate reconciliation of application events with system-layer accesses. lprof [42] and Stitch [41] observe that programmers will output sufficient information to logs so as to be able to reconstruct runtime execution flows. Based on the observation, they analyze application logs to provide semantic contexts for a single request without instrumenting any distributed application. However, all those works highly rely on the quality of application logs. It means that those works cannot work on applications which do not provide rich and sufficient application logs. Furthermore, lprof and OmegaLog require binary static analysis which is not available for binary codes built dynamically at runtime. In contrast, our system provides a general way based on general system events to recover high-level application behaviors without binary analysis. UIScope [40] correlates low-level system events with high-level UI events to provide high visibility. However, UIScope can only work on GUI applications while our system can work on both GUI and non-GUI applications. On the other hand, some works [11,29] map low-level system events to high-level Tactics, Techniques, and Procedures (TTPs) and connect them on generated provenance graphs to accelerate attack investigation. Those works leverage domain knowledge to generate rules to do mapping. In contrast, our work provides a general and accurate way to automatically identify high-level behaviors, which can supplement those works. RATScope [39] also leverages call-stacks to recover high-level behaviors for a specific kind of malware (i.e., Remote Access Trojans), while our work provides a semantic labeling system for benign applications. Furthermore, RATScope relies on complex behavior models (i.e., graph) which makes them non-realtime while our work can perform real-time labeling.

9 Conclusion

We develop SEMFLOW, which uses system-level data that is manually labeled by the activity that was run, then finds events that are responsible and used in a specific activity. Then let the ETW collector know about the label of each event it receives in realtime. The overhead for labeling is negligible as the collector can use set matching to perform labeling on individual events. We then implemented a prototype of the system and showed that it can expand and improve the robustness of existing work in detection and forensics by being able to distinguish between events.

References

1. Hardening Windows 10 with zero-day exploit mitigations (2017). https://bit.ly/2KdiTiv. Accessed 10 June 2017
2. Taintgrind. https://github.com/wmkhoo/taintgrind (2017). Accessed 10 Dec 2017
3. Windows-10-Mitigation-Improvement (2018). https://ubm.io/2IIVwtn Accessed 10 Apr 2018
4. APT1 (2019). https://bit.ly/2D7RNHI. Accessed 4 May 2019
5. Living off the Land: Attackers Leverage Legitimate Tools for Malicious Ends (2020). https://symantec-enterprise-blogs.security.com/blogs/threat-intelligence/living-land-legitimate-tools-malicious. Accessed 10 Oct 2020
6. Living off the Land: Turning Your Infrastructure Against You (2020). https://docs.broadcom.com/doc/living-off-the-land-turning-your-infrastructure-against-you-en. Accessed 10 Oct 2020
7. Attariyan, M., Flinn, J.: Automating configuration troubleshooting with dynamic information flow analysis. In: OSDI, vol. 10, pp. 1–14 (2010)
8. Gao, P., et al.: SAQL: a stream-based query system for real-time abnormal system behavior detection. In: USENIX Security (2018)
9. Gao, P., Xiao, X., Li, Z., Xu, F., Kulkarni, S.R., Mittal, P.: AIQL: enabling efficient attack investigation from system monitoring data. In: USENIX ATC (2018)
10. Harang, R., Kott, A.: Burstiness of intrusion detection process: Empirical evidence and a modeling approach. IEEE Trans. Inf. Forensics Secur. **12**(10), 2348–2359 (2017)
11. Hassan, W.U., Bates, A., Marino, D.: Tactical provenance analysis for endpoint detection and response systems. In: Proceedings of the IEEE Symposium on Security and Privacy (2020)
12. Hassan, W.U., et al.: Nodoze: combatting threat alert fatigue with automated provenance triage. In: NDSS (2019)
13. Hassan, W.U., Noureddine, M.A., Datta, P., Bates, A.: Omegalog: high-fidelity attack investigation via transparent multi-layer log analysis. In: Proceedings of NDSS (2020)
14. Hofmeyr, S.A., Forrest, S., Somayaji, A.: Intrusion detection using sequences of system calls. J. Comput. Secur. **6**(3), 151–180 (1998)
15. Hossain, M.N., et al.: {SLEUTH}: Real-time attack scenario reconstruction from {COTS} audit data. In: 26th USENIX Security Symposium (USENIX Security 2017), pp. 487–504 (2017)

16. Hu, W., Liao, Y., Vemuri, V.R.: Robust anomaly detection using support vector machines. In: Proceedings of the International Conference on Machine Learning, pp. 282–289. Citeseer (2003)

17. Jee, K., Portokalidis, G., Kemerlis, V.P., Ghosh, S., August, D.I., Keromytis, A.D.: A general approach for efficiently accelerating software-based dynamic data flow tracking on commodity hardware. In: NDSS (2012)

18. Kim, C.H., Rhee, J., Lee, K.H., Zhang, X., Xu, D.: Perfguard: binary-centric application performance monitoring in production environments. In: Proceedings of the 2016 24th ACM SIGSOFT International Symposium on Foundations of Software Engineering, pp. 595–606 (2016)

19. Kim, C.H., Rhee, J., Zhang, H., Arora, N., Jiang, G., Zhang, X., Xu, D.: Introperf: transparent context-sensitive multi-layer performance inference using system stack traces. ACM SIGMETRICS Perform. Eval. Rev. $42(1)$, 235–247 (2014)

20. King, S.T., Chen, P.M.: Backtracking intrusions. ACM Trans. Comput. Syst. (TOCS) $23(1)$, 51–76 (2005)

21. Kwon, Y., et al.: LDX: causality inference by lightweight dual execution. In: Proceedings of the Twenty-First International Conference on Architectural Support for Programming Languages and Operating Systems, pp. 503–515 (2016)

22. Kwon, Y., et al.: MCI: modeling-based causality inference in audit logging for attack investigation. In: NDSS (2018)

23. Lee, K.H., Zhang, X., Xu, D.: High accuracy attack provenance via binary-based execution partition. In: NDSS (2013)

24. Lee, K.H., Zhang, X., Xu, D.: LogGC: garbage collecting audit log. In: Proceedings of the 2013 ACM SIGSAC Conference on Computer & Communications Security, pp. 1005–1016 (2013)

25. Lee, W., Stolfo, S.: Data mining approaches for intrusion detection (1998)

26. Liu, Y., et al.: Towards a timely causality analysis for enterprise security. In: NDSS (2018)

27. Ma, S., Lee, K.H., Kim, C.H., Rhee, J., Zhang, X., Xu, D.: Accurate, low cost and instrumentation-free security audit logging for windows. In: Proceedings of the 31st Annual Computer Security Applications Conference, pp. 401–410 (2015)

28. Ma, S., Zhai, J., Wang, F., Lee, K.H., Zhang, X., Xu, D.: {MPI}: multiple perspective attack investigation with semantic aware execution partitioning. In: 26th USENIX Security Symposium (USENIX Security 2017), pp. 1111–1128 (2017)

29. Milajerdi, S.M., Gjomemo, R., Eshete, B., Sekar, R., Venkatakrishnan, V.: Holmes: real-time apt detection through correlation of suspicious information flows. In: 2019 IEEE Symposium on Security and Privacy (SP), pp. 1137–1152. IEEE (2019)

30. Song, D., et al.: BitBlaze: a new approach to computer security via binary analysis. In: Sekar, R., Pujari, A.K. (eds.) ICISS 2008. LNCS, vol. 5352, pp. 1–25. Springer, Heidelberg (2008). https://doi.org/10.1007/978-3-540-89862-7_1

31. Tandon, G., Chan, P.K.: On the learning of system call attributes for host-based anomaly detection. Int. J. Artif. Intell. Tools $15(06)$, 875–892 (2006)

32. Tang, Y., et al.: Nodemerge: template based efficient data reduction for big-data causality analysis. In: Proceedings of the 2018 ACM SIGSAC Conference on Computer and Communications Security, pp. 1324–1337 (2018)

33. Tiwari, M., Li, X., Wassel, H.M., Chong, F.T., Sherwood, T.: Execution leases: a hardware-supported mechanism for enforcing strong non-interference. In: Proceedings of the 42nd Annual IEEE/ACM International Symposium on Microarchitecture, pp. 493–504 (2009)

34. Tiwari, M., Wassel, H.M., Mazloom, B., Mysore, S., Chong, F.T., Sherwood, T.: Complete information flow tracking from the gates up. In: Proceedings of the 14th International Conference on Architectural Support for Programming Languages and Operating Systems, pp. 109–120 (2009)

35. Wang, F., Kwon, Y., Ma, S., Zhang, X., Xu, D.: Lprov: practical library-aware provenance tracing. In: Proceedings of the 34th Annual Computer Security Applications Conference, pp. 605–617 (2018)

36. Wu, J., Peng, D., Li, Z., Zhao, L., Ling, H.: Network intrusion detection based on a general regression neural network optimized by an improved artificial immune algorithm. PloS One $10(3)$, e0120976 (2015)

37. Xiong, C., et al.: Conan: a practical real-time apt detection system with high accuracy and efficiency. IEEE Trans. Dependable Secure Comput. (2020)

38. Xu, Z., et al.: High fidelity data reduction for big data security dependency analyses. In: Proceedings of the 2016 ACM SIGSAC Conference on Computer and Communications Security, pp. 504–516 (2016)

39. Yang, R., et al.: Ratscope: recording and reconstructing missing rat semantic behaviors for forensic analysis on windows. IEEE Trans. Dependable Secure Comput. (2020)

40. Yang, R., Ma, S., Xu, H., Zhang, X., Chen, Y.: UIscope: accurate, instrumentation-free, and visible attack investigation for GUI applications. In: Network and Distributed Systems Symposium (2020)

41. Zhao, X., Rodrigues, K., Luo, Y., Yuan, D., Stumm, M.: Non-intrusive performance profiling for entire software stacks based on the flow reconstruction principle. In: 12th USENIX Symposium on Operating Systems Design and Implementation (OSDI 2016), pp. 603–618 (2016)

42. Zhao, X., et al.: lprof: A non-intrusive request flow profiler for distributed systems. In: 11th USENIX Symposium on Operating Systems Design and Implementation (OSDI 2014), pp. 629–644 (2014)

Author Index

Abadia, German   I-499
Abazari, Farzaneh   I-374
Abla, Parhat   II-407
Acosta, Jaime C.   I-82
Akbar, Monika   I-82
Akiyama, Mitsuaki   II-3
Amich, Abderrahmen   I-207
Anastasova, Mila   II-441
Ashena, Narges   I-187
Ashouri, Mohammadreza   I-144
Aspinall, David   I-456
Azarderakhsh, Reza   II-424, II-441, II-475
Azhar, M. A. Hannan Bin   I-499

Barenghi, Alessandro   II-458
Bernstein, Abraham   I-187
Bisheh-Niasar, Mojtaba   II-441
Blasco, Jorge   II-252
Bordeanu, Octavian Ciprian   II-164
Branca, Enrico   I-374
Buccafurri, Francesco   II-43

Cai, Lijun   I-3
Carranza, Ronald Rivera   I-374
Chen, Bo   II-495
Chen, Yan   I-513
Cheng, Feng   I-25
Cheng, Zelei   II-394
Chiba, Daiki   II-3
Chowdhury, Badrul   II-338
Clarke, Luisana   I-82
Clausen, Henry   I-456
Cruz, Breno Dantas   II-273
Cui, Mingxin   I-418
Curtmola, Reza   II-143

Danda, Shashank Reddy   II-495
Davies, Toby   II-164
De Angelis, Vincenzo   II-43
Dell'Aglio, Daniele   I-187
Dong, Jian   II-64
Duan, Xiaoyi   I-270

Elkhatib, Rami   II-475
Eshete, Birhanu   I-207

Fejrskov, Martin   I-476
Flood, Robert   I-456
Free-Nelson, Frederica   I-82
Fukushi, Naoki   II-3

Gaber, Tarek   II-509
Giron, Alexandre Augusto   II-363
Gogineni, Kailash   I-100
Gou, Gaopeng   I-418
Guan, Yangyang   I-418

Han, Xiao   II-295
Haque, Nur Imtiazul   II-338
He, Daojing   I-287
He, Siman   I-270
Hell, Martin   II-207
Hering, Till   I-123
Hu, Chengbin   II-295
Huff, Philip   I-62, I-164

Idone, Maria Francesca   II-43
Ivanov, Nikolay   II-99

Jung, Taeho   I-311, I-332, I-352

Karagoz, Emrah   II-424
Karl, Ryan   I-311, I-332, I-352, II-372
Kavousi, Mohammad   I-513
Kermani, Mehran Mozaffari   II-441
Koide, Takashi   II-3
Koziel, Brian   II-475

Labrini, Cecilia   II-43
Lan, Tian   I-100
Langenberg, Brandon   II-475
Lau, Wing Cheong   II-79
Leith, Douglas J.   II-231
Li, Peng   II-185
Li, Qinghua   I-62, I-164
Li, Qun   I-229

Li, Xiuying   I-270
Li, You   I-270
Li, Zuotian   II-394
Lin, Jingqiang   I-249
Liu, Chang   I-418
Liu, Yao   II-295
Liu, Yin   II-273
Liu, Zhengyu   II-64
Lu, Zhuo   II-295

Ma, Shiqing   I-513
Mannan, Mohammad   II-120
Medina, Stephanie   I-82
Mei, Yongsheng   I-100
Meinel, Christoph   I-25
Meng, Dan   I-3
Mitseva, Asya   I-123
Mohammed, Alamin   I-332, I-352
Mozaffari-Kermani, Mehran   II-424

Najafi, Pejman   I-25
Nakano, Hiroki   II-3
Nikbakht Bideh, Pegah   II-207

Ouyang, Linshu   II-384

Paladi, Nicolae   II-207
Pan, Kaiyun   I-287
Panchenko, Andriy   I-123
Pang, Chenbin   II-185
Pedersen, Jens Myrup   I-476
Pelosi, Gerardo   II-458
Perriello, Simone   II-458
Poll, Erik   II-317

Rahman, Mohammad Ashiqur   II-338

Salloum, Said   II-509
Sanal, Pakize   II-424
Seo, Hwajeong   II-424
Shaalan, Khaled   II-509
Shahriar Hossain, Mahmud   I-82
Shahriar, Md Hasan   II-338
Shen, Yun   II-164
Shi, Shangcheng   II-79
Shi, Yiming   I-399
Silva, Carlos   I-438
Sivakumaran, Pallavi   II-252
Sousa, Bruno   I-438
Stakhanova, Natalia   I-374

Striegel, Aaron   I-332, I-352
Stringhini, Gianluca   II-164

Takeshita, Jonathan   I-311, I-332, I-352
Tang, Yong   II-23
Tao, Jing   II-23
Tao, Zeyi   I-229
Tilevich, Eli   II-273
Tiloca, Marco   II-207
Tong, Jianmin   I-270
Triandopoulos, Nikolaos   II-185

Uddin, Md Shahab   II-120

Vadera, Sunil   II-509
Van Aubel, Pol   II-317
Vasilomanolakis, Emmanouil   I-476
Venkataramani, Guru   I-100
Vilela, João P.   I-438

Wan, Lipeng   I-249
Wang, Bin   II-64
Wang, Enze   II-23
Wang, Mingsheng   II-407
Wang, Xianbo   II-79
Wang, Yifan   II-185
Wang, Zhaoyuan   II-64
Wang, Zhenhua   II-23
Wei, Renzheng   I-3
Wei, Yuheng   I-44
Whisenant, Steven G.   II-338

Xia, Qi   I-229
Xiao, Xin   I-399
Xie, Lijia   I-399
Xie, Wei   II-23
Xiong, Gang   I-418
Xiong, Junjie   II-295
Xu, Chuan   I-287
Xu, Jun   II-185
Xu, Xiaojie   II-64

Yan, Qiben   II-99
Yang, Jin   II-64
Yang, Ronghai   II-79
Yang, Runqing   I-513
Youssef, Amr   II-120
Yu, Aimin   I-3
Yuan, Xiaoyong   II-495

Zaheri, Mojtaba   II-143
Zeng, Kyle   II-79
Zhang, Peishu   I-270
Zhang, Xiao   I-399
Zhang, Yongzheng   II-384
Zhang, Yuchen   II-185
Zhao, Lixin   I-3

Zhao, Panpan   I-418
Zhao, Shangqing   II-295
Zhao, Shuang   I-399
Zheng, Fangyu   I-249
Zheng, Zhiming   I-399
Ziemann, Torsten   I-123
Zou, Futai   I-44